DAVII H'S SONY® α SLT-A57

GUIDE TO DIGITAL PHOTOGRAPHY

David D. Busch

Course Technology PTR
A part of Cengage Learning

COURSE TECHNOLOGY
CENGAGE Learning®

Australia, Brazil, Japan, Korea, Mexico, Singapore, Spain, United Kingdom, United States

COURSE TECHNOLOGY
CENGAGE Learning

David Busch's Sony® α SLT-A57 Guide to Digital Photography
David D. Busch

Publisher and General Manager, Course Technology PTR:
Stacy L. Hiquet

Associate Director of Marketing:
Sarah Panella

Manager of Editorial Services:
Heather Talbot

Senior Marketing Manager:
Mark Hughes

Executive Editor:
Kevin Harreld

Project Editor:
Jenny Davidson

Series Technical Editor:
Michael D. Sullivan

Interior Layout Tech:
Bill Hartman

Cover Designer:
Mike Tanamachi

Indexer:
Katherine Stimson

Proofreader:
Sara Gullion

Library of Congress Control Number: 2012940151

ISBN-13: 978-1-285-17128-9

ISBN-10: 1-285-17128-4

Course Technology, a part of Cengage Learning
20 Channel Center Street
Boston, MA 02210
USA

Cengage Learning is a leading provider of customized learning solutions with office locations around the globe, including Singapore, the United Kingdom, Australia, Mexico, Brazil, and Japan. Locate your local office at: **international.cengage.com/region**.

Cengage Learning products are represented in Canada by Nelson Education, Ltd.

For your lifelong learning solutions, visit **courseptr.com**.

Visit our corporate website at **cengage.com**.

Printed in the United States of America
1 2 3 4 5 6 7 14 13 12

For Cathy

Acknowledgments

Once again thanks to the folks at Course Technology PTR, who have pioneered publishing digital imaging books in full color at a price anyone can afford. Special thanks to executive editor Kevin Harreld, who always gives me the freedom to let my imagination run free with a topic, as well as my veteran production team, including project editor, Jenny Davidson and technical editor, Mike Sullivan. Also thanks to Bill Hartman, layout; Katherine Stimson, indexing; Sara Gullion, proofreading; Mike Tanamachi, cover design; and my agent, Carole Jelen, who has the amazing ability to keep both publishers and authors happy.

Also, big thanks to the folks at Campus Camera (www.campuscamera.net), who obtained a Sony SLT-A57 for me when even Sony had none to provide. Their help made it possible for me to be using this great camera and putting together this book while most Sonyphiles were still waiting for delivery.

Thanks again to master photographer Nancy Balluck for the back cover photo of yours truly (www.nancyballuckphotography.com).

About the Author

With more than a million books in print, **David D. Busch** is the #1 bestselling camera guide author, and the originator of popular series like *David Busch's Pro Secrets, David Busch's Compact Field Guides,* and *David Busch's Quick Snap Guides.* He has written more than 50 hugely successful guidebooks for Sony and other digital SLR models, including the all-time #1 bestsellers for several different cameras, additional user guides for other camera models, as well as many popular books devoted to dSLRs, including *Mastering Digital SLR Photography, Third Edition* and *Digital SLR Pro Secrets.* As a roving photojournalist for more than 20 years, he illustrated his books, magazine articles, and newspaper reports with award-winning images. He's operated his own commercial studio, suffocated in formal dress while shooting weddings-for-hire, and shot sports for a daily newspaper and upstate New York college. His photos have been published in magazines as diverse as *Scientific American* and *Petersen's PhotoGraphic,* and his articles have appeared in *Popular Photography & Imaging, Rangefinder, The Professional Photographer,* and hundreds of other publications. He's also reviewed dozens of digital cameras for CNet and *Computer Shopper.*

When About.com named its top five books on Beginning Digital Photography, debuting at the #1 and #2 slots were Busch's *Digital Photography All-In-One Desk Reference for Dummies* and *Mastering Digital Photography.* In the last week of 2011, he had a total of 18 books listed in the Top 100 of Amazon.com's Digital Photography Bestseller list—simultaneously! Busch's 150-plus other books published since 1983 include bestsellers like *David Busch's Quick Snap Guide to Using Digital SLR Lenses.*

Busch is a member of the Cleveland Photographic Society (www.clevelandphoto.org), which has operated continuously since 1887.

Visit his website at http://www.dslrguides.com/blog.

Contents

Chapter 3
Setting Up Your Sony Alpha SLT-A57 69

Chapter 4
Getting the Right Exposure 125

Chapter 5
Mastering Autofocus Options 161

Chapter 6
Advanced Techniques for Your Sony Alpha SLT-A57 183

Chapter 10
Downloading and Editing Your Images 307

Chapter 11
Sony Alpha SLT-A57: Troubleshooting and Prevention 321

Glossary 345

Index 357

Preface

A camera with 16 megapixels of resolution, continuous shooting at 12 frames per second, and full high-definition movie making for under $800—with lens? No wonder you're excited about the new Sony SLT-A57 camera! You don't expect to take good pictures with such a camera—you demand *outstanding* photos. After all, this Alpha model is one of the most innovative cameras that Sony has ever introduced. But your gateway to pixel proficiency is dragged down by the slim little book included in the box as a manual. You know everything you need to know is in there, somewhere, but you don't know where to start. In addition, the camera manual doesn't offer much information on photography or digital photography. Nor are you interested in spending hours or days studying a comprehensive book on digital SLR photography that doesn't necessarily apply directly to your Alpha.

What you need is a guide that explains the purpose and function of the Alpha's basic controls, how you should use them, and *why*. Ideally, there should be information about file formats, resolution, aperture/priority exposure, and special autofocus modes available, but you'd prefer to read about those topics only after you've had the chance to go out and take a few hundred great pictures with your new camera. Why isn't there a book that summarizes the most important information in its first two or three chapters, with lots of full-color illustrations showing what your results will look like when you use this setting or that?

Now there is such a book. If you want a quick introduction to the Alpha's focus controls, flash synchronization options, how to choose lenses, or which exposure modes are best, this book is for you. If you can't decide on what basic settings to use with your camera because you can't figure out how changing ISO or white balance or focus defaults will affect your pictures, you need this guide.

Introduction

Sony continues to amaze the photo world with its constant upgrading of its innovative SLT (single lens translucent) camera line. It's packaged up the most alluring features of advanced digital SLRs and stuffed them into a compact, highly affordable body in the Alpha SLT-A57, which boasts some features you won't find on other cameras. These include an innovative semi-transparent mirror that makes it possible to use live view and advanced phase detection autofocus *all the time.*

You'll find your new camera is loaded with capabilities that few would have expected to find in such an affordable camera. Indeed, the Alpha retains the ease of use that smoothes the transition for those new to digital photography. For those just dipping their toes into the digital pond, the experience is warm and inviting. The A57 isn't a snapshot camera—it is a point-and-shoot (if you want to use it in that mode) for the thinking photographer.

Nor will you easily outgrow this camera. It's neatly positioned between the new entry-level SLT-A37 and its "pro" stablemates, including the A77, with enough features to satisfy the most avid photographer. The A57 model has 16.2 megapixels of resolution, autofocus that's improved over its predecessors, and lots of customization options. Sony must love fledgling photographers, because it seems to work extra hard to give them incredible value for their money.

But once you've confirmed that you made a wise purchase decision, the question comes up, *how do I use this thing?* All those cool features can be mind numbing to learn, if all you have as a guide is the manual furnished with the camera. Help is on the way. I sincerely believe that this book is your best bet for learning how to use your new camera, and for learning how to use it well.

If you're a Sony Alpha SLT owner who's looking to learn more about how to use this great camera, you've probably already explored your options. There are DVDs and online tutorials—but who can learn how to use a camera by sitting in front of a television or computer screen? Do you want to watch a movie or click on HTML links, or do you want to go out and take photos with your camera? Videos are fun, but not the best answer.

There's always the manual furnished with the Alpha. It's compact and filled with information, but there's really very little about *why* you should use particular settings or features, and its organization may make it difficult to find what you need. Multiple cross-references may send you flipping back and forth between two or three sections of the book to find what you want to know. The basic manual is also hobbled by black-and-white line drawings and tiny monochrome pictures that aren't very good examples of what you can do.

Also available are third-party guides to the Alpha, like this one. I haven't been happy with some of these guidebooks, which is why I wrote this one. The existing books range from skimpy and illustrated with black-and-white photos to lushly illustrated in full color but too generic to do much good. Photography instruction is useful, but it needs to be related directly to the Sony Alpha SLT as much as possible.

I've tried to make *David Busch's Sony Alpha SLT-A57 Guide to Digital Photography* different from your other Alpha learn-up options. The roadmap sections use larger, color pictures to show you where all the buttons and dials are, and the explanations of what they do are longer and more comprehensive. I've tried to avoid overly general advice, including the two-page checklists on how to take a "sports picture" or a "portrait picture" or a "travel picture." Instead, you'll find tips and techniques for using all the features of your Sony Alpha SLT to take *any kind of picture* you want. If you want to know where you should stand to take a picture of a quarterback dropping back to unleash a pass, there are plenty of books that will tell you that. This one concentrates on teaching you how to select the best autofocus mode, shutter speed, f/stop, or flash capability to take, say, a great sports picture under any conditions.

This book is not a lame rewriting of the manual that came with the camera. Some folks spend five minutes with a book like this one, spot some information that also appears in the original manual, and decide "Rehash!" without really understanding the differences. Yes, you'll find information here that is also in the owner's manual, such as the parameters you can enter when changing your Alpha's operation in the various menus. Basic descriptions—before I dig in and start providing in-depth tips and information—may also be vaguely similar. There are only so many ways you can say, for example, "Hold the shutter release down halfway to lock in exposure." But not *everything* in the manual is included in this book. If you need advice on when and how to use the most important functions, you'll find the information here.

David Busch's Sony Alpha SLT-A57 Guide to Digital Photography is aimed at both Sony veterans as well as newcomers to digital photography and digital SLRs. Both groups can be overwhelmed by the options the Alpha offers, while underwhelmed by the explanations they receive in their user's manual. The manuals are great if you already know what you don't know, and you can find an answer somewhere in a booklet arranged by menu listings and written by a camera vendor employee who last threw together instructions on how to operate a camcorder.

Once you've read this book and are ready to learn more, I hope you pick up one of my other guides to interchangeable lens digital photography. Four of them are offered by Course Technology PTR, each approaching the topic from a different perspective. They include:

Quick Snap Guide to Digital SLR Photography
Consider this a prequel to the book you're holding in your hands. It might make a good gift for a spouse or friend who may be using your Alpha, but who lacks even basic knowledge about digital photography, digital SLR photography, and Sony Alpha photography. It serves as an introduction that summarizes the basic features of digital cameras in general (not just the Alpha), and what settings to use and when, such as continuous autofocus/single autofocus, aperture/shutter priority, EV settings, and so forth. The guide also includes recipes for shooting the most common kinds of pictures, with step-by-step instructions for capturing effective sports photos, portraits, landscapes, and other types of images.

David Busch's Quick Snap Guide to Using Digital SLR Lenses
A bit overwhelmed by the features and controls of interchangeable lenses, and not quite sure when to use each type? This book explains lenses, their use, and lens technology in easy-to-access two- and four-page spreads, each devoted to a different topic, such as depth-of-field, lens aberrations, or using zoom lenses.

Mastering Digital SLR Photography, Third Edition
Although your A57 is not a digital SLR (the viewing system is the chief difference) it behaves a lot like one, so this book is a useful, in-depth introduction to digital photography for Sony Alpha SLT owners, with nuts-and-bolts explanations of the technology, more in-depth coverage of settings, and whole chapters on the most common types of photography. While not specific to the Alpha, this book can show you how to get more from its capabilities.

Digital SLR Pro Secrets
This is my more advanced guide to digital photography with greater depth and detail about the topics you're most interested in. If you've already mastered the basics in *Mastering Digital SLR Photography*, this book will take you to the next level.

Why the Sony Alpha Needs Special Coverage

There are many general digital photography books on the market. Why do I concentrate on books about specific cameras like the Alpha?

When I started writing digital photography books in 1995, digital SLRs cost $30,000 and few people other than certain professionals could justify them. Most of my readers a dozen years ago were stuck using the point-and-shoot, low-resolution digital cameras of the time—even if they were advanced photographers. I took tons of digital pictures with an Epson digital camera with 1024 × 768 (less than 1 megapixel!) resolution, and which cost $500.

As recently as 2003 (years before the original Alpha was introduced), the lowest-cost dSLRs were priced at $3,000 or more. Today, anyone with around $600 can afford one of these basic cameras, and around $800 buys you a sophisticated model like the Sony Alpha SLT-A57 (with lens). The digital SLR is no longer the exclusive bailiwick of the professional, the wealthy, or the serious photography addict willing to scrimp and save to acquire a dream camera. Digital SLRs have become the favored camera for anyone who wants to go beyond point-and-shoot capabilities. And Sony cameras (and the Minolta models that preceded them) have enjoyed a favored position among digital SLRs because of Sony's innovation in introducing affordable cameras with interesting features, such as SteadyShot image stabilization, and outstanding performance. It doesn't hurt that Sony also provides both full-frame cameras (like the SLT-A99) and smaller format digital cameras and a clear migration path between them (if you stick to the Sony lenses that are compatible with both).

Who Are You?

When preparing a guidebook for a specific camera, it's always wise to consider exactly who will be reading the book. Indeed, thinking about the potential audience for *David Busch's Sony Alpha SLT-A57 Guide to Digital Photography* is what led me to taking the approach and format I use for this book. I realized that the needs of readers like you had to be addressed both from a functional level (what you will use the Sony Alpha SLT-A57 for) as well as from a skill level (how much experience you may have with digital photography, dSLRs, or Sony cameras specifically).

From a functional level, you probably fall into one of these categories:

- Professional photographers who understand photography and digital cameras, and simply want to learn how to use the Sony Alpha SLT-A57 as a backup camera, or as a camera for their personal "off-duty" use.
- Individuals who want to get better pictures, or perhaps transform their growing interest in photography into a full-fledged hobby or artistic outlet with a Sony Alpha and advanced techniques.
- Those who want to produce more professional-looking images for their personal or business website, and feel that the Sony Alpha will give them more control and capabilities.
- Small business owners with more advanced graphics capabilities who want to use the Sony Alpha SLT-A57 to document or promote their business.

- Corporate workers who may or may not have photographic skills in their job descriptions, but who work regularly with graphics and need to learn how to use digital images taken with a Sony Alpha for reports, presentations, or other applications.
- Professional webmasters with strong skills in programming (including Java, JavaScript, HTML, Perl, etc.) but little background in photography, but who realize that the Sony Alpha can be used for sophisticated photography.
- Graphic artists and others who already may be adept in image editing with Photoshop or another program, but who need to learn more about digital photography and the special capabilities of the Sony Alpha.

Addressing your needs from a skills level can be a little trickier, because the Sony Alpha is such a great camera that a full spectrum of photographers will be buying it, from absolute beginners who have never owned a digital camera before up to the occasional professional with years of shooting experience who will be using the Sony Alpha as a backup body.

Before tackling this book, it would be helpful for you to understand the following:

- **How digital photography differs from film:** The image is stored not on film (which I call the *first* write-once optical media), but on a memory card as pixels that can be transferred to your computer, and then edited, corrected, and printed without the need for chemical processing.
- **What the basic tools of correct exposure are:** Don't worry if you don't understand these; I'll explain them later in this book. But if you already know something about shutter speed, aperture, and ISO sensitivity, you'll be ahead of the game. If not, you'll soon learn that shutter speed determines the amount of time the sensor is exposed to incoming light; the f/stop or aperture is like a valve that governs the quantity of light that can flow through the lens; the sensor's sensitivity (ISO setting) controls how easily the sensor responds to light. All three factors can be varied individually and proportionately to produce a picture that is properly exposed (neither too light nor too dark).

It's tough to provide something for everybody, but I am going to try to address the needs of each of the following groups and skill levels:

- **Digital photography newbies:** If you've used only point-and-shoot digital cameras, or have worked only with non-SLR film cameras, you're to be congratulated for selecting one of the very best intermediate digital cameras as your first. This book can help you understand the controls and features of your Sony Alpha, and lead you down the path to better photography with your camera. I'll provide all the information you need, but if you want to do some additional reading for extra credit, you can also try one of the other books I mentioned earlier. They complement this book well.

- **Advanced point-and-shooters moving on up:** There are some quite sophisticated pocket-sized digital cameras available, including those with many user-definable options and settings, so it's possible you are already a knowledgeable photographer, even though you're new to the world of the digital SLR. You've recognized the limitations of the point-and-shoot camera: even the best of them have more noise at higher sensitivity (ISO) settings than a camera like the Sony Alpha; the speediest still have an unacceptable delay between the time you press the shutter and when the photo is actually taken; even a non-interchangeable super-zoom camera with 12X to 20X magnification often won't focus close enough, include an aperture suitable for low-light photography, or take in the really wide view you must have. Interchangeable lenses and other accessories available for the Sony Alpha are another one of the reasons you moved up. Because you're an avid photographer already, you should pick up the finer points of using the Sony Alpha from this book with no trouble.
- **Experienced dSLR users broadening their experience to include the Sony Alpha SLT-A57:** Perhaps you started out with another Sony or Konica Minolta digital SLR. You may have used a digital SLR from another vendor and are making the switch. You understand basic photography, and want to learn more. And, most of all, you want to transfer the skills you already have to the Sony Alpha, as quickly and seamlessly as possible.
- **Pro photographers and other advanced shooters:** I expect my most discerning readers will be those who already have extensive experience with advanced dSLR cameras. I may not be able to teach you folks much about photography. But, even so, an amazing number of Sony Alpha SLT-A57 cameras have been purchased by those who feel it is a good complement to their favorite, more advanced camera.

Who Am I?

After spending years as the world's most successful unknown author, I've become slightly less obscure in the past few years, thanks to a horde of camera guidebooks and other photographically oriented tomes. You may have seen my photography articles in *Popular Photography & Imaging* magazine. I've also written about 2,000 articles for magazines like *Petersen's PhotoGraphic* (which is now defunct through no fault of my own), plus *Rangefinder*, *Professional Photographer*, and dozens of other photographic publications. But, first, and foremost, I'm a photojournalist and made my living in the field until I began devoting most of my time to writing books. Although I love writing, I'm happiest when I'm out taking pictures, which is why during the past 12 months I've taken off chunks of time to travel to southwest Ireland, Prague in the Czech Republic, and a week in Valencia, Spain. You'll find photos of many of these visual treats within the pages of this book.

Like all my digital photography books, this one was written by someone with an incurable photography bug. One of my first SLRs was a Minolta SRT-101, from the company whose technology was eventually absorbed by Sony in 2006. I've used a variety of newer models since then. I've worked as a sports photographer for an Ohio newspaper and for an upstate New York college. I've operated my own commercial studio and photo lab, cranking out product shots on demand and then printing a few hundred glossy 8 × 10s on a tight deadline for a press kit. I've served as a photo-posing instructor for a modeling agency. People have actually paid me to shoot their weddings and immortalize them with portraits. I even prepared press kits and articles on photography as a PR consultant for a formerly dominant Rochester, N.Y., company, which shall remain nameless. My trials and travails with imaging and computer technology have made their way into print in book form an alarming number of times, including a few dozen on scanners and photography.

Like you, I love photography for its own merits, and I view technology as just another tool to help me get the images I see in my mind's eye. But, also like you, I had to master this technology before I could apply it to my work. This book is the result of what I've learned, and I hope it will help you master your Alpha digital SLR, too.

In closing, I'd like to ask a special favor: let me know what you think of this book. If you have any recommendations about how I can make it better, visit my website at www.dslrguides.com/blog, click on the E-Mail Me tab, and send your comments, suggestions on topics that should be explained in more detail, or, especially, any typos. (The latter will be compiled on the Errata page you'll also find on my website.) I really value your ideas, and appreciate it when you take the time to tell me what you think! Some of the content of the book you hold in your hands came from suggestions I received from readers like yourself. If you found this book especially useful, tell others about it. Visit http://www.amazon.com/ and leave a positive review. Your feedback is what spurs me to make each one of these books better than the last. Thanks!

1

Getting Started with Your Sony Alpha SLT-A57

I once read a camera guide that began with the author advising the Gentle Reader to resist the temptation to go out and take pictures until the proper amount of time had been spent Setting Up The Camera, apparently to avoid wasting electrons on shots that were doomed to failure if the arcane operational knowledge that was forthcoming wasn't first absorbed. What universe was he from?

Relax! I fully expect that you took several hundred or a thousand (or two) photos before you ever cracked the cover of this book—for several reasons. First, and foremost, the Sony Alpha SLT-A57 is incredibly easy to use, especially for the absolute beginner. Even the newest digital camera owner can rotate the mode dial to the aqua Auto position and go out and begin taking great pictures. Getting to that point by charging the battery, mounting a lens, and inserting a Secure Digital or Memory Stick memory card isn't exactly rocket science, either. Sony has cleverly marked the power switch (located concentrically with the shutter release button) with large ON and OFF labels, and the bright red button labeled MOVIE will provide a major clue for anyone interested in taking advantage of these cameras' advanced motion-picture capabilities.

So, budding photographers are likely to muddle their way through getting the camera revved up and working well enough to take a bunch of still pictures or video sequences without the universe collapsing. Eventually, though, many may turn to this book when they realize that they can do an even better job with a little guidance.

Second, I know that many of you will be previous owners of one of the predecessors of this camera, such as the Alpha DSLR-A390, Alpha SLT-A33, or even one of the much earlier Minolta Maxxum dSLR models. Most of the basic operations of the Alpha

SLT-A57 are quite similar to those of the older models. It's true that the SLT-series uses a different mirror technology called Single Lens Translucent, rather than SLR, for Single Lens Reflex. But, as you may be able to tell by its outward appearance and by its operation, for our purposes as photographers it functions in very much the same way as dSLRs do—only better, when it comes to rapid focusing, as I'll discuss in Chapter 5. So, veteran Sony/Minolta dSLR owners can venture out, shoot first, and ask questions later, with confidence that their dSLR experience will translate well to the new world of the SLT.

The A57's semi-transparent mirror (*not* translucent, despite Sony's nomenclature) does not swing up and down like the mirror in a typical SLR. Rather, it stays put and it allows 70 percent of the light that strikes it to pass through to the 16.2 MP CMOS sensor while the remaining light is reflected upwards to a large 15-point phase detection AF area. This AF area always receives light and as a result these cameras can focus with lightning speed for both still photography and movies, even during exposure. The penalty for this magic is about 1/3 EV reduction in light for live view and image capture but without a swinging mirror and related optical system, the sensor is always receiving light.

Finally, I realize that most of you didn't buy this book at the same time you purchased your Sony Alpha. As much as I'd like to picture thousands of avid photographers marching out of their camera stores with an Alpha box under one arm, and my book in hand, I know that's not going to happen *all* the time. A large number of you had your camera for a week, or two, or a month, became comfortable with it, and sought out this book in order to learn more. So, a chapter on "setup" seems like too little, too late, doesn't it?

In practice, though, it's not a bad idea, once you've taken a few orientation pictures with your camera, to go back and review the basic operations of the camera from the beginning, if only to see if you've missed something. This chapter is my opportunity to review the setup procedures for the camera for those among you who are already veteran users, and to help ease the more timid (and those who have never worked with a digital SLR before) into the basic preflight checklist that needs to be completed before you really spread your wings and take off. For the uninitiated, as easy as it is to use initially, the Sony Alpha *does* have lots of dials, buttons, and settings that might not make sense at first, but will surely become second nature after you've had a chance to review the instructions in this chapter.

But don't fret about wading through a manual to find out what you must know to take those first few tentative snaps. I'm going to help you hit the ground running with this chapter (or keep on running if you've already jumped right in). If you *haven't* had the opportunity to use your Alpha yet, I'll help you set up your camera and begin shooting in minutes. You won't find a lot of detail in this chapter. Indeed, I'm going to tell you just what you absolutely *must* understand, accompanied by some interesting tidbits that will help you become acclimated. I'll go into more depth and even repeat some of what

I explain here in later chapters, so you don't have to memorize everything you see. Just relax, follow a few easy steps, and then go out and begin taking your best shots—ever.

Your Out-of-Box Experience

Your Sony Alpha SLT-A57 comes in an impressive box filled with stuff, including connecting cords, booklets, a CD, and lots of paperwork. The most important components are the camera and lens, battery, battery charger, and, if you're the nervous type, the neck strap. You'll also need a Secure Digital or Memory Stick card, as one is not included. If you purchased your Alpha from a camera shop, as I did, the store personnel probably attached the neck strap for you, ran through some basic operational advice that you've already forgotten, tried to sell you a Secure Digital card, and then, after they'd given you all the help you could absorb, sent you on your way with a handshake.

Perhaps you purchased your Sony Alpha from one of those mass merchandisers that also sell washing machines and vacuum cleaners. In that case, you might have been sent on your way with only the handshake, or, maybe, not even that if you resisted the efforts to sell you an extended warranty. You save a few bucks at the big-box stores, but you don't get the personal service a professional photo retailer provides. It's your choice. There's a third alternative, of course. You might have purchased your camera from a mail order or Internet source, and your camera arrived in a big brown (or purple/red) truck. Your only interaction when you took possession of your camera was to scrawl your signature on an electronic clipboard.

In all three cases, the first thing to do is to carefully unpack the camera and double-check the contents with the checklist on one side of the box (and at page 12 of the instruction manual). While this level of setup detail may seem as superfluous as the instructions on a bottle of shampoo, checking the contents *first* is always a good idea. No matter who sells a camera, it's common to open boxes, use a particular camera for a demonstration, and then repack the box without replacing all the pieces and parts afterwards. Someone might actually have helpfully checked out your camera on your behalf—and then mispacked the box. It's better to know *now* that something is missing so you can seek redress immediately, rather than discover two months from now that the USB cable you thought you'd never use (but now *must* have) was never in the box.

So, check the box at your earliest convenience, and make sure you have (at least) the following:

- **Sony Alpha SLT-A57 camera.** This is hard to miss. The camera is the main reason you laid out the big bucks, and it is tucked away inside a nifty bubble-wrap envelope you should save for protection in case the Alpha needs to be sent in for repair. It almost goes without saying that you should check out the camera immediately, making sure the color LCD on the back isn't scratched or cracked, the memory card and battery compartment door opens properly, and, when a charged battery is inserted and lens mounted, the camera powers up and reports for duty. Out-of-the-box defects in these areas are rare, but they can happen. It's probably more common that your dealer played with the camera or, perhaps, it was a customer return. That's why it's best to buy your Alpha from a retailer you trust to supply a factory-fresh camera.

- **Rubber eyecup.** This slide-on soft-rubber eyecup should be attached to the viewfinder when you receive the camera. It helps you squeeze your eye tightly against the window, excluding extraneous light, and also protects your eyeglasses (if you wear them) from scratching.
- **Body cap.** The plastic twist-off body cap keeps dust from entering the camera when no lens is mounted. Even with automatic sensor cleaning built into the Alpha, you'll want to keep the amount of dust to a minimum. The body cap belongs in your camera bag if you contemplate the need to travel with the lens removed.
- **Lens (if purchased).** The Sony Alpha may come in a kit with the SAL-1855 DT 18-55mm f/3.5-5.6 zoom lens. Or, you may purchase the camera with another lens. The lens will come with a lens cap on the front, and a rear lens cap aft.
- **Battery pack NP-FM500H.** The power source for your Sony Alpha is packaged separately. The battery should be charged as soon as possible (as described next) and inserted in the camera. It's smart to have more than one battery pack (a spare costs about $60, although the Sony list price is about $80), so you can continue shooting when your main battery is discharged or, after many uses, peters out entirely. Make sure you get this model number of battery; it is different from the batteries used in some earlier Sony cameras (though it's the same one used by the Sony SLT-A77, A55, DSLR-A560/A580, and a few other models).
- **Battery charger BC-VM10A.** This battery charger will be included. Outside of the United States and Canada, the camera ships with a power cord that attaches to the charger (which allows Sony to package each charger with a cord that fits the specific power outlets of the country where it's sold). In the United States, the charger is plugged in using its integrated US-style AC plug.
- **Shoulder strap.** Sony provides you with a suitable neck or shoulder strap, emblazoned with Sony advertising. While I am justifiably proud of owning a fine Sony camera, I never attach the factory straps to my cameras, and instead opt for a more serviceable strap from UPstrap (www.upstrap-pro.com). If you carry your camera over one shoulder, as many do, I particularly recommend UPstrap (shown in Figure 1.1). It has a patented non-slip pad that offers reassuring traction and eliminates the contortions we sometimes go through to keep the camera from slipping off. I know several photographers who refuse to use anything else. If you do purchase an UPstrap, be sure to tell photographer-inventor Al Stegmeyer that I sent you hence.

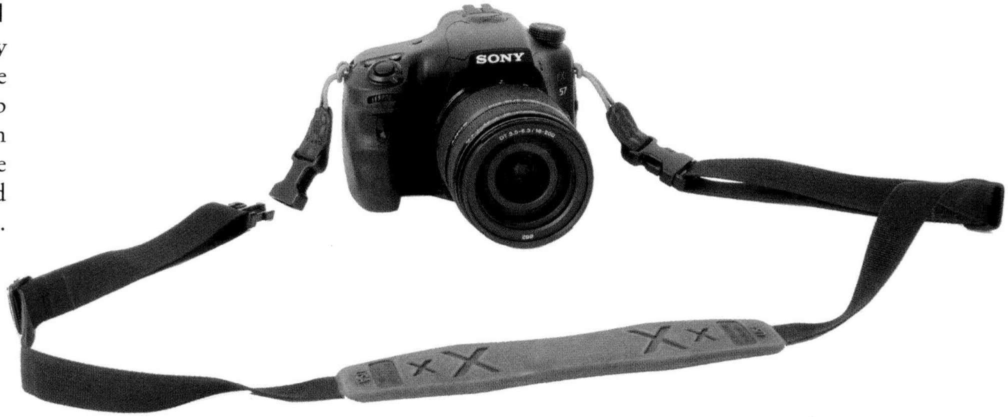

Figure 1.1
Third-party neck straps, like this UPstrap model, are often preferable to the Sony-supplied strap.

- **USB cable.** This is a USB cable that can be used to link your Sony Alpha SLT to a computer, and it is especially useful when you need to transfer pictures but don't have a card reader handy.
- **Application software CD.** The disc contains useful software that will be discussed in more detail in Chapter 10.
- **Printed instruction manuals.** These include a basic instruction manual for the camera and a folded instruction sheet for the lens, if you bought the camera in a kit with the lens. There will also be assorted pamphlets listing accessories, lenses, and warranty and registration information.

Initial Setup

The initial setup of your Sony Alpha SLT is fast and easy. Basically, you just need to charge the battery, attach a lens, and insert a memory card. I'll address each of these steps separately, but if you already feel you can manage these setup tasks without further instructions, feel free to skip this section entirely. You should at least skim its contents, however, because I'm going to list a few options that you might not be aware of.

Battery Included

Your Sony Alpha SLT is a sophisticated hunk of machinery and electronics, but it needs a charged battery to function, so rejuvenating the NP-FM500H lithium-ion battery pack furnished with the camera should be your first step. A fully charged power source should be good for approximately 510 shots under normal temperature conditions, based on standard tests defined by the Camera & Imaging Products Association (CIPA) document DC-002. If most of your pictures use the built-in flash, you can expect somewhat fewer shots before it's time for a recharge. While those figures sound like a lot of shooting, activities like picture review can use up more power than you might expect. If your pictures are important to you, always take along one spare, fully charged battery.

And remember that all rechargeable batteries undergo some degree of self-discharge just sitting idle in the camera or in the original packaging. Lithium-ion power packs of this type typically lose a small amount of their charge every day, even when the camera isn't turned on. Li-ion cells lose their power through a chemical reaction that continues when the camera is switched off. So, it's very likely that the battery purchased with your camera, even if charged at the factory, has begun to poop out after the long sea voyage on a banana boat (or, more likely, a trip by jet plane followed by a sojourn in a warehouse), so you'll want to revive it before going out for some serious shooting.

Charging the Battery

When the battery is inserted into the charger properly (it's impossible to insert it incorrectly), a Charge light begins glowing yellow-orange, without flashing. It continues to glow until the battery completes the charge and the lamp turns off. (See Figure 1.2.) It should take about 175 minutes to completely rejuvenate a fully discharged battery.

If the charging lamp flashes when you insert the battery, that flashing indicates an error condition. Make sure you have the correct model number battery and that the charger's contacts (the shiny metal prongs that connect to the battery) are clean.

When the battery is charged, slide the latch on the bottom of the camera, open the battery door, and ease the battery in with the three contact openings facing down into the compartment so they will meet up with the contacts at the bottom of the compartment (see Figure 1.3). To remove the battery, you must press a blue lever in the battery compartment that prevents the pack from slipping out when the door is opened.

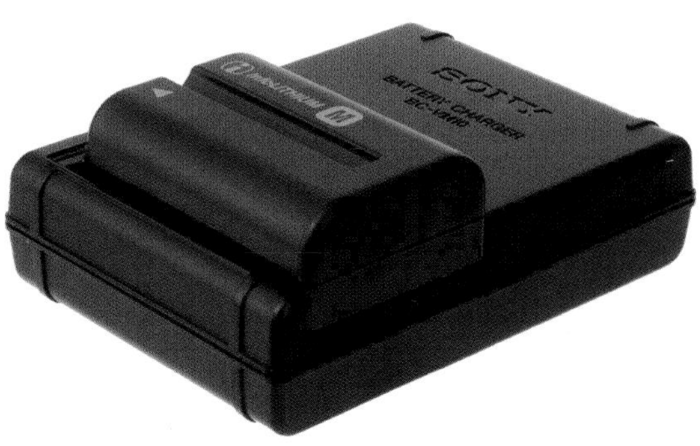

Figure 1.2 The BC-VM10A charger takes about three hours to provide a normal charge to the battery pack.

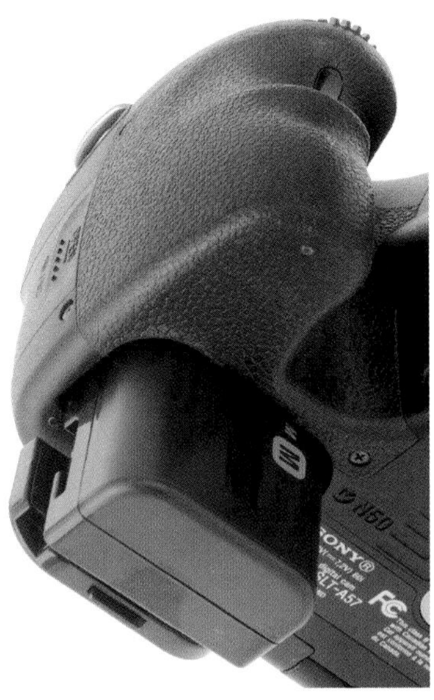

Figure 1.3 Insert the battery in the camera; it only fits one way.

Final Steps

Your Sony Alpha SLT is almost ready to fire up and shoot. You'll need to select and mount a lens, adjust the viewfinder for your vision, and insert a memory card. Each of these steps is easy, and if you've used any Sony camera in the past, you already know exactly what to do. I'm going to provide a little extra detail for those of you who are new to the Sony or digital SLR/SLT worlds.

Mounting the Lens

As you'll see, my recommended lens mounting procedure emphasizes protecting your equipment from accidental damage, and minimizing the intrusion of dust. If your Alpha has no lens attached, select the lens you want to use and loosen (but do not remove) the rear lens cap. I generally place the lens I am planning to mount vertically in a slot in my camera bag, where it's protected from mishaps but ready to pick up quickly. By loosening the rear lens cap, you'll be able to lift it off the back of the lens at the last instant, so the rear element of the lens is covered until then.

After that, remove the body cap by rotating the cap towards the shutter release button. You should always mount the body cap when there is no lens on the camera, because it helps keep dust out of the interior of the camera, where it can settle on the mirror, and potentially find its way past the shutter onto the sensor. (While the Alpha's automatic sensor cleaning mechanism works fine, the less dust it has to contend with, the better.) The body cap also protects the vulnerable mirror from damage caused by intruding objects (including your fingers, if you're not cautious).

Once the body cap has been removed, remove the rear lens cap from the lens, set it aside, and then mount the lens on the camera by matching the red-orange alignment indicator on the lens barrel with the red-orange dot on the camera's lens mount (see Figure 1.4). Rotate the lens clockwise, until the lens seats securely. (Don't press the lens release button during mounting.) If a lens hood is bayoneted on the lens in the reversed position (which makes the lens/hood combination more compact for transport), twist it off and remount with the rim facing outward (see Figure 1.5). A lens hood protects the front of the lens from accidental bumps, and reduces flare caused by extraneous light arriving at the front element of the lens from outside the picture area.

Adjusting Diopter Correction

Those of us with less than perfect eyesight can often benefit from a little optical correction in the viewfinder. Your contact lenses or glasses may provide all the correction you need, but if you are a glasses wearer and want to use the Sony Alpha without your glasses, you can take advantage of the camera's built-in diopter adjustment correction to match that of your glasses or your eyesight with your glasses on. Turn on the camera, look into the electronic viewfinder, focus your eye on the numbers and other indicators on the viewfinder's screen, then rotate the diopter adjustment wheel (see Figure 1.6) while looking into the viewfinder until the numbers and indicators appear sharp.

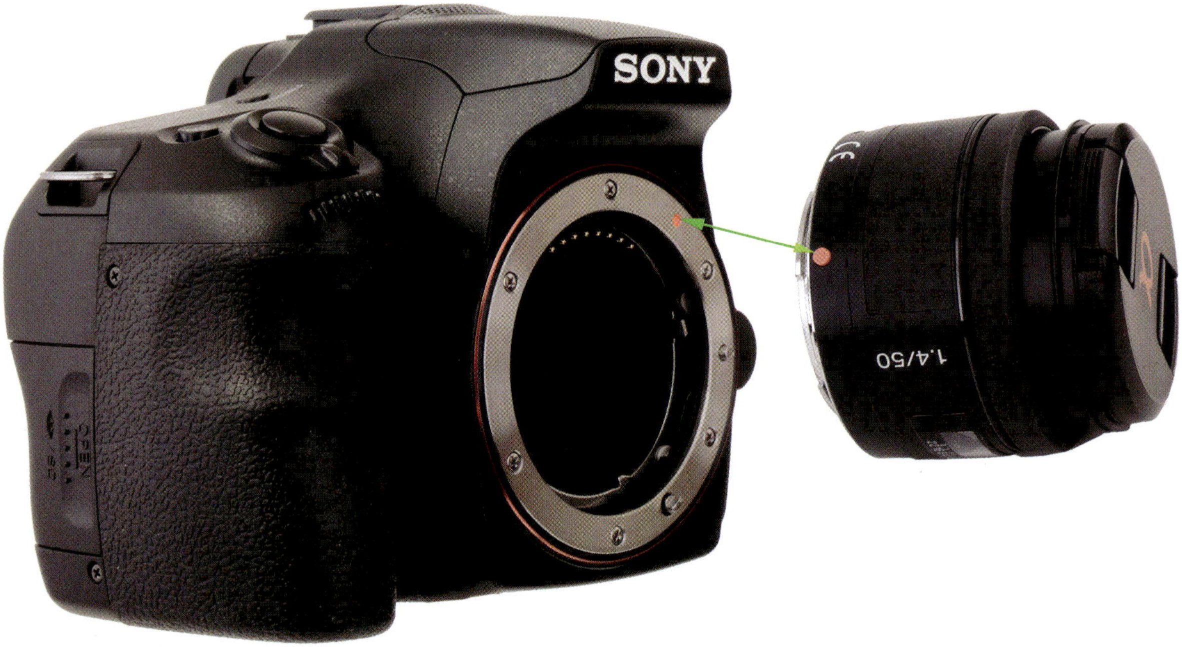

Figure 1.4 Match the red-orange dot on the lens with the red-orange dot on the camera mount to properly align the lens with the bayonet mount.

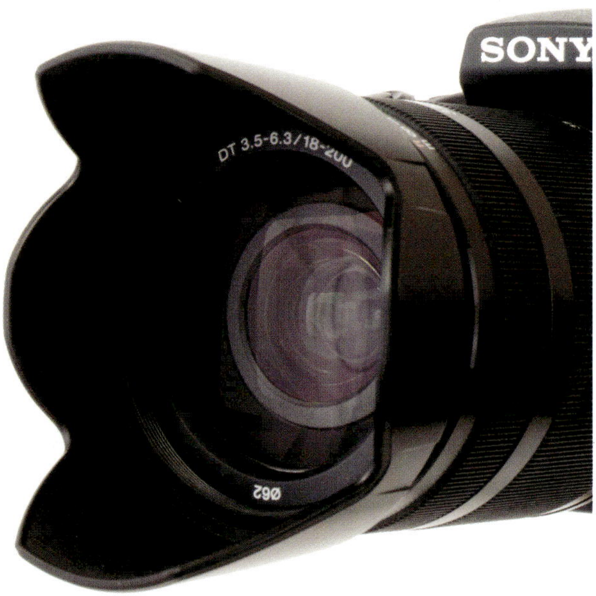

Figure 1.5 A lens hood protects the lens from extraneous light and accidental bumps.

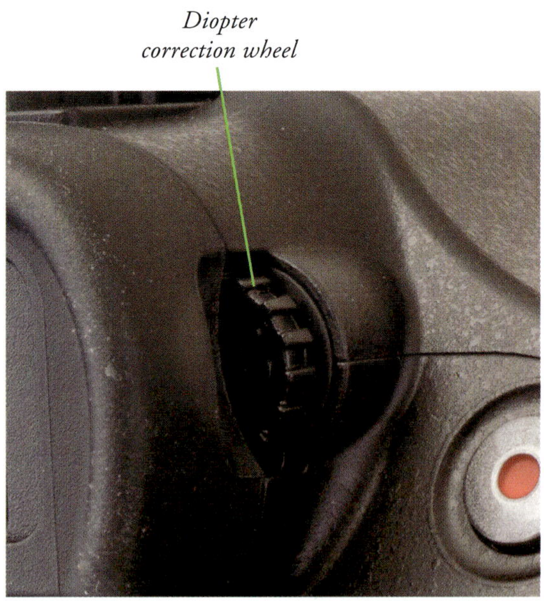

Figure 1.6 Viewfinder diopter correction can be dialed in.

Inserting a Memory Card

You can't take actual photos without a memory card inserted in your Sony Alpha. If you don't have a card installed, the camera will upbraid you with a flashing No Card warning shown at the upper left of the LCD and viewfinder. If you press the shutter button, though, the shutter will operate and it will sound as if a picture has been taken. If you didn't notice the No Card warning, you will be faced with a sad situation when you try to play back the image you thought you had recorded. So, your final step will be to insert a memory card.

The Alpha accepts both Secure Digital (or Secure Digital High Capacity) and Sony Memory Stick PRO Duo (or Memory Stick PRO-HG Duo) cards. It doesn't matter which type you use, but you can only use one or the other; there is only one memory card slot in the camera. If you decide on the Sony Memory Stick option, you probably want a PRO-HG Duo card, which you can get in a capacity of up to 32GB. If you go the Secure Digital (SD) route, there are several options. The standard SD card comes in sizes only up to 2GB. The next step up, the SDHC (high capacity) card, comes in sizes from 4GB to 32GB. If you really want to flex your storage muscles, you can spring for one of the newest types of SD card, called the SDXC, for extended capacity. SDXC cards are currently available in capacities of 48GB, 64GB, and 128GB, which is more than enough for any application, except maybe doing photo IDs for the entire population of a small city. Theoretically, these cards can be made in capacities up to 2TB (terabytes), the equivalent of about 2,000GB.

Nowadays, all new computers should be compatible with SDHC cards. You might need to get a new card reader if you are using a reader more than a year or two old, because the older SD card readers cannot read SDHC cards. If you feel like splurging (which you'll have to do at current prices of at least $200) for an SDXC card, you need to be careful about compatibility, not just with the card reader (you'll likely need a new one), but with your computer. At this writing, SDXC cards can be read by most Macintosh computers and PCs using Windows 7.

Luckily, my computer has an ExpressCard/34 slot to accommodate the reader; many computers don't have that type of slot. Also, I had to download a special driver from Sonnet's website to enable the computer to read the SDXC card, even with that new reader. Once I downloaded the driver, though, the MacBook Pro could read the card even when the images were transferred to the computer through a USB connection to the camera. The message here is to be very careful about computer compatibility before investing in an SDXC card.

Finally, there's one other option you may want to consider for your storage card. The Sony Alpha SLT-A57 provides compatibility with the Eye-Fi card, a special type of SDHC card that includes a tiny transmitter for transferring images directly to your computer over a wireless (Wi-Fi) network. The card works just like any other SDHC card, but, once the camera records an image (or video), the card immediately connects to your network and starts sending the image to your computer; you will see a little window open up on your computer's screen, and the file will be available for editing or viewing within a number of seconds or minutes, depending on its size. This is a terrific technology that can provide a real boost to your productivity if you shoot a lot of images, such as in a studio or laboratory environment.

Whether you ultimately opt for a Memory Stick PRO Duo or a variety of SD card, either type of card fits in the same slot underneath the door on the right side of the camera. You should only remove the memory card when the camera is switched off. Insert the memory card with the label facing the back of the camera (for a Secure Digital card), or toward the front of the camera if inserting a Memory Stick. In either case, the card should be oriented so the edge with the metal contacts goes into the slot first. (See Figure 1.7.)

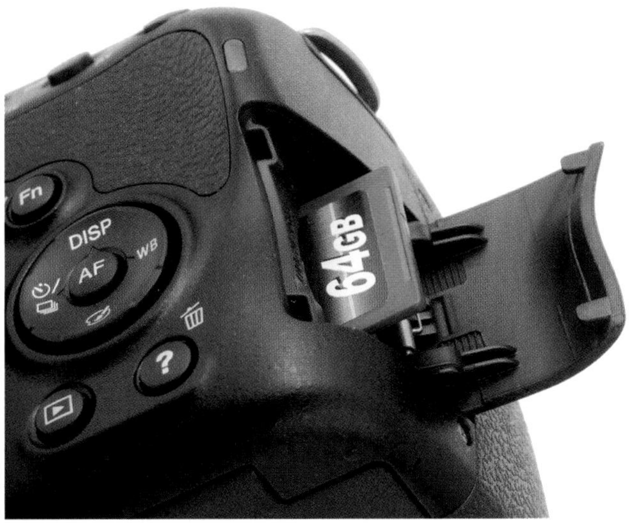

Figure 1.7
The memory card is inserted in the slot on the right side of the camera.

Close the door, and your preflight checklist is done! (I'm going to assume you remember to remove the lens cap when you're ready to take a picture!) When you want to remove the memory card later, just press down on the card edge that protrudes from the slot, and it will pop right out.

Turn on the Power

Slide the On/Off switch that surrounds the shutter release button clockwise, to the On position. The camera will remain on or in a standby mode until you manually turn it off. After one minute of idling, the Alpha goes into the standby mode to save battery power. Just tap the shutter release button to bring it back to life. (The one-minute time is the default; you can adjust this setting through the menu system, as I discuss in Chapter 3.)

When the camera first powers up, you may be asked to set the date and time. The procedure is fairly self-explanatory (although I'll explain it in detail in Chapter 3). You can use the left/right controller keys to navigate among the Daylight Savings Time setting, date, year, time, and date format; and you can use the up/down keys to enter the correct settings. When finished, press the center controller button, choose Enter on the screen that pops up, and press the center controller button again to confirm the date.

TAKING CONTROL

Sony's nomenclature for the Alpha's controls can be confusing. The large pad on the back of the camera is officially called the control button, even though it includes five separate buttons or keys within it. The directional/function keys at the north, south, east, and west positions of this pad are referred to only by triangle icons pointing in the requisite directions. The button in the center of the pad that activates your choices is called the control button (Enter)/AF button. For this book, I've elected to refer to the overall thumbpad as the controller; the "Enter" button will be called the center controller button; and the directional keys will be referred to as the left/right/up/down cursor buttons, or keys, or by their separate functions (DISP, WB, ISO, and drive mode). Oh, and that small wheel on the front of the camera is the control dial.

Once the Sony Alpha is satisfied that it knows what time it is, the recording information display should appear on the LCD, overlaid over the Live View of the scene in front of the camera. Press the DISP button (up cursor button) to produce this screen if you want to activate this display when it has gone dark. There are five versions: a graphic display (Figure 1.8), a standard display (Figure 1.9), a display with just basic information (Figure 1.10), a display showing the digital electronic level (Figure 1.11), and a screen with live histogram (not shown).

When you're looking through the electronic viewfinder instead of at the LCD, the camera presents you with displays that are similar to the LCD displays, but with some differences. For one thing, the display with just basic information is not shown in the viewfinder. For another, the icons showing the settings for items such as flash, white balance, and autofocus mode that appear at the left and right edges of the LCD are not shown in the viewfinder displays, except when the Function menu is activated. (I discuss the Function menu in detail in Chapter 3.) You can switch among the three viewfinder displays and the four LCD displays independently of each other, so you may see different amounts of information in the viewfinder than on the LCD at any given time.

The recording information displays show the basic settings of the camera, including current shutter speed and lens opening, shooting mode, ISO sensitivity, and other parameters. I'll explain these features in more detail in later chapters of this book (especially in Chapter 4, which deals with exposure).

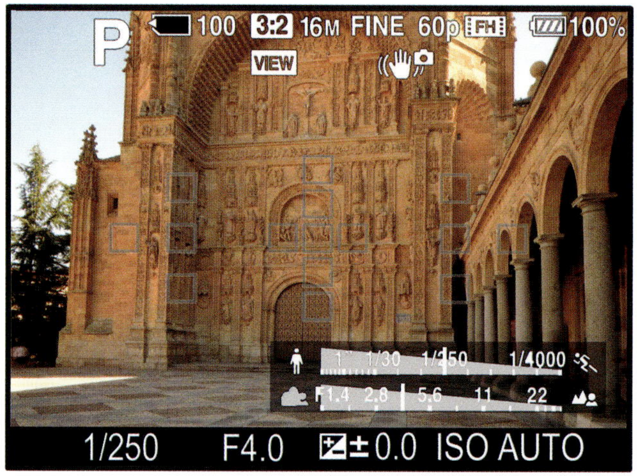

Figure 1.8

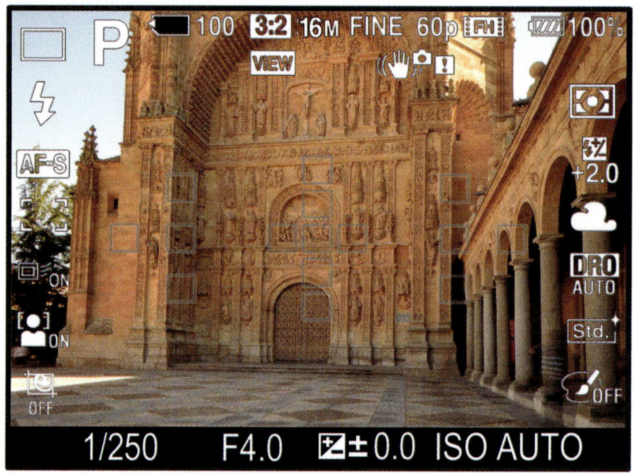

Figure 1.9

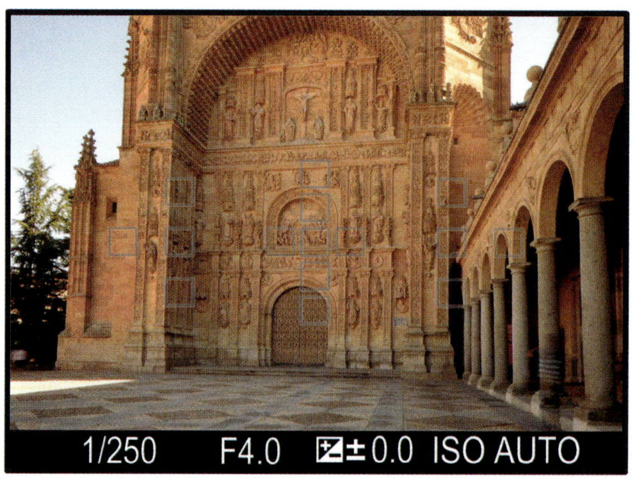

Figure 1.10

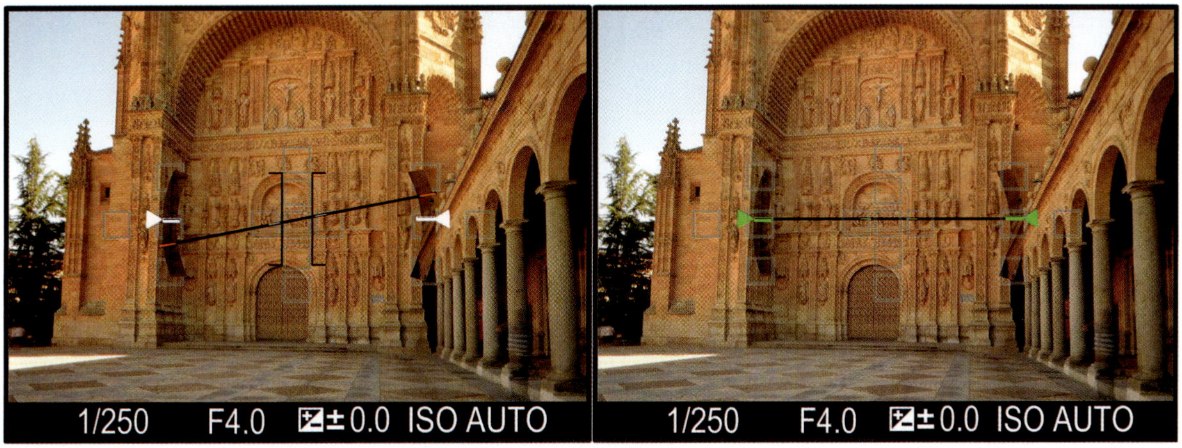

Figure 1.11 In the image on the left, the electronic level shows that the camera is tilted to the right and is leaning forward, by the outer and inner brown indicators. In the image on the right, the green indicators show that the camera is level in both directions.

Formatting a Memory Card

There are three ways to create a blank Secure Digital or Memory Stick PRO Duo card for your Sony Alpha, and two of them are at least partially wrong. Here are your options, both correct and incorrect:

- **Transfer (move) files to your computer.** When you transfer (rather than copy) all the image files to your computer from the memory card (either using a direct cable transfer or with a card reader and appropriate software, as described later in this chapter), the old image files can, at your option, be erased from the card, leaving the card blank. Theoretically. Unfortunately, this method does *not* remove files that you've labeled as Protected (by choosing Protect from the Playback menu during playback), nor does it identify and lock out parts of your card that have become corrupted or unusable since the last time you formatted the card. Therefore, I recommend always formatting the card, rather than simply moving the image files, each time you want to make a blank card. The only exception is when you *want* to leave the protected/unerased images on the card for a while longer, say, to share with friends, family, and colleagues.
- **(Don't) Format in your computer.** With the memory card inserted in a card reader or card slot in your computer, you can use Windows or Mac OS to reformat the memory card. Don't! The operating system won't necessarily arrange the structure of the card the way the Alpha likes to see it (in computer terms, an incorrect *file system* may be installed). The only way to ensure that the card has been properly formatted for your camera is to perform the format in the camera itself. The only exception to this rule is when you have a seriously corrupted memory card that your

camera refuses to format. Sometimes it is possible to revive such a corrupted card by allowing the operating system to reformat it first, then trying again in the camera.

- **Playback menu format.** To use the recommended method to format a memory card, press the MENU button, and use the left/right buttons of the controller pad to choose the Memory Card Tool menu (which is represented by the memory card icon). The Format entry, which is the top line of this menu, should already be highlighted. Press the center controller button, and select Enter from the screen that appears. Press the center controller button once more to begin the format process.

HOW MANY SHOTS?

The Sony Alpha SLT provides a fairly accurate estimate of the number of shots remaining on the LCD. It is only an estimate, because the actual number will vary, depending on the capacity of your memory card, the file format(s) you've selected (more on those later), the aspect ratio (proportions) of the image (the Alpha can use both traditional 3:2 proportions and 16:9—HDTV—aspect ratios), and the content of the image itself. (Some photos may contain large areas that can be more efficiently squeezed down to a smaller size.)

Table 1.1 shows the typical number of shots you can expect using a good-sized 16GB SD memory card (which I expect will be a popular size card among Alpha SLT users as prices continue to plummet during the life of this book). Take those numbers and double them if you're using a 32GB card; cut them in half if you're using an 8GB SD card; and multiply by 25 percent if you're using a lowly 4GB card.

Table 1.1 Typical Shots with a 16GB Memory Card

	3:2 Aspect Ratio			16:9 Aspect Ratio		
	Large	Medium	Small	Large	Medium	Small
JPEG Standard	2,868	4,277	5,669	3,186	4,599	5,946
JPEG Fine	1,735	3,105	4,473	1,974	3,409	4,827
RAW	627	N/A	N/A	623	N/A	N/A
RAW+JPEG	460	N/A	N/A	473	N/A	N/A

Selecting a Shooting Mode

You can choose a shooting method from the mode dial located on the top left of the Sony Alpha SLT (see Figure 1.12). There are eight special shooting modes (including two Auto modes), in some of which the camera makes many or most of the decisions for you (apart from when to press the shutter), and four semi-automatic and manual modes, which allow you to provide the maximum input over the exposure and settings the camera uses. You'll find a complete description of the special, automatic, and semi-automatic and manual modes in Chapter 4.

Turn your camera on by flipping the power switch to ON. Next, you need to select which shooting mode to use. If you're very new to digital photography, you might want to set the camera to an automatic mode (either the Auto or the Auto+ setting on the mode dial) or the P (Program mode) setting and start snapping away. Any of these modes will make all the appropriate settings for you for many shooting situations. If you have a specific type of picture you want to shoot, you can turn the mode dial to one of several specialized settings that suit various types of photographic situations. For specific types of subject matter, you may want to turn the mode dial to the SCN setting and try out one of the scene types by scrolling down the list of options using the front dial or the down button, as shown in Figure 1.13. You can also browse the scene types

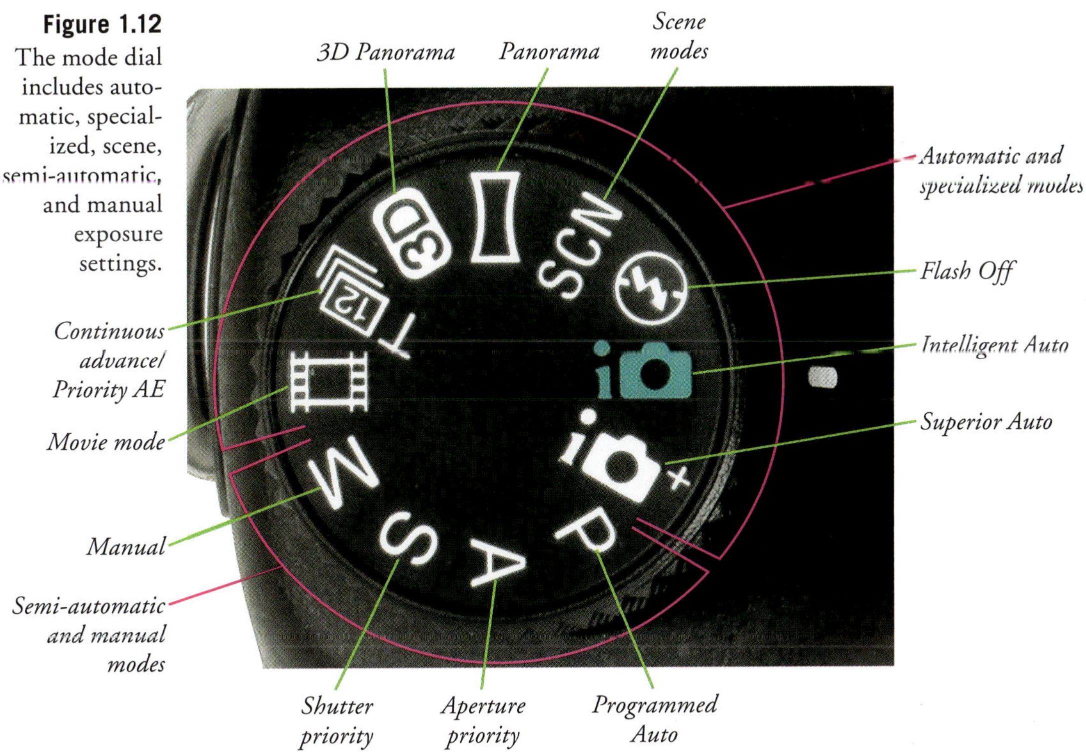

Figure 1.12 The mode dial includes automatic, specialized, scene, semi-automatic, and manual exposure settings.

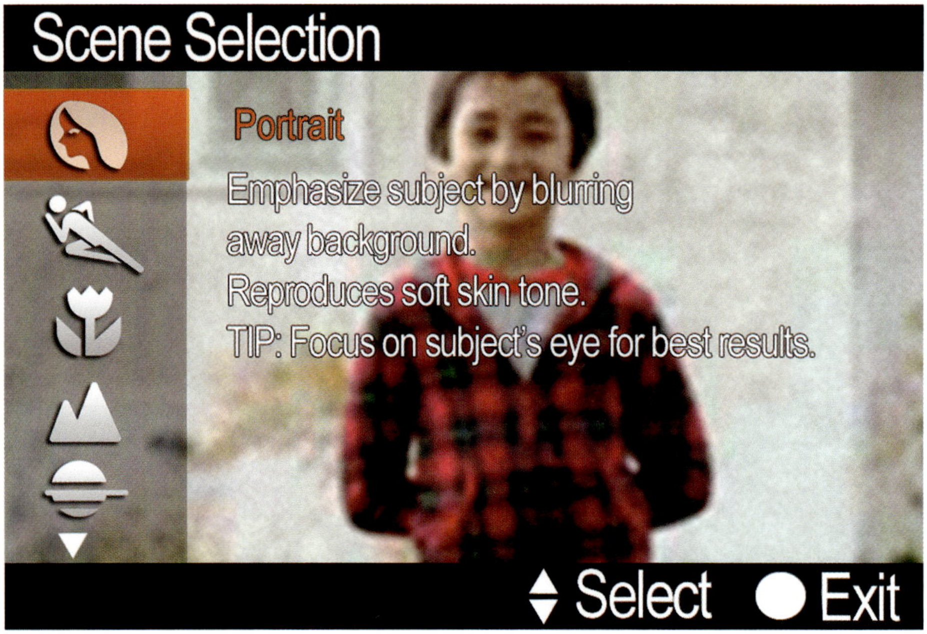

Figure 1.13
The Scene mode types appear on the screen when you turn the mode dial to the SCN setting. You can choose one of these settings to fit the particular type of subject you are trying to photograph. Shown here, top to bottom, are Portrait, Sports Action, Macro, Landscape, and Sunset; not shown are Night View, Hand-held twilight, and Night Portrait.

with this camera by setting the mode dial to SCN, pressing the FN button and highlighting the scene selection then scrolling the list using the control dial or the down button.

- **Movie.** Choose this mode when you want to shoot video clips.
- **Continuous Advance Priority AE.** This shooting mode, the last of the automatic or specialized modes, is marked on the mode dial by the letter T and a stack of rectangles containing the number 12, indicating the maximum number of continuous shots per second that the camera will take in this mode. The camera initially sets itself to optimize continuous shooting by choosing a high ISO setting and other options, but you can change most of the settings if you want to, as I'll discuss later.
- **Sweep Shooting.** When you turn the dial to this next setting, marked by the icon of a stretched rectangle, the camera presents a brief menu at the left side of the screen or viewfinder with two options for shooting in-camera panoramas. The two choices are discussed below.
  - **3D Sweep Panorama.** With this setting, which is a subset of the Sweep Panorama mode, the camera takes a sweeping panorama that can be displayed in 3D on a compatible 3D Sony (naturally) HDTV. You can also convert the camera's 3D images to a format that can be printed out or viewed on a computer screen or non-3D TV using ordinary red/blue 3D glasses. I'll explain how to do that in Chapter 4.

- **Sweep Panorama.** This special mode lets you "sweep" the camera across a scene that is too wide for a single image. The camera takes multiple pictures and combines them in the camera into a single, wide panoramic final product.

- **SCN.** When you turn the mode dial to this setting, the left side of the LCD (or viewfinder) presents you with a menu of scene types to select from. Scroll through this list using the control dial or the direction buttons to choose from among the eight options listed below. If the camera is already set to SCN mode, press the Fn button on the back of the camera to activate the Function menu, then highlight the scene selection icon at the upper left of the screen, press the center controller button, and scroll through the choices to select a different scene type.
  - **Portrait.** Use this mode when you're taking a portrait of a subject positioned relatively close to the camera and want to de-emphasize the background, maximize sharpness of the subject, and produce flattering skin tones.
  - **Sports Action.** Use this mode to freeze fast-moving subjects. The camera uses a fast shutter speed and shoots continuously while you hold down the shutter button, to capture the action as it unfolds.
  - **Macro.** This mode is helpful when you are shooting close-up pictures of a subject from about one foot away or less.
  - **Landscape.** Select this mode when you want extra sharpness and rich colors of distant scenes.
  - **Sunset.** This is a great mode to accentuate the reddish hues of a sunrise or sunset.
  - **Night Scene.** This mode is suited for nighttime scenes at a distance, such as city skylines. The camera will use a slow shutter speed and will not fire the flash, so it is a good idea to use a tripod to avoid blur from camera movement during the exposure.
  - **Hand-held Twilight.** Use this mode for night scenes when it's not practical to use a tripod. The camera sets itself to use a higher ISO (light sensitivity) setting so that it can use a faster shutter speed. It takes a continuous burst of several images, then processes them together internally into a single image that removes the visual "noise" that can result from high ISO settings.
  - **Night Portrait.** Choose this mode when you want to illuminate a subject in the foreground with flash, but still allow the background to be exposed properly by the available light. Be prepared to use a tripod or to rely on the SteadyShot feature to reduce the effects of camera shake. (You'll find more about image stabilization and camera shake in Chapter 8.) If there is no foreground subject that needs to be illuminated, you may do better by using the Night View mode.

- **Flash Off.** This is the mode to use in museums and other locations where the use of flash is forbidden or inappropriate. It otherwise operates exactly like the Auto setting but disables the pop-up internal flash.
- **Auto.** In this mode, the Alpha makes all the exposure decisions for you, and will pop up the flash if necessary under low-light conditions.
- **Auto+.** In this mode, the Alpha makes all the exposure decisions for you, and will pop up the flash if necessary under low-light conditions. In addition, it will use its programming to select certain additional functions as indicated by the shooting conditions. In particular, in certain situations the camera will take multiple shots and then combine them internally in order to achieve an improved final image. Using these techniques, the camera attempts to recognize certain Scene types: Night View, Hand-held Twilight, Landscape, Backlight Portrait, Portrait, Tripod Night View, Backlight, Macro, and Night Portrait.

If you have more photographic experience, you might want to opt for one of the semi-automatic or manual modes, also shown in Figure 1.12. These, too, are described in more detail in Chapter 4. These modes let you apply a little more creativity to your camera's settings. These modes are indicated on the mode dial by the letters P, A, S, and M:

- **P (Program auto).** This mode allows the Alpha to select the basic exposure settings, but you can still override the camera's other choices to fine-tune your image.
- **A (Aperture priority).** Choose this mode when you want to use a particular lens opening, especially to control sharpness, isolate a background using a wide lens opening, or to manage how much of your image is in focus. The Alpha will select the appropriate shutter speed for you.
- **S (Shutter priority).** This mode is useful when you want to use a particular shutter speed to stop action or produce creative blur effects. The Alpha will select the appropriate f/stop for you.
- **M (Manual).** Select this mode when you want full control over the shutter speed and lens opening, either for creative effects or because you are using a studio flash or other flash unit not compatible with the Alpha's automatic flash metering. In Manual mode, the camera will still display a suggested exposure.

Choosing a Metering Mode

You might want to select a particular metering mode for your first shots, although the default Multi segment metering (which is set automatically when you choose a Scene mode) is probably the best choice as you get to know your camera. To change metering modes (you must not be using one of the Auto or SCN modes), press the Fn button (located on the back of the camera to the right of the LCD) and, using the controller's

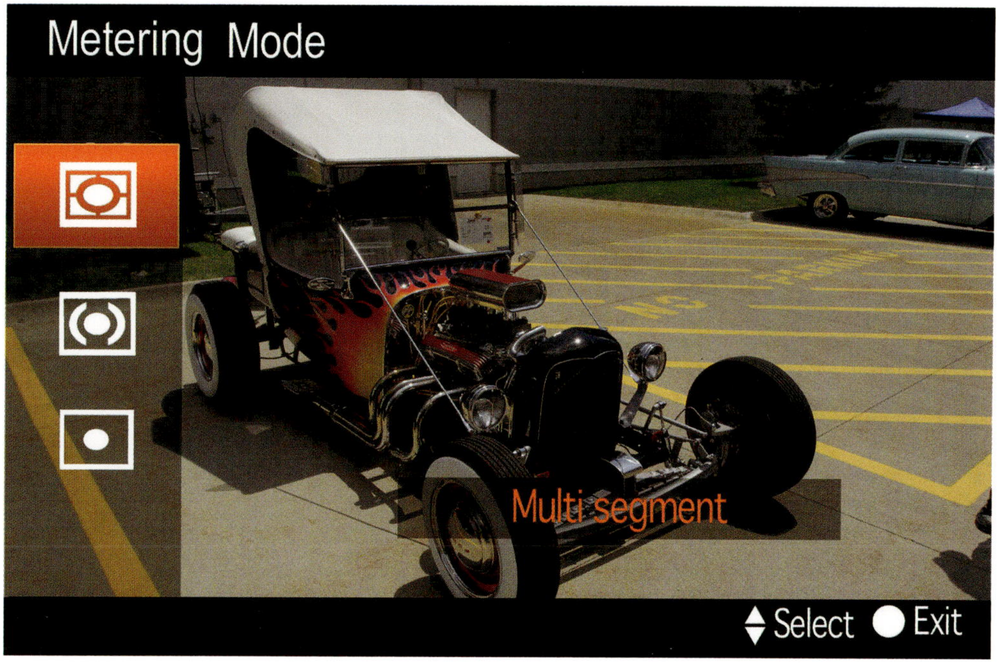

Figure 1.14
Metering modes (top to bottom): Multi segment, Center weighted, and Spot.

up/down and left/right buttons, navigate to the right side of the screen and select Metering Mode from the Function menu by pressing the center controller button while that icon is highlighted. Then, use the up/down keys or turn the control dial, and select one of the three modes described below. Press the center controller button or press halfway down on the shutter button to confirm your choice. The three metering options are shown in Figure 1.14:

- **Multi segment metering.** The standard metering mode, and the only choice available in Auto or Scene modes; the Alpha attempts to intelligently classify your image and choose the best exposure based on readings from 1,200 different zones in the frame. You can read about these zones in Chapter 4.
- **Center weighted metering.** The Alpha meters the entire scene, but gives the most emphasis to the central area of the frame.
- **Spot metering.** Exposure is calculated from a smaller central spot.

You'll find a detailed description of each of these modes in Chapter 4.

Choosing a Focus Mode

You can easily switch between automatic and manual focus by moving the AF/MF switch on the lens mounted on your camera. (If the lens doesn't have this switch, then you need to use the switch on the camera.) However, if you set this switch to AF, you'll still need to choose an appropriate focus mode on the camera, as discussed below.

(You can read more on selecting focus parameters in Chapter 5.) If you're using a Scene, Auto, or Panorama shooting mode, the focus method is set for you automatically, and the AF mode selection will be grayed out and unavailable for selection.

To set the camera's autofocus mode, press the Fn button and navigate with the controller buttons to Autofocus mode on the left side of the Function menu. Then select the mode you want from the screen that pops up (see Figure 1.15) using the up/down controller keys or the control dial. Press the center controller button to confirm your selection. The three choices are as follows:

- **Single-shot (AF-S).** This mode, sometimes called *single autofocus,* locks in a focus point when the shutter button is pressed down halfway, and the green focus confirmation circle glows in the viewfinder or on the LCD. The focus will remain locked until you release the shutter button or take the picture. If the camera is unable to achieve sharp focus, the focus confirmation light will blink. This mode is best when your subject is relatively motionless.
- **Automatic AF (AF-A).** In this mode, the Alpha switches between Single-shot and Continuous AF as appropriate. That is, it locks in a focus point when you partially depress the shutter button (Single-shot mode), but switches automatically to Continuous AF if the subject begins to move. This mode is handy when photographing a subject, such as a child at quiet play, who might move unexpectedly.

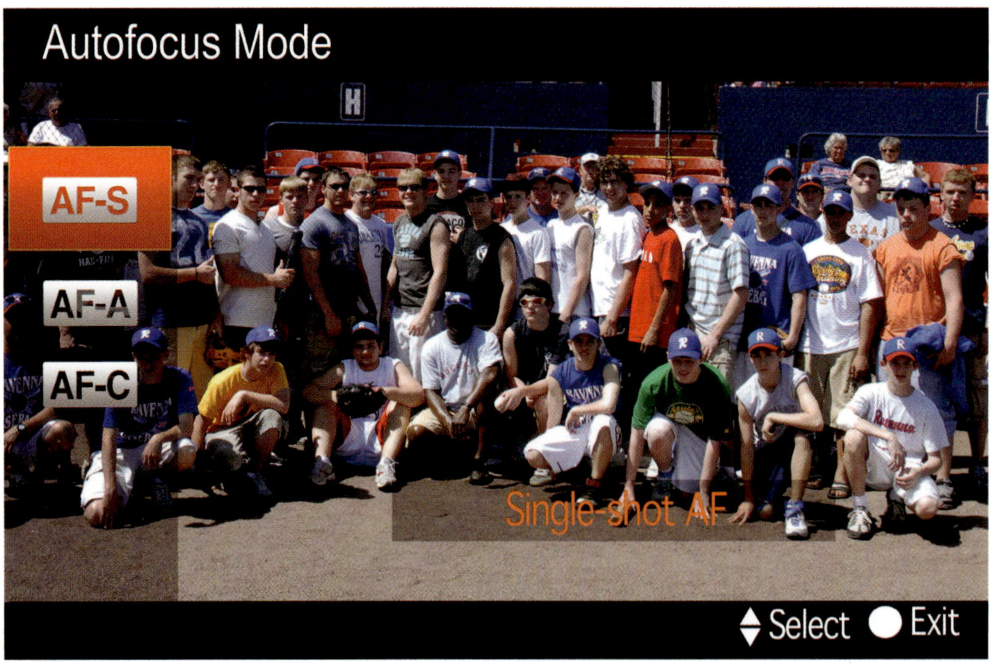

Figure 1.15
Set Autofocus mode from the Function menu. The choices from top to bottom are Single-shot AF, Automatic AF, and Continuous AF.

- **Continuous AF (AF-C).** This mode, sometimes called *continuous servo,* sets focus when you partially depress the shutter button, but continues to monitor the frame and refocuses if the camera or subject is moved. This is a useful mode for photographing sports and moving subjects.

Selecting a Focus Point

The Sony Alpha SLT uses 15 different focus points to calculate correct focus. In the Auto and SCN modes, as well as the Sweep Panorama mode, or when the Smile Shutter is activated, the focus point is selected automatically by the camera. In the semi-automatic and manual modes, you can allow the camera to select the focus point automatically, or you can specify which focus point should be used.

You make your decision about how the focus point is chosen by setting the AF area through the Function menu. There are four AF area options, shown in Figure 1.16, and also described in Chapter 5. Press the Fn button, navigate to the AF area selection on the left side of the screen, press the center controller button, and select one of these four choices. Press the center controller button again to confirm.

- **Wide.** The Alpha chooses the appropriate focus zone from the 15 AF areas on the screen.

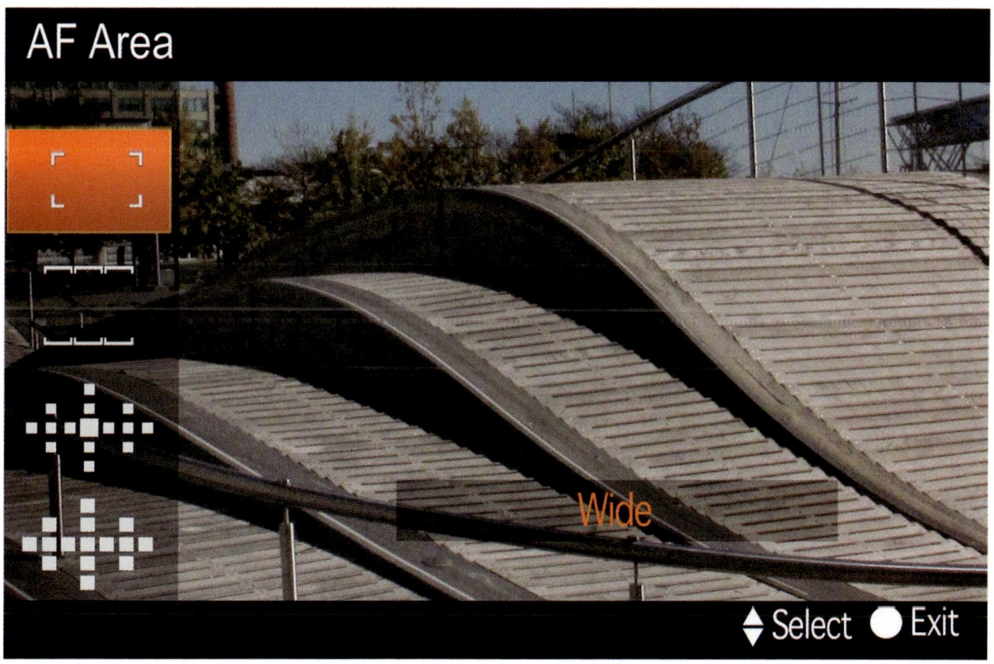

Figure 1.16 Select from Wide (the Alpha selects one of the 15 AF areas); Zone (the Alpha chooses which AF area from left, center, or right zones); Spot (only the center focus spot is used); or Local (you can choose which of the 15 areas to use).

- **Zone.** Choose from the left, center, or right zones (represented by the three clusters of boxes shown in the viewfinder/LCD). The camera will select which of the four AF areas in the left or right zones, or which of the seven AF areas in the center zone will be used. When shooting, press the center controller/AF button and use the left/right directional buttons to choose the zone to be used.
- **Spot.** The Alpha always uses the center, cross-type focus zone (as described in Chapter 5) to calculate correct focus.
- **Local.** Use the controller's direction buttons or the control dial to move the focus zone to any single position among the 15 focus zones, and press the center controller button or press the shutter button halfway to exit to the shooting screen. If you want to return to the screen to move the focus point, press the center controller/AF button to bring the selection screen back, and move the focus point as before. I'll discuss this topic again in Chapter 5, where I explain your focus options in more detail.

Other Settings

There are a few other settings you can make if you're feeling ambitious, but don't feel bad if you postpone using these features until you've racked up a little more experience with your Sony Alpha.

Adjusting White Balance and ISO

If you like, you can custom-tailor your white balance (color balance) and ISO sensitivity settings, as long as you're not using one of the Auto or SCN shooting modes. In the Sweep Panorama modes, you can adjust white balance but not ISO. To start out, it's best to set white balance (WB) to Auto, and ISO to ISO 200 for daylight photos, and to ISO 400 for pictures in dimmer light. White balance and ISO both have direct-setting buttons located on the controller panel. Or, if you prefer, you can get access to both settings by pressing the Fn button and navigating to these settings on the Function menu.

Using the Self-Timer

If you want to set a short delay before your picture is taken, you can use the self-timer. Press the drive button (which doubles as the left cursor button on the back of the camera), and use the up/down cursor buttons or the control dial to highlight the self-timer icon, then press the left/right cursor buttons to select from either the 10-second or 2-second self-timer. Press the center controller button to confirm your choice (see Figure 1.17) and a self-timer icon will appear on the recording information display on

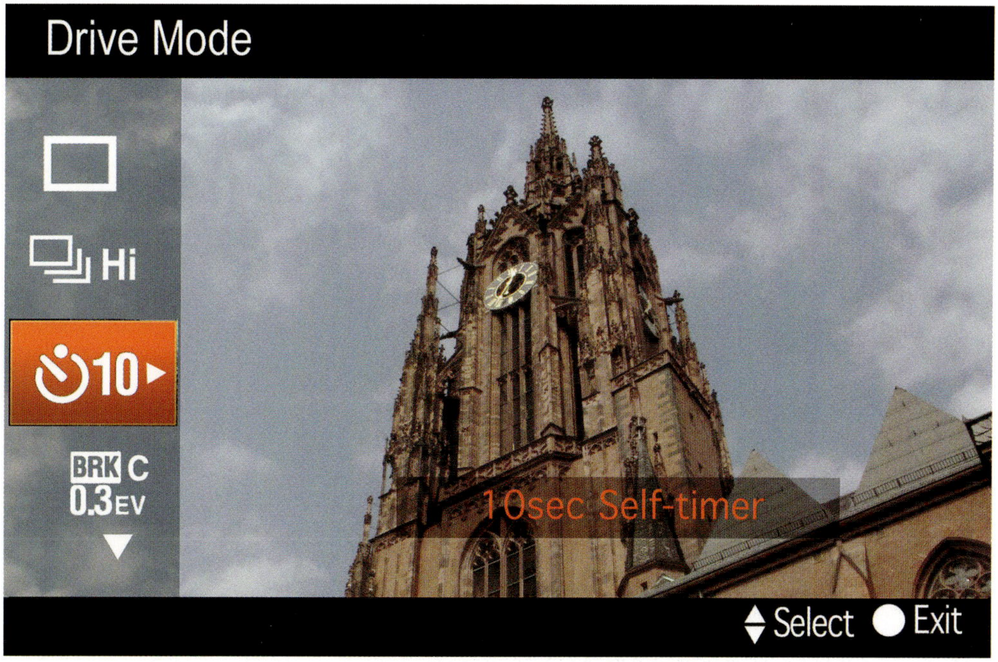

Figure 1.17 The Drive modes include (top to bottom) Single-shot, Continuous, Self-timer, and Exposure Bracketing. The White Balance Bracketing and Remote Commander options are not shown.

the back of the Sony Alpha. (It won't appear in the viewfinder.) Press the shutter release to lock focus and exposure and start the timer. The red self-timer lamp in the hand grip will flash and the beeper will count down (unless you've silenced it in the menus) until the final two seconds (in 10-second mode), when the lamp stays lit and the beeper beeps more rapidly. In the 2-second mode, the lamp stays lit and the beeper sounds off rapidly for the entire time.

In addition to the Self-timer, Continuous shooting, and Single-shot choices in the Drive menu, there are also bracketing and infrared remote control options (not shown in the figure).

Using the Alpha SLT's Flash

Working with the SLT-A57's built-in flash unit deserves a chapter of its own, and I'm providing one. (See Chapter 9.) But the SLT's flash is easy enough to work with that you can begin using it right away, either to provide the main lighting of a scene or as supplementary illumination to fill in the shadows. (See Figure 1.18.) The camera will automatically balance the amount of light emitted from the flash so that it illuminates the shadows nicely, without overwhelming the highlights and producing a glaring "flash" look. (Think *Baywatch* when they're using too many reflectors on the lifeguards!)

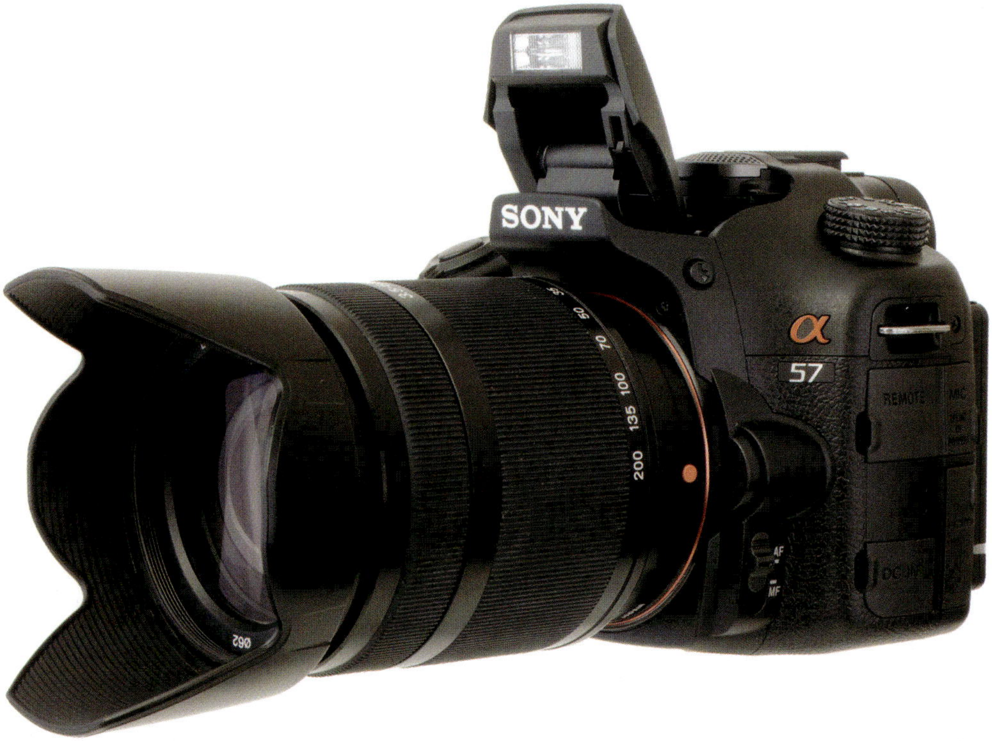

Figure 1.18
The Alpha SLT-A57 has a built-in flash unit that pops up automatically or on your command when it is needed to provide extra illumination for a scene.

Your options for using the flash depend on what shooting mode the camera is set to. For example, in the two Auto modes, the SCN modes, and the Sweep Panorama modes, the camera decides whether or not to pop up the flash, and you can't pop it up even if you press the round Flash button on the side of the camera below the flash unit. If the camera's programming determines that flash is needed, it will pop up the unit. Once it is popped up though, you will have some options for controlling it, by pressing the Fn key and selecting Flash Control from the Function menu. You can choose to leave the flash on its initial setting of Autoflash, to force it off, or to force it on, for fill flash. (In the Flash Off shooting mode, not surprisingly, the camera will not pop up the flash unit and neither can you.)

In the other shooting modes—P, A, S, M, and Continuous Advance Priority AE—you have more control over the built-in flash. The camera will not use it unless you manually pop it up by pressing the Flash button. Once it is popped up, you can use the Flash Control item on the Function menu to select from various flash options available to choose: Forced on (Fill-flash), Slow Sync, and Rear Sync, which I'll explain in Chapter 9. In those shooting modes, you don't have the Forced off or Auto-flash options available. You also have one other setting available—Wireless, which enables you to fire a remote flash unit using the SLT's flash as the controller.

You can read about all of the above settings, as well as flash exposure compensation, red-eye reduction options, and other flash features in Chapter 9.

An Introduction to Movie Making

I'm going to talk in more detail about your movie-making options with the SLT-A57 in Chapter 7. For now, though, I'll give you enough information to get started, in case a cinematic subject wanders into your field of view before you get to that chapter.

The SLT cameras have advanced motion-picture capabilities, including the ability to produce excellent quality high-definition (HD) movies. You can adjust several shooting settings, including exposure compensation, white balance, AF area, and others. The SLT cameras also provide a breakthrough ability in that they can continuously autofocus on your scene using Phase Detection focusing with Live View. No other camera in this class has had this ability, which greatly enhances the sharpness and quality of your video footage.

You get access to the settings for the movie file formats through the Recording menu in the main menu system. For now, just press the MENU button at the left of the camera's top, make sure the movie menu list at the left is highlighted (it has a "film" icon), and, using the control dial or the down direction button, scroll down to highlight the File Format line. Make sure the AVCHD/60i/60p option is selected. If it isn't, use the direction buttons and the center controller button to scroll to that option and highlight it, then exit from the menu by pressing the MENU button again.

Now let's just make a basic movie. With the camera turned on in any shooting mode, aim at your subject and locate the red Movie button just to the right of the viewfinder, angled toward the back of the camera. Press that button once to start the recording, and again to stop it; don't hold down the button. You can record for up to about 29 minutes consecutively if you have sufficient storage space on your memory card and charge in your battery, if you have the SteadyShot image stabilizing system turned off. If SteadyShot is turned on, the continuous-shooting limit is about 9 minutes for the SLT-A57.

The camera will adjust the focus and exposure automatically, and you can zoom while recording, if you have a zoom lens attached to the camera. When the movie has been recorded, you can press the Play button on the back of the camera to view it immediately. (To play a movie after you have taken some still photos, so the movie is not the latest item available to play, you need to use the index screen; see the last bullet of the section below on "Reviewing the Images You've Taken" for that procedure.) While a movie is playing, the buttons on the control wheel act like VCR buttons, as follows:

- **Pause/Resume.** Press the center controller button.
- **Fast-forward.** Press the right direction button while the movie is playing.

- **Fast-reverse.** Press the left direction button while the movie is playing.
- **Slow-forward.** Turn the control dial to the right while the movie is paused.
- **Fast-reverse.** Press the control dial to the left while the movie is paused.
- **Adjust sound volume.** Press the bottom direction button to bring up the volume control on the screen, then raise or lower the volume by using the top and bottom buttons or by turning the control dial.
- **Turn recording information on or off.** Press the DISP button (up cursor button).

Reviewing the Images You've Taken

The Sony Alpha SLT-A57 has a broad range of playback and image review options. Here is all you really need to know at this time, as shown in Figure 1.19:

- Press the Playback button (the bottom button immediately to the lower right of the LCD, marked with a hard-to-see dark blue right-pointing triangle) to display the most recent image on the LCD.
- Press the left cursor button, or scroll the control dial on the front of the camera to the left, to view a previous image.
- Press the right cursor button, or scroll the control dial to the right, to view the next image.
- Press the Trash button to delete the currently displayed image.
- Press the Fn button, followed by the center controller button, to rotate the image 90 degrees. Successive presses of the center button rotate it 90 degrees each time. (You won't likely need this feature unless you have disabled automatic rotation, which causes the camera to display your vertically oriented pictures already rotated. I'll explain how to activate/deactivate automatic rotation in Chapter 3.)
- Press the Zoom In/AEL and Zoom Out/Index buttons at the top of the camera's back to select zoomed and full-screen views. Press either button repeatedly to change the zoom level. You can press the Playback button to resume normal viewing quickly.
- Rotate the control dial located on the front of the camera to display a different image at the same zoom level.
- Use the left/right/up/down keys to scroll around within a magnified image. An inset box shows the relationship of the magnified image to the entire frame.

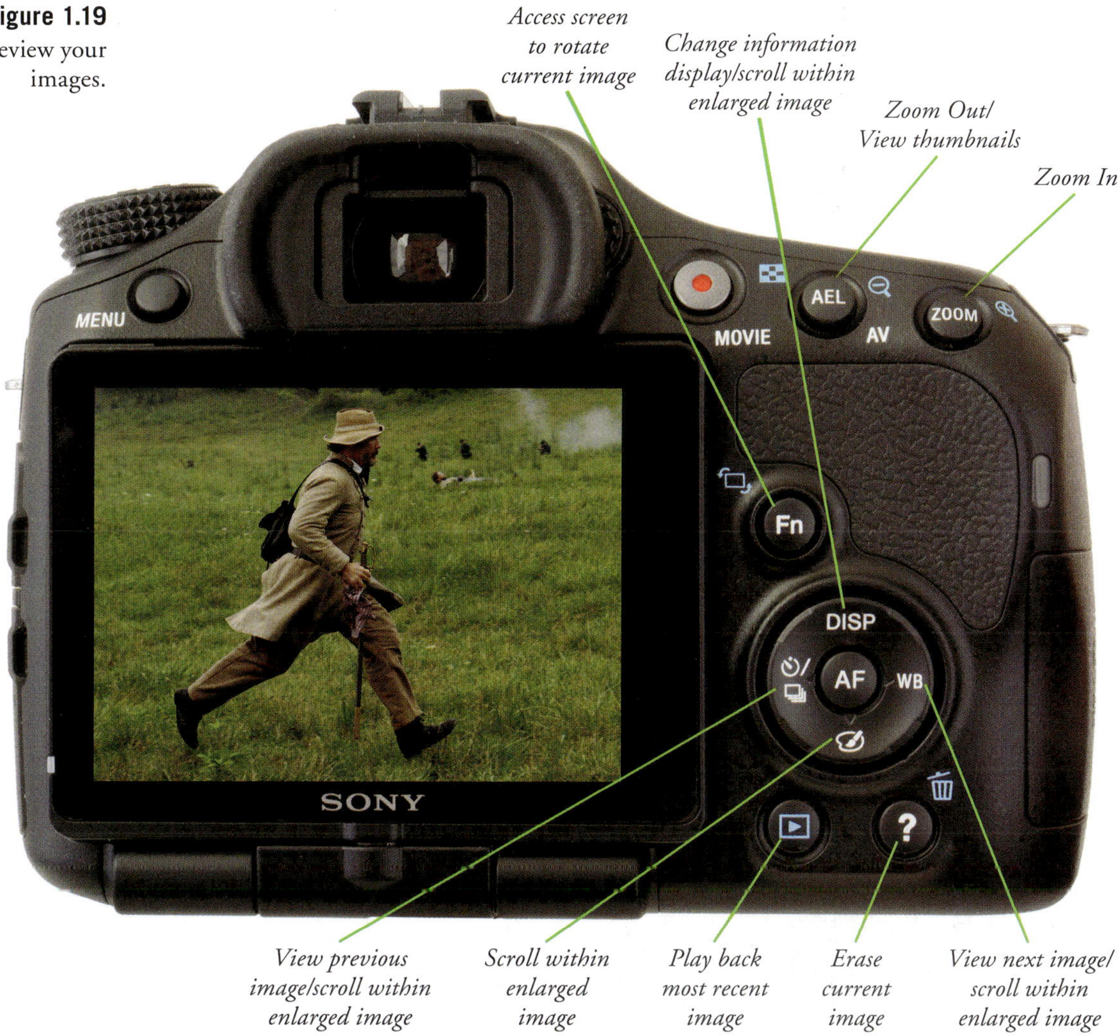

Figure 1.19 Review your images.

- Press the DISP button repeatedly to cycle among views that have no recording data, full recording data (f/stop, shutter speed, image quality/size, etc.), and a thumbnail image with histogram display. (I'll explain all these in Chapter 2.)
- Press the Zoom Out/Index button to display an index screen showing 4 or 9 thumbnail images. (You can select 4 or 9 images using the Playback menu, as I'll discuss in Chapter 3.) Press the AV button again to return to the single-image display.

You'll find more information on viewing thumbnail indexes of images and other image review functions in Chapter 2.

Transferring Photos to Your Computer

The final step in your picture-taking session will be to transfer the photos you've taken to your computer for printing, further review, or image editing. (You can also take your memory card to a retailer for printing if you don't want to go the do-it-yourself route.) Your Alpha allows you to print directly to PictBridge-compatible printers and to create print orders right in the camera, plus you can select which images to transfer to your computer. I'll outline those options in Chapter 10.

For now, you'll probably want to transfer your images by either using a cable transfer from the camera to the computer or removing the memory card from the Alpha and transferring the images with a card reader (shown in Figure 1.20). The latter option is usually the best, because it's usually much faster and doesn't deplete the battery of your camera. However, you can use a cable transfer when you have the cable and a computer but no card reader (perhaps you're using the computer of a friend or colleague, or you're at an Internet café).

To transfer images from a memory card to the computer using a card reader:

1. Turn off the camera.
2. Slide open the memory card door, and press on the card, which causes it to pop up so it can be removed from the slot.
3. Insert the memory card into a memory card reader that is plugged into your computer. Your installed software detects the files on the card and offers to transfer them. (You'll find descriptions of your transfer software options in Chapter 10.) The card can also appear as a mass storage device on your desktop, which you can open and then drag and drop the files to your computer.

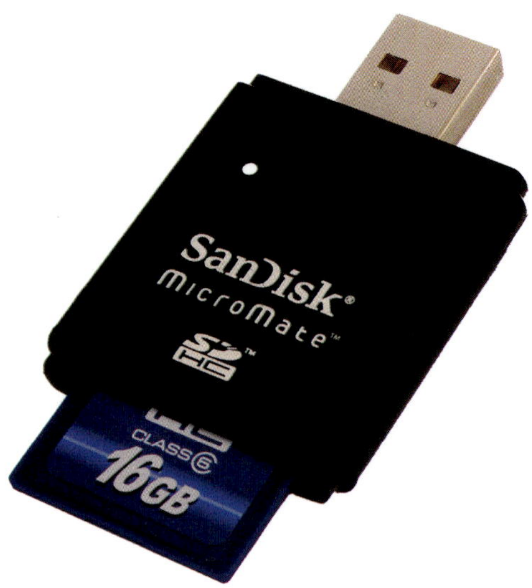

Figure 1.20
A card reader is the fastest way to transfer photos.

To transfer images from the camera to a Mac or PC computer using the USB cable:

1. Turn off the camera.
2. Open the port door on the left side of the camera and plug the USB cable furnished with the camera into the USB port, the lower of the two openings inside that door. (See Figure 1.21.)
3. Connect the other end of the USB cable to a USB port on your computer.
4. Turn on the camera. Your installed software usually detects the camera and offers to transfer the pictures, or the camera appears on your desktop as a mass storage device, enabling you to drag and drop the files to your computer. I'll cover using the Sony Alpha's bundled software to transfer images in Chapter 10.

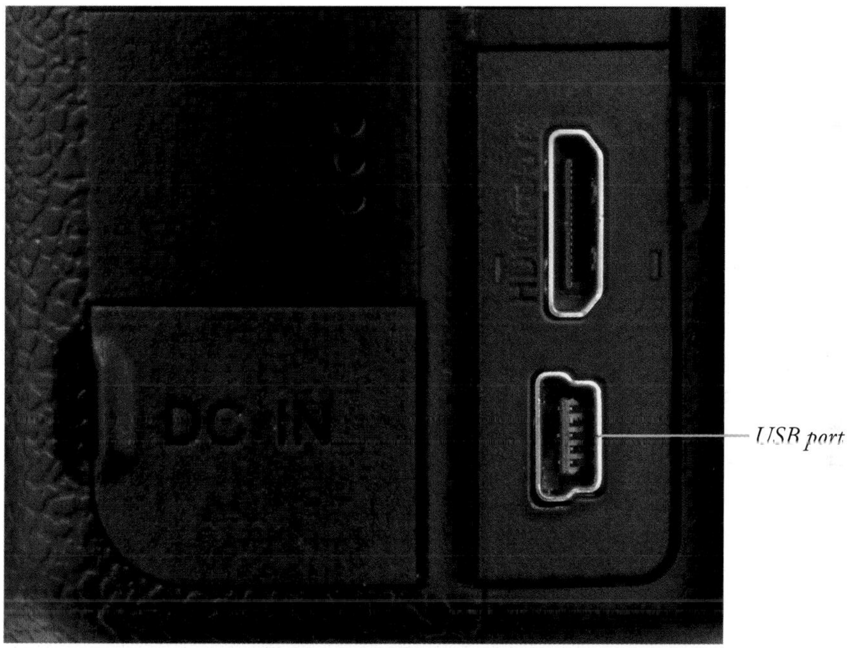

Figure 1.21 Images can be transferred to your computer using a USB cable plugged into the USB port.

Finally, if you are a die-hard technophile and don't mind spending a little extra money to use the coolest method for transferring your photos to your computer, go out and get an Eye-Fi card. (See Figure 1.22.) This relatively recent entry on the digital scene looks and acts exactly like an ordinary SDHC card, but with a big difference—once you have the card set up with your local Wi-Fi (wireless) network, whenever you take a picture with this card in the camera, the card wirelessly connects to your computer over that network and transmits the image file to any location you have specified. For example, my Eye-Fi card sends any new pictures directly to the Pictures/Eye-Fi folder on my computer.

I have tested this system with the Sony SLT, and it works beautifully. Now, I will admit that it's no trouble at all to just take an ordinary card out of the camera and pop it into a card reader, or to hook up a USB cable to the camera and the computer. The Eye-Fi card has to be classified as a bit of a luxury. But it will save you a few moments, and you can amaze your friends as your photos almost instantly show up on your computer, as if by magic.

If you want to explore this option, I strongly recommend you look for the Pro X2 version of the Eye-Fi card, shown in Figure 1.22, which can upload RAW files. The other models of the card, at this writing, are capable of handling only JPEG files.

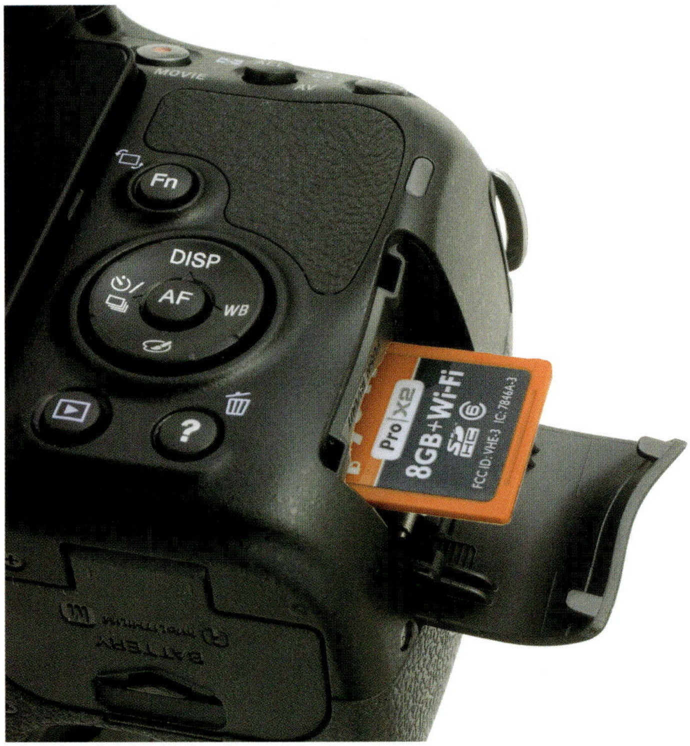

Figure 1.22
With an Eye-Fi card, you can have your images transmitted wirelessly to your computer as soon as your camera is in range of your local wireless network.

2

Sony Alpha SLT-A57 Roadmap

One thing that always surprises new owners of the Sony Alpha SLT-A57 is that the camera has a total of 397 buttons, dials, switches, levers, latches, and knobs bristling from its surface. Okay, I lied. Actually, the real number is closer to two dozen controls and adjustments, but that's still a lot of components to master, especially when you consider that many of these controls serve double-duty to give you access to multiple functions.

Traditionally, there have been two ways of providing a roadmap to guide you through this maze of features. One approach uses two or three tiny black-and-white line drawings or photos impaled with dozens of callouts labeled with cross-references to the actual pages in the book that tell you what these components do. You'll find this tactic used in the pocket-sized manual Sony provides with the Alpha A57, and most of the other third-party guidebooks as well. Deciphering one of these miniature camera layouts is a lot like being presented with a world globe when what you really want to know is how to find the capital of Belgium.

I originated a more useful approach in my field guides, providing you, instead of a satellite view, a street-level map that includes close-up, full-color photos of the camera from several angles, with a smaller number of labels clearly pointing to each individual feature. And, I don't force you to flip back and forth among dozens of pages to find out what a particular component does. Each photo is accompanied by a *brief* description that summarizes the control, so you can begin using it right away. Only when a particular feature deserves a lengthy explanation do I direct you to a more detailed write-up later in the book.

So, if you're wondering what the Fn button does, I'll tell you up front, rather than have you flip to pages 53 and 55 as the main Sony instruction manual does. This book is not a scavenger hunt. But after I explain how to use the ISO button to change the sensitivity of the Alpha, I *will* provide a cross-reference to a longer explanation later in the book that clarifies noise reduction, ISO, and its effects on exposure. I've had some readers write me and complain about even my minimized cross-reference approach; they'd like to open the book to one page and read everything there is to know about bracketing, for example. Unfortunately, it's impossible to understand some features without having a background in what related features do. So, I'll provide you with introductions in the earlier chapters, covering simple features completely, and relegating some of the really in-depth explanations to later chapters. I think this kind of organization works best for a camera as sophisticated as the Sony Alpha.

By the time you finish this chapter, you'll have a basic understanding of every control and what it does. I'm not going to delve into menu functions here—you'll find a discussion of your Recording, Setup, Playback, and other menu options in Chapter 3. Everything here is devoted to the button pusher and dial twirler in you.

Front View

When we picture a given camera, we always imagine the front view. That's the view that your subjects see as you snap away, and the aspect that's shown in product publicity and on the box. The frontal angle is, essentially, the "face" of a camera like the Sony Alpha. But, not surprisingly, most of the "business" of operating the camera happens *behind* it, where the photographer resides. The front of the Alpha actually has very few controls and features to worry about. In Figure 2.1, you can see the components revealed when the lens is removed:

- **Translucent mirror.** This semi-transparent (*not* translucent) mirror allows 70 percent of the light passing through the lens to continue on to the sensor. The remaining 30 percent is reflected upward toward the camera's autofocus sensor. This system gives the A57 the ability to automatically focus at all times, even while providing a live view of the sensor image and when shooting movies.
- **Electrical contacts.** These contacts mate with matching electrical components on the back of the lens to allow the camera and lens to communicate focus and exposure information.
- **Lens mounting index mark.** Match up this mark with an indicator on the lens to align the two when attaching a lens to the camera.
- **Lens mount.** This bayonet mount holds the lens securely.

Figure 2.1

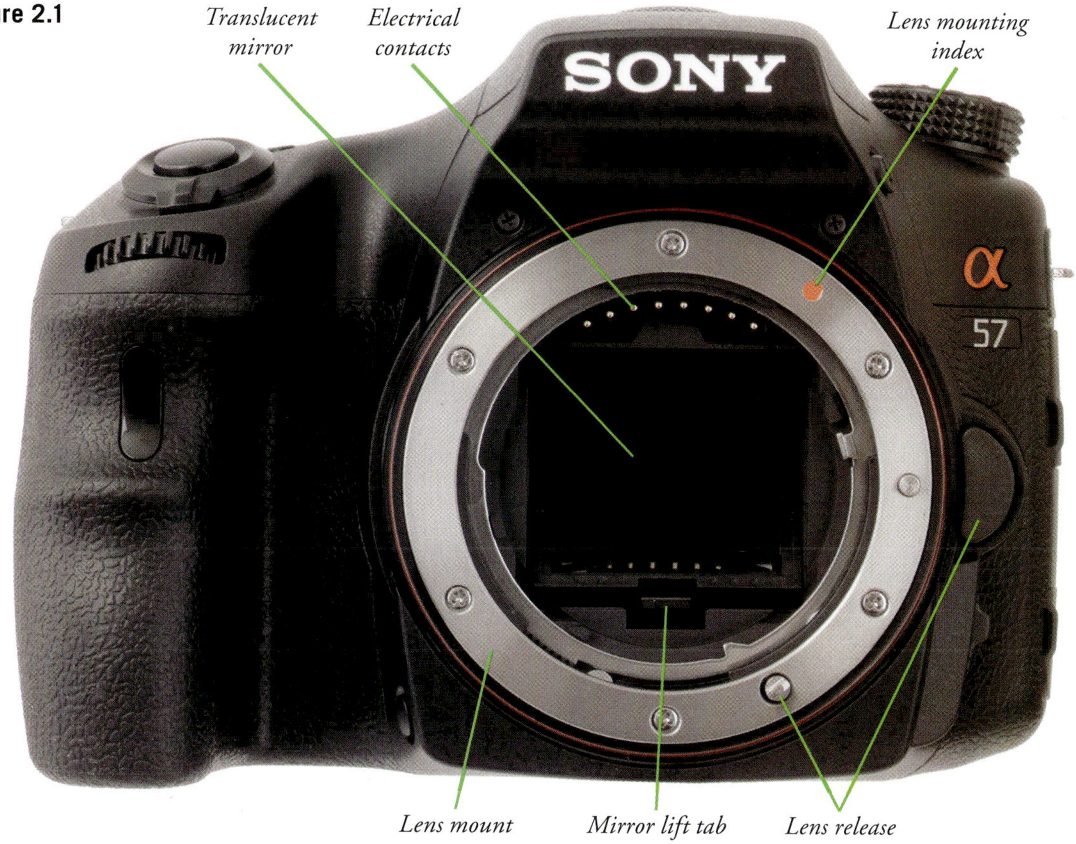

- **Mirror lift tab.** Grip this tab with a fingertip to gently flip up the mirror for manual sensor cleaning.
- **Lens release.** Press the button on the side of the lens mount to drop the lens lock tab down to allow removing the lens.

Other components are located on the side of the camera that's gripped by your right hand when holding the A57 in the shooting position. They include:

- **Shutter release button.** Angled on top of the hand grip is the shutter release button. Press this button down halfway to lock exposure and focus (in Single-shot mode and Continuous autofocus mode with non-moving subjects). The Alpha assumes that when you tap or depress the shutter release, you are ready to take a picture, so the release can be tapped to activate the exposure meter or to exit from most menus.
- **Power switch.** Rotate clockwise to turn the camera on; counter-clockwise to power down.

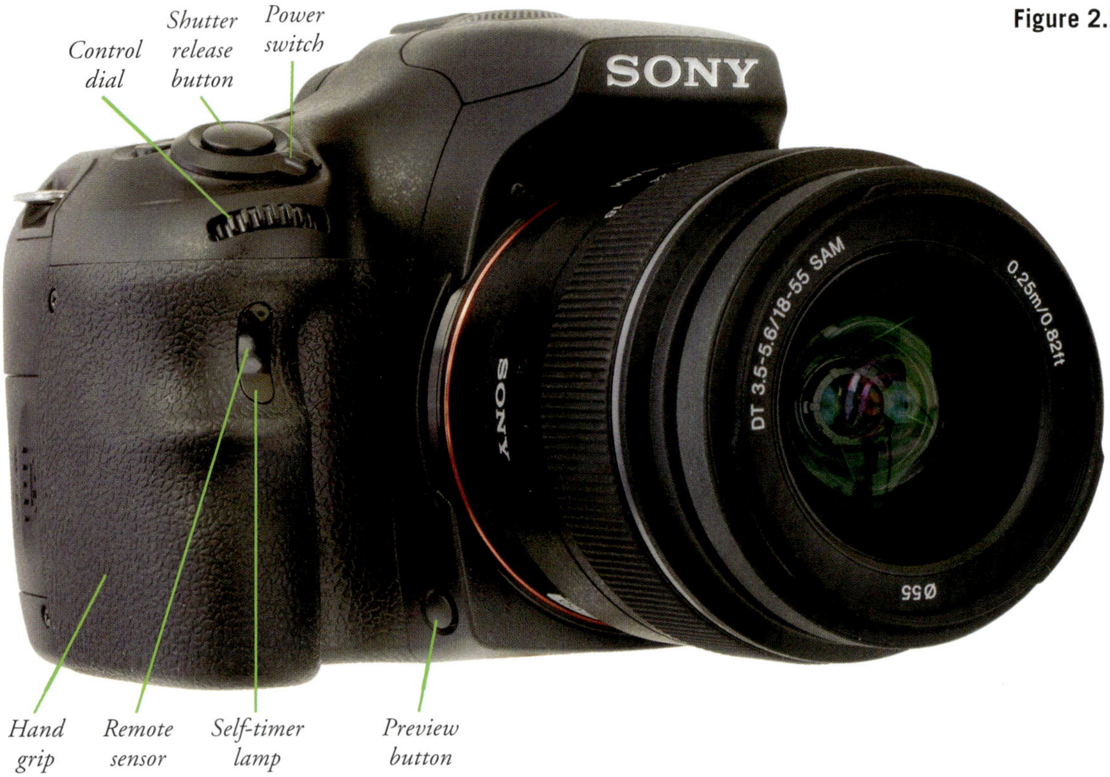

Figure 2.2

- **Control dial.** This dial is used to change shooting settings. When settings are available in pairs (such as shutter speed/aperture), this dial will be used to make one type of setting, such as shutter speed. The other setting, the aperture, is made using an alternate control, such as spinning the control dial while holding down the AEL/AV button (which resides conveniently under the thumb near the viewfinder window on the back of the camera). This dial also advances through your images in Playback mode.
- **Self-timer lamp.** This LED flashes red while your camera counts down the 10-second self-timer, flashing steadily at first, then switching to a constant glow in the final moments of the countdown. With the 2-second self-timer, the lamp stays lit during the entire countdown.
- **Remote sensor.** This small window in the hand grip shares space with the self-timer lamp, and is where you aim an infrared remote control, such as Sony's RMT-DSLR1 Remote Commander, an optional accessory. The remote control can trigger the camera's shutter, so you can avoid camera shake during delicate exposures.
- **Hand grip.** This provides a comfortable hand-hold, and also contains the Alpha's battery and memory card.

- **Preview button.** This control, sometimes known as a depth-of-field preview button, lets you see how your image will look with the aperture stopped down to its actual value, before you press the shutter button. Normally, when you are viewing the image on the LCD or in the viewfinder in Recording mode, the lens is at its widest aperture, such as f/3.5, for example. Because the depth-of-field changes as the aperture gets smaller (with a larger number, such as f/8), viewing through the wide-open lens does not let you judge how much of the image will be in focus when the picture is actually recorded. When you press the Preview button, the lens stops down to the actual shooting aperture so you can judge what areas of the image will be in sharp focus at that aperture.

You'll find more controls on the other side of the Alpha, shown in Figure 2.3.

- **Lens release button.** Press and hold this button to unlock the lens so you can rotate it and remove it from the camera.
- **Lens mounting index.** Match this recessed, red-orange index button on the lens with a red-orange indicator on the camera's lens mount to line the two up for attaching the lens to the Alpha's body.

Figure 2.3

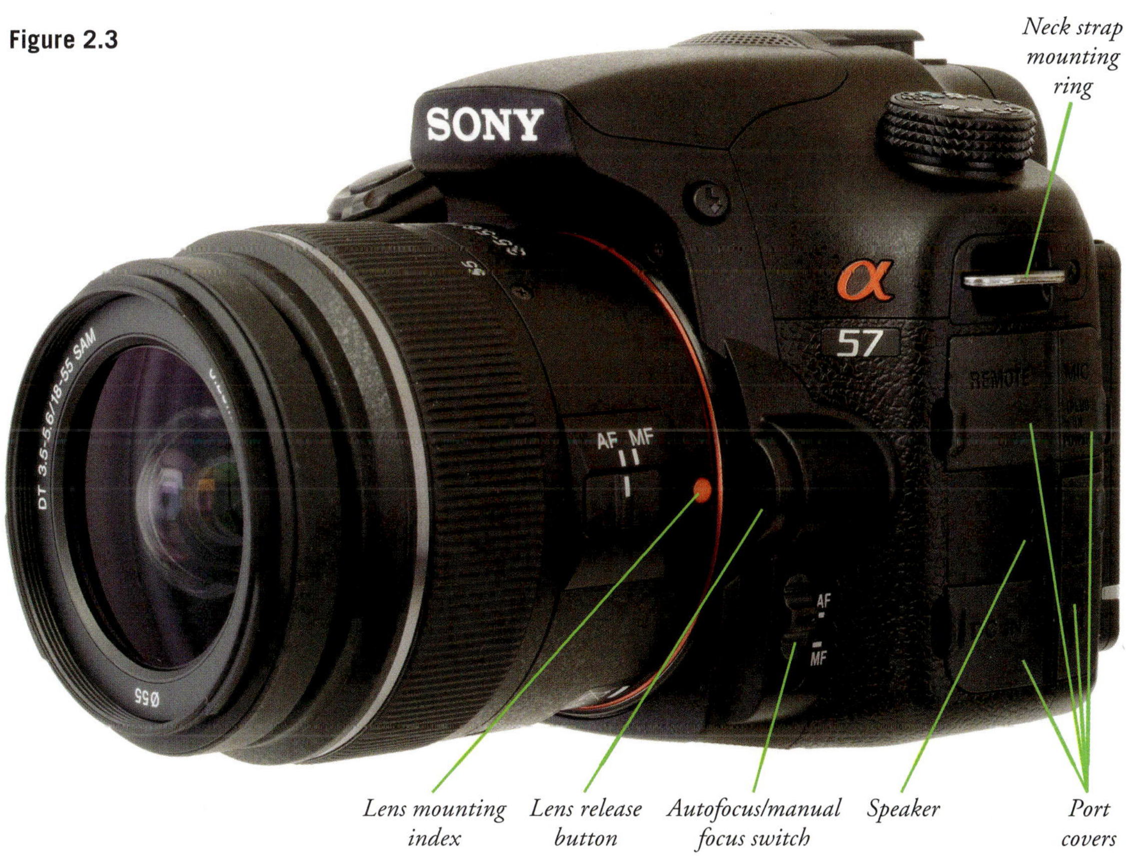

- **Focus mode switch.** Slide this switch up to set the Alpha for automatic focus; slide it down if you want to focus manually. How you use this switch depends on what lens is attached to your camera. If you're using a Sony lens with its own AF/MF switch, then you always leave the camera's switch set to AF, and select AF or MF with the switch on the lens. If you're using a lens that does not have its own switch, then you select AF or MF with the switch on the camera. So, you need to be careful; you might reasonably believe that setting the camera's switch to MF will put the camera into manual focus mode, but that is the case only if there is no AF/MF switch on the lens.
- **Neck strap mounting ring.** Attach the strap that comes with your Alpha to this ring, or use a third-party strap of your choice.
- **Port covers.** The A57's connectors for remote controls, microphones, DC power, HDMI output, and USB cables are stowed under these four covers.
- **Speaker.** Sound emitted by your camera emanates from this speaker on the side.
- **Pop-up flash.** This is your Alpha's internal flash. (See Figure 2.4.) It pops up automatically when needed while using any of the Auto or most Scene modes including (not surprisingly) Flash Off, and may be manually flipped up by pressing the Flash button on the left side of the camera when you're using the Program, Aperture priority, Shutter priority, Manual exposure, and Continuous Advance Priority AE modes. In the Scene and Auto modes, you cannot pop up the flash using the Flash button; the camera will give you an error message if you try.
- **Flash button.** This is the button you push to pop up the camera's built-in flash unit. As noted above, you can do this manually only when the camera is set to Program auto, Aperture priority, Shutter priority, Manual, or Continuous Advance Priority AE mode.

The main features on the left side of the Sony Alpha are four hinged doors that provide a modicum of protection for the ports underneath from dust and moisture. The connectors hidden under those doors, shown in Figure 2.5, are as follows:

- **HDMI terminal.** If you'd like to see the images from your camera on a television screen, you'll need to buy an HDMI cable (not included with the camera) to connect this port to an HDTV set or monitor. Be sure to get a cable that has a male mini-HDMI connector at the camera end and a standard male HDMI connector at the TV end. Once the cable is connected, you can not only view your stored images on the TV in Playback mode, you can also use the camera in Recording mode and see on your TV screen what the camera sees. So, in effect, you can use your HDTV set as a large monitor to help with composition, focusing, and the like.

  One unfortunate point is that these Alpha models no longer support video output to an old-style TV's yellow composite video jack. If for some reason it's important to you to connect the camera to one of those inputs, you'll need to find a device that can "down-scale" the HDMI signal to composite video. I have done this successfully with a device by Gefen called the HDMI to Composite Scaler, which costs somewhat more than $200 at Amazon.com, svideo.com, and other sites. It's likely you'd have to *really* need a converter like that to justify the cost.

The good news is that if you own a TV that supports Sony's Bravia sync protocol, you can use your Bravia remote control to control image display, mark images for printing, switch to index view, or perform other functions.

Figure 2.4

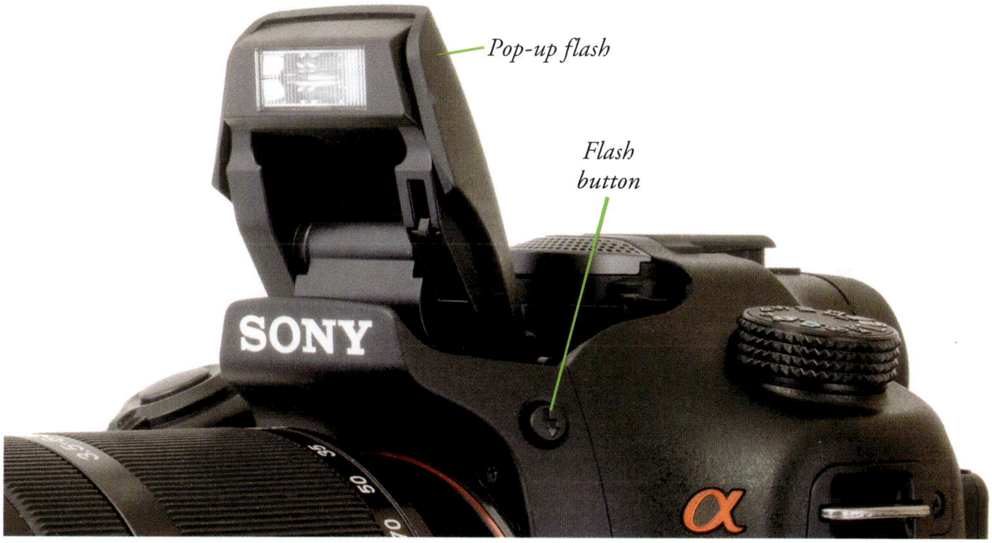

Figure 2.5

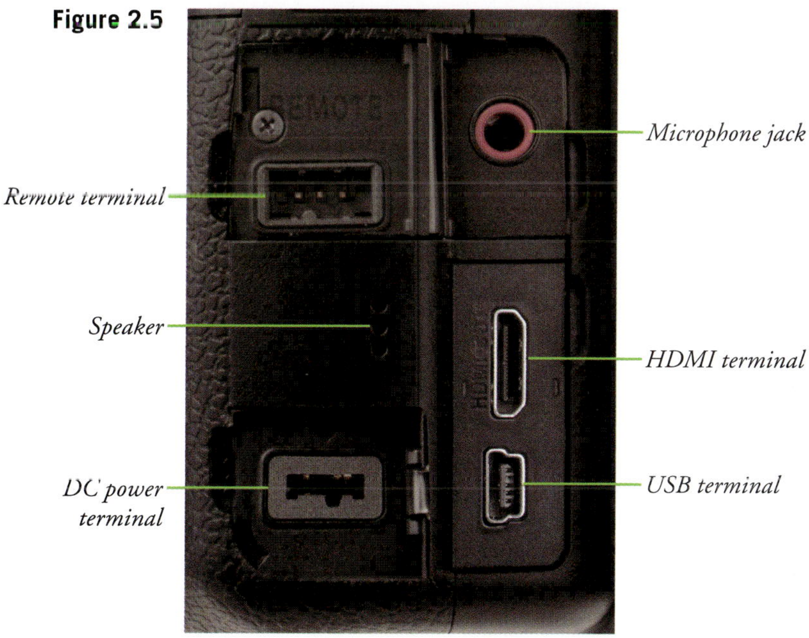

- **USB terminal.** Connect your camera to your computer by means of this port, using the USB cable that is supplied with the camera.
- **Remote control terminal.** This port is where you connect a wired remote control such as Sony's RM-S1AM, which lets you actuate the camera's shutter without causing the camera shake that can result from pressing the shutter button on the camera. I'll discuss remote control options in more detail in Chapter 6.
- **DC power terminal.** You can plug the optional AC-PW10AM adapter into this connector to provide continuous power to the camera.
- **External microphone jack.** This small opening is of considerable value to those who want to delve into high-quality videography with the SLT cameras. This port accepts a stereo mini-plug from a standard external microphone, allowing you to achieve considerably higher audio quality for your movies than is possible with the camera's built-in microphones. The port also can provide plug-in power for microphones that can take their power from this sort of outlet rather than from a battery in the microphone. Sony provides optional compatible microphones such as the ECM-ALST1 and the ECM-CG50; you also may find suitable microphones from companies such as Shure and Audio-Technica, which can be mounted using an adapter for Sony's proprietary accessory shoe. When a microphone is plugged into this port, the internal microphones are disabled.

The Sony Alpha's Business End

The back panel of the Sony Alpha bristles with more than a dozen different controls, buttons, and knobs (see Figure 2.6). That might seem like a lot of controls to learn, but you'll find, as I noted earlier, that it's a lot easier to press a dedicated button and spin a dial than to jump to a menu every time you want to change a setting.

Most of the controls on the back panel of the Alpha are clustered on the right side of the body, with the exception of the MENU button perched on the back slope, just northwest of the LCD, and a few other items of note. The key components labeled in Figure 2.6 include:

- **MENU button.** Summons/exits the menus displayed on the rear LCD and electronic viewfinder display of the Alpha. When you're working with submenus, this button also serves to exit a submenu and return to the main menu.
- **Viewfinder eyepiece.** You can frame your composition and see the information on the electronic viewfinder's display, including shooting settings, recorded images, and menu screens, by peering into this eyepiece. It's surrounded by a removable soft rubber frame that seals out extraneous light when pressing your eye tightly up to the viewfinder, and it also protects your eyeglass lenses (if worn) from scratching.

Figure 2.6

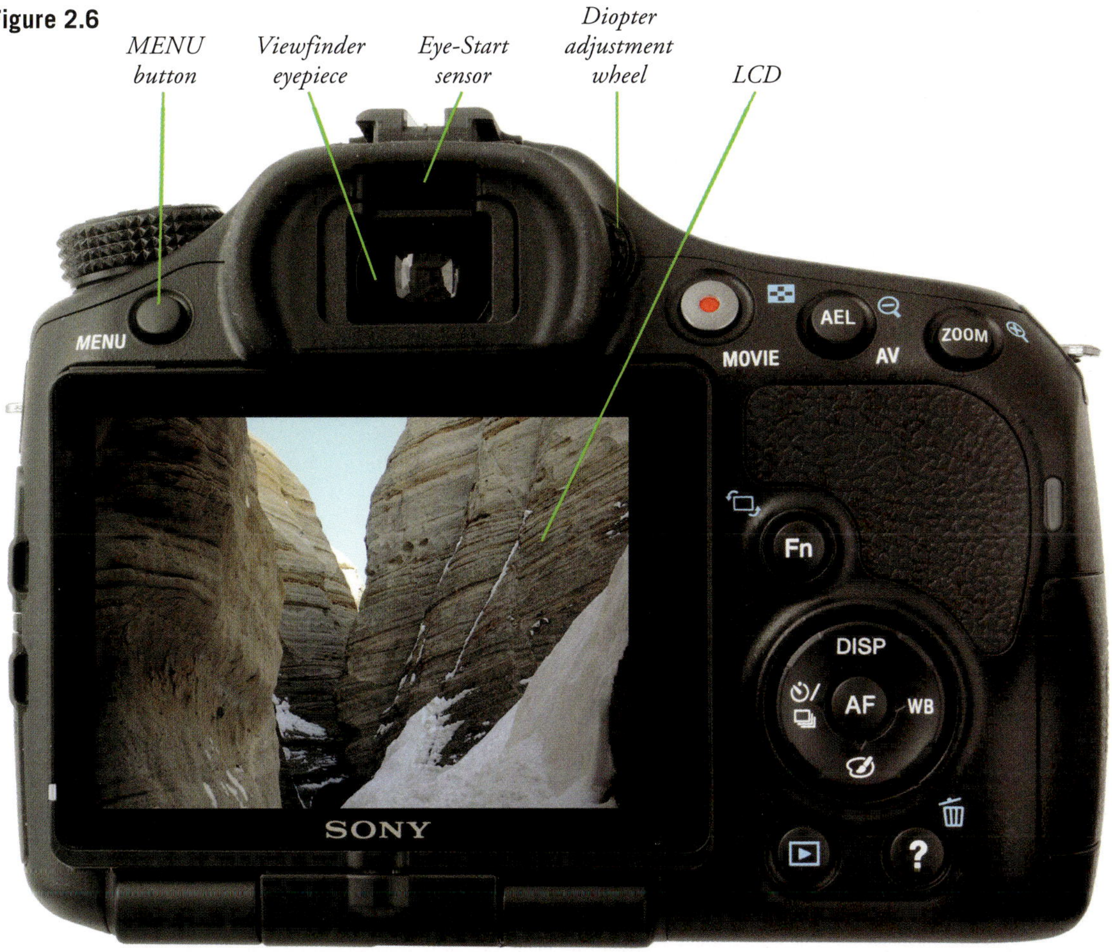

- **Eye-Start sensors.** These sensors detect when your face or some other object approaches the viewfinder, and activates automatic focusing while turning off the LCD display. Some find this feature annoying, because it can be triggered by other objects (such as your body when carrying the camera, switched on, over your shoulder or around your neck). In Chapter 3, I'll show you how to disable this function. You might also want to turn it off when using the optional FDA-M1AM magnifying eyepiece or FDA-A1AM right-angle finder, because these accessories could activate the sensors.
- **Diopter correction wheel.** Rotate this to adjust eyesight correction applied when looking through the Alpha's viewfinder.
- **LCD.** This is the 3-inch display that shows your Live View preview; image review after the picture is taken; recording information display before the photo is snapped; and all the menus used by the Sony Alpha.

The control cluster on the right side of the back of the camera includes these buttons, shown in Figure 2.7:

- **Movie button.** This red button is your gateway to movie making with the A57 cameras. Its operation is about as simple as it gets—just press the button once to start recording a movie, and press it again to stop the recording. The more involved aspects of video recording are handled through the menu system. I'll discuss your movie making options in Chapter 7.
- **Auto Exposure Lock/Zoom Out/Playback Index button.** This button has several functions, which differ depending on the camera's active mode.
  - **Shooting mode.** In any exposure mode other than Manual, press this button to lock the exposure. A * symbol appears on the display to indicate that the exposure is locked. If you continue to hold the button while shooting, subsequent images will be taken using the same exposure. Exposure lock is released when the button is no longer depressed. In Shooting mode, pressing this button locks your exposure setting. With the exposure locked, you can first aim the camera at a

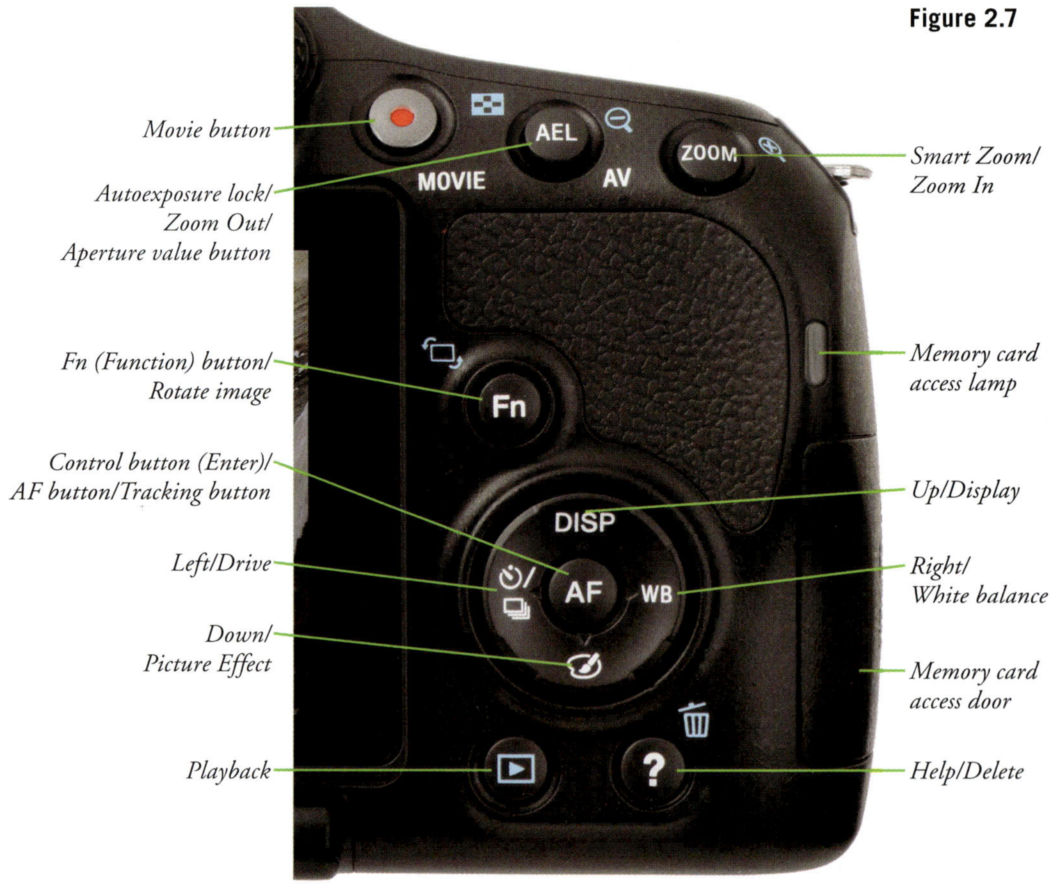

Figure 2.7

subject whose brightness will yield your desired results. Once you have made that exposure reading by pressing the shutter button halfway, press the AEL button, and that exposure reading will remain locked in. Now, aim the camera at your actual subject, and press the shutter button to re-focus and take the picture, using the locked-in exposure setting.

- You can change the behavior of the AEL button in Shooting mode using the Custom 3 menu, and choosing the AEL Hold item. If you set it to Hold, you have to hold the button down to keep the exposure locked; if you set it to Toggle, you can press and release it to lock exposure; then press it again to cancel that setting. Either way, whenever you have exposure locked with this button, an asterisk (*) appears in the viewfinder or on the LCD.
- **Manual exposure.** When using Manual exposure, hold this button and rotate the control dial to adjust the aperture value.
- **Playback mode.** Press this button to display an index screen showing 4 or 9 of your images at a time (select 4 or 9 through the Playback menu), and press again to return to full screen view. When the image being played back is zoomed in, press this button to zoom it back out. Each press zooms the image out one more step, until it is back to normal size. If you press the button one more time after that, the index screen is displayed.

- **Zoom In/Focus magnifier button.** This button has two functions:
  - **Shooting mode.** Press this button to zoom in on your subject, from about 1.4X to 8X, depending on the Clear Image Zoom and Digital Zoom settings of the camera, as well as image size settings. The section that follows describes your options.
  - **Playback mode.** Press this button to zoom in on the image during picture review. The controller directional buttons can be used to move the zoomed area around within the frame. Use the AEL/Zoom Out button to zoom back out again.
- **Memory card access lamp.** When lit or blinking, this lamp indicates that the memory card is being read from or written to. Do not remove the battery, turn off the power, or remove the card while this lamp is lit, or your image data could be corrupted.
- **Fn (Function) button.** In Shooting mode, pressing this button pops up a screen on the LCD or in the viewfinder with options for selecting various settings, depending on what Shooting mode the camera is set to. When you're shooting in one of the semi-automatic or manual modes (P, A, S, or M), you have the greatest number of settings available: Drive mode, Flash mode, Autofocus mode, AF area, Face Detection, Smile Shutter, ISO, Metering mode, Flash Exposure

Compensation, White Balance (color bias), the Dynamic Range Optimizer (to improve highlight/shadow detail), and a Creative Style (such as Vivid, Portrait, or Sunset). (See Figure 2.8.)

In Playback mode, press the Fn button to pop up a screen that allows you to rotate the current image by 90 degrees each time you press the center controller button. (See Figure 2.9.)

- **Controller/Enter/AF button.** The center controller button can be used as an Enter key to confirm menu choices when a menu is shown on the screen. In any autofocus mode, pressing this button causes the camera to autofocus on the subject, unless the AF area is set to Zone or Local. In that case, pressing this button brings up a screen to let you adjust the location of the focusing area. If you've activated Object Tracking, pressing the button also tells the camera to follow a moving subject to retain focus. (I'll discuss autofocus options in detail in Chapter 5.)
- **Directional buttons.** Press the left/right/up/down keys to navigate menus and to move the viewing area around within magnified images and to navigate within displays of image thumbnails during playback. In addition, when the AF area is set to Zone or Local, you can use the directional keys to select any of the zones or positions for the autofocus sensor. The left/right keys also move to the previous/next image on your memory card in Playback mode

In addition to their duties as navigational buttons, each of the four directional buttons has another identity, as set forth on its label. Those other functions are discussed next for each of the four buttons.

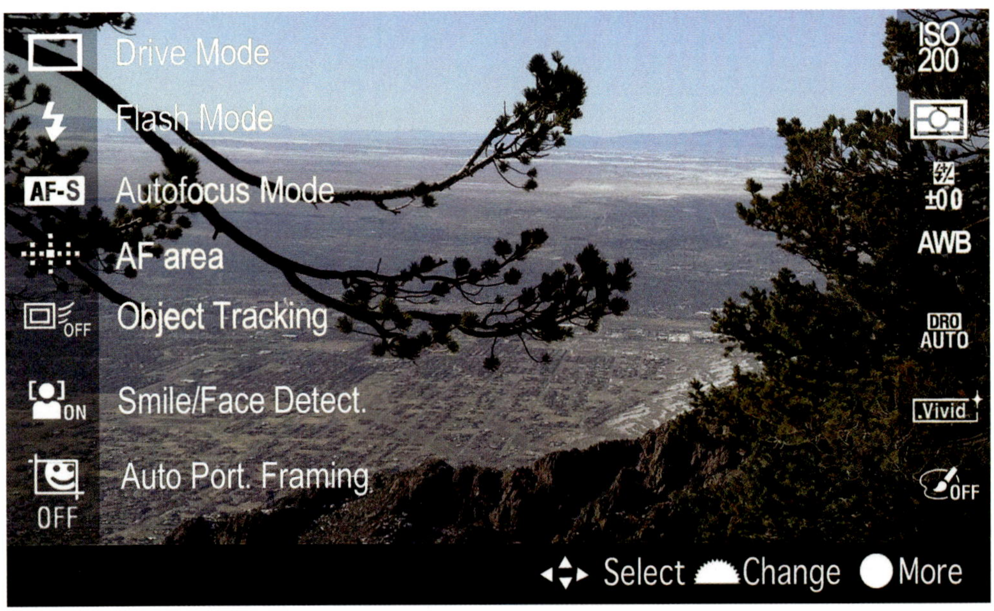

Figure 2.8

Figure 2.9

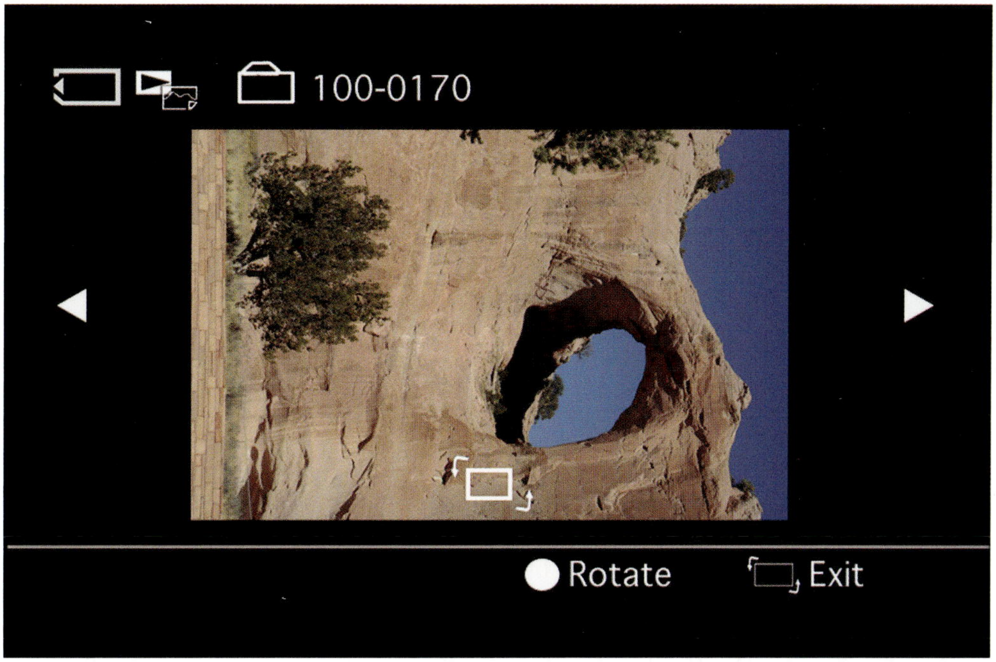

- **Up/DISP button.** When in Shooting mode and using the LCD, press the DISP button repeatedly to cycle among the four recording information displays available while you are taking photos. I'll describe the data shown in these displays and additional options in the next section.

  In Playback mode, press the DISP button to cycle among the three available playback screens for showing your images: full recording data; histogram with recording data; and no recording data. (For movies, there are only two playback screens; there is no histogram screen.)

- **Right/WB button.** This button gives you immediate access to an important function that otherwise would require a trip to the Function menu using the Fn button. With this button, one push takes you straight to the screen for selecting among the various white balance options: Auto, Daylight, Shade, Cloudy, Incandescent, Fluorescent, Flash, Color Temperature, Color Filter, and Custom. You navigate through these choices with the up/down direction buttons or with the control dial. Use the left/right direction buttons to make further adjustments to any of the individual settings. I'll discuss white balance in more detail in Chapter 6.

- **Down/Picture Effect button.** You can choose any of the eleven Picture Effects discussed in Chapter 6, ranging from Toy Camera, Pop Color, Posterization, and Retro Photo to Soft High-Key, Partial Color, High Contrast monochrome, Soft Focus, HDR Painting, Rich-tone monochrome, and Miniature.

- **Left/Drive mode button.** Press this button to produce a screen that lets you choose a drive mode. Then use the up/down buttons or the control dial to select from Single-shot advance; Continuous advance (with high- and low-speed options selectable with the left/right buttons); Self-timer (with 10- and 2-second options available with the left/right buttons); Continuous exposure bracketing (three shots with one shutter press, with exposure interval chosen using left/right buttons); White Balance bracketing (a series of three shots with a specified variation in white balance, selectable with left/right buttons); and Remote Commander shooting when using the optional RMT-DSLR1 Wireless Remote Commander. You'll find more about bracketing in Chapter 4; the Self-timer, Continuous advance, and the Remote Commander are discussed in Chapter 6. Here again, the drive mode button is a convenient shortcut; you can get to the same options by pressing the Fn button and navigating through the Function menu.
- **Trash/Help button.** In Shooting mode, this button summons the A57's In-Camera Guide, a listing of shooting tips you can access whenever this book or my *Compact Field Guide* condensed version is not at hand. You can page through listings for Portraits, Landscapes, Night Scenes, Close-up, Macro, and Subject in Motion scenes. When viewing a menu item, the Help button displays some information about the highlighted entry.

  In Playback mode, press this button once if you want to delete the image displayed on the LCD. Then press the up/down cursor buttons to choose Delete (to confirm your action) or Cancel (if you change your mind). Press the center controller button (Enter) to confirm your choice.
- **Playback button.** Displays the last picture taken. Thereafter, you can move back and forth among the available images by pressing the left/right cursor buttons or spinning the control dial to advance or reverse one image at a time. To quit playback, press this button again. The Alpha also exits Playback mode automatically when you press the shutter button (so you'll never be prevented from taking a picture on the spur of the moment because you happened to be viewing an image).

Zoom, Zoom, Zoom

Your SLT-A57 offers several ways to zoom in on an image as you capture a photo, including old-fashioned optical zoom (when you have a zoom lens attached). There are some interesting new permutations on the often-reviled *digital zoom* capability, too, which doesn't actually produce any new detail but, instead, creates a magnified image by manipulating pixels to include only those that capture the zoomed area. The next few sections will explain each of your options. Table 2.1 provides a summary.

Table 2.1 Zoom Factors

Zoom Mode	Zoom Settings	Image Size	Zoom Range
Optical Zoom	Clear Image Zoom: Off Digital Zoom: Off	Large Medium Small	Zoom range of lens.
Smart Zoom	Clear Image Zoom: Off Digital Zoom: Off	Large	Smart Zoom not available.
		Medium	1X-1.4X
		Small	1X-2X
Clear Image Zoom	Clear Image Zoom: On Digital Zoom: Off	Large	1X-2X
		Medium	1X-1.3X (Smart Zoom) 1.4X-2.8X (Clear Image Zoom)
		Small	1X-1.9X (Smart Zoom) 2X-4X (Clear Image Zoom)
Digital Zoom	Clear Image Zoom: On Digital Zoom: On	Large	1X-2X (Clear Image Zoom) 2.1x-4X (Digital Zoom)
		Medium	1X-1.3X (Smart Zoom) 1.4X-2.9X (Clear Image Zoom) 3X-5.5X (Digital Zoom)
		Small	1X-1.9X (Smart Zoom) 2X-4X (Clear Image Zoom) 4.1X-8X (Digital Zoom)

Optical Zoom

Settings: Clear Image Zoom: Off; Digital Zoom: Off; Image Size: Large

This option is available only when you have a zoom lens mounted on your A57. In the Shooting 2 menu, set Clear Image Zoom and Digital Zoom both to Off. Then, simply turn the zoom ring on the lens to zoom in and out of your image. This mode provides the best image quality, because the full 16 megapixels of the Alpha's sensor are used (when Large Image Size is selected in the Shooting 1 menu) to record the photo. The magnification range is determined by the lens itself. For example, the 18-55mm kit lens allows a roughly 1X to 3X zoom range.

You should always use the optical zoom to magnify your image first, before resorting to one of the digital zoom options, because optical zoom produces the least amount of image degradation. Indeed, with a good-quality zoom lens, you may notice little, if any, loss in sharpness as you zoom in and out.

Smart Zoom

Settings: Clear Image Zoom: Off; Digital Zoom: Off; Image Size: Medium or Small

Large Image Size. Smart Zoom not available.

Medium/Small Image Size. Smart zoom becomes available when you select Medium (8.4 megapixels) or Small (4 megapixels) as your Image Size in the Shooting 2 menu. When either of those resolutions are activated, pressing the Zoom button produces a scale at the lower right corner of the display. The magnifying glass icon has an "S" next to it when zooming in to indicate that you're using the Smart Zoom feature. Use the left/right directional buttons to zoom from 1X to 1.4X at Medium resolution or 1X to 2X at Small resolution.

In this mode, the image is cropped to produce a "magnified" 8.4 or 4 megapixel version, with no other image processing required.

Clear Image Zoom

Settings: Clear Image Zoom: On; Digital Zoom: Off; Image Size: Large, Medium, or Small

Large Image Size. When Clear Image Zoom is activated in the Shooting 2 menu, the A57 will use image processing to magnify the image, if required. When Image Size is set to Large, that processing is applied to create a full-resolution image at 1X to 2X magnification. The magnifying glass icon has a "C" next to it to show that Clear Image Zoom is being applied. (See Figure 2.10.) Press the left/right directional buttons to zoom in and out, and the up/down buttons to zoom in larger steps. The center button exits the zoom process when you're finished.

Medium/Small Image Size. However, if you choose Medium or Small Image Size, the camera will first simply trim the image (without processing) from 1X to 1.2X (Medium) or 1X to 1.9X (Small). If you continue zooming, then image processing will be used to provide additional zooming from 1.4X to 2.8X (Medium) or 2X to 4X (Small). The magnifying glass icon will display a "C" or "S" to show which processing mode is being used.

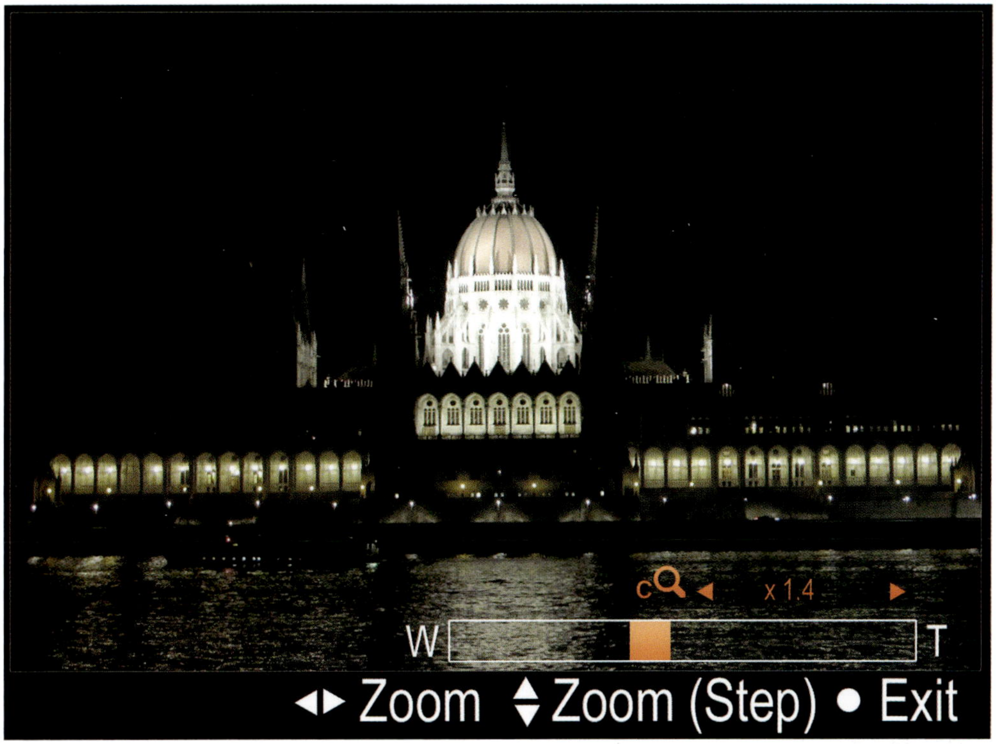

Figure 2.10
Zoom status is shown on the display.

Digital Zoom

Settings: Clear Image Zoom: On; Digital Zoom: On; Image Size: Large, Medium, or Small

Large Image Size. Digital Zoom deploys all three non-optical zooming methods. When Large is selected, Clear Image Zoom magnification, a high-quality image processing algorithm, will be used from 1X to 2X, while from 2.1X to 4X, the reduced image quality process, Digital Zoom, will be applied.

Medium Image Size. Select Medium resolution, and the highest quality Smart Zoom trimming will be applied from 1X to 1.3X; Clear Image Zoom from 1.4X to 2.9X; and Digital Zoom from 3X to 5.6X.

Small Image Size. Select Small and Smart Zoom trimming will be applied from 1X to 1.9; Clear Image Zoom from 2.0 to 4.0; and Digital Zoom from 4.1 to 8X.

What You See, and What You Get

Your SLT-A57 has two display screens, of course: the internal, 1.44 megapixel electronic viewfinder, and the external three-inch 921,600-dot back-panel color LCD. You can use either of them at any time. The A57 will be kind enough to switch back and forth automatically by using its Eye-Start sensors to decide whether the camera is held up to your eye (thereby activating the EVF), or held at arm's length (in which case, you probably want to work with the back-panel LCD). Although you can alternate between them, these two viewing systems are not completely interchangeable. Each has its own advantages and disadvantages.

LCD vs. EVF

Whether you use the LCD or EVF in a given shooting situation is largely a matter of personal preference and/or convenience. But there are some things to consider about your two viewing systems:

- **EVF has higher resolution.** The resolution of the electronic viewfinder is 1.44 megapixels when set to Maximum magnification, or 1.2 megapixels if you choose Standard magnification. The back-panel LCD has a resolution of roughly 922,000 dots. So, the EVF has more effective resolution, making it a slightly better choice for examining small details while framing and composing an image and, especially, when manually focusing. The LCD has plenty of detail for framing an image, and, in fact, has more resolution than the first generation of 3-inch LCDs, which had as few as one-third as many dots.
- **LCD prone to washout.** The back-panel LCD is exposed to ambient lighting and can, in fact, be washed out or reduced in contrast when used under bright lighting conditions. The internal EVF, on the other hand, is shielded from ambient light, and is usually the better choice when photographing outdoors. But keep in mind that you can adjust the brightness of either display to suit the shooting environment.
- **LCD has better viewing angles.** The internal EVF must be viewed more or less from directly behind the viewfinder window, although your eye needn't be pressed right up against the frame. Your eye can be as far as 23mm from the removable viewfinder frame, and 25mm from the window itself (this is known as the *eyepoint* distance), which is a benefit for eyeglass wearers. The swiveling LCD, on the other hand, can be viewed from any distance that allows you to view the detail you need to see, and can be canted at a variety of angles.

  For example, you can fold the LCD downward and reverse it, so that it's facing the *front* of the camera, making it easy to capture a self-portrait without use of a mirror to compose your smiling visage, or to allow your subject to preview the image before it's taken. You can also hold the camera overhead and use the angled LCD like a periscope to capture a parade or shoot over the heads of the other paparazzi.

  Moreover, the LCD can be viewed by several people simultaneously. When taking an advertising product shot, both you and the art director can view the image before the exposure (although this is a bit of a far-fetched scenario). More likely, you'll be using the back-panel LCD to show off the images you've already taken to a third party or group, which is more convenient than asking each person, in turn, to peer through the viewfinder.

- **EVF encourages solid shooting stance.** Using the EVF, with the A57 pressed up against your forehead, helps steady the camera and reduce potential blur at slow shutter speeds. (SteadyShot is *not* a panacea and, actually, works even better when the camera is fairly stable to begin with.) When taking several pictures in succession, the EVF and camera held at eye level provide a familiar shooting platform. Most sports photos, for example, are best captured with the camera pressed tightly to your eye. The LCD's shooting stance, especially when you hold the camera out at arm's length, tends to increase the unsteadiness of hand-held photography. The LCD might be your preferred viewfinder for casual or stealth photography.

TIP

Here's a really cool technique that takes advantage of the Eye-Start sensor. Flip the LCD forward facing your subject, as seen in Figure 2.11. The LCD allows your victim to summon up her best smile, or check her hair. Then, when you're ready to take the picture, just bring the camera to your eye and view through the EVF. There's no need to turn the LCD back around. The Eye-Start sensor will switch the display from the LCD to the viewfinder automatically, so, even though you've given your subject a preview of the picture you're going to take, you can still use the EVF immediately.

Figure 2.11 Flipping the LCD forward allows you—or your subject—to preview the image the camera is about to take.

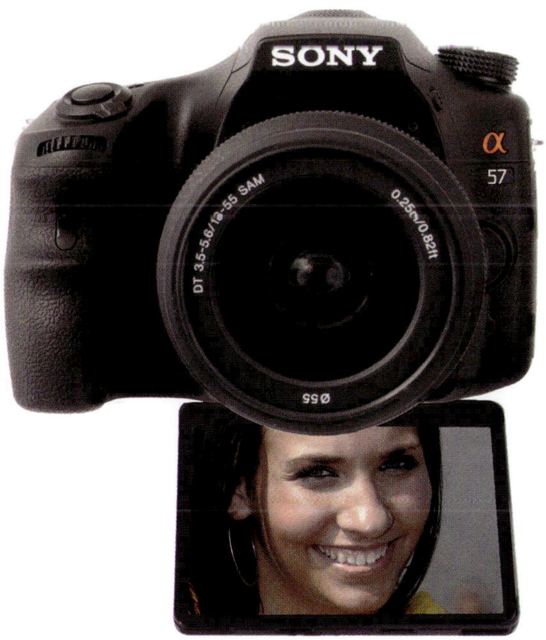

EVF/LCD VS. OPTICAL VIEWFINDERS

- **Adjustable brightness.** You can adjust the viewfinder's relative brightness in the Setup 1 menu (I'll show you how later) to produce a view that's as bright or as dim as you like (the brightness of the back-panel LCD can also be adjusted separately).
- **Gain, no pain.** The EVF can automatically amplify the image for better viewing under dim lighting conditions, unlike an optical viewfinder, which grows dimmer as the illumination decreases.
- **Preview effects.** The EVF and LCD can be set to show the effects of your settings, such as exposure or color balance, as you view the image prior to taking the picture. With an optical viewfinder, what you see is not necessarily what you get.
- **Live histogram.** Some cameras offer a live histogram display during preview on their back-panel LCD, so you can use the histogram's chart to judge exposure. (I'll explain how to use histograms in Chapter 4.) However, no eye-level optical viewfinder is able to show a histogram under any circumstances. You can easily enable your A57's optional EVF histogram display (and I'll show you how later in this chapter).

Choosing Your View

When reviewing images, the A57 provides three views, which you can cycle through by pressing the DISP button. Press the Playback button and you'll see a plain vanilla, no-information full-screen display with nothing but the image; a full-screen display with basic shooting information overlaid; and a more detailed display that includes more shooting data, a reduced-size thumbnail of your image, and a quartet of histograms (one each for brightness, red, green, and blue color channels). (See Figure 2.12.) I'm going to leave the discussion of using histograms for Chapter 4, which deals with the wonders of exposure.

The shooting mode displays are a little more complicated. When you're in shooting mode, both the EVF and LCD show a preview of the image you've framed with the camera, as well as a recording information display of relevant shooting data, such as exposure information, focus point, and other settings. The amount of information shown varies, and can be changed from one display to the next by pressing the DISP (up) button on the control pad. The EVF and LCD can be set individually, and each can show a different information display. That's very handy, as you can have a detailed display on the back-panel LCD, and minimal information overlaid on the EVF if you want a cleaner display while framing and shooting your image with the viewfinder. There are five different displays for the EVF and LCD, and several optional informational variations. You can enable or disable each of these displays individually, so if you decide you no longer want to view the graphic display in the EVF, you can turn it off

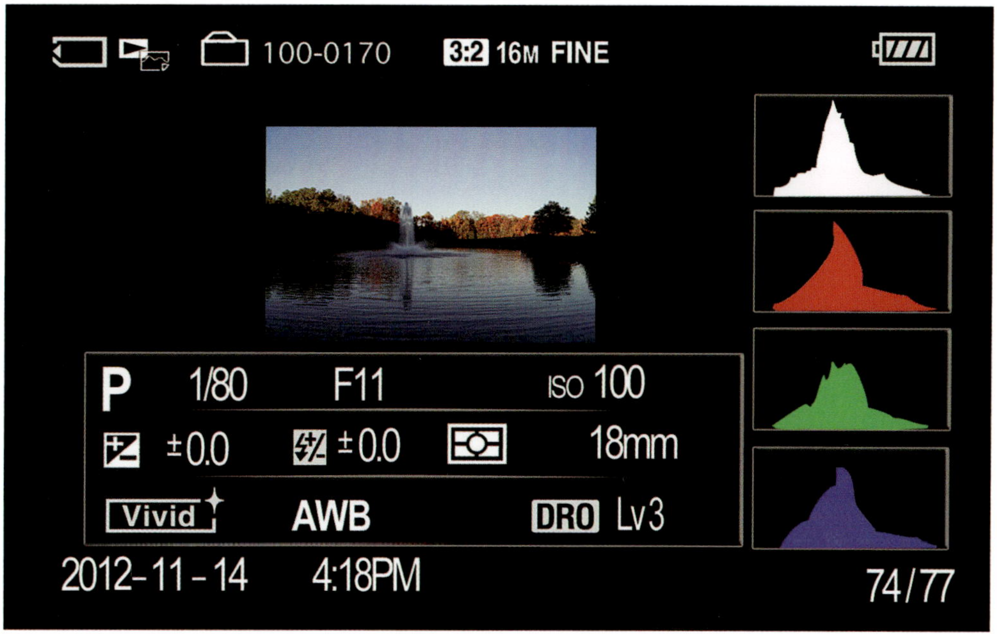

Figure 2.12
Histogram display.

there, while retaining that display option on the LCD. I'll show you how to do that shortly. But first, a discussion of the available displays:

- **Graphic display.** This display is graphic to the extent that the shutter speed and aperture value settings are shown as graphs, with indicators pointing to the current values. The LCD version is shown in Figure 2.13. The EVF version is similar, but has a black background band at the top of the frame to make the information displayed in the top row of icons more easily visible. In addition, the +/–EV (exposure compensation) icon on the bottom row of the LCD is replaced by a scale showing the amount of exposure compensation you've dialed in.

  The graphic display is an excellent choice for beginners who are just learning about shutter speeds and f/stops. Notice that the shutter speed graph has icons of a standing figure at left, and a running figure at right, providing a quick clue that faster shutter speeds are better for movement and action. Similarly, the aperture graph has a cloud at the "wide" end (because wider, larger apertures are best for dimmer conditions), and a landscape icon at the right that brings typical brightly lit scenes to mind. Unless you find the complete graphic display helpful, you'll probably abandon it as you become more proficient with your A57. The callouts for Figure 2.13 show what kind of information is presented at the top, bottom, and middle of the screen. Not all of these indicators will be displayed at once.

- **Display all information.** This display (the LCD version is shown in Figure 2.14) really clutters up your screen, although, fortunately, not all of this information is overlaid on your image at once. The top rows and bottom row are the same as in the graphic display, and two columns of additional information are stacked at left and right of the frame.

  These are reminders of the settings you can change by pressing the Fn button, and indicate their current values. To change any of them, press the Fn button, use the

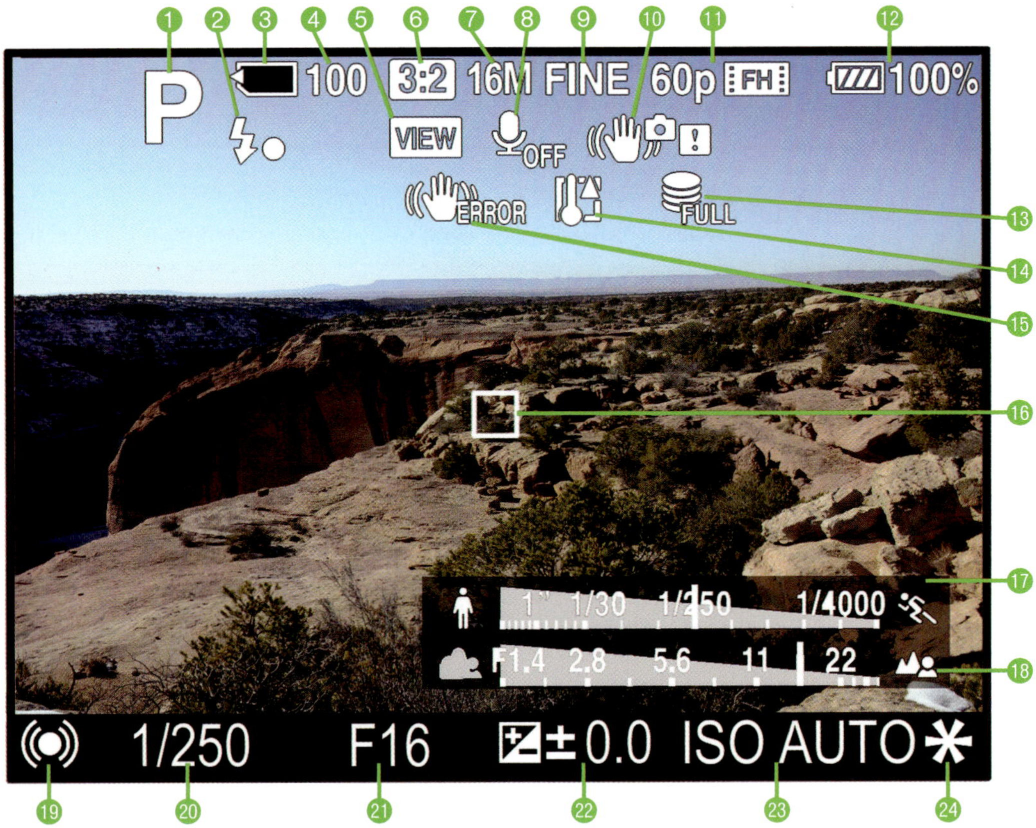

1 *Exposure mode*
2 *Flash charge progress*
3 *Memory card*
4 *Images remaining*
5 *Setting effect off*
6 *Aspect ratio*
7 *Image resolution*
8 *Sound mode*
9 *Image quality*
10 *SteadyShot status*
11 *Movie resolution*
12 *Battery status*
13 *Database file full/error*
14 *Overheating warning*
15 *SteadyShot warning*
16 *AF Focus area*
17 *Aperture indicator*
18 *Shutter speed indicator*
19 *Focus*
20 *Shutter speed*
21 *Aperture*
22 *Exposure compensation*
23 *ISO sensitivity*
24 *AE lock*

Figure 2.13 Graphic display.

left/right directional buttons to navigate from one column to the other, and then the up/down buttons to highlight the icon of the setting you want to adjust. Press the center OK button, and a screen will appear with that setting's options. Select, and press the OK button to confirm and exit.

As with the graphic display, the EVF version is almost identical, with the addition of the black background band at the top of the frame, and the EV scale at the bottom.

- **No Display info.** This display minimizes the clutter on the LCD or EVF. The LCD version, shown in Figure 2.15, has just a narrow band of information at the bottom. The EVF rendition adds a black band with exposure mode, shots remaining, and image quality at the top. This display mode eliminates the distractions of the first two screens I described.
- **Electronic level display.** This display makes it easy to level the A57 along the side-to-side (horizontal) axis while adjusting for forward or backward tilt at the same time. The sidebar, "Using the Level" explains how to work with this useful tool.

Figure 2.14 Display all information.

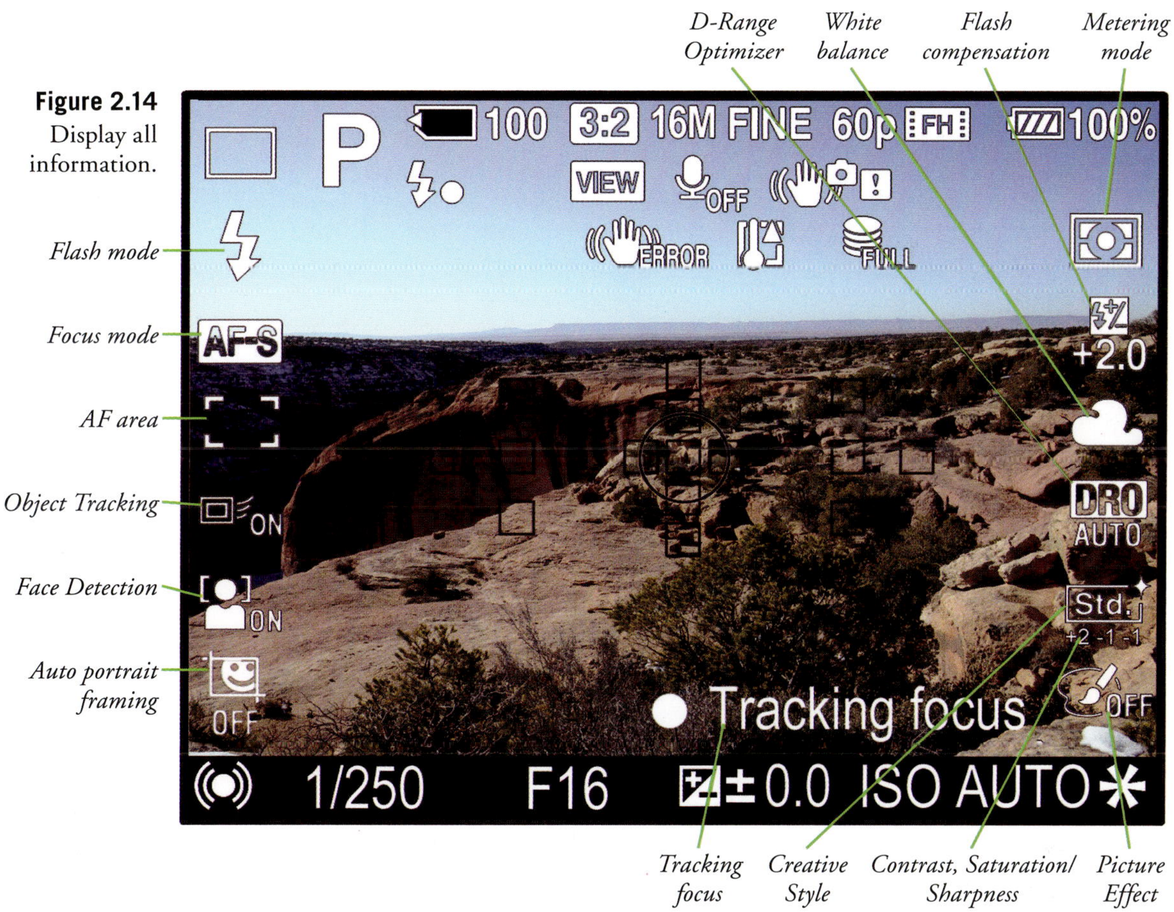

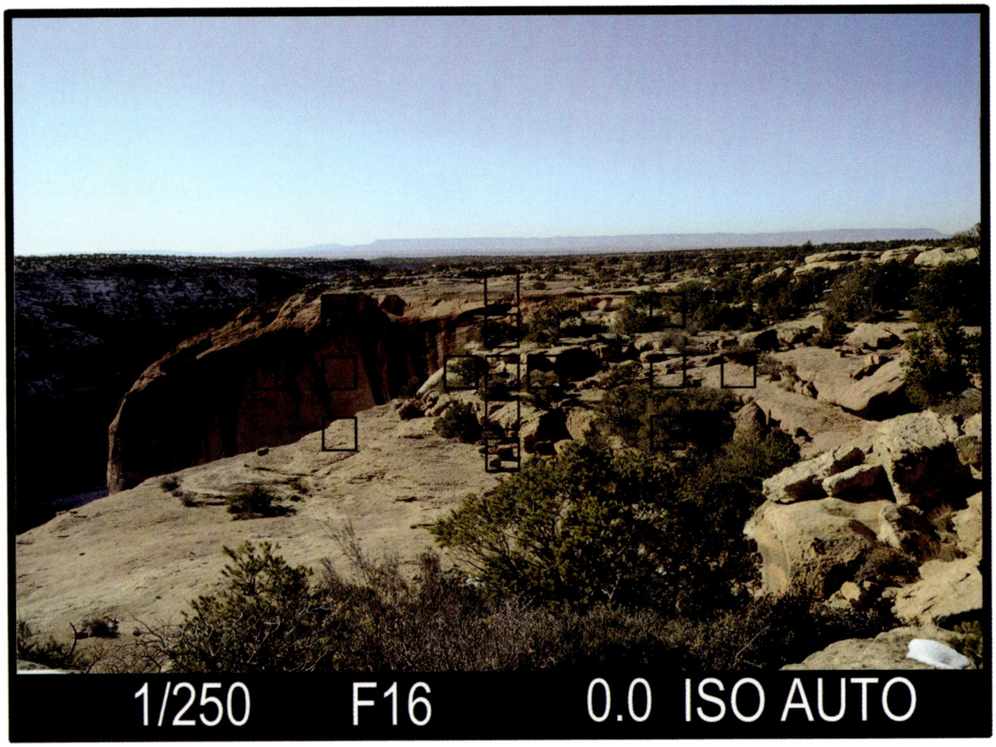

Figure 2.15
Minimal information display.

- **Grids.** You can add any of three types of grids to the display screens as an aid for alignment and composition. These grids include Rule of Thirds, Square Grid, and Diagonal+Square Grid, and can be activated from the Custom 2 menu. I'll show you what these grids look like and how to access them in the next chapter.
- **Histograms.** These charts help you judge how the tonal values are being captured. I'll show you how to work with histograms in Chapter 4.
- **For Viewfinder mode.** There is one more optional screen which, despite its misleading name, is available *only* for display on the back-panel LCD. It's a non-live view mode that shows no image at all. Only your current settings information is displayed. It's a useful screen for those times when you want to use the EVF exclusively to frame and evaluate your image (which Sony calls Viewfinder mode), and would prefer that the LCD display only shooting information. The data is shown large and in an easy-to-read display, as you can see in Figure 2.16, which illustrates the display as seen when using PASM modes, or Continuous Advance Priority AE mode. The screen is slightly simplified for Intelligent Auto, Superior Auto, and Scene selection modes, displaying only the settings that the user can adjust. I'll explain how to activate this option, as well as other display options, in the next section.

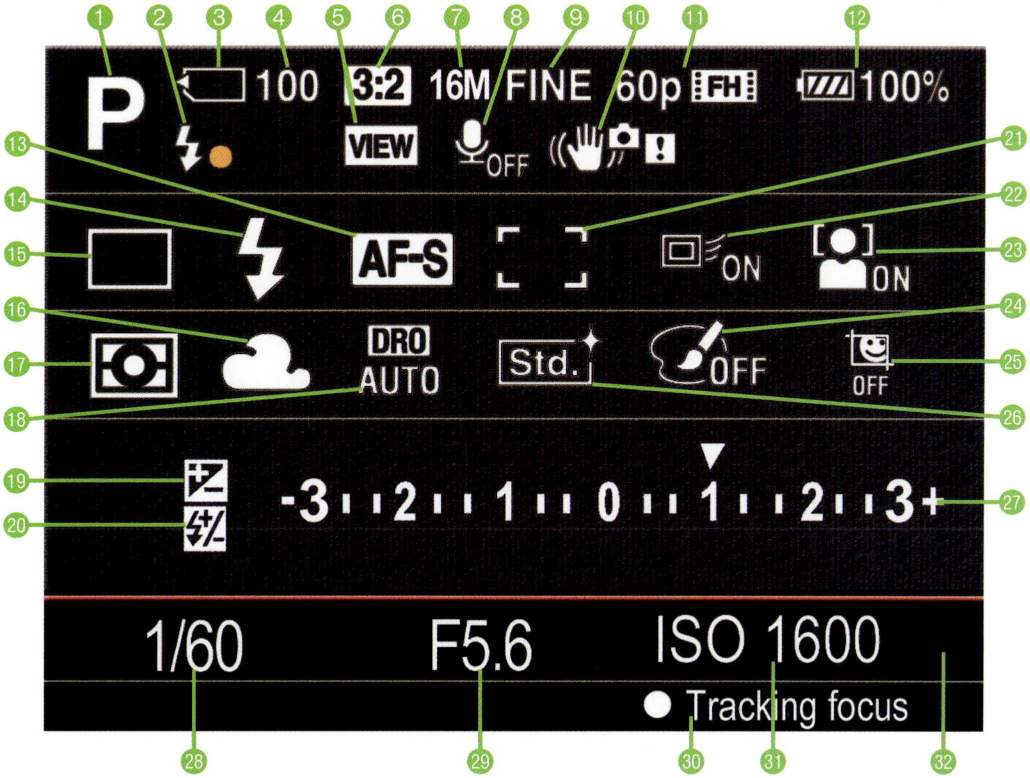

1 *Exposure mode*
2 *Flash ready*
3 *Memory card*
4 *Images remaining*
5 *View On*
6 *Aspect ratio*
7 *Resolution*
8 *Sound mode*
9 *Image quality*
10 *SteadyShot*
11 *Movie resolution*
12 *Battery status*
13 *Autofocus mode*
14 *Flash mode*
15 *Drive mode*
16 *White balance*
17 *Metering mode*
18 *D-Range Optimizer*
19 *Exposure compensation*
20 *Flash exposure compensation*
21 *Autofocus area*
22 *Object Tracking*
23 *Face Detection*
24 *Picture Effect*
25 *Auto cropping*
26 *Creative Style*
27 *EV scale*
28 *Shutter speed*
29 *Aperture*
30 *Focus Tracking*
31 *ISO setting*
32 *AE lock*

Figure 2.16 LCD display for Viewfinder mode.

USING THE LEVEL

When you activate the electronic level, a set of indicators appears on the display, as shown in Figure 2.17. The horizontal bar with red tips shows the horizontal orientation of the camera. As you rotate the camera to level it, the tips will eventually intersect with the white indicators overlaid on the arcs placed left and right of center. The red tips and the white indicators will turn green to show that the camera has been leveled horizontally.

At the same time, you'll see red tilt indicators hovering above or below the white bars clustered near the center of the frame. As you tilt the camera forward or back, the red indicators will eventually match up with the white bars, showing that the camera is level on that axis, as well. When the camera is completely level, the indicators will look like those shown in Figure 2.18.

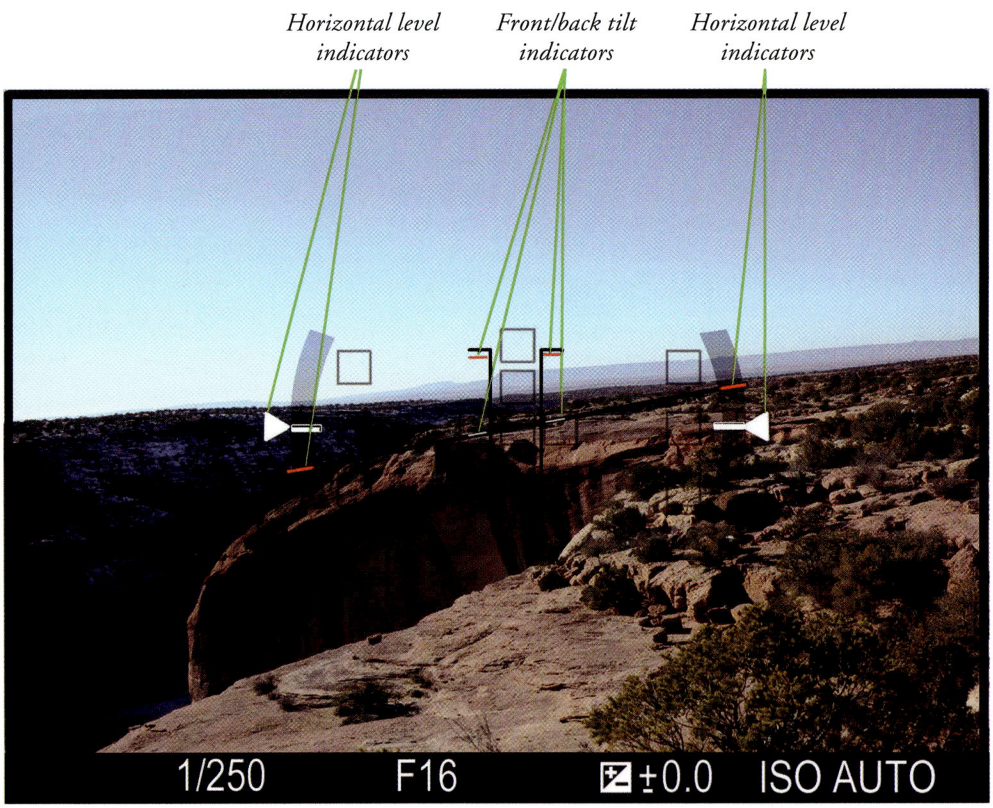

Figure 2.17
Display when camera is not level.

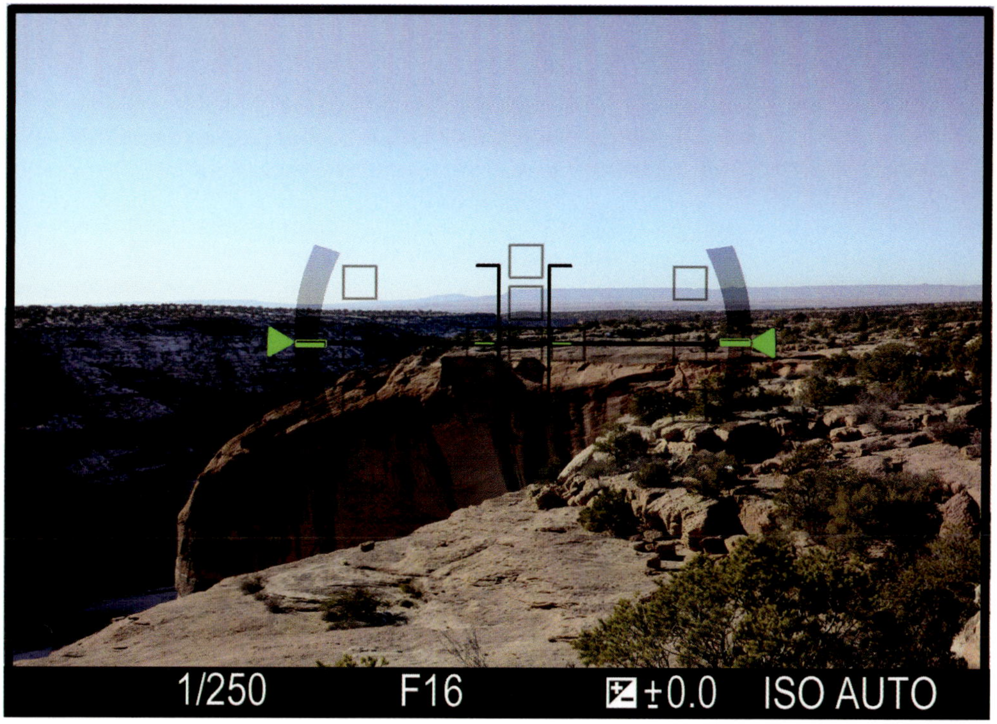

Figure 2.18
Display when camera is level.

Typical Information Display

As you work your way through this book, you'll learn how to use and work with all the information shown in a typical information display. The indicators you'll find, called out in Figures 2.13 and 2.14, include:

- **Exposure mode.** Shows whether you're using Program auto, Aperture priority, Shutter priority, Manual, or one of the Auto, Scene, or specialized modes. (If the camera is set to Auto or any of the other Scene modes, the information shown on the two recording information displays is considerably less than the full amount that appears in the P, A, S, or M modes.)
- **Image quality.** Your image quality setting (JPEG Fine, JPEG Standard, RAW, or RAW & JPEG).
- **Image size/Aspect ratio.** Shows whether you are shooting Large, Medium, or Small resolution images, and whether the Alpha is set for the 3:2 aspect ratio or wide-screen 16:9 aspect ratio (the image size icon changes to a "stretched" version when the aspect ratio is set to 16:9). If you're shooting RAW images, there is no symbol shown, because all RAW images are the same size and no size choice is available.

- **Memory card.** This icon appears when a memory card (either SD or Memory Stick) is present in the camera.
- **Remaining exposures.** Shows the approximate number of shots available to be taken on the memory card, assuming current conditions, such as image size and quality.
- **Movie resolution.** This icon gives the movie file format and resolution. The choices are: FH, for Full High Definition (AVCHD) at 1920 × 1080 pixels; 1080, for MP4 at 1440 × 1080; and VGA, for MP4 at 640 × 480.
- **Battery status.** Remaining battery life is indicated by this icon.
- **Flash mode.** Provides flash mode information. The possible choices are Flash Off, Autoflash, Fill-flash, Slow Sync, Rear Sync, and Wireless. Not all of these choices are available at all times.
- **Drive mode.** Shows whether camera is set for Single-shot, Continuous shooting (Low- or High-speed), Self-timer, Exposure Bracketing, White Balance Bracketing, or Remote Commander.
- **Autofocus mode.** Tells whether AF-S, AF-C, or AF-A autofocus mode is active, as described in Chapter 1 and discussed in more detail in Chapter 5.
- **Autofocus area.** Shows the AF area mode in use: Wide (the camera chooses one or more of the 15 AF areas to use); Zone (you select which group of AF areas to use); Spot (the camera uses the center AF area exclusively); or Local (you select which of the 15 areas to use). I'll explain autofocus options in more detail in Chapter 5.
- **White balance.** Shows current white balance setting. The choices are Auto White Balance, Daylight, Shade, Cloudy, Incandescent, Fluorescent, Flash, Color Temperature, and Custom.
- **D-Range Optimizer.** Indicates the type of D-Range optimization (highlight/shadow enhancement) in use, either Off, Auto, Level 1 through 5, or Auto HDR, as described in Chapter 6.
- **Creative Style.** Indicates which of the six Creative Style settings (Standard, Vivid, Portrait, Landscape, Sunset, or Black and White) is being applied. This setting is discussed in Chapter 6.
- **Picture effects.** Various special effects can be applied to your image as you shoot.
- **ISO setting.** Indicates the sensor ISO sensitivity setting, either Auto ISO or a numerical value from 100 to 16000. This icon also may indicate that Multi Frame Noise Reduction is in effect, in which case the ISO icon includes a stack of multiple rectangular frames.

- **Metering mode.** The icons represent Multi segment, Center weighted, or Spot metering. (See Chapter 4 for more detail.)
- **Flash exposure compensation.** This icon is shown whenever the built-in flash is popped up or a compatible external flash is attached to the hot shoe.
- **Exposure value scale.** On both the standard and graphic displays when viewing through the EVF, this scale is displayed along with an indicator to show the amount of exposure compensation that is being applied. In Manual exposure mode, on the display without Live View, the icon next to this scale changes to the M.M. icon, meaning that manual metering is in effect.
- **Shutter speed.** Shows the current shutter speed.
- **Aperture.** Displays the current f/stop.
- **Exposure compensation.** On all of the information displays, the amount of exposure compensation, even if zero, is shown by an indicator on the EV scale. On the full display without Live View, if there is some exposure compensation, in addition to the scale, a number appears at the bottom right of the screen indicating the positive or negative amount of compensation.
- **AEL button status.** An asterisk is displayed whenever the AEL button is used to lock the exposure setting.
- **SteadyShot status.** Shows whether the Alpha's anti-shake features are turned on or off.
- **Shutter speed indicator (graphic display only).** Graphically illustrates that faster shutter speeds are better for action/slower for scenes with less movement.
- **Aperture indicator (graphic display only).** Icons indicate that wider apertures produce less depth-of-field (represented by a "blurry" background icon).
- **Face Detection.** When this feature is activated, the camera attempts to detect faces in the scene, and, if it does, it adjusts autofocus and exposure accordingly. I'll discuss this feature in Chapter 5.
- **Smile Shutter.** With this feature turned on, the camera will automatically trigger the shutter when the subject smiles. I discuss its operation in Chapter 3.

Enabling/Disabling LCD/EVF Displays

Once you've gotten used to your SLT-A57, you will probably develop some preferences as to which of the displays are available when pressing the DISP button. You can activate or deactivate any of them, so that only those you prefer are shown. You'll need to visit the Setup menu, which I'll explain in more detail in Chapter 3, but the process is easy.

Just follow these steps:

1. **View menus.** Press the MENU button, located on the upper-left corner of the back of the A57. Use the left/right directional buttons to highlight the Custom 2 menu. The tab with the four Custom menu listings is represented by a gear icon, as you can see in Figure 2.19.
2. **Choose either DISP button (Monitor) or DISP button (Finder).** Use the up/down buttons to highlight either choice; the former controls the displays offered for the LCD monitor, while the latter is used to set the displays for the EVF. Press OK to view the selection screen, like the one in Figure 2.20, which shows the LCD version.
3. **Use the up/down buttons to highlight any of the six display choices.** Press the OK button to mark or unmark any of them. You must have at least one display option selected, however. Five of the options, Graphic Display, Display All Info., No Disp. Info., Level, and For Viewfinder should be familiar to you from the discussion in the previous section. The sixth, Histogram, adds a screen that is similar to the No Disp. Info screen, but with a histogram chart lodged in the lower-right corner of the screen. The histogram provides a live view of exposure data, representing the number of black, white, and gray tones that will be captured in your image. I'll show you how to work with histograms in Chapter 4 (their use is beyond the scope of this Roadmap chapter).

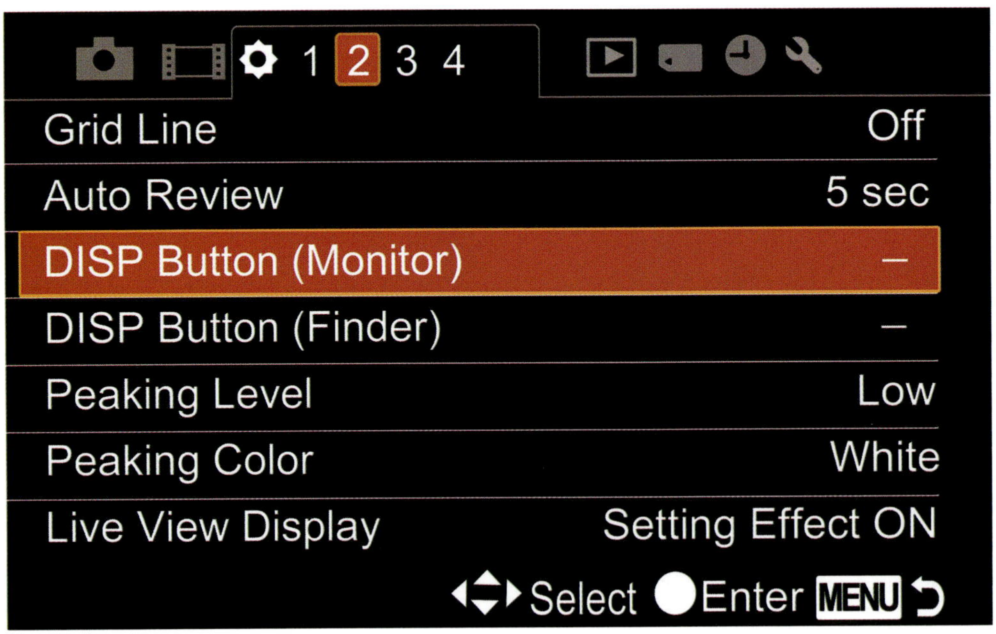

Figure 2.19
Navigate to the Custom 2 menu.

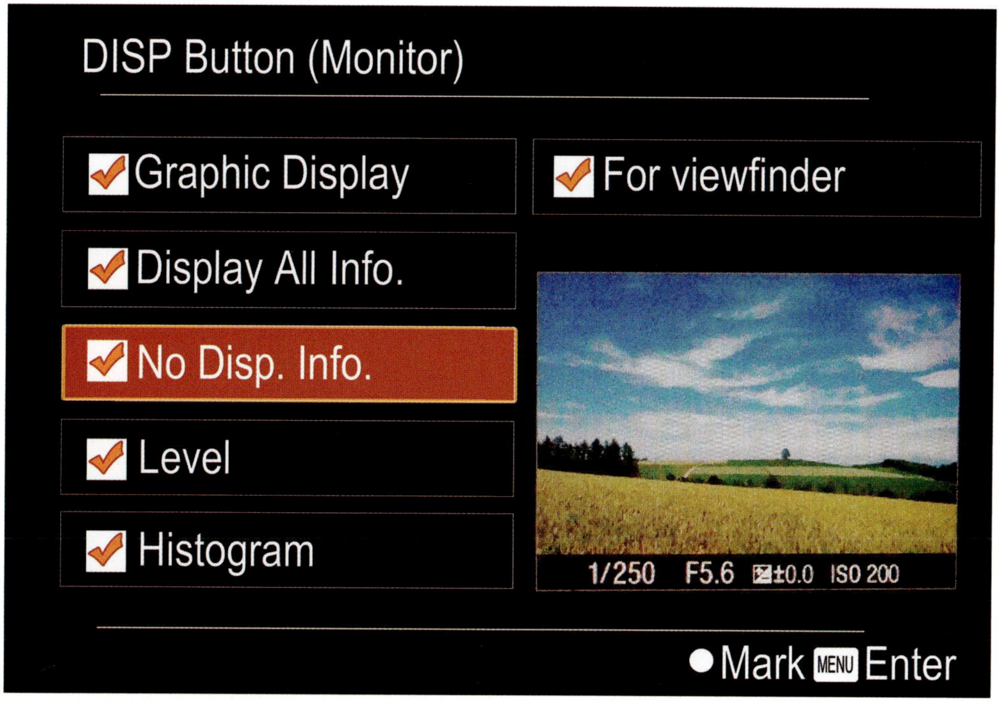

Figure 2.20
Mark or unmark the displays.

4. **Confirm your choice.** When you've finished marking/unmarking the display screens, press the MENU button to confirm and exit.

5. **Repeat for the other type of display.** You may want a different set of choices for the EVF and LCD. The setup screens for each are identical, except that the For Viewfinder option is not available for the electronic viewfinder.

Swiveling the Screen

With the SLT-A57, the LCD monitor can be pulled away from the camera body and swiveled up or down to provide a variety of views from different viewing positions. The screen on these models does not merely move up and down, though—it is fully articulated and can swivel completely on two axes. This means, for example, that you can store or transport the camera with the LCD screen in its "closed" position (see Figure 2.21). In this position, the screen is folded in against the back of the camera, with its display surface hidden from view.

This "closed" configuration is a great way to protect the screen from damage, dirt, or the elements. Many other cameras have their screens exposed to possible harm whenever they're out of their cases. The ability to fold the screen in provides a built-in screen protection system. In addition, in some situations you may want to take your pictures in as discreet a way as possible, such as at concerts or religious ceremonies, and you may

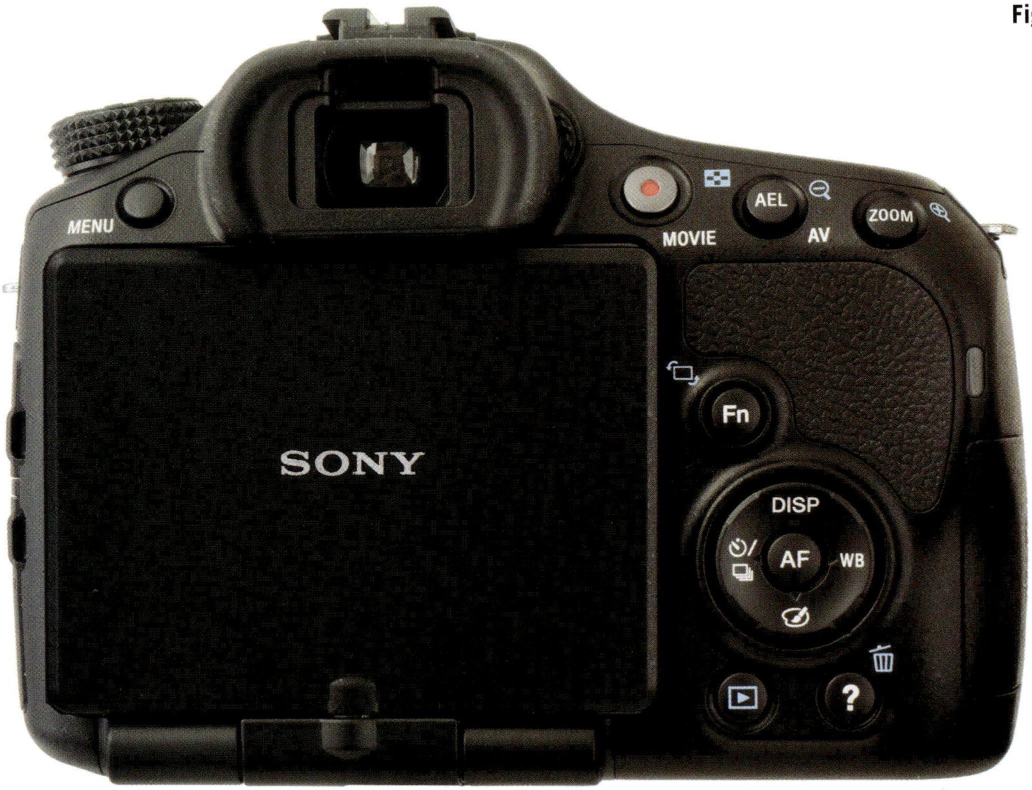

Figure 2.21

not want to distract persons near you by having the LCD display showing. Of course, you can turn off the display of other digital cameras—at least those that have viewfinders, so you won't be shooting blind. But it may be easier and more effective to just fold it in against the camera.

Flip open the LCD on your Sony Alpha SLT and take a look at what it has to offer in the way of photographic versatility. First, check out Figure 2.22. In this position, the screen is swiveled out from the camera and facing up at you from a low angle. From here, you can swivel the screen right or left. These positions give you several options. With the screen swiveled down as shown, you can easily hold the camera down at waist level and compose your image without bending over. In this way, you can compose a photograph that looks better when taken from a low angle, and you don't have to get down on your belly or crouch in a squat. If you swivel the screen to the left or right from this angle, you can shoot at an angle, or even around a corner.

On the other hand, if you flip the screen so it aims downward, as shown in Figure 2.23, you can hold the camera above your head to peer over the tops of crowds or physical obstructions, and compose the image in the LCD, sort of like submarine commanders with their raised periscopes. I appreciate this mode at concerts, because I can raise the camera up over the heads of the multitude milling around in front of me.

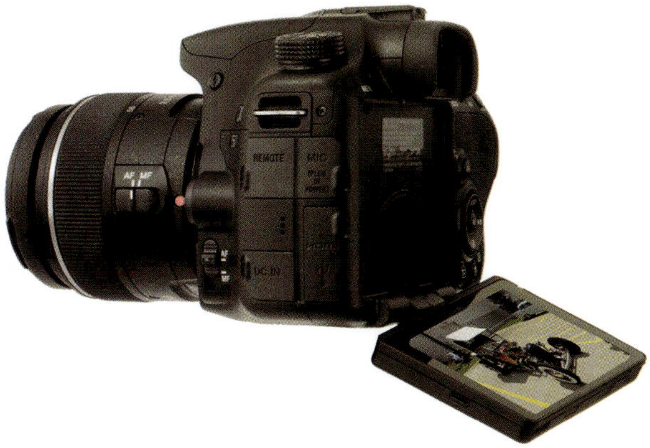

Figure 2.22

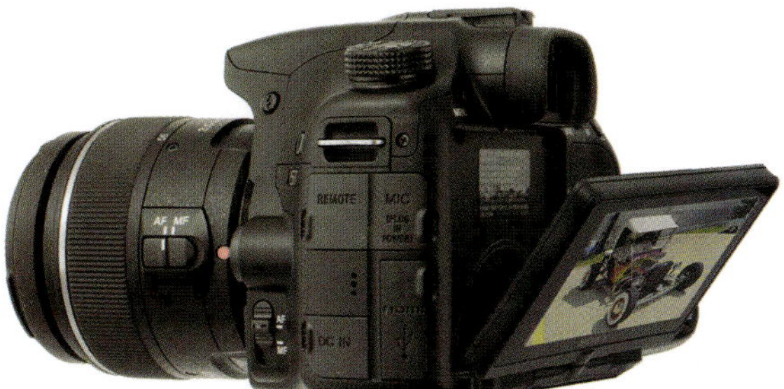

Figure 2.23

Going Topside

The top surface of the Sony Alpha SLT-A57 has several frequently accessed controls of its own. They are labeled in Figure 2.24:

- **Mode dial.** Rotate this dial to switch among Scene modes and semi-automatic and manual exposure modes. You'll find these exposure modes and options described in more detail in Chapter 4.
- **ISO button.** This button gives you access to a menu for specifying ISO sensor sensitivity settings, from ISO 100 to ISO 12800, plus Auto and Multi Frame Noise Reduction. Some of these settings may not be available, depending on the camera's other settings, including shooting mode and image quality. Scroll down through the list of these choices one line at a time using the up/down buttons or the control dial. If you prefer not to use this button, you can get to the same selection screen by using the Fn button and navigating through the Function menu. I'll provide more details about ISO settings in Chapter 4.
- **Exposure button.** In Shooting mode, with the mode dial set to Program, Aperture priority, Shutter priority, Sweep Panorama, or Continuous Advance Priority AE, press this button to produce the exposure compensation display. Then, press the left/right controller keys or turn the control dial to add or subtract from the camera's exposure setting.
- **Flash/Accessory shoe.** Slide an electronic flash into this mount when you need a more powerful speedlight. A dedicated flash unit, like those from Sony, can use the multiple contact points shown to communicate exposure, zoom setting, white balance information, and other data between the flash and the camera. There's more on using electronic flash in Chapter 9. Unfortunately, Sony, like its Minolta

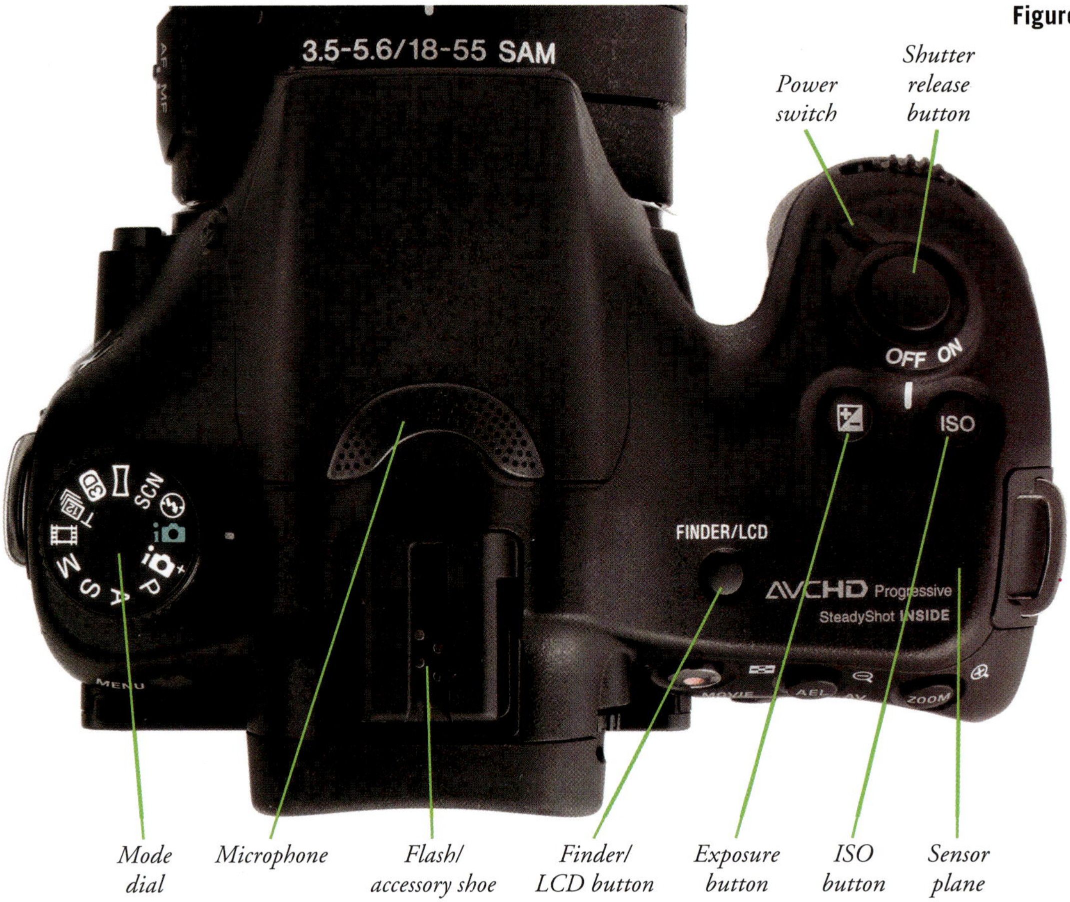

Figure 2.24

predecessor (since 1988), uses a non-standard accessory/flash shoe mount, rather than the industry standard ISO 518 configuration. This keeps you from attaching electronic flash units, radio triggers, and other accessories built for the standard shoe, unless you use one of the adapters that are available.

- **Microphones.** These openings just aft of the flip-up flash house the right and left microphones that record the stereo sound for your movies. Be careful not to cover these holes with your hand or anything else while recording a movie.
- **Finder/LCD button.** This control switches the display between the EVF and LCD. If you've disabled automatic switching using the Eye-Start sensor, you can manually toggle between the two displays with this button.
- **Power switch.** Rotate all the way clockwise to turn the Alpha on; in the opposite direction to switch it off.

- **Shutter release button.** Partially depress this button to lock in exposure and focus. Press all the way to take the picture. Tapping the shutter release when the camera has turned off the autoexposure and autofocus mechanisms reactivates both. When a review image is displayed on the back-panel color LCD, tapping this button removes the image from the display and reactivates the autoexposure and autofocus mechanisms.
- **Sensor focal plane.** Precision macro and scientific photography sometimes requires knowing exactly where the focal plane of the sensor is. The symbol etched on the top of the camera marks that plane.

Underneath Your Sony Alpha

The bottom panel of your Sony Alpha is pretty bare. You'll find a tripod socket, which secures the camera to a tripod, and the door to the battery/memory card compartment, which has a smaller door inset for plugging in an AC adapter. Figure 2.25 shows the underside view of the camera.

Figure 2.25

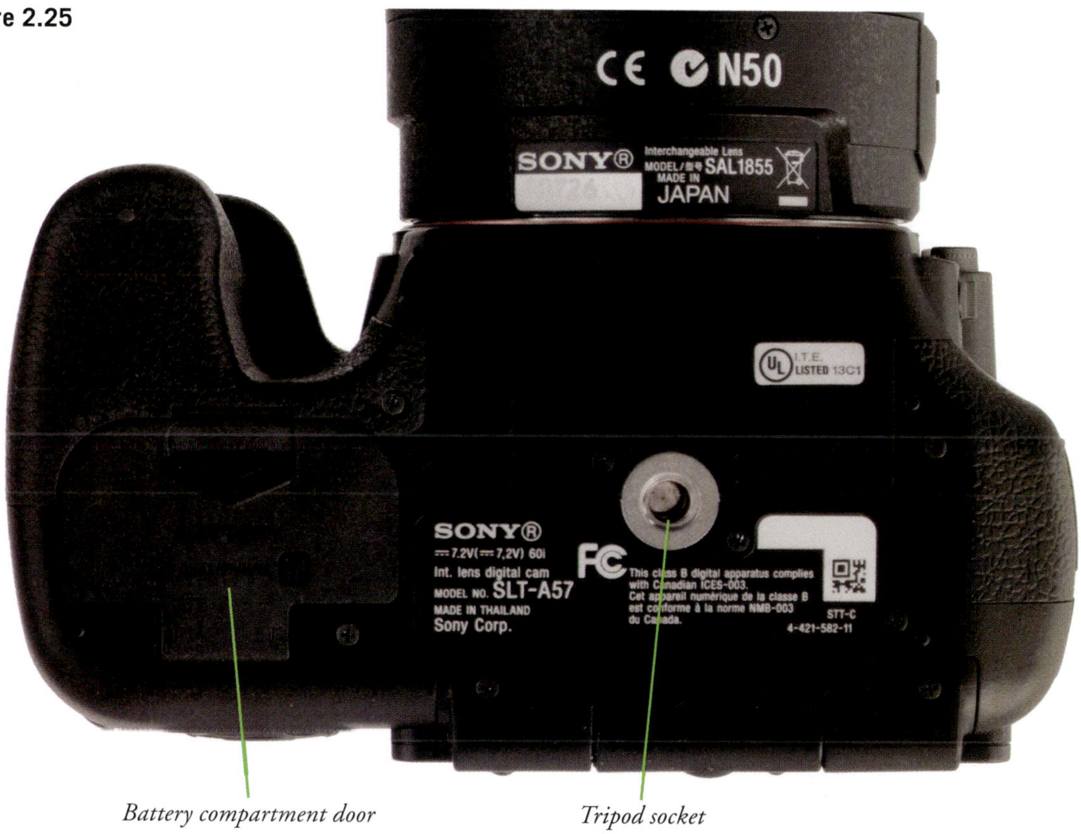

- **Battery compartment slot cover.** This hinged panel protects your battery compartment from dust and dirt. Keep it closed except when you're inserting or removing a battery.
- **Tripod socket**. Attach the camera to a flash/microphone bracket, tripod, monopod, or other support using this standard receptacle.

Lens Components

There's not a lot going on with most Sony lenses in terms of controls because, in the modern electronic age, most of the functions previously found in lenses in the ancient film era, such as autofocus options, are taken care of by the camera itself. Nor do Sony lenses require an on/off switch for image stabilization, because SteadyShot is built into the sensor components. Not every lens has every feature or component, so I've illustrated two common types—a zoom and a fixed focal length ("prime") lens that contain many of the basic components, in Figure 2.26.

- **Lens hood bayonet.** This is used to mount the lens hood for lenses that don't use screw-mount hoods (the majority).
- **Zoom ring.** Turn this ring to change the zoom setting.

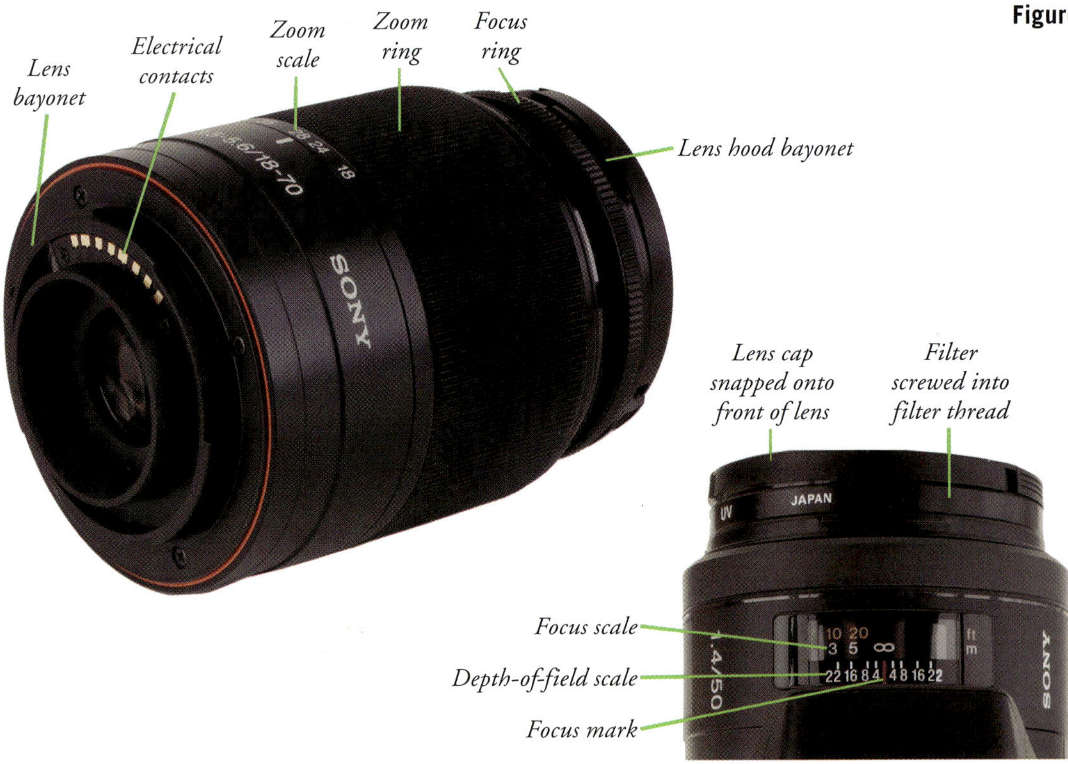

Figure 2.26

- **Zoom scale.** These markings on the lens show the current focal length selected.
- **Focus ring.** This is the ring you turn when you manually focus the lens.
- **Electrical contacts.** On the back of the lens are electrical contacts that the camera uses to communicate focus, aperture setting, and other information.
- **Lens bayonet.** This mount is used to attach the lens to a matching bayonet on the camera body.
- **Filter thread.** Lenses (including those with a bayonet lens hood mount) have a thread on the front for attaching filters and other add-ons. Some also use this thread for attaching a lens hood (you screw on the filter first, and then attach the hood to the screw thread on the front of the filter). A filter is shown screwed into the filter thread at lower right in Figure 2.26.
- **Distance scale/Depth-of-field scale.** Some lenses, especially prime lenses like the one at lower right in the figure, have this readout that rotates in unison with the lens's focus mechanism to show the distance at which the lens has been focused. It's a useful indicator for double-checking autofocus, roughly evaluating depth-of-field, and for setting manual focus guesstimates.
- **AF/MF switch (not shown).** Some Sony lenses have a switch to choose between autofocus and manual focus; some do not. With the Sony Alpha SLT-A57, you need to switch focus modes on the lens, if it has such a switch. In that case, leave the AF/MF switch on the camera set to AF at all times, and switch to MF or AF using the switch on the lens. If the lens does not have such a switch, then you need to use the switch on the camera to change from autofocus to manual focus and vice-versa.

3

Setting Up Your Sony Alpha SLT-A57

The Sony Alpha A57 has a remarkable number of options and settings you can use to customize the way your camera operates. Not only can you change shooting settings used at the time the picture is taken, but you can adjust the way your camera behaves. This chapter will help you sort out the settings for all the Alpha's menus. These include the Still Shooting and Playback menus, which determine how the Alpha uses many of its shooting features to take a photo and how it displays images on review. I'll also show you how to use the Setup and Custom menus to adjust power-saving timers, specify LCD brightness, and adjust options like Eye-Start autofocus and red-eye reduction. And, I'll discuss two categories that Sony has added to the menu lineup with its recent cameras: the Memory Card Tool and Clock setup menus.

This book isn't intended to replace the manual you received with your Alpha, nor have I any interest in rehashing its contents. You'll still find the original manual useful as a standby reference that lists every possible option in exhaustive (if mind-numbing) detail—without really telling you how to use those options to take better pictures. There is, however, some unavoidable duplication between the Sony manual and this chapter, because I'm going to explain all the key menu choices and the options you may have in using them. You should find, though, that I will give you the information you need in a much more helpful format, with plenty of detail on why you should make some settings that are particularly cryptic.

I'm not going to waste a lot of space on some of the more obvious menu choices in these chapters. For example, you can probably figure out, even without my help, that the Format command in the Memory Card Tool menu erases the content of your memory card. In this chapter, I'll devote no more than a sentence or two to the blatantly obvious settings and concentrate on the more confusing aspects of Alpha setup, such as autofocus. I'll start with an overview of using the Alpha's menus themselves.

Anatomy of the Sony Alpha's Menus

The Alpha has one of the best-designed menu systems of any digital camera in its price class, with a significant amount of consistency with other cameras in the Sony current product line. The Sony Alpha SLT-A57 has a series of fifteen separate tabbed menus, each with a single screen of entries, arranged in rows. (The main categories are shown in Figure 3.1.)

You'll never need to scroll within a menu to see all the entries; however, if you scroll down to the bottom of any given menu, and then past the last entry, you'll be taken automatically to the first entry in the next tab. Just press the MENU button, located in the upper-left corner of the back of the camera, use the left/right cursor buttons to highlight the menu tab you want to access, and then use the up/down buttons or spin the control dial to highlight the menu entry you want. What could be easier?

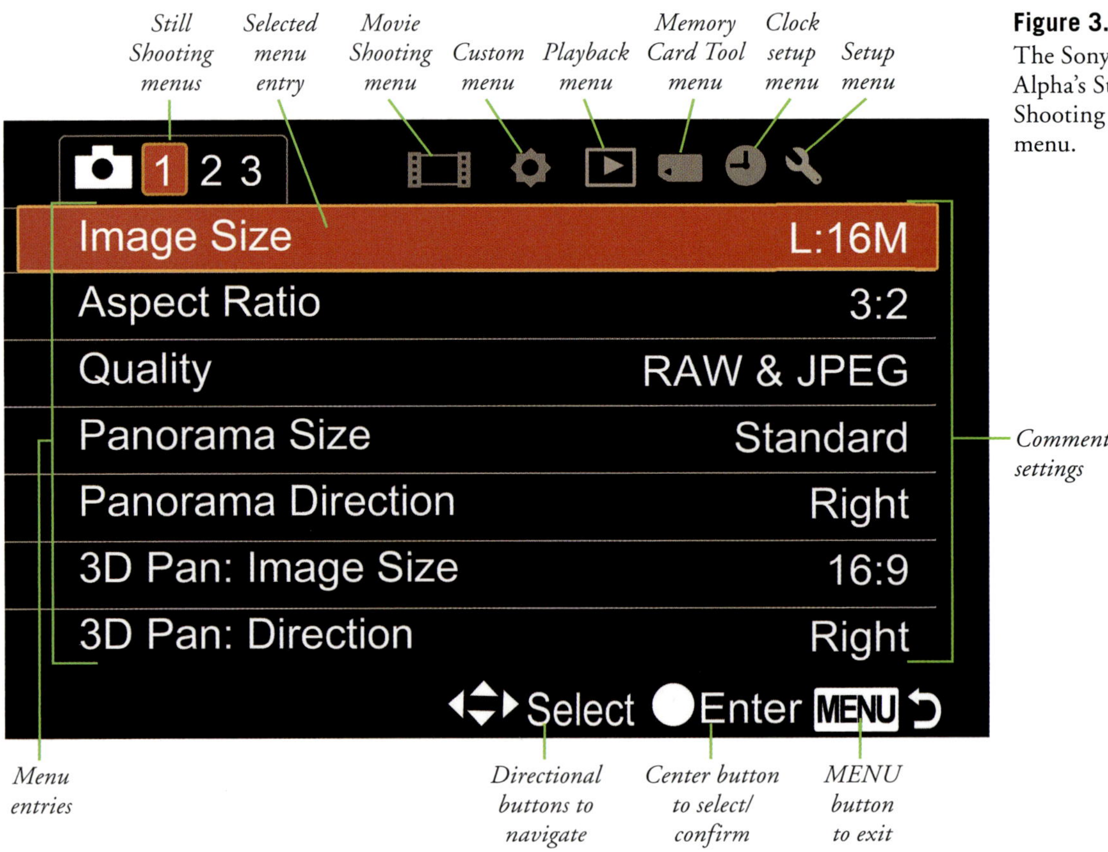

Figure 3.1 The Sony Alpha's Still Shooting 1 menu.

Pressing the MENU button brings up a typical menu. (If the camera goes to "sleep" because of the Power Save feature while you're reviewing a menu, you can wake it up again by tapping the MENU button.) The 15 menu tabs are Still Shooting 1, Still Shooting 2, Still Shooting 3, Movie Shooting 1, Custom 1, Custom 2, Custom 3, Custom 4, Playback 1, Playback 2, Memory Card Tool 1, Clock setup 1, Setup 1, Setup 2, and Setup 3.

Of course, not everything is set using these menus. The Alpha also has very convenient direct setting controls, such as the drive mode, exposure compensation, white balance, and ISO buttons that bypass the multilayered menu system to provide quick access to some features. Even more direct access adjustment screens are available when you press the Fn (Function) button, which produces the Function menu and submenus, introduced in Chapters 1 and 2 and discussed in more detail later in this chapter.

When working with any of these menus, after you've moved the highlighting bar with the up/down buttons (or the control dial) to the menu item you want to work with, press the center controller button to select it. In most cases, a submenu with a list of options for the selected menu item will appear. Within the submenu options, you can scroll with the up/down buttons or with the control dial to choose a setting, and then press the center controller button to confirm the choice you've made. Press the MENU button again to exit. Or, if you prefer, you can press halfway down on the shutter button to exit the menu system and go directly into Still Shooting mode, ready to snap a photo with your new menu settings.

At times you will notice that some lines on various menu screens are "grayed out," so you can read them, but they cannot be selected. This means that item is not available for adjustment with your current settings. For example, if you have set Quality to RAW, the Image Size line will be grayed out, because RAW files are all the same size, and no size setting is possible.

Still Shooting 1/2/3 Menu

The various settings accessed through the buttons on the Alpha for drive mode, ISO, white balance, and exposure compensation are likely to be the most common settings you change. Some of the settings that are accessible through the Fn button are also very useful ones that you may change frequently, such as metering mode, autofocus mode, and autofocus area. Several of the camera's most important settings, however, are available only through the menu system, including image size, quality, and aspect ratio. You'll probably find that these and other Still Shooting menu options are among those that you access frequently when you're using your Sony Alpha. You might make such adjustments as you begin a shooting session, or when you move from one type of subject to another. Sony makes accessing these changes very easy. Figure 3.1 shows the Still Shooting 1 menu.

This section explains the options of the two Still Shooting menu screens and how to use them. The choices you'll find on these screens include the following:

- Image: Size
- Image: Aspect Ratio
- Image: Quality
- Panorama: Size
- Panorama: Direction
- 3D Pan.: Image Size
- 3D Pan.: Direction
- Clear Image Zoom
- Digital Zoom
- Long Exposure NR
- High ISO NR
- Flash Control
- AF Illuminator
- Color Space
- SteadyShot
- Shooting Tip List

Image: Size

Options: Large, Medium, and Small

Default: L (Large)

Here you can choose from the A57's Large, Medium, and Small image settings. Select the menu option, and use the up/down cursor buttons or the control dial to choose L, M, or S. Then press the center controller button to confirm your choice. Of course, the resolution of each of these options depends on whether you're working with the standard 3:2 aspect ratio or the optional 16:9 HDTV aspect ratio (described next). Table 3.1 provides a comparison.

There are few reasons to use anything other than the Large setting with either of these cameras, even if reduced resolution is sufficient for your application, such as photo ID cards or web display. Starting with a full-size image gives you greater freedom for cropping and fixing problems with your image editor. An 800 × 600-pixel web image created from a full-resolution original often ends up better than one that started out at a lower resolution.

Of course, the Medium and Small settings make it possible to squeeze more pictures onto your memory card, and an 8.4 MP or 7.1 MP image (the Medium sizes for A57 and images at the 3:2 aspect ratio) is nothing to sneeze at—either one is a resolution

Table 3.1 Image Sizes Available

Image Size	Megapixels 3:2 Aspect Ratio	Resolution 3:2 Aspect Ratio	Megapixels 16:9 Aspect Ratio	Resolution 16:9 Aspect Ratio
Large (L)	16 MP	4912 × 3264	14 MP	4912 × 2760
Medium (M)	8.4 MP	3568 × 2368	7.1 MP	3568 × 2000
Small (S)	4.0 MP	2448 × 1624	3.4 MP	2448 × 1376

that approaches the maximum of some very fine cameras of the last few years. Smaller image sizes might come in handy in situations where your storage is limited and/or you don't have the opportunity to offload the pictures you've taken to your computer. For example, if you're on vacation and plan to make only 4 × 6-inch snapshot prints, a lower resolution can let you stretch your memory card's capacity. The A57 can fit 928 of those 8.4 MP Medium shots at the 3:2 aspect ratio in JPEG Fine quality mode onto a 4GB memory card. Most of the time, however, it makes more sense to simply buy more memory cards and use your camera at its maximum resolution.

Image: Aspect Ratio

Options: 3:2, 16:9 aspect ratios

Default: 3:2

The aspect ratio is simply the proportions of your image as stored in your image file. The standard aspect ratio for digital photography is approximately 3:2; the image is two-thirds as tall as it is wide, as shown by the outer green rectangle in Figure 3.2. These proportions conform to those of the most common snapshot size in the USA, 4 × 6 inches. Of course, if you want to make a standard 8 × 10-inch enlargement, you'll need to trim some image area from either end, or use larger paper and end up with an 8 × 12-inch print. Aspect ratios are nothing new for 35mm film photographers (or those who own a "full-frame" digital SLR). The 36 × 24mm (or 24 × 36mm) frame of those cameras also has a 3:2 (2:3) aspect ratio.

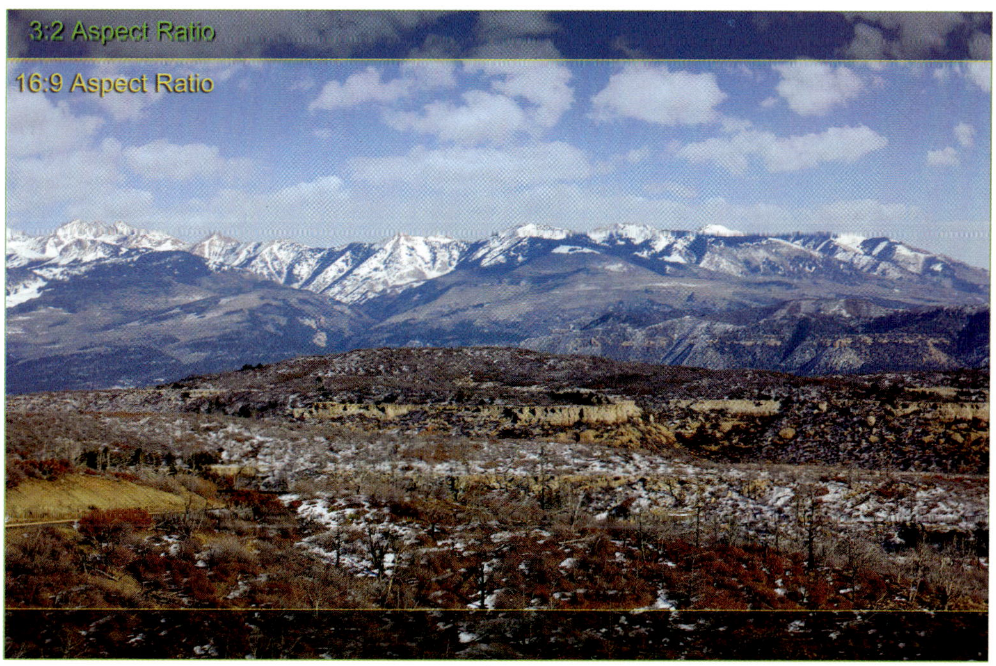

Figure 3.2
The 3:2 aspect ratio is shown by the outer green box. The yellow bars indicate the 16:9 aspect ratio cropping.

If you're looking for images that will "fit" a wide-screen computer display or a high-definition television, the Alpha models can be switched to a 16:9 aspect ratio that is much wider than it is tall. The camera performs this magic by cutting off the top and bottom of the frame, and storing a reduced resolution image (as shown in Table 3.1). Your 16 MP image becomes a 14 MP shot. If you need the wide-screen look, the 16:9 aspect ratio will save you some time in image editing, but you can achieve the same proportions (or any other aspect ratio) by trimming a full-resolution image in your editor. As with the other basic menu choices in this chapter, just navigate to the entry, press the center controller button, choose the option you want, and press the center controller button again to confirm your choice.

Image: Quality

Options: RAW, RAW & JPEG, Fine, Standard

Default: Fine

You can choose the image quality settings used by the Alpha to store its files. You have several choices to select from within this menu entry: RAW, RAW & JPEG, Fine, and Standard. (The two latter options are JPEG formats.) Here's what you need to know to choose intelligently:

- **JPEG compression.** To reduce the size of your image files and allow more photos to be stored on a given memory card, the Alpha uses JPEG compression to squeeze the images down to a smaller size. This compacting reduces the image quality a little, so you're offered your choice of Fine compression and Standard compression. Fine should really be your *standard*, because it offers the best image quality of the two JPEG options.
- **JPEG, RAW, or both.** You can elect to store only JPEG versions of the images you shoot (Fine or Standard), or you can save your photos as RAW files, which consume several times as much space on your memory card. Or, you can store both file types at once as you shoot. Many photographers elect to save *both* a JPEG and a RAW file (RAW & JPEG), so they'll have a JPEG version that might be usable as-is, as well as the original "digital negative" RAW file in case they want to do some processing of the image later. You'll end up with two different versions of the same file: one with a .jpg extension, and one with the .arw extension that signifies a Sony RAW file. Note that if you choose either RAW or RAW & JPEG, the Image Size menu option will no longer be available. With either setting, the A57 always stores a RAW image at full resolution, and with RAW & JPEG stores a full resolution (Large) image using JPEG Fine compression as well.

As I noted under Image: Size, there are some limited advantages to using the Medium and Small resolution settings, and similar space-saving benefits accrue to the Standard JPEG compression setting. They all allow stretching the capacity of your memory card so you can shoehorn quite a few more pictures onto a single memory card. That can be useful when you're on vacation and are running out of storage, or when you're shooting non-critical work that doesn't require full resolution (such as photos taken for real estate listings, web page display, photo ID cards, or similar applications). Some photographers like to record RAW & JPEG Fine so they'll have a JPEG file for review and minor adjustments, while retaining access to the original RAW file for serious editing.

But for most work, using lower resolution and extra compression is false economy. You never know when you might actually need that extra bit of picture detail. Your best bet is to have enough memory cards to handle all the shooting you want to do until you have the chance to transfer your photos to your computer or a personal storage device.

JPEG vs. RAW

You'll sometimes be told that RAW files are the "unprocessed" image information your camera produces, before it's been modified. That's nonsense. RAW files are no more unprocessed than your camera film is after it's been through the chemicals to produce a negative or transparency. A lot can happen in the developer that can affect the quality of a film image—positively and negatively—and, similarly, your digital image undergoes a significant amount of processing before it is saved as a RAW file. Sony even applies a name (BIONZ) to the digital image processing (DIP) chip used to perform this magic in the Sony Alpha.

A RAW file is more similar to a film camera's processed negative. It contains all the information, with no compression, no sharpening, no application of any special filters or other settings you might have specified when you took the picture. Those settings are *stored* with the RAW file so they can be applied when the image is converted to a form compatible with your favorite image editor. However, using RAW conversion software such as Adobe Camera Raw or Sony's Image Data Converter SR, you can override those settings and apply settings of your own. You can select essentially the same changes there that you might have specified in your camera's picture-taking options.

RAW exists because sometimes we want to have access to all the information captured by the camera, before the camera's internal logic has processed it and converted the image to a standard file format. RAW doesn't save as much space as JPEG. What it does do is preserve all the information captured by your camera after it's been converted from analog to digital form.

So, why don't we always use RAW? Although some photographers do save only in RAW format, it's more common to use either RAW plus the JPEG option or to just shoot JPEG and eschew RAW altogether. While RAW is overwhelmingly helpful when an image needs to be fine-tuned, in other situations working with a RAW file can slow you down significantly. RAW images take longer to store on the memory card and require more post-processing effort, whether you elect to go with the default settings in force when the picture was taken or make minor adjustments.

MANAGING LOTS OF FILES

The only long-term drawback to shooting everything in RAW & JPEG is that it's easy to fill up your computer's hard drive if you are a prolific photographer. Here's what I do. My most recent photos are stored on my working hard drive in a numbered folder, say Alpha-01, with subfolders named after the shooting session, such as 130202Groundhog, for pictures of groundhogs taken on February 2, 2013. An automatic utility called Allway Sync (allwaysync.com) copies new and modified photos to a different hard drive for backup as soon as they appear.

When the top-level folder accumulates about 30GB of images, I back it up to multiple DVDs and then move the folder to a drive dedicated solely for storage of folders that have already been backed up onto DVD. Then I start a new folder, such as Alpha-02, on the working hard drive and repeat the process. I always have at least one backup of every image taken, either on another hard drive or on a DVD (or both).

As a result, those who depend on speedy access to images or who shoot large numbers of photos in one session may prefer JPEG over RAW. Wedding photographers, for example, might expose several thousand photos during a bridal affair and offer hundreds to clients as electronic proofs for inclusion in an album. Wedding shooters take the time to make sure that their in-camera settings are correct, minimizing the need to post-process photos after the event. Given that their JPEGs are so good, there is little need to get bogged down shooting RAW. Sports photographers also avoid RAW files for similar reasons.

JPEG was invented as a more compact file format that can store most of the information in a digital image, but in a much smaller size. JPEG predates most digital SLRs, and was initially used to squeeze down files for transmission over slow dialup connections. Even if you were using an early dSLR with 1.3 megapixel files for news photography, you didn't want to send them back to the office over a modem at 1,200 bps.

But, as I noted, JPEG provides smaller files by compressing the information in a way that loses some image data. JPEG remains a viable alternative because it offers several different quality levels. At the highest quality Fine level, you might not be able to tell the difference between the original RAW file and the JPEG version. With Standard compression, you'll usually notice a quality loss when making big enlargements or cropping your image tightly.

In my case, I shoot virtually everything in RAW & JPEG. Most of the time, I'm not concerned about filling up my memory cards, as I usually have a minimum of three 32GB memory cards with me. If I know I may fill up all those cards, I have a tiny battery-operated personal storage device that can copy a typical card in about 15 minutes. As I mentioned earlier, when shooting sports I'll shift to JPEG Fine (with no RAW file) to squeeze a little extra speed out of my Alpha's continuous shooting mode, and to reduce the need to wade through long series of photos taken in RAW format. On the other hand, on my last trip to Europe, I took only RAW photos and transferred more images onto my netbook, as I planned on doing at least some post-processing on many of the images for a travel book I was working on.

Panorama: Size

Options: Standard, Wide

Default: Standard

This setting is available only when the shooting mode is set to Sweep Panorama. In this case, there are only two options—the default choice of Standard, or the optional setting of Wide. With the Standard setting, if you are shooting a horizontal panorama, the size of your images will be 8192 × 1856 pixels; if your shots are vertical, the size will be 2160 × 3872 pixels. With the Wide setting, horizontal panoramas will be at a size of 12416 × 1856 pixels, and vertical shots will be 2160 × 5536 pixels.

Panorama: Direction

Options: Right, Left, Up, Down

Default: Right

When the shooting mode is set to Sweep Panorama, you have four options for the direction in which the camera will prompt you to pan or tilt the camera: Right, Left, Up, or Down. You have to select one of these so the camera will know ahead of time how to perform its in-camera processing of the images that it will stitch together into the final panorama. The default, Right, is probably the most natural to sweep the camera, but you may have occasions to use the others, depending on the scene to be photographed. You can set this option only when the shooting mode is set to Sweep Panorama.

3D Pan.: Image Size

Options: 16:9, Standard, Wide

Default: Standard

This setting is available only when the camera's shooting mode is set to 3D Panorama. Select from 16:9, Standard, and Wide for the size of the resulting panoramic image. Note that with this mode you get the additional ability to shoot with the 16:9 aspect ratio, as opposed to just the Wide and Standard options that are available for non-3D panoramas. This option lets you shoot normal-sized images in 3D, rather than only panoramas. With the 16:9 setting, the panorama's size is 1920 × 1080 pixels; with the Standard setting, the size is 4912 × 1080 pixels; with the Wide setting, the size is 7152 × 1080 pixels. The orientation is limited to horizontal in all cases. I'll discuss this shooting mode in more detail in Chapter 4.

3D Pan.: Direction

Options: Right, Left

Default: Right

This menu option is available only if you have set your shooting mode to 3D Panorama. The choice here is very simple: select either right or left for the direction in which the camera will prompt you to pan when shooting a 3D Panorama. (Unlike the normal Sweep Panorama mode, 3D Panorama images cannot be shot vertically.) I'll discuss various aspects of panorama shooting in Chapter 4.

Clear Image Zoom/Digital Zoom

Options: On, Off

Default: Clear: On; Digital Zoom: Off

These menu options, the first two on Still Shooting 2 menu (see Figure 3.3), allow you to disable/enable the A57's smart zooming features. I provided an entire section on using optical and non-optical zoom in Chapter 2, and won't repeat those instructions here.

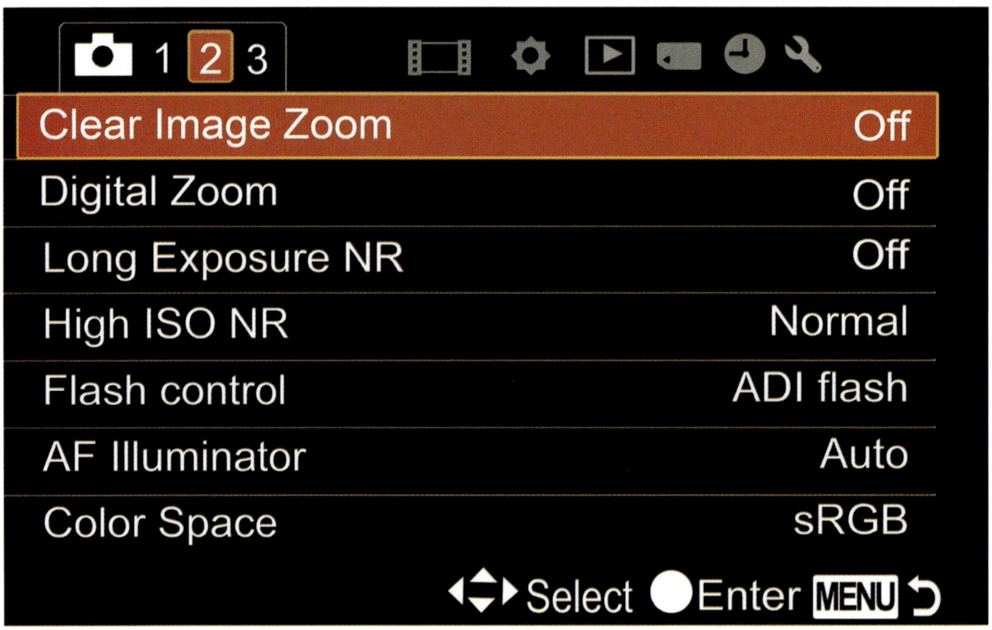

Figure 3.3
The Sony Alpha's Still Shooting 2 menu.

Long Exposure NR/High ISO NR

Options: Long Exp.: On/Off; Default: On

Options: High ISO NR: High/Normal/Low; Default: Normal

I've grouped these two options together because they work together, each under slightly different circumstances. Moreover, the causes and cures for noise involve some overlapping processes.

Your Alpha can reduce the amount of grainy visual noise in your photo, but, at the same time, eliminate some of the detail along with the noise. These two menu choices let you choose whether or not to apply noise reduction to exposures of one second or longer and how much noise reduction to apply to exposures made at high ISO settings (ISO 1600 and above). Although noise reduction is usually a good thing, it's helpful to have the option to turn it off or minimize it when you want to preserve detail, even if it means putting up with a little extra noise.

Visual noise is that awful graininess that shows up as multicolored specks in images, and these settings help you manage it. In some ways, noise is like the excessive grain found in some high-speed photographic films. However, while photographic grain is sometimes used as a special effect, it's rarely desirable in a digital photograph.

The visual noise-producing process is something like listening to a CD in your car, and then rolling down all the windows. You're adding sonic noise to the audio signal, and while increasing the CD player's volume may help a bit, you're still contending with an unfavorable signal to noise ratio that probably mutes tones (especially higher treble notes) that you really want to hear.

The same thing happens when the analog signal is amplified: You're increasing the image information in the signal, but boosting the background fuzziness at the same time. Tune in a very faint or distant AM radio station on your car stereo. Then turn up the volume. After a certain point, turning up the volume further no longer helps you hear better. There's a similar point of diminishing returns for digital sensor ISO increases and signal amplification as well.

These processes create several different kinds of noise. As I noted, noise can be produced from high ISO settings. As the captured information is amplified to produce higher ISO sensitivities, some random noise in the signal is amplified along with the photon information. Increasing the ISO setting of your camera raises the threshold of sensitivity so that fewer and fewer photons are needed to register as an exposed pixel. Yet, that also increases the chances of one of those phantom photons being counted among the real-life light particles, too.

A second way noise is created is through longer exposures. Extended exposure times allow more photons to reach the sensor, but increase the likelihood that some photosites will react randomly even though not struck by a particle of light. Moreover, as the sensor remains switched on for the longer exposure, it heats, and this heat can be mistakenly recorded as if it were a barrage of photons. Figure 3.4 shows a pair of images taken at about 15 seconds at f/11 and ISO 3200. The top version suffers from both long exposure and high ISO noise; the bottom version, taken a few seconds later, had both types of noise reduction applied, producing an image with less visual grain.

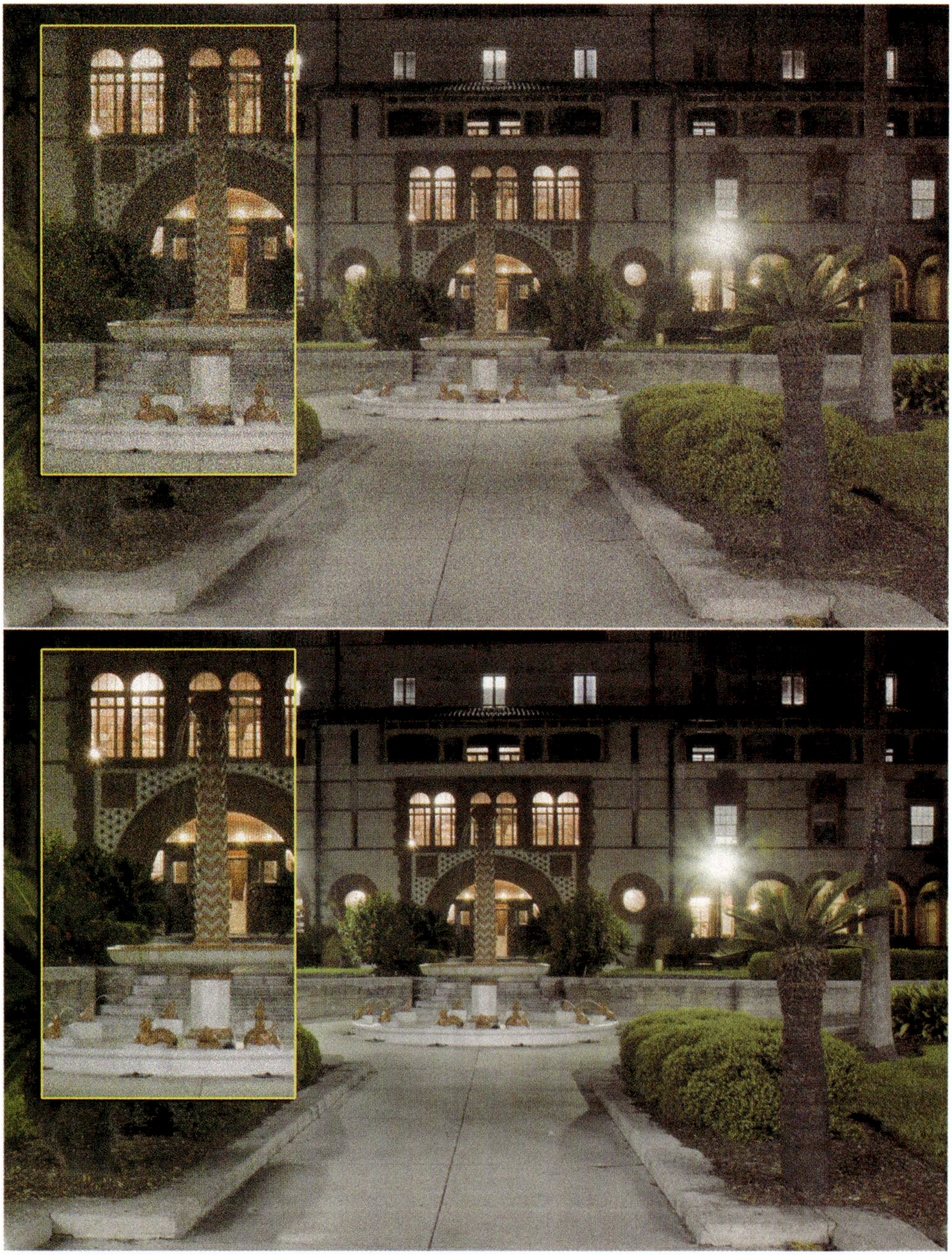

Figure 3.4
Top: Image taken at high ISO with a long exposure, and no noise reduction. Bottom: Same scene with Long Exposure NR and High ISO NR applied.

However, you might want to turn off noise reduction for long exposures and minimize it for high ISOs to preserve image detail, and when the delay caused by the noise reduction process (it can take roughly the same amount of time as the exposure itself) interferes with your shooting. Or, you simply may not need NR in some situations. For example, you might be shooting waves crashing into the shore at ISO 100 with the camera mounted on a tripod, using a neutral-density filter and long exposure to cause the pounding water to blur slightly. To maximize detail in the non-moving portions of your photos, you can switch off long exposure noise reduction.

TIP

- **Long exposure noise reduction** is disabled, even if the menu option is turned on, if the shooting mode is set to Sweep Panorama, 3D Sweep Panorama Continuous Advance Priority AE, Continuous shooting, Continuous bracketing, or if either Sports Action, or Hand-held Twilight scene modes are active. Long exposure noise reduction also does not operate when ISO is set to Multi Frame Noise Reduction.

On the other hand, when the shooting mode is set to any of the Auto or Scene modes, long exposure noise reduction cannot be turned *off.*

- **High ISO noise reduction.** The menu option for setting the amount of high ISO noise reduction is grayed out and unavailable when shooting in RAW quality. (If you shoot in RAW & JPEG, the JPEG images, but not the RAW files, will be affected by this setting.)

High ISO noise reduction is automatically set to Low during continuous shooting or continuous bracketing (in order to reduce the amount of processing lag that might slow down your continuous sequence). You cannot adjust High ISO NR when the A57 is set for Auto, Auto+, Scene, or either Sweep Panorama shooting modes.

Flash Control

Options: ADI flash, Pre-flash TTL

Default: ADI flash

This is a technical setting that can be left untouched unless you happen to know you have a need to change it. ADI stands for Advanced Distance Integration. When you are using a lens that includes a distance encoder, this function may result in more accurate computation of the flash output. I discuss this option in Chapter 9.

AF Illuminator

Options: Auto, Off

Default: Auto

The AF illuminator is a pre-flash that fires when there is insufficient light for the Alpha's autofocus mechanism to zero in. This light emanates from either the built-in flash unit or a compatible external flash, if one is attached to the hot shoe. In the automatic and Scene modes, the built-in flash will pop up on its own if necessary for this purpose. The extra blast from the AF illuminator helps the camera focus sharply. The default setting, Auto, allows the AF illuminator to work any time the camera judges that it is necessary. Turn it off when you want to use flash but would prefer not to use this feature. For example, the AF illuminator doesn't work when using AF-C focus mode, or when AF-A autofocus is used with a moving subject (which means it has shifted into AF-C mode). Nor will it work when the Smile Shutter is turned on, or with lenses with focal lengths and zoom settings of 300mm or longer.

Color Space

Options: sRGB/Adobe RGB

Default: sRGB

The Alpha's Color Space option gives you the choice of two different color spaces (also called *color gamuts*), named Adobe RGB (because it was developed by Adobe Systems in 1998), and sRGB (supposedly because it is the *standard* RGB color space). These two color gamuts define a specific set of colors that can be applied to the images your Alpha captures.

You're probably surprised that the Alpha doesn't automatically capture *all* the colors we see. Unfortunately, that's impossible because of the limitations of the sensor and the filters used to capture the fundamental red, green, and blue colors, as well as that of the LEDs used to display those colors on your camera and computer monitors. Nor is it possible to *print* every color our eyes detect, because the inks or pigments used don't absorb and reflect colors perfectly.

Instead, the colors that can be reproduced by a given device are represented as a color space that exists within the full range of colors we can see. That full range is represented by the odd-shaped splotch of color shown in Figure 3.5, as defined by scientists at an international organization back in 1931. The colors possible with Adobe RGB are represented by the larger, black triangle in the figure, while the sRGB gamut is represented by the smaller white triangle.

Regardless of which triangle—or color space—is used by the Alpha, you end up with 16.8 million different colors that can be used in your photograph. (No one image will contain all 16.8 million!) But, as you can see from the figure, the colors available will be *different*.

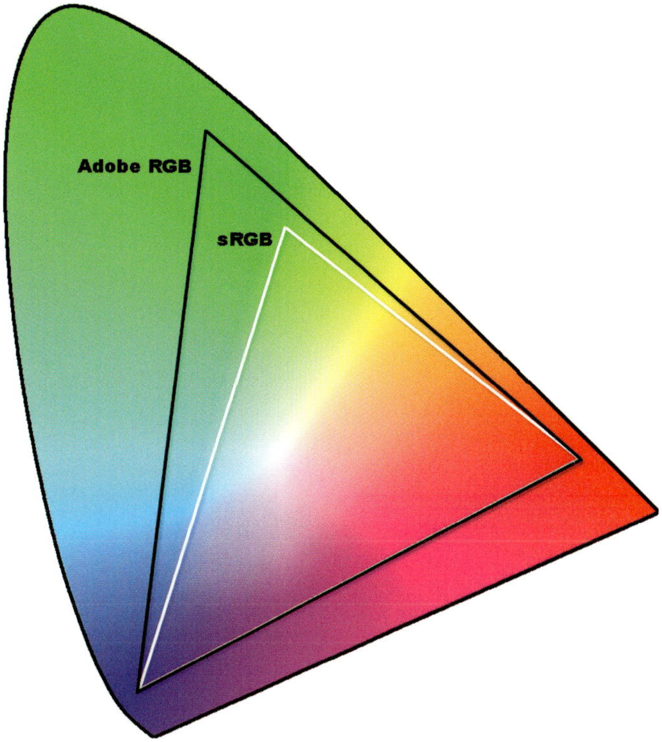

Figure 3.5
The outer figure shows all the colors we can see; the two inner outlines show the boundaries of Adobe RGB (black triangle) and sRGB (white triangle).

ADOBE RGB vs. sRGB

You might prefer sRGB, which is the default for the Sony Alpha cameras, as it is well suited for the colors displayed on a computer screen and viewed over the Internet. The sRGB setting is recommended for images that will be output locally on the user's own printer, or at a retailer's automated kiosk.

Adobe RGB is an expanded color space useful for commercial and professional printing, and it can reproduce a wider range of colors. It can also be useful if an image is going to be extensively retouched within an image editor. You don't need to automatically "upgrade" your camera to Adobe RGB, because images tend to look less saturated on your monitor and, it is likely, significantly different from what you will get if you output the photo to your personal inkjet printer.

Strictly speaking, both sRGB and Adobe RGB can reproduce the exact same absolute *number* of colors (16.8 million when reduced to 8 bits per channel from the original capture). Adobe RGB spreads those colors over a larger space, much like a giant box of crayons in which some of the basic colors have been removed and replaced with new hues not in the original box. The "new" gamut contains a larger proportion of "crayons" in the cyan-green portion of the box, a better choice for reproduction with cyan, magenta, yellow, and black inks at commercial printers, rather than the red, green, and blue hues of your computer display.

Adobe RGB is what is often called an *expanded* color space, because it can reproduce a range of colors that is spread over a wider range of the visual spectrum. Adobe RGB is useful for commercial and professional printing.

SteadyShot

Options: On/Off

Default: On

This entry, one of only two on the Still Shooting 3 tab (not illustrated), can be used to switch off the SteadyShot image stabilization feature. You might want to do that when the camera is mounted on a tripod, as the additional anti-shake feature is not needed in that situation, and slight movements of the tripod can sometimes "confuse" the system. However, it's rarely necessary to turn SteadyShot off, and I recommend leaving it turned on at all times unless you find that it causes problems in some specific situations.

Shooting Tip List

Options: View list of entries

Default: None

Your Alpha SLT-A57 has a built-in Help system that can provide a limited amount of useful information whenever this book or my Compact Field Guide condensed version is not handy. As I noted in Chapter 2, you can summon Help by pressing the Trash/Help button. There are three versions, one each for still shooting, movie shooting, and menu viewing. When the camera is set to a still shooting mode, including Scene modes, a screen of help topics appears suited to the kind of picture you're trying to capture. For example, you can page through listings for Portraits, Landscapes, Night Scenes, Close-up, Macro, and Subject in Motion scenes. In movie mode, a Help menu of choices related to movie making is displayed. If you're viewing a menu, either within the main menu system or a menu selection from among the options produced by the Function menu (press the Fn button to view it), a brief description of that menu entry appears.

This menu entry is for informational purposes only. You can't use it to turn the Help system on or off; the tips will always be available when you press the Trash/Help button. What you can do is scroll down the list that pops up when you select this menu entry, and view *all* the available tips.

1. **Choose a topic.** Scroll down the list of tips and press the OK button to view the text associated with that tip.
2. **View topic.** Some help topics are longer than one screen. Press the up/down directional buttons to scroll within a particular tip.
3. **View next topic.** Press the right directional button to advance to the next tip, or the left button to go back to the previous tip.

4. **Return to tip listing.** Press the MENU button to retreat to the list of tips, where you can scroll to find another tip to view.
5. **Exit Help system.** Press the Trash/Help button to exit the Help system and return to shooting mode.

Movie Menu

This menu, shown in Figure 3.6, has five entries that control movie-making options. It's available at all times; you don't need to switch the mode dial to the Movie mode to set these options.

- File Format
- Record Setting
- Movie: Audio Recording
- Wind Noise Reduct.
- SteadyShot

File Format

Options: AVCHD, MP4

Default: AVCHD

The Sony Alpha SLT-A57 offers full high-definition video recording in the AVCHD format in addition to the somewhat lesser quality MP4 format. If you select AVCHD, which is the default choice, you have no other choices to make for the movie image

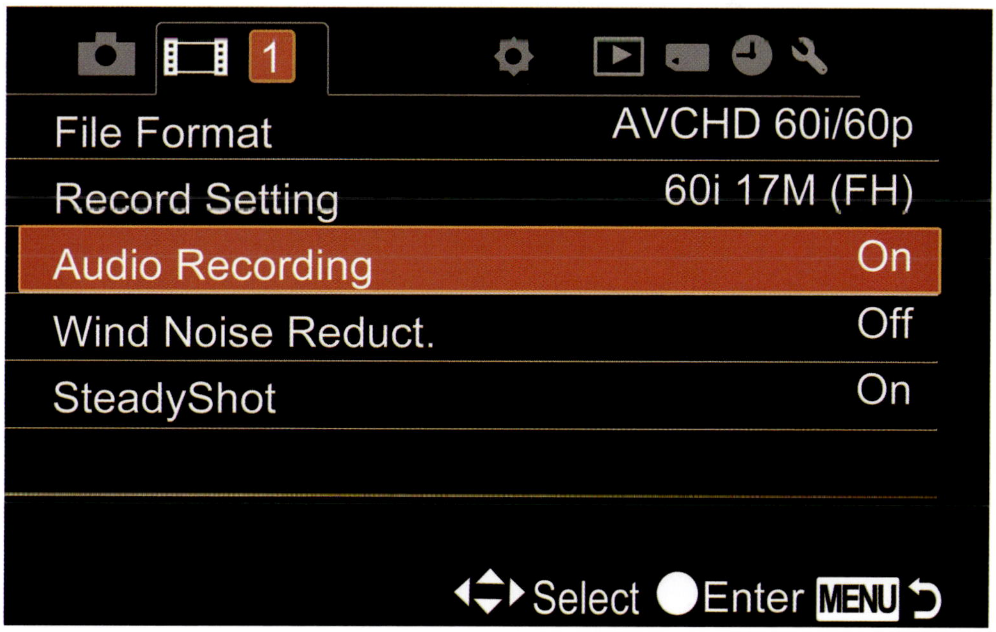

Figure 3.6 The Movie menu.

parameters—AVCHD 60i/60p provides only one image size of 1920 × 1080 pixels. If you select MP4, you have two choices of image size (see below).

Record Setting

Options (AVCHD): 60i 24M (FX), 60i 17M (FH), 60p 28M (PS), 24p 24M (FX), 24p 17M (FH)

Default: 60i 17M (FH)

Options (MP4): 1440 × 1080, VGA (640 × 480)

Default: 1440 × 1080

This setting offers different options, depending on whether you've selected the AVCHD or MP4 format. The default setting for AVCD is 60i 17M (FH), a high-quality format. The *i* in some format names stands for *interlaced scan* while the *p* in other format names stands for *progressive scan*. The figures represent the number of fields or frames captured per second (60 or 24), plus the capture speed in megabits per second (28, 24, or 17M). If you selected MP4, you can choose between 1440 × 1080 and 640 × 480 resolutions. I'll explain these options and how to choose between them in a great deal more detail in Chapter 7.

Audio Recording

Options: On, Off

Default: On

This setting lets you turn off the audio recording for your movies. You might want to do this if you are certain you don't want to have any sound recorded, or if you believe you might be bothered by sounds from the operation of the camera or lens that might be recorded. In my case, I always leave audio recording enabled, because you can always erase a soundtrack that you don't want or replace it with a new one, but you can never recover sounds that you didn't record in the first place.

Wind Noise Reduct.

Options: On/Off

Default: Off

Activates or disables in-camera processing of your audio to remove the whistling sound produced by wind passing over the built-in microphones. (This entry has no effect on external microphones.) As you'll learn in Chapter 7, wind noise reduction does degrade sound quality a little by emphasizing bass tones when recording at low volume, so you'll want to use it only when you have wind noises to contend with.

SteadyShot

Options: On/Off

Default: On

This entry can be used to switch off the SteadyShot image stabilization feature for movie making, separately from the stabilization used for still images (available in the Still Shooting 2 menu). You might want to do that when the camera is mounted on a tripod, as the additional anti-shake feature is not needed in that situation, and slight movements of the tripod can sometimes "confuse" the system. However, it's rarely necessary to turn SteadyShot off, and I recommend leaving it turned on at all times unless you find that it causes problems in some specific situations.

Custom 1/2/3/4 Menu

The options on the four Custom menu screens allow you to specify how your Alpha operates. If you find the Eye-Start autofocus feature distracting, you can change it here. If you'd like to change the length of time that a newly captured image is displayed on the LCD, you can choose that behavior. There are 25 menu entries overall in the Custom menu. The first screen is shown in Figure 3.7.

- Eye-Start AF
- FINDER/LCD Setting
- Viewfinder Magnification
- Red Eye Reduction
- Release w/o Lens
- S. Auto+ Cont. Shooting
- S. Auto+ Image Extract
- Grid Line
- Auto Review
- DISP Button (Monitor)
- DISP Button (Finder)
- Peaking Level
- Peaking Color
- Live View Display
- Func. of AEL Button
- ISO Button
- Preview Button
- Focus Hold Button
- MOVIE Button
- Lens Comp: Shading
- Lens Comp: Chro. Aber
- Lens Comp: Distortion
- Front Curtain Shutter
- Face Registration
- Face Priority Tracking

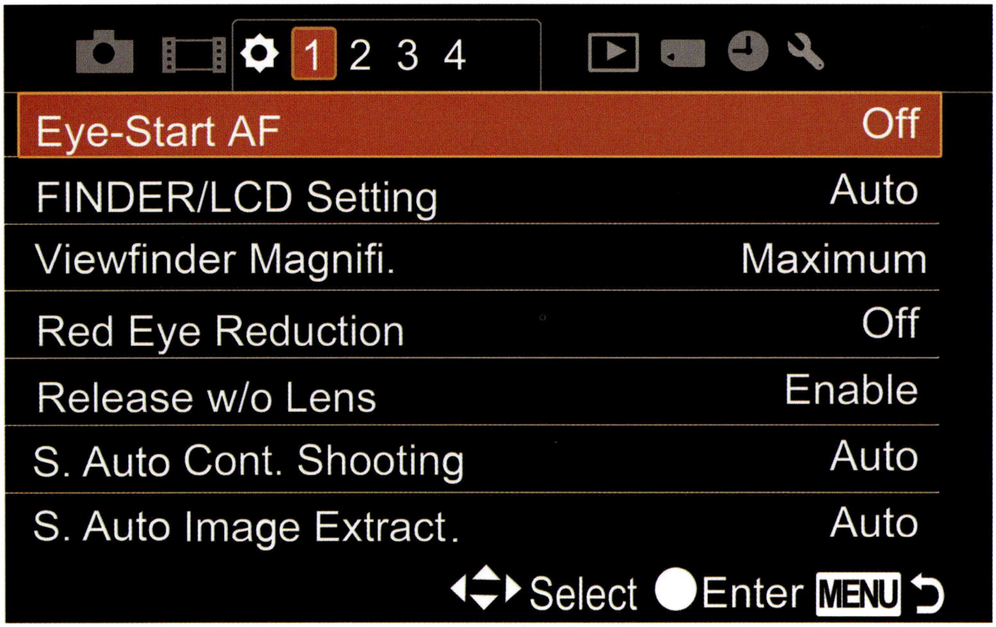

Figure 3.7
The Sony Alpha's Custom 1 menu.

Eye-Start AF

Options: On, Off

Default: Off

It's great how the Sony Alpha is able to read your mind and start autofocusing the instant you move the viewfinder to your eye. The image on the LCD vanishes, the camera adjusts autofocus, and, if you've selected any exposure mode other than Manual, it sets shutter speed and/or aperture for you. You don't even have to partially depress the shutter release. Of course, it's not magic. There are two sensors just above the viewfinder window that detect when your face (or anything else) approaches the finder. (See Figure 3.8.)

On the one hand, Eye-Start AF can be convenient, especially when you're shooting fast-moving subjects and want to take pictures quickly. Indeed, you discover that focus is frequently achieved more rapidly than when Eye-Start AF is switched off and the Alpha defaults to the boring old behavior of not initiating focus until you partially depress the shutter button. On the other hand, some people find this feature annoying. The camera may turn off the LCD and switch on autofocus when a stray hand or other object passes near the viewfinder. Also, if you're wearing the camera around your neck, you may hear a continuous clicking as the camera rubs against your body, triggering the focusing mechanism. One other consideration is that this feature does use a significant amount of battery power. If you choose to, you can turn off Eye-Start AF using this menu setting.

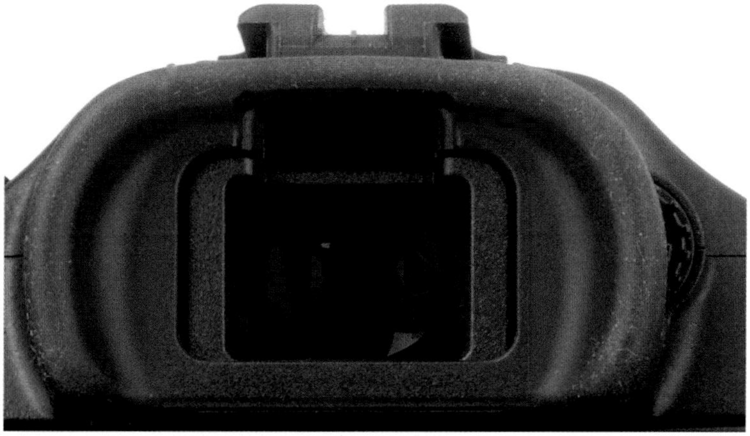

Figure 3.8
The Eye-Start sensors just above the viewfinder window detect when your head (or another object) gets close to the viewfinder's eyepiece.

FINDER/LCD Setting

Options: Auto, Manual

Default: Auto

This option is somewhat similar to the Eye-Start setting, above, though this setting controls only whether the camera turns off the LCD and switches the view to the viewfinder when your eye comes near the viewfinder. With the default setting of Auto, the screen goes blank and the viewfinder activates when your eye approaches the Eye-Start sensors. With the Manual setting, you have to use the FINDER/LCD button, to the right of the viewfinder, to switch the view. You might want to use this setting if you are doing work involving critical focusing, and you need to examine the LCD closely without having it turn off whenever your face gets too close to the screen.

Viewfinder Magnification

Options: Maximum, Standard

Default: Maximum

This unusual option changes the size of the display seen through the EVF viewfinder window. Ordinarily, you would like the largest EVF image possible for framing, focusing, and previewing details in your image. The SLT-A57 has a relatively large viewfinder image with 1.04X magnification and a 100% view of the frame, compared to some other cameras, which may show only 95-98% of the image at a magnification of 0.73-0.86X. However, some folks, particularly glasses wearers, have difficulty seeing all of the A57's large frame. If that's the case, you can reduce the magnification from the default Maximum setting (1,440,000 dots, and 1.04X) to Standard magnification (1,253,280 dots, and 0.97X). Vendors calculate "magnification" as the relative size of an image in real life compared to the size of the image seen through the viewfinder with a 50mm lens.

Red Eye Reduction

Options: On, Off

Default: Off

Unfortunately, your camera is unable, on its own, to *eliminate* the red-eye effects that occur when an electronic flash (or, rarely, illumination from other sources) bounces off the retinas of your subject's eyes and into the camera lens. Animals seem to suffer from yellow or green glowing pupils, instead; the effect is equally undesirable. The effect is worst under low-light conditions (exactly when you might be using a flash) as the pupils expand to allow more light to reach the retinas. The best you can hope for is to *reduce* or minimize the red-eye effect.

It's fairly easy to remove red-eye effects in an image editor (some image importing programs will do it for you automatically as the pictures are transferred from your camera or memory card to your computer). But, it's better not to have glowing red eyes in your photos in the first place.

When this feature is activated, the Alpha's flip-up flash issues a few brief bursts prior to taking the photo, theoretically causing your subjects' pupils to contract, reducing the effect (assuming the person is looking at the camera during the bursts). (See Figure 3.9.) This option works only with the built-in flash, and doesn't produce any prebursts if you have an external flash attached. In most cases, the higher elevation of the external flash effectively prevents red eye anyway.

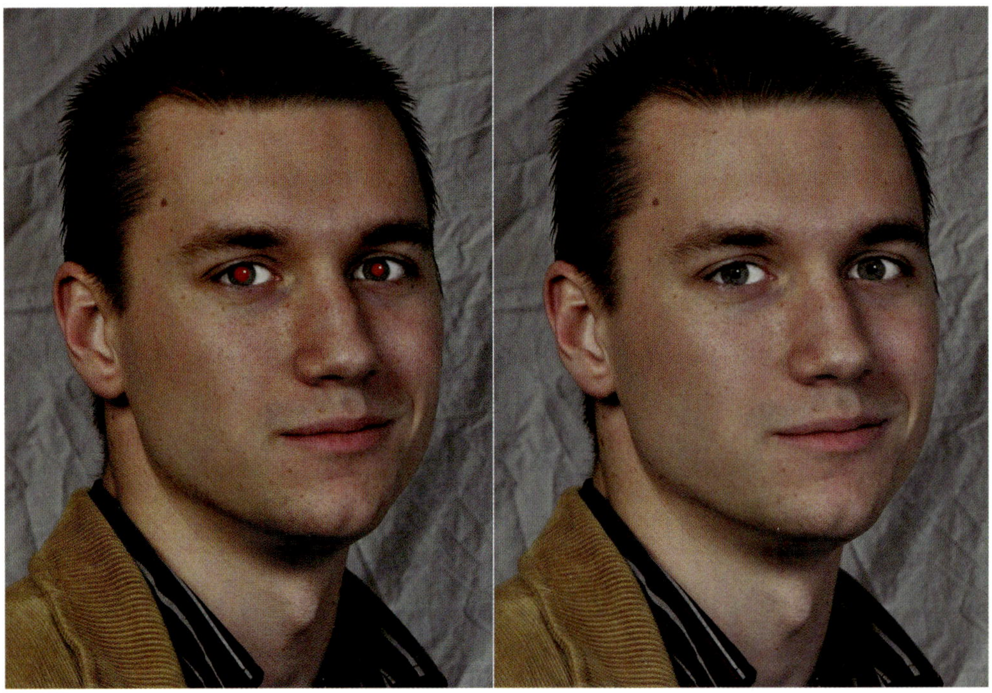

Figure 3.9
The Alpha's flip-up flash can emit bursts that cause your subject's pupils to contract (right), reducing the effects of red-eye.

Release w/o Lens

Options: Enable, Disable

Default: Disable

When this option is enabled, it's possible to release the shutter when no lens is attached to the camera. This feature is needed when you have attached the camera body to some other piece of equipment, such as a telescope, for astrophotography or a similar activity. If you're not doing something that clearly requires this option, you should leave it disabled to avoid causing problems for your camera's delicate inner workings.

Superior Auto Cont. Advance

Options: Auto, Off

Default: Auto

When the camera's shooting mode is set to S. Auto, for Superior Auto (AUTO+ on earlier SLT models), the camera recognizes various scene types and other shooting situations. With this menu option set to its default setting of Auto, the camera will automatically take multiple shots in that shooting mode when appropriate, such as when motion is detected. With this option turned off, the camera will not automatically take multiple shots in the Superior Auto mode. (You can still set continuous shooting through the drive mode option on the Function menu, but continuous shooting will not take place automatically.)

Superior Auto Image Extract

Options: Auto, Off

Default: Auto

As noted above, in the S. Auto/Superior Auto shooting mode, the Alpha SLT automatically detects various Scene types and shooting environments, and may take multiple shots in certain situations. This menu option gives you two choices for how the images are stored when the Superior Auto setting triggers multiple shots. With the default setting of Auto, the camera selects what it deems to be the most appropriate image of all those that were shot and stores only that one image, as a sort of "best shot" mode. With the Off setting, the camera stores all of the multiple shots, leaving it up to you to select whichever one(s) you want to keep. (However, if the recognized scene type is Hand-held Twilight, the camera saves just a single combined image, even if this menu item is set to Off.)

Grid Line

Options: Off, Rule of 3rds Grid, Square Grid, Diag. + Square Grid

Default: Off

This feature, the first item on the Custom 2 menu screen (see Figure 3.10), lets you choose from three possible configurations of composition aids on the camera's screen. The Rule of 3rds Grid option puts two pairs of parallel lines on the screen, dividing the image into 9 parts. If you place the most important part of your composition near the intersections of these lines, you will be observing the Rule of Thirds, which calls for locating the main features of the photograph away from the center of the image. The Square Grid uses five vertical lines and four horizontal lines, in each direction, yielding 24 blocks, which allows for more precise placement of the components of your shot. Finally, the Diag. + Square Grid option uses the same square grid with diagonal lines intersecting in the center of the image, giving you a few more options for alignment of the elements of your composition. (See Figure 3.11.)

Auto Review

Options: Off, 2 seconds, 5 seconds, 10 seconds

Default: 2 seconds

The Sony Alpha can display an image on the LCD for your review after the photo is taken. (When you shoot a continuous or bracketed series of images, only the last picture exposed is shown.) During this display, you can delete a disappointing shot by pressing

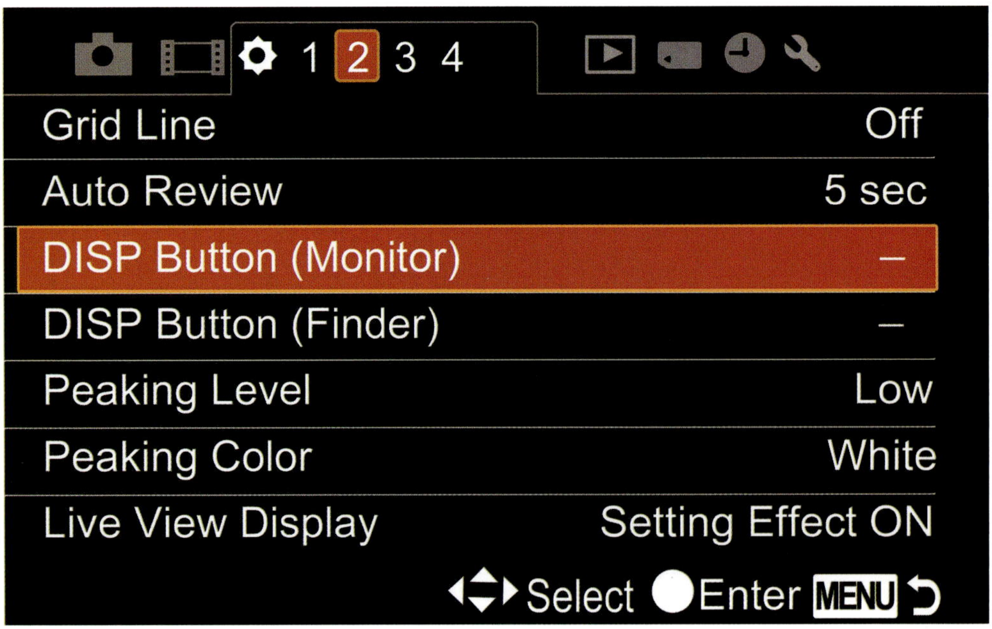

Figure 3.10 The Sony Alpha's Custom 2 menu.

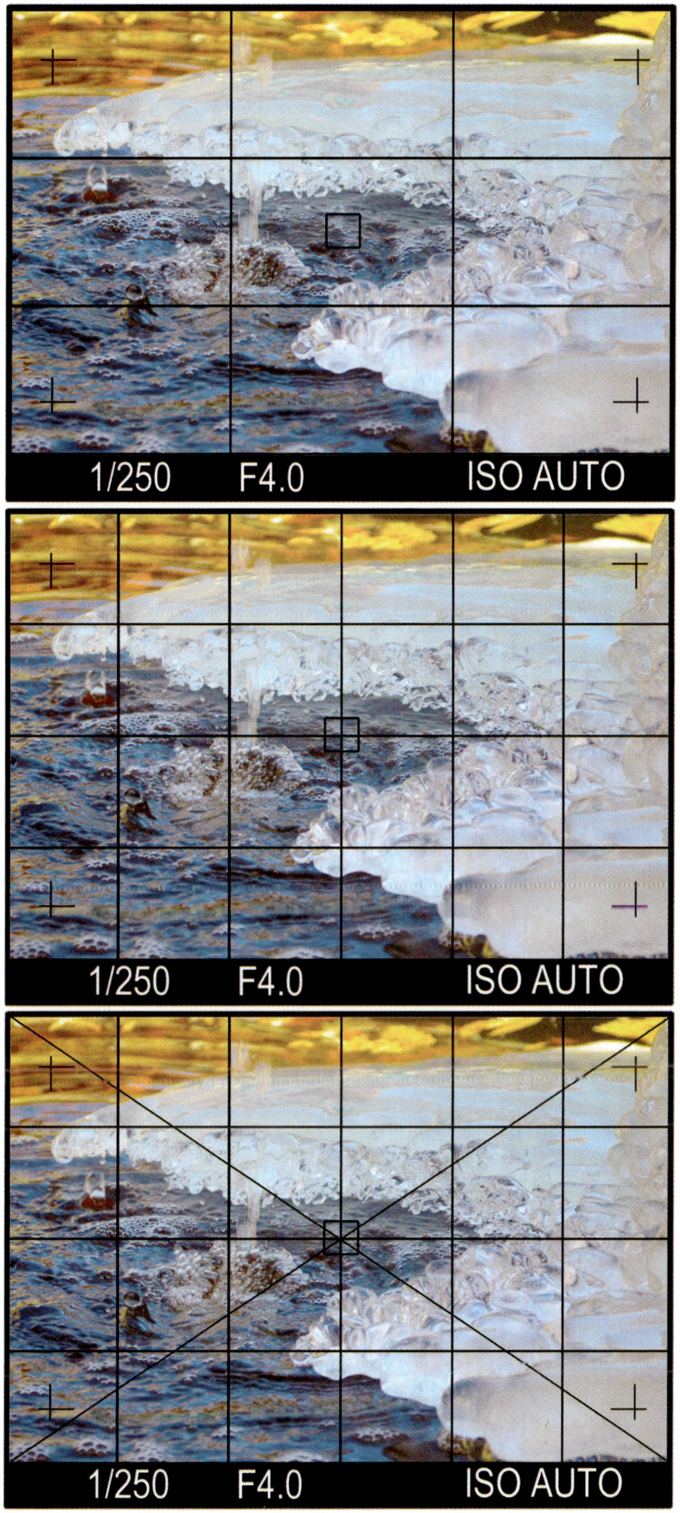

Figure 3.11
Rule of 3rds Grid (top), Square Grid (middle), Diagonal plus Square Grid (bottom).

the Trash button, or cancel picture review by tapping the shutter release, or performing another function. (You'll never be prevented from taking another picture because you were reviewing images on your LCD.) This option can be used to specify whether the review image appears on the LCD for 2, 5, or 10 seconds, or not at all. Even if you have Auto Review turned on, if Eye-Start is activated and the camera is near your eye, the LCD remains off until you remove your eye from the viewfinder.

Depending on how you're working, you might want a quick display (especially if you don't plan to glance at each picture as it's taken), or might prefer a more leisurely examination (when you're carefully checking compositions). Other times, you might not want to have the review image displayed at all, such as when you're taking photos in a darkened theater or concert venue, and the constant flashing of images might be distracting to others. Turning off picture review or keeping the duration short also saves power. You can always review the last picture you took at any time by pressing the Playback button.

DISP Button (Monitor)

Options: Graphic Display, Display All Info., No Disp. Info, Level, Histogram, For Viewfinder (Choose any one, or all)

Default: Display All Info.+Graphic Display+No Disp. Info+Level

As mentioned in Chapter 2, you can select which of the information displays are shown on the back-panel LCD (monitor) and EVF (finder) separately. This entry specifies the screens that will be shown when you press the DISP button repeatedly. You must choose at least one, but can activate or deactivate as many of the others as you prefer. To mark an option for display, use the up/down buttons to highlight your choice. A thumbnail preview of the screen that will be displayed is shown as a thumbnail in the lower-right corner of the screen. Press the OK button to mark/unmark a given screen, then press the MENU button to confirm your choices and exit. For a recap of what the available screens look like and their contents, see Figures 2.11 to 2.16 in the previous chapter.

DISP Button (Finder)

Options: Graphic Display, Display All Info., No Disp. Info, Level, Histogram

Default: Graphic Display+No Disp. Info+Level

This item has the exact same function as the previous menu entry, and functions exactly the same way, except the adjustment applies to the electronic viewfinder display instead.

Peaking Level

Options: Off, Low, Mid, High

Default: Off

"Peaking" is a manual focus aid that helps you visually determine when an image is in focus by outlining the areas that are in sharp focus with a contrasting color. When the color outline (red, yellow, or white) is maximized around the subject you want to emphasize, focus is sharpest. You can select low, medium, or high peaking effects, depending on how much aid you think you need. (High peaking tends to obscure details in your subject while viewing the image, but doesn't affect the actual captured image, of course.)

Peaking Color

Options: Red, Yellow, White

Default: White

This entry allows you to specify which color is used to indicate peaking. White is the default value, but if that color doesn't provide enough contrast with a similarly hued subject, you can switch to a more contrasting color, such as red or yellow (see Figure 3.12).

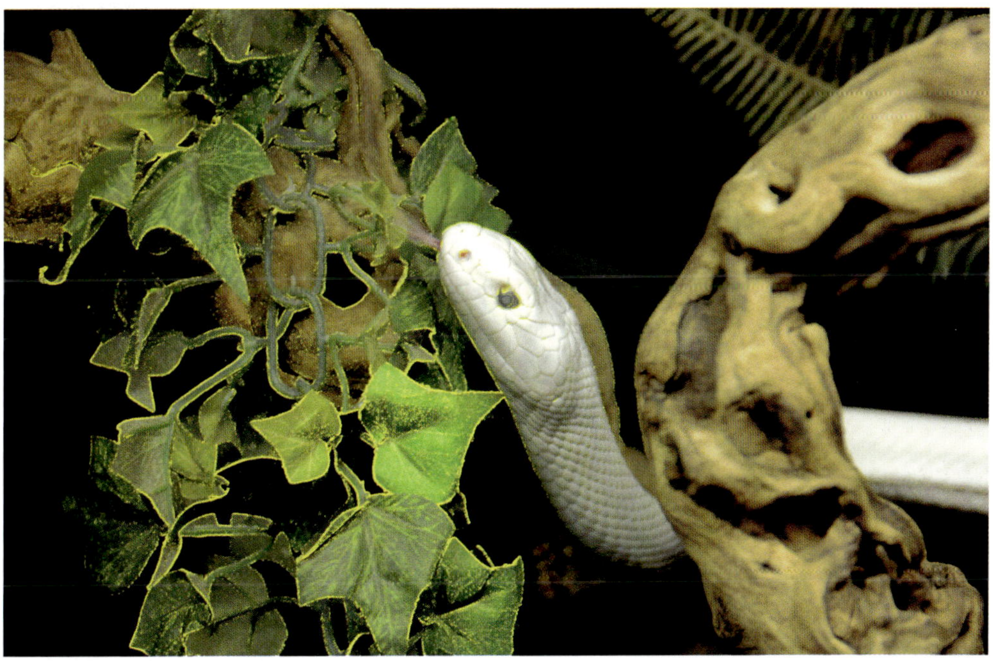

Figure 3.12
The peaking color can be set to red, yellow, or white.

Live View Display

Options: Setting Effect ON, Setting Effect OFF

Default: Setting Effect ON

This entry allows you to specify whether the effects of any settings you make (for, say, exposure compensation, white balance, Creative Effects, or Picture Effects) are reflected in the image displayed on the LCD and EVF, or whether the displays ignore these adjustments and show just the standard, unmodified live view. While this capability is useful, it poses some hidden dangers, which I'll explain shortly.

When Setting Effect On is chosen (the default), the LCD and EVF display will change to reflect your current settings, which can be especially helpful when you're using any of the Picture Effects, because you can preview the exact rendition that the effect you've dialed in produces. You'll also find the On option helpful when working with exposure compensation, as you can visually see how much lighter or darker your adjustment makes the image. If you're trying to achieve correct color balance, it's useful to be able to preview how a particular white balance setting affects your image.

Unfortunately, the default On setting has caused more than a few minutes of head scratching among new users who switch to Manual exposure mode and find themselves with a completely black (or utterly white) screen. The black screen, especially, may fool you into thinking your camera has malfunctioned.

It happened to me the first time I used my A57 in the studio. I attached the radio control that triggered my studio flash to the camera's accessory/hot shoe (using an adapter), flipped into Manual exposure mode (because the A57 doesn't provide auto flash exposure with studio flash units), set the shutter speed to 1/160th second (the maximum speed that can be synchronized with electronic flash), and the aperture of my macro lens to f/22 (so I could get maximum depth-of-field for the tabletop setup I was shooting). Both the LCD and EVF were completely black, and, having had the A57 for only a few hours, I had no idea what was going on.

With the feature activated, the modeling lights in my studio didn't provide enough illumination to produce an image on the LCD at ISO 100, f/22, and 1/160th second—the camera had no idea I was going to use flash. All was well when I switched to Setting Effect OFF, however, and the standard image at full brightness was displayed. I've had about a dozen e-mails since then from readers with the same problem, so I know I'm not alone in needing to remedy this vexing complication.

Func. of AEL Button

Options: Exposure Comp., Drive Mode, Flash Mode, Autofocus Mode, AF area, Smile/Face Detection, Auto Portrait Framing, ISO, Metering Mode, Flash Comp., White Balance, DRO/Auto HDR, Creative Style, Picture Effect, Image Size, Quality, AEL Hold, AEL Toggle, AEL Hold (Spot metering), AEL Toggle (Spot metering), Object Tracking, AF Lock, Aperture Preview, Shot Result Preview, Zoom, Focus Magnifier

Default: AEL hold

This option, the first in the Custom 3 menu (see Figure 3.13), affects the operation of the Zoom Out/AEL (auto exposure lock) button, located at the top of the camera's back, at the right side next to the red Movie button. Sony's gone overboard in providing optional functions for this button beyond the usual auto exposure lock options. If you decide you don't want or need an AEL function, you can redefine this button to perform any of several dozen other functions.

Most users like the AEL function and will choose between the default setting AEL Hold and its variation, AEL Toggle. With the AEL Hold setting, when you press the AEL button your exposure is locked only as long as you hold down the button. If you set this option to AEL Toggle, then you can just press the button and release it, and the exposure will stay locked until you press and release it again. Use this setting if you want to lock in exposure and then reframe extensively or even point the camera at another subject you want to photograph using the same exposure settings. You can also

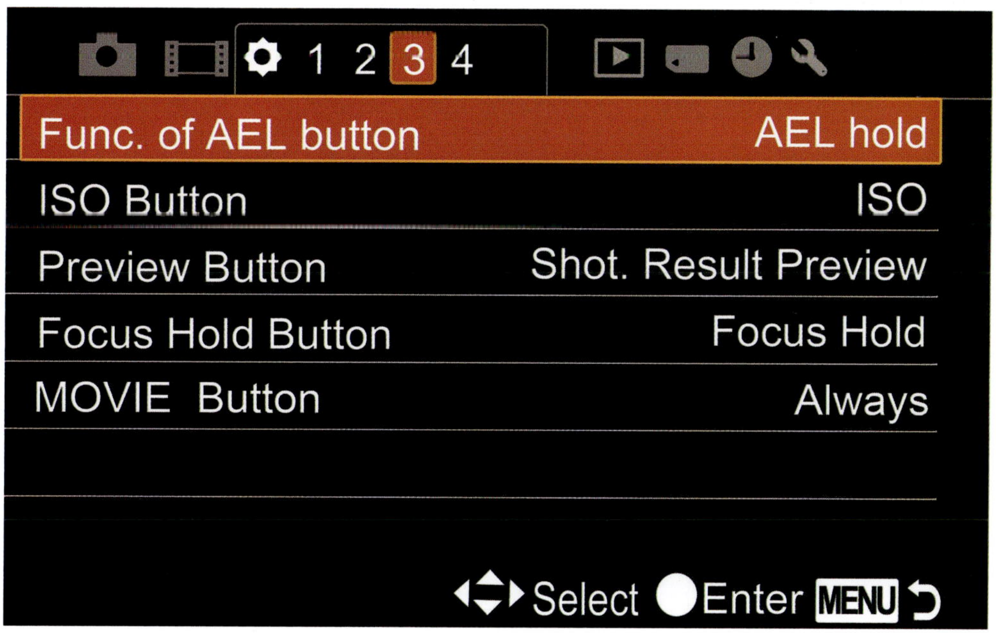

Figure 3.13
The Custom 3 menu.

select from two additional variations: AEL Hold (Spot Metering) and AEL Toggle (Spot Metering) which, as you might guess, perform the same functions but switch the camera into Spot metering mode (if you have another metering mode activated). In all these cases, when exposure is locked, the asterisk symbol appears at lower right in the LCD and EVF.

The other settings transform the AEL button into another function button of your choice from the list shown above. Most of them are self-explanatory, except for Aperture Preview (which is actually a depth-of-field preview that stops the lens down to the f/stop that will be used to take the picture), and Shot Result Preview (which shows you how your shutter speed and f/stop settings will affect your image).

ISO Button

Options: Exposure Comp., Drive Mode, Flash Mode, Autofocus Mode, AF area, Smile/Face Detection, Auto Portrait Framing, ISO, Metering Mode, Flash Comp., White Balance, DRO/Auto HDR, Creative Style, Picture Effect, Image Size, Quality, AEL Hold, AEL Toggle, AEL Hold (Spot metering), AEL Toggle (Spot metering), Object Tracking, AF Lock, Aperture Preview, Shot Result Preview, Zoom, Focus Magnifier

Default: ISO

This option allows you to retain the ISO button's function for adjusting ISO, or redefine the button to one of the other functions listed above.

Shot. Result Preview

Options: Shot Result Preview/Aperture Preview/Focus Magnifier

Default: Shot. Result Preview

The Preview button can be set to provide depth-of-field preview when pressed, or any of the other functions listed above.

Focus Hold Button

Options: Focus Hold, D.O.F. Preview

Default: Focus Hold

This function is of use only when you are using a lens equipped with a focus hold button. This setting specifies the effect of pressing that button. With the default option, Focus Hold, pressing the button on the lens holds the focus at its current setting. The other setting, D.O.F. Preview, lets you use that button to activate a depth-of-field preview, which causes the lens to stop down to the actual shooting aperture so you can more accurately judge the depth-of-field that will be obtained at that aperture.

MOVIE Button

Options: Always, Movie Mode Only

Default: Always

You can set the Movie button to activate movie capture anytime the button is pressed, regardless of the mode selected on the mode dial, or to begin shooting movies *only* when the Mode dial is set to the Movie position. The Always setting will allow you to capture video on the spur of the moment, while Movie Mode Only will prevent you from accidentally shooting a movie when using non-movie modes.

Lens Comp: Shading/Chro. Aber/Distortion

Options: Auto, Off

Default: Auto (Shading, Chro. Aber); Off for Distortion

These are the first three entries in the Custom 4 menu (see Figure 3.14). All of them compensate for lens defects when working with A-mount lenses (they serve no function when using other lenses with adapters).

- **Shading.** This is an anti-vignetting correction feature, which can fully or partially compensate for darkened corners produced by some types of lenses. Because the default setting is Auto, you may never know that this feature is at work—until you turn it off. Figure 3.15 shows an example of an image with and without shading correction.

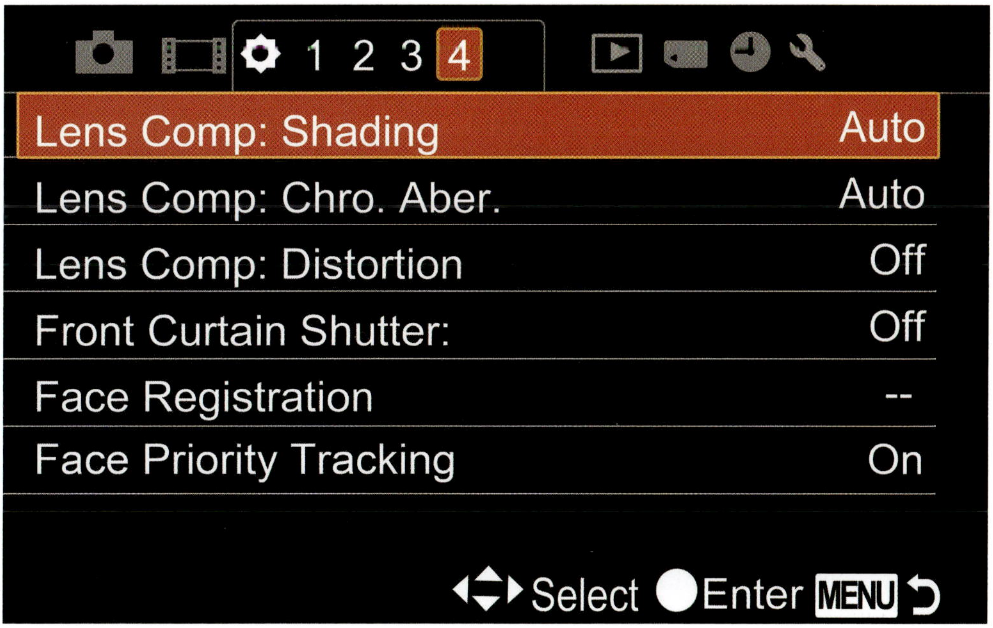

Figure 3.14
The Custom 4 menu.

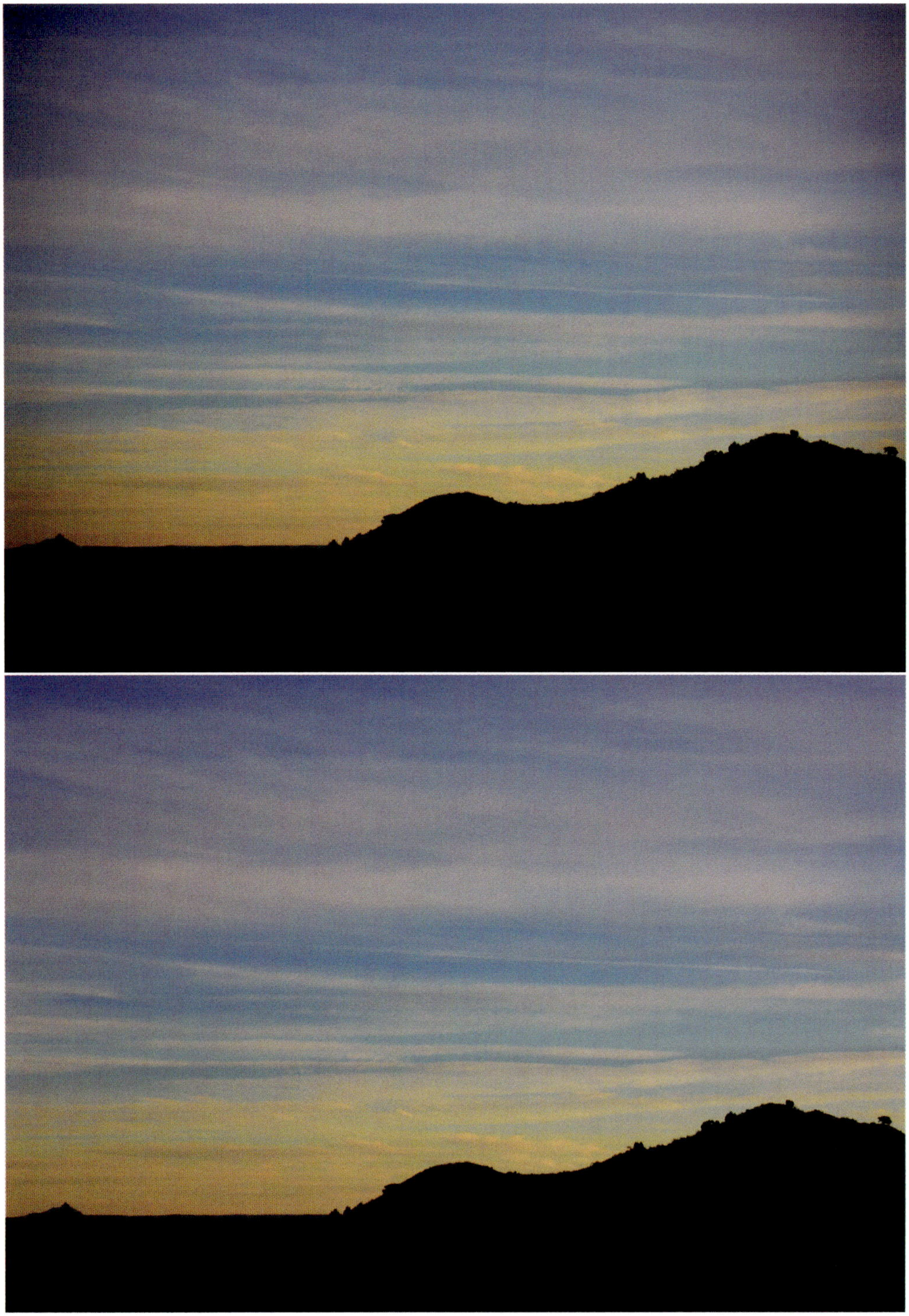

Figure 3.15
No shading (vignetting) correction (top); shading corrected (bottom).

- **Chro. Aber.** Chromatic Aberration correction reduces color distortion at the corners of the image. Its default setting is Auto. Figure 3.16 shows an example of an image with and without chromatic aberration correction.
- **Distortion.** This lens compensation feature fixes inward or outward bowing of lines at the edges of images, caused by wide-angle and telephoto lenses (respectively). I'll show you more about this type of distortion in Chapter 8.

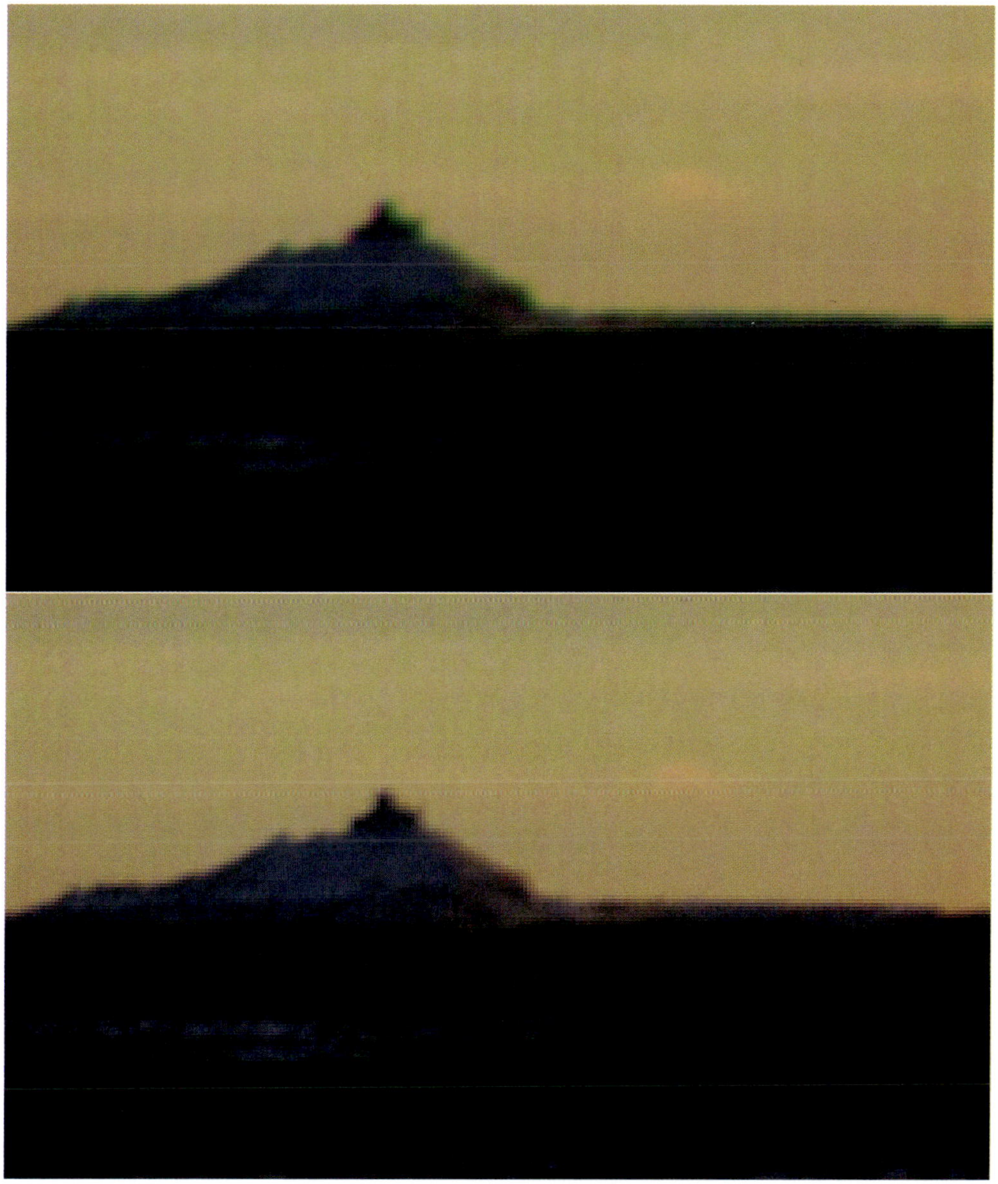

Figure 3.16 Chromatic aberration displayed as green fringe (top); chromatic aberration corrected (bottom).

Front Curtain Shutter

Options: On, Off

Default: On

As a translucent mirror camera, your SLT-A57's sensor is normally exposed to incoming light until just before the moment of exposure, when the shutter closes, the image that had been on the sensor is electronically "dumped" to make way for your actual exposure, and then the shutter opens again to take the picture. That takes time and introduces a certain amount of shutter lag time. This option reduces that lag by electronically "closing" the shutter (and dumping the existing image), so the mechanical shutter can close and open immediately. Use this setting when taking action shots and other types of images where even a small amount of shutter lag is objectionable. By default, it's on, so you won't have to think about it unless you want to use rear curtain shutter mode (set using Flash Options). I'll explain the differences between and applications for front and rear shutter modes in Chapter 9.

Face Registration

Options: New Registration, Order Exchanging, Delete, Delete All

Default: None

This menu entry is used to log into your camera's face detection memory the visages of those you photograph often. New Registration allows you to log up to eight different faces. Line up your victim (subject) against a brightly lit background, to allow easier detection of the face. Use the directional buttons to align the green frame that appears with the face, and press the shutter button. A confirmation message appears, and you press the center OK button to confirm.

The Order Exchanging option allows you to review and change the priority in which the faces appear, from 1 to 8. The A57 will use your priority setting to determine which face to focus on if several registered faces are detected in a scene.

You can also select a specific face and delete it from memory (say, you broke up with your significant other!) or delete *all* faces from the registry (your SO got custody of the camera).

Face Priority Tracking

Options: On, Off

Default: On

Use this option to turn Face Priority autofocus tracking, described in more detail in Chapter 5, on or off.

Playback 1/2 Menu

The Playback menu controls functions for deleting, protecting, displaying, and printing images. You can bring it up on your screen quickly by pressing the Playback button first, then the MENU button. Otherwise, you have to start with the Still Shooting menu and scroll over the tabs to the right. The first of the two screens of the Playback menu is shown in Figure 3.17.

- Delete
- View Mode
- Slide Show
- Image Index
- 3D Viewing
- Protect
- Specify Printing
- Volume Settings
- Auto Rotate

Delete

Options: Multiple Images, All in Folder/All AVCHD View Files

Default: None

All of us sometimes take pictures that we know should never see the light of day. Maybe you were looking into the lens and accidentally tripped the shutter. Perhaps you really goofed up your settings. You want to erase that photo *now,* before it does permanent damage. While you can delete a photo immediately after you take it by pressing the Trash button, sometimes you need to wait for an idle moment to erase pictures. This menu choice makes it easy to remove selected photos (Multiple Images), or to erase all the photos in a folder on a memory card (All in Folder). Note that neither function removes images marked Protected (described below in the section on "Protect").

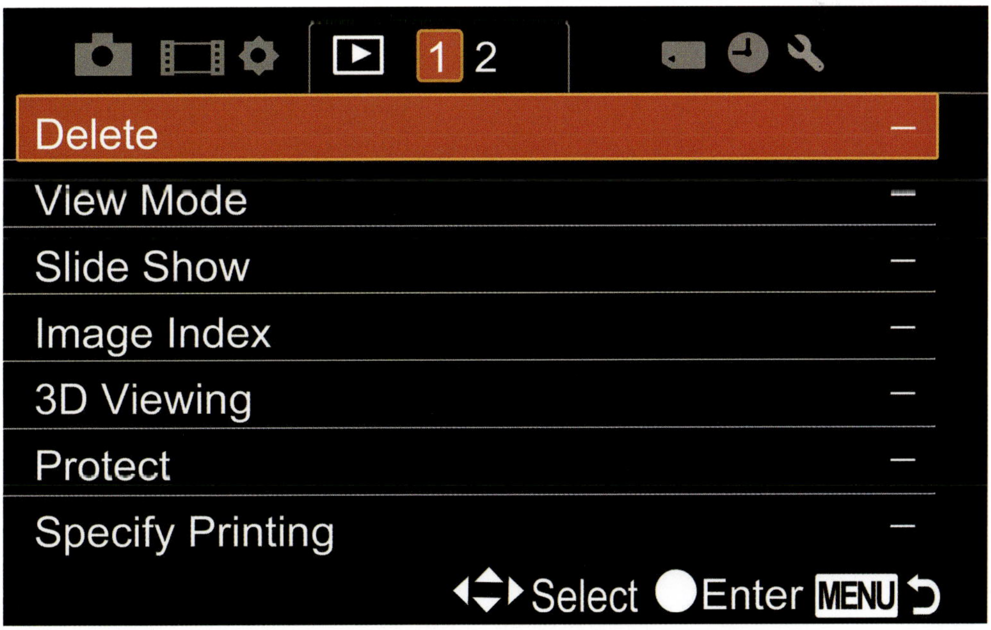

Figure 3.17 The Sony Alpha's Playback 1 menu.

To remove selected images, select the Delete menu item, and use the up/down keys or the control dial to choose the Multiple Images option from the submenu. Press the center controller button, and the most recent image appears on the LCD. Scroll through your images using the left/right direction keys or the control dial, and press the center controller button while an image that you want to delete is displayed; a green trash can icon is superimposed over each marked image. The number of images marked for deletion is incremented in the indicator at the lower left of the LCD, with a check mark icon. When you're satisfied (or have expressed your dissatisfaction with the really bad images), press the MENU button to go back, where you can choose Delete to erase the images you've marked.

While you can also use this menu choice to delete all the images in the current folder on the memory card by selecting the All in Folder option (All AVCHD View Files will appear if you've shot movies) instead of the Multiple Images option, the process can take some time. If you have a large number of images on your memory card, you're better off using the Format command on the Memory Card Tool menu, described later in this chapter.

View Mode

Options: Folder View (Still), Folder View (MP4), AVCHD View

Default: Folder View (Still)

Selects the type of images to be displayed when the Playback button is pressed. Choose from Still images by folder, MP4 movies by folder, or AVCHD movies.

Slide Show

Menu Options: Enter, Cancel

Slide Show Options:

Interval: 1 second, 3 seconds, 5 seconds, 10 seconds, 30 seconds;
Default: 3 seconds

Repeat: On, Off; Default: Off

Image Type: All, Display 3D Only; Default: All

This menu option allows you to display all the images on your memory card in a continuous show, using a three-second delay between images, or another delay period you select by choosing the Interval suboption. Choose 1, 3, 5, 10, or 30 seconds for your interval. Set the Repeat option to On to make the show repeat continuously. If you have 3D images on your memory card, you can elect to include only those images in the show, or include all images. You cannot play back both still images and movies in the same slide show; you have to select one or the other, using the Still/Movie select methods discussed above, before setting up the slide show.

During the show you can:

- Move forward or reverse in the show by pressing the controller left/right keys.
- Press the DISP button to toggle between full screen images and the same images overlaid with date, time, and image number.
- Stop the show at any time by pressing the MENU button, the Play button, or the center controller button. (There is no way to pause and resume the show.)

Image Index

Options: 4 Images, 9 Images

Default: 4 Images

Use this option to set the number of thumbnail images to be displayed when you press the Zoom Out/Index button during playback. After you have set the number to 4 or 9, you can press the MENU button to return to the menu, or you can press the center controller button if you want to go ahead and view the screen of thumbnail images.

3D Viewing

This option is not available unless you have connected your Sony Alpha to a 3D-capable HDTV to display your 3D Sweep Panorama images. You need to select this menu item to view 3D images, and when you select it, only 3D images will be viewed on the HDTV. To view other images, you need to exit from this viewing option.

Protect

Options: Multiple Images, Cancel All Images

Default: None

You might want to protect images on your memory card from accidental erasure, either by you or by others who may use your camera from time to time. This menu choice enables you to protect multiple marked images (using a procedure similar to the Delete Multiple Images process described earlier) or to cancel protection for all images, which unmarks and unprotects any photos you have previously marked for protection.

To protect selected images, select the Protect menu item, and choose Multiple Images. Press the center controller button, and the images appear one by one on your LCD or EVF as you browse through them with the left/right cursor buttons or with the control dial. When an image you want to protect is displayed, press the center controller button to mark it for protection (or to unmark an image that has already been marked). An orange check mark appears in a box next to each marked image. When you've marked all the images you want to protect, press the MENU button to return to the menu screen, and then choose Enter to finish the protection operation.

Specify Printing

Options (DPOF Setup): Multiple Images, Cancel All (unmark all images)

Options (Date Imprint): On, Off

Defaults: Off

Most digital cameras are compatible with the DPOF (Digital Print Order Format) protocol, which enables you to mark in your camera which of the JPEG images on the memory card (but not RAW files) you'd like to print, and specify the number of copies of each that you want. You can then transport your memory card to your retailer's digital photo lab or do-it-yourself kiosk, or use your own compatible printer to print out the marked images and quantities you've specified. You can access the Specify Printing options from this menu choice.

- **DPOF Setup.** You can choose to print Multiple Images or to Cancel All. Selecting images is similar to the method you use to mark images for deletion or protection. To print selected images, select the DPOF Setup option, press the center controller button, and choose Marked images from the submenu. Then scroll down to the Enter option, and press the center controller button to select it. You can then browse through the images you want to print, using the left/right direction keys or the control dial. Press the center controller button to mark the image; an orange check mark appears in the lower-left corner to indicate you've selected that image. You can't select the number of copies printed for each image (only one copy is available).

  When finished marking images, press the MENU button to exit picture selection. The Cancel All option at the top of the screen removes all DPOF print selection marks. This entry is useful if you print photos from a memory card, but then leave the images on the card while you shoot additional pictures. Removing the DPOF markings clears the card of print requests so you can later select additional or different images for printing from the same collection.

- **Date Imprint.** Choose this menu option to superimpose the current date onto images when they are printed. Select On to add the date; Off (the default value) skips date imprinting. The date is added during printing by the output device, which controls its location on the final print.

Volume Settings

Options: 0-7

Default: 2

This menu option is the first one on the Playback 2 menu. (See Figure 3.18.) It is available for selection only when you have at least one movie saved on your memory card, and the Still/Movie selection is set to Movie. Set the volume for movie playback to any setting from 0 (no sound) to 7 (loudest sound). You also can adjust the volume while a movie is playing, by pressing the down cursor button, which pops up an on-screen volume control. You can then raise or lower the volume with the up/down keys or the control dial.

Auto Rotate

Options: Auto Rotate, Manual Rotate

Default: Auto Rotate

When this item is set to Auto Rotate, the Sony Alpha rotates pictures taken in vertical orientation on the LCD screen so you don't have to turn the camera to view them comfortably. However, this orientation also means that the longest dimension of the image is shown using the shortest dimension of the LCD, so the picture is reduced in size. (See Figure 3.19.) Choose Manual Rotate instead, and you can rotate only those photos you want to re-orient, by pressing the Fn button when the image is displayed and choosing Rotate from the resulting screen.

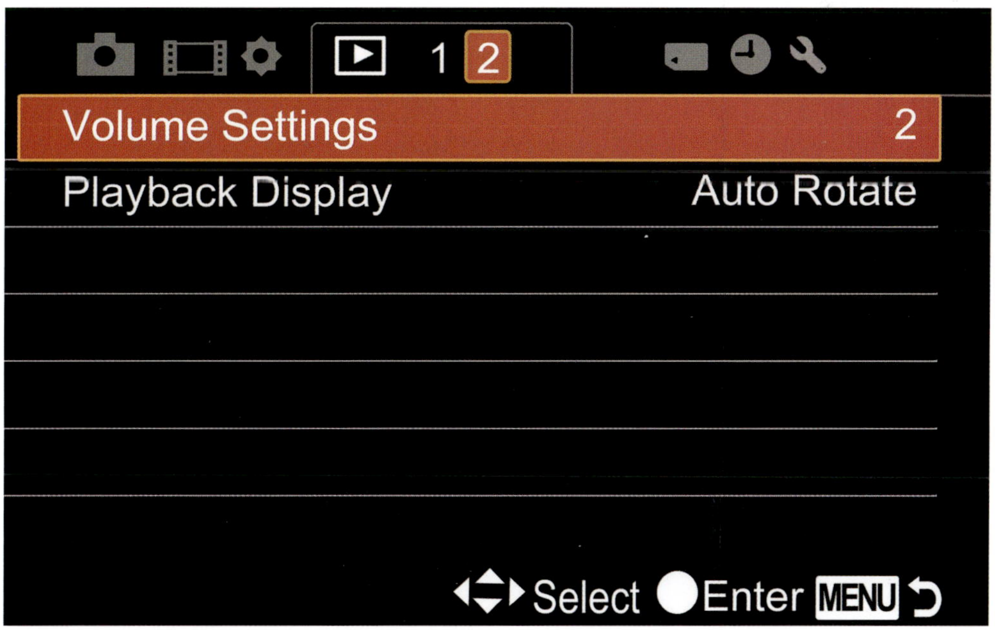

Figure 3.18 The Sony Alpha's Playback 2 menu.

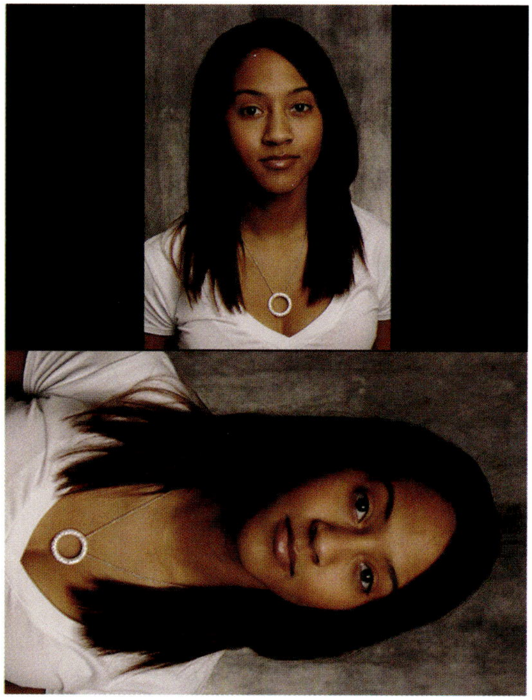

Figure 3.19
Unrotated (top); rotated (bottom).

Memory Card Tool Menu

With its SLT-series cameras, Sony has branched out somewhat in its menu structure. Rather than limiting these cameras to the standard array of Still Shooting, Custom, Playback, and Setup menus, Sony has broken out some functions that may need to be accessed more often or separately, and created new menu categories for them, instead of cluttering up a very long Setup menu with functions of varying usefulness. The first of these new menus is the single-screen Memory Card Tool menu, which gives you ready access to several options that are all related to the storage of images on your SD or Memory Stick card. (See Figure 3.20.)

- Format
- File Number
- Folder Name
- Select REC Folder
- New Folder
- Recover Image DB

Format

Options: Enter, Cancel

Default: Cancel

To reformat your memory card, choose the Format menu entry and press the center controller button. Choose Enter when the "All data will be deleted. Format?" message appears.

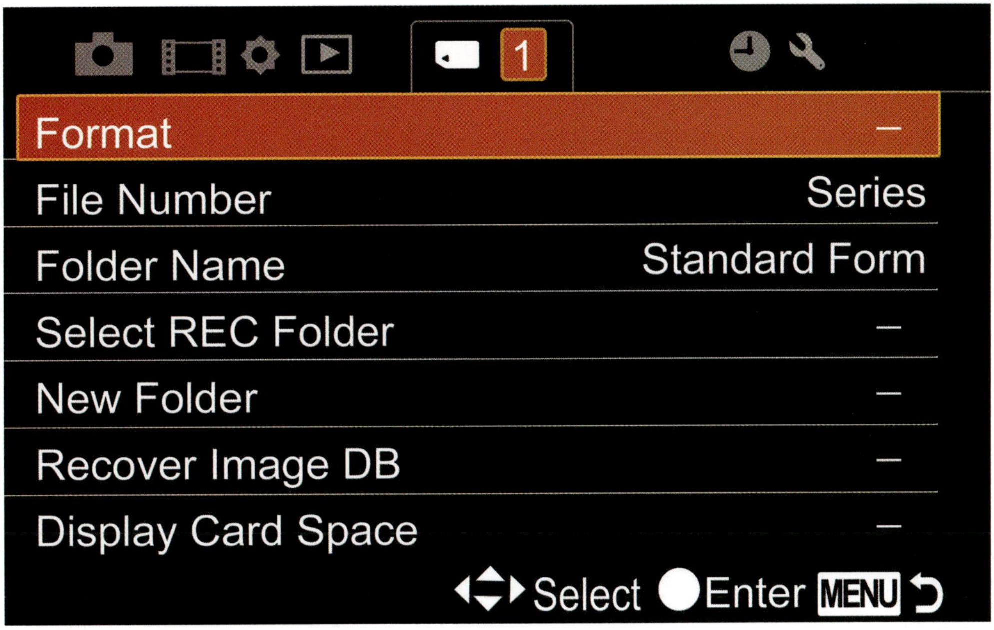

Figure 3.20 The Sony Alpha's Memory Card Tool menu.

Use this option to erase everything on your memory card, including Protected images, and set up a fresh file system ready for use. The Format command removes all the images on the memory card, and reinitializes the card's file system by defining anew the areas of the card available for image storage, locking out defective areas, and creating a new folder in which to deposit your images. It's usually a good idea to reformat your memory card in the camera (not in your camera's card reader using your computer's operating system) before each use. Formatting is generally much quicker than deleting images one by one.

File Number

Options: Series, Reset

Default: Series

The File Number option controls how the camera sets up the file numbers for your images. The Sony Alpha will automatically apply a file number to each picture you take when this option is set to Series, using consecutive numbering for all your photos over a long period of time, spanning many different memory cards, and even if you reformat a card. Numbers are applied from 0001 to 9999, at which time the camera starts back at 0001. The camera keeps track of the last number used in its internal memory. So, you could take pictures numbered as high as 100-0240 on one card, remove the card and insert another, and the next picture will be numbered 100-0241 on the new card.

Reformat either card, take a picture, and the next image will be numbered 100-0242. Use the Series option when you want all the photos you take to have consecutive numbers (at least, until your camera exceeds 9999 shots taken).

If you want to restart numbering back at 0001 on a more frequent basis, use the Reset option. In that case, the file number will be reset to 0001 *each* time you format a memory card or delete all the images in a folder, insert a different memory card, or change the folder name format (as described in the next menu entry).

Folder Name

Options: Standard Form, Date Form

Default: Standard Form

If you have viewed one of your memory cards' contents on a computer using a card reader, you noticed that the top-level folder on the card is always named DCIM. Inside that folder is another folder created by your camera. Different cameras use different folder names, and they can coexist on the same card. For example, if your memory card is removed from your Sony camera and used in, say, a camera from another vendor that also accepts Secure Digital or Memory Stick cards, the other camera will create a new folder using a different folder name within the DCIM directory.

By default, the Alpha creates its folders using a three-number prefix (starting with 100), followed by MSDCF. As each folder fills up with 999 images, a new folder with a prefix that's one higher (say, 101) is used. So, with the "Standard Form," the folders on your memory card will be named 100MSDCF, 101MSDCF, and so forth.

You can select Date Form instead, and the Alpha will use a *xxxymmdd* format, such as 10030204, where the 100 is the folder number, 1 is the last digit of the year, 02 is the month, and 04 is the day of that month. If you want your folder names to be more date-oriented, rather than generic, use the Date Form option instead of Standard Form.

Select REC Folder

Options: Select folder

Default: Current folder

If you have opted for the Standard Form for your storage folders using the above option, then you can use the Select REC Folder option to choose which folder to use for storage of your still images. (If you use Date Form, the images will be stored in folders according to their dates.) This option applies only to storage of still images, not movies.

New Folder

Options: New Folder

Default: None

This option gives you the ability to create a new folder for storing still images and movies. Select this menu item by pressing the center controller button on the New Folder menu line, and a message like "10110114 folder created" or "103MSDCF folder" appears on the LCD, depending on whether the Date Form or Standard Form for folders is in effect. Press the center controller button again to dismiss the screen and return to the menu.

Recover Image DB

Options: Enter, Cancel

Default: None

The Recover Image DB function is provided in case errors crop up in the camera's database that records information about your movies. (You may notice that the first time you use a memory card in your Alpha that was used in a different non-Sony camera, you'll be urged to create a new Image Database file.) According to Sony, a corrupted image database may develop if you have processed or edited movies on a computer and then re-saved them to the memory card that's in your camera. I have never had this problem, so I'm not sure exactly what it would look like. But, if you find that your movies are not playing correctly in the camera, go ahead and try this operation. Highlight this menu option and press the center controller button, and the camera will prompt you, "Check Image Database File?" Press the center controller button to confirm, or the MENU key to cancel.

Clock Setup Menu

The other new branch of the menu system added by Sony for these cameras is the very short Clock setup menu, which has only two entries. If you travel a good deal, you may find it convenient to be able to get quick access to these settings to adjust your current location so that the dates and times of your images and videos will be recorded accurately. This brief menu screen is shown in Figure 3.21.

- Date/Time Setup
- Area Setting

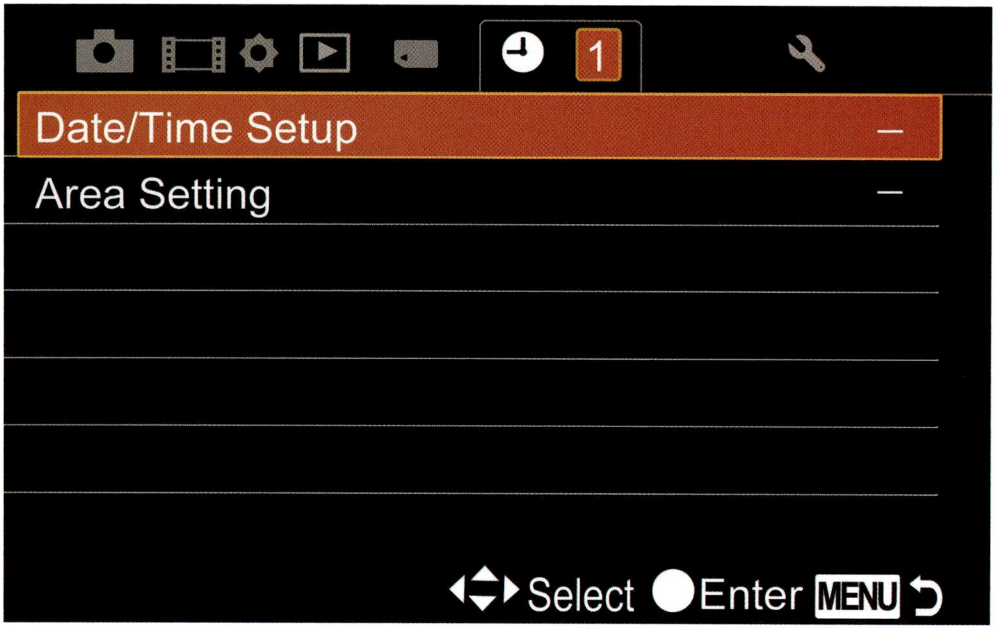

Figure 3.21
The Sony Alpha's Clock setup menu.

Date/Time Setup

Options: Daylight Savings Time, Year, Month, Day, Time, Date Format

Default: None

Use this option to specify the date and time that will be embedded in the image file along with exposure information and other data. You can select whether Daylight Savings Time is in effect or not, year, day, month, hour, minute, and date format, but you cannot choose AM/PM specifically. To set, say 2:32 AM or 2:32 PM, you'll have to pretend you're using a digital clock and cycle past midnight or noon to get to the AM/PM hours, respectively.

Area Setting

Options: World Time Zones

Default: None

When you select this option, you are presented with a world map on the LCD. Use the control wheel or the left/right direction buttons to scroll until you have highlighted the time zone that you are. Once the camera is set up with the correct date and time in your home time zone, you can use this setting to change your time zone during a trip, so you will record the local time with your images without disrupting your original date and time settings. Just scroll back to your normal time zone once you return home.

Setup 1/2/3 Menus

Finally, the three screens of the Setup menu are populated with the less frequently changed settings, such as language, LCD brightness, and power saving settings. The Setup 1 menu is shown in Figure 3.22.

- Menu Start
- LCD Brightness
- Viewfinder Bright.
- Eco Mode
- Power Save
- HDMI Resolution
- CTRL FOR HDMI
- Upload Settings (appears only when an Eye-Fi card is installed)
- USB Connection
- Audio Signals
- Cleaning Mode
- Version
- Language
- Mode Dial Guide
- Demo Mode
- Initialize

Menu Start

Options: Top, Previous

Default: Top

This menu option, first in the first Setup screen (see Figure 3.22), lets you determine which menu position is used by default when you press the MENU button. If you select Top, then the first tab, the Still Shooting 1 menu, appears. Select Previous, and the last menu you accessed will be shown. I find the Previous option is the most convenient, because it's very likely that the last setting I made will be the one I want to access the

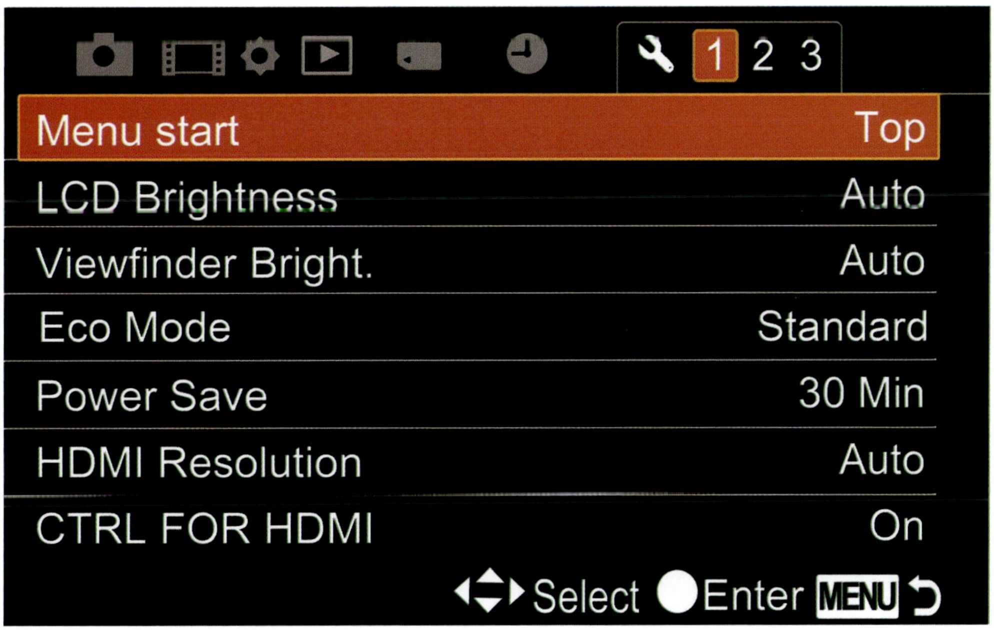

Figure 3.22 The Sony Alpha's Setup 1 menu.

next time (say, to turn off an option I wanted to use only temporarily), and the other menu tabs can be selected quickly even if the most recently used choice is not the one I want next time.

LCD Brightness

Options: Auto/Manual: Plus or minus 2

Default: Auto

When you access this menu choice, a pair of grayscale steps and a color chart appear on the screen, allowing you to see the effects of your brightness changes on the dark, light, and middle tones as well as colors. Select Auto to have the Alpha choose screen brightness for you. Choose Manual instead and a scale appears. Use the left/right cursor buttons to adjust the brightness by plus or minus two (arbitrary) increments. If you find you have no trouble viewing the dimmed screen, you can set the brightness manually to –2 increments, and save some battery power.

Viewfinder Bright.

Options: Auto/Manual: Plus or minus 1

Default: Auto

This menu item is similar to the LCD Brightness option discussed above. The difference is that, because the viewfinder is shaded from the sun or other bright lights, there is no need to enhance its brightness to a high level, as there is with the LCD. So, your only options here are to opt for the Auto setting or to choose Manual and adjust the brightness by one unit in either direction. The camera reminds you with a message on the LCD that you should be looking through the viewfinder while making this adjustment.

Eco Mode

Options: Max, Standard

Defaults: Standard

When you choose Max, Power Save (described below) is set to 10 seconds.

Power Save

Options: 10 seconds, 20 seconds, 1 minute, 5 minutes, 30 minutes

Default: 1 minute

This setting determines the length of time before the Alpha switches to Power Save mode. Then, the display vanishes but can be restored by tapping the shutter release button or certain other controls, such as the MENU button. The choices are 10 or 20 seconds, or 1, 5, or 30 minutes. (If the camera is connected to a TV or the drive mode is set to Remote Commander, the time period will be 30 minutes, no matter what setting is made here.)

SAVING POWER WITH THE Sony Alpha

There are several settings and techniques you can use to help you stretch the longevity of your Alpha's battery. These include setting the Auto Review, LCD Brightness, Viewfinder Brightness, and Power Save options to reduce power usage as much as possible. That big 3-inch LCD uses a lot of juice, so reducing its brightness or the amount of time it is used (either for automatic review or for manually playing back your images) can boost the effectiveness of your battery. If you're willing to shade the LCD with your hand, you can often get away with lower LCD brightness settings outdoors. The techniques? Use the built-in flash as little as possible; no flash at all or fill flash uses less power than a full blast. Turn off SteadyShot and GPS if you feel you don't need them. When transferring pictures from your Alpha to your computer, use a card reader instead of the USB cable. Linking your camera to your computer and transferring images using the cable takes longer and uses a lot more power.

HDMI Resolution

Options: Auto, 1080p, 1080i

Default: Auto

Adjusts the camera's output for display on a high-definition television. Usually, Auto will work with any HDTV. If you have trouble getting the image to display correctly, you can set the resolution manually here.

CTRL for HDMI

Options: On, Off

Default: On

You can view the display output of your Alpha on a high-definition television (HDTV) if you make the investment in an HDMI cable with a mini-HDMI connector on the camera end (which Sony does not supply) and you own an HDTV (which Sony does not supply with the camera, either). When connecting HDMI-to-HDMI, the camera automatically selects the correct image settings, including color broadcast system, for viewing. (Earlier Alpha models, which used a composite video connection instead of HDMI, had to be set to either NTSC or PAL broadcast standards.)

If you're lucky enough to own a TV that supports the Sony Bravia synchronization protocol, you can operate the camera using that TV's remote control. Just press the

Link Menu button on the remote, and then use the device's controls to delete images, display an image index of photos in the camera, display a slide show, protect/unprotect images in the camera, specify printing options, and play back single images on the TV screen.

The CTRL for HDMI option on the Setup menu is intended for use when you have connected the camera to a non-Sony HDTV and find that the TV's remote control produces unintended results with the camera. If that happens, try turning this option off, and see if the problem is resolved.

Upload Settings

Options: On, Off

Default: On

This option, the first in the Setup 2 menu (see Figure 3.23), provides for Eye-Fi setup. This menu option appears only if you have an Eye-Fi card inserted in the memory card slot. As I mentioned in Chapter 1, an Eye-Fi card is a special type of SD card that connects to an available wireless (Wi-Fi) network and uploads the images from your memory card to a computer on that network. The Upload Settings option on the Setup menu lets you either enable or disable the use of the Eye-Fi card's transmitting capability. So, if you want to use an Eye-Fi card just as an ordinary SD card, for example, when no wireless network is available, you can turn this option off and save whatever power

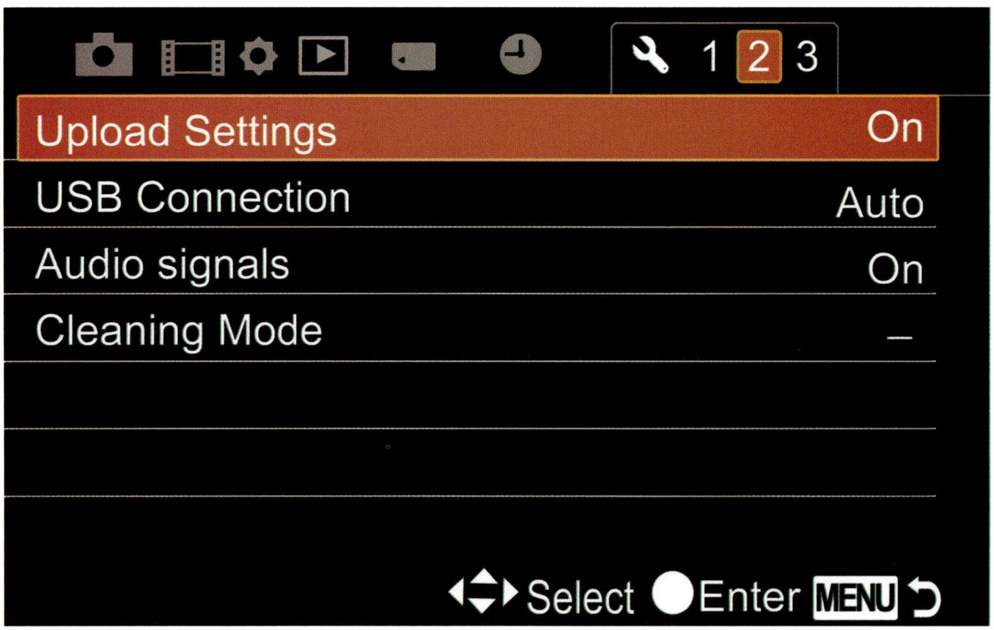

Figure 3.23 The Sony Alpha's Setup 2 menu.

the camera uses to enable the Eye-Fi card to transmit. If you are using an Eye-Fi card to upload images, make sure this option is turned on.

I have found that A57 movies upload quite nicely to my PC and Macintosh using an Eye-Fi Pro X2 8GB card. The movies ended up in a Movies/Eye-Fi folder instead of the Pictures/Eye-Fi folder where the still images went, but they uploaded with no problems.

This menu item appears only when an Eye-Fi wireless (Wi-Fi) card is loaded into the camera. This option enables/disables the upload function of the Eye-Fi card. The functions of the card itself are set, not in the camera, but using the Eye-Fi manager software supplied with the card. Follow the instructions that came with the Eye-Fi card to set up the access points, networks, and where/if uploaded pictures are to be forwarded to another location, such as Flickr or Facebook.

USB Connection

Options: Auto, Mass Storage, MTP

Default: Auto

This option allows you to switch your USB connection protocol between the default Mass Storage setting (used when you transfer images from your camera to your computer), and MTP (Media Transfer Protocol), which you'd use to connect your camera to a PictBridge-compatible printer. In Mass Storage mode, your camera appears to the computer as just another storage device, like a disk drive. You can drag and drop files between them. In MTP mode, the device you're connected to recognizes your camera as a camera and can communicate with it, which is what happens when you use a PictBridge printer.

Most of the time, you'll want to leave this setting at Auto, changing it only when you're communicating with a PictBridge printer that requires an MTP connection.

Audio Signals

Options: On, Off

Default: On

The Sony Alpha's internal beeper provides a helpful chirp to signify various functions, such as the focus lock and the countdown of your camera's self-timer. You can switch it off if you want to avoid the beeps because they are annoying, impolite, or distracting (at a concert or museum), or undesired for any other reason. (I've had new dSLR owners ask me how to turn off the "shutter sound" the camera makes; such an option was available in the point-and-shoot camera they'd used previously.) You can't turn off all sounds made by an SLT camera because, even though the mirror doesn't move, it still has moving shutters. Select Audio Signals from the Setup 2 menu, choose On or Off, and press the center controller button.

Cleaning Mode

Options: Enter (perform cleaning), Cancel

Default: None

One of the Sony Alpha's best features is the automatic sensor cleaning system that reduces or eliminates the need to clean your camera's sensor manually using brushes, swabs, or bulb blowers (you'll find instructions on how to do that in Chapter 11). Sony has applied anti-static coatings to the image sensor and other portions of the camera body interior to counter charge build-ups that attract dust. The sensor vibrates ultrasonically each time the Alpha is powered off, shaking loose any dust, which is captured by a sticky strip beneath the sensor.

If you believe there is dust on the sensor and you want the camera to perform an automatic cleaning procedure, select this menu option. Make sure you have a fully charged battery or are using an optional AC adapter. Then, select this menu option and press Enter. You will hear a brief buzzing sound, during which the camera does its automatic vibration process to dislodge dust. The camera will then prompt you to turn off the power.

At that point, you can proceed to the manual cleaning procedure if necessary, as discussed in Chapter 11.

Version

Options: None

Select this menu option to display the version number of the firmware (internal operating software) installed in your camera. (See Figure 3.24.) From time to time, Sony will update the original Version 1.00 firmware with a newer version that adds or enhances features or corrects operational bugs. In fact, the version in my camera when I purchased it was 1.01, which indicates that some changes had already been made to the original firmware. When a new version is released, such as the 1.02 version update available within a week after I bought my camera, it will be accompanied by instructions, which generally involve downloading the update to your computer, transferring it to a memory card, and then inserting that card into your camera using a specified procedure. In some cases, the update is done by connecting the camera by USB cable to a computer that has had the update file downloaded to it. It's a good idea to check the Sony website occasionally, http://esupport.sony.com, to see if a new version of the camera's firmware is available for download. (You can also go to that site to download updates to the software that came with the camera, and to get general support information.)

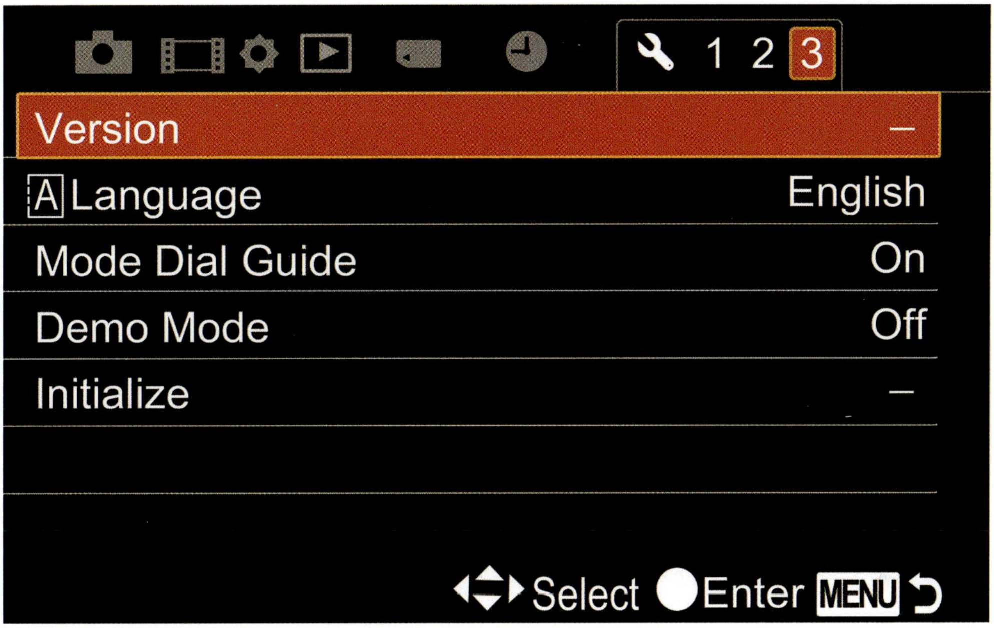

Figure 3.24
The Setup 3 menu.

Language

Options: English, French, Spanish, Italian, Japanese, Chinese languages

Default: Language of country where camera is sold

If you accidentally set a language you don't read and find yourself with incomprehensible menus, don't panic. Just choose the second option from the top of the Setup 3 menu, and select the idioma, lingua, or langue of your choice. Also, Sony has placed a symbol that looks like an alphabet block "A" at the beginning of this menu item, no matter which language is selected, so you can recognize this menu item even if it's in a language that you're not familiar with.

Mode Dial Guide

Options: On, Off

Default: On

The Alpha's Help Guide display provides quick snippets of information about various functions as you select them using the Fn button, direct-access buttons, or the mode dial, and then removes the information from the screen when you press the center controller button or shutter release. Once you've become comfortable with the operations of the camera, you may find that these factoids slow down your operation of the Alpha. You can turn them off with this menu option.

Demo Mode

Options: On, Off

Default: Off

The only purpose of this menu option is to let you set the camera in a "demo mode," in which the camera will start to play a movie if it is left idle for about one minute. There is no built-in demo movie; you have to record your own movie for this function.

Initialize

Options: Reset Default, Rec mode reset, Custom reset

Default: None

If you've made a lot of changes to your Alpha's settings, you may want the camera to return to the factory settings so you can start over without manually going back through the menus and restoring everything. This menu selection lets you do that with the press of a few buttons. You can see the default values that will be reset at pages 170-173 of the Sony instruction manual.

Reset Default resets everything for all menus and shooting settings; Rec Mode Reset initializes shooting settings, Still Shooting menu, and Movie Shooting menu settings; Custom Reset only resets the Custom menu settings.

Function Menu

It's time to drag out the Alpha's Fn (Function) menu again, mentioned in Chapters 1 and 2, but not explained in a great amount of detail in either. That's because several of the functions deserve complete descriptions within the context of their respective applications. For example, Autofocus mode, AF area, and metering mode are best deferred to the chapters that explain those features in exhaustive detail. This section will provide an overview that points you to the parts of the book that delve into the functions available from this menu.

The Function menu appears when you press the Fn button when the camera is in Shooting mode or in the main menu system (that is, when you're not reviewing an image on the LCD). (If the camera is in Playback or Auto Review mode, pressing the Fn button produces a screen that lets you rotate the image on display 90 degrees each time you press the center controller button.)

This menu (see Figure 3.25) has up to 14 options, depending on the context. All 14 options are available when the Shooting mode is Program auto, Aperture priority, Shutter priority, or Manual. In other shooting modes, some of these items will not appear on the Function menu screen or will be grayed out and unavailable.

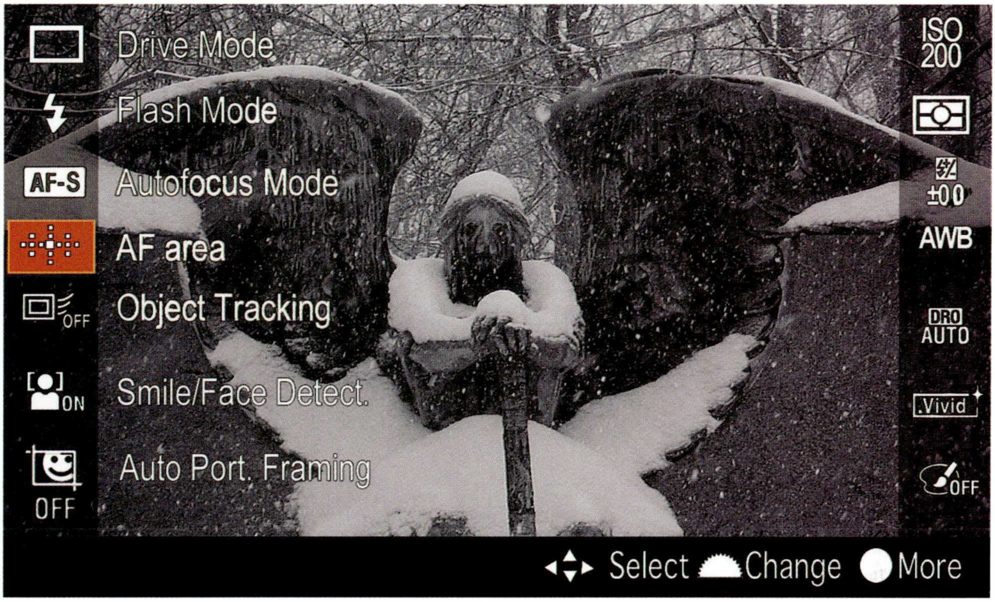

Figure 3.25
The Function menu.

After you press the Fn button, the camera will show all of the available options on the LCD or viewfinder screen. Use the four direction buttons to scroll up and down and left and right among the various options. When the option you want is highlighted, you can press the center controller button to activate a submenu with the settings for that option. Or, if you want to take a quicker route, once the option is highlighted, just spin the control dial left or right to change the settings directly, without having to get into the submenu.

- **Drive mode.** This is the first option on the top left. There are several choices available through this single item on the screen: continuous shooting mode at high or low speed; self-timer; exposure bracketing; white balance bracketing; and Remote Commander. I discuss bracketing in Chapter 4, and continuous shooting and the other topics in Chapter 6.
- **Flash mode.** This entry calls forth a submenu that allows you to choose among the several flash modes that are available when the flash is popped up or an external flash is attached: Flash Off, Autoflash, Fill flash, Slow Sync, Rear Sync, and Wireless. Not all of these modes are available at all times. I'll describe the use of flash in detail in Chapter 9.
- **Autofocus mode.** This entry summons a terse submenu that allows you to choose *when* the Alpha locks in focus—AF-S (single autofocus), AF-C (continuous autofocus), or AF-A (automatic autofocus). These were described in Chapter 1, and will be explained more completely in the autofocus section of Chapter 5.

- **AF area.** The Alpha includes 15 autofocus sensors arranged around the central portion of the viewfinder. You can elect to have the Alpha always choose which of the sensors to use, you can select any one of the 15 sensors yourself, or you can set the camera to always use the center autofocus point. You'll find tips for choosing the best AF area mode, from among Wide, Spot, or Local, for the kind of shooting you are doing, in Chapter 5.
- **Object Tracking.** Used to tell the A57 to follow focus on moving objects. You'll learn more about this in Chapter 5 as well.
- **Smile/Face Detection.** This option causes the camera to search for faces in the scene being photographed. If it detects a face, it adjusts the focus and exposure to produce the best possible image with one or more faces in sharp focus and properly exposed. I introduced this feature in Chapter 2, and will have some more to say about it in Chapter 5, which covers focus and related topics.

  Smile Shutter is related to Face Detection; when you turn Smile Shutter on, Face Detection is automatically turned on also. With Smile Shutter, the camera watches for a smile, and fires the shutter automatically each time it sees one. This is an interesting high-tech feature, because the subject's smile acts as a sort of remote control. Each time a person smiles, the camera clicks the shutter and takes a picture. There is no limit to the number of smiles and images; you, or whoever is in front of the camera, can keep smiling repeatedly, and the camera will keep taking more pictures, until it runs out of memory storage or battery power. Of course, the main purpose of this feature is not to act as a remote control; it's really intended to make sure your subject is smiling before the shutter fires. When you first activate Smile Shutter, you can use the right/left cursor buttons to adjust the smile sensitivity for a slight, normal, or big smile.
- **Auto Portrait Framing.** When the A57 is in Face Detection mode, when a picture is contained containing a single human face, the original shot is saved to your memory card, and an additional version is stored that has been cropped to just the face. During picture review, the cropping used appears on the screen. The Auto Port. Framing indicator on the display is highlighted in green when this feature is active. You can choose Auto or Off.

  There's a long list of modes in which this function cannot be used. You must have activated Face Detection and selected Auto for Auto Port. Framing. It is not available when using RAW or RAW & JPEG image quality settings. It can be enabled only when using P, S, A, or M modes, and certain scene modes, and is disabled when using Sweep/3D Sweep Panorama, Continuous Advance Priority AE Mode, Movie mode, or Hand-held Twilight and Sports Action Scene modes. Nor is it possible when using Continuous shooting, continuous bracketing, Multi Frame Noise Reduction, Auto HDR, any of the Zoom modes, manual focus, soft focus, and Picture Effects including HDR Painting, Rich-tone monochrome, or Miniature.

- **ISO sensitivity.** In addition to using the direct-access ISO button (the down cursor button), you have the option of using the Fn menu to set the camera's ISO to Auto, or to various values from 100 to 16000. You also can choose Multi Frame Noise Reduction from this menu, in which case the ISO can be set as high as 25600 using the up/down buttons. ISO is discussed in detail in Chapter 4.
- **Metering mode.** The metering mode determines what part of the image is used to determine correct exposure. The Alpha can be set to evaluate multiple points within the image, concentrate only on the center portion of the frame, or measure a small spot in the middle of the shot. You'll learn how metering mode affects exposure in Chapter 4, which is devoted exclusively to exposure topics.
- **Flash compensation.** This feature works like exposure compensation (discussed in Chapter 4), and allows you to dial in more or less exposure when using the flash. If your flash photo (such as a test shot) is too dark or too light, access this menu entry. Press the left/right cursor buttons or spin the control dial to reduce or increase flash exposure by up to two steps; then press the center controller button to confirm your choice. This and other flash-related topics are discussed in detail in Chapter 9.
- **White balance.** The different light sources you shoot under have differing color balances. Indoor light, for example, is much redder than outdoor illumination, which tends to have a bluish bias. The Alpha lets you choose the color/white balance that's appropriate, or it can make this adjustment automatically. You can choose Auto White Balance, and let the camera select the proper setting, or you can select from several preset options for commonly encountered lighting situations: Daylight, Shade, Cloudy, Incandescent (standard light bulbs), Fluorescent, Flash, Color Temperature, and Custom. I'll discuss the last two settings in Chapter 6, in the discussion of more advanced shooting options. The Auto White Balance setting works very well on the A57, and one advantage of using it is that you don't have to worry about changing it for your next shooting session; there's no risk of having the camera set for, say, Daylight, when you're shooting indoors. If you shoot in RAW quality, though, you don't have to worry about white balance at all, because you can easily adjust it in your software after the fact.
- **D-Range Optimizer/Auto HDR.** The brightness/darkness range of many images is so broad that the sensor has difficulty capturing both the brightest highlight areas and the darkest shadow areas. The Alpha is able to expand its *dynamic range* using the D-Range Optimizer feature available from this menu entry. You can leave DRO turned off, set it to Auto, letting the camera decide how much processing to apply, or set it manually to any level of processing from 1 (weak) to 5 (strong).

  In addition, this feature of the Alpha offers an Auto HDR setting. If you select Auto HDR, the camera takes three exposures at different exposure levels using an interval that you select, from 1.0 to 6.0 EV. It then combines the three exposures so as to lighten the shadows and darken the highlights of the resulting image, producing an enhanced dynamic range. I'll provide tips and examples in Chapter 6.

- **Creative Style.** This option gives you six different combinations of contrast, saturation, and sharpness: Standard, Vivid, Portrait, Landscape, Sunset, and B/W (black-and-white). The Creative Style option is not available in the AUTO or Scene modes, though it is available in all other shooting modes, including Sweep Panorama and Continuous Advance Priority AE. I explain the "looks" of each of these styles in Chapter 6.
- **Picture Effects.** These are interesting special effects you can apply to photos as you shoot them, right in the camera. I'll explain these and show you some examples of what images look like when they are used, in Chapter 6.

4

Getting the Right Exposure

When you bought your Sony Alpha SLT-A57, you probably thought your days of worrying about getting the correct exposure were over. To paraphrase an old Kodak tagline dating back to the 19th Century—the goal is, "you press the button, and the camera does the rest." For the most part, that's a realistic objective. The Alpha is one of the smartest cameras available when it comes to calculating the right exposure for most situations. You can generally choose one of the Auto or Scene modes, or spin the mode dial to Program (P), Aperture priority (A), or Shutter priority (S) and shoot away.

So, why am I including an entire chapter on exposure? As you learn to use your Alpha creatively, you're going to find that the right settings—as determined by the camera's exposure meter and intelligence—need to be *adjusted* to account for your creative decisions or special situations.

For example, when you shoot with the main light source behind the subject, you end up with *backlighting*, which can result in an overexposed background and/or an underexposed subject. The Sony Alpha recognizes backlit situations nicely, and can properly base exposure on the main subject, producing a decent photo. Features like D-Range Optimizer (discussed in Chapter 6) can fine-tune exposure to preserve detail in the highlights and shadows.

But what if you *want* to underexpose the subject, to produce a silhouette effect? Or, perhaps, you might want to flip up the Alpha's built-in flash unit to fill in the shadows on your subject. The more you know about how to use your Alpha, the more you'll run into situations where you want to creatively tweak the exposure to provide a different look than you'd get with a straight shot.

This chapter shows you the fundamentals of exposure, so you'll be better equipped to override the Sony Alpha's default settings when you want to, or need to. After all, correct exposure is one of the foundations of good photography, along with accurate focus and sharpness, appropriate color balance, freedom from unwanted noise and excessive contrast, as well as pleasing composition.

The Sony Alpha gives you a great deal of control over all of these, although composition is entirely up to you. You must still frame the photograph to create an interesting arrangement of subject matter, but all the other parameters are basic functions of the camera. You can let your Alpha set them for you automatically, you can fine-tune how the camera applies its automatic settings, or you can make them yourself, manually. The amount of control you have over exposure, sensitivity (ISO settings), color balance, focus, and image parameters like sharpness and contrast make the Alpha a versatile tool for creating images.

In the next few pages, I'm going to give you a grounding in one of those foundations, and explain the basics of exposure, either as an introduction or as a refresher course, depending on your current level of expertise. When you finish this chapter, you'll understand most of what you need to know to take well-exposed photographs creatively in a broad range of situations.

Getting a Handle on Exposure

In the most basic sense, exposure is all about light. Exposure can make or break your photo. Correct exposure brings out the detail in the areas you want to picture, providing the range of tones and colors you need to create the desired image. Poor exposure can cloak important details in shadow, or wash them out in glare-filled featureless expanses of white. However, getting the perfect exposure requires some intelligence—either that built into the camera or the smarts in your head—because digital sensors can't capture all the tones we are able to see. If the range of tones in an image is extensive, embracing both inky black shadows and bright highlights, we often must settle for an exposure that renders most of those tones—but not all—in a way that best suits the photo we want to produce.

For example, look at two exposures presented in Figure 4.1. For the image at the top, the highlights (chiefly the clouds at upper left and the top-left edge of the skyscraper) are well exposed, but everything else in the shot is seriously underexposed. The version at the bottom, taken an instant later with the tripod-mounted camera, shows detail in the shadow areas of the buildings, but the highlights are completely washed out. The camera's sensor simply can't capture detail in both dark areas and bright areas in a single shot.

With digital camera sensors, it's often tricky to capture detail in both highlights and shadows in a single image, because the number of tones, the *dynamic range* of the sensor, is limited. The solution, in this particular case, was to resort to a technique called High Dynamic Range (HDR) photography, in which the two exposures from Figure

4.1 were combined in an image editor such as Photoshop, or a specialized HDR tool like Photomatix (about $100 from www.hdrsoft.com). The resulting shot is shown in Figure 4.2. I'll explain more about HDR photography in Chapter 6, including the Auto HDR feature of the Sony Alpha, which lets you accomplish a decent approximation of HDR processing right in the camera. For now, though, I'm going to concentrate on showing you how to get the best exposures possible without resorting to such tools, using only the ordinary exposure-related features of your Alpha SLT-A57.

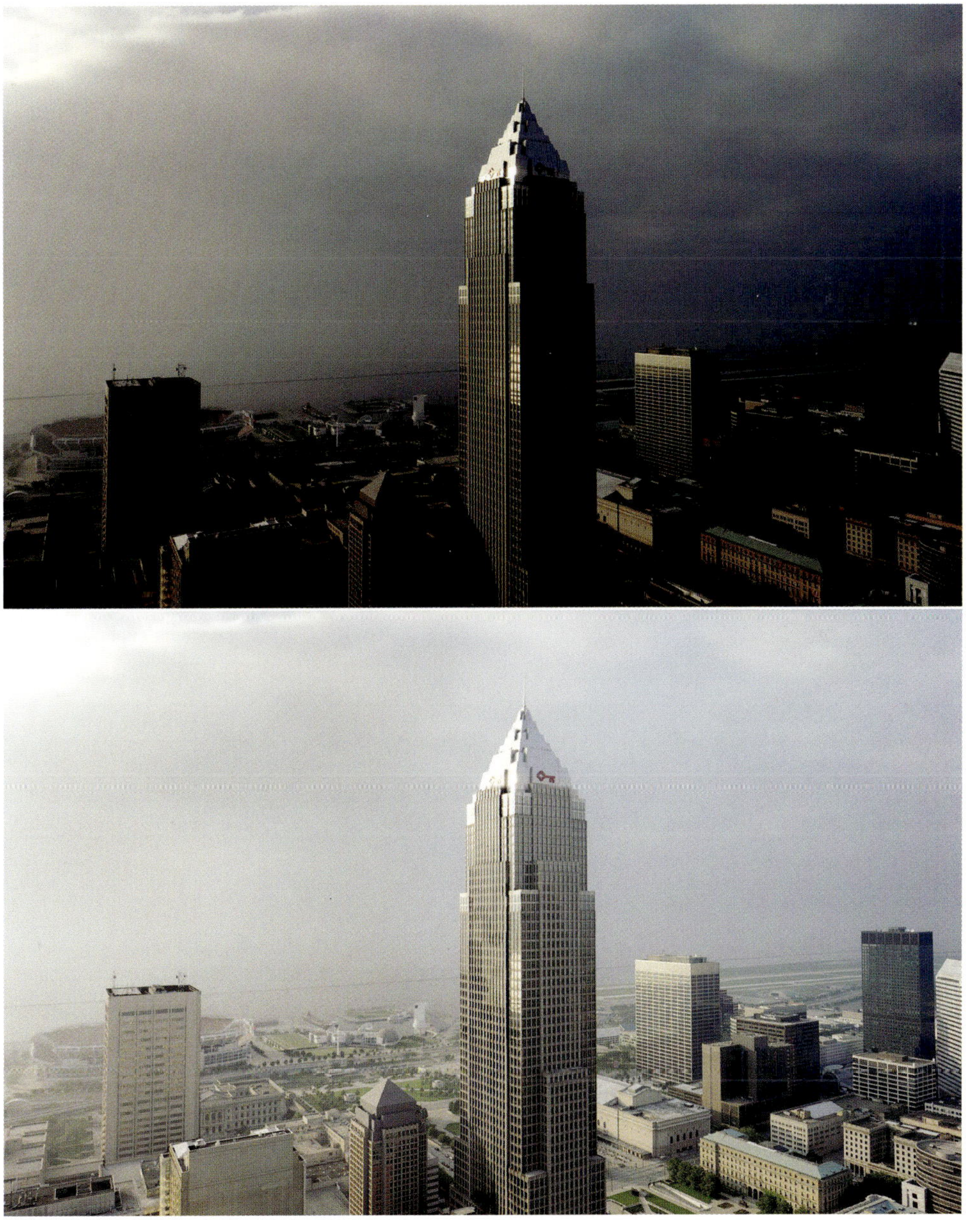

Figure 4.1
At top, the image is exposed for the highlights, losing shadow detail. At bottom, the exposure captures detail in the shadows, but the highlights are washed out.

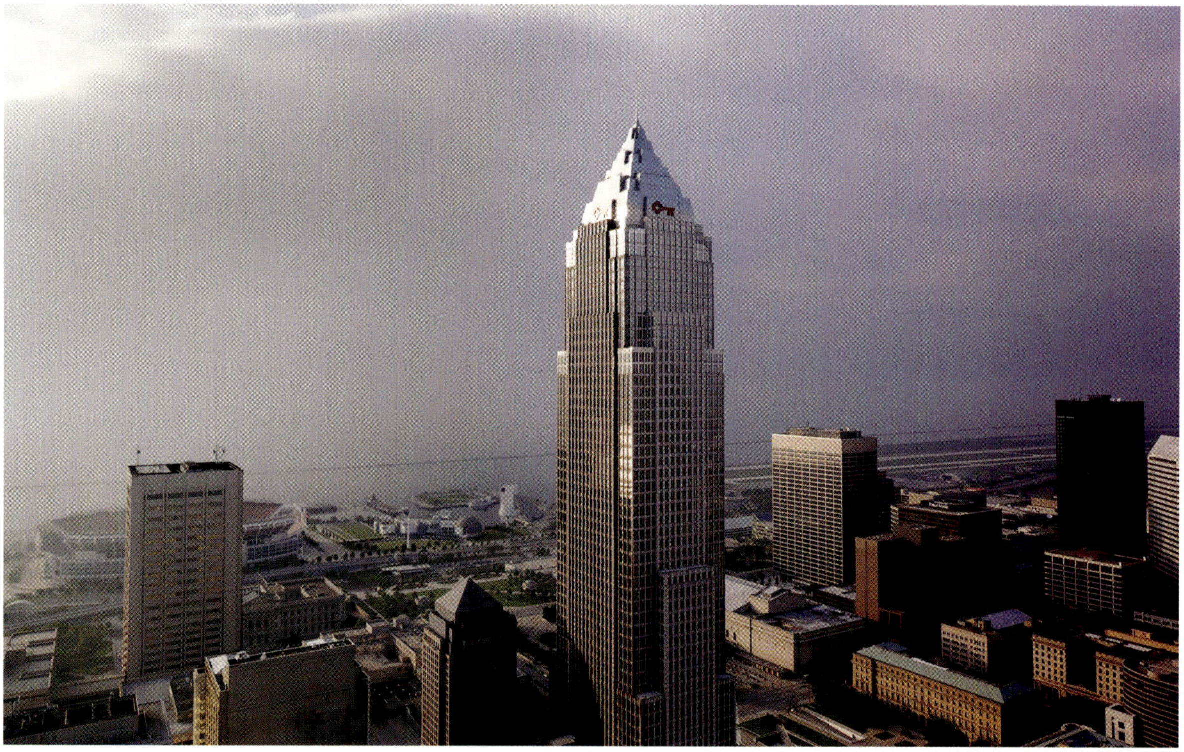

Figure 4.2 Combining the two exposures produces the best compromise image.

To understand exposure, you need to understand the six aspects of light that combine to produce an image. Start with a light source—the sun, an interior lamp, or the glow from a campfire—and trace its path to your camera, through the lens, and finally to the sensor that captures the illumination. Here's a brief review of the things within our control that affect exposure, listed in "chronological" order (that is, as the light moves from the subject to the sensor):

- **Light at its source.** Our eyes and our cameras—film or digital—are most sensitive to that portion of the electromagnetic spectrum we call *visible light.* That light has several important aspects that are relevant to photography, such as color and harshness (which is determined primarily by the apparent size of the light source as it illuminates a subject). But, in terms of exposure, the important attribute of a light source is its *intensity.* We may have direct control over intensity, which might be the case with an interior light that can be brightened or dimmed. Or, we might have only indirect control over intensity, as with sunlight, which can be made to appear dimmer by introducing translucent light-absorbing or reflective materials in its path.

- **Light's duration.** We tend to think of most light sources as continuous. But, as you'll learn in Chapter 9, the duration of light can change quickly enough to modify the exposure, as when the main illumination in a photograph comes from an intermittent source, such as an electronic flash.
- **Light reflected, transmitted, or emitted.** Once light is produced by its source, either continuously or in a brief burst, we are able to see and photograph objects by the light that is reflected from our subjects towards the camera lens; transmitted (say, from translucent objects that are lit from behind); or emitted (by a candle or television screen). When more or less light reaches the lens from the subject, we need to adjust the exposure. This part of the equation is under our control to the extent we can increase the amount of light falling on or passing through the subject (by adding extra light sources or using reflectors), or by pumping up the light that's emitted (by increasing the brightness of the glowing object).
- **Light passed by the lens.** Not all the illumination that reaches the front of the lens makes it all the way through. Filters can remove some of the light before it enters the lens. Inside the lens barrel is a variable-sized diaphragm that dilates and contracts to produce an opening called an *aperture* that controls the amount of light that enters the lens. You, or the Alpha's autoexposure system, can control exposure by varying the size of the aperture. The relative size of the aperture is called the *f/stop*. (See Figure 4.3.)
- **Light passing through the shutter.** Once light passes through the lens, the amount of time the sensor receives it is determined by the Alpha's shutter, which can remain open for as long as 30 seconds (or even longer if you use the Bulb setting) or as briefly as 1/4,000th second.
- **Light captured by the sensor.** Not all the light falling onto the sensor is captured. If the number of photons reaching a particular photosite doesn't pass a set threshold, no information is recorded. Similarly, if too much light illuminates a pixel in the sensor, then the excess isn't recorded or, worse, spills over to contaminate adjacent pixels. We can modify the minimum and maximum number of pixels that contribute to image detail by adjusting the ISO setting. At higher ISOs, the incoming light is amplified to boost the effective sensitivity of the sensor.

These four factors—quantity of light, light passed by the lens, the amount of time the shutter is open, and the sensitivity of the sensor—all work proportionately and reciprocally to produce an exposure. That is, if you double the amount of light, increase the aperture by one stop, make the shutter speed twice as long, or boost the ISO setting 2X, you'll get twice as much exposure. Similarly, you can increase any of these factors while decreasing one of the others by a similar amount to keep the same exposure.

F/STOPS AND SHUTTER SPEEDS

If you're *really* new to more advanced cameras (and I realize that some ambitious amateurs do purchase the Alpha SLT-A57 as their first digital interchangeable-lens camera), you might need to know that the lens aperture, or f/stop, is a ratio, much like a fraction, which is why f/2 is larger than f/4, just as 1/2 is larger than 1/4. However, f/2 is actually *four times* as large as f/4. (If you remember your high school geometry, you'll know that to double the area of a circle, you multiply its diameter by the square root of two: 1.4.)

Lenses are usually marked with intermediate f/stops that represent a size that's twice as much/half as much as the previous aperture. So, a lens might be marked:

f/2, f/2.8, f/4, f/5.6, f/8, f/11, f/16, f/22, with each larger number representing an aperture that admits half as much light as the one before, as shown in Figure 4.3.

Shutter speeds are actual fractions (of a second), so that 1/60, 1/125, 1/250, 1/500, 1/1000, and so forth represent 1/60th, 1/125th, 1/250th, 1/500th, and 1/1,000th second. To avoid confusion, the Sony Alpha uses quotation marks to signify longer exposures: 2", 2.5", 4", and so forth representing 2.0, 2.5, and 4.0-second exposures, respectively.

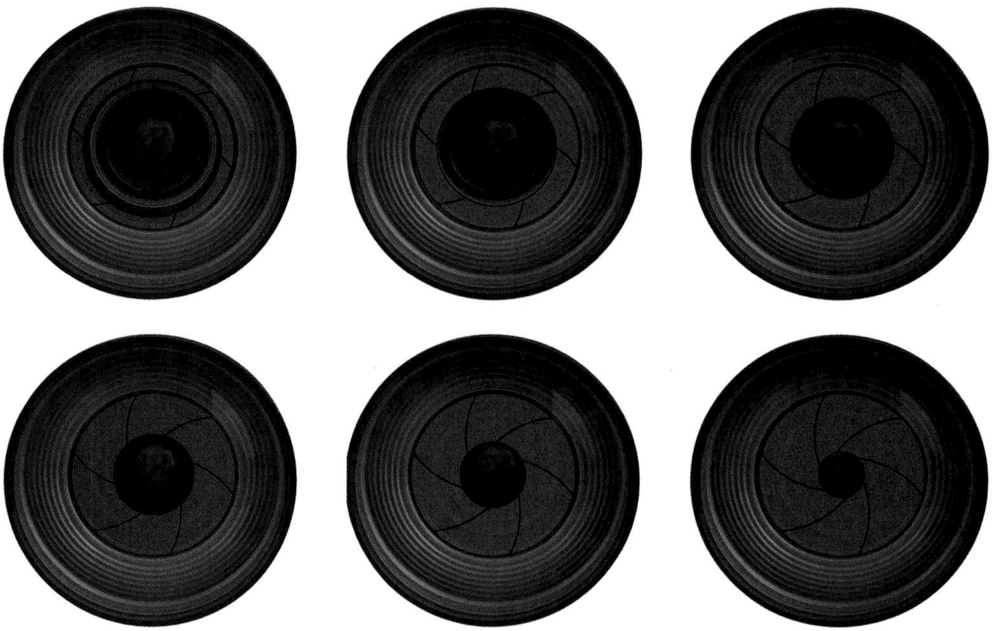

Figure 4.3
Top row (left to right): f/2, f/2.8, f/4; bottom row, f/5.6, f/8, f11.

Most commonly, exposure settings are made using the aperture and shutter speed, followed by adjusting the ISO sensitivity if it's not possible to get the preferred exposure (that is, the one that uses the "best" f/stop or shutter speed for the depth-of-field or action stopping we want). Table 4.1 shows equivalent exposure settings using various shutter speeds and f/stops.

When the Alpha is set for P mode, the metering system automatically selects the aperture and shutter speed that will result in what the camera judges to be the correct exposure. You can change the shutter speed and aperture value combination by rotating the control dial to achieve Program Shift in P mode. You cannot change the shutter speed or aperture individually, although you can cause the camera to do so by dialing in exposure compensation or by changing the ISO setting. In Aperture priority (A) and Shutter priority (S) modes, you can change to an equivalent exposure, but only by adjusting either the aperture (the camera chooses the shutter speed) or shutter speed (the camera selects the aperture). I'll cover all these exposure modes later in the chapter.

Table 4.1 Equivalent Exposures

Shutter speed	f/stop	Shutter speed	f/stop
1/30th second	f/22	1/500th second	f/5.6
1/60th second	f/16	1/1,000th second	f/4
1/125th second	f/11	1/2,000th second	f/2.8
1/250th second	f/8	1/4,000th second	f/2

How the Sony Alpha Calculates Exposure

Your A57 calculates exposure by measuring the light that passes through the lens to reach the sensor, based on the assumption that each area being measured reflects about the same amount of light as a neutral gray card that reflects a "middle" gray of about 12- to 18-percent reflectance. (The photographic "gray cards" you buy at a camera store have an 18-percent gray tone; your camera is calibrated to interpret a somewhat darker 12-percent gray; I'll explain more about this later.) That "average" 12- to 18-percent gray assumption is necessary, because different subjects reflect different amounts of light. In a photo containing, say, a white cat and a dark gray cat, the white cat might reflect five times as much light as the gray cat. An exposure based on the white cat will cause the gray cat to appear to be black, while an exposure based only on the gray cat will make the white cat washed out.

This is more easily understood if you look at some photos of subjects that are dark (they reflect little light), those that have predominantly middle tones, and subjects that are highly reflective. The next few figures show some images of actual cats (actually, the *same* cat rendered in black, gray, and white varieties through the magic of Photoshop), with each of the three strips exposed using a different cat for reference.

Correctly Exposed

The three pictures shown in Figure 4.4 represent how the black, gray, and white cats would appear if the exposure were calculated by measuring the light reflecting from the middle, gray cat, which, for the sake of illustration, we'll assume reflects approximately 12 to 18 percent of the light that strikes it. The exposure meter sees an object that it thinks is a middle gray, calculates an exposure based on that, and the feline in the center of the strip is rendered at its proper tonal value. Best of all, because the resulting exposure is correct, the black cat at left and white cat at right are rendered properly as well.

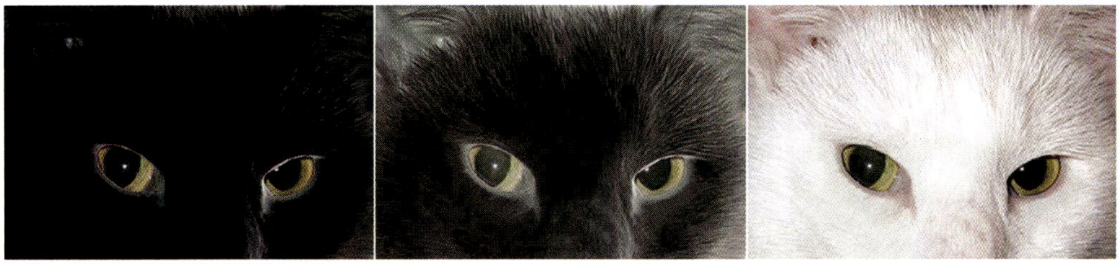

Figure 4.4
When exposure is calculated based on the middle-gray cat in the center, the black and white cats are rendered accurately, too.

When you're shooting pictures with your A57, and the meter happens to base its exposure on a subject that averages that "ideal" middle gray, then you'll end up with similar (accurate) results. The camera's exposure algorithms are concocted to ensure this kind of result as often as possible, barring any unusual subjects (that is, those that are backlit, or have uneven illumination). The A57 has three different metering modes (described next), plus Scene modes, each of which is equipped to handle certain types of unusual subjects, as I'll outline.

Overexposed

The strip of three images in Figure 4.5 show what would happen if the exposure were calculated based on metering the leftmost, black cat. The light meter sees less light reflecting from the black cat than it would see from a gray middle-tone subject, and so figures, "Aha! I need to add exposure to brighten this subject up to a middle gray!" That lightens the black cat, so it now appears to be gray.

But now the cat in the middle that was *originally* middle gray is overexposed and becomes light gray. And the white cat at right is now seriously overexposed, and loses detail in the highlights, which have become a featureless white.

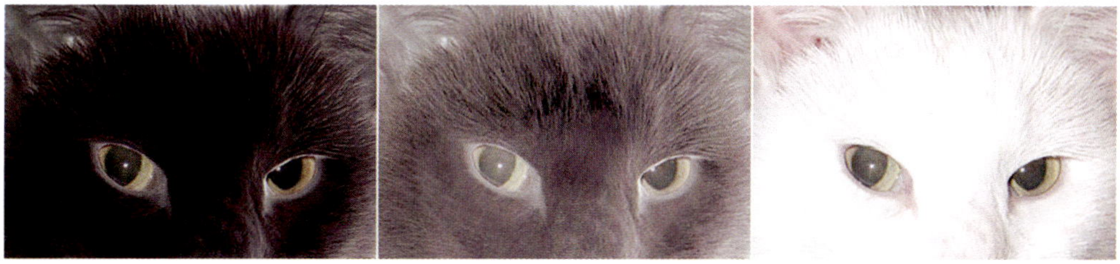

Figure 4.5
When exposure is calculated based on the black cat at the left, the black cat looks gray, the gray cat appears to be a light gray, and the white cat is seriously overexposed.

Underexposed

The third possibility in this simplified scenario is that the light meter might measure the illumination bouncing off the white cat, and try to render that feline as a middle gray. A lot of light is reflected by the white kitty, so the exposure is *reduced*, bringing that cat closer to a middle gray tone. The cats that were originally gray and black are now rendered too dark. Clearly, measuring the gray cat—or a substitute that reflects about the same amount of light—is the only way to ensure that the exposure is precisely correct. (See Figure 4.6.)

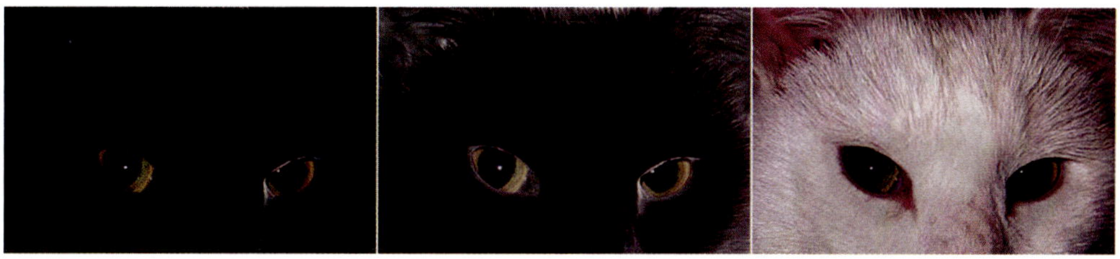

Figure 4.6
When exposure is calculated based on the white cat on the right, the other two cats are underexposed.

As you can see, the ideal way to measure exposure is to meter from a subject that reflects 12 to 18 percent of the light that reaches it. If you want the most precise exposure calculations, if you don't have a gray cat handy, the solution is to use a stand-in, such as the evenly illuminated gray card I mentioned earlier. But, because the standard Kodak gray card reflects 18 percent of the light that reaches it and, as I said, your camera is calibrated for a somewhat darker 12-percent tone, you would need to add about one-half stop *more* exposure than the value metered from the card.

Another substitute for a gray card is the palm of a human hand (the backside of the hand is too variable). But a human palm, regardless of ethnic group, is even brighter than a standard gray card, so instead of one-half stop more exposure, you need to add one additional stop. That is, if your meter reading is 1/500th of a second at f/11, use 1/500th second at f/8 or 1/250th second at f/11 instead. (Both exposures are equivalent.)

If you actually wanted to use a gray card, place it in your frame near your main subject, facing the camera, and with the exact same even illumination falling on it that is falling on your subject. Then, use the Spot metering function (described in the next section) to calculate exposure. Of course, in most situations, it's not necessary to do this. Your camera's light meter will do a good job of calculating the right exposure, especially if you use the exposure tips in the next section. But, I felt that explaining exactly what is going on during exposure calculation would help you understand how your A57's metering system works.

In most cases, your camera's light meter will do a good job of calculating the right exposure, especially if you use the exposure tips in the next section. But if you want to double-check, or feel that exposure is especially critical, take the light reading off an object of known reflectance, such as a gray card. To meter properly, you'll want to choose both the *metering method* (how light is evaluated) and *exposure method* (how the appropriate shutter speeds and apertures are chosen). I'll describe both in the following sections.

WHY THE GRAY CARD CONFUSION?

Why are so many photographers under the impression that cameras and meters are calibrated to the 18-percent "standard," rather than the true value, which may be 12 to 14 percent, depending on the vendor? You'll find this misinformation in an alarming number of places. I've seen the 18-percent "myth" taught in camera classes; I've found it in books, and even been given this wrong information from the technical staff of camera vendors. (They should know better—the same vendors' engineers who design and calibrate the cameras have the right figure.)

The most common explanation is that during a revision of Kodak's instructions for its gray cards in the 1970s, the advice to open up an extra half stop was omitted, and a whole generation of shooters grew up thinking that a measurement off a gray card could be used as-is. The proviso returned to the instructions by 1987, it's said, but by then it was too late. Next to me is a (c)2006 version of the instructions for KODAK Gray Cards, Publication R-27Q, and the current directions read (with a bit of paraphrasing from me in italics):

- For subjects of normal reflectance increase the indicated exposure by 1/2 stop.
- For light subjects use the indicated exposure; for very light subjects, decrease the exposure by 1/2 stop. (*That is, you're measuring a cat that's lighter than middle gray.)*
- If the subject is dark to very dark, increase the indicated exposure by 1 to 1-1/2 stops. *(You're shooting a black cat.)*

Choosing a Metering Method

The Alpha has three different schemes for evaluating the light received by its exposure sensors. You can choose among them by pressing the Fn button and choosing Metering Mode from the screen that pops up (see Figure 4.7).

- **Multi segment.** The Alpha SLT-A57 has an advantage over many earlier models because of its unique internal structure. The translucent mirror allows light to reach the image sensor constantly, so the camera uses the entire image sensor to evaluate the exposure of your shots. So, instead of the more usual 40 or 49 metering zones, the SLT models use the whole sensor surface, which is considered to consist of 1,200 separate zones, as shown in Figure 4.8. The camera evaluates the measurements to make an educated guess about what kind of picture you're taking, based on examination of exposure data derived from thousands of different real-world photos. For example, if the top sections of a picture are much lighter than the bottom portions, the algorithm can assume that the scene is a landscape photo with lots of sky. This mode is the best all-purpose metering method for most pictures, like the typical scene in Figure 4.9.

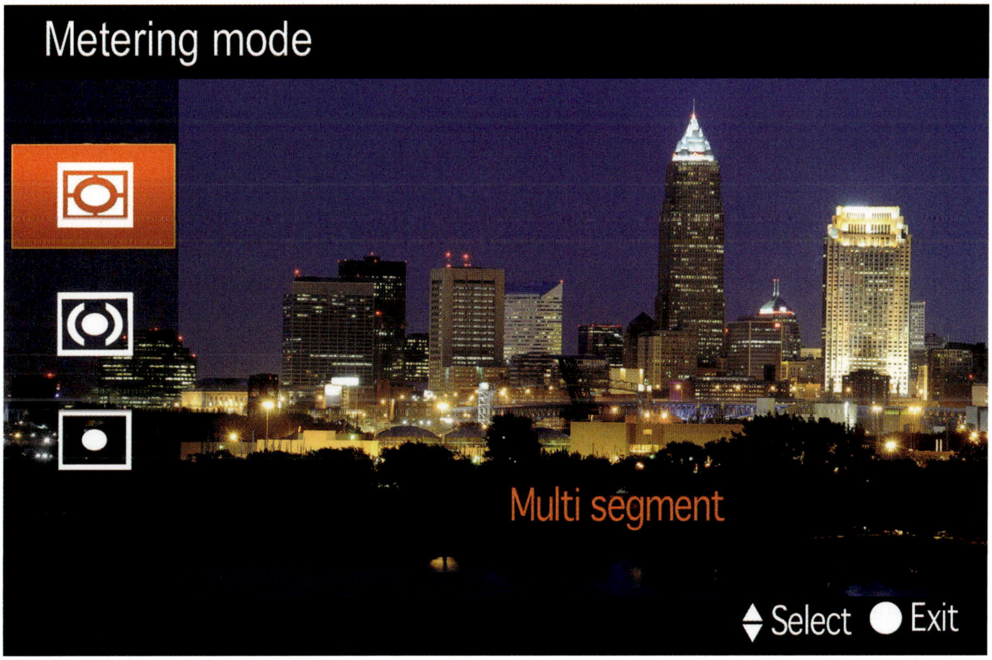

Figure 4.7 Choose a metering mode.

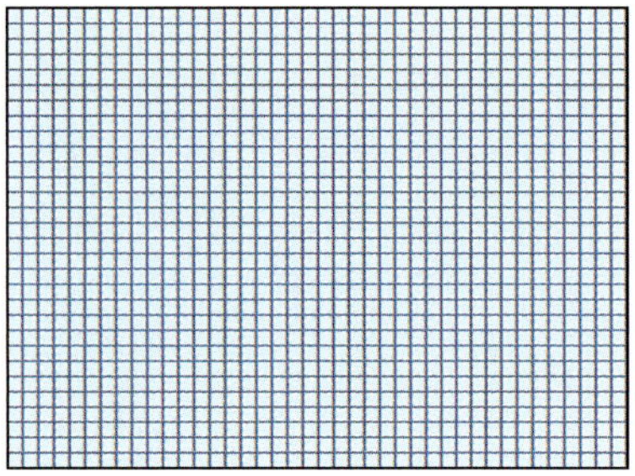

Figure 4.8 Multi segment metering uses the entire surface of the image sensor, divided into 1,200 individual zones.

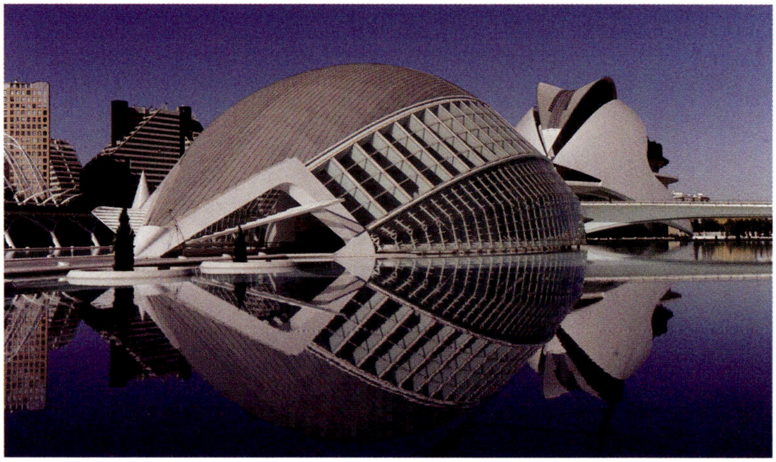

Figure 4.9 Multi segment metering does a good job of interpreting scenes like this one.

- **Center weighted.** In this mode, the exposure meter emphasizes a zone in the center of the frame to calculate exposure, as shown in Figure 4.10, on the theory that, for most pictures, the main subject will be located in the center. Center weighting works best for portraits, architectural photos, and other pictures in which the most important subject is located in the middle of the frame. As the name suggests, the light reading is *weighted* towards the central portion, but information is also used from the rest of the frame. If your main subject is surrounded by very bright or very dark areas, the exposure might not be exactly right. However, this scheme works well in many situations if you don't want to use one of the other modes, such as scenes like the one seen in Figure 4.11.
- **Spot.** This mode confines the reading to a limited area in the center of the viewfinder, as shown in Figure 4.12. This mode is useful when you want to base exposure on a small area in the frame. If that area is in the center of the frame, so much the better. If not, you'll have to make your meter reading on that area and then lock exposure by pressing the shutter release halfway (or by pressing the AEL button), before re-aiming the camera at your actual subject. This mode works well for scenes like the one shown in Figure 4.13.

Choosing an Exposure Method

You'll find four methods for choosing the appropriate shutter speed and aperture semi-automatically or manually. Just spin the mode dial to choose the method you want to use (see Figure 4.14). Your choice of which is best for a given shooting situation will depend on things like your need for lots of (or less) depth-of-field, a desire to freeze

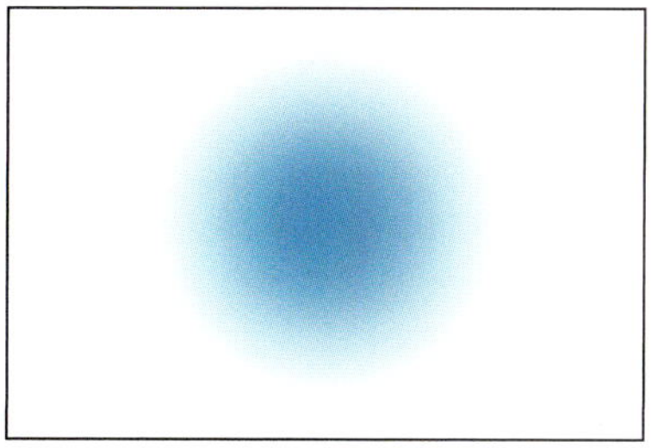

Figure 4.10 Center weighted metering calculates exposure based on the full frame, but emphasizes the center area.

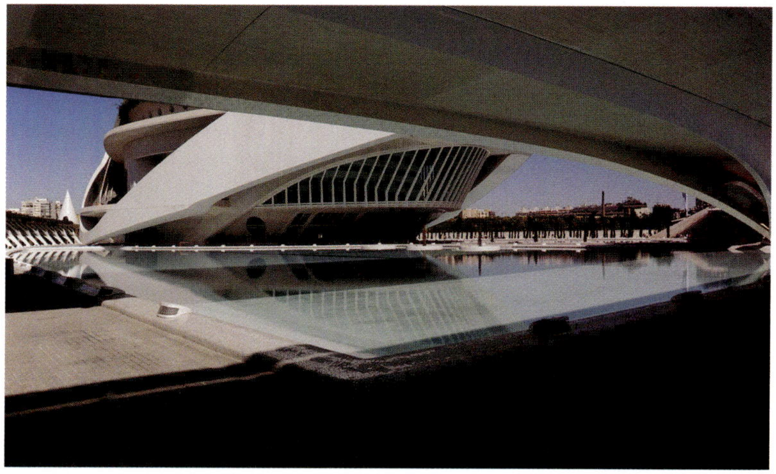

Figure 4.11 Center weighted metering is suitable for scenes like this one.

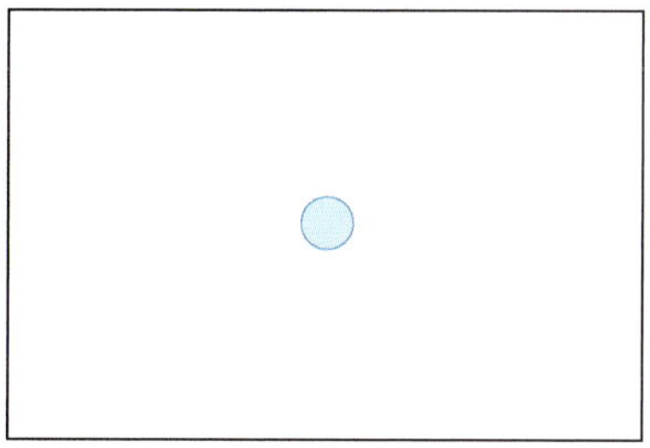

Figure 4.12 Spot metering calculates exposure based on a center spot that's only a small percentage of the image area.

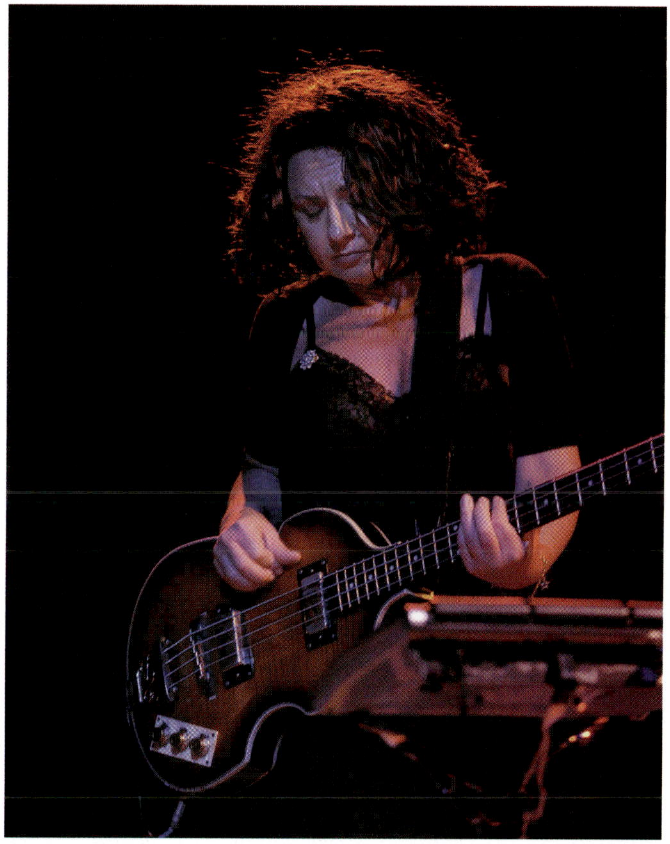

Figure 4.13 Spot metering allowed calculating exposure on the bass player's face.

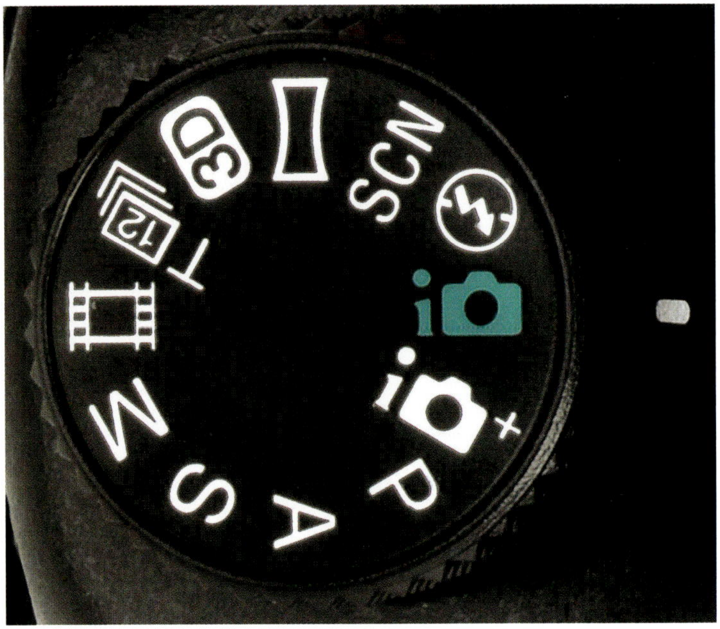

Figure 4.14
Choose exposure modes by spinning the mode dial.

action or allow motion blur, or how much noise you find acceptable in an image. Each of the Sony Alpha's semi-automatic and manual exposure methods emphasizes one aspect of image capture or another. This section introduces you to all four.

Aperture Priority

In Aperture priority mode, you specify the lens opening used, and the Alpha selects the shutter speed. Aperture priority is especially good when you want to use a particular lens opening to achieve a desired effect. Perhaps you'd like to use the smallest f/stop possible to maximize depth-of-field in a close-up picture. Or, you might want to use a large f/stop to throw everything except your main subject out of focus, as in Figure 4.15. Maybe you'd just like to "lock in" a particular f/stop because it's the sharpest available aperture with that lens. Or, you might prefer to use, say, f/2.8 on a lens with a maximum aperture of f/1.4, because you want the best compromise between speed and sharpness.

Aperture priority can even be used to specify a *range* of shutter speeds you want to use under varying lighting conditions, which seems almost contradictory. But think about it. You're shooting a soccer game outdoors with a telephoto lens and want a relatively high shutter speed, but you don't care if the speed changes a little should the sun duck behind a cloud. Set your Alpha to A, and adjust the aperture until a shutter speed of, say, 1/1,000th second is selected at your current ISO setting. (In bright sunlight at ISO 400, that aperture is likely to be around f/11.) Then, go ahead and shoot, knowing that your Alpha will maintain that f/11 aperture (for sufficient depth-of-field as the soccer

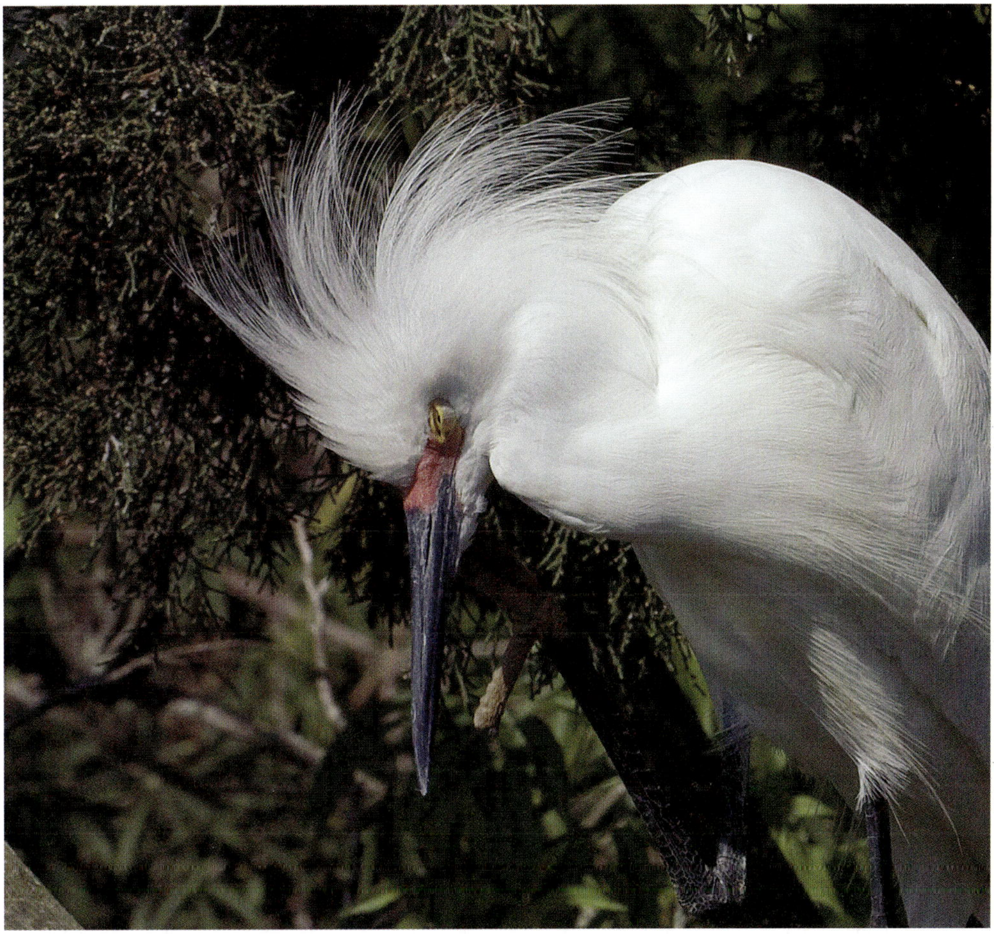

Figure 4.15
Use Aperture priority mode to "lock in" a large f/stop when you want to blur the background.

players move about the field), but will drop down to 1/800th or 1/500th second if necessary should the lighting change a little.

A blinking shutter speed indicator in the viewfinder and on the LCD indicates that the Alpha is unable to select an appropriate shutter speed at the selected aperture and that over- or underexposure will occur at the current ISO setting. That's the major pitfall of using Aperture priority: you might select an f/stop that is too small or too large to allow an optimal exposure with the available shutter speeds. For example, if you choose f/2.8 as your aperture and the illumination is quite bright (say, at the beach or in snow), even your camera's fastest shutter speed might not be able to cut down the amount of light reaching the sensor to provide the right exposure. Or, if you select f/8 in a dimly lit room, you might find yourself shooting with a very slow shutter speed that can cause blurring from subject movement or camera shake. Aperture priority is best used by those with a bit of experience in choosing settings. Many seasoned photographers leave their Alpha set on Aperture priority all the time.

Shutter Priority

Shutter priority is the inverse of Aperture priority: you choose the shutter speed you'd like to use, and the camera's metering system selects the appropriate f/stop. Perhaps you're shooting action photos and you want to use the absolute fastest shutter speed available with your camera; in other cases, you might want to use a slow shutter speed to add some blur to a sports photo that would be mundane if the action were completely frozen (see Figure 4.16). Shutter priority mode gives you some control over how much action-freezing capability your digital camera brings to bear in a particular situation.

You'll also encounter the same problem as with Aperture priority when you select a shutter speed that's too long or too short for correct exposure under some conditions. I've shot outdoor soccer games on sunny Fall evenings and used Shutter priority mode to lock in a 1/1,000th second shutter speed, only to find that my Alpha refused to produce the correct exposure when the sun dipped behind some trees and there was no longer enough light to shoot at that speed, even with the lens wide open.

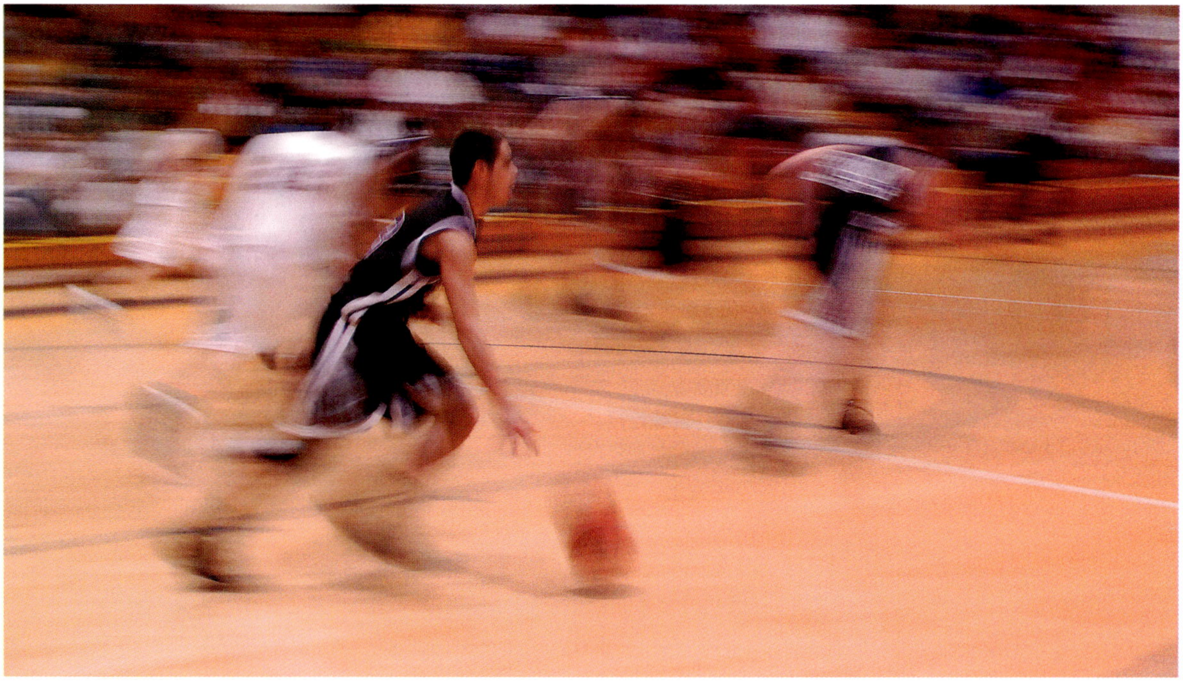

Figure 4.16 Lock the shutter at a slow speed to introduce blur into an action shot, as with this panned image of a basketball player.

As with Aperture priority mode, it's possible to choose an inappropriate shutter speed. If that's the case, the maximum aperture of your lens (to indicate underexposure) or the minimum aperture (to indicate overexposure) will blink in the viewfinder and on the LCD.

Program Auto Mode

Program auto mode, often just called Program mode (P), uses the Alpha's built-in smarts to select the correct f/stop and shutter speed using a database of picture information that tells it which combination of shutter speed and aperture will work best for a particular photo. The camera will not pop the flash up automatically in this mode, so if you want to use flash, you need to press the flash button to pop the unit up (or attach an external flash unit).

Making Exposure Value Changes

Sometimes you'll want more or less exposure than indicated by the Sony Alpha's metering system. Perhaps you want to underexpose to create a silhouette effect, or overexpose to produce a high-key look. It's easy to use the Alpha's exposure compensation system to override the exposure recommendations. It's available only in the Program auto, Aperture priority, Shutter priority, Sweep Panorama/3D Panorama, and Continuous Advance Priority AE shooting modes.

Press the exposure compensation button (located on the top surface, just southwest of the shutter release button), then press the right direction button or rotate the control dial to the right to make the image brighter (add exposure); use the left button or move the dial to the left to make the image darker (subtract exposure). The exposure scales in the viewfinder (if the viewfinder is in use) and on the LCD indicate the EV change you've made. Also, separate orange displays appear, showing the amount of the change, and the image lightens or darkens as you dial in more or less compensation. Any adjustment you've made remains for the exposures that follow, even after you've turned the camera off and back on, until you manually zero out the EV setting with the exposure compensation button and the control dial or direction buttons. (See Figure 4.17.)

Manual Exposure

Part of being an experienced photographer comes from knowing when to rely on your Sony Alpha's automation (including Auto, P mode, and Scene mode settings), when to go semi-automatic (with Shutter priority or Aperture priority), and when to set exposure manually (using M). Some photographers actually prefer to set their exposure manually, as the Alpha will be happy to provide an indication of when its metering system judges your manual settings provide the proper exposure, using the analog exposure scale at the bottom of the viewfinder and on the LCD.

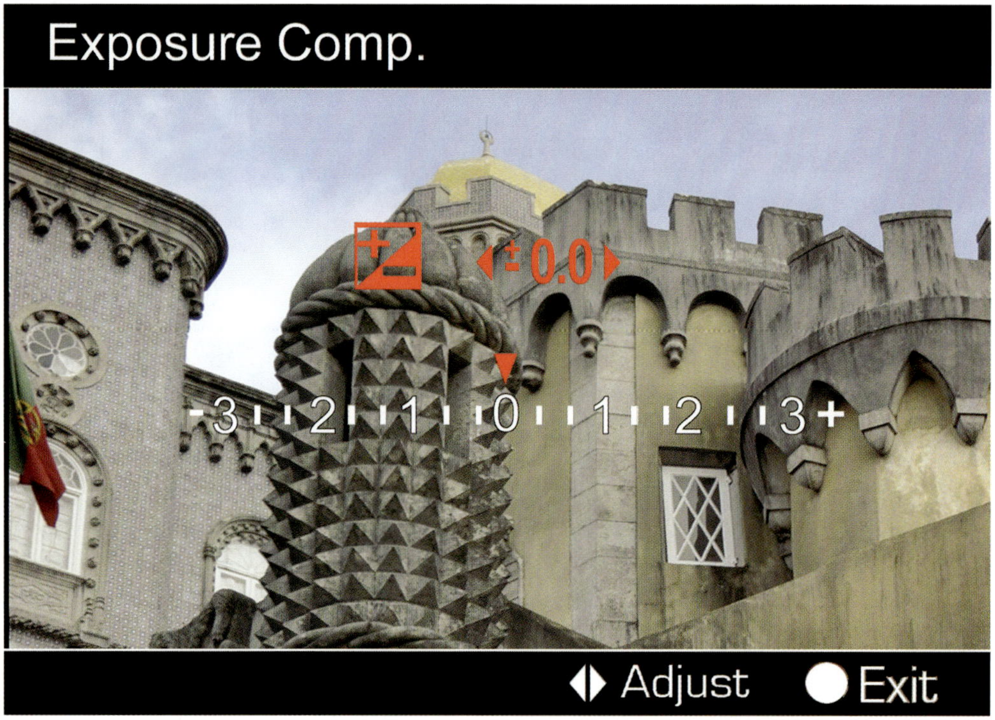

Figure 4.17
EV changes are displayed on the screen as you dial them in.

Manual exposure can come in handy in some situations. You might be taking a silhouette photo and find that none of the exposure modes or EV correction features gives you exactly the effect you want. For example, when I shot the windmill in Figure 4.18, there was no way any of my Sony Alpha's exposure modes would be able to interpret the scene the way I wanted to shoot it. So, I took a couple test exposures, and set the exposure manually to use the exact shutter speed and f/stop I needed. You might be working in a studio environment using multiple flash units. The additional flash units are triggered by slave devices (gadgets that set off the flash when they sense the light from another flash, or, perhaps from a radio or infrared remote control). Your camera's exposure meter doesn't compensate for the extra illumination, and can't interpret the flash exposure at all, so you need to set the aperture manually.

Although, depending on your proclivities, you might not need to set exposure manually very often, you should still make sure you understand how it works. Fortunately, the Sony Alpha makes setting exposure manually very easy. Just set the mode dial to M, turn the control dial to set the shutter speed, and hold down the AV/AEL (aperture value) button while rotating the control dial to adjust the aperture. Press the shutter release halfway, and the indicator above the exposure scale in the viewfinder (or LCD) reveals how far your chosen setting diverges from the metered exposure. If your settings go beyond 3 EV greater or less than the metered exposure, the indicator will change to a triangle pointing off the scale, or flashing for even greater differences. If you want to

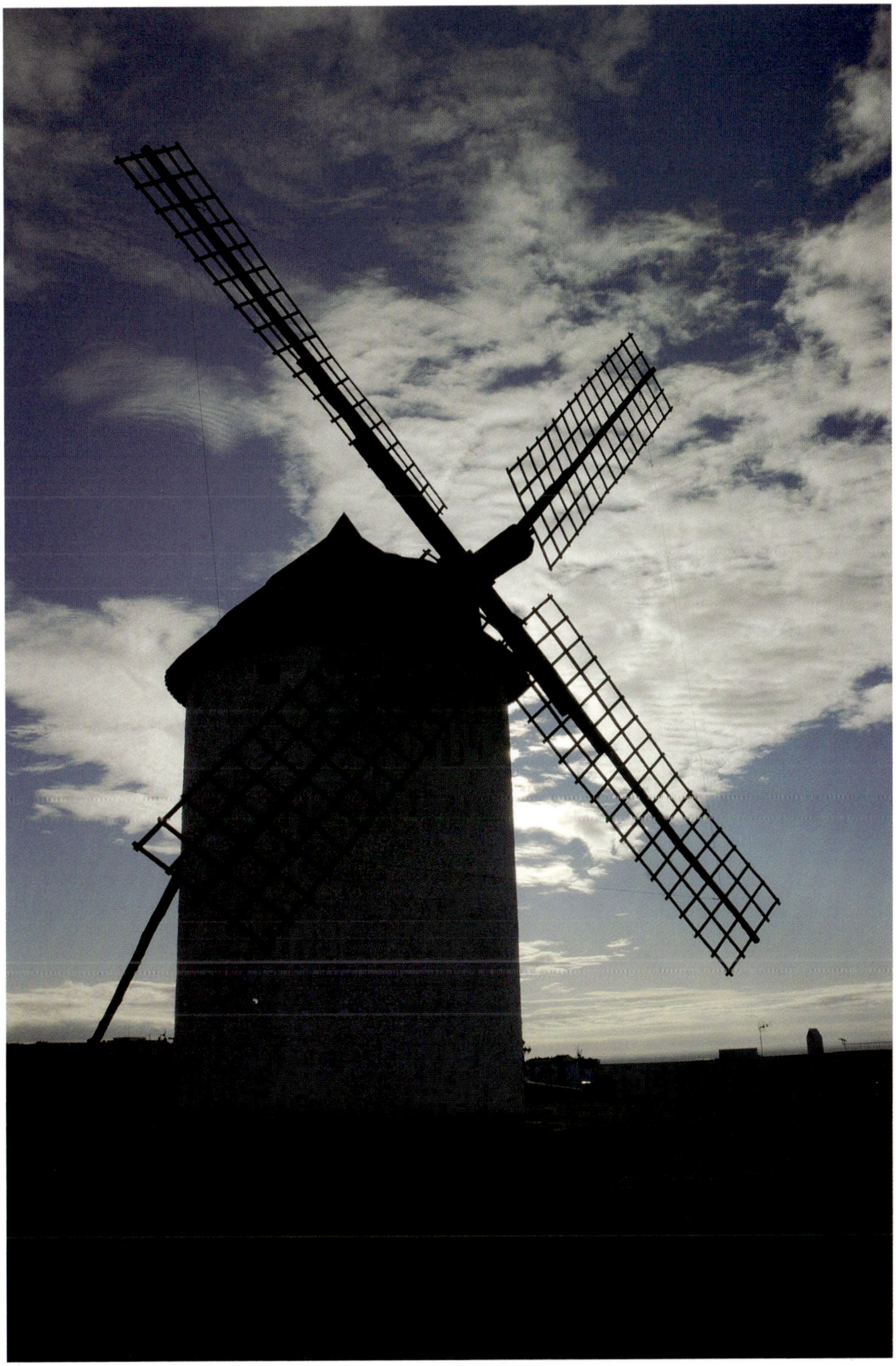

Figure 4.18
Manual mode allowed setting the exact exposure for this silhouette shot.

set the exposure according to the camera's metering, adjust the aperture or shutter speed, or both, until the indicator is directly above the zero mark in the center of the scale. If you are using the viewfinder and have the LCD display set to show recording information only (with no Live View), the recording information display on the LCD will show the letters M.M. to the left of the EV scale, indicating that the camera is in Manual Metered mode.

Adjusting Exposure with ISO Settings

Another way of adjusting exposures is by changing the ISO sensitivity setting. Sometimes photographers forget about this option, because the common practice is to set the ISO once for a particular shooting session (say, at ISO 100 for bright sunlight outdoors, or ISO 800 when shooting indoors) and then forget about ISO. The reason for that is that ISOs higher than ISO 100 are sometimes seen as "bad" or "necessary evils." However, changing the ISO is a valid way of adjusting exposure settings, particularly with the Sony Alpha, which produces good results at ISO settings that create grainy, unusable pictures with some other camera models.

Indeed, I find myself using ISO adjustment as a convenient alternate way of adding or subtracting EV (exposure values) when shooting in Manual mode, and as a quick way of choosing equivalent exposures when in automatic or semi-automatic modes. For example, I've selected a manual exposure with both f/stop and shutter speed suitable for my image using, say, ISO 400. I can change the exposure in full-stop increments by pressing the ISO button (down cursor button), and spinning the control dial one click at a time. The difference in image quality/noise at the base setting of ISO 400 is negligible if I dial in ISO 200 to reduce exposure a little, or change to ISO 800 to increase exposure. I keep my preferred f/stop and shutter speed, but still adjust the exposure.

Or, perhaps, I am using Shutter priority mode and the metered exposure at ISO 400 is 1/500th second at f/11. If I decide on the spur of the moment I'd rather use 1/500th second at f/8, I can press the ISO button, and spin the control dial to switch to ISO 200. Of course, it's a good idea to monitor your ISO changes, so you don't end up at ISO 6400 or higher accidentally, likely resulting in more graininess in your image than you would like. ISO settings can, of course, also be used to boost or reduce sensitivity in particular shooting situations, such as in deeply shaded or brightly illuminated areas.

The camera can adjust the ISO automatically as appropriate for various lighting conditions. In Auto and Scene modes, in which Auto ISO is the only available option, the camera normally sets the ISO between 200 and 800, but the setting varies depending on the particular mode. When you set the camera to Auto ISO in Program, Aperture priority, or Shutter priority modes, sensitivity will be set within the range of ISO 100-1600. If you want to use a higher ISO setting in those modes, you must select it manually. In Manual exposure mode, you have to select your ISO setting manually; the camera will not accept an Auto ISO setting, and it will initially set the ISO to 100 if it had been set to Auto ISO before you switched into Manual mode. You can then reset the ISO to any numerical value you want, but not to Auto ISO.

Over the past few years, there has been something of a competition among the manufacturers of digital cameras to achieve the highest ISO ratings—sort of a non-military version of the "missile gap" of years gone by. The highest announced ISO numbers keep rising annually, from 1600 to 3200, and recently to 6400 and beyond. Sony has not stood on the sidelines during this race—the SLT-A57 has a top ISO setting of an impressive 16000 under normal conditions, which can be set at any time. And it can even go one step higher under certain circumstances, as discussed below.

Multi Frame Noise Reduction

If you have a particular need for an even higher ISO level, the SLT-A57 can reach the stratospheric plateau of ISO 25600, but with some caveats. In order to reach that level, you have to use a special setting called Multi Frame Noise Reduction. This setting is actually akin to a separate shooting mode, but Sony has placed it on the ISO menu as an ISO setting. In order to set the sensitivity that high, you must be shooting JPEG images, not RAW, and you have to be shooting in one of the P, A, S, or M shooting modes. Also, you cannot use D-Range Optimizer settings or flash. Otherwise, though, all normal settings are available.

You get access to the Multi Frame Noise Reduction option through the ISO menu, using the ISO button (on top of the camera, just southeast of the shutter release) or the Function menu. Scroll to the top of the list of ISO values, and select the value that is above AUTO in the list. The icon for that option has the label ISO on a stack of frames, indicating a multi-shot mode. Scroll right and left with the cursor buttons to select a value from ISO 100 to ISO 25600 for Multi Frame Noise Reduction. When you press the shutter button, the camera will take multiple images and combine them in the camera to produce one composite image with reduced noise to compensate for the high ISO that was used. (You don't have to use a high ISO, but the whole point of this setting is to allow you to use a high value, so you might as well do so. If you want to use, say, ISO 100, there's really no need to use this special setting.) Also, it takes the camera some time to perform all this magic, so if you are in a hurry to take another shot, best to not use this setting. Keep in mind that the setting is "sticky" and should be turned off when no longer wanted.

Later in this chapter, I'll discuss the specialized shooting modes, including a Scene mode called Hand-held Twilight. In that mode, the camera also takes multiple shots at a higher ISO setting and combines them in the camera to produce one clear image with lower noise than a single high-ISO shot would have. Because that feature is one of the Scene modes, however, you are very limited in your ability to adjust the camera's other settings. If you want to shoot multiple high ISO shots with in-camera processing to reduce noise, and you want the flexibility of adjusting most of your other settings as well, remember to look for the Multi Frame Noise Reduction option on the ISO menu.

Bracketing

Bracketing is a method for shooting several consecutive exposures of the same scene automatically using different settings, as a way of improving the odds that one of the images will be exactly right for your needs. Before digital and electronic film cameras took over the universe, it was common to bracket exposures, shooting, say, a series of three photos at 1/125th second, but varying the f/stop from f/8 to f/11 to f/16. In practice, smaller than whole-stop increments were used for greater precision. Plus, it was just as common to keep the same aperture and vary the shutter speed, although in the days before electronic shutters, film cameras often had only whole increment shutter speeds available.

Today, cameras like the Alpha can bracket exposures much more precisely. When this feature is activated, the Alpha takes three consecutive photos: one at the metered "correct" exposure, one with less exposure, and one with more exposure, in your choice of 1/3 or 2/3 stop increments. Figure 4.19 shows an image with the metered exposure (center), flanked by exposures of 2/3 stop more (left), and 2/3 stop less (right).

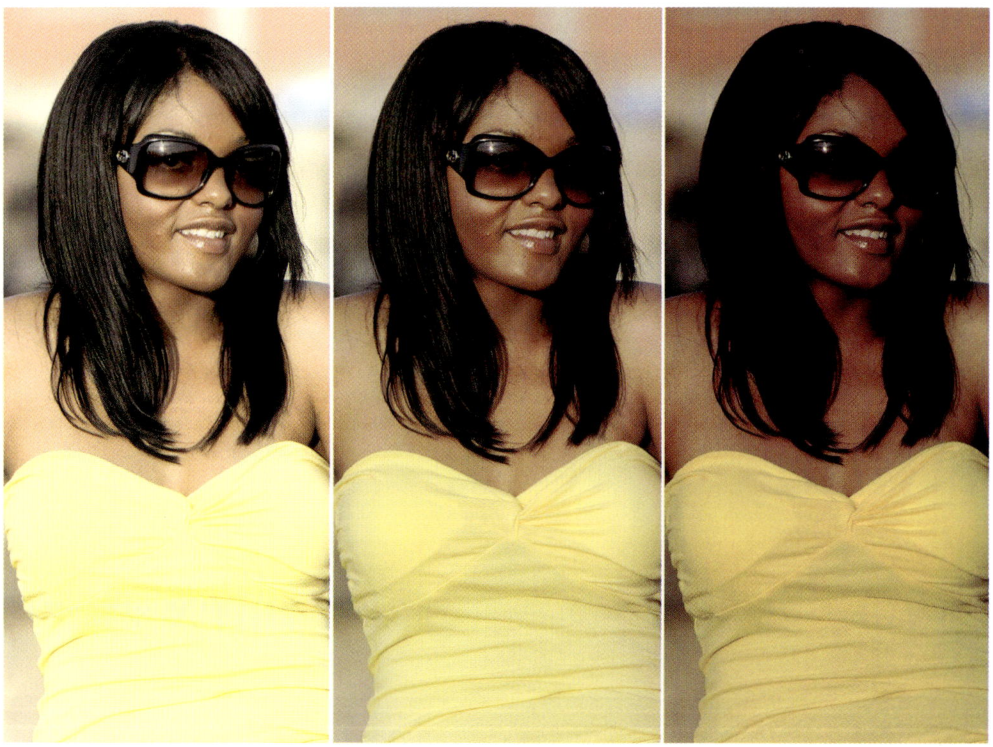

Figure 4.19
Metered exposure (center) accompanied by bracketed exposures of 2/3 more (left) and 2/3 stop less (right).

Bracketing cannot be performed when using the Auto, either Sweep or 3D Panorama modes, Continuous Advance Priority AE, or Scene exposure modes; you must be working with Program, Aperture priority, Shutter priority, or Manual exposure to use this feature. The Alpha SLT-A57 camera has two exposure bracketing modes: Continuous (BRK C), in which three exposures at the adjusted settings are taken when you hold down the shutter button; and Single (BRK S). When exposure bracketing is set, three small inverted triangles appear above the center of the exposure scale in the viewfinder or on the LCD (if activated in the Custom 2 menu), showing how many shots remain to be shot in the set. When you begin, you'll see all three triangles, then two, then one, and zero, as the bracket set is exposed.

In addition to bracketing exposures, the Alpha A57 has the ability to take a bracketed sequence of images with varied white balance values (BRK WB), in case you're uncertain what value is best for the lighting conditions you're faced with. With white balance bracketing, the camera takes three images with one shutter activation; you will hear only one shutter sound, but three different images are recorded electronically. You will not see the three triangles on the LCD or in the viewfinder, as you do with exposure bracketing.

Here are some points to keep in mind about bracketing:

- **Drive, he said.** You'll find the bracketing choices on the Drive menu. For exposure bracketing, press the drive button on the left of the controller pad (or press the Fn button then navigate to the Drive mode icon) and choose BRK C or BRK S. Then press the left/right directional buttons to switch between 0.3 and 0.7 bracket increments. Use 0.3 if you want to fine-tune exposure, or 0.7 if you'd like more dramatic changes between shots.

  To select white balance bracketing, select Drive mode as before, then scroll down to the BRKWB option, and use the left/right direction buttons to choose either the Hi or the Lo option. With Hi, the camera varies the white balance by 20 mired (a measure of color temperature); with Lo, the interval is 10 mired.

- **HDR isn't hard.** The 0.7 stop setting is the best choice for exposure bracketing if you plan to perform High Dynamic Range magic later on in Photoshop or another image editor. The Merge to HDR command in later versions of Photoshop allows you to combine three or more images with different exposures into one photo with an amazing amount of detail in both highlights and shadows. To get the best results, mount your camera on a tripod, shoot in RAW format, use BRK C, and set the exposure increment to 0.7 stops. Of course, with these Alpha models, you also have the option of using the Auto HDR feature, discussed in Chapter 6, which can achieve excellent results in the camera without the need to use any special HDR software.

- **Adjust the base value.** You can bracket your exposures based on something other than the base (metered) exposure value. Make an adjustment for extra or less exposure with the exposure compensation button and the control dial. Bracketing will be over, under, and equal to the *compensated* value.
- **What changes?** In Aperture priority mode, exposure bracketing will be achieved by changing the shutter speed; in Shutter priority mode, bracketing will be done using different f/stops; in Manual exposure mode, bracketing is applied using the shutter speed. (If you're shooting bracketed exposures for later merging using HDR, use Aperture priority so the focus/depth-of-field will remain the same for all shots.) In Program mode, the Alpha will vary both shutter speed and aperture, as appropriate for your scene.
- **Flash works, too.** With some cameras, exposure bracketing can't be used when working with the flash. That's not a problem with the Sony Alpha SLT-A57. When you have the built-in flash popped up or a compatible flash unit attached that communicates through the camera's hot shoe, the camera will take multiple shots, but you have to press the shutter for each shot and you won't see the three triangles in the viewfinder or on the LCD. The camera will vary the exposure by changing the intensity of the flash for the successive exposures.

  The camera will also perform white balance bracketing with flash. In that case, as is the case with or without flash, the camera takes three exposures with one press of the shutter, but only one shutter activation takes place; the three exposures are recorded electronically.

Dealing with Noise

Image noise is that random grainy look that some like to use as a visual effect, but which, most of the time, is objectionable because it robs your image of detail even as it adds that "interesting" texture. Noise is caused by two different phenomena: high ISO settings and long exposures.

High ISO noise commonly appears when you raise your camera's sensitivity setting above ISO 400. With Sony cameras, which generally have good ISO noise characteristics, noise may become visible at ISO 800, and is usually fairly noticeable at ISO 1600 and above. This kind of noise appears as a result of the amplification needed to increase the sensitivity of the sensor. While higher ISOs do pull details out of dark areas, they also amplify non-signal information randomly, creating noise. The Sony Alpha SLT-A57 automatically applies noise reduction that is strong enough to be visible as a reduction of sharpness in the image for any exposures taken when the ISO is set at ISO 1600 or higher. Figure 4.20 shows two pictures shot during different at-bats at the same baseball game. Both were exposed at ISO 1600, but with noise reduction applied in the version at top, and with no noise reduction at bottom. (I've exaggerated the differences

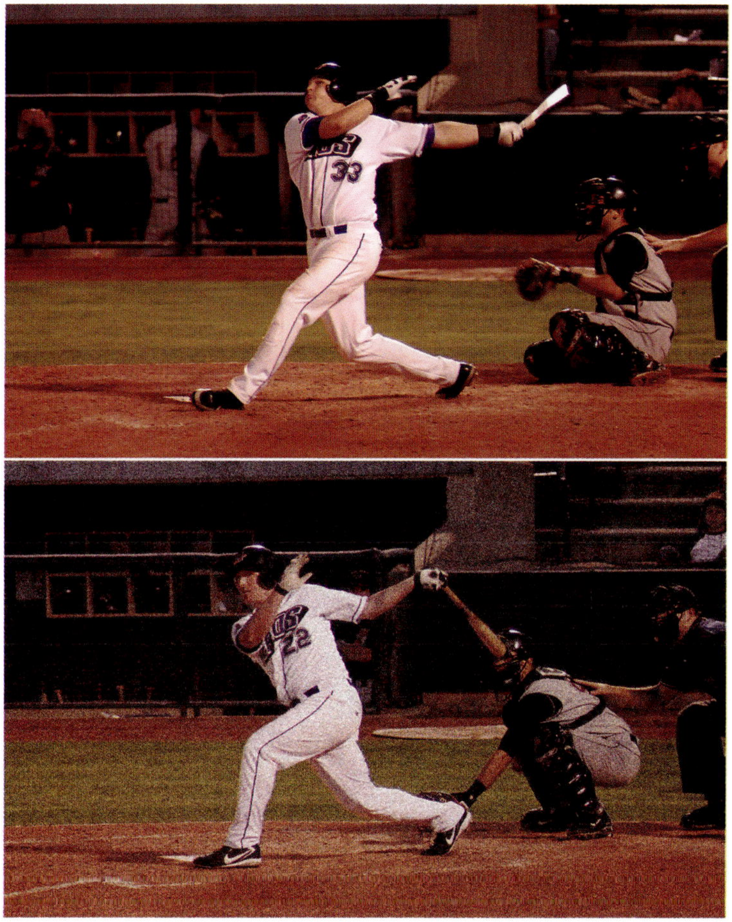

Figure 4.20 Noise reduction applied (top) produces a less grainy image than the version at bottom, which has no noise reduction.

between the two so the grainy/less grainy images are more evident on the printed page. The halftone screen applied to printed photos tends to mask these differences.)

A similar noisy phenomenon occurs during long time exposures, which allow more photons to reach the sensor, increasing your ability to capture a picture under low-light conditions. However, the longer exposures also increase the likelihood that some pixels will register random phantom photons, often because the longer an imager is "hot" the warmer it gets, and that heat can be mistaken for photons.

With a CCD like the one used in some other cameras in the Alpha series, the entire signal is conveyed off the chip and funneled through a single amplifier and analog-to-digital conversion circuit. Any noise introduced there is, at least, consistent. CMOS imagers like the ones in the Alpha SLT-A57, on the other hand, contain millions of individual amplifiers and A/D converters, all working in unison. Because these circuits don't necessarily all process in precisely the same way all the time, they can introduce something called fixed-pattern noise into the image data.

These Sony Alpha cameras perform long exposure noise reduction for any exposures longer than one full second. Fortunately, Sony's electronics geniuses have done an exceptional job minimizing noise. Even so, there are situations in which you might want to adjust your camera's automatic noise reduction features. For example, noise reduction can mask some detail as it removes random pixels from your image. Some of the image-making pixels are unavoidably vanquished at the same time. To change the settings for either type of noise reduction, navigate to the Still Recording 2 menu and turn Long Exposure NR on or off or set High ISO NR to either High, Normal, or Low. The menu settings for both types of NR are overridden by the camera any time you are using continuous shooting or continuous bracketing. In that case, High ISO NR is automatically set to Low and Long Exposure NR is disabled, even if it was previously turned on in the menu. No noise reduction settings are available for RAW images.

You can also apply noise reduction to a lesser extent using Photoshop, and when converting RAW files to some other format, using your favorite RAW converter, or using an industrial-strength product like Noise Ninja (www.picturecode.com) to wipe out noise after you've already taken the picture.

Finally, as discussed above, you can use the special Multi Frame Noise Reduction setting, which tackles the noise situation from a different angle, by taking several shots and combining them with in-camera processing to produce a single composite image with markedly reduced noise.

Fixing Exposures with Histograms

While you can often recover poorly exposed photos in your image editor, your best bet is to arrive at the correct exposure in the camera, minimizing the tweaks that you have to make in post-processing. However, you can't always judge exposure just by viewing the image on your Alpha's LCD after the shot is made. Nor can you get a 100-percent accurately exposed picture by using the Alpha's continuous Live View feature. Ambient light may make the LCD difficult to see, and the brightness level you've set can affect the appearance of the playback image.

Instead, you can use a histogram, which is a chart displayed on the Sony Alpha's LCD that shows the number of tones being captured at each brightness level. One variety of histogram can be displayed for images that are being viewed in Playback mode; that histogram screen shows overall brightness levels for the image as well as for the red, green, and blue channels combined. (See Figure 4.21.) In addition, any areas of the image on that screen that are either underexposed or overexposed will flash ("blinkies"), alerting you that you may need to change your settings to avoid blowing highlights or losing detail in the shadows. You can use the histogram information along with the flashing alerts to guide your settings for the next shots you take.

DISPLAYING HISTOGRAMS

To view histograms on your screen (either in Playback mode or in Still Recording mode using live view), press the DISP button while an image appears on the LCD. Keep pressing the button until the histogram screen appears. The Playback histogram screen shows overall brightness levels as well as levels for each of the red, green, and blue channels (Figure 4.21). On that histogram display, you'll also see a thumbnail at the top left of the screen with your image displayed. In Still Recording mode, the histogram display is less detailed; all that is shown is a basic chart representing the overall brightness levels of the image, superimposed over the live view image (Figure 4.22).

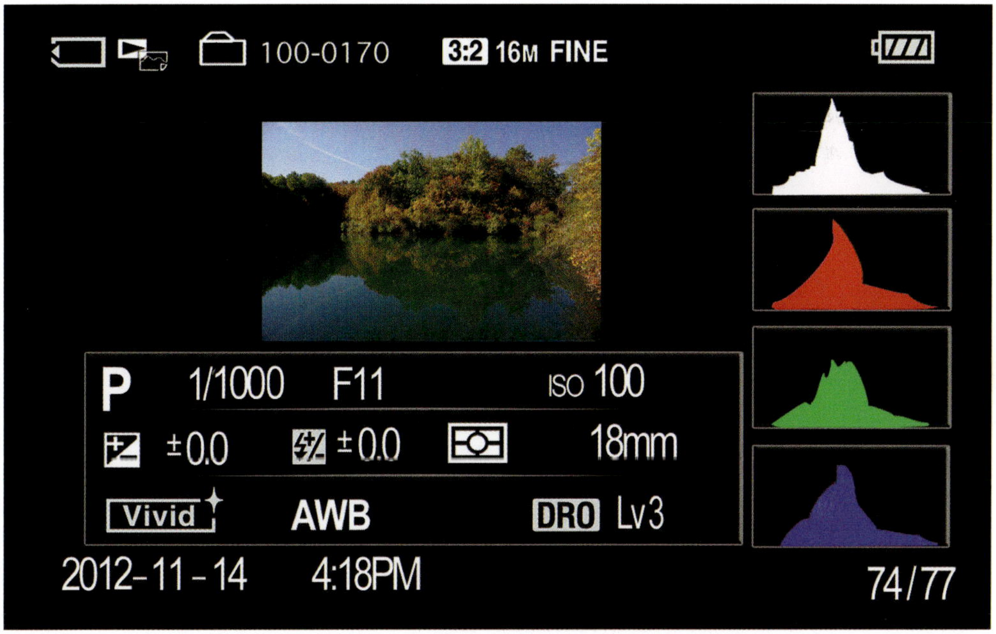

Figure 4.21 The Playback histogram screen shows the relationship of tones in an image, including brightness (top right), and red, green, and blue tones (middle and bottom right).

When the camera is in Shooting mode, one of the screens that is produced in the viewfinder or on the LCD by pressing the DISP button is the live view of the current scene, with a small, basic histogram that shows the brightness levels of the image, given the current values of aperture, shutter speed, exposure compensation, and other settings (see Figure 4.22). If you don't see the histogram, turn it on with the Histogram option in the Custom 2 DISP Button (Monitor) and/or DISP Button (Finder) menu options.

Both types of histograms are charts that include a representation of up to 256 vertical lines on a horizontal axis that show the number of pixels in the image at each brightness level, from 0 (black) on the left side to 255 (white) on the right. (The 3-inch LCD doesn't have enough pixels to show each and every one of the 256 lines, but, instead,

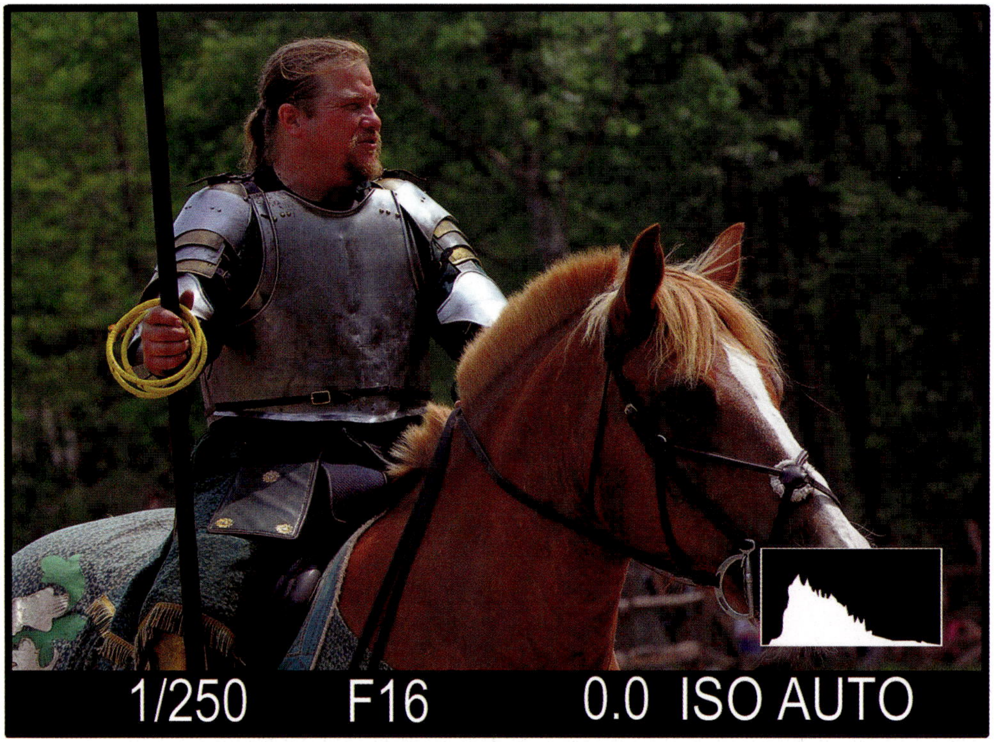

Figure 4.22
The Still Recording histogram screen provides a basic display showing the overall brightness levels of the image being viewed in Live View mode.

provides a representation of the shape of the curve formed.) The more pixels at a given level, the taller the bar at that position. If no bar appears at a particular position on the scale from left to right, there are no pixels at that particular brightness level.

A typical histogram produces a mountain-like shape, with most of the pixels bunched in the middle tones, with fewer pixels at the dark and light ends of the scale. Ideally, though, there will be at least some pixels at either extreme, so that your image has both a true black and a true white representing some details. Learn to spot histograms that represent over- and underexposure, and add or subtract exposure using an EV modification to compensate.

For example, Figure 4.23 shows the histogram for an image that is badly underexposed. You can guess from the shape of the histogram that many of the dark tones to the left of the graph have been clipped off. There's plenty of room on the right side for additional pixels to reside without having them become overexposed. Or, a histogram might look like Figure 4.24, which is overexposed. In either case, you can increase or decrease the exposure (either by changing the f/stop or shutter speed in Manual mode or by adding or subtracting an exposure compensation value in P, S, or A modes) to produce the corrected histogram shown in Figure 4.25. See "Making Exposure Value Changes," above, for information on dialing in exposure compensation.

Figure 4.23
This histogram shows an underexposed image.

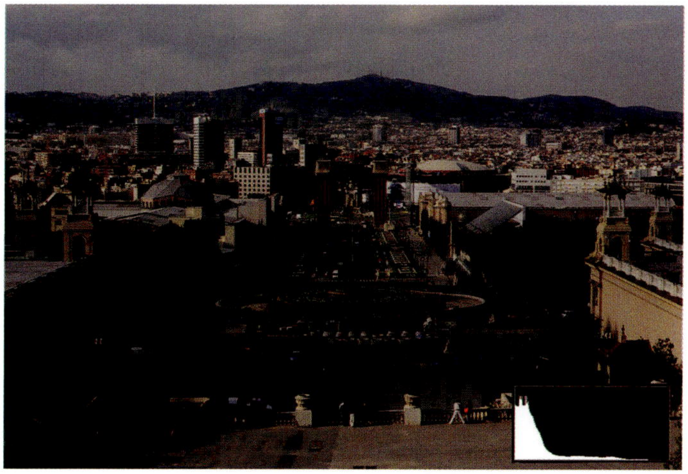

Figure 4.24
This histogram reveals that the image is overexposed.

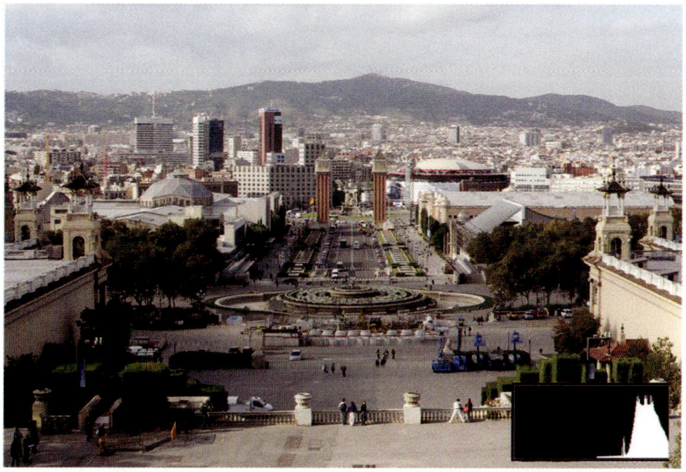

Figure 4.25
A histogram for a properly exposed image should look like this.

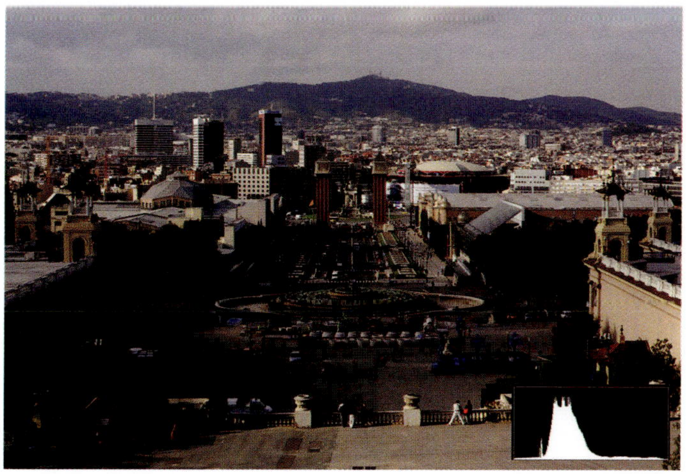

The histogram can also be used to aid in fixing the contrast of an image, although gauging incorrect contrast is more difficult. For example, if the histogram shows all the tones bunched up in one place in the image, the photo will be low in contrast. If the tones are spread out more or less evenly, the image is probably high in contrast. In either case, your best bet may be to switch to RAW (if you're not already using that format) so you can adjust contrast in post-processing.

Automatic and Specialized Shooting Modes

Although, as you've seen from the discussion so far, the Sony Alpha SLT-A57 is a sophisticated camera with a full range of adjustments available to the serious photographer, it also comes equipped with automatic or special-purpose shooting modes that can do a lot of the photographic heavy lifting for you, if you so choose. These include eight Scene modes, which automatically make all the basic settings needed for certain types of shooting situations, such as portraits, landscapes, close-ups, sports, night portraits, and sunsets. If you choose the standard Auto mode or the more sophisticated Auto+ mode, the camera will use its programmed intelligence to try to identify the type of scene and set itself accordingly. These "autopilot" modes are useful when you suddenly encounter a picture-taking opportunity and don't have time to decide exactly which semi-automatic or manual mode (P, A, S, or M) you want to use. Instead, you can spin the mode dial to the Auto or the Auto+ (Superior Auto) setting, or, if you have a little more time, to an appropriate Scene mode, and fire away, knowing that you have a fighting chance of getting a good or usable photo.

Finally, the Alpha SLT-A57 offers you three more specialized modes, for use in particular situations: Continuous Advance Priority AE, Sweep Panorama, and 3D Sweep Panorama. Those modes provide special capabilities, and give you a bit more leeway in adjusting the camera's settings than the Intelligent Auto and Scene modes do.

Auto and Scene Modes

The Auto and Scene modes are especially helpful when you're just learning to use your Alpha SLT, because they let you get used to composing and shooting, and obtaining excellent results, without having to struggle with unfamiliar controls to adjust things like shutter speed, aperture, ISO, and white balance. Once you've learned how to make those settings, you'll probably prefer one of the PASM modes that provide more control over shooting options. The Auto and Scene modes may give you few options for making your own settings, or none at all. For example, the AF mode, AF area, ISO, white balance, Dynamic-Range Optimizer, and metering mode are all set for you. In most modes, you can select the drive setting and the flash mode, though not all settings for those options are available. You cannot adjust exposure compensation or Creative Styles in any of these modes.

Here are some essential points to note about the Auto and Scene modes:

- **Intelligent Auto.** This is the setting to use when you hand your camera to a total stranger and ask him or her to take your picture posing in front of the Eiffel Tower. All the photographer has to do is press the shutter release button. Every other decision is made by the camera's electronics, and many settings, such as ISO, white balance, metering mode, and autofocus mode, are not available to you for adjustment. However, you still are able to set the drive mode to Continuous shooting, Self-timer, or Remote Commander (but not to Bracketing), and you can set the flash mode to Autoflash or Flash Off.
- **Flash Off.** This shooting mode, represented on the mode dial by the icon showing the flash-off symbol, is exactly the same as the Auto setting, except that the flash is forced off and cannot be turned on. This mode is the one to use when you're in a museum or other location where the use of flash is not permitted.
- **Superior Auto.** This mode can be considered a sort of "super-Auto" setting. The camera evaluates the image and makes settings that it calculates to be appropriate, including selecting one of the Scene modes, but it goes further, and will take multiple shots if appropriate for a particular situation, such as a scene involving motion or wide ranges of light and darkness. For example, the camera may turn on continuous shooting or Auto HDR. It will only take multiple shots, though, if the S. Auto Cont. Shooting option is set to Auto in the Custom 2 menu.
- **Portrait.** When you turn the mode dial to the SCN setting, you are presented with a menu of eight icons representing the various scene types. Portrait, the first of these settings, tends to use wider f/stops and faster shutter speeds, providing blurred backgrounds and images with no camera shake. The drive mode cannot be set to Continuous shooting, though you can use the Self-timer or the Remote Commander, and you can set the flash mode to Autoflash, Fill-flash, or Flash Off.
- **Sports action.** In this mode, the Alpha tries to use high shutter speeds to freeze action, switches to Continuous drive mode to let you take a quick sequence of pictures with one press of the shutter release, and uses Continuous Autofocus to continually refocus as your subject moves around in the frame. You can find more information on autofocus options in Chapter 5.
- **Macro.** This mode is similar to the Portrait setting, with wider f/stops to isolate your close-up subjects, and high shutter speeds to eliminate the camera shake that's accentuated at close focusing distances. However, if you have your camera mounted on a tripod or are using SteadyShot, you might want to use Aperture priority mode instead, so you can specify a smaller f/stop with additional depth-of-field.

- **Landscape.** The Alpha tries to use smaller f/stops for more depth-of-field, and boosts saturation slightly for richer colors. You can use the Self-timer or the Remote Commander; most other settings are not available in this mode.
- **Sunset.** Increases saturation to emphasize the red tones of a sunrise or sunset. You can use the Self-timer or Remote Commander, but most other adjustments are unavailable to you.
- **Night Scene.** For shooting portraits in low light without flash; the flash is forced off. Use a tripod if possible, because the camera is likely to use a slow shutter speed. Most settings are not available, other than the Self-timer and Remote Commander.
- **Hand-held Twilight.** This mode is designed to let you take hand-held shots in dark conditions without a tripod. The camera takes a burst of six exposures and then combines them in the camera into a single image. Depending on how dark the scene is, the camera may set the ISO to a high level so it can use a fast shutter speed to avoid blur from camera shake. Taking six images and combining them in the camera allows the camera to use the multiple sets of image information to reduce the noise that would otherwise be produced by the high ISO setting. Almost no settings are available for you to adjust when using this mode. (If you would like to have the benefits of this mode and still be able to adjust most of your settings, you can use the Multi Frame Noise Reduction feature instead. That feature is not considered a shooting mode, because you get access to it through the ISO setting. It is discussed earlier in this chapter, in the section on ISO.)
- **Night Portrait.** Pops up the flash and sets Flash mode to the Slow Sync setting, which combines flash with ambient light to produce an image that is mainly illuminated by the flash, but with the background exposed by the available light. This mode uses longer exposures, so a tripod, monopod, or SteadyShot (if available with your lens) is a must. You can use the Self-timer or the Remote Commander.

Continuous Advance Priority AE and Panorama Modes

Finally, the A57 has three other shooting modes with specific capabilities for particular situations.

Continuous Advance Priority AE

This next shooting mode is a very special creature—it transforms your very capable, high-quality interchangeable-lens camera into a Speed Monster. Really, it's difficult to over-emphasize what a big deal this mode is in the overall evolution of consumer-level cameras. Until now, you basically had two choices when it came to high-speed continuous shooting: You could pay, say, $5,000 for a professional-level dSLR like the Canon EOS-1D Mark IV (body only) and shoot at a steady rate of 10 frames per second, or you could purchase a lesser camera for about $1,000 and shoot at 5 or 6 frames per second, often with compromises in image quality and flexibility. With the SLT-A57, Sony has delivered a game-changing entry in the rapid-shooting sweepstakes. Because of this camera's innovative use of the fixed translucent mirror, it can take a series of full-resolution images at a blazing 12 frames per second with only minimal compromises in quality or flexibility.

It's worth taking a moment to explain the mechanics of this feature. As I've discussed earlier, the mirror in your SLT camera is translucent, so it constantly transmits light from the lens directly to the image sensor, and, at the same time, to the autofocus sensor. In a standard dSLR, there is a mirror that reflects all of the light to the autofocus sensor during focusing, but the mirror then has to flip up out of the way during the actual exposure, so the light can bypass the mirror and travel to the image sensor in the back of the camera. In the SLT camera, the time saved by not having to wait for the mirror to move back and forth allows the camera to snap off a rapid volley of shots, while going through the full process of phase-detection autofocusing at the same time. The result is a professional-level ability to fire rapidly at full resolution (including RAW if desired), with full autofocusing between shots.

The Continuous Advance Priority AE shooting mode is selected by turning the mode dial to the icon of multiple frames containing T and the number 12, representing the maximum rate of shooting in frames per second. Use the Fn button to choose Tele (at 12 fps) or Continuous (at 10 fps) using the control dial.

This shooting mode is specially designed to maximize the speed of continuous shooting. If you use the drive button to set continuous shooting in another shooting mode, the fastest firing you can achieve is about 6 frames per second. With the Continuous Advance Priority AE mode, in order to maximize speed of shooting, the camera imposes a few compromises. For one thing, you do not see the actual Live View image between shots; instead, the camera displays the image that was just captured, so you are actually viewing on the LCD the recorded image from a split second earlier. Also, if you set the autofocus mode to AF-C, for continuous autofocus, the aperture will be locked at its widest-open value and neither aperture nor ISO can be adjusted. However, if you set the camera to manual focus or to AF-S (single autofocus), you are then free to adjust both the aperture and the ISO sensitivity using the normal controls (control dial for the aperture and ISO button or Function menu for ISO). However, in this case the focus will be fixed at the focus for the first image, because continuous autofocus is not in effect.

Those few compromises are not serious impediments to using this shooting mode to great advantage, not just for capturing fast-breaking action, but also for catching fleeting expressions on the faces of playing children or even serious adults. This feature is a real breakthrough, so make good use of it if it suits your purposes.

Sweep Panorama

With other cameras, you can shoot a series of overlapping shots of a panoramic vista, and then "stitch" them together in special software programs to make a single, very wide, panoramic image. Some cameras can even do this for you with in-camera processing if you use a tripod and are quite careful about how much the images overlap. The Sony SLT models, though, are particularly adept at creating panoramas from hand-held shots. Here are a few tips to consider:

- **Choose a direction.** You can select four directions for your panorama: left, right, up, or down. You make this choice on the Still Shooting menu, using the Panorama Direction setting; you can't set it unless the camera is set to Sweep Panorama mode. The default setting, right, is probably the most natural for many people, but it's good to have options. Of course, up or down motion is what you will need for certain subjects, including skyscrapers and nearby mountains.
- **Change settings while in Panorama mode.** When you select this shooting mode, the camera presents you with a large arrow and urgent-sounding instructions to press the shutter button and move the camera in the direction of the arrow. Don't let the camera intimidate you with this demand; what it is neglecting to tell you is that you can take all the time you want, and that you are free to change certain settings before you shoot. Just press the MENU button, the Fn button, or some of the direct-setting buttons, and you will find several items that can be adjusted, including panorama image size, white balance, exposure compensation, and metering mode. Once you have those settings fine-tuned to your satisfaction, *then* go ahead and press the shutter button.
- **Smooth and steady does it.** Press the shutter button and immediately start moving the camera smoothly and steadily around in an arc, and keep going until the shutter stops clicking. If you went too fast or too slow, you'll get an error message and the camera will prompt you to start over.
- **Beware of moving objects.** The Sweep Panorama shooting mode is best used for stationary subjects, such as mountain ranges, city skylines, or expansive gardens. Figure 4.26 is an example of a panorama taken in a nature preserve. There's nothing to stop you from shooting a scene that contains moving cars, people, or other objects, but be aware of problems that can arise in that situation. Because you're taking multiple overlapping shots that are then stitched into a single image, the camera may capture the same car or person twice (or more) in slightly different positions, which can result in a truncated or otherwise distorted picture of that particular subject. You may want to experiment with that type of image for creative purposes, but if you want an accurate depiction of the scene, be sure to scrutinize the finished product to see that it doesn't contain any unwelcome surprises.

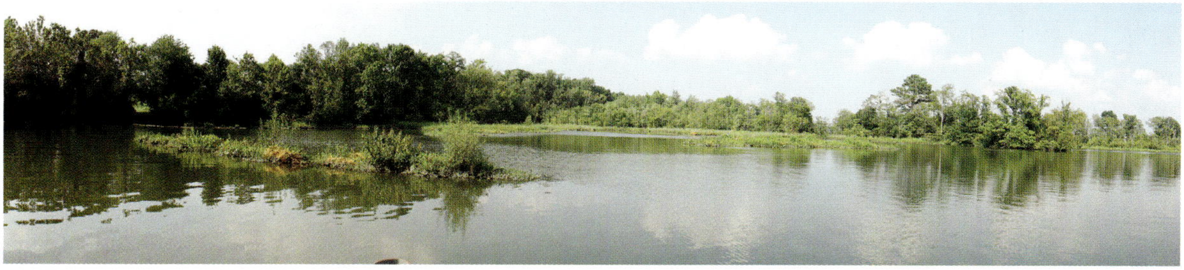

Figure 4.26 This image was taken with the in-camera Sony Sweep Panorama mode using the Standard image size for panoramas.

3D Sweep Panorama

The 3D Sweep Panorama mode, which appears as a suboption of the Sweep Panorama mode, was designed to create panoramas that will appear in 3D on certain models of Sony Bravia 3D HDTV sets, such as the Bravia NX810. However, if you're the experimenting type, you can enjoy the benefits of 3D images without shelling out $2,800 or so for a new TV. The 3D panoramas taken by the SLT-A57 create image files with an extension of MPO. You can download software that will convert these files to JPEG images in the "anaglyph" 3D format, which will look blurry to the naked eye, but will appear in 3D if you view them through standard-issue 3D glasses (with a red filter over the left eye and a blue one over the right). Here are some pointers for dealing with 3D images taken with these Sony cameras:

- **Choose right or left.** You can select only two directions for a 3D panorama: left or right. Make this setting on the Still Shooting 1 menu while the camera is set to 3D Panorama shooting mode.
- **Create a non-panoramic panorama.** In 3D Panorama mode, the camera offers you one additional option for image size, in addition to the Standard and Wide options that are available with the normal Sweep Panorama mode. You can select 16:9, which, of course, is the same aspect ratio as that of normal still images taken using the 16:9 settings. In other words, a non-panoramic image! So, if you just want to take a 3D image that is not a super-wide panorama, you can do so by selecting the 16:9 Image Size setting from the Recording 1 menu while in 3D Panorama shooting mode. The camera will still direct you to pan around, but the image will be considerably less wide than the standard panorama, and you will not need to scroll it on the camera's screen to view the whole image, as you do with standard panoramas.
- **View 3D with no 3D TV.** I appreciate the benefits of 3D images and enjoy viewing them, but I would prefer to view them without shelling out $2,800 or so to acquire a 3D HDTV. You can accomplish this fairly easily if you're willing to

take a few steps to process the 3D MPO files that the SLT-A57 generates. Go to http://stereo.jpn.org/eng/stphmkr and download a free program for Windows called Stereo Photo Maker. From the program's File menu, select Open Stereo Image. Check the box for file type Anaglyph Color, and open your MPO file. You should now see two images on the screen. Go to the Stereo menu and select Color Anaglyph—Dubois (red/cyan). Now you should see a single image that is blurry, like any other 3D image that needs to be viewed through red and blue lenses. You can then save that image by going to the File menu. Choose Save Stereo Image and save the image using file type JPEG. (See Figure 4.27.) Now go find a pair of 3D glasses that came with a DVD or comic book, open your saved file, and voilà! You're viewing your image in 3D and just saved $2,800! (Note to Mac users: There is a downloadable program called Anaglyph Workshop that might accomplish the same result, but I have not tested it. It is available at www.tabberer.com/sandyknoll/more/3dmaker/anaglyph-software.html.)

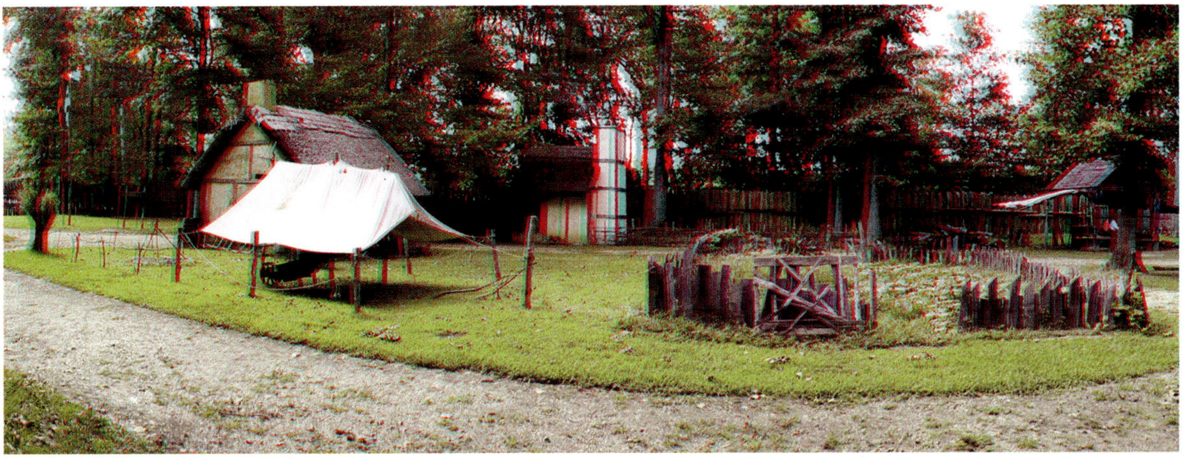

Figure 4.27 This JPEG version of a 3D image taken using the Sony 3D Sweep Panorama mode will look blurry until you find a pair of red/blue 3D glasses to view it with!

5

Mastering Autofocus Options

One of the most useful and powerful features of modern digital cameras is their ability to lock in sharp focus faster than the blink of an eye. Sometimes. Although autofocus has been with us for more than 20 years, it continues to be problematic. While vendors like Sony are giving us faster and more precise autofocus systems—like the full-time autofocus possible with the SLT series' translucent mirror technology—it's common for the sheer number of options to confuse even the most advanced photographers.

One key problem is that the camera doesn't really know, for certain, what subject you want to be in sharp focus. It may select an object and lock in focus with lightning speed—even though the subject is not the one that's the center of interest of your photograph. Or, the camera may lock focus too soon, or too late. This chapter will help you choose the options available with your Sony SLT-A57 that will help the camera understand what you want to focus on, when, and maybe even why.

Getting into Focus

Learning to use the Sony SLT's modern autofocus system is easy, but you do need to fully understand how the system works to get the most benefit from it. Once you're comfortable with autofocus, you'll know when it's appropriate to use the manual focus option, too. The important thing to remember is that focus isn't absolute. For example, some things that look in sharp focus at a given viewing size and distance might not be in focus at a larger size and/or closer distance. In addition, the goal of optimum focus isn't always to make things look sharp. Not all of an image will be or should be sharp. Controlling exactly what is sharp and what is not is part of your creative palette. Use of depth-of-field characteristics to throw part of an image out of focus while other parts are sharply focused is one of the most valuable tools available to a photographer. But selective focus works only when the desired areas of an image are in focus properly. For the digital SLR (or SLT) photographer, correct focus can be one of the trickiest parts of the technical and creative process.

To make your job easier, the Sony Alpha SLT-A57 has a precision 15-point autofocus system that uses a separate sensor in the viewing system to measure the contrast of the image. When the contrast is highest at the active autofocus point(s), that part of the image is in sharp focus. The active focus points are actually 15 sets of lines of pixels represented by boxes visible in the display (see Figure 5.1), and can be selected automatically by the camera, or manually by you, the photographer. Three of these autofocus points are of the advanced "cross" type (that is, they measure in both horizontal and vertical directions) that work with all Sony lenses having a maximum aperture of f/5.6 or larger, but have enhanced sensitivity when used with faster lenses.

The camera also looks for these contrast differences among pixels to determine relative sharpness. There are two ways that sharp focus is determined: Phase Detection and Contrast Detection. The primary method used by the Sony Alpha SLT is Phase Detection, so I'll discuss it first; then I'll explain how Contrast Detection differs and when it is used with this camera.

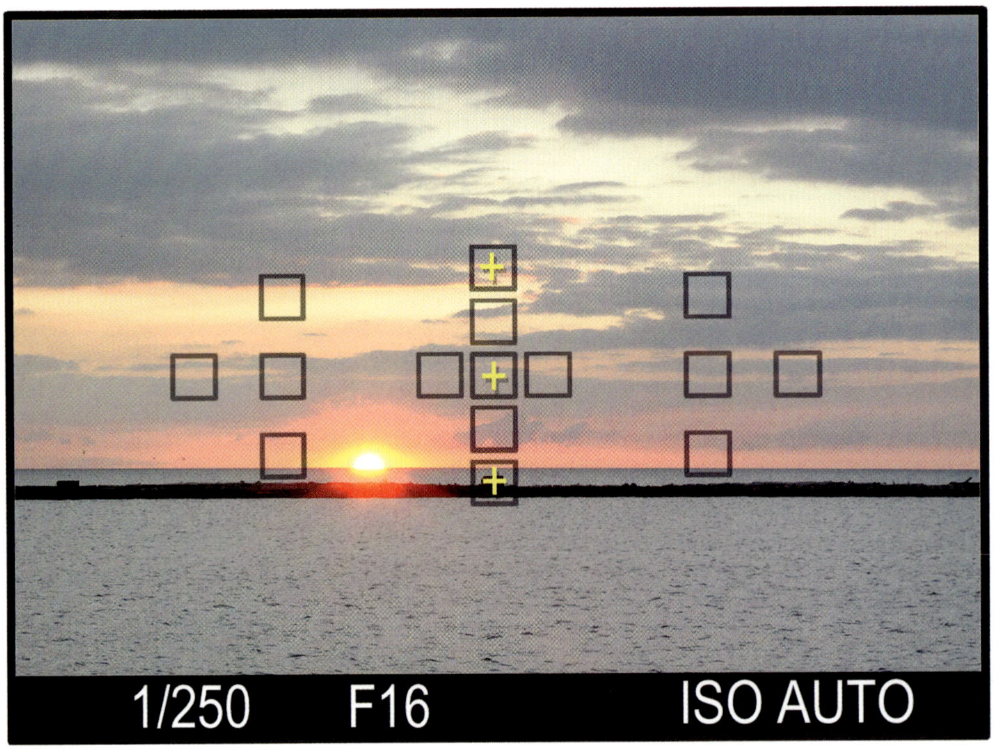

Figure 5.1
Any of the 15 autofocus points can be selected by the photographer manually or by the camera automatically. The three blocks marked with yellow plus signs represent the more advanced "cross" type focus sensors.

Phase Detection

In this mode, the autofocus sampling area is divided into two halves by a lens in the focus sensor. The two halves are compared, much like (actually, exactly like) a two-window rangefinder used in surveying, weaponry, and non-SLR cameras like the venerable Leica M film models. The contrast between the two images changes as focus is moved in or out, until sharp focus is achieved when the images are "in phase," or lined up.

You can visualize how Phase Detection autofocus works if you look at Figures 5.2 and 5.3. (However, your camera's actual autofocus sensors don't look *anything* like this; I'm providing a greatly simplified view just for illustration.) In Figure 5.2, a typical horizontally oriented focus sensor is looking at a series of parallel vertical lines in a weathered piece of wood. The lines are broken into two halves by the sensor's rangefinder prism, and you can see that they don't line up exactly; the image is slightly out of focus.

Fortunately, the rangefinder approach of Phase Detection tells the Alpha exactly how badly out of focus the image is, and in which direction (focus is too near, or too far) thanks to the amount and direction of the displacement of the split image. The camera can quickly and precisely snap the image into sharp focus and line up the vertical lines, as shown in Figure 5.3. Of course, this scenario—vertical lines being interpreted by a horizontally oriented sensor—is ideal. When the same sensor is asked to measure focus

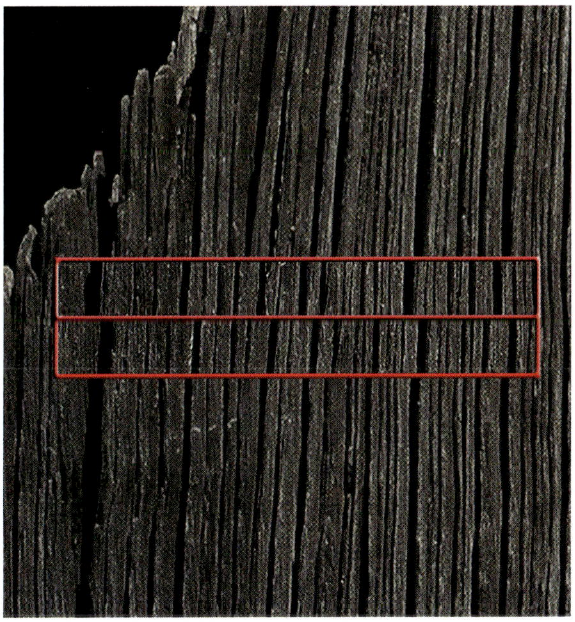

Figure 5.2 When an image is out of focus, the split lines don't align precisely.

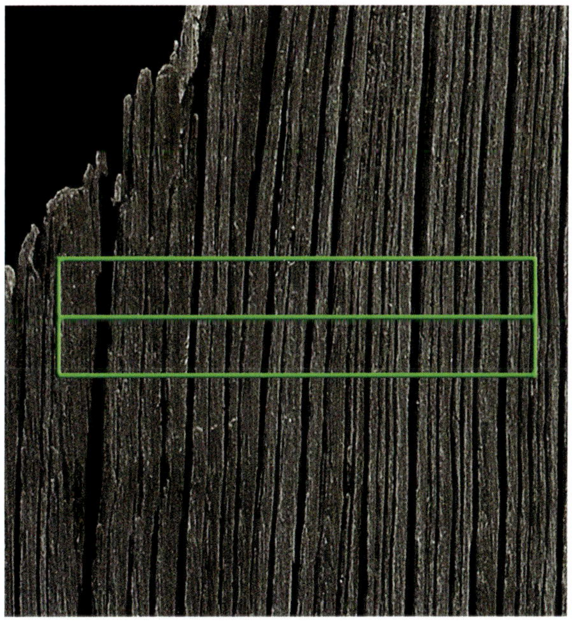

Figure 5.3 Using Phase Detection, the Alpha is able to align the features of the image and achieve sharp focus quickly.

for, say, horizontal lines that don't split up quite so conveniently, or, in the worst case, subjects such as the sky (which may have neither vertical or horizontal lines), focus can slow down drastically, or even become impossible.

Phase Detection is the focusing mode used at all times by the Alpha SLT for autofocus, no matter whether you are viewing the Live View in the electronic viewfinder or on the LCD. As with any rangefinder-like function, accuracy is better when the "base length" between the two images is larger. (Think back to your high school trigonometry; you could calculate a distance more accurately when the separation between the two points where the angles were measured was greater.) For that reason, Phase Detection autofocus is more accurate with larger (wider) lens openings—especially those with maximum f/stops of f/2.8 or better—than with smaller lens openings, and may not work at all when the f/stop is smaller than f/5.6. As I noted, the Alpha is able to perform these comparisons very quickly.

Improved Cross-Type Focus Points

Besides the camera's ability to use Phase Detection autofocus at all times, another important feature of the Alpha SLT-A57 is the use of cross-type focus points at three central positions. Why is this important? It helps to take a closer look at the Phase Detection system when presented with a non-ideal subject.

Figure 5.4 shows the same weathered wood shown earlier, except in this case we've chosen to rotate the camera 90 degrees (say, because we want a vertically oriented composition). In the illustration, the image within the focus sensor's area is split in two and displaced slightly side-to-side, but the amount and direction of the misalignment is far from obvious. A horizontally oriented focus sensor will be forced to look for less obvious vertical lines to match up. Our best-case subject has been transformed into a *worst*-case subject for a horizontal focus sensor.

The value of the cross-type focus sensors, which can interpret contrast in both horizontal and vertical directions, can be seen in Figure 5.5. The horizontal lines are still giving the horizontal portion of the cross sensor fits, but the vertical bar can easily split and align the subject to achieve optimum focus. Cross-type sensors can handle horizontal and vertical lines with equal aplomb and, if you think about it, lines at any diagonal angle as well. In lower light levels, with subjects that were moving, or with subjects that have no pattern and less contrast to begin with, the cross-type sensor not only works faster but can focus subjects that a horizontal- or vertical-only sensor can't handle at all.

So, you can see that having a central cross-type focus sensor that is extra sensitive with faster lenses is a definite advantage. Having three of these sensors, when many digital cameras have only one, if any, is a great leap forward for the SLT.

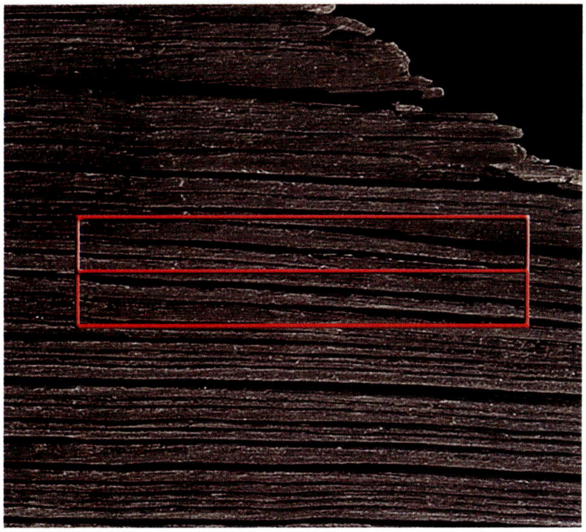

Figure 5.4 A horizontal focus sensor doesn't handle horizontal lines very well.

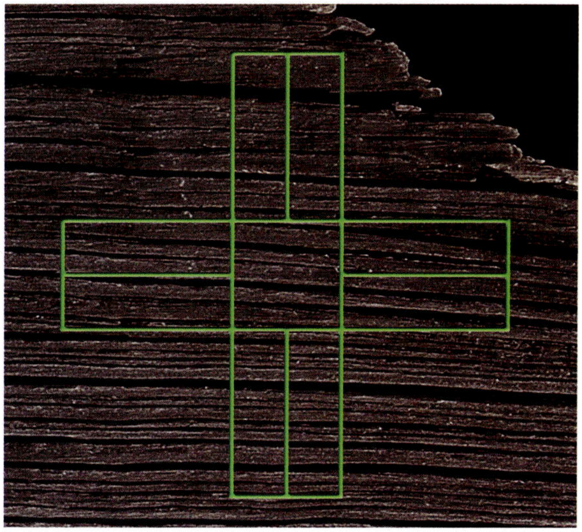

Figure 5.5 Cross-type sensors can evaluate contrast in both horizontal and vertical directions, as well as diagonally.

Contrast Detection

This is a slower mode, suitable for static subjects, which comes into play with the Alpha SLT-A57 *only* when the camera is set to manual focus mode. When autofocusing, the Alpha A57 always uses the Phase Detection system described above, which is able to autofocus continuously because of the camera's translucent mirror. This is unusual, because most cameras that have Live View must use Contrast Detection to focus when Live View is active. Some have a mode that interrupts Live View to flip up the mirror, focus using Phase Detection, and then flip the mirror back down to resume Live View. That's not necessary with the SLT-A57.

Contrast Detection still can come into play with these cameras. It is the system your eye uses to focus on the image on the LCD or in the electronic viewfinder when you're focusing manually. It's a bit easier to understand than Phase Detection, and is illustrated by Figure 5.6. At top in the figure, the transitions between the edges found in the image are soft and blurred because of the low contrast between them. Although the illustration uses the same vertical lines used with the Phase Detection example, the orientation of the features doesn't matter. The focus system looks only for contrast between edges, and those edges can run in any direction.

At the bottom of Figure 5.6, the image has been brought into sharp focus, and the edges have much more contrast; the transitions are sharp and clear. Although this example is a bit exaggerated so you can see the results on the printed page, it's easy to understand that when maximum contrast in a subject is achieved, it can be deemed to be in sharp focus. Although achieving focus with Contrast Detection is generally quite

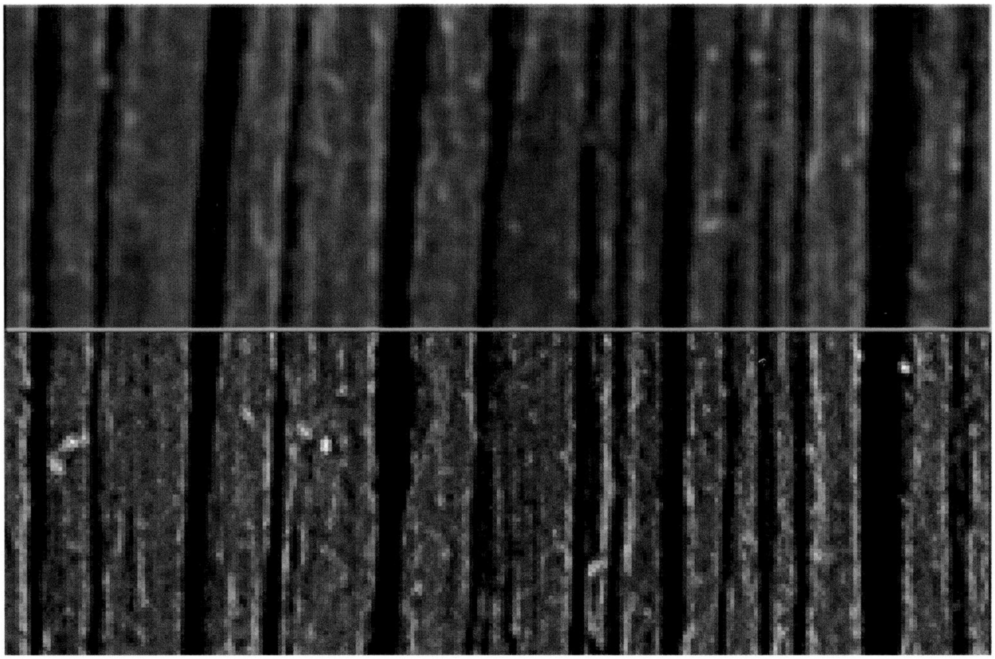

Figure 5.6
Manual focus in Contrast Detection mode allows you to evaluate the increase in contrast in the edges of subjects, starting with a blurry image (top) and producing a sharp, contrasty image (bottom).

a bit slower, because you're doing it manually, there are several advantages to this method:

- **Works with more image types.** Contrast Detection doesn't require subject matter rotated 90 degrees from the sensor's orientation for you to use it to focus manually. Any subject that has edges will work.
- **Focus on any point.** While Phase Detection focus can be achieved *only* at the points that fall under one of the 15 autofocus sensors, with Contrast Detection, any portion of the image can be used as you view the image. Focus is achieved with the actual sensor image, so focus point selection is simply a matter of choosing which part of the sensor image to use.
- **Potentially more accurate.** Phase Detection can fall prey to the vagaries of uncooperative subject matter: if suitable lines aren't available, the system may have to hunt for focus or achieve less than optimal focus. Contrast Detection is more clear-cut. Your eye can clearly see when the highest contrast has been achieved.

The Alpha's autofocus mechanism, like all such Phase Detection systems found in digital cameras, evaluates the degree of focus, but, unlike the human eye, it is able to remember the progression perfectly, so that autofocus can lock in much more quickly and, with an image that has sufficient contrast, more precisely. Many of the techniques for using autofocus effectively involve telling the Sony Alpha exactly what it should be focusing on, by choosing a focus zone or by allowing the camera to choose a focus zone for you. I'll address that topic shortly.

As the camera collects focus information from the sensors, it then evaluates it to determine whether the desired sharp focus has been achieved. The calculations may include whether the subject is moving, and whether the camera needs to "predict" where the subject will be when the shutter release button is fully depressed and the picture is taken. The speed with which the camera is able to evaluate focus and then move the lens elements into the proper position to achieve the sharpest focus determines how fast the autofocus mechanism is.

Focus Modes

The Sony Alpha has three AF modes: Single-shot AF (also known as single autofocus, or AF-S), Continuous AF (or AF-C), and Automatic AF (AF-A), which switches between the other two as appropriate. I'll explain all of these in more detail later in this section.

MANUAL FOCUS

With manual focus activated by sliding the switch on the side of the lens (or on the camera body if there's no switch on the lens), your Sony Alpha lets you set the focus yourself. There are some advantages and disadvantages to this approach. While your batteries will last slightly longer in manual focus mode, it will take you longer to focus the camera for each photo, a process that can be tricky. Modern digital cameras, even dSLRs, depend so much on autofocus that the viewfinders of models that have less than full-frame-sized sensors are no longer designed for optimum manual focus. Their viewfinders offer an image that's usually just 65 to 75 percent of life size. The electronic viewfinder in the Alpha SLT-A57 provides 1.09X magnification in Max mode (see Chapter 3's section on Viewfinder Magnification for more on that). That means that with a 50mm focal length, the image appears to be 109 percent of life size, and is a joy to focus on. I'll address some manual focus issues later in this chapter.

Focus Pocus

Prior to the introduction of dSLR autofocus capabilities in the 1980s, back in the day of film cameras, focusing was always done manually. Honest. Even though viewfinders were bigger and brighter than they are today, special focusing screens, magnifiers, and other gadgets were often used to help the photographer achieve correct focus. Imagine what it must have been like to focus manually under demanding, fast-moving conditions such as sports photography. Minolta, which pioneered the technology now used in Sony Alpha cameras and lenses, led the way in developing autofocus systems.

Manual focusing is problematic because our eyes and brains have poor memory for correct focus, which is why your eye doctor must shift back and forth between sets of lenses and ask "Does that look sharper—or was it sharper before?" in determining your correct prescription. Similarly, manual focusing involves jogging the focus ring back and forth as you go from almost in focus, to sharp focus, to almost focused again. The little clockwise and counterclockwise arcs decrease in size until you've zeroed in on the point of correct focus. As I mentioned earlier in this chapter, what you're looking for is the image with the most contrast between the edges of elements in the image.

The Sony Alpha SLT-A57's autofocus mechanism, like all such systems found in SLR cameras, also evaluates these increases and decreases in sharpness, but it is able to remember the progression perfectly, so that autofocus can lock in much more quickly and, with an image that has sufficient contrast, more precisely. Unfortunately, while the Sony Alpha's focus system finds it easy to measure degrees of apparent focus at each of the focus points in the viewfinder, it doesn't really know with any certainty *which object* should be in sharpest focus. Is it the closest object? The subject in the center? Something lurking *behind* the closest subject? A person standing over at the side of the picture? Using autofocus effectively involves telling the Sony Alpha exactly what it should be focusing on.

Adding Circles of Confusion

But there are other factors in play, as well. You know that increased depth-of-field brings more of your subject into focus. But more depth-of-field also makes autofocusing (or manual focusing) more difficult because the contrast is lower between objects at different distances. So, autofocus with a 200mm lens (or zoom setting) may be easier than at a 28mm focal length (or zoom setting) because the longer lens has less apparent depth-of-field. By the same token, a lens with a maximum aperture of f/1.8 will be easier to autofocus (or manually focus) than one of the same focal length with an f/4 maximum aperture, because the f/4 lens has more depth-of-field *and* a dimmer view. That's why lenses with a maximum aperture smaller than f/5.6 can give your Sony Alpha's autofocus system fits, because the largest f/stop is the lens opening the camera uses to focus.

To make things even more complicated, many subjects aren't polite enough to remain still. They move around in the frame, so that even if the Alpha is sharply focused on your main subject, it may change position and require refocusing. An intervening subject may pop into the frame and pass between you and the subject you meant to photograph. You (or the Alpha SLT) have to decide whether to lock focus on this new subject, or remain focused on the original subject. Finally, there are some kinds of subjects that are difficult to bring into sharp focus because they lack enough contrast to allow the Sony Alpha's AF system (or our eyes) to lock in. Blank walls, a clear blue sky, or other subject matter may make focusing difficult.

If you find all these focus factors confusing, you're on the right track. Focus is, in fact, measured using something called a *circle of confusion*. An ideal image consists of zillions of tiny little points, which, like all points, theoretically have no height or width.

There is perfect contrast between the point and its surroundings. You can think of each point as a pinpoint of light in a darkened room. When a given point is out of focus, its edges decrease in contrast and it changes from a perfect point to a tiny disc with blurry edges (remember, blur is the lack of contrast between boundaries in an image). (See Figure 5.7.)

If this blurry disc—the circle of confusion—is small enough, our eye still perceives it as a point. It's only when the disc grows large enough that we can see it as a blur rather than a sharp point that a given point is viewed as out of focus. You can see, then, that enlarging an image, either by displaying it larger on your computer monitor or by making a large print, also enlarges the size of each circle of confusion. Moving closer to the image does the same thing. So, parts of an image that may look perfectly sharp in a 5 × 7-inch print viewed at arm's length, might appear blurry when blown up to 11 × 14 and examined at the same distance. Take a few steps back, however, and it may look sharp again.

To a lesser extent, the viewer also affects the apparent size of these circles of confusion. Some people see details better at a given distance and may perceive smaller circles of confusion than someone standing next to them. For the most part, however, such differences are small. Truly blurry images will look blurry to just about everyone under the same conditions.

Technically, there is just one plane within your picture area, parallel to the back of the camera (or sensor, in the case of a digital camera) that is in sharp focus. That's the plane in which the points of the image are rendered as precise points. At every other plane in front of or behind the focus plane, the points show up as discs that range from slightly blurry to extremely blurry. In practice, the discs in many of these planes will still be so small that we see them as points, and that's where we get depth-of-field. Depth-of-field is just the range of planes that include discs that we perceive as points rather than blurred splotches. The size of this range increases as the aperture is reduced in size and is allocated roughly one-third in front of the plane of sharpest focus, and

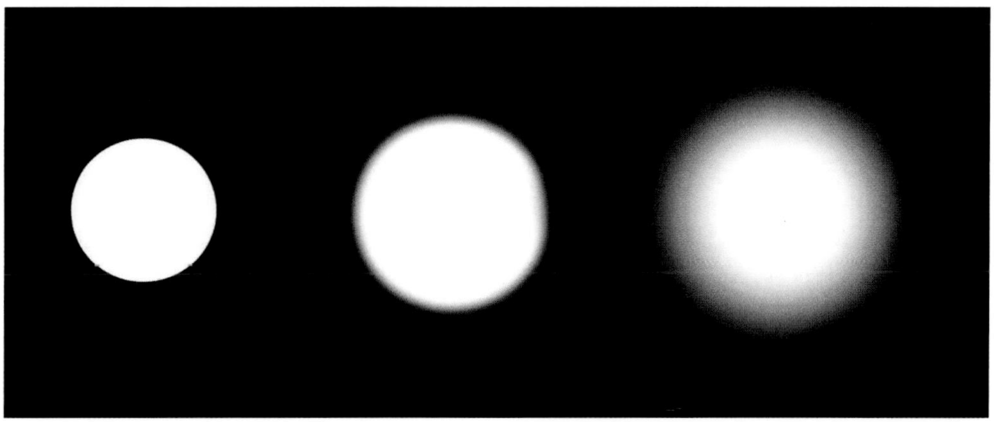

Figure 5.7 When a pinpoint of light (left) goes out of focus, its blurry edges form a circle of confusion (center and right).

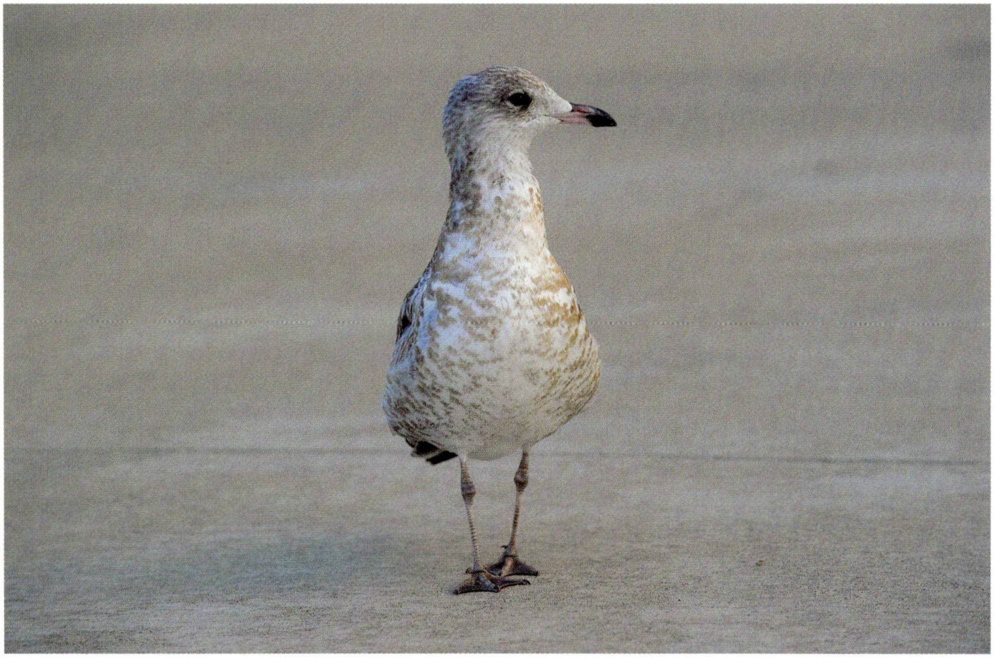

Figure 5.8
Only the bird is in focus, but the area behind him appears blurry because the depth-of-field is limited.

two-thirds behind it. The range of sharp focus is always greater behind your subject than in front of it—although in many cases, depth-of-field will be very shallow, as shown in Figure 5.8.

Making Sense of Focus Sensors

The number and type of autofocus sensors can affect how well the system operates. As I mentioned, the Sony Alpha SLT-A57 has 15 AF points. These focus sensors can consist of vertical or horizontal lines of pixels, cross-shapes, and often a mixture of these types within a single camera. As I noted earlier, the Sony Alpha SLT includes three cross-type sensors at central positions. The more AF points available, the more easily the camera can differentiate among areas of the frame, and the more precisely you can specify the area you want to be in focus if you're manually choosing a focus spot.

As the camera collects focus information from the sensors, it evaluates it to determine whether the desired sharp focus has been achieved. The calculations may include whether the subject is moving, and whether the camera needs to "predict" where the subject will be when the shutter release button is fully depressed and the picture is taken. The speed with which the camera is able to evaluate focus and then move the lens elements into the proper position to achieve the sharpest focus determines how fast the autofocus mechanism is. Although your Sony Alpha will almost always focus more quickly than a human, there are types of shooting situations where that's not fast enough.

For example, if you're having problems shooting sports because the Sony Alpha's autofocus system manically follows each moving subject, a better choice might be to switch autofocus modes or shift into manual focus and prefocus on a spot where you anticipate the action will be, such as a goal line or soccer net. At night football games, for example, when I am shooting with a telephoto lens almost wide open, I often focus manually on one of the referees who happens to be standing where I expect the action to be taking place (say, a halfback run or a pass reception). When I am less sure about what is going to happen, I may switch to Continuous (AF-C) AF and let the camera decide.

Your Autofocus Mode Options

Choosing the right autofocus mode and the way in which focus points are selected is your key to success. Using the wrong mode for a particular type of photography can lead to a series of pictures that are all sharply focused—on the wrong subject. When I first started shooting sports with an autofocus SLR (back in the film camera days), I covered one baseball game alternating between shots of base runners and outfielders with pictures of a promising young pitcher, all from a position next to the third base dugout. The base runner and outfielder photos were great, because their backgrounds didn't distract the autofocus mechanism. But all my photos of the pitcher had the focus tightly zeroed in on the fans in the stands behind him. Because I was shooting film instead of a digital camera, I didn't know about my gaffe until the film was developed. A simple change, such as locking in focus or focus zone manually, or even manually focusing, would have done the trick.

To save battery power, your Sony Alpha doesn't start to focus the lens until you partially depress the shutter release, or your face approaches the Eye-Start sensors (if you have that feature switched on). But, autofocus isn't some mindless beast out there snapping your pictures in and out of focus with no feedback from you after you press that button. There are several settings you can modify that return at least a modicum of control to you. In order to make these settings, you have to be shooting in Program, Aperture priority, Shutter priority, Manual, or Continuous Advance Priority AE exposure mode. (In the latter mode, you can only select either Continuous AF or Single-shot AF.) If you're shooting in Auto, Auto+, or one of the Scene or Panorama modes, the camera will make all focus settings for you.

If you're shooting in one of the modes that gives you these focusing options, your first decision should be whether to set the Sony Alpha to Single-shot AF (AF-S), Continuous AF (AF-C), or Automatic AF (AF-A). Press the Fn button (on the back of the camera, just above the controller pad) and use the direction buttons to highlight and select Autofocus mode, and then the up/down buttons to choose from among AF-S, AF-A, and AF-C, as shown in Figure 5.9. (If you want to skip a step, you can spin the control dial to cycle through the three choices once the AF mode icon is highlighted.) Press the center controller button to confirm your choice. The camera does not need to be set to

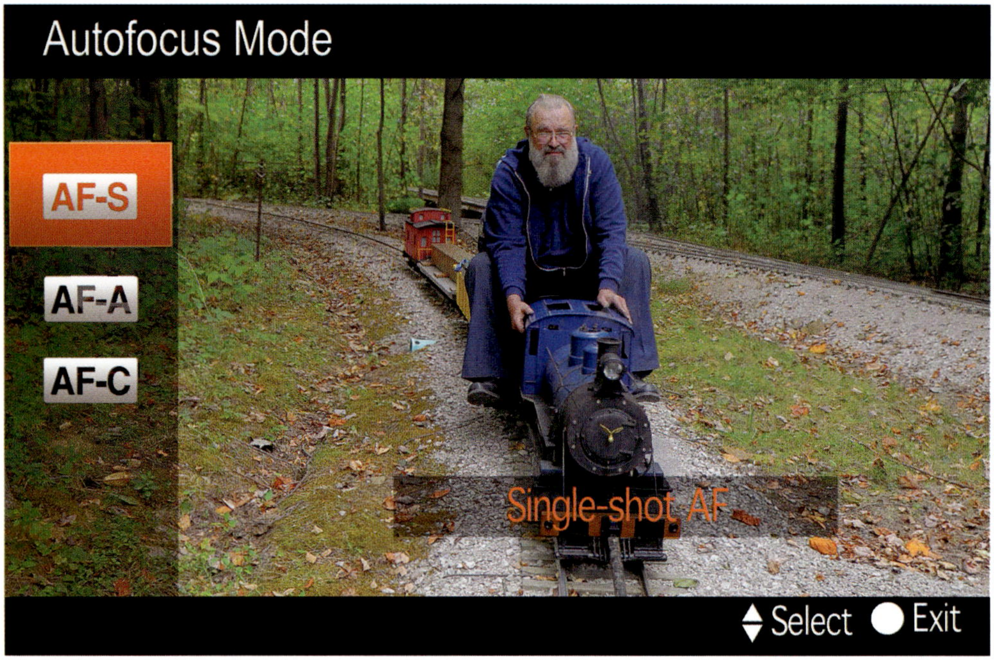

Figure 5.9
Press the up/down controller keys until the AF mode choice you want is selected from the Function menu.

AF before you can change autofocus mode, but the mode will not be activated until you switch to AF as opposed to MF. If the lens you are using has an AF/MF switch, you must set that switch to AF; the switch on the camera will have no effect. If the lens does not have a switch, then you must set the switch on the camera.

When the image under the current focus area (described later) is in sharp focus, the focus confirmation indicator in the viewfinder or on the LCD will glow a steady green; the camera is ready to shoot. If the green light framed by parentheses-like brackets is illuminated, focus is set, and the focus point will follow a moving subject. You can take a picture at any time. When only the green brackets are illuminated, the Alpha is still seeking focus, and the shutter is locked. A flashing green indicator dot indicates that the Alpha is unable to focus. The shutter is locked. You may need to switch to manual focus to get this shot.

Single-Shot AF

In this mode, also called *single autofocus*, focus is set once and remains at that setting until the button is fully depressed, taking the picture, or until you release the shutter button without taking a shot. Activate by pressing the shutter release halfway down. For non-action photography, this setting is usually your best choice, as it minimizes out-of-focus pictures (at the expense of spontaneity). The drawback here is that you might not be able to take a picture at all while the camera is seeking focus; you're locked out until the autofocus mechanism is happy with the current setting. Single autofocus is sometimes referred to as *focus priority* for that reason. Because of the small delay while the camera zeroes in on correct focus, you might experience slightly more shutter lag. This mode uses less battery power. When sharp focus is achieved, the selected focus point(s) will turn green in the viewfinder or on the LCD, and the focus confirmation light at the lower left will glow green.

Continuous AF

This mode is the one to use for sports and other fast-moving subjects. With Continuous AF, once the shutter release is partially depressed, the camera sets the focus but continues to monitor the subject, so that if it moves or you move, the lens will be refocused to suit. Focus and exposure aren't really locked until you press the shutter release down all the way to take the picture. As I mentioned, the focus confirmation indicator in the viewfinder or on the LCD is flanked by parentheses-like brackets, which indicates that the image is in focus, but the Alpha will change focus as your subject moves. Continuous AF uses the most battery power, because the autofocus system operates as long as the shutter release button is partially depressed. (It also operates when your eye or another object approaches the viewfinder, if you're using the viewfinder and have the Eye-Start AF option turned on. In that case, there's even more risk of battery drain.)

Continuous AF uses a technology called *predictive AF*, which allows the camera to calculate the correct focus if the subject is moving toward or away from the camera at a constant rate. It uses either the automatically selected AF point or the point you select manually to set focus.

Automatic AF

This setting is actually a combination of the first two. When AF-A is selected, the camera focuses using Single-shot AF and locks in the focus setting. But, if the subject begins moving, it will switch automatically to Continuous AF and change the focus to keep the subject sharp. Automatic AF is a good choice when you're shooting a mixture of action pictures and less dynamic shots and want to use Single-shot AF when possible. The camera will default to that mode, yet switch automatically to Continuous AF when it would be useful for subjects that might begin moving unexpectedly.

Setting the AF Area

You can specify which of the 15 focus points the Sony SLT uses to calculate correct focus, or allow the camera to select the point for you. Note that the Alpha SLT-A57 camera has its autofocus points clustered in the central portion of the screen, which indicates the general AF area. That means that you (or the camera) can focus only on subjects that fall under one of the autofocus marks. To focus somewhere else in the frame, you'll need to place your subject under the appropriate autofocus area, focus, and then lock focus by pressing the shutter release button halfway. You can then reframe your photo with the focus locked in.

To choose the AF area mode, press the Fn button and navigate to the AF area choice at the left side of the screen, and press the center controller button. (See Figure 5.10.) The screen shown in Figure 5.11 appears, with four basic AF area options. (Additional options, not available from this screen, include Face Detection and Object Tracking, which I'll discuss shortly.) Make your selection, and press the center controller button again to confirm. Note: If you're using Intelligent Auto, Superior Auto, Sweep Panorama, 3D Sweep Panorama, Scene Selection, Smile Shutter, or Object Tracking, AF Area is locked at Wide.

- **Wide.** The Alpha chooses the appropriate focus zone or zones from the 15 AF areas on the screen.
- **Zone.** You can use the left/right controller buttons to specify whether the group of four focus zones on the left or right of the frame, or the seven zones in the center are used. The camera chooses the exact zone.
- **Spot.** The Alpha always uses the center, cross-type focus zone to calculate correct focus.
- **Local.** Use the left/right/up/down controller buttons to choose the focus zone from among the 15 available zones. When the AF area is initially set to Local, you can use the cursor buttons or the control dial to move the focus zone around the screen; press the center controller button or press the shutter button halfway to lock in the location. If you want to move the focus zone again later, press the center controller/AF button to activate the Local AF area mode again, allowing you to move the focus zone once more.

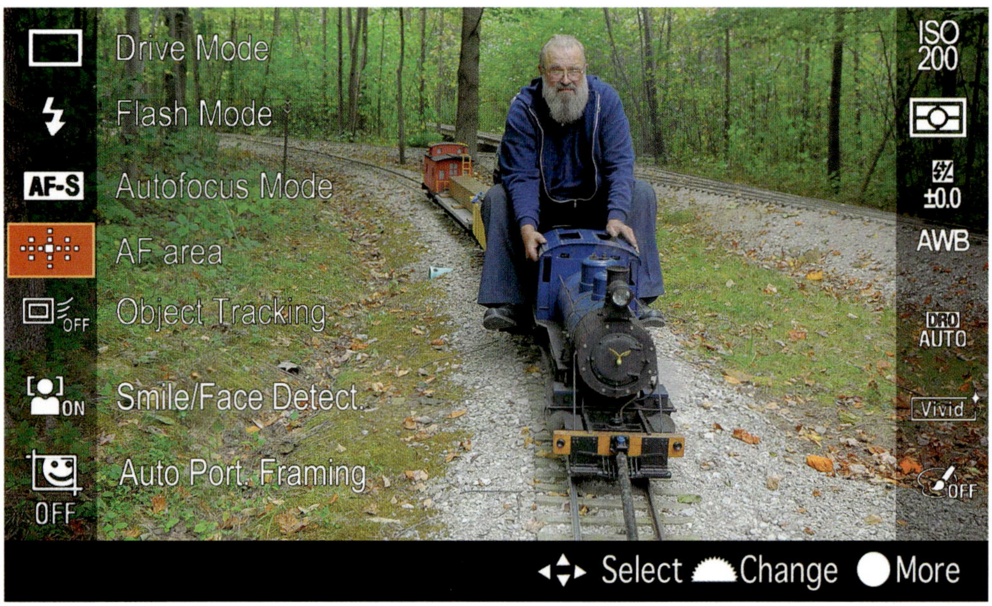

Figure 5.10
Press the Fn button and choose AF Area.

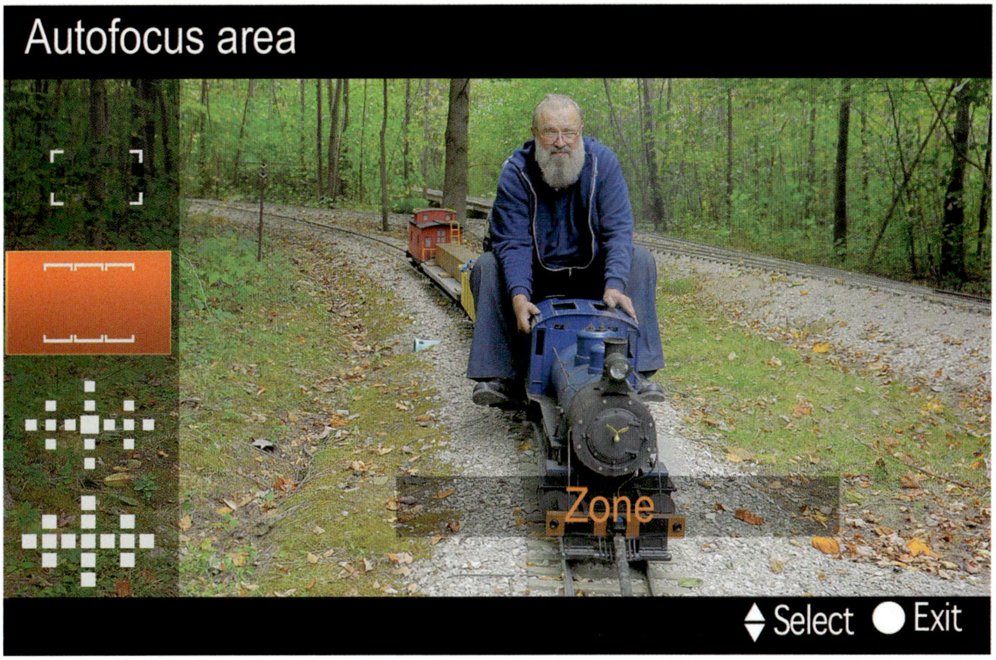

Figure 5.11 Choose from Wide (the selected setting, in which the Alpha selects one or more of the 15 AF areas); Zone (you choose which of the three zones the camera will use); Spot (only the center focus spot is used); or Local (you can choose which of 15 areas to use).

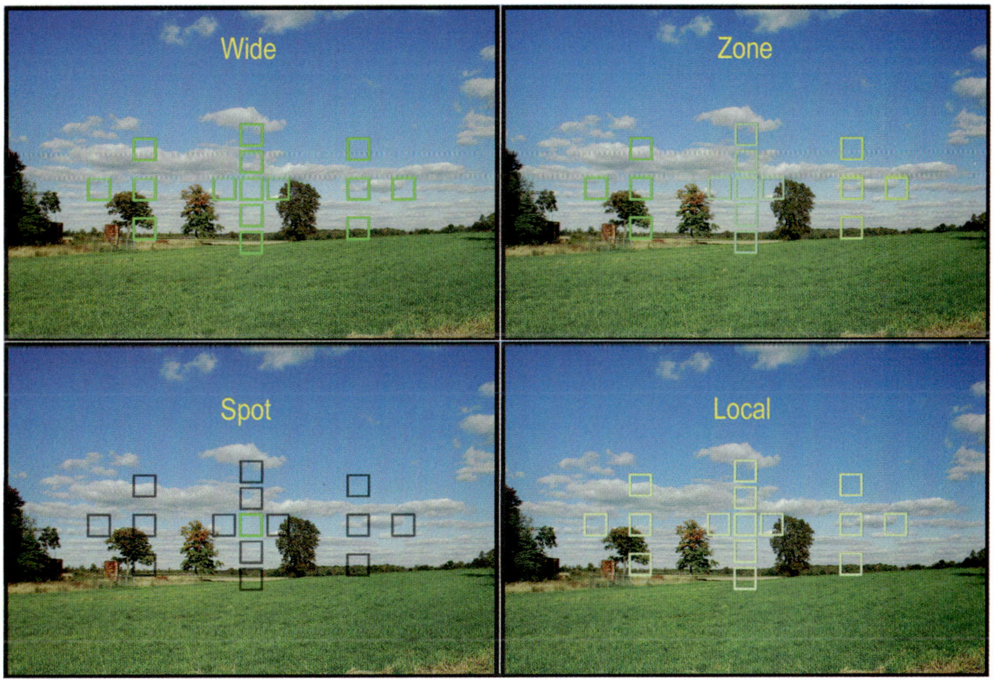

Figure 5.12 In the Wide area mode the camera will select any one of the 15 AF areas shown in green (upper left). In Zone mode, you choose the zone from the left, center, and right areas, and the camera selects the exact focus zone (upper right). In Spot mode the camera uses only the center focus spot; in Local mode, you select which of the 15 areas to use.

Face Detection/Smile Detection

The Sony Alpha SLT-A57 has a couple more tricks up its sleeve for setting the AF area. If you activate Face Detection mode (the next-to-bottom option on the left side of the Function menu), the camera will try to identify any human faces in the scene. If it does, it will surround each one (up to eight in all) with a frame (see Figure 5.13). If it judges that autofocus is possible for one or more faces, it will turn the frames around those faces orange. Then, when you press the shutter halfway down to autofocus, the frames will turn green once they are in focus. The camera will also attempt to adjust exposure, including using the pop-up flash, as appropriate for the scene. If no faces are detected, the camera will choose a focus point using whichever of the three basic AF areas has been set: Wide, Spot, or Local.

Face Detection is available at all times, except when you are using either the Sweep Panorama or the Continuous Priority AE shooting mode, or shooting a movie. Personally, I prefer to exercise my own control over what parts of a scene to focus on, but this feature could come in handy if you need to hand the camera to a stranger to photograph you and your family or friends at an outing in the park.

As I explained in Chapter 3, you can refine the A57's Face Detection operation by registering familiar faces so they'll be easier for the camera to detect. Once you've

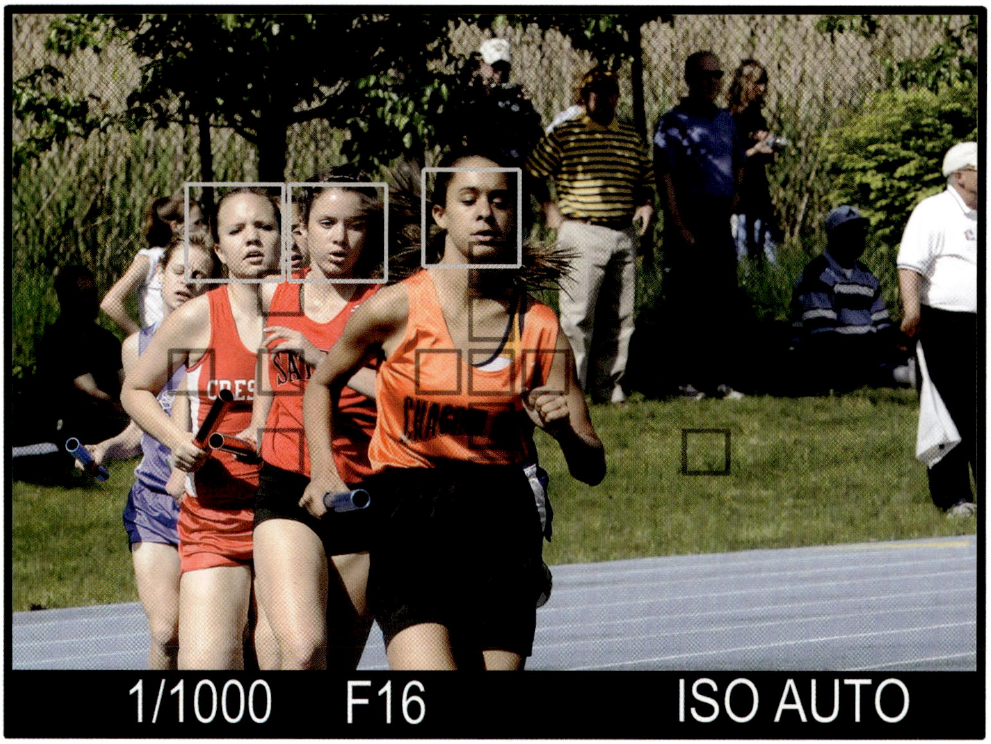

Figure 5.13
In Face Detection mode, the camera will attempt to identify as many as eight human faces in a scene, and focus on the one nearest the camera.

activated Face Detection using the Fn menu, this Custom 4 menu entry has several options. New Registration allows you to log up to eight different faces. Line up your subject against a brightly lit background, to allow easier detection of the face. Use the directional buttons to align the green frame that appears with the face, and press the shutter button. A confirmation message appears, and you press the center OK button to confirm. Thereafter, primary registered faces will be surrounded by a magenta frame; unregistered primary faces will be surrounded by a white frame.

Also available is the Order Exchanging Option, which allows you to review and change the priority in which the faces will be recognized, from 1 (your youngest child) to 8 (your brother-in-law). The A57 will use your priority setting to determine which face to focus on if several registered faces are detected in a scene. You can also select a specific face and delete it from memory or delete *all* faces from the registry.

Smile detection can be set for Slight Smile, Normal Smile, and Big Smile (actually measuring the whiteness of the teeth appearing on the face). A Smile Detection Sensitivity indicator appears at the left side of the frame, and when the smile exceeds the threshold point (marked with a left-pointing triangle), the picture will be taken. If you've also selected Auto for Auto Port. Framing, a second image will be stored on your memory card trimmed to include only the face in the photo.

Object Tracking

The final AF magic the SLT-A57 can perform is called *Object Tracking*. You can choose a moving subject to lock focus on, and as it moves around the frame, the A57 will attempt to retain focus on that subject. Changes in lighting, lack of contrast with the background, extra small or extra large subjects, and anything moving very rapidly can confuse Object Tracking, but it generally does a good job.

Object Tracking is activated from the Fn menu, with the option that's third from the bottom on the left side. Choose On to enable, or Off to disable the feature. When active, in shooting mode you can press the center controller button to produce the target frame (object selection screen) shown in Figure 5.14. The target box appears in the center of the frame. Move the camera until the object to be tracked is within the box, and then press the center controller button a second time. You can then reframe and the A57 begins tracking the subject as it moves within the image area. (See Figure 5.15.)

There are some special considerations when using this feature if the target subject is a human face. The A57 "remembers" the face selected, so if the subject disappears from the frame and then returns, the camera locks in on that face again. If you're using the Smile Shutter function, then the A57 will not only track the individual's face, but release the shutter and take a picture if your subject smiles!

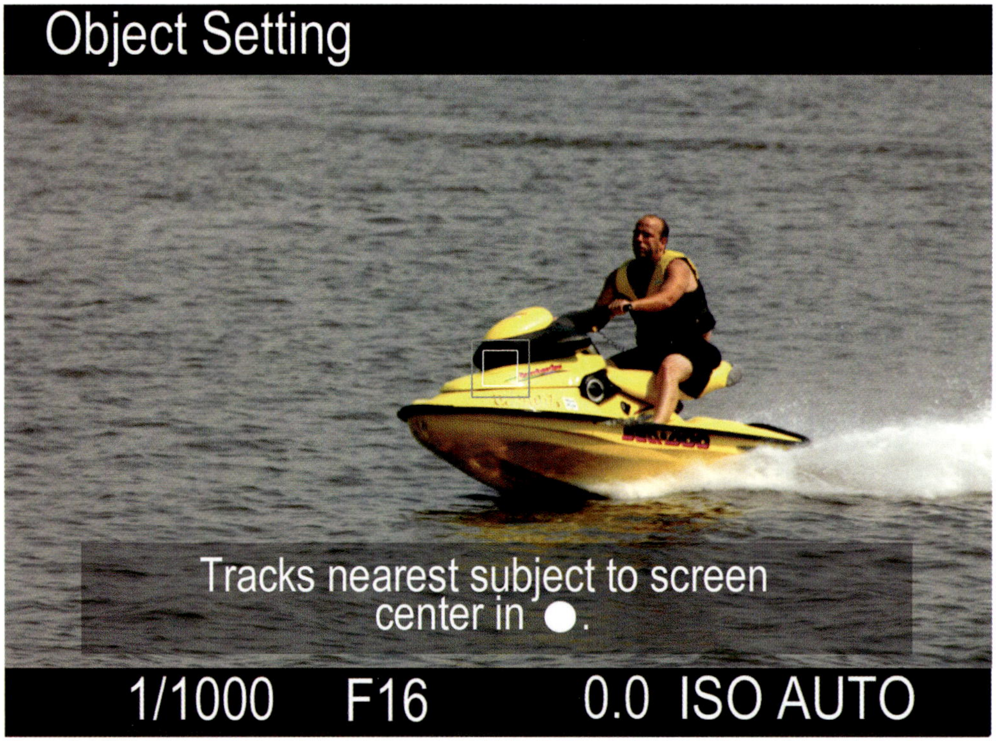

Figure 5.14
Place the object to be tracked within the box and then press the center controller button to activate tracking.

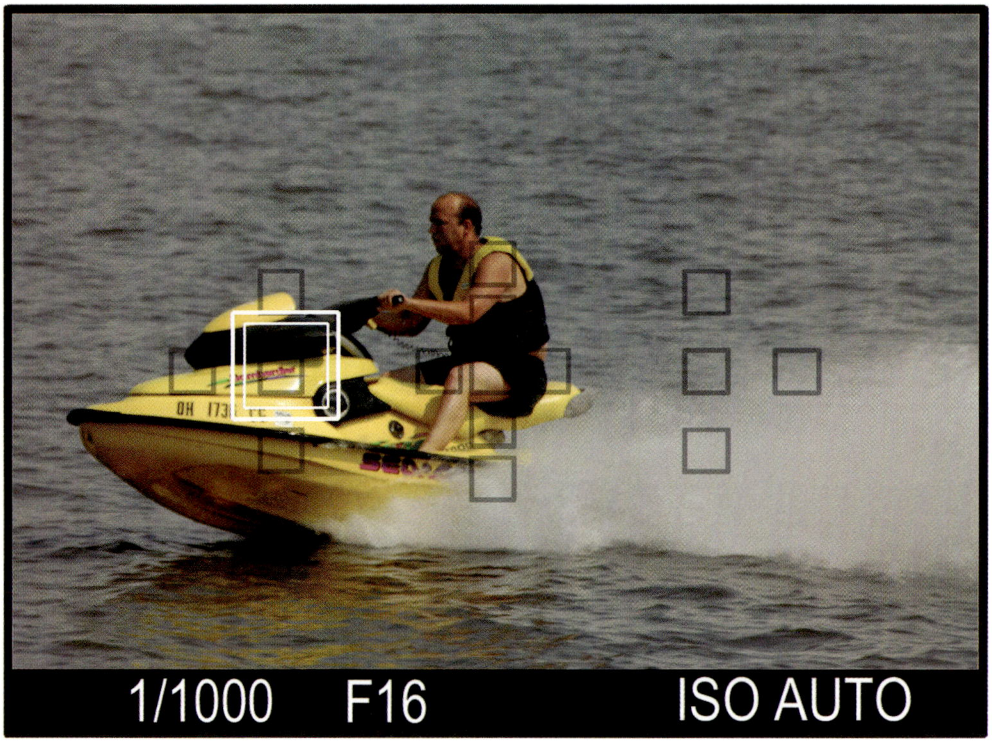

Figure 5.15
The camera will continue tracking the subject as it moves within the frame.

Manual Focus

Although the autofocus capabilities of modern digital cameras at times seem to border on the miraculous in their features, such as deciding where to focus, focusing in low light, detecting faces, and tracking moving subjects, there are times when manual focus is your best option for getting the picture made the way you want it. For example, when shooting through glass, shooting a complex scene with many possible focus points, or shooting extreme close-ups (macro photography), there may be no viable substitute for adjusting the focus by hand.

Here's a brief reminder of the basic procedure for using manual focus, after which I'll discuss a couple of specific options that can help you achieve sharp focus manually in particular situations. In focusing manually with the Sony Alpha SLT-A57, you first have to consider what lens you are using. If you're using a standard kit lens such as the Sony 18-55mm f/3.5-5.6 SAM DT zoom lens, you will see an AF/MF switch on the lens itself. In order to use manual focus mode in that case, you have to set the switch on the lens to MF; if you leave it set to AF and set the switch on the camera to MF, the camera will still autofocus with the lens. In other words, when the lens has an AF/MF switch, always use the switch on the lens to change focus modes, and leave the switch on the camera set to AF at all times.

If you're using a lens that does not have an AF/MF switch, such as the Sony SAL 100mm f/2.8 macro lens, then you need to use the switch on the camera to switch between manual focus and autofocus.

Once you have selected manual focus using the proper switch, just turn the focusing ring on the lens until the image appears sharp. The camera will give you confirmation as you focus: As you view the image in the electronic viewfinder or on the LCD, the focus confirmation and focus bracket both turn green to confirm focus, once the camera has determined that the image is sharp. If you're having difficulty getting the image into the best possible focus, there are a couple of techniques you can use to improve your results:

- **Zoom in.** If you're using a zoom lens, but are not composing the shot at the longest zoom setting, zoom all the way in before focusing so you can see the focus point on your subject more clearly. If the focus is sharp at the longest focal length, it will also be sharp when you zoom back out to the focal length at which the picture is taken.
- **Use the Focus Magnifier button.** If you're finding it difficult to achieve a sharp image using manual focus, you can use the Focus Magnifier option, which can be set as the alternate function of the AEL, ISO, or Preview buttons in the Custom 3 menu, as described in Chapter 3. Press the button once to activate the feature, and move the small orange frame over the area of most critical focus. Then press the button again to enlarge the image to about 7 times normal and once more to about 15 times. Press it a final time to return to the normal view.

- **Use Focus Peaking.** I love this feature, especially when I am trying to manually focus in dim light. Set up the feature using the Peaking Level and Peaking Color settings in the Custom 2 menu, as described in Chapter 3. Then rotate the focus ring until the subject area you want in sharp focus is outlined in white, red, or yellow (depending on the Peaking Color you've selected).

Focus Stacking

If you are doing macro (close-up) photography of insects, flowers, or other small objects at short distances, the depth-of-field often will be extremely narrow. In some cases, it will be so narrow that it will be impossible to keep the entire subject in focus in one photograph. Although having part of the image out of focus can be a pleasing effect for a portrait of a person, it is likely to be a hindrance when you are trying to make an accurate photographic record of a flower, insect, or small piece of precision equipment. One solution to this problem is focus stacking, a procedure that can be considered like HDR translated for the world of focus—taking multiple shots with different settings, and, using software as explained below, combining the best parts from each image in order to make a whole that is better than the sum of the parts.

For example, see Figures 5.16 through 5.18, in which I took photographs of three colorful crayons using a Sony Alpha with the Sony SAL f/2.8 100mm macro lens, which has an effective focal length of 150mm when used with the camera's APS-C-sized sensor. As you can see from these images, the depth-of-field was extremely narrow, and only a small part of the subject was in focus for each shot.

Now look at Figure 5.19, in which the entire subject is in reasonably sharp focus. This image is a composite, made up of the three shots above, as well as 10 others, each one focused on the same scene, but at very gradually increasing distances from the camera's lens. All 13 images were then combined in Adobe Photoshop using the focus stacking procedure. Here are the steps you can take to combine shots for the purpose of achieving sharp focus in this sort of situation:

1. Set the camera firmly on a solid tripod. A tripod or other equally firm support is absolutely essential for this procedure.
2. Connect a wired remote control or use an infrared remote control if possible. If not, consider using the self-timer to avoid any movement of the camera when images are captured.
3. Set the camera to manual focus mode.
4. Set the exposure, ISO, and white balance manually, using test shots if necessary to determine the best values. This step will help prevent visible variations from arising among the multiple shots that you'll be taking.

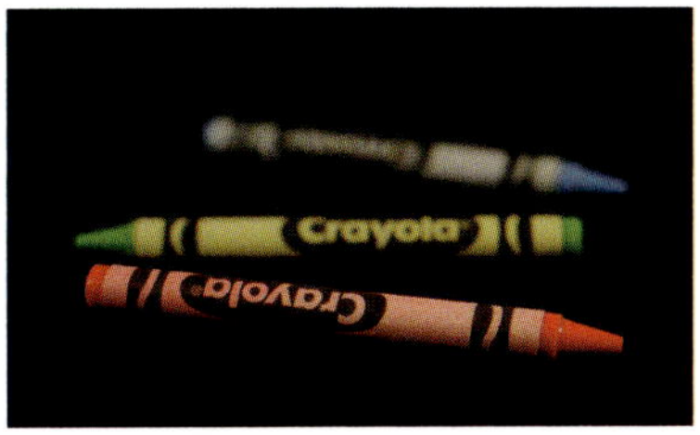

Figure 5.16

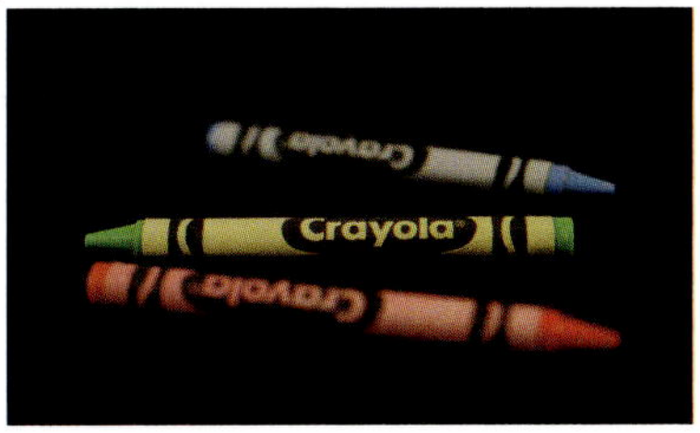

Figure 5.17

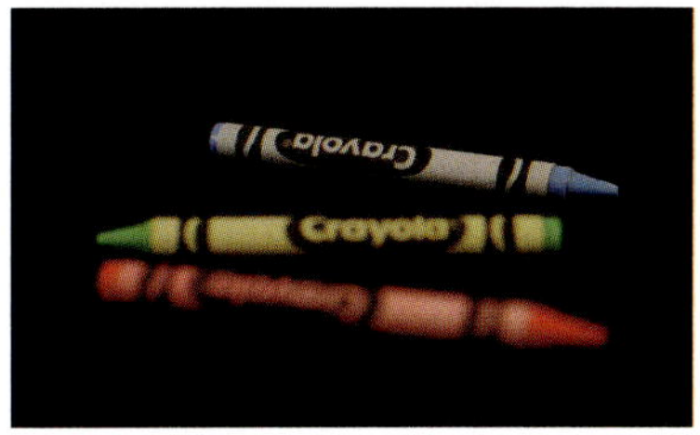

Figure 5.18

These three shots were all focused on different distances within the same scene. No single shot could bring the entire subject into sharp focus.

Figure 5.19
Three partially out-of-focus shots have been merged, along with ten others, through a focus stacking procedure in Adobe Photoshop, to produce a single image with the entire subject in focus.

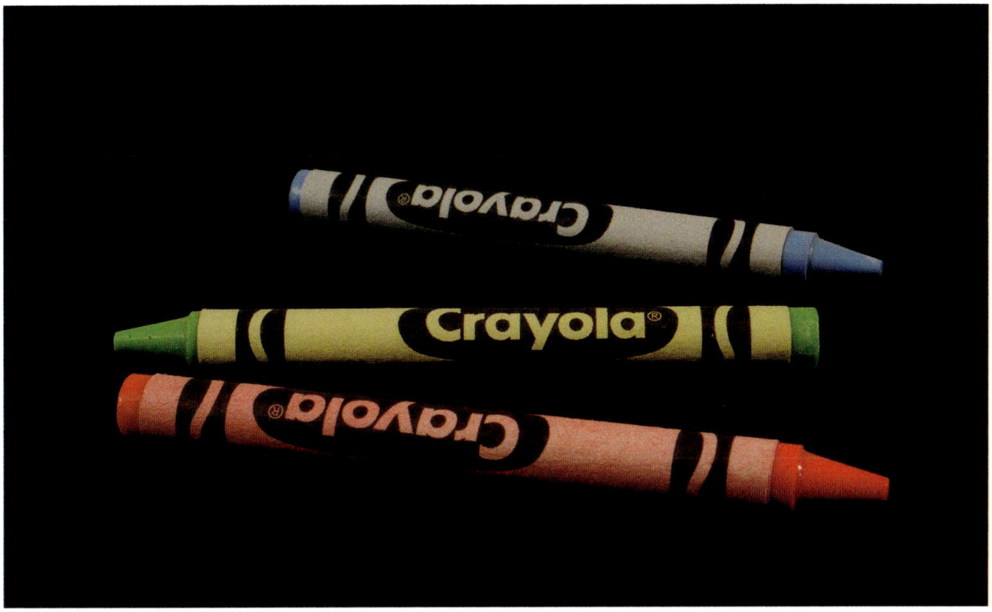

5. Set the quality of the images to RAW & JPEG or FINE.
6. Focus manually on the very closest point of the subject to the lens. Trip the shutter, using the remote control or self-timer.
7. Focus on a point slightly farther away from the lens and trip the shutter again.
8. Continue taking photographs in this way until you have covered the entire subject with in-focus shots.
9. In Photoshop, select Files > Scripts > Load Files into Stack. In the dialog box that then appears, navigate on your computer to find the files for the photographs you have taken, and highlight them all.

10. At the bottom of the next dialog box that appears, check the box that says, "Attempt to Automatically Align Source Images," then click OK. The images will load; it may take several minutes for the program to load the images and attempt to arrange them into layers that are aligned based on their content.
11. Once the program has finished processing the images, go to the Layers panel and select all of the layers. You can do this by clicking on the top layer and then Shift-clicking on the bottom one.
12. While the layers are all selected, in Photoshop go to Edit > Auto-Blend Layers. In the dialog box that appears, select the two options, Stack Images and Seamless Tones and Colors, then click OK. The program will process the images, possibly for a considerable length of time.
13. If the procedure worked well, the result will be a single image made up of numerous layers that have been processed to produce a sharply focused rendering of your subject. If it did not work well, you may have to take additional images the next time, focusing very carefully on small slices of the subject as you move progressively farther away from the lens.

Although this procedure can work very well in Photoshop, you also may want to try it with programs that were developed more specifically for focus stacking and related procedures, such as Helicon Focus (www.heliconsoft.com), PhotoAcute (www.photo-acute.com), or CombineZM (www.hadleyweb.pwp.blueyonder.co.uk).

6

Advanced Techniques for Your Sony Alpha SLT-A57

Of the primary foundations of great photography, only one of them—the ability to capture a compelling image with a pleasing composition—takes a lifetime (or longer) to master. The art of *making* a photograph, rather than just *taking* a photograph, requires an aesthetic eye that sees the right angle for the shot, as well as a sense of what should be included or excluded in the frame; a knowledge of what has been done in the medium before (and where photography can be taken in the future); and a willingness to explore new areas. The more you pursue photography, the more you will learn about visualization and composition. When all is said and done, this is what photography is all about.

The other basics of photography—equally essential—involve more technical aspects: the ability to use your camera's features to produce an image with good tonal and color values; to achieve sharpness (where required) or unsharpness (when you're using selective focus); and to master appropriate white/color balance. It's practical to learn these technical skills in a time frame that's much less than a lifetime, although most of us find there is always room for improvement. You'll find the basic information you need to become proficient in each of these technical areas in this book.

You've probably already spent a lot of time learning your Sony Alpha's basic features, and setting it up to take decent pictures automatically, with little input from you. It probably felt great to gain the confidence to snap off picture after picture, knowing that a large percentage of them were going to be well exposed, in sharp focus, and rich with color. The Sony Alpha SLT-A57 is designed to produce good, basic images right out of the box.

But after you were comfortable with your camera, you began looking for ways to add your own creativity to your shots. You explored ways of tweaking the exposure, using selective focus, and, perhaps, experimenting with the different looks that various lens zoom settings (*focal lengths*) could offer.

The final, and most rewarding, stage comes when you begin exploring advanced techniques that enable you to get stunning shots that will have your family, friends, and colleagues asking you, "How did you *do* that?" These more advanced techniques deserve an entire book of their own (and I have one for you called *Digital SLR Pro Secrets*, also from Course Technology). But there is plenty of room in this chapter to introduce you to some clever things you can do with your Sony Alpha SLT.

Exploring Ultra-Fast Exposures

Fast shutter speeds stop action because they capture only a tiny slice of time. Electronic flash also freezes motion by virtue of its extremely short duration—as brief as 1/50,000th second or less. The Sony Alpha SLT has a top shutter speed of 1/4,000th second and its built-in flash unit fires off brief bursts that can give you more of these ultra-quick glimpses of moving subjects. An external flash, such as one of the Sony HVL-series strobes, offers even more versatility. You can read more about using electronic flash to stop action in Chapter 9.

In this section, I'm going to emphasize the use of short exposures to capture a moment in time. The Sony Alpha is fully capable of immobilizing all but the fastest movement using only its shutter speeds, which range all the way up to that impressive 1/4,000th second. Some cameras, such as the stablemate Alpha SLT-A77, have speeds up to 1/8,000th second, but those ultra-fast shutters are generally overkill when it comes to stopping action, and are rarely needed for achieving the exposure you desire. For example, the image shown in Figure 6.1 required a shutter speed of just 1/2,000th second to freeze the high jumper clearing the bar.

When it comes to stopping action, most sports can be frozen at 1/2,000th second or slower, and for many sports a slower shutter speed is actually preferable—for example, to allow the wheels of a racing automobile or motorcycle, or the propeller on a helicopter, to blur realistically.

In practice, shutter speeds faster than 1/4,000th second are rarely required. If you wanted to use an aperture of f/1.8 at ISO 200 outdoors in bright sunlight, say to throw a background out of focus with a wide aperture's shallow depth-of-field, a shutter speed of 1/4,000th second would more than do the job. You'd need a faster shutter speed only if you moved the ISO setting to a higher sensitivity, and you probably wouldn't do that if your goal were to use the widest f/stop possible. Under *less* than full sunlight, 1/4,000th second is more than fast enough for any conditions you're likely to encounter.

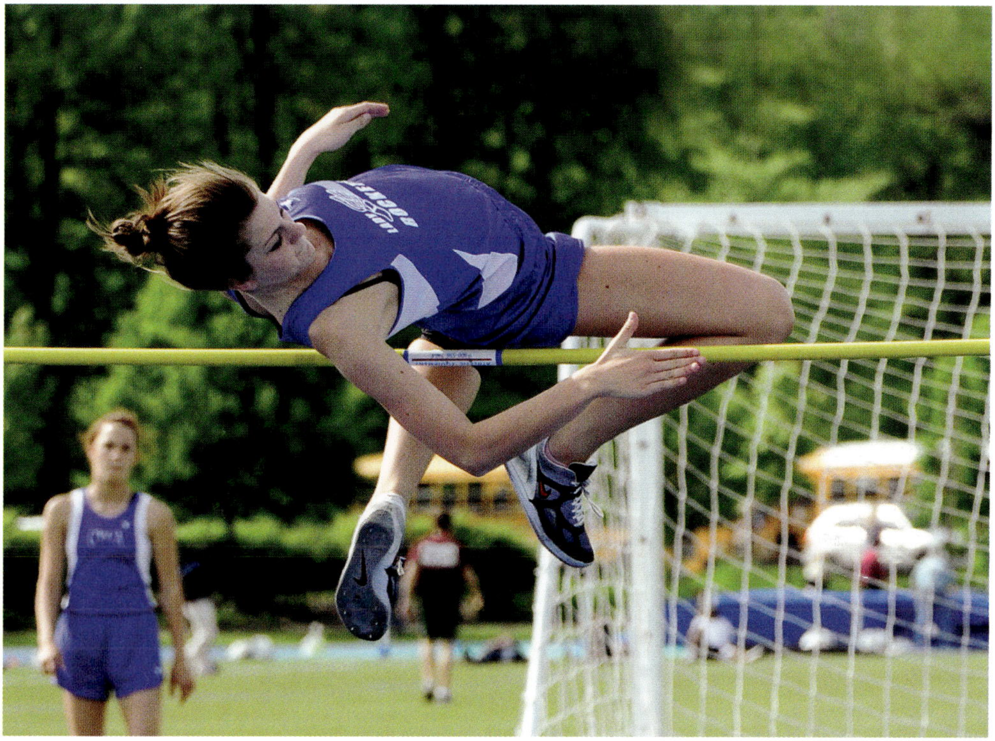

Figure 6.1
A shutter speed of 1/2,000th second will stop most action.

That's why electronic flash units work so well for high-speed photography when used as the only source of illumination: they provide both the effect of a very brief shutter speed and the high levels of light needed for an exposure.

Of course, as you'll see, the tiny slices of time extracted by the millisecond duration of an electronic flash exact a penalty. To use flash at its full power setting, you have to use a shutter speed equal to or slower than the *maximum sync speed* of your Alpha camera. With the A57, the top speed usable for flash is 1/160th second (unless you're using the special High-speed sync mode I'll describe in Chapter 9). The sync speed is the fastest speed at which the camera's focal plane shutter is completely open. At shorter speeds, the camera uses a "slit" passed in front of the sensor to make an exposure. The flash will illuminate only the portion of the slit exposed during the duration of the flash.

Indoors, that shutter speed limitation may cause problems: at 1/160th second, there may be enough existing ("ambient") light to cause ghost images. Outdoors, you may find it difficult to achieve a correct exposure. In bright sunlight at the lowest ISO settings available with the Alpha cameras, an exposure of 1/160th second at f/13 might be required. So, even if you want to use daylight as your main light source, and work with flash only as a fill for shadows, you can have problems. I'll explain the vagaries of electronic flash in more detail in Chapter 9.

You can have a lot of fun exploring the kinds of pictures you can take using very brief exposure times, whether you decide to take advantage of the action-stopping capabilities of your built-in or external electronic flash or work with the motion-freezing capabilities of the Sony Alpha SLT's faster shutter speeds (between 1/1,000th and 1/4,000th second). Here are a few ideas to get you started:

- **Take revealing images.** Fast shutter speeds can help you reveal the real subject behind the façade, by freezing constant motion to capture an enlightening moment in time. Legendary fashion/portrait photographer Philippe Halsman used leaping photos of famous people, such as the Duke and Duchess of Windsor, Richard Nixon, and Salvador Dali, to illuminate their real selves. Halsman said, "*When you ask a person to jump, his attention is mostly directed toward the act of jumping and the mask falls so that the real person appears.*" Try some high-speed portraits of people you know in motion to see how they appear when concentrating on something other than the portrait.
- **Create unreal images.** High-speed photography can also produce photographs that show your subjects in ways that are quite unreal. A helicopter in mid-air with its rotors frozen or a motocross cyclist leaping over a ramp, but with all motion stopped so that the rider and machine look as if they were frozen in mid-air, makes for an unusual picture. (See the frozen rotors at top in Figure 6.2.) When we're accustomed to seeing subjects in motion, seeing them stopped in time can verge on the surreal.

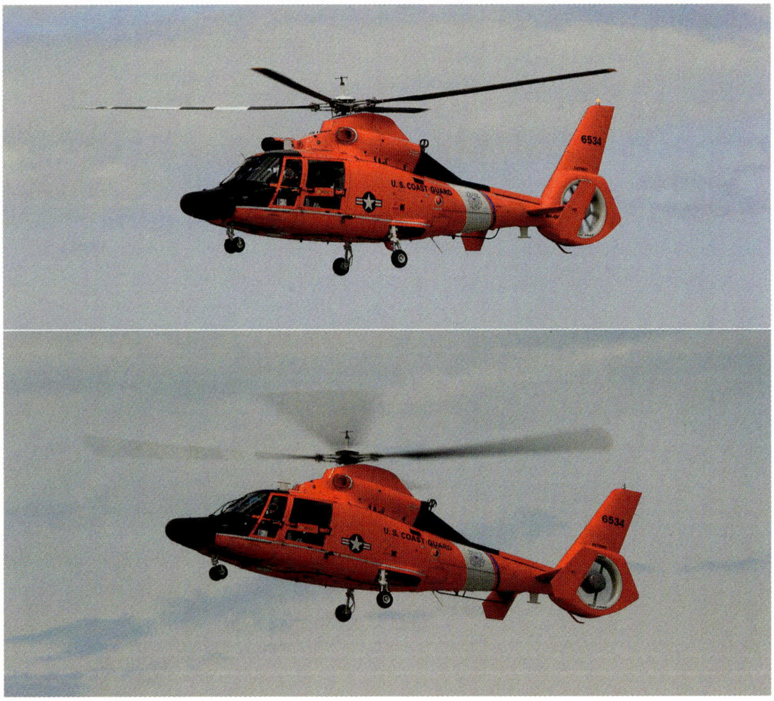

Figure 6.2
Freezing a helicopter's rotors with a fast shutter speed makes for an image that doesn't look natural (top); a little blur helps convey a feeling of motion (bottom).

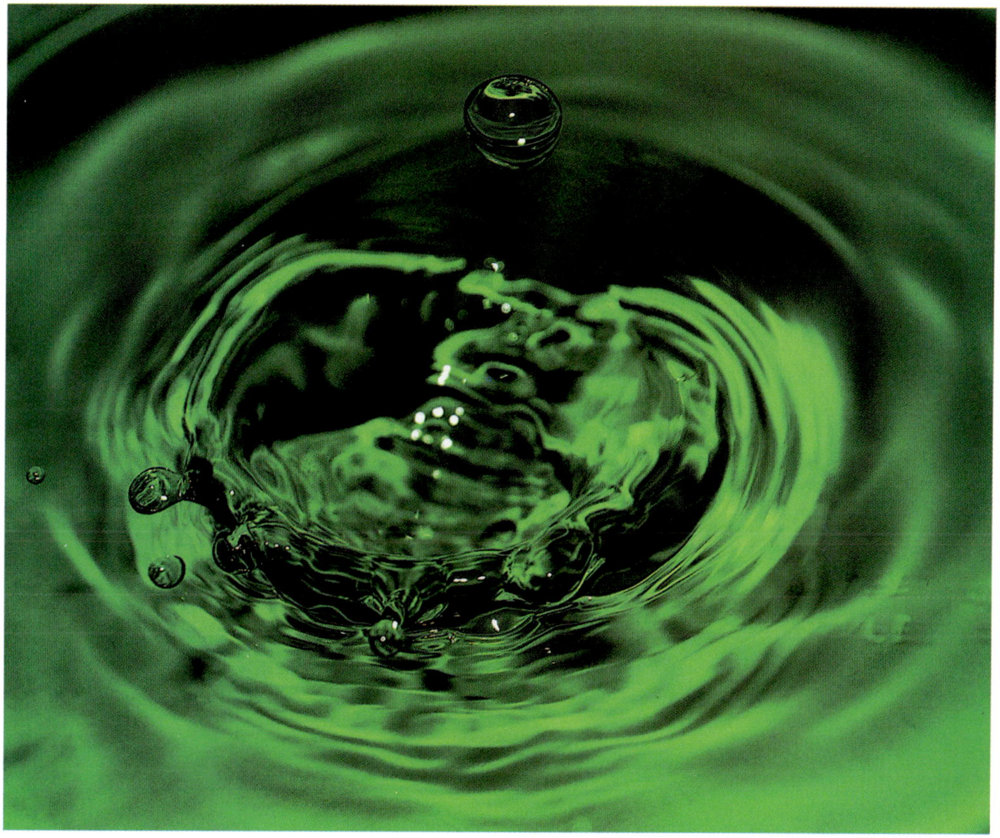

Figure 6.3
A large amount of artificial illumination and an ISO 1600 sensitivity setting allowed capturing this shot at 1/2,000th second without use of an electronic flash.

- **Capture unseen perspectives.** Some things are *never* seen in real life, except when viewed in a stop-action photograph. M.I.T. professor Dr. Harold Edgerton's famous balloon burst photographs were only a starting point for the inventor of the electronic flash unit. Freeze a hummingbird in flight for a view of wings that never seem to stop. Or, capture the splashes as liquid falls into a bowl, as shown in Figure 6.3. No electronic flash was required for this image (and wouldn't have illuminated the water in the bowl as evenly). Instead, a clutch of high-intensity lamps bounced off a green card and an ISO setting of 1600 allowed the Sony Alpha to capture this image at 1/2,000th second.

Long Exposures

Longer exposures are a doorway into another world, showing us how even familiar scenes can look much different when photographed over periods measured in seconds. At night, long exposures produce streaks of light from moving, illuminated subjects like automobiles or amusement park rides. Or, you can move the camera or zoom the lens to get interesting streaks from non-moving light sources, such as the holiday lights shown in Figure 6.4. Extra-long exposures of seemingly pitch-dark subjects can reveal

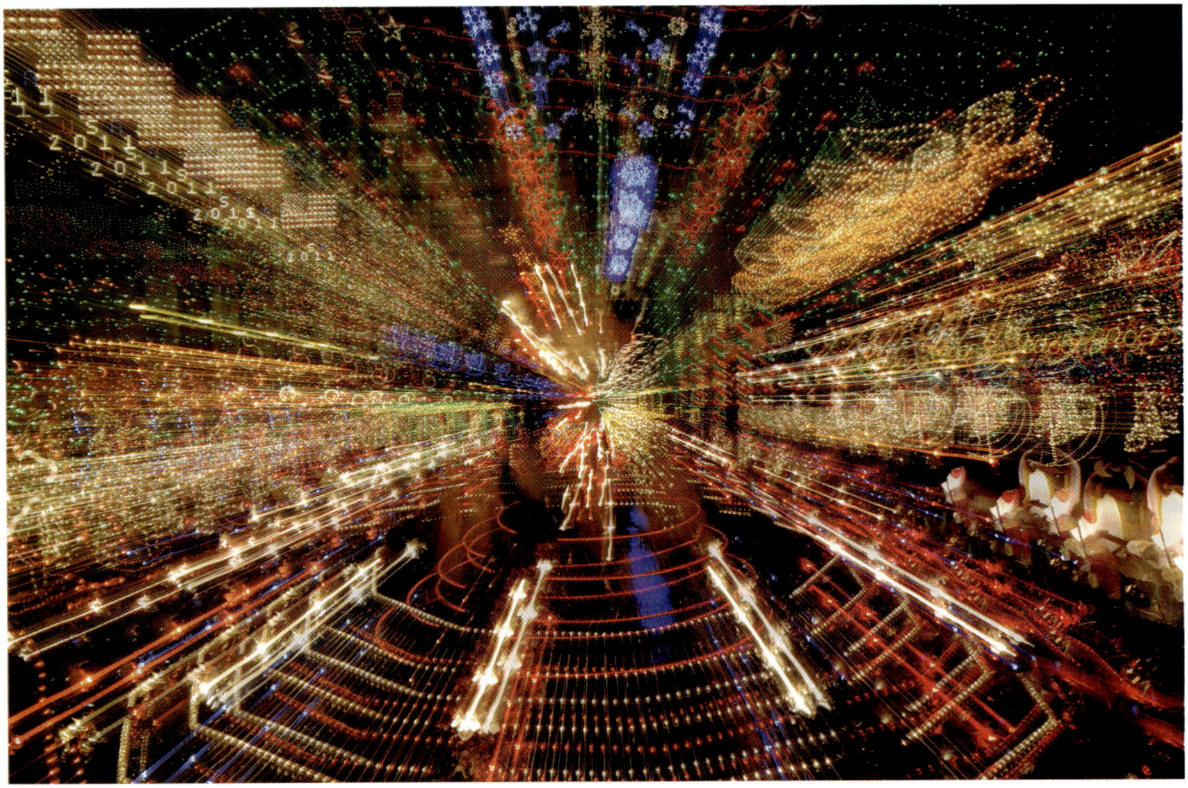

Figure 6.4 Long exposures can produce interesting streaks of light, particularly if you zoom during the exposure.

interesting views using light levels barely bright enough to see by. At any time of day, including daytime (in which case you'll often need the help of neutral-density filters (described below) to make the long exposure practical), long exposures can cause moving objects to vanish entirely, because they don't remain stationary long enough to register in a photograph.

Three Ways to Take Long Exposures

There are actually three common types of lengthy exposures: *timed exposures*, *bulb exposures*, and *time exposures*. Because of the length of the exposure, all of the following techniques should be used with a tripod to hold the camera steady.

- **Timed exposures.** These are long exposures, from 1 second to 30 seconds, measured by the camera itself. To take a picture in this range, simply use Manual or Shutter priority mode and use the control dial to set the shutter speed to the length of time you want, choosing from several preset speeds ranging from 1.0 to 30.0 seconds. The advantage of timed exposures is that the camera does all the calculating for you. There's no need for a stopwatch. If you review your image on the EVF or LCD and decide to try again with the exposure doubled or halved, you can dial in the correct exposure with precision. The disadvantage of timed exposures is that you can't take a photo for longer than 30 seconds.

- **Bulb exposures.** This type of exposure is so-called because in the olden days the photographer squeezed and held an air bulb attached to a tube that provided the force necessary to keep the shutter open. Traditionally, a bulb exposure is one that lasts as long as the shutter release button is pressed; when you release the button, the exposure ends. To make a bulb exposure with the Sony Alpha, set the camera on Manual mode and use the control dial to select the shutter speed immediately after 30 seconds. BULB will be displayed on the LCD and in the viewfinder. (You can't set the shutter speed to BULB when using the Smile Shutter, Auto HDR, or Multi Frame Noise Reduction ISO settings.)

  Then, press the shutter to start the exposure, and release it to close the shutter. If you'd like to minimize camera shake, you can use the self-timer or the Sony wired or infrared remote control. With the wired remote, RM-S1AM, you can press and hold the release button to open the shutter and then release it to close the shutter. Or, you can lock the release button in place to open the shutter, and press it again later to end the exposure. With the infrared remote, RMT-DSLR1, you press the remote's shutter release once to open the shutter, and press it one more time to close the shutter.

- **Time exposures.** This is a setting found on some cameras to produce longer exposures. With cameras that implement this option, the shutter opens when you press the shutter release button, and remains open until you press the button again. Usually, you'll be able to close the shutter using a mechanical cable release or, more commonly, an electronic release cable. The advantage of this approach is that you can take an exposure of virtually any duration without the need for special equipment. You can press the shutter release button, go off for a few minutes, and come back to close the shutter (assuming your camera is still there). The disadvantages of this mode are exposures must be timed manually, and with shorter exposures it's possible for the vibration of manually opening and closing the shutter to register in the photo. For longer exposures, the period of vibration is relatively brief and not usually a problem—and there is always the release cable option to eliminate photographer-caused camera shake entirely. While the Sony Alpha SLT A57 does not have a built-in time exposure capability, you can still get lengthy exposures using the RMT-DSLR1 Remote Commander, the infrared remote control. As I discussed above, that unit has a shutter button that you press once to start the exposure, and press a second time to end it, so you can leave the shutter open for any length of time you want. (This remote can also be used to control playback of your images when the Alpha is connected to an HDTV.) You can also use the wired remote, the RM-S1AM, which has a shutter release that you can leave locked for any length of time, and then release to end the exposure.

Working with Long Exposures

Because the Sony Alpha produces such good images at longer exposures, and there are so many creative things you can do with long-exposure techniques, you'll want to do some experimenting. Get yourself a tripod or another firm support and take some test shots with long exposure noise reduction both enabled and disabled (to see whether you prefer low noise or high detail) and get started. Here are some things to try:

- **Make people invisible.** One very cool thing about long exposures is that objects that move rapidly enough won't register at all in a photograph, while the subjects that remain stationary are portrayed in the normal way. That makes it easy to produce people-free landscape photos and architectural photos at night or, even, in full daylight if you use a neutral-density filter (or two or three) to allow an exposure of at least a few seconds. At ISO 100, f/22, and a pair of 8X (three-stop) neutral-density filters, you can use exposures of nearly two seconds; overcast days and/or even more neutral-density filtration would work even better if daylight people-vanishing is your goal. They'll have to be walking *very* briskly and across the field of view (rather than directly toward the camera) for this to work. At night, it's much easier to achieve this effect with the 20- to 30-second exposures that are possible.
- **Create streaks.** If you aren't shooting for total invisibility, long exposures with the camera on a tripod can produce some interesting streaky effects. Even a single 8X ND filter will let you shoot at f/22 and 1/6th second in daylight. Indoors, you can achieve interesting streaks with slow shutter speeds, as shown in Figure 6.5. I shot the dancers using a 1/2-second exposure, triggering the shot at the beginning of a movement.

> **Tip**
>
> Neutral-density filters are gray (non-colored) filters that reduce the amount of light passing through the lens, without adding any color or effect of their own.

- **Produce light trails.** At night, car headlights, taillights, and other moving sources of illumination can generate interesting light trails. Your camera doesn't even need to be mounted on a tripod; hand-holding the Sony Alpha for longer exposures adds movement and patterns to your trails. If you're shooting fireworks, a longer exposure—with a tripod—may allow you to combine several bursts into one picture, as shown in Figure 6.6.

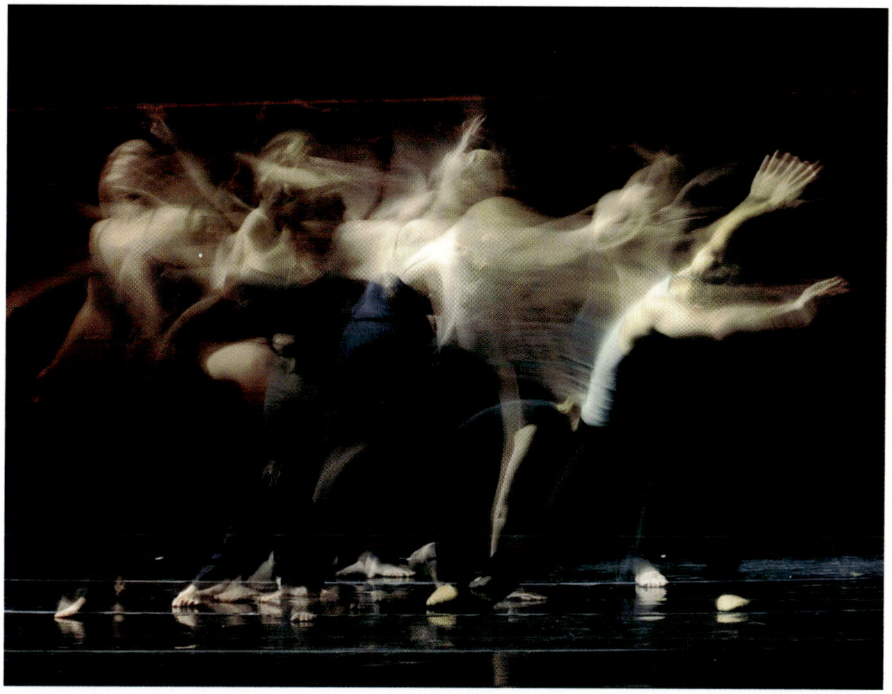

Figure 6.5
The shutter opened as the dancers began their movement from a standing position, and finished when they had bent over and paused.

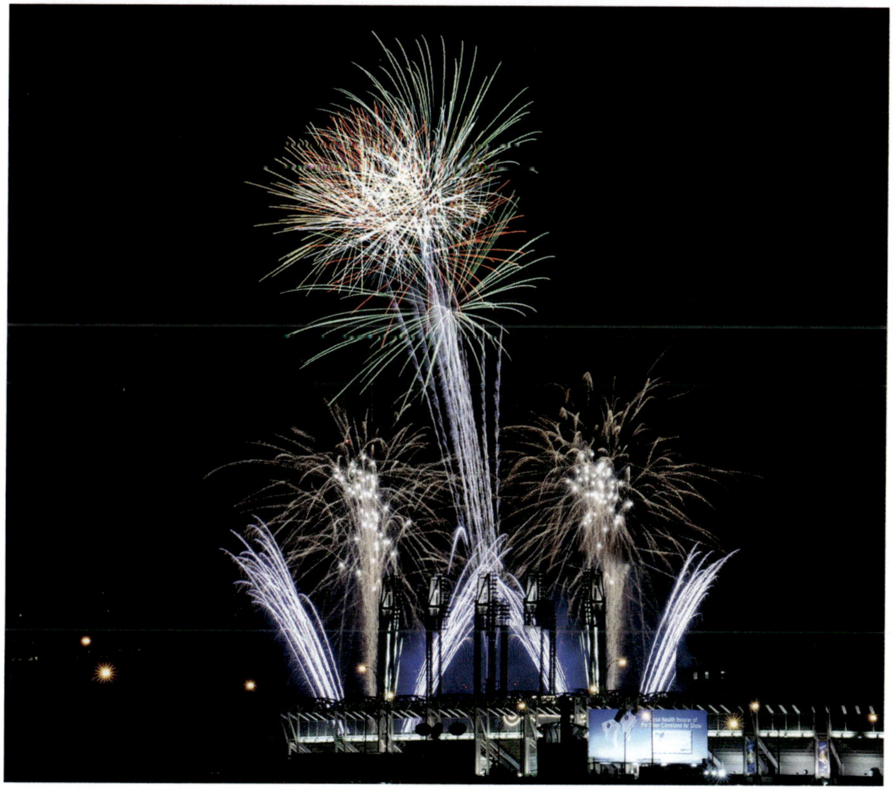

Figure 6.6
I caught the fireworks after a baseball game from a half-mile away, using a four-second exposure to capture several bursts in one shot.

- **Blur waterfalls, etc.** You'll find that waterfalls and other sources of moving liquid produce a special type of long-exposure blur, because the water merges into a fantasy-like veil that looks different at different exposure times, and with different waterfalls. Cascades with turbulent flow produce a rougher look at a given longer exposure than falls that flow smoothly. Although blurred waterfalls have become almost a cliché, there are still plenty of variations for a creative photographer to explore, as you can see in Figure 6.7. For that shot, I incorporated the flowing stream in the background.
- **Show total darkness in new ways.** Even on the darkest, moonless nights, there is enough starlight or glow from distant illumination sources to see by, and, if you use a long exposure, there is enough light to take a picture, too. I was visiting a Great Lakes park hours after sunset, but found that a several-second exposure revealed the skyline scene shown in Figure 6.8, even though in real life, there was barely enough light to make out the boats in the distance. Although the photo appears as if it were taken at twilight or sunset, in fact the shot was made at 10 p.m.

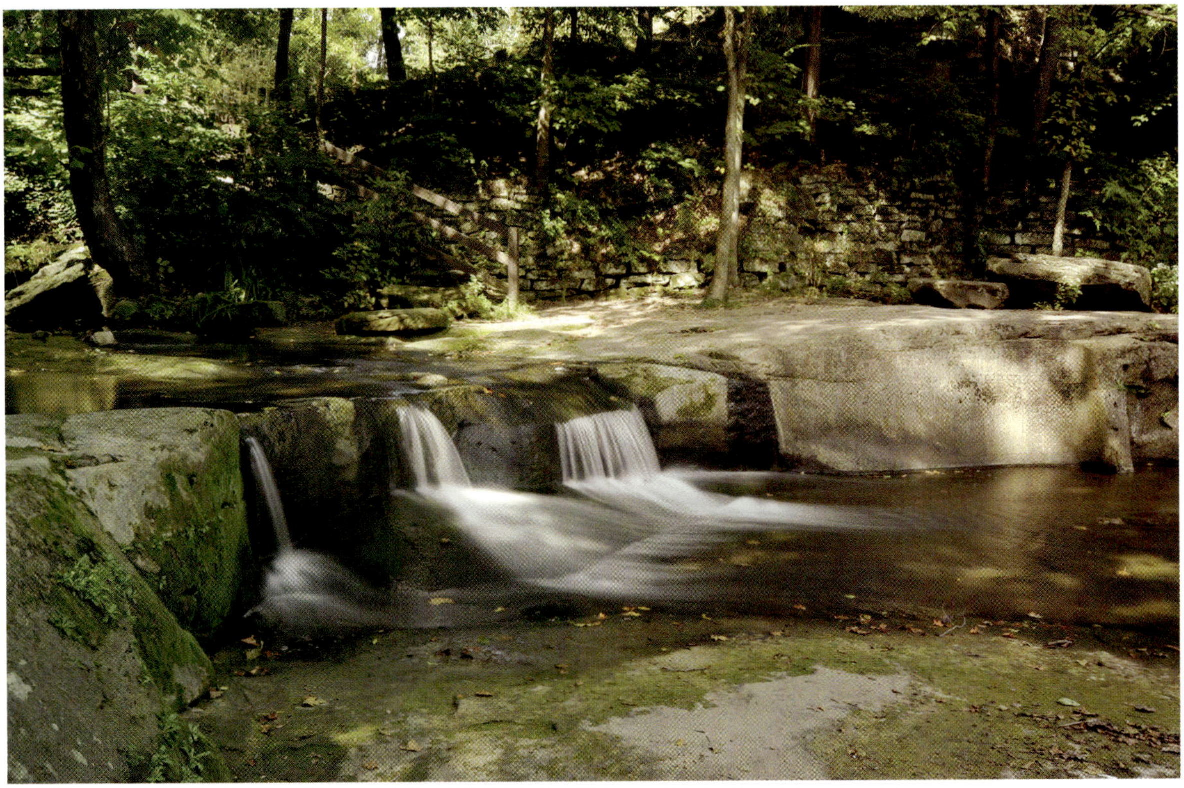

Figure 6.7 Long exposures can transform a waterfall and stream into a display of flowing silk.

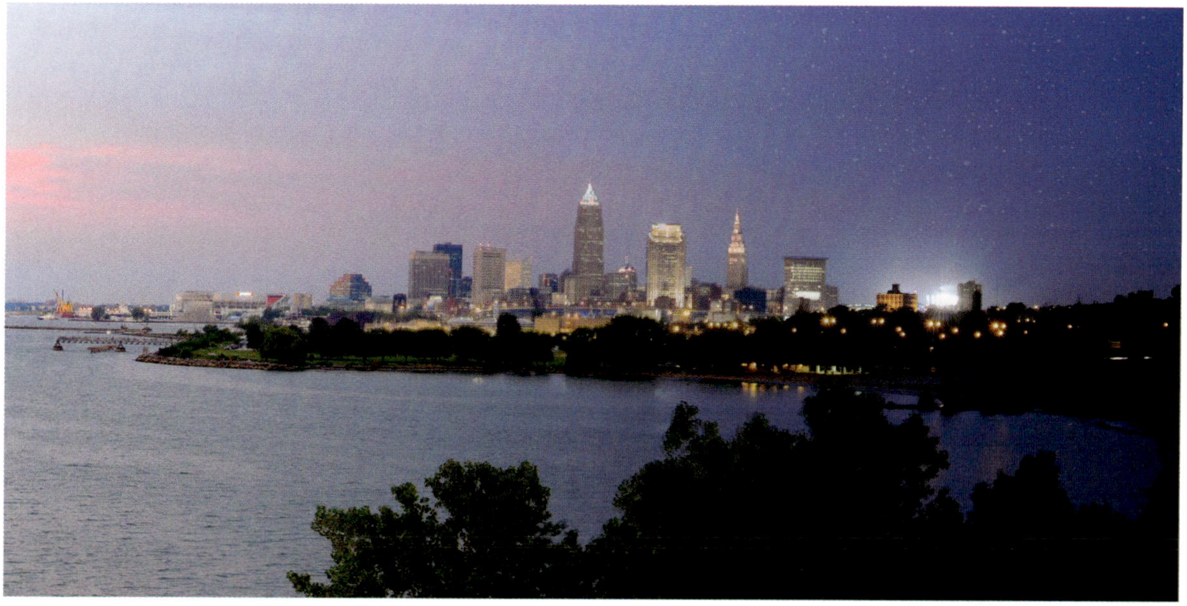

Figure 6.8 A long exposure transformed this night scene into a picture apparently taken at dusk.

Delayed Exposures

Sometimes it's desirable to have a delay of some sort before a picture is actually taken. Perhaps you'd like to get in the picture yourself, and would appreciate it if the camera waited 10 seconds after you press the shutter release to actually take the picture. Maybe you want to give a tripod mounted camera time to settle down and damp any residual vibration after the release is pressed to improve sharpness for an exposure with a relatively slow shutter speed. It's possible you want to explore the world of time-lapse photography. The next sections present your delayed exposure options.

Self-Timer

The Sony Alpha SLTs have a built-in self-timer with 10-second and 2-second delays. Activate the timer by pressing the drive button (left cursor button) and navigating with the up/down controller buttons or the control dial to choose the self-timer icon. Then, press the left/right controller buttons to toggle between 2-second and 10-second exposures. Press the center controller button to lock in your choice.

Then, press the shutter release button halfway to lock in focus on your subjects (if you're taking a self-portrait, focus on an object at a similar distance using manual focus). When you're ready to take the photo, continue pressing the shutter release the rest of the way. The lamp on the front of the camera hand grip will blink slowly for eight seconds (when using the 10-second timer) and the beeper will chirp (if you haven't disabled it). During the final two seconds, the beeper sounds more rapidly and the lamp remains on until the picture is taken. (With the 2-second timer, you get continuous rapid chirping along with a steadily lit lamp until the picture is taken.)

One other way to get a self-timer effect is to use the infrared remote, RMT-DSLR1, which has a 2-second delay shutter release. Set the Drive mode to Remote Commander, set up the shot as you want it, then aim the remote at the camera's infrared sensor in the hand grip and press the "2 sec" button. The self-timer lamp will light up and you'll hear a series of beeps, similar to the self-timer's behavior, but with a different pattern. The shutter will release at the end of the two seconds, giving you time to put the remote control out of the picture or make other last-second adjustments before the shutter fires.

Continuous Shooting

The Sony Alpha SLT's continuous shooting modes remind me how far digital photography has brought us. The first accessory I purchased when I worked as a sports photographer some years ago was a motor drive for my film SLR. It enabled me to snap off a series of shots at a three frames-per-second rate, which came in very handy when a fullback broke through the line and headed for the end zone. Even a seasoned action photographer can miss the decisive instant when a crucial block is made, or a baseball superstar's bat shatters and pieces of cork fly out. Continuous shooting simplifies taking a series of pictures, either to ensure that one has more or less the exact moment you want to capture or to capture a sequence that is interesting as a collection of successive images.

The Sony Alpha's "motor drive" capabilities are, in many ways, much superior to what you get with a film camera. For one thing, a motor-driven film camera can eat up film at an incredible pace, which is why many of them are used with cassettes that hold hundreds of feet of film stock. At three frames per second (typical of film cameras), a short burst of a few seconds can burn up as much as half of an ordinary 36-exposure roll of film. Digital cameras like the Alpha, in contrast, have reusable "film," so if you waste a few dozen shots on non-decisive moments, you can erase them and shoot more.

The increased capacity of digital memory cards gives you a prodigious number of frames to work with. At a baseball game I covered a while back, I took more than 1,000 images in a couple hours. Yet, even with my Alpha SLT-A57's 16-megapixel resolution I was able to cram more than 500 JPEG Fine images on a single 8GB memory card. That's a lot of shooting. Given an average burst of about eight frames per sequence (nobody really takes 15-20 shots or more of one play in a baseball game), I was able to capture more than 60 different sequences before I needed to swap cards. Figure 6.9 shows a typical short burst of three shots taken at a basketball game as a player drove in for a lay-up.

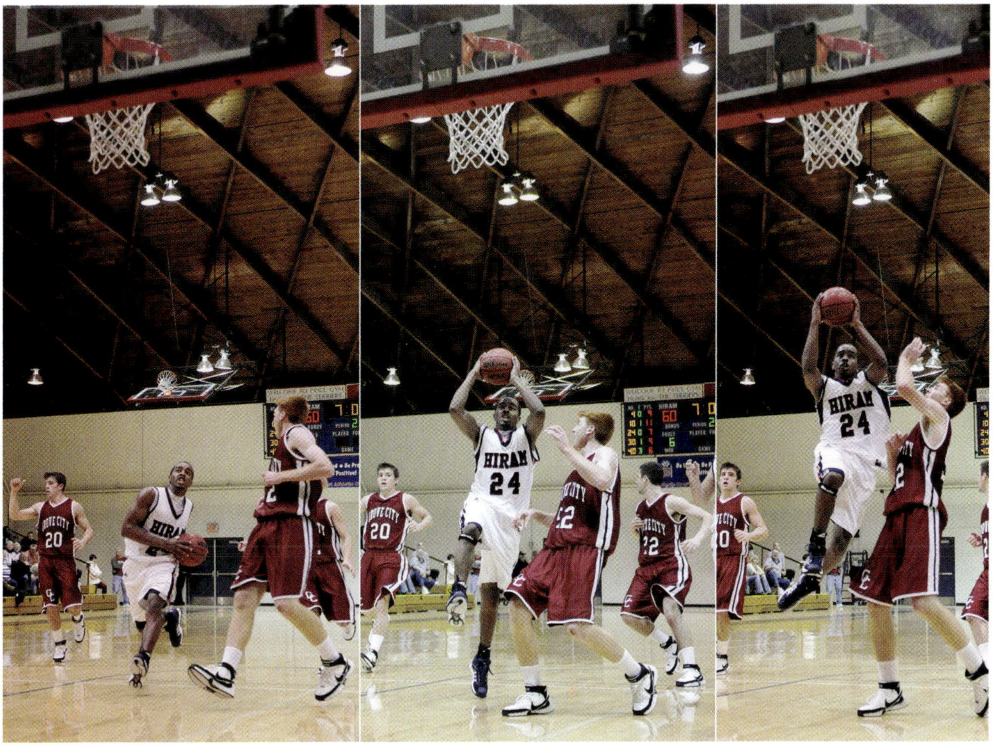

Figure 6.9
Continuous shooting allows you to capture an entire sequence of exciting moments as they unfold.

On the other hand, for some sports (such as football) the longer bursts came in handy, because running and passing plays often last 5 to 10 seconds, and change in character as the action switches from the quarterback dropping back to pass or hand off the ball, then to the receiver or running back trying to gain as much yardage as possible.

Because of the special capabilities made possible by their fixed-mirror internal construction, these SLT models are especially adept at snapping rapid sequences of full-resolution shots. To take full advantage of these capabilities, Sony has equipped the cameras with a special shooting mode that is optimized for super-fast shooting, which I'll discuss in a moment. First, though, I'll discuss the standard continuous shooting feature of the cameras.

To use the Sony Alpha's normal continuous shooting option, press the drive button (left cursor button). Then navigate down the list with the up/down controller keys until the Continuous Adv. (continuous advance) mode is selected, and navigate left or right with the controller buttons to choose between Lo and Hi speeds. The maximum output at Lo speed is about 3 images per second; the maximum for Hi speed is about 8 images per second. (For even faster frame rates, up to 12 fps, see Continuous Advance Priority AE, described below.) These speeds will be reduced by various conditions, such as dim ambient light that requires slow shutter speeds, the use of flash, and the size of your images. When you choose the Hi speed, the camera does not display the Live View between shots; instead, it displays the last recorded image. So, if it's important to you to keep viewing the live scene before you while you're shooting, you may want to set the continuous shooting speed to Lo. You can't use continuous advance when using Scene modes, other than Sports Action.

Once you have decided on a continuous shooting mode and speed, press the center controller button to confirm your choice. (See Figure 6.10.) As long as you hold down the shutter button, the Alpha will fire continuously until it reaches the limit of its capacity to store images, given the image size you have selected.

You can considerably increase the number of continuous shots by using an image-quality setting of JPEG Standard. The reason the size of your bursts is limited is that continuous images are first shuttled into the Sony Alpha's internal memory buffer, then doled out to the memory card as quickly as they can be written to the card. Technically, the Sony Alpha takes the RAW data received from the digital image processor and converts it to the output format you've selected—either JPEG or RAW—and deposits it in the buffer ready to store on the card.

This internal "smart" buffer can suck up photos much more quickly than the memory card and, indeed, some memory cards are significantly faster or slower than others. When the buffer fills, you can't take any more continuous shots until the Sony Alpha has written some of them to the card, making more room in the buffer. Keep an eye on the red memory card access light at the bottom of the camera's back, and wait until it turns off before trying for another stream of speedy shots. (You should keep in mind

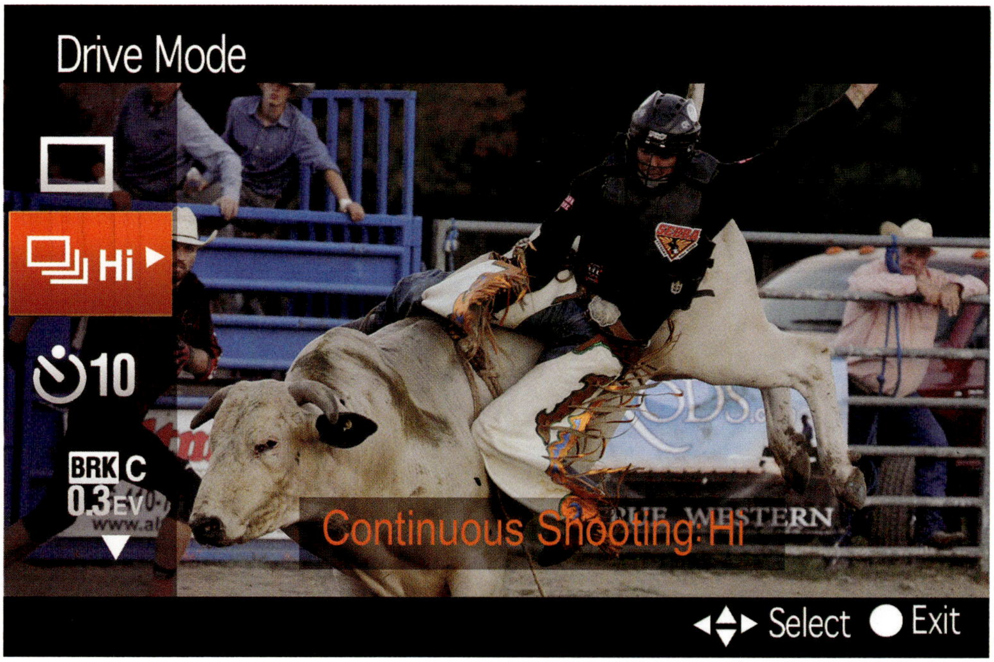

Figure 6.10
Press the drive button and use the up/down controller keys to select Continuous Adv., here shown with its Hi-speed option selected.

that faster memory cards, rated at least 40X or 6 megabits per second, write images more quickly, freeing up buffer space faster.) The camera does not provide any display showing how many images can be shot in continuous mode.

Continuous Advance Priority AE

Sony has paid extra attention to the aptitude of the SLT models to fire off rapid bursts of images. The A57 is equipped with a special shooting mode that occupies its own slot on the mode dial, called Continuous Advance Priority AE. When you turn the dial to this position, marked with the letter T and a 12 label, the camera is optimized for the greatest speed of shooting possible, while still letting you record your images in RAW quality and full resolution, with continuous autofocusing. There are some tradeoffs in return for achieving maximum speed, but they still leave you with an extremely powerful photographic tool in your hands.

In the Tele-zoom Continuous Advance Priority AE mode, the A57 can fire at a rate of up to 12 images per second, rivaling the capability of professional-level dSLRs. You can set the Autofocus mode to AF-C, and the camera will focus continuously while shooting, but in that case you cannot adjust the aperture or ISO; the camera locks the aperture at its widest value in order to achieve the increased shooting speed, and adjusts the exposure automatically. If you set the focus mode to manual or AF-S, the camera will fix the focus with the first image, and not vary it for later images. However, in that case you are free to set the aperture (using the control dial) and the ISO (using the ISO button or Function menu).

The Sony Alpha SLT's continuous shooting abilities, particularly the Continuous Advance Priority AE mode, give you a phenomenal tool for expanding your capacity for making stunning images. Take some time to experiment with these features. You will find that they can be of great use not just for stopping action in sports and other action shots, but for capturing fleeting expressions on your subjects' faces or for recording a scene at the "decisive moment" immortalized by the great French photographer Henri Cartier-Bresson.

Setting Image Parameters

You can fine-tune the appearance of the images that you take in several different ways. For example, if you don't want to choose a predefined white balance (see Chapter 3) or use white balance bracketing (see Chapter 4), you can set a custom white balance based on the illumination of the site where you'll be taking photos, or choose a white balance based on color temperature. With the Creative Style options, you can set up customized saturation, contrast, and sharpness for various types of pictures. This section shows you how to use the available image parameters.

Customizing White Balance

Back in the film days, color films were standardized, or balanced, for a particular "color" of light. Digital cameras like the Sony SLT use a "white balance" that is, ideally, correctly matched to the color of light used to expose your photograph. The proper white balance is measured using a scale called *color temperature.* Color temperatures were assigned by heating a theoretical "black body radiator" and recording the spectrum of light it emitted at a given temperature in degrees Kelvin. So, daylight at noon has a color temperature in the 5,500 to 6,000 degree range. Indoor illumination is around 3,400 degrees. Hotter temperatures produce bluer images (think blue-white hot) while cooler temperatures produce redder images (think of a dull-red glowing ember). Because of human nature, though, bluer images are actually called "cool" (think wintry day) and redder images are called "warm" (think ruddy sunset), even though their color temperatures are reversed.

If a photograph is exposed indoors under warm illumination with a digital camera sensor balanced for cooler daylight, the image will appear much too reddish. An image exposed outdoors with the white balance set for incandescent illumination will seem much too blue. These color casts may be too strong to remove in an image editor from JPEG files, although if you shoot RAW you can change the WB setting to the correct value when you import the image into your editor.

Mismatched white balance settings are easier to achieve accidentally than you might think, even for experienced photographers. I'd just arrived at a concert after shooting some photos indoors with electronic flash and had manually set WB for flash. Then, as the concert began, I resumed shooting using the incandescent stage lighting—which looked white to the eye—and ended up with a few shots like Figure 6.11. Eventually, I caught the error during picture review, and changed my white balance. Another time, I was shooting outdoors, but had the camera white balance still set for incandescent illumination. The excessively blue image shown in Figure 6.12 resulted. (I suppose I should salvage my reputation as a photo guru by admitting that both these images were taken "incorrectly" deliberately, as illustrations for this book; in real life, I'm excessively attentive to how my white balance is set. You do believe me, don't you?)

The Auto White Balance (AWB) setting, available by pressing the Fn key and navigating to the White Balance menu, examines your scene and chooses an appropriate value based on your scene and the colors it contains. However, the Sony Alpha's selection process is not foolproof. Under bright lighting conditions, it may evaluate the colors in the image and still assume the light source is daylight and balance the picture accordingly, even though, in fact, you may be shooting under extremely bright incandescent illumination. In dimmer light, the camera's electronics may assume that the illumination is tungsten, and if there are lots of reddish colors present, set color balance for that type of lighting. Sony notes that with mercury vapor or sodium lamps, correct white

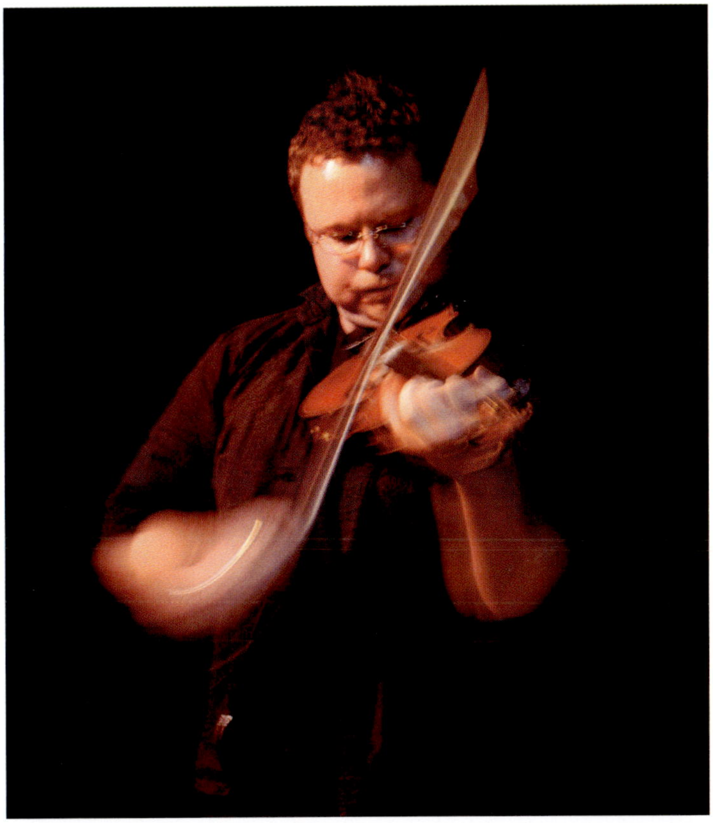

Figure 6.11
An image exposed indoors with the WB set for daylight or electronic flash will appear too reddish.

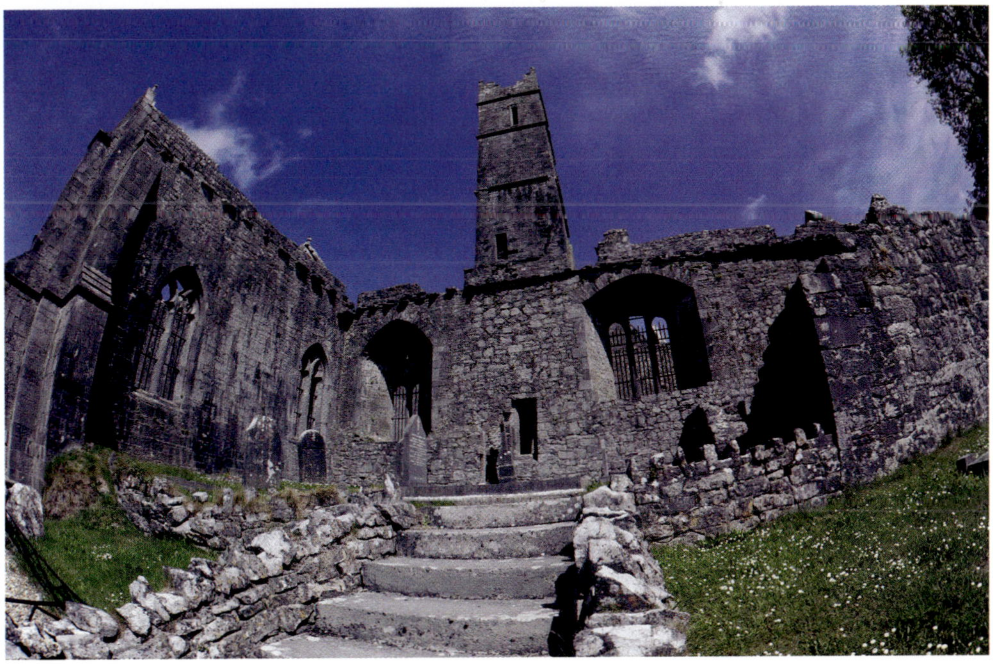

Figure 6.12
An image exposed under daylight illumination with the WB set for tungsten illumination will appear too blue.

balance is virtually impossible to achieve; in that case, you should use flash instead, or shoot in RAW and make your corrections when importing the file into your image editor.

Of course, flash isn't completely consistent in white balance, either. However, some electronic flash units, such as the Sony HVL-series dedicated flash units, can report to the camera the particular white balance that they are outputting, since a flash's color temperature can vary depending on how brief the flash exposure is. The Alpha can adjust its own white balance setting automatically, based on the information it receives from the flash.

The other presets in the WB list apply to specific lighting conditions. You can choose from Daylight, Shade, Cloudy, Incandescent, four types of Fluorescent (Warm White, Cool White, Day White, and Daylight—shown in Figure 6.13), plus Flash, Color Temperature/Filter, and Custom. When any is selected, you can fine-tune the white balance by pressing the right controller button to reveal the Fine Adjustment screen shown in Figure 6.14.

Then, use the left/right controller buttons to change the bias of the color. Pressing the right button makes the image more red/amber; the left button makes the image bluer. The up button produces a greener bias, and the down button more magenta balance. Use all four to place the center balance indicator anywhere in the grid for a customized white balance. You can choose plus/minus 7 increments (although Sony doesn't reveal exactly what those increments are) in any of the four directions. A readout just above

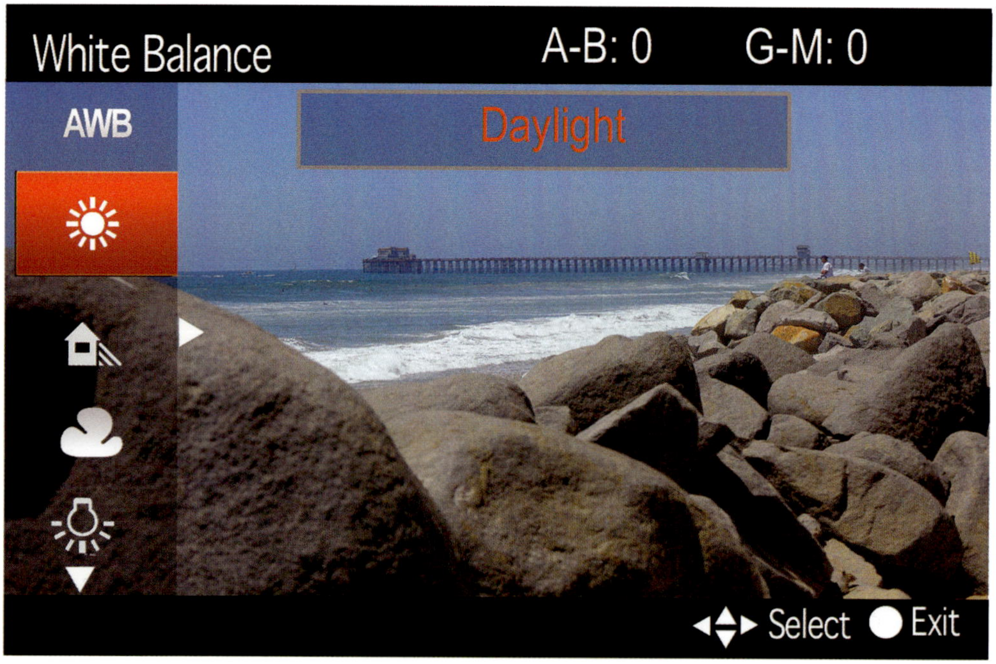

Figure 6.13 Your white balance preset selections include (top to bottom): Automatic, Daylight, Shade, Cloudy, and Incandescent, plus (not shown) four types of fluorescent illumination (Warm White, Cool White, Day White, Daylight). Also not shown are the Flash, Color Temperature/Filter, and Custom settings.

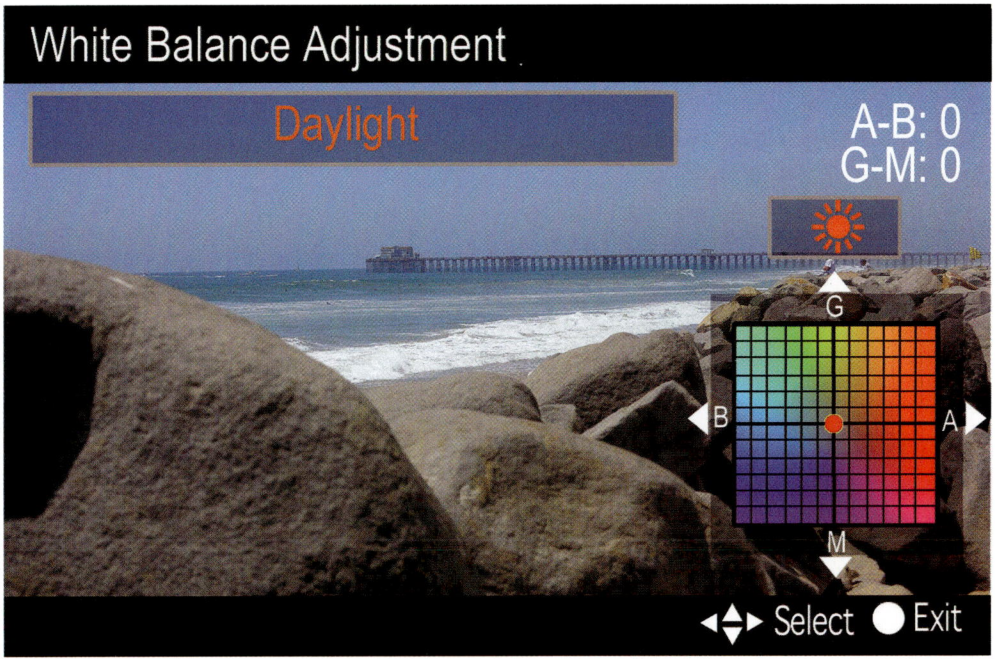

Figure 6.14
Fine-tune white balance here.

the color grid shows the current Amber-Blue and Green-Magenta bias. (Yes, I know the Amber-Blue readout is opposite the Blue-Amber scale on the grid.)

The Daylight setting puts WB at 5,200K, while the Shade setting uses a much bluer 7,000K. The chief difference between direct daylight and shade or even incandescent light sources is nothing more than the proportions of red and blue light. The spectrum of colors used by the A57 is continuous, but it is biased toward one end or the other.

However, some types of fluorescent lights produce illumination that has a severe deficit in certain colors, such as only *particular* shades of red. If you looked at the spectrum or rainbow of colors encompassed by such a light source, it would have black bands in it, representing particular wavelengths of light that are absent. You can't compensate for this deficiency by adding all tones of red. That's why the fluorescent setting of your Sony Alpha may provide less than satisfactory results with some kinds of fluorescent bulbs. If you take many photographs under a particular kind of non-compatible fluorescent light, you might want to investigate specialized fluorescent light filters for your lenses, available from camera stores, or learn how to adjust for various sources in your image editor. However, you might also get acceptable results using the four choices on the WB list.

If you find that none of the presets fits your lighting conditions, and the Automatic setting is not able to set the white balance adequately, you have two other options—using the color temperature option, or setting a custom white balance.

Setting White Balance by Color Temperature

If you want to set your white balance by color temperature, you have the option of setting it anywhere from 2,500K (resulting in bluish images) to 9,900K (resulting in reddish images). Of course, if you have instrumentation or reliable information that gives you a precise reading of the color temperature of your lighting, this option is likely to be your best bet. Even if you don't have that information, you may want to experiment with this setting, especially if you are trying to achieve creative effects with color casts along the spectrum from blue to red. To use this setting, just highlight it on the white balance menu and use the left/right direction buttons to scroll through the numerical color temperature scale.

Sony has had a sub-option to this setting called Color Temp/Color Filter, which corresponds to the use of CC (Color Compensation) filters that are used to compensate for various types of lighting when shooting with film. It has been folded into the fine adjustment screen, and now has adjustments in both the green/magenta and blue/amber directions. When you use this option, as with any fine adjustment, the color filter value you set takes effect in conjunction with the color temperature you have set. In other words, both of these settings work together to give you very precise control over the degree of color correction you are using.

Setting a Custom White Balance

Setting a custom white balance expressly for the scene you want to shoot may be the most accurate way of getting the right color balance, short of having a special meter that gives you a precise reading of color temperature. It's easy to do with the Sony Alpha SLT-A57. Just follow these steps:

1. **Access menu.** Press the WB button to produce the White Balance menu. Or, press the Fn button and then use the controller up/down/left/right keys to navigate to the White Balance menu selection, and press the center controller button to produce the White Balance menu.
2. **Select Custom.** Scroll down the list of white balance options until the Custom entry is highlighted. Press the right controller key to bring up the "Custom setup" screen, then press the center controller button.
3. **Aim at neutral target.** The camera will prompt you to "Use spot focus area data. Press shutter to load." Point the camera at a neutral white object large enough to fill the small frame in the center of the viewfinder.
4. **Press the shutter release.** The picture you took, as well as the custom white balance calculated, appears on the LCD.
5. **Exit.** Press the center controller button or press the shutter button halfway to return to the recording information display.

The Alpha SLT-A57 will retain the custom setting you just captured until you repeat the process to replace the setting with a new one. Thereafter, you can activate this custom setting by scrolling down to Custom in the White Balance menu and pressing the controller center button to confirm your choice.

Image Processing

As I mentioned in Chapter 3, the Sony Alpha SLT camera offers two more very powerful ways of customizing the rendition of your images. You can use the Dynamic Range Optimizer (aka, D-Range Optimizer and DRO), and you can specify certain changes to contrast, saturation, and sharpness in the Creative Style menu.

D-Range Optimizer and In-Camera HDR

This innovative tool helps you adjust the relative brightness range of your JPEG images as they are taken. The DRO has no effect on RAW images. (To apply dynamic range effects to RAW files, use the bundled Image Data Converter SR program described in Chapter 10.) In addition, DRO processing is available only when you are shooting in the Program, Aperture priority, Shutter priority, or Manual exposure mode.

Although DRO has been around for a while on Sony Alpha dSLRs, the A57 offers a particularly broad range of options with this feature, well beyond the plain vanilla DRO processing of some earlier models. The most dramatic enhancement is that this model provides an Auto HDR function, with which the camera does a very reasonable job of producing a High Dynamic Range image of your scene, strictly with in-camera processing with one click of the shutter.

The DRO feature, available by choosing DRO/Auto HDR from the Function menu, has three basic settings: Off, DRO, and Auto HDR, with several sub-settings for the last two. Once you have selected either DRO or Auto HDR, you can select further options for those choices by pressing the right directional button. Figure 6.15 shows how DRO settings affect your image processing at four of its settings: Off, Auto, 3 EV, and 6EV. Here is how the DRO and Auto HDR settings work:

- **Off.** No optimization. You're on your own. But if you have the foresight to shoot RAW (or RAW & JPEG), you can apply DRO effects to your RAW image when converting it with the Image Data Converter SR software, as I mentioned earlier. Use this setting when shooting subjects of normal contrast, or when you want to capture an image just as you see it, without modification by the camera.
- **DRO.** Choose Auto, or Level 1 EV through Level 5. With the Auto setting, the camera dives into your image, looking at various small areas to examine the contrast of highlights and shadows, making modifications to each section to produce the best combination of brightness and tones with detail. If you choose a specific

level of DRO from 1 through 5, the camera again makes changes in the shadows and highlights to improve the lighting of the image, making progressively stronger changes with each higher numbered setting. (See Figure 6.15.)

- **Auto HDR.** In this mode, the Alpha takes three exposures at different exposure settings, then combines these exposures in the camera and processes them together to achieve a final image with increased dynamic range, using the best-exposed areas from each image. Using the left/right direction buttons, you can set this option to Auto, in which case the camera analyzes the scene and decides on an interval between the exposures, or you can select an interval from 1.0 EV to 6.0 EV (one EV equals one stop of exposure).

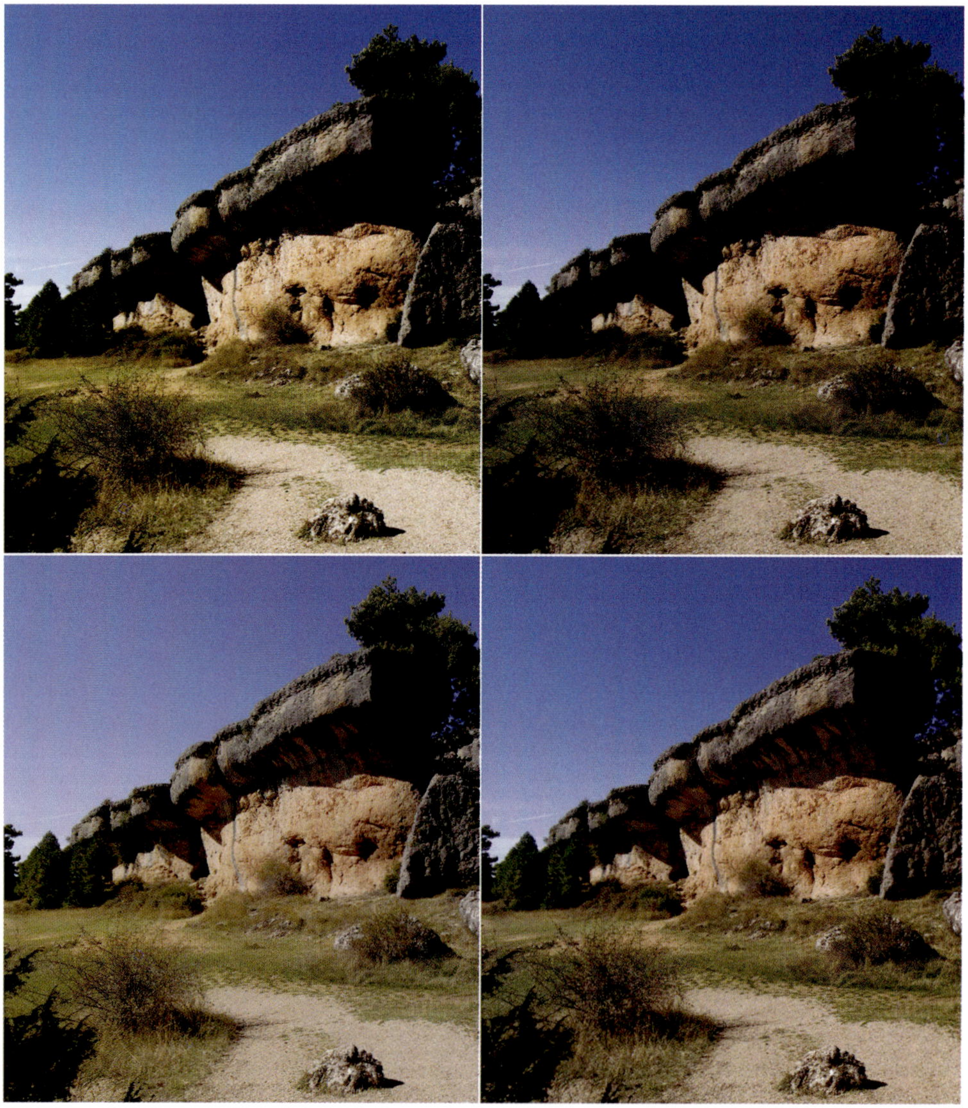

Figure 6.15
This scene was shot with the Sony Alpha A57 with settings of DRO Off (upper left), DRO Auto (upper right), DRO Level 3 (lower left), and DRO Level 5.

When using the in-camera HDR feature, whether you use the Auto setting or a specific exposure interval, you should use a tripod or other solid support, and your subject should be a non-moving one. The camera will be taking three shots, and you don't want there to be significant differences between the three views of the scene. Also, note that the Auto HDR feature, like DRO processing, is not available when shooting RAW images.

HDR in Post-Processing

While my goal in this book is to show you how to take great photos *in the camera* rather than how to fix your errors in Photoshop, the Merge to HDR Pro feature in Adobe Photoshop and Photoshop Elements is too cool to ignore. Using this tool, you can usually get much better HDR results than you can with the A57's in-camera HDR feature.

The ability to have a bracketed set of exposures that are identical except for exposure is key to getting good results with this feature, which allows you to produce images with a full, rich dynamic range that includes a level of detail in the highlights and shadows that is almost impossible to achieve with digital cameras. In contrasty lighting situations, even the A57 has a tendency to blow out highlights when you expose solely for the shadows or midtones.

Suppose you wanted to photograph a dimly lit room that had a bright window showing an outdoors scene. Proper exposure for the room might be on the order of 1/60th second at f/2.8 at ISO 200, while the outdoors scene probably would require f/11 at 1/400th second. That's almost a 7 EV step difference (approximately 7 f/stops) and well beyond the dynamic range of any digital camera, including the A57.

When you're using Merge to HDR Pro, you'd take four pictures, one for the shadows, one for the highlights, and perhaps two for the midtones. (You could also take more than four pictures, but for this example, I'm going to assume you're working with just four.) Then, you'd use the Merge to HDR Pro command to combine all of the images into one HDR image that integrates the well-exposed sections of each version. Because the A57 allows you to take only *three* bracketed images, and with no more than 0.7EV difference between them, you'll need to adjust your exposures manually. (The Auto HDR feature does allow up to 6 steps between just three exposures, but is less versatile than doing HDR manually.)

The images should be as identical as possible, except for exposure. So, it's a good idea to mount the A57 on a tripod, use a remote release, and take all the exposures one after another. Just follow these steps:

1. **Set up the camera.** Mount the A57 on a tripod.
2. **Set the camera for Manual exposure.** Use the mode dial to select Manual exposure.

3. **Choose an f/stop.** Select an aperture that will provide a correct exposure at your initial manual settings for the series of manually bracketed shots. *And then leave this adjustment alone!* You don't want the aperture to change for your series, as that would change the depth-of-field. You want to adjust exposure *only* with the shutter speed.
4. **Choose a shutter speed for the initial exposure.** For this exercise, we'll be shooting four different bracketed exposures, so set the shutter speed such that the image will be two stops underexposed. If necessary, take a test shot to find the "correct" exposure and adjust from there.
5. **Choose manual focus.** You don't want the focus to change between shots, so set the A57 to manual focus, and carefully focus your shot.
6. **Choose RAW exposures.** Set the camera to take RAW files, which will give you the widest range of tones in your images.
7. **Take the first shot.** Press the button on the remote (or carefully press the shutter release) and take the first exposure, which will be two stops underexposed.
8. **Adjust shutter speed to give one stop more exposure.** For example, if your first shot was at 1/500th second at f/11, *gently* change to 1/250th second.
9. **Take the second shot.** Press the button on the remote or press the shutter release and take the second exposure, which will be one stop underexposed.
10. **Repeat steps 8 and 9 twice more.** Create exposures at the metered exposure and one stop overexposed. You'll end up with a set of photos like those shown in Figure 6.16.
11. **Continue with the Merge to HDR Pro steps listed next.** You can also use a different program, such as Photomatix, if you know how to use it. Note that these steps could also be carried out using Aperture priority, and rotating the right control dial to provide exposure compensation over the same range. I find manual bracketing to be just as fast.

The next steps show you how to combine the separate exposures into one merged high dynamic range image. The sample images in Figure 6.16 show the results you can get from a four-shot bracketed sequence.

1. **Copy your images to your computer.** If you use an application to transfer the files to your computer, make sure it does not make any adjustments to brightness, contrast, or exposure. You want the real raw information for Merge to HDR Pro to work with.
2. **Activate Merge to HDR Pro.** Choose File > Automate > Merge to HDR Pro.

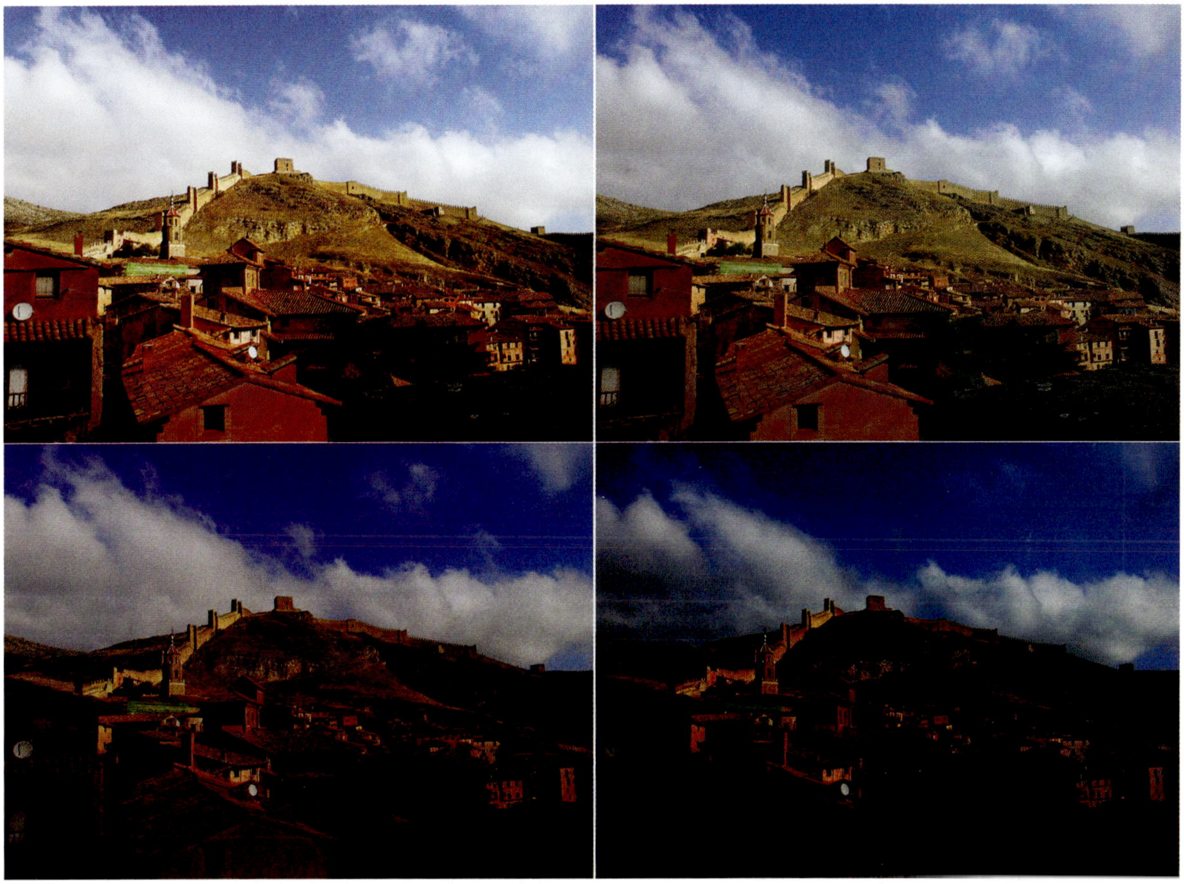

Figure 6.16 Your bracketed photos should look like this.

3. **Select the photos to be merged.** Use the Browse feature to locate and select your photos to be merged. You'll note a checkbox that can be used to automatically align the images if they were not taken with the camera mounted on a rock-steady support. This will adjust for any slight movement of the camera that might have occurred when you changed exposure settings.
4. **Choose parameters (optional).** The first time you use Merge to HDR Pro, you can let the program work with its default parameters. Once you've played with the feature a few times, you can read the Adobe help files and learn more about the options than I can present in this non-software-oriented camera guide. (See Figure 6.17.)
5. **Click OK.** The merger begins.
6. **Save.** Once HDR merge has done its thing, save the file to your computer.

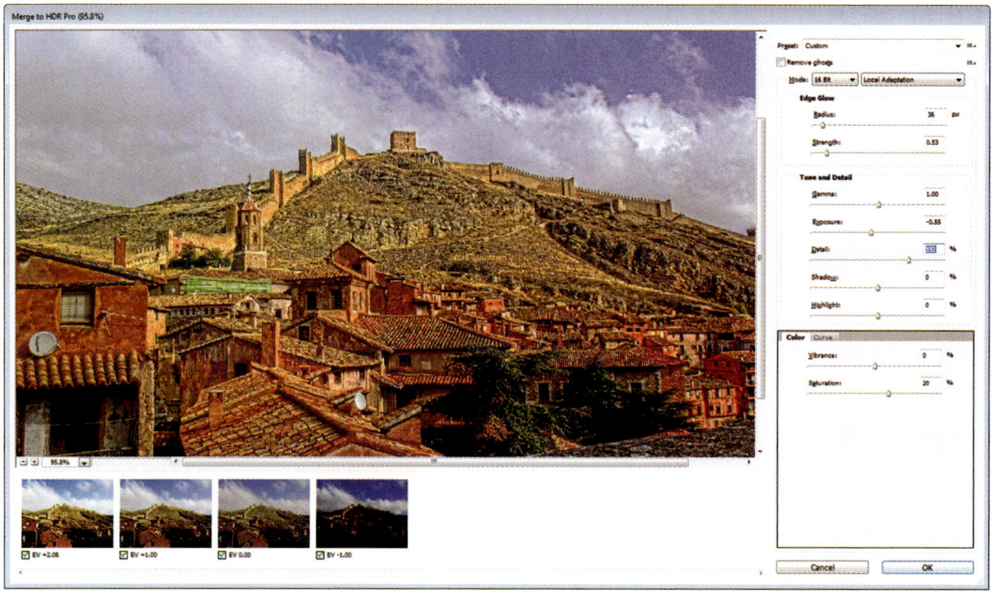

Figure 6.17
Use the Merge to HDR Pro command in Photoshop or Photoshop Elements to combine the four images.

If you do everything correctly, you'll end up with a photo like the one shown in Figure 6.18, which has the properly exposed foreground of the first shot, and the well-exposed rocks of the second and third images. Note that, ideally, nothing should move between shots.

What if you don't have the opportunity, inclination, or skills to create several images at different exposures, as described? If you shoot in RAW format, you can still use Merge to HDR, working with a *single* original image file. What you do is import the image into Photoshop several times, using Adobe Camera Raw to create multiple copies of the file at different exposure levels.

For example, you'd create one copy that's too dark, so the shadows lose detail, but the highlights are preserved. Create another copy with the shadows intact and allow the highlights to wash out. Then, you can use Merge to HDR to combine the two and end up with a finished image that has the extended dynamic range you're looking for. (This concludes the image-editing portion of the chapter. We now return you to our alternate sponsor: photography.)

Using Creative Styles

This option, found in the Function menu, gives you six different combinations of contrast, saturation, and sharpness: Standard, Vivid, Portrait, Landscape, Sunset, and B/W (black-and-white). Those are useful enough that you should make them a part of your everyday toolkit. You can apply Creative Styles *only* when you are not using one of the

Figure 6.18
You'll end up with an extended dynamic range photo like this one.

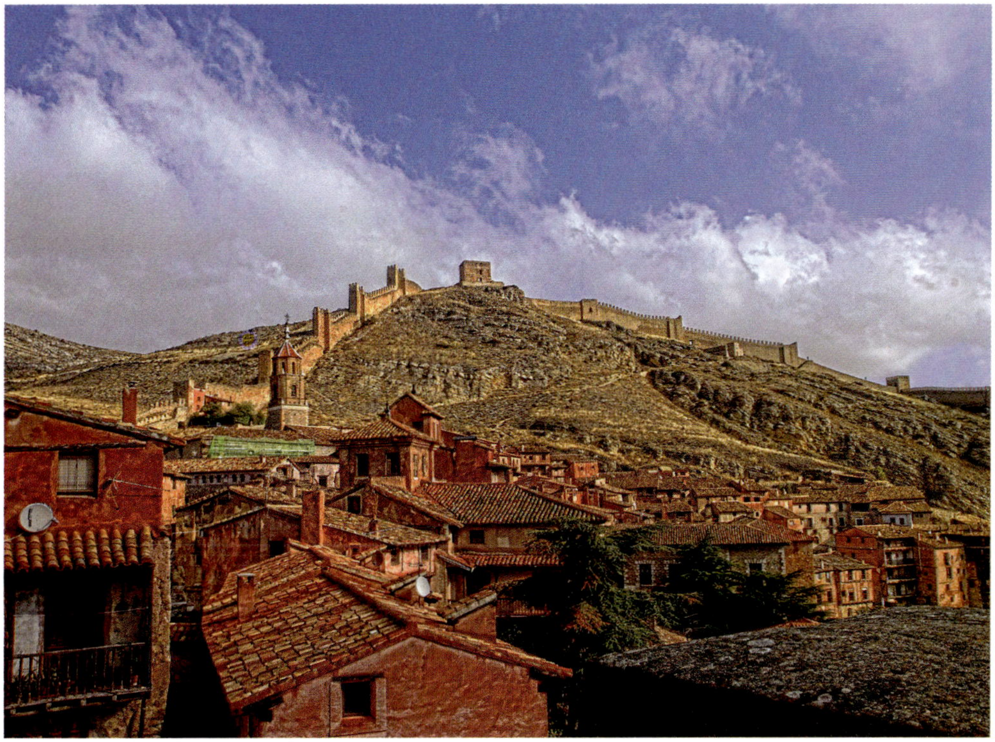

Alpha's Auto or Scene modes. (That is, you're shooting in Program, Aperture priority, Shutter priority, or Manual exposure mode.) But wait, as they say, there's more. When working with Creative Styles, you can *adjust* those parameters within each preset option to fine-tune the rendition. First, look at the "stock" creative styles:

- **Standard.** This is, as you might expect, your default setting, with a good compromise of sharpness, color saturation, and contrast. Choose this, and your photos will have excellent colors, a broad range of tonal values, and standard sharpness that avoids the "oversharpened" look that some digital pictures acquire.
- **Vivid.** If you want more punch in your images, with richer colors, heightened contrast that makes those colors stand out, and moderate sharpness, this setting is for you. It's good for flowers, seaside photos, any picture with expanses of blue sky, and on overcast days where a punchier image can relieve the dullness.
- **Portrait.** Unless you're photographing a clown, you don't want overly vivid colors in your portraits. Nor do you need lots of contrast to emphasize facial flaws and defects. This setting provides realistic, muted skin tones, and a softer look that flatters your subjects.

- **Landscape.** As with the Vivid setting, this option boosts saturation and contrast to give you rich scenery and purple mountain majesties, even when your subject matter is located far enough from your camera that distant haze might otherwise be a problem. There's extra sharpness, too, to give you added crispness when you're shooting Fall colors.
- **Sunset.** Accentuates the red tones found in sunrise and sunset pictures.
- **B/W.** If you're shooting black-and-white photos in the camera, this setting allows you to change the contrast and sharpness (only).

To customize any of these settings, after you press the Fn button, choose Creative Styles from the right-hand column of the Fn menu, highlight the style you want to change, and press the right direction key to move over to the "business" side of the menu, at the bottom of the right side of the LCD screen. Then, use the left/right controller keys to choose from (left to right) contrast, saturation, and sharpness. With the parameter you want to modify highlighted, press the up/down controller keys or turn the control dial to change the values up to three increments higher or lower than normal. (See Figure 6.19.)

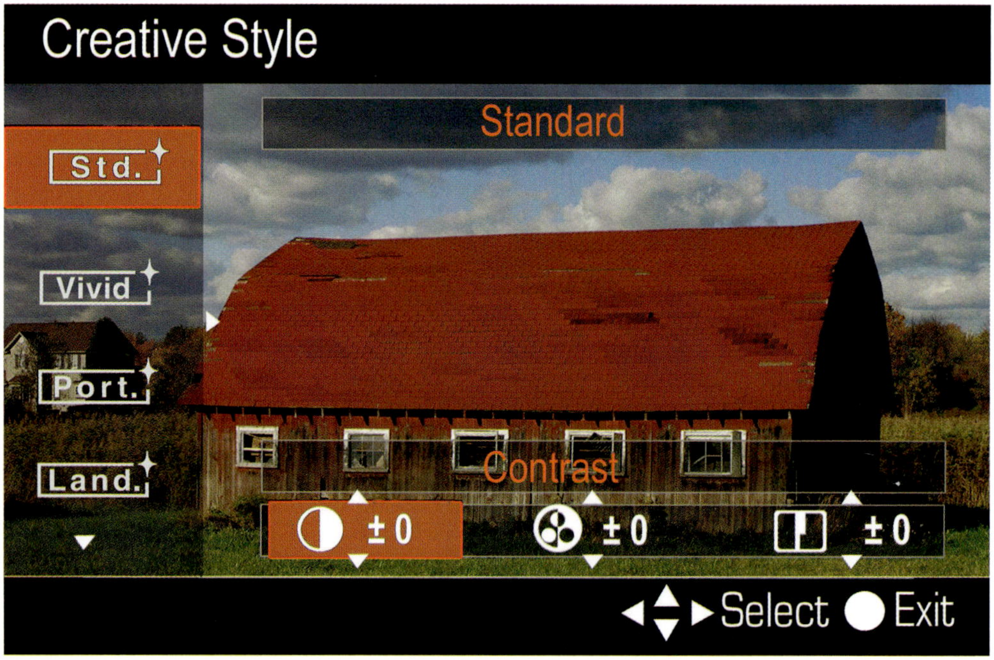

Figure 6.19
You can customize the sharpness, contrast, and color saturation of any of the six Creative Styles.

Here is a summary of how the parameters you can change with Creative Styles affect your images:

- **Sharpness.** Increases or decreases the contrast of the edge outlines in your image, making the photo appear more or less sharp, depending on whether you've selected 0 (no sharpening), +3 (extra sharpening), to –3 (softening). Remember that boosting sharpness also increases the overall contrast of an image, so you'll want to use this parameter in conjunction with the contrast parameter with caution.
- **Contrast.** Compresses the range of tones in an image (increase contrast from 0 to +3) or expands the range of tones (from 0 to –3) to decrease contrast. Higher contrast images tend to lose detail in both shadows and highlights, while lower contrast images retain the detail but appear more flat and have less snap.
- **Color saturation.** You can adjust the richness of the color from low saturation (0 to –3) to high saturation (0 to +3). Lower saturation produces a muted look that can be more realistic for certain kinds of subjects, such as humans. Higher saturation produces a more vibrant appearance, but can be garish and unrealistic if carried too far. Boost your saturation if you want a vivid image, or to brighten up pictures taken on overcast days. As I noted, this setting cannot be changed for the B/W Creative Style.

Picture Effects

All the Picture Effects modes perform significant image processing on your photos before saving them to the memory card. Picture Effects cannot be used when shooting RAW or RAW & JPEG; Soft Focus, HDR Painting, Rich-Tone Monochrome, and Miniature cannot be used when shooting movies. Your choices available when you press the Picture Effect position on the control button include:

- **Toy Camera.** Produces images like you might get with a Diana or Holga "plastic" camera, with vignetted corners, image blurring, and bright, saturated colors.
- **Pop Color.** This setting adds a lot of saturation to the colors, making them especially vivid and rich looking. When used with subjects that have a lot of bright colors, the effect can be dramatic. Duller subjects gain a more "normal" appearance (try using this setting on an overcast day to see what I mean).
- **Posterization.** This option produces a vivid, high-contrast image that emphasizes the primary colors (as shown in Figure 6.20), or in black-and-white, with a reduced number of tones, creating a poster effect.
- **Retro Photo.** Adds a faded photo look to the image, with sepia overtones.
- **Soft High Key.** Produces bright images.

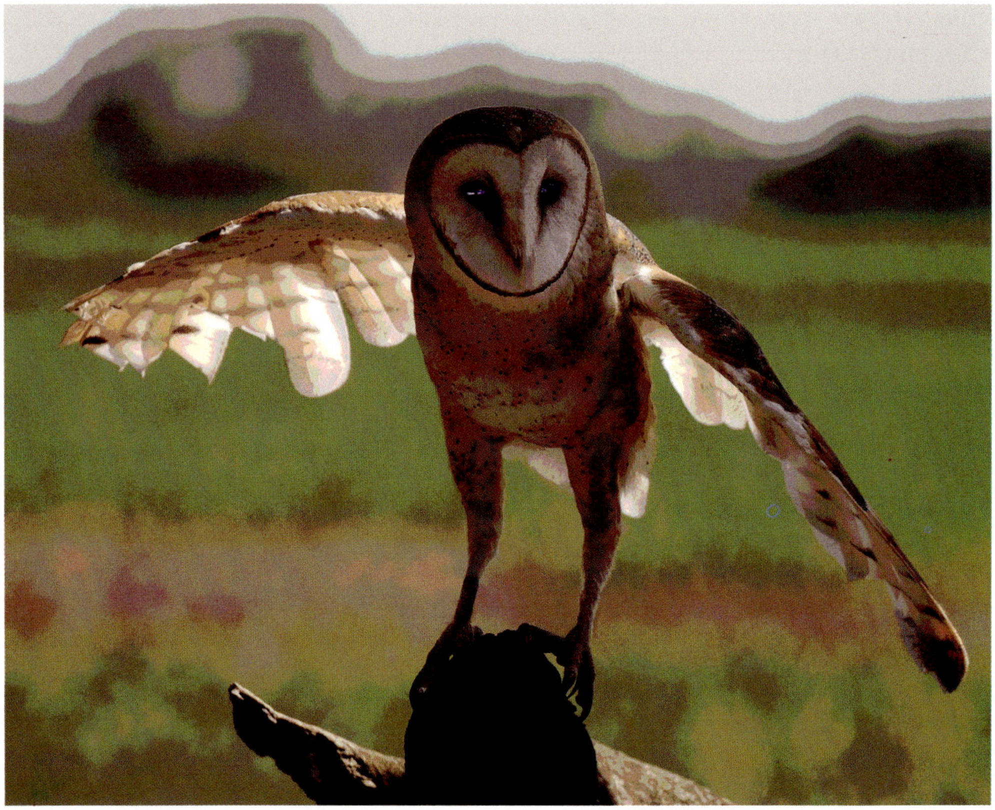

Figure 6.20
Posterization effect.

- **Partial Color.** Attempts to retain the selected color of an image, while converting other hues to black-and-white. Use the left/right control buttons to select a color, from red, green, blue, or yellow. (See Figure 6.21.)
- **High contrast monochrome.** Converts the image to black-and-white and boosts the contrast to give a stark look to the image.
- **Soft Focus.** Creates a soft, blurry effect. Use the left/right control buttons to choose low, mid, or high intensity.
- **HDR Painting.** Produces a painted look by taking three pictures consecutively and then using HDR techniques to enhance color and details. The Option button allows specifying the intensity of the effect (low, mid, high).
- **Rich-tone monochrome.** Also uses HDR processes to create a long-gradation image from three consecutive exposures.
- **Miniature.** You select the area to be rendered in sharp focus using the left/right control buttons. You can select from horizontal areas (top, middle, bottom) or vertical sections (left, middle, right) or choose Auto. The effect is similar to the tilt-shift look used to photograph craft models. (See Figure 6.22.)

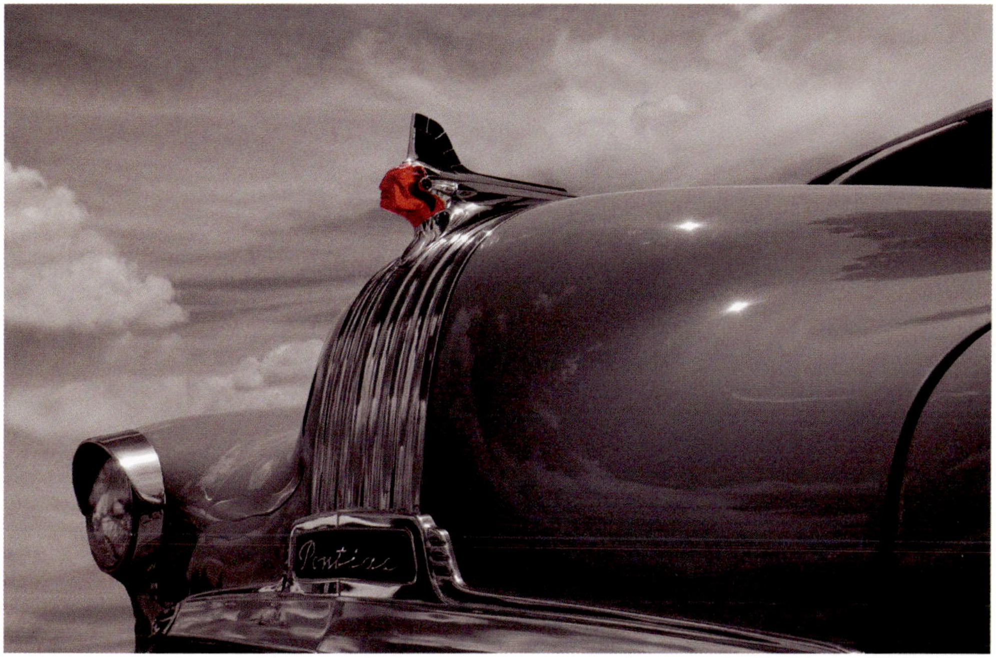

Figure 6.21
Partial Color effect.

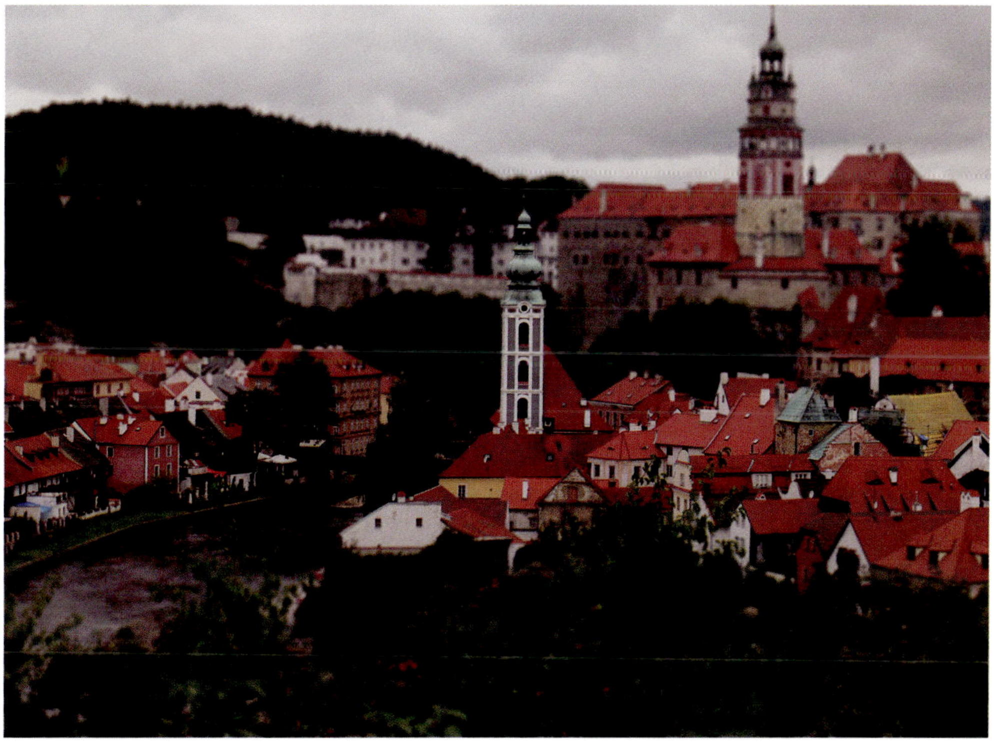

Figure 6.22
Miniature effect.

Wi-Fi

These days, GPS and Wi-Fi capabilities work together with your A57 in interesting new ways. Wireless capabilities allow you to upload photos directly from your A57 to your computer at home or in your studio, or, through a hotspot at your hotel or coffee shop back to your home computer or to a photo sharing service like Facebook or Flickr. A special Wi-Fi-enabled memory card that you slip in the SD slot of your camera performs the magic. GPS capabilities—built right into some of those Wi-Fi cards—allow you to mark your photographs with location information, so you don't have to guess where a picture was taken.

Both capabilities are very cool. Wi-Fi uploads can provide instant backup of important shots and sharing. And, as noted in the previous section, geotagging is most important as a way to associate the geographical location where the photographer was when a picture was taken, with the actual photograph itself. It can be done with the location-mapping capabilities of the Wi-Fi card, or through add-on devices that third parties make available for your A57.

A relatively affordable solution is offered by Eye-Fi (www.eye.fi). The Eye-Fi card (see Figure 6.23) is an SDHC memory card with a wireless transmitter built in. You insert it in your camera just as with any ordinary card, and then specify which networks to use. You can add as many as 32 different networks. The next time your camera is on within range of a specified network, your photos and videos can be uploaded to your computer and/or to your favorite sharing site. During setup, you can customize where you want your images uploaded. The Eye-Fi card will only send them to the computer and to the sharing site you choose. Upload to any of 25 popular sharing websites, including Flickr, Facebook, MobileMe, Costco, Adorama, Smugmug, YouTube, Shutterfly, or Walmart. Online Sharing is included as a lifetime, unlimited service with all X2 cards.

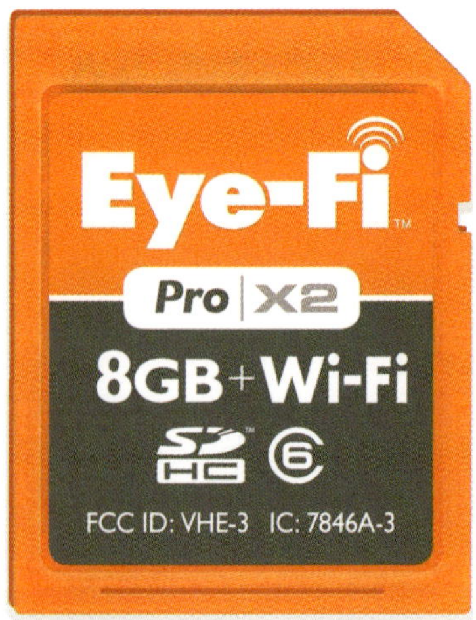

Figure 6.23
The Eye-Fi card is an SD card with built-in Wi-Fi features.

When uploading to online sites, you can specify not just where your images are sent, but how they are organized, by specifying preset album names, tags, descriptions, and even privacy preferences on certain sharing sites. Some Eye-Fi cards also include geotagging service, which help you view uploaded photos on a map, and sort them by location. Eye-Fi's geotagging uses Wi-Fi Positioning System (WPS) technology. Using built-in Wi-Fi, the Eye-Fi card senses surrounding Wi-Fi networks as you take pictures. When photos are uploaded, the Eye-Fi service then adds the geotags to your photos. You don't need to have the password or a subscription for the Wi-Fi networks the card accesses; it can grab the location information directly without the need to "log in." You don't need to set up or control the Eye-Fi card from your camera. Software on your computer manages all the parameters. (See Figure 6.24.)

Your A57 has an Upload Settings entry in the Setup 2 menu (it appears when a Wi-Fi card is inserted) that allows you to enable or disable this capability. You'll want to turn off Eye-Fi when traveling on an airplane (just as you disable your cell phone, tablet, or laptop's wireless capabilities when required to do so). In addition, use of Wi-Fi cards may be restricted or banned outside the United States, because the telecommunications laws differ in other countries.

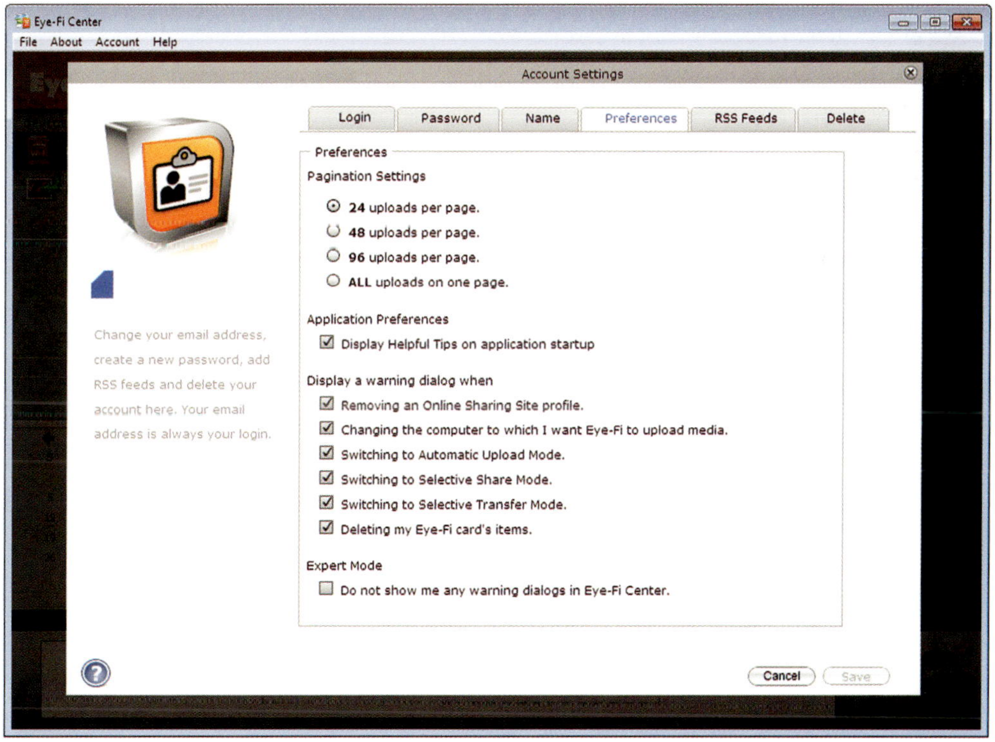

Figure 6.24
Functions of the Eye-Fi card can be controlled from your computer.

If you frequently travel outside the range of your home (or business) Wi-Fi network, an optional service called Hotspot Access is available, allowing you to connect to any AT&T Wi-Fi hotspot in the USA. In addition, you can use your own Wi-Fi accounts from commercial network providers, your city, even organizations you belong to such as your university.

The card has another interesting feature called Endless Memory. When pictures have been safely uploaded to an external site, the card can be set to automatically erase the oldest images to free up space for new pictures. You choose the threshold where the card starts zapping your old pictures to make room.

Eye-Fi currently offers several models, including basic versions for about $50, which can be used to transmit your photos from the dSLR to a computer on your home network (or any other network you set up somewhere, say, at a family reunion). You can also upload your images from your camera through your computer network directly to websites and digital printing services already mentioned. The most sophisticated option is Eye-Fi Pro X2, an 8GB SDHC card that adds geographic location labels to your photo (so you'll know where you took it), and frees you from your own computer network by allowing uploads from more than 10,000 Wi-Fi hotspots around the USA. Very cool, and the ultimate in picture backup.

Tablets, Smart Phones, and the Sony SLT-A57

Although tablets and smart phones are still in their infancies, in the future, your iPhone, iPad/tablet computer, iPod Touch/MP3 player, smart phone, or Google Android portable device will be one of the most important accessories you can have for your A57 (or other) digital camera. We're only now seeing the beginnings of the trend. The relevant platforms are these:

- **Old-style smart phones.** I include in this category all smart phones that are *not* iPhones or phones based on Google's Android operating system. You can buy lots of interesting apps for these phones, although not many applications specifically for photography. This type of phone should be on its way out, too, with iPhone and Android smart phones dominating, simply because it's easier to write applications for the iPhone's iOS and Android than to create them for multiple "old" smart phone platforms.
- **Android smart phones.** There are already more Android-based smart phones on the market than for all other types, including iOS. Although Apple had a head start, the number of Android applications is rapidly catching up.
- **iPhones.** It might sound strange to say that the skyrocketing sales of iPhones has been held in check, but it's true. The real or imagined short-comings of AT&T's

data network—which only got worse as more users grabbed iPhones—have kept many from switching to the iOS platform. The difficulties may even have contributed to the rapid growth of Android-based phones, which have been offered by Verizon and other suppliers seen as having "better" communications networks. Even so, iOS leads in number of applications, especially for photography apps. When my first app was developed, it appeared for the iOS platform first.

- **iPod Touch.** Basically, the latest iPod Touch is an iPhone that can't make phone calls. (Although there are some hacks around that limitation.) Virtually all of the apps that run on the iPhone under iOS also run on the iPod Touch. You need a Wi-Fi connection to access features that use network capabilities, but, these days, Wi-Fi hot spots aren't that difficult to find. Tethering and Mi-Fi (which allow another device to serve as a hot spot for non-connected gadgets like the Touch), and *automobiles* that include built-in Wi-Fi (!) make connectivity almost universal. In my travels through Europe in the last year, I found free Wi-Fi connections in the smallest towns. (Indeed, the only time I was asked to pay for it was when staying in an upscale hotel.) So, for many who are tied to a non-iPhone cell phone, the iPod Touch is a viable alternative.
- **Tablet computers.** I've been welded to my iPad (shown alongside my iPhone in Figure 6.25) since I bought it the first day they became available. I use them to access e-mail, useful apps, and as a portable portfolio. Today, there are alternative tablet computers running Android. I recently picked up an Amazon Kindle Fire, which also does e-mail and a limited number of apps, and which has a Gallery feature (see Figure 6.26) that transforms it onto a compact portfolio almost as useful for that purpose as an iPad. (However, only 6 of the Kindle Fire's 8GB of storage are available to the user, so you'll have to limit the size of your portfolio.)

I use the Kindle Fire and both an iPhone and iPad. (If I'm traveling overseas where my iPhone can't be used, I usually take along the iPod Touch instead.) The iPhone/iPod slips in a pocket and can be used anywhere. I don't even have to think about taking it with me, because I always have one or the other. I have to remember to tote along the iPad or Kindle Fire, and, I do, to an extent you'd probably find surprising. (After the movie finally starts in the theater, I fold them into their cases and use them as a tray for my popcorn bucket.) Tablet computers can do everything a pocket-sized device can do, and are easier to read/view/type on. When I am out shooting, I prefer to have all my apps in a smaller device that I can slip in the camera bag, but if there's room, the iPad goes along instead. Because my iPad (unlike the Kindle Fire) has 3G connectivity, I don't need a Wi-Fi connection to use it almost anywhere. I do have a Wi-Fi hot spot built into my iPhone that I can use to connect the Kindle Fire to the net if I need to.

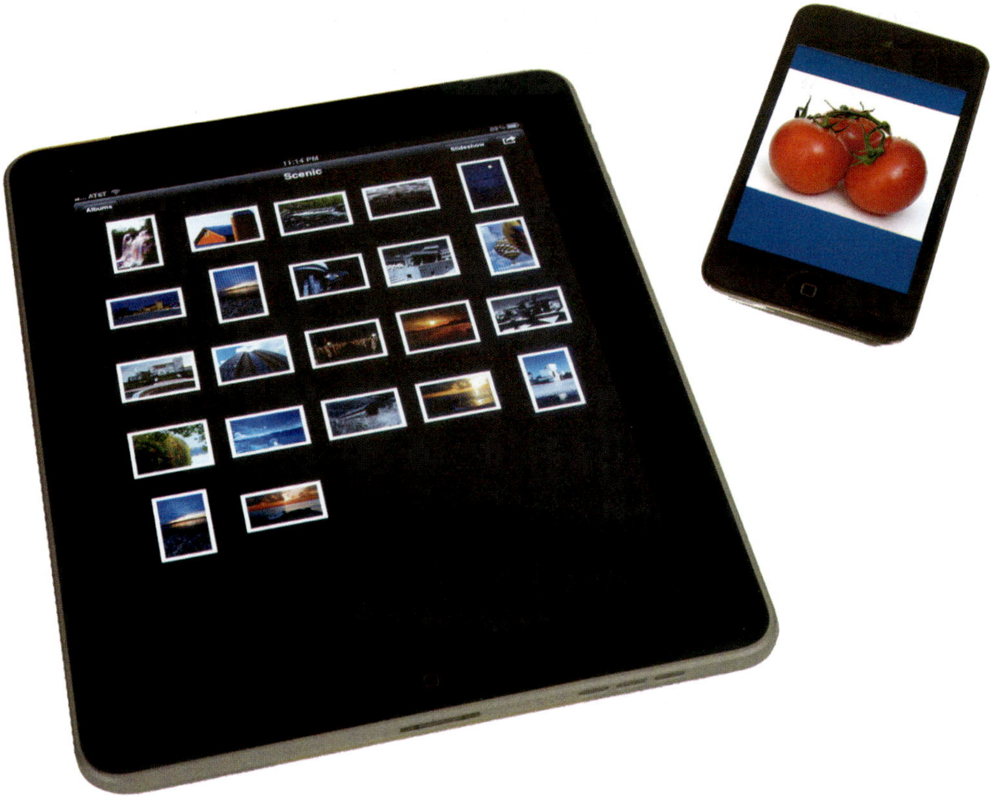

Figure 6.25
The iPad, iPod, and other devices open a whole world of useful apps to the photographer.

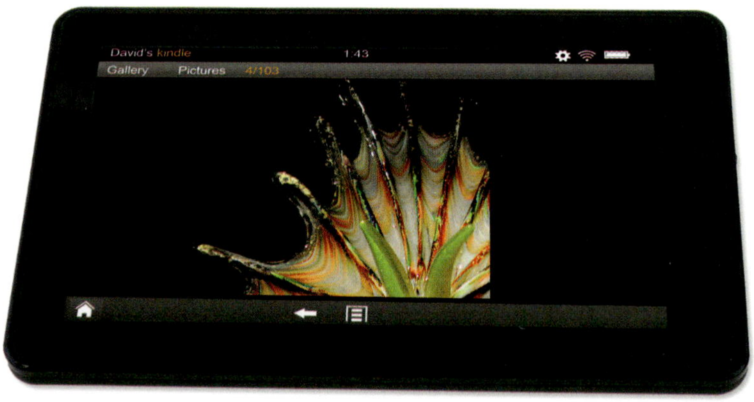

Figure 6.26
The Kindle Fire is a smaller, more affordable alternative to the iPad.

What Else Can You Do with Them?

Many of these devices can serve as a backup for your A57's memory cards. I've got Apple's camera connection kit, and can offload my pictures to my iPad's 64GB of memory, then upload them to Flickr or Facebook, or send to anyone through e-mail. My iPad also makes a perfect portable portfolio, too. I have hundreds of photos stored on mine, arranged into albums ready for instant display, either individually or in slide shows. I have the same photo library on my iPhone and iPod Touch, and more than a few pictures available for showing on my Kindle Fire.

But the real potential for using these devices comes from specialized apps written specifically to serve photographic needs. Here are some of the kinds of apps you can expect in the future. (I'm working on more than a few of them myself.)

- **Camera guides.** Even the rotten manual that came with your camera is too large to carry around in your camera bag all day. I'm converting many of my own camera-specific guides to app form, while adding interactive elements, including hyperlinks and videos. You can already put a PDF version of your camera manual on your portable device and read it, if you like. In the future, you should be able to read any of the more useful third-party guides anywhere, anytime.
- **Lens selector.** Wonder what's the best lens to use in a specific situation? Enter information about your scene, and your app will advise you.
- **Exposure estimator.** Choose a situation and the estimated exposure will be provided. Useful as a reality check and in difficult situations, such as fireworks, where the camera's meters may falter.
- **Shutter speed advisor.** The correct shutter speed for a scene varies depending on whether you want to freeze action, or add a little blur to express motion. Other variables include whether the subject is crossing the frame, moving diagonally, or headed toward you. The photographer also needs to consider the focal length of the lens, and presence/absence of image-stabilization features, tripod, monopod, etc. This app will allow you to tap in all the factors and receive advice about what shutter speed to use.
- **Hyperfocal length calculator.** In any given situation, set the focus point at the distance specified for your lens's current focal length setting, and everything from half that distance to infinity will be in focus. But the right setting differs at various focal lengths. This app tells you, and is a great tool for grab shots.
- **Accessory selector.** Confused about what flash, remote control, battery grip, lens hood, filter, or other accessory to use with your camera or lens? This selector lists the key gadgets, which ones fit which cameras, and explains how to use them.

- **Before and after.** Images showing before/after versions of dozens of situations with and without corrective/in-camera special effects applied.
- **Fill light.** Pesky shadows on faces from overhead lighting indoors? This turns your iPod/iPhone or (best of all) iPad into a bright, diffuse fill light panel. Choose from white fill light, or *colors* for special effects. Makes good illumination for viewing your camera's buttons and dials in dark locations, too. Some of these apps use the iPhone's flash for an especially bright light.
- **Gray card.** Turn your i-device into an 18-percent gray card for metering and color balance.
- **Super links.** If you don't find your answer in the Toolkit, you can link to websites, including mine, with more information.
- **How It's Made.** A collection of inspiring photos, with details on how they were taken in camera—or manipulated in Photoshop (if that's your thing).
- **Quickie guides.** Small apps that lead you, step-by-step, through everything you need to photograph lots of different types of scenes. Typical subjects would be sports, landscape photography, macro work, portraits, concerts/performances, flowers, wildlife, and nature.

As you can see, the potential for apps is virtually unlimited. You can expect your smart phone, tablet computer, or other device to be a mainstay in your camera bag within a very short time.

7

Shooting Movies

As we've seen in our exploration of its features so far, the Sony Alpha SLT-A57 is superbly equipped for taking still photographs of very high quality in a wide variety of shooting environments. But this camera's superior level of performance is not limited to stills. The Alpha SLT camera is capable in the movie-making arena as well. So, even though you may have bought your Alpha primarily for shooting stationary scenes, you acquired a device that is equipped with a cutting-edge set of features for recording high-quality video clips. It can record high-definition (HD) video with stereo sound, and it is quite versatile in its feature set. Whether you're looking to record informal clips of the family on vacation, the latest viral video for YouTube, or a set of scenes that will be painstakingly crafted into a cinematic masterpiece using editing software, the Alpha SLT-A57 will perform admirably.

When you set out to record video with the Alpha SLT, remember that, although a large memory card, such as a 16GB SDHC card, can hold about two hours of the highest-quality (AVCHD) video, the camera is limited in its ability to record continuous movie sequences. With SteadyShot turned off, the camera can record about 29 minutes of video continuously. The maximum movie file size is 2GB, though, and the camera will stop if that limit is reached while recording an MP4 file. If the camera is recording an AVCHD file, it will create a new file automatically when the 2GB limit is reached. Note that the maximum movie length may vary depending on ambient temperature and camera settings. Your movie recording time may be reduced if you're shooting in a hot environment. The A57's SteadyShot feature also can cause the sensor to heat up, which is why Sony includes the option to turn image stabilization on and off separately for stills and movie shooting.

Some Fundamentals

Recording a video with the Sony Alpha SLT-A57 is extraordinarily easy to accomplish—just press the prominent red button at the upper right of the camera's back to start, and press it again to stop. As explained in Chapter 3, you can set the camera (in the Custom 3 menu) so that the MOVIE button *always* activates movie shooting, regardless of what shooting mode you're using, or *only* initiates video capture when the mode dial is set to the Movie position. Your preference may be that you prefer to avoid accidentally shoot movies (use "Movie Mode Only") or have movie shooting available for spur-of-the-moment capture (use "Always" mode).

Before you press that button, though, there are some settings to prepare the camera to record the scene the way you want it to. Setting up the camera for recording video can be a bit tricky, because it's not immediately obvious, either from the camera's menus or from Sony's manuals, which settings apply to video recording and which do not. I will unravel that mystery for you, and throw in a few other tips to help improve your movies.

I'll show you how to optimize your settings before you start shooting video, but here are some considerations to be aware of as you get started. Many of these points will be covered in more detail later in this chapter:

- **Use the right card.** You'll want to use an SD or SDHC card with Class 6 or higher speed; if you use a slower card, like a Class 4 or especially Class 2, the recording may stop after a minute or two. Choose a memory card with at least 4GB capacity; 8GB or 16GB are even better. If you're going to be recording a lot of HD video, that could be a good reason to take advantage of the ability to use SDXC cards of 64GB capacity. Just make sure your memory card reader is SDXC compatible and your computer can read the files from that type of card. I've standardized on fast Class 6 or Class 10 16GB SDHC cards when I'm shooting movies; one of these cards will hold at least three hours of video. However, the camera cannot shoot a continuous movie scene for more than 29 minutes. You can start shooting the next clip right away, though, missing only about 30 seconds of the action. Of course that assumes there's enough space on your memory card and adequate battery power.

  One aspect that doesn't always occur to new movie shooters is that the capacity of the card matters only with respect to the number and length of video clips you intend to shoot. Larger cards let you capture more and longer sequences. You don't need to upgrade the size of your card because you've upgraded the resolution of your camera. A 16-megapixel SLT-A57 and a 24-megapixel SLT-A65 or A77 *all* record full HD movies using the exact same 1920 × 1080-pixel resolution. The upscale models may outperform your A57 in other respects, but when it comes to HD movie making, the playing field is level.

WHY THE 29-MINUTE LIMITATION?

Vendors are really cagey about revealing the reason for the seemingly arbitrary/non-arbitrary 29 minute, 59 second limitation on the length of a single video clip—not only with Sony still cameras, but with other brands as well. So, various theories have emerged.

- The sensor will overheat when you shoot continuously. In a camera like the SLT-A57, the sensor is active virtually all the time the camera is being used to view or capture images, so that idea doesn't hold water. Plus, you can shoot one 29-minute clip, then immediately begin another one. Thermal protection seems to be a problem only when shooting in high ambient temperatures, or when features like SteadyShot give the sensor mechanism an extra workout.
- The European Union classifies cameras that capture clips longer than 29 minutes, 59 seconds as camcorders and subject them to higher duties. Informal talks are underway to remove this limitation in the World Trade Organization's Information Technology Agreement—but don't hold your breath.
- The FAT32 file format limits the size of video clips to 4GB, and the FAT16 file format (used in pre-SDHC memory cards) had a 2GB limitation. My 64GB SDXC card allows files of up to 2 terabytes in size, but when I insert one into my SLT-A57, I still can't exceed 29 minutes, 59 seconds.
- Theories aside, the only people who want to shoot clips longer than 30 minutes are the proud parents who plop the SLT-A57 down on a tripod and capture an entire Spring Pageant or high school musical. Those who want to go beyond camcorder ennui will shoot segments of only a few seconds each and, perhaps, piece them together into an effective production using easy-to-master editing software.

- **Add an external mic.** For the best sound quality, and to avoid picking up the sound of the autofocus motor, get an external stereo mic. If you get a Sony microphone, like the ECM-ALST1, it will slide right into the non-standard Sony/Minolta accessory shoe on top of the camera and can be plugged into the A57's microphone jack. Other brands will require an adapter to mount onto the accessory shoe. I'll have more advice about capturing sound later in this chapter.
- **Minimize zooming.** While it's great to be able to use the zoom for filling the frame with a distant subject, think twice before zooming during the shot. Unless you are using an external mic, the sound of the zoom ring being spun will be picked up and it will be audible when you play a movie. Any more than the occasional minor zoom will be very distracting to friends who watch your videos. And digital zoom will definitely degrade image quality. Don't use the digital zoom if quality is more important than recording a specific subject such as a famous movie star far from a distance.

- **Use a fully charged battery.** A fresh battery will allow about one hour of filming at normal (non-Winter) temperatures, but that can be shorter if there are many focus adjustments. Individual clips can be no longer than 29 minutes, however.
- **Keep it cool.** Video quality can suffer terribly when the imaging sensor gets hot so keep the camera in a cool place. When shooting on hot days especially, the sensor can get hot more quickly than usual; when there's a risk of overheating, the camera will stop recording and it will shut down about five seconds later. Give it time to cool down before using it again.
- **Press the Movie button.** You don't have to hold it down. Press it again when you're done to stop recording.

Preparing to Shoot Video

Before you start, you'll want to review the special movie settings first discussed in Chapter 3. These options are as follows.

File Format

The file format is the type of video file you capture and store on your memory card. Your choice of file format affects image quality, image characteristics, and, potentially, your editing and output options. Your choices in the Movie 1 menu's File Format listings include only AVCHD 60i/60p (the default), or MP4. Outside North America and other countries that use the NTSC video system, you may see AVCDH 50i/60p offered instead.

The AVCHD format is the highest quality option available with the A57, and produces movies recorded at 1920 × 1080 pixels, with five additional choices of size/quality selected in the Record Setting menu entry, described next. If you select MP4, you have two choices of image size, 1440 × 1080 and 640 × 480 pixels, both of lower image quality.

OKAY, WHAT'S AVCHD?

Even if you're not new to movie making, the video format known as AVCHD (Advanced Video Coding High Definition) may be unknown to you. The format was developed by Sony and Panasonic for use in producing high-definition video for both professional and consumer use. It uses the MPEG-4 AVC/H.264 (AVC) standard for video compression, which may be familiar to those with some video-shooting experience. It supports a variety of resolutions and scanning methods (I'll explain those in more detail later in this chapter), and can be used to produce Blu-ray, AVCHD, and DVD-Video discs using the supplied PMB (Picture Motion Browser) software, assuming you have compatible recording and playback equipment, as described in a later section.

Record Setting

Here you'll select the image quality of your 60i/60p and MP4 movies, and, with AVCHD video, the type of scanning used—either progressive scan or interlaced scan. (See the sections which follow for an explanation of the difference between the two.) For AVCHD video, your five choices for 1920 × 1080 (full HD movies) include:

- **60i 24M (FX).** This setting produces high-quality video, but also puts stiffest demands on your memory card and, when editing, on your computer equipment. It records movies at a 24 megabits per second rate with 60 interlaced fields (30 odd-numbered fields alternating with 30 even-numbered fields) recorded per second. (The section which follows explains interlacing and fields.) You can use this setting if you have a fast SD card, preferably Class 10 or better.
- **60i 17M (FH).** This default setting produces standard image quality video at a slightly less demanding 17Mbps recording rate, with 60 interlaced fields recorded per second. You'll want to use this setting most of the time.
- **60p 28M (PS).** This setting produces the highest quality video at a 28Mbps recording rate, and uses *progressive scan*, which captures all the horizontal lines in an image in the correct order, 60 times per second.
- **24p 24M (FX).** This setting captures high-quality video at a rate of 24 fields/frames per second, captured progressively at a 24Mbps capture rate, and is said to produce the most cinema-like appearance in the final movie image. I'll explain why this is important shortly.
- **24p 17M (FH).** This setting captures standard quality cinema-style video at 24fps with a 17Mbps capture rate.

You might elect to use the MP4 file format instead to produce AVC movies if your video requirements are not as demanding, and you don't plan on creating a playable disc using the supplied PMB software. You can select either of two image qualities, both of which use progressive scanning:

- **1440 × 1080 12M.** This option provides medium-quality video that may be good enough for many applications, such as display on a laptop or other small screen. Its 12Mbps average bit rate is compatible with virtually all memory cards.
- VGA **3M (640 × 480).** If you're planning on sending your video by e-mail, displaying your movie on a web page or uploading to YouTube, this image quality setting may be ideal.

Understanding Interlacing and Progressive Scan

TECH ALERT

The A57 is aimed at still photographers who are upgrading their equipment and goals, and at more advanced photographers who want to shoot stills and video without making too many compromises feature-wise. That's why the A57 offers the resolution and frame rate options it has. This next section is aimed at more advanced moviemakers who want to understand some of the nuts and bolts behind their choices. To understand which resolution and frame rate you might want to use, it's necessary to understand the difference between interlaced and progressive scans. I'll make the explanation as painless as possible. Those of you who just want to shoot movies can opt to choose 60i 17M in the Record Setting section of the Movie 1 menu, and jump to the next section.

As you probably know, video images as you see them on your TV or monitor consist of a series of lines which are displayed, or *scanned* at a fixed rate. When captured by your A57, the images are also grabbed, using what is called a *rolling shutter,* which simply means that the image is grabbed one line at a time at the same fixed rate that will be used during playback. (There is a more expensive option, not used in the A57, called a *global shutter* that captures all the lines at one time.)

Line-by-line scanning during capture and playback can be done in one of two ways. With *interlaced scanning,* odd-numbered lines (lines 1, 3, 5, 7… and so forth) are captured with one pass, and then the even-numbered lines (2, 4, 6, 8…and so forth) are grabbed. With the AVCHD 60i format, roughly 60 pairs of odd/even line scans, or 60 *fields* are captured each second. (The actual number is 59.94 fields per second.) Interlaced scanning was developed for and works best with analog display systems such as older television sets. It was originally created as a way to reduce the amount of bandwidth required to transmit television pictures over the air. Modern LCD, LED, and plasma-based HDTV displays must de-interlace a 1080i image to display it. (See Figure 7.1.)

Newer displays work better with a second method, called *progressive scanning* or *sequential scanning.* Instead of two interlaced fields, the entire image is scanned as consecutive lines (lines 1,2,3,4…and so forth). This happens at a rate of about 60 frames per second (not fields). (All these numbers apply to the NTSC television system used in the United States, Canada, Japan, and some other countries; other places use systems like PAL, where the nominal scanning figures are 50.)

One problem with interlaced scanning appears when capturing video of moving subjects. Half of the image (one set of interlaced lines) will change to keep up with the movement of the subject while the other interlaced half retains the "old" image as it waits to be refreshed. Flicker or *interline twitter* results. That makes your progressive scan options of 60p or 24p a better choice for action photography.

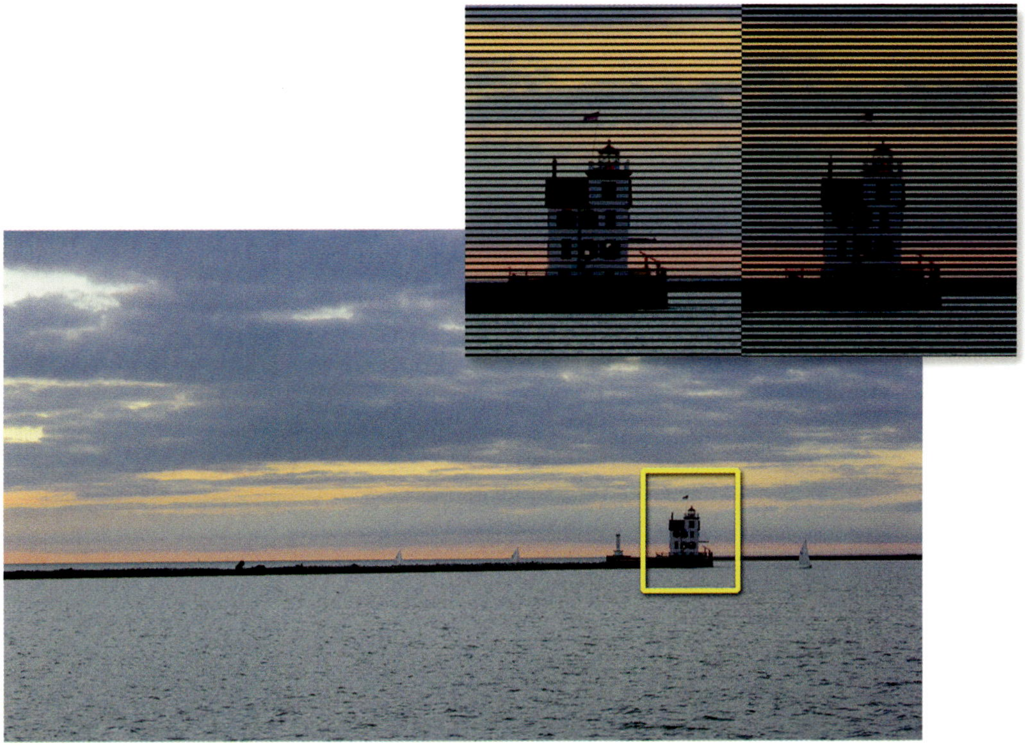

Figure 7.1
The inset shows how lines of the image alternate between odd and even in an interlaced video capture.

Which to Choose?

If you're shooting a relatively static image, you can choose 60p 28M for the best combination of resolution and image quality, if you can accept the high demands of a 28Mbps transfer rate, and have a TV that can display 60p video (otherwise, the video will be converted before output to the television). Use 60i 24M or 60i 17M if you know you'll be mixing your video with existing 60i footage, or if you happen to be shooting for NBC, CBS, or The CW. (Ha!) Keep in mind that if you use the supplied PMB software instead of another movie-editing package, your 60p, 60i, or 24p video will be converted before it can be written to an AVCHD disc, and that can take a long time and reduces image quality. To preserve all the detail you shot, you must write your movie to a Blu-ray disc (and most of us don't have Blu-ray disc writers). For action shooting, choose 24p M or 24p 17 to get the smoothest-looking image—one that's more film-like.

Audio Recording

This setting lets you turn audio recording for your movies on or off. You might want to disable audio recording if you are certain you don't want to have any sound recorded, or if you believe you might be bothered by sounds from the operation of the camera or lens that might be recorded. In my case, I always leave audio recording enabled, because you can always erase a soundtrack that you don't want or replace it with a new one, but you can never recover sounds that you didn't record in the first place.

Wind Noise Reduct

This setting activates or disables in-camera processing of your audio to remove the whistling sound produced by wind passing over the built-in microphones. (This entry has no effect on external microphones.) Wind noise reduction does degrade sound quality a little by emphasizing bass tones when recording at low volume, so you'll want to use it only when you have wind noises to contend with.

SteadyShot

This entry can be used to switch off the SteadyShot image stabilization feature for movie making, separately from the stabilization used for still images (available in the Still Shooting 3 menu). You might want to do that when the camera is mounted on a tripod, as the additional anti-shake feature is not needed in that situation, and slight movements of the tripod can sometimes "confuse" the system. However, it's rarely necessary to turn SteadyShot off, and I recommend leaving it turned on at all times unless you find that it causes problems in some specific situations, such as when shooting in high ambient temperatures to avoid sensor overheating.

Recording Video

Here are some additional points to consider before you press that Movie button. Here's what I recommend you do to prepare for your recording session:

- **Set the camera's aspect ratio.** The aspect ratio setting (3:2 or 16:9, accessed through the Image Size menu) won't affect your video recording, but it will affect how you frame your images using the live view on the LCD screen prior to pressing the movie button. So, if you want to know approximately how your video will be framed on the screen, set the aspect ratio to 3:2 if you're going to be recording in VGA; set it to 16:9 if you'll be using any of the other formats. (For another way to get a visual preview of how a video will be framed with the current settings, turn on the Grid Line options in the Custom 2 menu, which will place a set of four small movie frame brackets on the screen; those brackets will show you the size of the movie frame before you press the red button to start recording.)
- **Turn on autofocus.** Make sure autofocus is turned on using the AF/MF switch on the lens or on the camera, as discussed in Chapter 5 (assuming you're using a Sony lens that will autofocus with this camera). You have the option of using manual

focus if you want, but in most cases there is no reason not to rely on the camera's excellent ability to autofocus during movie making. You also can set the Autofocus Area using the Function menu; if you set it to Zone or Local, you can move the active focus sensor or zone while you're recording your video.

- **Set white balance, Creative Style, and metering mode as you want them.** These are three exposure-related functions that will work for your video shooting, so take advantage of them. Of course, for many purposes you may be content with Auto White Balance, the Standard Creative Style, and the Multi segment metering mode, but be aware that these settings are available if you want to use them for creative purposes. If you want to adjust any of these three settings, be sure to set the camera to a shooting mode, such as Program, in which those settings can be made; if you switch back to an Auto or Scene mode, the camera will revert back to its automatic settings. Make the settings before you start recording the movie, because you cannot adjust them during the recording. Don't worry about setting other exposure-related items, such as DRO, which will have no effect.
- **Choose Aperture priority mode if you want to control the aperture.** In most cases, when you press the red Movie button, the camera will adjust the exposure for you automatically, no matter what shooting mode the camera is set to—Auto, Program, Manual, or even 3D Panorama or Continuous Advance Priority AE. The camera just records the movie, adjusting the aperture, shutter speed, and ISO to achieve a correct exposure. However, Sony provided the ability to maintain a fixed aperture if you want to. In order to do so, you need to use Aperture priority mode, and set your chosen aperture before starting to record the movie. If you then press the red Movie button, the camera will keep the aperture you have set, and do its best to expose the footage correctly using that aperture. The idea with this feature is to give you a way to achieve a defocused background by maintaining a wide aperture setting.

GETTING INFO

The information display shown on the LCD screen when shooting movies is fairly sparse, because there are not too many settings you can make. The screen will show recording time elapsed and time remaining and the REC indicator to show that you are shooting a movie. It will also show you the format you are using and any exposure-related settings that are in effect, including white balance, Creative Style, and exposure compensation.

Steps During Movie Making

Once you have set up the camera for your video session and pressed the red button, you have done most of the technical work that's required of you. Now your task is to use your skills at composition, lighting, scene selection, and, perhaps, directing actors, to make a compelling video production. Later in this chapter I will have some advice to give you in those areas, but first there are a few technical points you should bear in mind as the camera is (figuratively) whirring away.

- **Zoom, autofocus, and autoexposure all work.** If you're new to the world of high-quality still cameras that also take video, you may just take it for granted that functions such as autofocus continue to work normally when you switch from stills to video. But until recently, most such cameras performed weakly in their video modes; they would lock their exposure and focus at the beginning of the scene, and you could not zoom while shooting the video. The Alpha SLT-A57 has no such handicaps, and, in fact, it is especially capable in these areas. Autoexposure works very well, and you can zoom to your heart's content (though, as I'll discuss later, I recommend that you zoom sparingly). Best of all, autofocus works like a charm; the camera can track moving subjects and quickly snap them back into sharp focus with the speedy phase-detection focusing mechanism made possible by the fixed translucent mirror. So don't limit yourself based on the weaknesses of past cameras; the A57 opens up new horizons of video freedom. Also, as I mentioned above, if the AF Area is set to Zone or Local, you have the ability to change to a different focus sensor while recording the movie.
- **Exposure compensation works while filming.** I found this feature to be quite remarkable. Although the autoexposure system works very well to vary the aperture when the ambient lighting changes, you also have the option of dialing in exposure compensation if you see a need for more or less brightness in a particular context. You could even use this function as a limited kind of "fade to black" in the camera, though you probably won't be able to fade quite all the way to black. Again, you may never need to adjust your EV manually while shooting video, but it's great to know that you have the option available.
- **Don't be a Flash in the pan.** With HD video, there is a possibility of introducing artifacts or distortion if you pan too quickly. That is, because of the way the lines of video are displayed in sequence, if the camera moves too quickly in a sideways motion, some of the lines may not show up on the screen quickly enough to catch up to the rest of the picture, resulting in a somewhat distorted effect and/or loss of detail. So, if at all possible, make your pans smooth and steady, and slow them down to a comfortable pace.

Tips for Shooting Better Video

Once upon a time, the ability to shoot video with a digital still camera was one of those "Gee whiz" gimmicks camera makers seemed to include just to have a reason to get you to buy a new camera. That hasn't been true for a couple of years now, as the video quality of many digital still cameras has gotten quite good. The A57 is a stellar example. It's capable of HD-quality video and is actually capable of outperforming typical modestly priced digital video camcorders, especially when you consider the range of lenses and other helpful accessories available for it.

Producing good-quality video is more complicated than just buying good equipment. There are techniques that make for gripping storytelling and a visual language the average person is very used to, but also pretty unaware of. While this book can't make you a professional videographer in half a chapter, there is some advice I can give you that will help you improve your results with the camera.

Producing high-quality videos can be a real challenge for amateur photographers. After all, by comparison we're used to watching the best productions that television, video, and motion pictures can offer. Whether it's fair or not, our efforts are compared to what we're used to seeing produced by experts. There are a number of different things to consider when planning a video shoot, and when possible, a shooting script and storyboard can help you produce a higher quality video.

Lens Craft

I'll cover the use of lenses with the A57 in more detail in Chapter 8, but a discussion of lens selection when shooting movies may be useful at this point. In the video world, not all lenses are created equal. The two most important considerations are depth-of-field, or the beneficial lack thereof, and zooming. I'll address each of these separately.

Depth-of-Field and Video

Have you wondered why professional videographers have gone nuts over still cameras that can also shoot video? The producers of *Saturday Night Live* could afford to have Alex Buono, their director of photography, use the niftiest, most expensive high-resolution video cameras to shoot the opening sequences of the program. Instead, Buono opted for a pair of digital SLR cameras. One thing that makes digital still cameras so attractive for video is that they have relatively large sensors, which provides improved low-light performance and results in the oddly attractive reduced depth-of-field, compared with most professional video cameras.

Figure 7.2 provides a comparison of the relative size of sensors. The typical size of a professional video camera sensor is shown at lower left. The APS-C sensor used in the A57 is shown just north of it. You can see that it is much larger, especially when compared with the sensor found in the typical point-and-shoot camera shown at right.

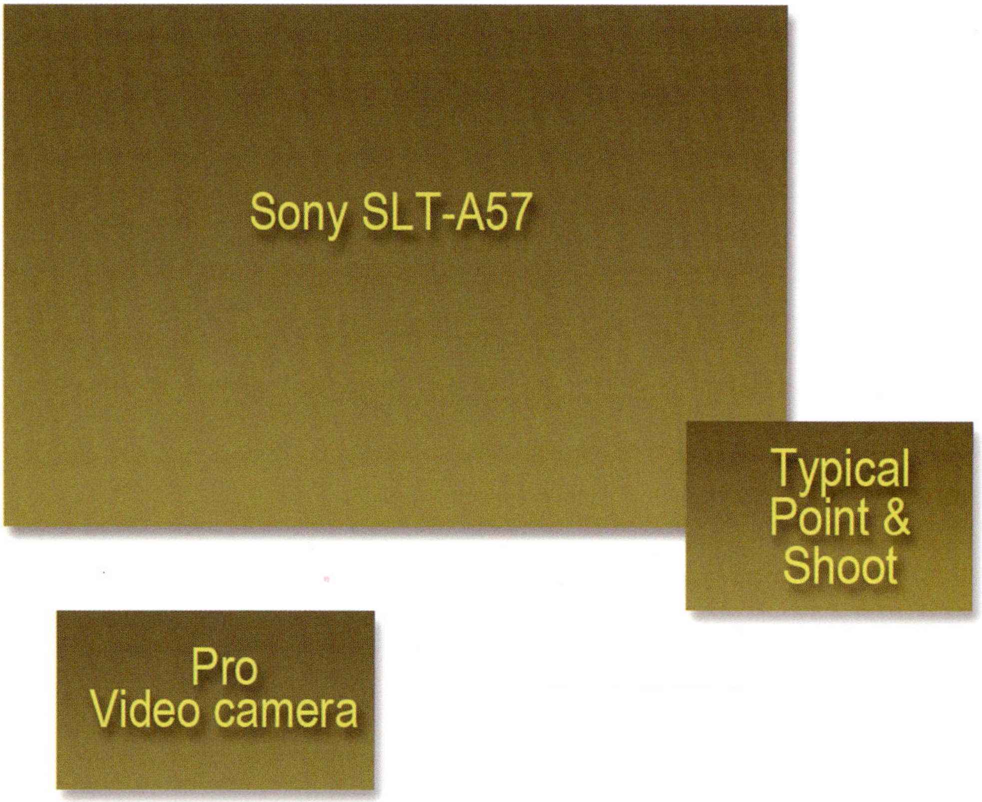

Figure 7.2
Sensor size comparison.

Compared with the sensors used in many pro video cameras and the even smaller sensors found in the typical computer camcorder, the A57's image-grabber is much larger.

As you'll learn in Chapter 8, a larger sensor calls for the use of longer focal lengths to produce the same field of view, so, in effect, a larger sensor has reduced depth-of-field. And *that's* what makes cameras like the A57 attractive from a creative standpoint. Less depth-of-field means greater control over the range of what's in focus. Your A57, with its larger sensor, has a distinct advantage over consumer camcorders in this regard, and even does a better job than many professional video cameras.

Zooming and Video

We're back to zooming (or not zooming) again! When shooting still photos, a zoom is a zoom is a zoom. The key considerations for a zoom lens used only for still photography are the maximum aperture available at each focal length ("How *fast* is this lens?), the zoom range ("How far can I zoom in or out?"), and its sharpness at any given f/stop ("Do I lose sharpness when I shoot wide open?").

When shooting video, the priorities may change, and there are two additional parameters to consider. The first two I listed, lens speed and zoom range, have roughly the same importance in both still and video photography. Zoom range gains a bit of importance in videography, because you can always/usually move closer to shoot a still photograph, but when you're zooming during a shot most of us don't have that option (or the funds to buy/rent a dolly to smoothly move the camera during capture). But, oddly enough, overall sharpness may have slightly less importance under certain conditions when shooting video. That's because the image changes in some way many times per second (24/60 times per second with the A57), so any given frame doesn't hang around long enough for our eyes to pick out every single detail. You want a sharp image, of course, but your standards don't need to be quite as high when shooting video.

Here are the remaining considerations:

- **Zoom lens maximum aperture.** The speed of the lens matters in several ways. A zoom with a relatively large maximum aperture lets you shoot in lower light levels, and a big f/stop allows you to minimize depth-of-field for selective focus. Keep in mind that the maximum aperture may change during zooming. A lens that offers an f/3.5 maximum aperture at its widest focal length, may provide only f/5.6 worth of light at the telephoto position.
- **Zoom range.** Use of zoom during actual capture should not be an everyday thing, unless you're shooting a kung-fu movie. However, there are effective uses for a zoom shot, particularly if it's a "long" one from extreme wide angle to extreme close-up (or vice versa). We all can recall those memorable long shots of a building, seen from a distance, followed by a quick zoom in on Steve McGarrett poised outside that building with a steely glint in his eye.

  But, most of the time, you'll use the zoom range to adjust the perspective of the camera *between* shots, and a longer zoom range can mean less trotting back and forth to adjust the field of view. Zoom range also comes into play when you're working with selective focus (longer focal lengths have less depth-of-field), or want to expand or compress the apparent distance between foreground and background subjects. A longer range gives you more flexibility.
- **Linearity.** Interchangeable lenses may have some drawbacks, as many photographers who have been using the video features of their digital SLRs have discovered. That's because, unless a lens is optimized for video shooting, zooming with a particular lens may not necessarily be linear. Rotating the zoom collar manually at a constant speed doesn't always produce a smooth zoom. There may be "jumps" as the elements of the lens shift around during the zoom. Keep that in mind if you plan to zoom during a shot, and are using a lens that has proved from experience to provide a non-linear zoom. (Unfortunately, there's no easy way to tell ahead of time whether you own a lens that is well-suited for zooming during a shot.)

Audio

When it comes to making a successful video, audio quality is one of those things that separates the professionals from the amateurs. We're used to watching top-quality productions on television and in the movies, yet the average person has no idea how much effort goes in to producing what seems to be "natural" sound. Much of the sound you hear in such productions is actually recorded on carefully controlled sound stages and "sweetened" with a variety of sound effects and other recordings of "natural" sound.

Tips for Better Audio

Since recording high-quality audio is such a challenge, it's a good idea to do everything possible to maximize recording quality. Here are some ideas for improving the quality of the audio your camera records:

- **Get the camera and its microphone close to the speaker.** The farther the microphone is from the audio source, the less effective it will be in picking up that sound. While having to position the camera and microphone closer to the subject affects your lens choices and lens perspective options, it will make the most of your audio source. Of course, if you're using a very wide-angle lens, getting too close to your subject can have unflattering results, so don't take this advice too far.
- **Use an external microphone.** Plug a stereo or monaural mic into the jack on the side of the camera, and you'll immediately enjoy better sound, because you won't be recording noises including autofocus motors or your own breathing.
- **Turn off any sound makers you can.** Little things like fans and air handling units aren't obvious to the human ear, but will be picked up by the microphone. Turn off any machinery or devices that you can plus make sure cell phones are set to silent mode. Also, do what you can to minimize sounds such as wind, radio, television, or people talking in the background.
- **Make sure to record some "natural" sound.** If you're shooting video at an event of some kind, make sure you get some background sound that you can add to your audio as desired in postproduction.
- **Consider recording audio separately.** Lip-syncing is probably beyond most of the people you're going to be shooting, but there's nothing that says you can't record narration separately and add it later. It's relatively easy if you learn how to use simple software video-editing programs like iMovie (for the Macintosh) or Windows Movie Maker (for Windows PCs). Any time the speaker is off-camera, you can work with separately recorded narration rather than recording the speaker on-camera. This can produce much cleaner sound.

External Microphones

The single most important thing you can do to improve your audio quality is to use an external microphone. The A57's internal stereo microphones mounted on the front of the camera will do a decent job, but have some significant drawbacks, partially spelled out in the previous section:

- **Camera noise.** The A57's shutter may be relatively quiet, but there are plenty of other noise sources emanating from the camera, including your own breathing and rustling around as the camera shifts in your hand. Manual zooming is bound to affect your sound, and your fingers will fall directly in front of the built-in mics as you change focal lengths. An external microphone isolates the sound recording from camera noise.
- **Distance.** Anytime your camera is located more than 6-8 feet from your subjects or sound source, the audio will suffer. An external unit allows you to place the mic right next to your subject.
- **Improved quality.** Obviously, Sony isn't going to install a super-high quality microphone on a non-professional camera. Decent external microphones can cost a significant percentage of the price of the A57, and you might want to spend $100-$150 or more on your own if you're serious about good sound.
- **Directionality.** The internal microphone generally records only sounds directly in front of it. An external microphone can be of the directional type or omnidirectional, depending on whether you want to "shotgun" your sound or record more ambient sound.

You can choose from several different types of microphones, each of which has its own advantages and disadvantages. If you're avid about movie making with your A57, you might want to own more than one. You can obtain a high-quality microphone made by a company such as Shure or Audio-Technica, and, if you are on a quest for really superior audio quality, you can even obtain a portable mixer that can plug into this jack, such as the affordable Rolls MX124 (around $150) (www.rolls.com), letting you use multiple high-quality microphones (up to four) to record your soundtrack.

An exciting new option designed specifically for still cameras like the SLT-A57 is the Beachtek DXA-SLR PRO HDSLR Audio Adapter. It's more expensive, at around $450, but has even more professional sound options and clips right onto the bottom of your camera using the tripod mounting socket. (See Figure 7.3.)

One advantage that a sound mixing device like the DSX-SLR PRO offers over the stock A57 is that it adds a headphone output jack to your camera, so you can monitor the sound being recorded (you can also listen to your soundtrack through the headphones during playback, which is *way* better than using the A57's built-in speaker). The adapter has two balanced XLR microphone inputs and can also accept line input (from another audio source), and provides cool features like AGC (automatic gain control), built-in limiting, and VU meters you can use to monitor sound input.

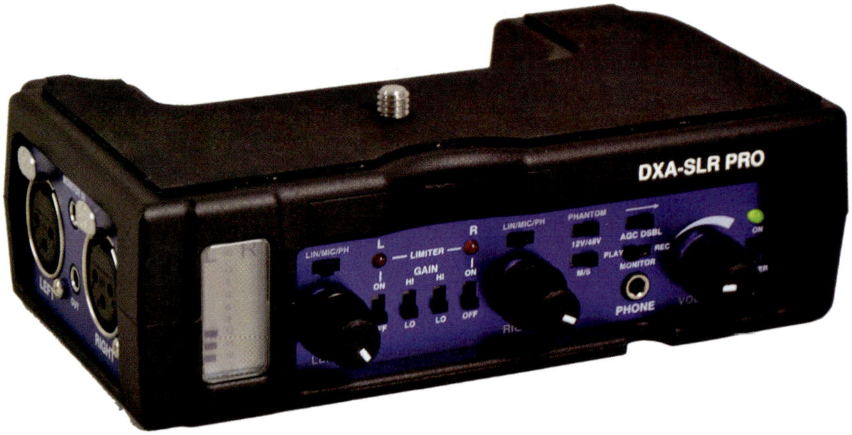

Figure 7.3
The Beachtek DXA-SLR PRO HDSLR Audio Adapter offers professional sound mixing options.

Common configurations of the microphones themselves include:

- **Shotgun microphones.** These can be mounted directly on your camera (with an adapter, if necessary). I prefer to use a bracket, originally intended for electronic flash units, which further isolates the microphone from any camera noise. Intended to pick up sound from the general direction in which it's pointed, such a microphone will provide decent pickup of ambient sound in its environment.
- **Lapel microphones.** Also called *lavalieres*, these microphones attach to the subject's clothing and picks up their voice with the best quality. You'll need a long enough cord or a wireless mic (described later). These are especially good for video interviews, so whether you're producing a documentary or grilling relatives for a family history, you'll want one of these.
- **Hand-held microphones.** If you're capturing a singer crooning a tune, or want your subject to mimic famed faux newscaster Wally Ballou, a hand-held mic may be your best choice. They serve much the same purpose as a lapel microphone, and they're more intrusive—but that may be the point. A hand-held microphone can make a great prop for your fake newscast! The speaker can talk right into the microphone, point it at another person, or use it to record ambient sound. If your narrator is not going to appear on-camera, one of these can be an inexpensive way to improve sound.
- **Wired and wireless external microphones.** This option is the most expensive, but you get a receiver and a transmitter (both battery powered, so you'll need to make sure you have enough batteries). The transmitter is connected to the microphone, and the receiver is connected to your A57. In addition to being less klutzy and enabling you to avoid having wires on view in your scene, wireless mics let you record sounds that are physically located some distance from your camera. Of course, you need to keep in mind the range of your device, and be aware of possible signal interference from other electronic components in the vicinity.

> **WIND NOISE REDUCTION**
>
> Always use the wind screen provided with an external microphone to reduce the effect of noise produced by even light breezes blowing over the microphone. Both the camera and many mics include a low-cut filter to further reduce wind noise. However, these can also affect other sounds. You can disable the low-cut filters for the A57's internal microphones by choosing Off for Wind Noise Reduction in the Movie 1 menu. Some external mics have their own low-cut filter switch.

Keep Things Stable and on the Level

Camera shake's enough of a problem with still photography, but it becomes even more of a nuisance when you're shooting video. While the A57's image-stabilization feature can help minimize this, it can't work miracles. Placing your camera on a tripod will work much better than trying to hand-hold it while shooting.

Shooting Script

A shooting script is nothing more than a coordinated plan that covers both audio and video and provides order and structure for your video. A detailed script will cover what types of shots you're going after, what dialogue you're going to use, audio effects, transitions, and graphics.

Storyboards

A storyboard is a series of panels providing visuals of what each scene should look like. While the ones produced by Hollywood are generally of very high quality, there's nothing that says drawing skills are important for this step. Stick figures work just fine if that's the best you can do. The storyboard just helps you visualize locations, placement of actors/actresses, props and furniture, and also helps everyone involved get an idea of what you're trying to show. It also helps show how you want to frame or compose a shot. You can even shoot a series of still photos and transform them into a "storyboard" if you want, such as in Figure 7.4.

Storytelling in Video

Today's audience is used to fast-paced, short-scene storytelling. In order to produce interesting video for such viewers, it's important to view video storytelling as a kind of shorthand code for the more leisurely efforts print media offers. Audio and video should always be advancing the story. While it's okay to let the camera linger from time to time, it should only be for a compelling reason and only briefly.

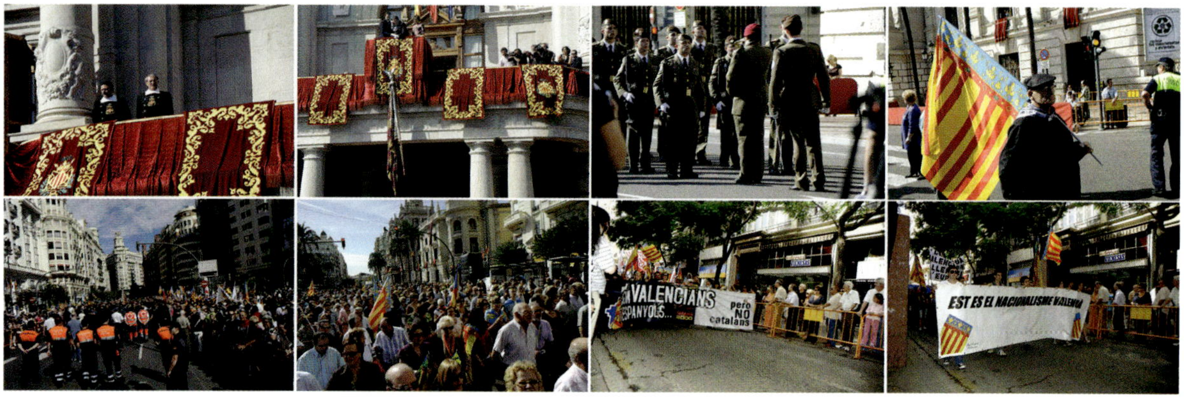

Figure 7.4 A storyboard is a series of simple sketches or photos to help visualize a segment of video.

It only takes a second or two for an establishing shot to impart the necessary information. For example, many of the scenes for a video documenting a model being photographed in a Rock and Roll music setting might be close-ups and talking heads, but an establishing shot showing the studio where the video was captured helps set the scene.

Provide variety too. Change camera angles and perspectives often and never leave a static scene on the screen for a long period of time. (You can record a static scene for a reasonably long period and then edit in other shots that cut away and back to the longer scene with close-ups that show each person talking.)

When editing, keep transitions basic! I can't stress this one enough. Watch a television program or movie. The action "jumps" from one scene or person to the next. Fancy transitions that involve exotic "wipes," dissolves, or cross fades take too long for the average viewer and make your video ponderous.

Composition

In movie shooting, several factors restrict your composition, and impose requirements you just don't always have in still photography (although other rules of good composition do apply). Here are some of the key differences to keep in mind when composing movie frames:

- **Horizontal compositions only.** Some subjects, such as basketball players and tall buildings, just lend themselves to vertical compositions. But movies are shown in horizontal format only. So if you're interviewing a local basketball star, you can end up with a worst-case situation like the one shown in Figure 7.5. If you want to show how tall your subject is, it's often impractical to move back far enough to show him full-length. You really can't capture a vertical composition. Tricks like getting down on the floor and shooting up at your subject can exaggerate the perspective, but aren't a perfect solution.

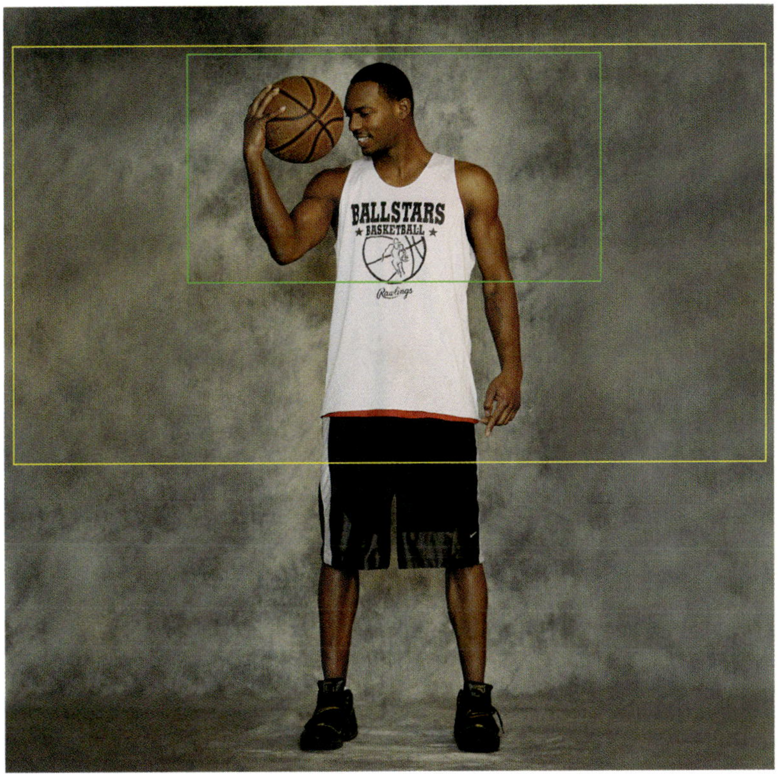

Figure 7.5
Movie shooting requires you to fit all your subjects into a horizontally oriented frame.

- **Wasted space at the sides.** Moving in to frame the basketball player as outlined by the yellow box in Figure 7.5 means that you're still forced to leave a lot of empty space on either side. (Of course, you can fill that space with other people and/or interesting stuff, but that defeats your intent of concentrating on your main subject.) So when faced with some types of subjects in a horizontal frame, you can be creative, or move in *really* tight. For example, if I was willing to give up the "height" aspect of my composition, I could have framed the shot as shown by the green box in the figure, and wasted less of the image area at either side.
- **Seamless (or seamed) transitions.** Unless you're telling a picture story with a photo essay, still pictures often stand alone. But with movies, each of your compositions must relate to the shot that preceded it, and the one that follows. It can be jarring to jump from a long shot to a tight close-up unless the director—you—is very creative. Another common error is the "jump cut" in which successive shots vary only slightly in camera angle, making it appear that the main subject has "jumped" from one place to another. (Although everyone from French New Wave director Jean-Luc Goddard to Guy Ritchie—Madonna's ex—has used jump cuts effectively in their films.) The rule of thumb is to vary the camera angle by at least 30 degrees between shots to make it appear to be seamless. Unless you prefer that your images flaunt convention and appear to be "seamy."

- **The time dimension.** Unlike still photography, with motion pictures there's a lot more emphasis on using a series of images to build on each other to tell a story. Static shots where the camera is mounted on a tripod and everything is shot from the same distance are a recipe for dull videos. Watch a television program sometime and notice how often camera shots change distances and directions. Viewers are used to this variety and have come to expect it. Professional video productions are often done with multiple cameras shooting from different angles and positions. But many professional productions are shot with just one camera and careful planning, and you can do just fine with your A57.

Here's a look at the different types of commonly used compositional tools:

- **Establishing shot.** Much like it sounds, this type of composition, as shown in Figure 7.6, establishes the scene and tells the viewer where the action is taking place. Let's say you're shooting a video of your offspring's move to college; the establishing shot could be a wide shot of the campus with a sign welcoming you to the school in the foreground. Another example would be for a child's birthday party; the establishing shot could be the front of the house decorated with birthday signs and streamers or a shot of the dining room table decked out with party favors and a candle-covered birthday cake. Or, in Figure 7.6, I wanted to show the studio where the video was shot.
- **Medium shot.** This shot is composed from about waist to head room (some space above the subject's head). It's useful for providing variety from a series of close-ups and also makes for a useful first look at a speaker. (See Figure 7.7.)

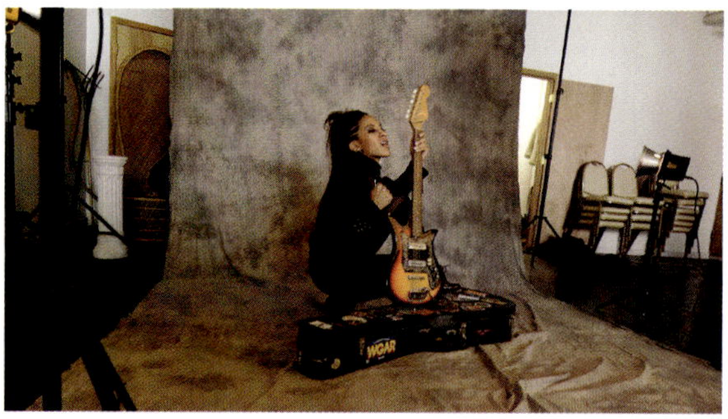

Figure 7.6 An establishing shot sets the stage for your video scene.

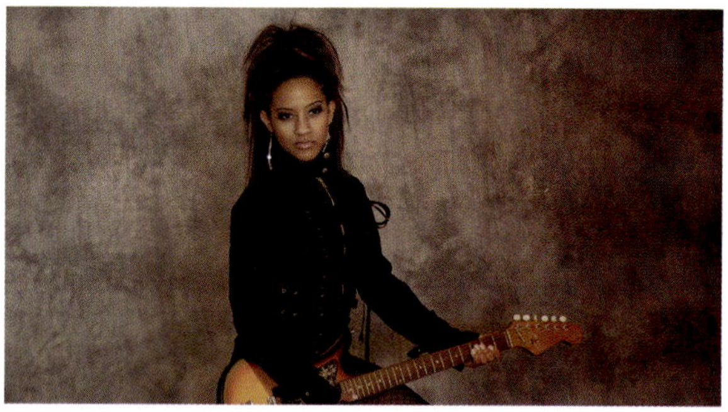

Figure 7.7 A medium shot is used to bring the viewer into a scene without shocking them. It can be used to introduce a character and provide context via their surroundings.

- **Close-up.** The close-up, usually described as "from shirt pocket to head room," provides a good composition for someone talking directly to the camera. Although it's common to have your talking head centered in the shot, that's not a requirement. In Figure 7.8 the subject was offset to the right. This would allow other images, especially graphics or titles, to be superimposed in the frame in a "real" (professional) production. But the compositional technique can be used with A57 videos, too, even if special effects are not going to be added.
- **Extreme close-up.** When I went through broadcast training back in the '70s, this shot was described as the "big talking face" shot and we were actively discouraged from employing it. Styles and tastes change over the years and now the big talking face is much more commonly used (maybe people are better looking these days?) and so this view may be appropriate. Just remember, the A57 is capable of shooting in high-definition video and you may be playing the video on a high-def TV; be careful that you use this composition on a face that can stand up to high definition. (See Figure 7.9.)

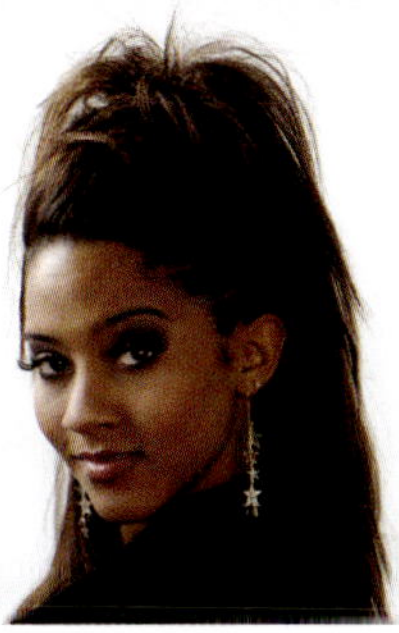

Figure 7.8 A close-up generally shows the full face with a little head room at the top and down to the shoulders at the bottom of the frame.

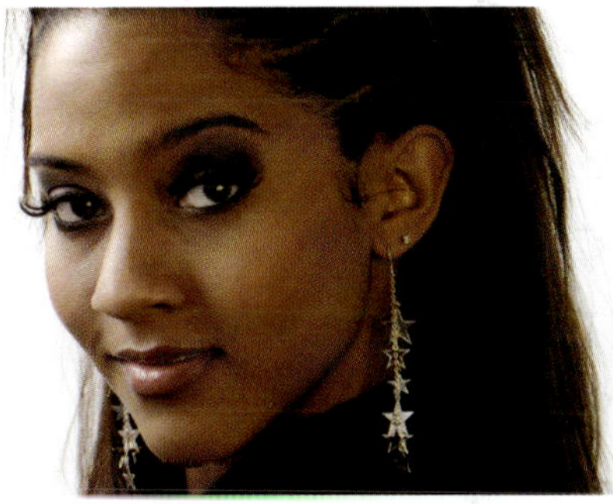

Figure 7.9 An extreme close-up is a very tight shot that cuts off everything above the top of the head and below the chin (or even closer!). Be careful using this shot since many of us look better from a distance!

- **"Two" shot.** A two shot shows a pair of subjects in one frame. (See Figure 7.10.) They can be side by side or one in the foreground and one in the background. This does not have to be a head to ground composition. Subjects can be standing or seated. A "three shot" is the same principle except that three people are in the frame.
- **Over-the-shoulder shot.** Long a composition of interview programs, the "over-the-shoulder shot" uses the rear of one person's head and shoulder to serve as a frame for the other person. This puts the viewer's perspective as that of the person facing away from the camera. (See Figure 7.11.)

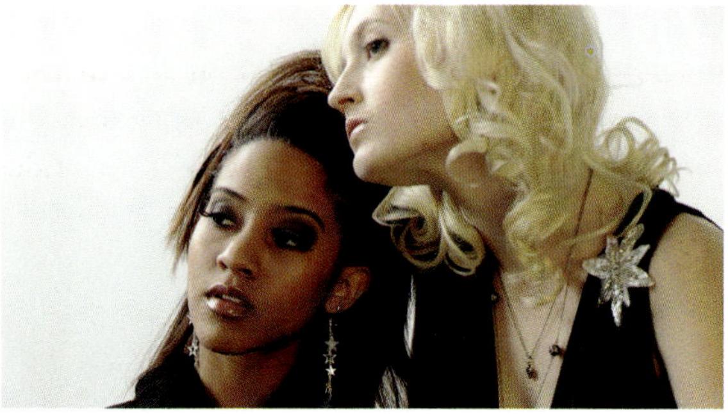

Figure 7.10 A "two-shot" features two people in the frame. This version can be framed at various distances such as medium or close-up.

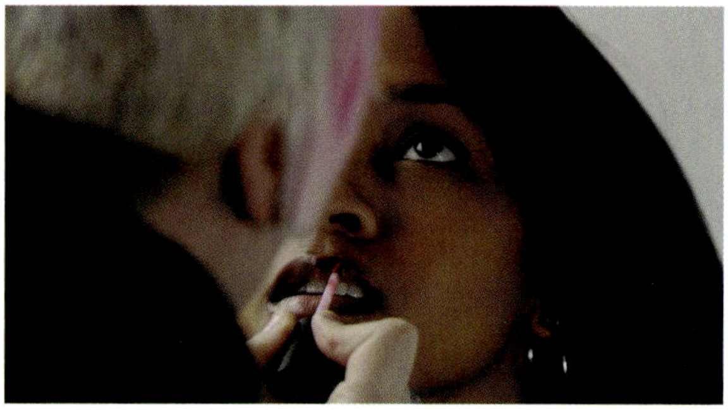

Figure 7.11 An "over-the-shoulder" shot is a popular shot for interview programs. It helps make the viewers feel like they're the ones asking the questions.

Lighting for Video

Much like in still photography, how you handle light pretty much can make or break your videography. Lighting for video can be more complicated than lighting for still photography, since both subject and camera movement is often part of the process.

Lighting for video presents several concerns. First off, you want enough illumination to create a useable video. Beyond that, you want to use light to help tell your story or increase drama. Let's take a closer look at both.

Illumination

You can significantly improve the quality of your video by increasing the light falling in the scene. This is true indoors or out, by the way. While it may seem like sunlight is more than enough, it depends on how much contrast you're dealing with. If your subject is in shadow (which can help him from squinting) or wearing a ball cap, a video light can help make him look a lot better.

Lighting choices for amateur videographers are a lot better these days than they were a decade or two ago. An inexpensive incandescent video light, which will easily fit in a camera bag, can be found for $15 or $20. You can even get a good-quality LED video light for less than $100. Work lights sold at many home improvement stores can also serve as video lights since you can set the camera's white balance to correct for any color casts. You'll need to mount these lights on a tripod or other support, or, perhaps, to a bracket that fastens to the tripod socket on the bottom of the camera.

Much of the challenge depends upon whether you're just trying to add some fill light on your subject versus trying to boost the light on an entire scene. A small video light will do just fine for the former. It won't handle the latter. Fortunately, the versatility of the A57 comes in quite handy here. Since the camera shoots video in Auto ISO mode, it can compensate for lower lighting levels and still produce a decent image. For best results though, better lighting is necessary.

Creative Lighting

While ramping up the light intensity will produce better technical quality in your video, it won't necessarily improve the artistic quality of it. Whether we're outdoors or indoors, we're used to seeing light come from above. Videographers need to consider how they position their lights to provide even illumination while up high enough to angle shadows down low and out of sight of the camera.

When considering lighting for video, there are several factors. One is the quality of the light. It can either be hard (direct) light or soft (diffused). Hard light is good for showing detail, but can also be very harsh and unforgiving. "Softening" the light, but diffusing it somehow, can reduce the intensity of the light but make for a kinder, gentler light as well.

While mixing light sources isn't always a good idea, one approach is to combine window light with supplemental lighting. Position your subject with the window to one side and bring in either a supplemental light or a reflector to the other side for reasonably even lighting.

Lighting Styles

Some lighting styles are more heavily used than others. Some forms are used for special effects, while others are designed to be invisible. At its most basic, lighting just illuminates the scene, but when used properly it can also create drama. Let's look at some types of lighting styles:

- **Three-point lighting.** This is a basic lighting setup for one person. A main light illuminates the strong side of a person's face, while a fill light lights up the other side. A third light is then positioned above and behind the subject to light the back of the head and shoulders. (See Figure 7.12.)
- **Flat lighting.** Use this type of lighting to provide illumination and nothing more. It calls for a variety of lights and diffusers set to raise the light level in a space enough for good video reproduction, but not to create a particular mood or emphasize a particular scene or individual. With flat lighting, you're trying to create even lighting levels throughout the video space and minimize any shadows. Generally, the lights are placed up high and angled downward (or possibly pointed straight up to bounce off of a white ceiling). (See Figure 7.13.)
- **"Ghoul lighting."** This is the style of lighting used for old horror movies. The idea is to position the light down low, pointed upwards. It's such an unnatural style of lighting that it makes its targets seem weird and ghoulish.

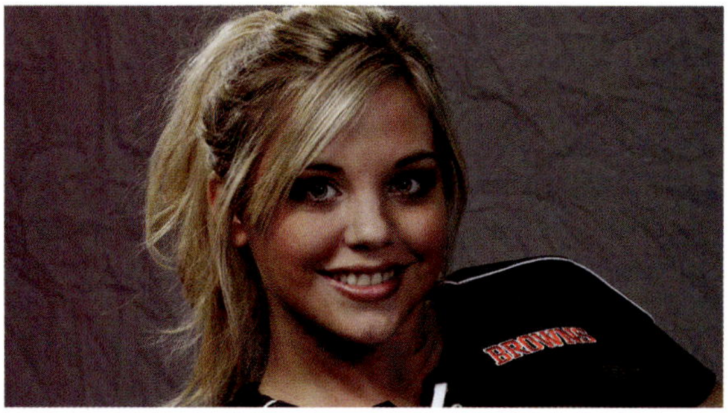

Figure 7.12 With three-point lighting, two lights are placed in front and to the side of the subject (45-degree angles are ideal) and positioned about a foot higher than the subject's head. Another light is directed on the background in order to separate the subject and the background.

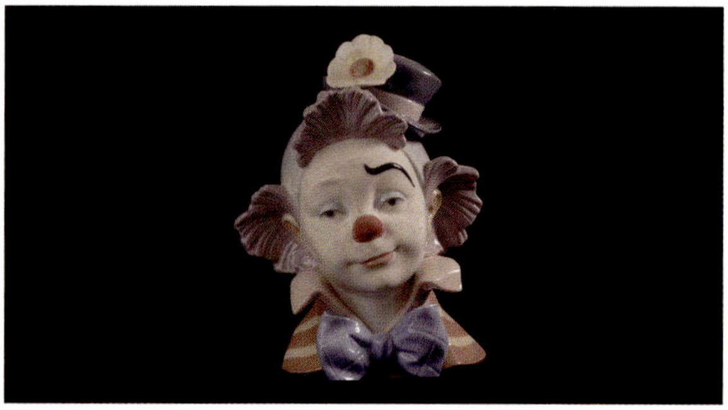

Figure 7.13 Flat lighting is another approach for creating even illumination. Here the lights can be bounced off of a white ceiling and walls to fill in shadows as much as possible. It is a flexible lighting approach since the subject can change positions without needing a change in light direction.

- **Outdoor lighting.** While shooting outdoors may seem easier because the sun provides more light, it also presents its own problems. As a general rule of thumb, keep the sun behind you when you're shooting video outdoors, except when shooting faces (anything from a medium shot and closer) since the viewer won't want to see a squinting subject. When shooting another human this way, put the sun behind her and use a video light to balance light levels between the foreground and background. If the sun is simply too bright, position the subject in the shade and use the video light for your main illumination. Using reflectors (white board panels or aluminum foil covered cardboard panels are cheap options) can also help balance light effectively.

8

Working with Lenses

Although it's sometimes alarming for those of us who have been taking pictures a very long time, the tendency for larger companies to absorb smaller vendors has paid some big dividends, most notably in the huge selection of lenses available for the Sony Alpha camera line.

In my youth, I managed a camera store for a while, and had access to a broad range of different models, and so used both Konica and Minolta cameras for many years—dating back to the Konica Autoreflex T (the first SLR with autoexposure/through-the-lens metering) and the legendary Minolta SRT-101. Only a few years into the digital SLR era, the two companies joined forces as Konica Minolta, and in turn saw their technology eventually taken over by Sony in 2006. Bye-bye Konica Minolta 7D, hello Sony Alpha models, like the company's first entry, the Alpha DSLR-A100, each with a legacy of hundreds of lenses from the sorely missed Minolta lineup.

Thanks to the head start provided by Konica and Minolta (and boosted by Minolta-compatible lenses from third parties), your Sony Alpha A57 camera can be used with a very broad range of high-quality lenses, suitable for a user base that extends from novice photo enthusiasts to advanced amateur and professional photographers. It's this mind-bending assortment of high-quality lenses available to enhance the capabilities of cameras like the Sony Alpha A57 that make the camera line so attractive. Hundreds of current and older lenses introduced by Minolta, Sony, and third-party vendors since the late 1980s can be used to give you a wider view, bring distant subjects closer, let you focus closer, shoot under lower light conditions, or provide a more detailed, sharper image for critical work.

My own collection of lenses for my SLT camera is a motley bunch that includes the 18-55mm kit lens, Sony-branded 50mm f/1.4, an 18-200mm f/3.5-f/6.3, a 30mm f/2.8

macro lens, and other recent-vintage Sony lenses. I also have a couple bargain-basement optics, including a Sigma 28-80mm f/3.5-5.6 Macro II and a Minolta-labeled 75-300mm f/4.5-5.6 macro lens. My favorite Lensbaby works just fine on my SLT-A57 (with an adapter), and I have other adapters that let me use even more lenses on the camera in manual focus/exposure mode.

All these choices are important because, other than the sensor itself, the lens you select for your camera is the most important component in determining image quality and perspective of your images. This chapter explains how to assemble the best lenses for the kinds of photography you want to do.

But Don't Forget the Crop Factor

From time to time you've heard the term *crop factor*, and you've probably also heard the term *lens multiplier factor*. Both are misleading and inaccurate terms used to describe the same phenomenon: the fact that cameras like the Sony Alpha (and most affordable interchangeable lens digital cameras) provide a field of view that's smaller and narrower than that produced by certain other (usually much more expensive) cameras, when fitted with exactly the same lens.

Figure 8.1 quite clearly shows the phenomenon at work. The outer rectangle, marked 1X, shows the field of view you might expect with a 100mm lens mounted on a so-called "full-frame" digital model like the Alpha SLT-A99, or a 35mm film camera, like

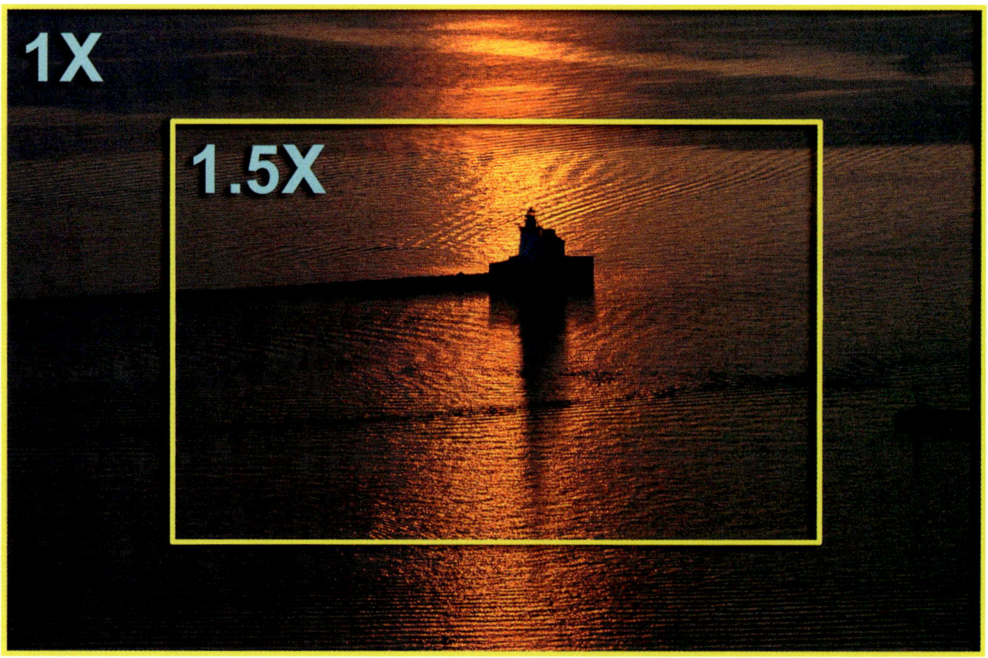

Figure 8.1
Sony offers digital SLRs with full-frame (1X) crops, as well as 1.5X crops.

the 1985 Minolta Maxxum 7000 (which happened to be the first SLR to feature both autofocus and motorized advance, something we take for granted in the digital SLR age). The rectangle marked 1.5X shows the field of view you'd get with that 100mm lens installed on a Sony Alpha SLT-A57. It's easy to see from the illustration that the 1X rendition provides a wider, more expansive view, while the other one is, in comparison, *cropped.*

The cropping effect is produced because the sensor of the Alpha A57 is smaller than the sensor of a full-frame camera. The "full-frame" camera has a sensor that's the size of the standard 35mm film frame, 24mm × 36mm. Your Sony Alpha's sensor does *not* measure 24mm × 36mm; instead, it specs out at roughly 24 × 16mm, or about 66 percent of the area of a full-frame sensor, as shown by the yellow boxes in the figure. You can calculate the relative field of view by dividing the focal length of the lens by .667. Thus, a 100mm lens mounted on a Sony Alpha A57 has the same field of view as a 150mm lens on a full-frame camera like the A850. We humans tend to perform multiplication operations in our heads more easily than division, so such field of view comparisons are usually calculated using the reciprocal of .667—1.5—so we can multiply instead. (100 / .667=150; 100 × 1.5=150.)

This translation is generally useful only if you're accustomed to using full-frame cameras (usually of the film variety) and want to know how a familiar lens will perform on a digital camera. I strongly prefer *crop factor* to *lens multiplier*, because nothing is being multiplied; a 100mm lens doesn't "become" a 150mm lens—the depth-of-field and lens aperture remain the same. (I'll explain more about these later in this chapter.) Only the field of view is cropped. But the term *crop factor* isn't much better, as it implies that the 24 × 36mm frame is "full" and anything else is "less." I get e-mails all the time from photographers who point out that they own full-frame cameras with 36mm × 48mm sensors (like the Mamiya 645ZD or Hasselblad H3D-39 medium format digitals). By their reckoning, the "half-size" sensors found in full-frame cameras like the Sony Alpha DSLR-A850 are "cropped."

If you're accustomed to using full-frame film cameras, you might find it helpful to use the crop factor "multiplier" to translate a lens's real focal length into the full-frame equivalent, even though, as I said, nothing is actually being multiplied. Throughout most of this book, I've been using actual focal lengths and not equivalents, except when referring to specific wide-angle or telephoto focal length ranges and their fields of view.

Your First Lens

The Sony Alpha is most frequently purchased with a lens, often the SAL-1855 DT 18-55mm f/3.5-5.6 zoom lens, which adds only about $100 to the price tag of the body alone, and is thus an irresistible bargain. You can also buy one of the Alpha bodies alone if you already have some lenses. So, you'll need to make a decision about what lens to buy, or decide what other kind of lenses you need to fill out your complement of Sony optics. This section will cover "first lens" concerns, while later in the chapter we'll look at "add-on lens" considerations.

When deciding on a first lens, there are several factors you'll want to consider:

- **Cost.** Even with a relatively low-cost camera body (especially for one with a 16MP sensor!), you might have stretched your budget a bit to purchase your Sony Alpha, so you might want to keep the cost of your first lens fairly low. Fortunately, there are excellent lenses available that will add from $100 to $300 to the price of your camera if purchased at the same time. Others cost a little more, but have very desirable features.
- **Zoom range.** If you have only one lens, you'll want a fairly long zoom range to provide as much flexibility as possible. Once you "graduate" from the 18-55mm kit lens, you'll find several other (pricey) options. For example, one of the most popular basic lenses for the Alpha, the DT 18-250mm f/3.5-6.3 and DT 18-200mm f/3.5-6.3 optics have 11.0X to an astounding 13.8X zoom ranges, with both extending from moderate wide-angle/normal out to long telephoto. These lenses are fine for everyday shooting, portraits, and some types of sports. They're not cheap, starting at about $529, but may be worth the cost to you if such a long range is desirable.
- **Adequate maximum aperture.** You'll want an f/stop of at least f/3.5 to f/4 for shooting under fairly low light conditions. The thing to watch for is the maximum aperture when the lens is zoomed to its telephoto end. You may end up with no better than an f/5.6 maximum aperture if you buy a kit lens. That's not great, but you can often live with it.
- **Image quality.** Your starter lens should have good image quality, because that's one of the primary factors that will be used to judge your photos. Even at a low price, the 18-55mm lens sold with the Alpha as a kit includes two aspherical elements that minimize distortion and chromatic aberration; it's plenty sharp enough for most applications.
- **Size matters.** A good walking-around lens is compact in size and light in weight.
- **Fast/close focusing.** Your first lens should have a speedy autofocus system. Close focusing (to 12 inches or closer) will let you use your basic lens for some types of macro photography.

You can find comparisons of the lenses discussed in the next section.

Buy Now, Expand Later

The Alpha is commonly available with several good, basic lenses that can serve you well as a "walk-around" lens (one you keep on the camera most of the time, especially when you're out and about without your camera bag). The number of options available to you is actually quite amazing when you consider third-party lenses, even if your budget is limited to about $100-$400 for your first lens. The most popular starter lens Sony offers for the Alpha is shown in Figure 8.2. Sony's best-bet first lenses, including some that have been discontinued but are still widely available, are as follows:

- **Sony SAL-1855 DT 18-55mm f/3.5-5.6 zoom lens.** This lens is sharp, small in size, and is fast enough at the wide-angle end of its zoom range for most available light shooting. Priced at around $220 if purchased separately, this lens is an all-around good choice.
- **Sony SAL-24105 24-105mm f/3.5-4.5 zoom lens.** This lens is not inexpensive at about $500, but, if you can find one, may be a smarter choice if you intend to shoot indoor or outdoor sports. It's faster at its longest focal length, and provides the equivalent of a moderate wide angle to short telephoto 5X zoom in one compact lens.
- **Sony SAL-18250 18-250mm f/3.5-6.3 high magnification zoom lens.** If you have $650 to spare, this lens is truly a do-everything lens with a near-14X zoom range that takes you from true wide angle to long telephoto in one swoop. It's great for sports, landscapes, and portraits, even though a bit slow at f/6.3 at the telephoto end. Sony also offers the similar, slightly smaller SAL-18200 18-200mm f/3.5-6.3 lens for $100 less. I purchased that version for myself, because I found a mint used copy for $350 at KEH Camera (www.keh.com). (See Figure 8.3.)
- **Sony SAL-16105 DT 16-105mm f/3.5-5.6 zoom lens.** Slightly wider and with twice as much telephoto reach as the kit lens, this one will let you shoot landscapes, portraits, and some sports with equal ease, and is more compact than the 18-250/18-200 tandem, while still being affordable to the serious photographer at $650. It focuses as close as 1.25 feet. This is another upgrade from the kit lens that serious photographers will appreciate.

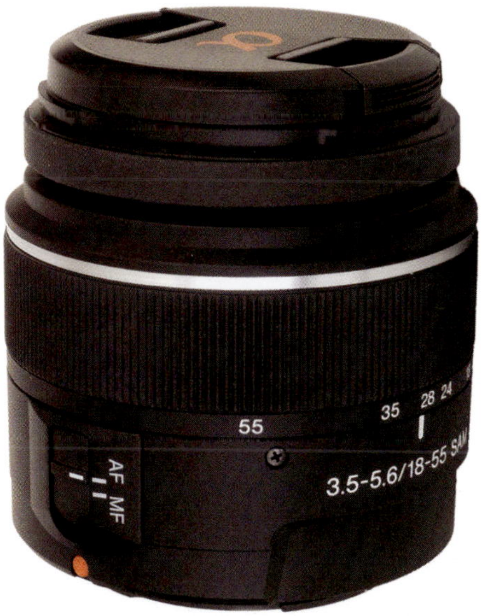

Figure 8.2
This 18-55mm lens is the most popular starter lens for Sony Alpha digital SLRs.

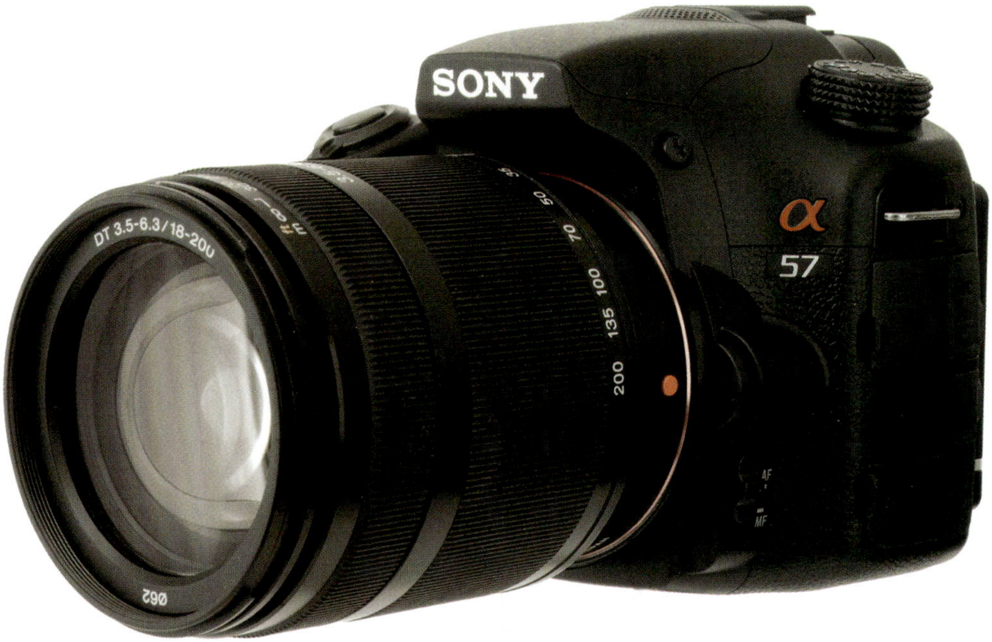

Figure 8.3
Sony's 18-200mm f/3.5-6.3 zoom is an excellent all-around lens.

- **Sony SAL-1680Z Carl Zeiss Vario-Sonnar T* DT 16-80mm f/3.5-4.5 zoom lens.** Slightly wider and longer than the kit lens, and a tad faster when fully zoomed, this one should be your first "pro" lens. It has the famed Carl Zeiss image quality and rugged mechanics. Buy this if you're looking to work your lenses hard without compromising quality, and are willing to compromise your budget with its $1,000 price tag.
- **Sony SAL-55200 DT 55-200mm f/4-5.6 telephoto zoom lens.** One main advantage of this lens is its low cost—about $200. Mated with the 18-55mm kit lens, you're covered for focal lengths from wide to long telephoto at a very attractive price.
- **Sony SAL-75300 75-300mm f/4.5-5.6 telephoto zoom lens.** This is another $250 bargain, slightly redesigned from its Minolta predecessor (which I happen to own). It sacrifices some of the short telephoto range (55-70mm) for a longer reach, out to a long 300mm. (Remember, a 300mm focal length on an Alpha is the equivalent of 450mm on a full-frame camera—truly super-telephoto range.) This is a compact lens (weighing just 18 ounces) that also can be used with any full-frame camera Sony might introduce in the future. It focuses as close as 5 feet at 300mm, which allows you to shoot skittish creatures (and humans) from a non-threatening distance.

- **Sony SAL-2470Z Carl Zeiss Vario-Sonnar T* 24-70mm f/2.8 zoom lens.** If you have $2,000 to spare, this lens is truly wonderful in terms of image quality and speed. It's great for sports, landscapes, and portraits.
- **Sony SAL-2875 28-75mm f/2.8 zoom lens.** Half the price of the 24-70mm Zeiss lens at around $900, this one weighs a third less, too, at 20 ounces, and makes a great all-around zoom.

Your Second (and Third...) Lens

There are really only two advantages to owning just a single lens. One of them is creativity. Keeping one set of optics mounted on your Alpha all the time forces you to be especially imaginative in your approach to your subjects. I once visited Europe with only a single camera body and a 35mm f/2 lens. The experience was actually quite exciting, because I had to use a variety of techniques to allow that one lens to serve for landscapes, available light photos, action, close-ups, portraits, and other kinds of images. Sony makes an excellent "35mm" lens (actually, it's the SAL-20F28 20mm f/2.8 wide-angle lens, which provides the roughly 30mm equivalent field of view on the Alpha cameras). At $750, this lens is expensive—and very sharp. It focuses down to 9.5 inches, and would be perfect for my Europe experiment today, although my personal choice would be the sublime SAL-35F15G 35mm f/1.4 lens, which is a little longer and a lot more expensive at $1,499.

Of course, it's more likely that your "single" lens is actually a zoom, which is, in truth, many lenses in one, taking you from, say, 16mm to 80mm (or some other range) with a rapid twist of the zoom ring. You'll still find some creative challenges when you stick to a single zoom lens's focal lengths.

The second advantage of the unilens camera is only a marginal technical benefit since the introduction of the Sony Alpha. If you don't exchange lenses, the chances of dust and dirt getting inside your Alpha and settling on the sensor are reduced (but *not* eliminated entirely). Although I've known some photographers who minimized the number of lens changes they made for this very reason, reducing the number of lenses you work with is not a productive or rewarding approach for most of us. The Alpha's automatic sensor cleaning feature has made this "advantage" much less significant than it was in the past.

It's more likely that you'll succumb to the malady known as *Lens Lust*, which is defined as an incurable disease marked by a significant yen for newer, better, longer, faster, sharper, anything-er optics for your camera. (And, it must be noted, this disease can *cost* you significant yen—or dollars, or whatever currency you use.) In its worst manifestations, sufferers find themselves with lenses that have overlapping zoom ranges or capabilities, because one or the other offers a slight margin in performance or suitability for specific tasks. When you find yourself already lusting after a new lens before you've really had a chance to put your latest purchase to the test, you'll know the disease has reached the terminal phase.

What Lenses Can Do for You

A saner approach to expanding your lens collection is to consider what each of your options can do for you and then choose the type of lens that will really boost your creative opportunities. Here's a general guide to the sort of capabilities you can gain by adding a lens to your repertoire.

- **Wider perspective.** Your 18-55mm f/3.5-5.6 lens has served you well for moderate wide-angle shots. Now you find your back is up against a wall and you *can't* take a step backward to take in more subject matter. Perhaps you're standing on the rim of the Grand Canyon, and you want to take in as much of the breathtaking view as you can. You might find yourself just behind the baseline at a high school basketball game and want an interesting shot with a little perspective distortion tossed in the mix. There's a lens out there that will provide you with what you need, such as the SAL-1118, DT 11-18mm f/4.5-5.6 super-wide zoom lens or SAL-16F28 16mm f/2.8 fisheye lens. Your extra-wide choices may not be abundant, but they are there. Figure 8.4 shows the perspective you get from an ultrawide-angle lens.
- **Bring objects closer.** A long lens brings distant subjects closer to you, offers better control over depth-of-field, and avoids the perspective distortion that wide-angle lenses provide. They compress the apparent distance between objects in your frame. In the telephoto realm, Sony is right in the ballgame, with lenses like the telephoto zooms I mentioned earlier to some super high-end models like the SAL-70200G 70-200mm f/2.8 G-series telephoto zoom. (You'll pay $2,000 for this baby.) Remember that the Sony Alpha's crop factor narrows the field of view of all these lenses, so your 70-200mm lens looks more like a 105mm-300mm zoom through the viewfinder. Figures 8.5 and 8.6 were taken from the same position as Figure 8.4, but with an 85mm and 500mm focal length, respectively.
- **Bring your camera closer.** Sony has three excellent close-up lenses, the SAL-30M28 30mm f/2.8 macro lens, the SAL-50M28 50mm f/2.8 macro lens, and the SAL-100M28 100mm f/2.8 macro lens. The 30mm lens is most reasonably priced at $200 (*very* inexpensive for a true macro), but paying $600 with the 50mm lens, or $800 for the 100mm version is not out of order for someone who wants to shoot close-up subjects but wants to stay farther away from a subject to provide more flexibility in lighting and enough distance to avoid spooking small wildlife.

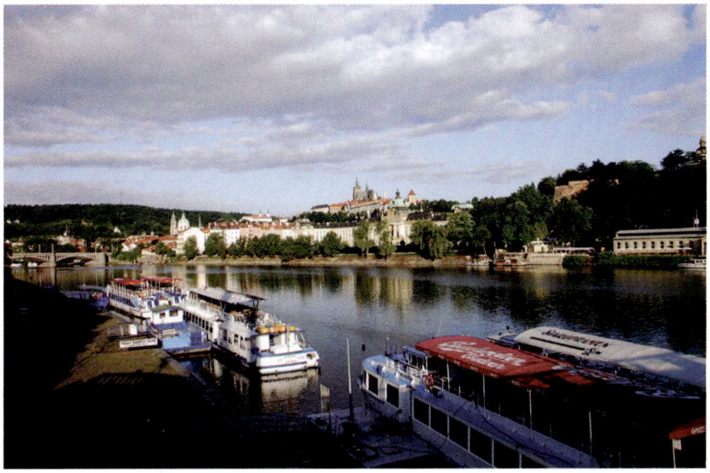

Figure 8.4
An ultrawide-angle lens provided this view of Prague Castle.

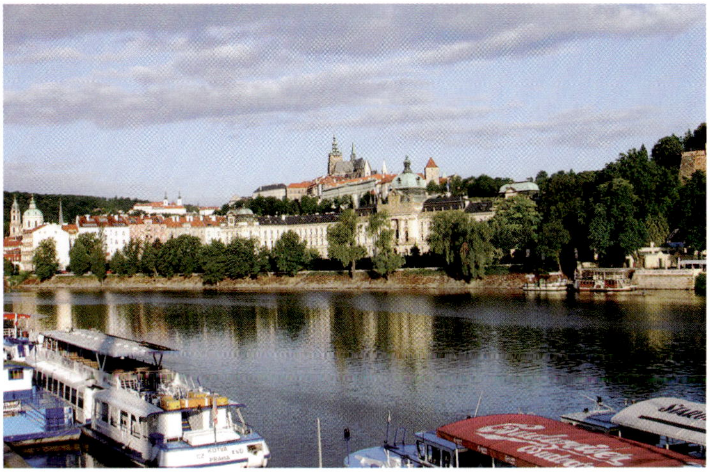

Figure 8.5
This photo, taken from roughly the same distance, shows the view using a short telephoto lens.

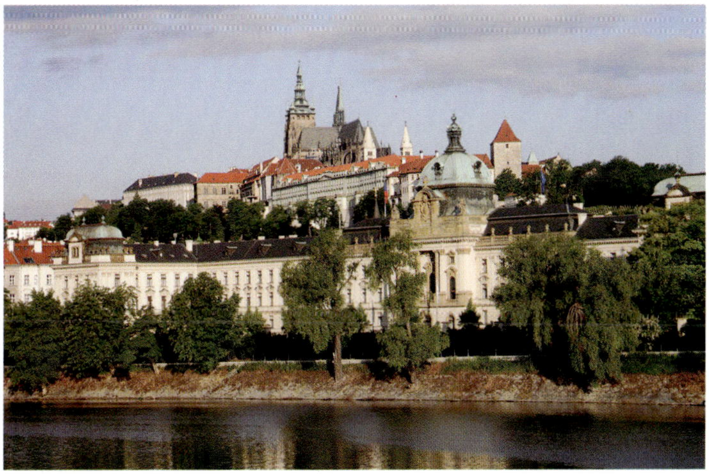

Figure 8.6
A longer telephoto lens captured this closer view from approximately the same shooting position.

- **Look sharp.** Many lenses, particularly the higher priced Sony optics, are prized for their sharpness and overall image quality. While your run-of-the-mill lens is likely to be plenty sharp for most applications, the very best optics are even better over their entire field of view (which means no fuzzy corners), are sharper at a wider range of focal lengths (in the case of zooms), and have better correction for various types of distortion. That, along with a constant f/2.8 aperture, is why the 70-200mm f/2.8 lens I mentioned earlier sells for $2,000.
- **More speed.** Your basic telephoto lens might have the perfect focal length and sharpness for sports photography, but the maximum aperture won't cut it for night baseball or football games, or, even, any sports shooting in daylight if the weather is cloudy or you need to use some ungodly fast shutter speed, such as 1/4,000th second. You might be happier with the Sony SAL-135F18Z Carl Zeiss Sonnar T* 135mm f/1.8 telephoto lens (if money is no object: it costs $1,800). But there are lower cost fast lens options, such as the SAL-50F14 50mm f/1.4 lens shown in Figure 8.7 ($500), which might be suitable for indoor sports such as basketball or volleyball, and can serve as a super fast 75mm-equivalent portrait/sports lens. (See Figure 8.8.)

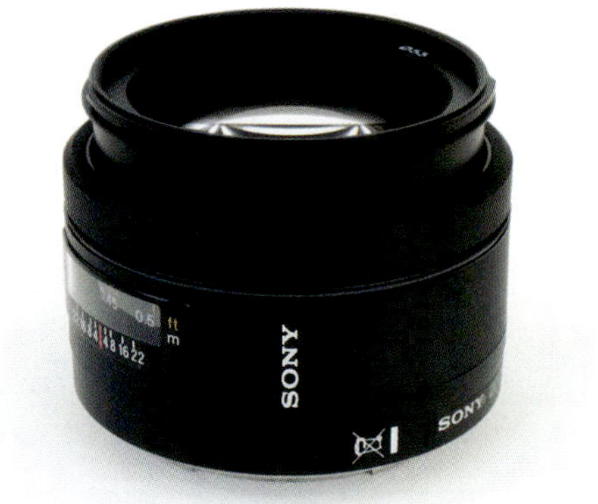

Figure 8.7 Sony's 50mm f/1.4 lens is a versatile lens for photography in low light.

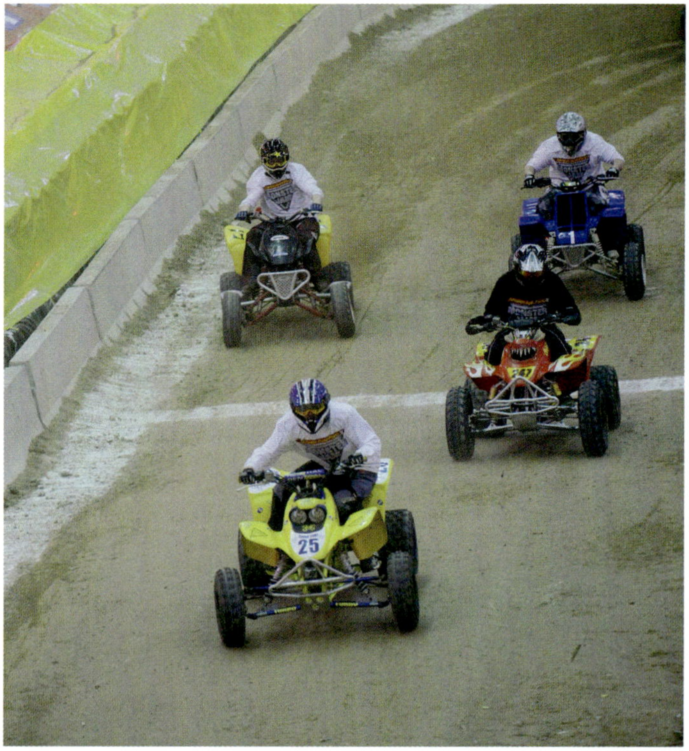

Figure 8.8 A fast lens can be useful for available light photography under dim conditions, indoors (as in this figure) or out.

Zoom or Prime?

Zoom lenses have changed the way serious photographers take pictures. One of the reasons that I own 12 SLR film bodies is that in ancient times it was common to mount a different fixed focal length prime lens on various cameras and take pictures with two or three cameras around your neck (or tucked in a camera case) so you'd be ready to take a long shot or an intimate close-up or wide-angle view on a moment's notice, without the need to switch lenses. It made sense (at the time) to have a bunch of bodies (two to use, one in the shop, one in transit, and a collection of backups). Zoom lenses of the time had a limited zoom range, were heavy, and not very sharp (especially when you tried to wield one of those monsters hand-held).

That's all changed today. Lenses like the sharp Sony lenses I've already described, including the top-of-the-line Carl Zeiss optics, have zoom ranges up to 13.8X, and are light in weight. The best zooms might seem expensive, but they are actually much less costly than the six or so lenses replaced. When selecting between zoom and prime lenses, there are several considerations to ponder. Here's a checklist of the most important factors. I already mentioned image quality and maximum aperture earlier, but those aspects take on additional meaning when comparing zooms and primes.

- **Logistics.** As prime lenses offer just a single focal length, you'll need more of them to encompass the full range offered by a single zoom. More lenses mean additional slots in your camera bag, and extra weight to carry. Even so, you might be willing to carry an extra prime lens or two in order to gain the speed or image quality that lens offers.
- **Image quality.** Prime lenses usually produce better image quality at their focal length than even the most sophisticated zoom lenses at the same magnification. Zoom lenses, with their shifting elements and f/stops that can vary from zoom position to zoom position, are in general more complex to design than fixed focal length lenses. That's not to say that the very best prime lenses can't be complicated as well. However, the exotic designs, aspheric elements, and other tweaks can be applied to improving the quality of the lens, rather than wasting a lot of it on compensating for problems caused by the zoom process itself. Figure 8.9 shows an image taken with an 85mm f/1.8 telephoto prime lens at f/4. With a zoom lens, shooting at f/4 would require using the maximum aperture, which is generally not the sharpest f/stop for a zoom. The same f/4 aperture on the prime lens allowed closing down the aperture more than one full stop, producing a sharper image under the same lighting conditions.
- **Maximum aperture.** Because of the same design constraints, zoom lenses usually have smaller maximum apertures than prime lenses, and the most affordable zooms have a lens opening that grows effectively smaller as you zoom to the telephoto position. The difference in lens speed verges on the ridiculous at some focal lengths.

For example, the 18mm-55mm basic zoom gives you a 55mm f/5.6 lens when zoomed all the way out, while prime lenses in that focal length commonly have f/1.8 or faster maximum apertures. Indeed, the fastest Sony lenses are all primes, and if you require speed, a fixed focal length lens is what you should rely on.

- **Speed.** Using prime lenses takes time and slows you down. It takes a few seconds to remove your current lens and mount a new one, and the more often you need to do that, the more time is wasted. If you choose not to swap lenses, when using a fixed focal length lens you'll still have to move closer or farther away from your subject to get the field of view you want. A zoom lens allows you to change magnifications and focal lengths with the twist of a ring and generally saves a great deal of time.

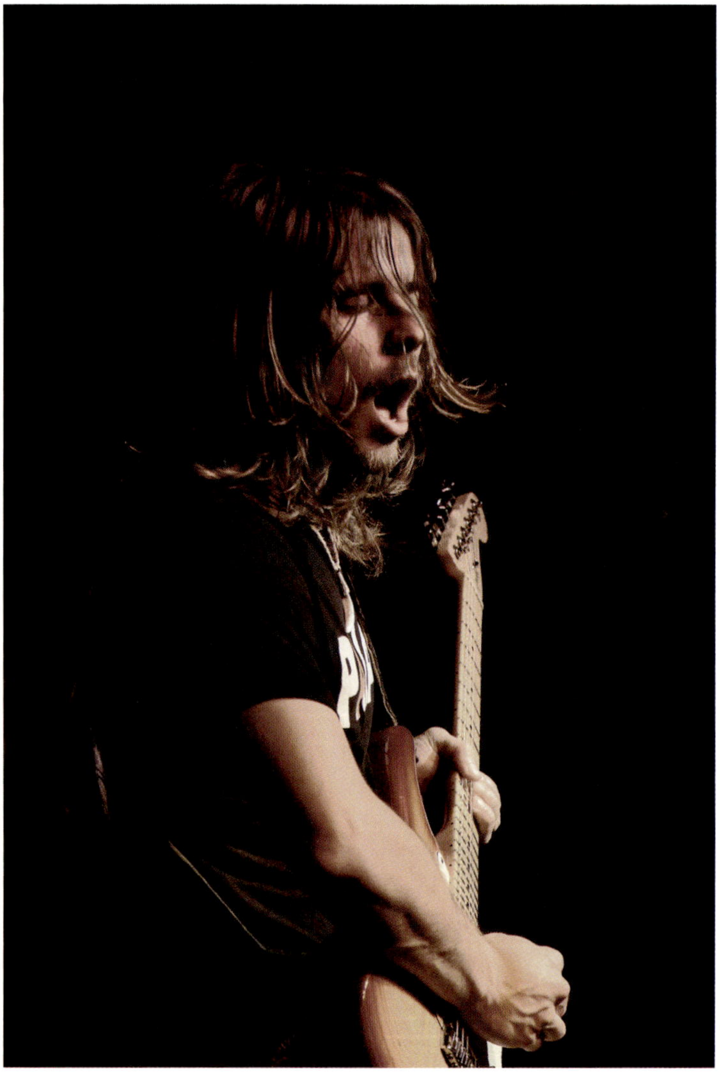

Figure 8.9
An 85mm f/1.8 lens was perfect for this hand-held photo of Willie Nelson's son Lukas.

Categories of Lenses

Lenses can be categorized by their intended purpose—general photography, macro photography, and so forth—or by their focal length. The range of available focal lengths is usually divided into three main groups: wide-angle, normal, and telephoto. Prime lenses fall neatly into one of these classifications. Zooms can overlap designations, with a significant number falling into the catchall wide-to-telephoto zoom range. This section provides more information about focal length ranges, and how they are used.

Any lens with an equivalent focal length of 10mm to 20mm is said to be an *ultrawide-angle lens*; from about 20mm to 40mm (equivalent) is said to be a *wide-angle lens. Normal lenses* have a focal length roughly equivalent to the diagonal of the film or sensor, in millimeters, and so fall into the range of about 45mm to 60mm (on a full-frame camera). *Telephoto lenses* usually fall into the 75mm and longer focal lengths, while those from about 300mm-400mm and longer often are referred to as *super telephotos.*

Using Wide-Angle and Wide-Zoom Lenses

To use wide-angle prime lenses and wide zooms, you need to understand how they affect your photography. Here's a quick summary of the things you need to know.

- **More depth-of-field.** Practically speaking, wide-angle lenses offer more depth-of-field at a particular subject distance and aperture. (But see the following sidebar for an important note.) You'll find that helpful when you want to maximize sharpness of a large zone, but not very useful when you'd rather isolate your subject using selective focus (telephoto lenses are better for that).
- **Stepping back.** Wide-angle lenses have the effect of making it seem that you are standing farther from your subject than you really are. They're helpful when you don't want to back up, or can't because there are impediments in your way.
- **Wider field of view.** While making your subject seem farther away, as implied above, a wide-angle lens also provides a larger field of view, including more of the subject in your photos.
- **More foreground.** As background objects retreat, more of the foreground is brought into view by a wide-angle lens. That gives you extra emphasis on the area that's closest to the camera. Photograph your home with a normal lens/normal zoom setting, and the front yard probably looks fairly conventional in your photo (that's why they're called "normal" lenses). Switch to a wider lens and you'll discover that your lawn now makes up much more of the photo. So, wide-angle lenses are great when you want to emphasize that lake in the foreground, but problematic when your intended subject is located farther in the distance.

- **Super-sized subjects.** The tendency of a wide-angle lens to emphasize objects in the foreground, while de-emphasizing objects in the background, can lead to a kind of size distortion that may be more objectionable for some types of subjects than others. Shoot a bed of flowers up close with a wide angle, and you might like the distorted effect of the larger blossoms nearer the lens. Take a photo of a family member with the same lens from the same distance, and you're likely to get some complaints about that gigantic nose in the foreground.
- **Perspective distortion.** When you tilt the camera so the plane of the sensor is no longer perpendicular to the vertical plane of your subject, some parts of the subject are now closer to the sensor than they were before, while other parts are farther away. So, buildings, flagpoles, or NBA players appear to be falling backwards (as in Figure 8.10). While this kind of apparent distortion (it's not caused by a defect in the lens) can happen with any lens, it's most apparent when a wide angle is used.

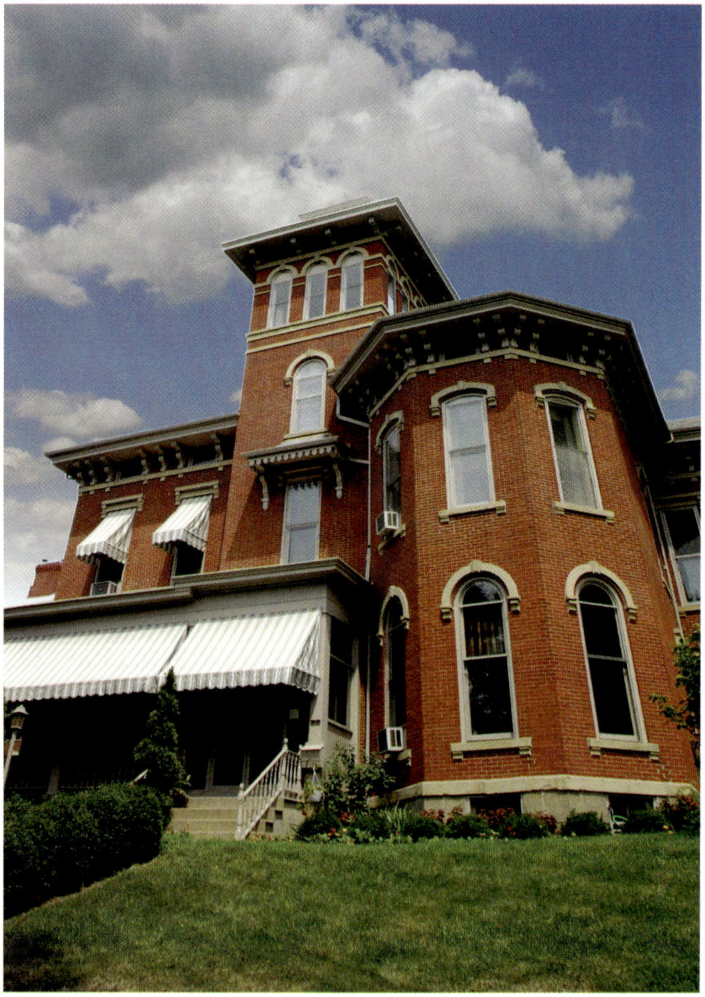

Figure 8.10
Tilting the camera back produces this "falling back" look in architectural photos.

- **Steady cam.** You'll find that you can hand-hold a wide-angle lens at slower shutter speeds easier than you can with a telephoto lens, without need for SteadyShot. The reduced magnification of the wide-lens or wide-zoom setting doesn't emphasize camera shake like a telephoto lens does.
- **Interesting angles.** Many of the factors already listed combine to produce more interesting angles when shooting with wide-angle lenses. Raising or lowering a telephoto lens a few feet probably will have little effect on the appearance of the distant subjects you're shooting. The same change in elevation can produce a dramatic effect for the much-closer subjects typically captured with a wide-angle lens or wide-zoom setting.

DOF IN DEPTH

The DOF advantage of wide-angle lenses is diminished when you enlarge your picture; believe it or not, a wide-angle image enlarged and cropped to provide the same subject size as a telephoto shot would have the *same* depth-of-field. Try it: take a wide-angle photo of a friend from a fair distance, and then zoom in to duplicate the picture in a telephoto image. Then, enlarge the wide shot so your friend is the same size in both. The wide photo will have the same depth-of-field (and will have much less detail, too).

Avoiding Potential Wide-Angle Problems

Wide-angle lenses have a few quirks that you'll want to keep in mind when shooting so you can avoid falling into some common traps. Here's a checklist of tips for avoiding common problems:

- **Symptom: converging lines.** Unless you want to use wildly diverging lines as a creative effect, it's a good idea to keep horizontal and vertical lines in landscapes, architecture, and other subjects carefully aligned with the sides, top, and bottom of the frame. That will help you avoid undesired perspective distortion. Sometimes it helps to shoot from a slightly elevated position so you don't have to tilt the camera up or down.
- **Symptom: color fringes around objects.** Lenses are often plagued with fringes of color around backlit objects, produced by *chromatic aberration*, which comes in two forms: *longitudinal/axial*, in which all the colors of light don't focus in the same plane; and *lateral/transverse*, in which the colors are shifted to one side. Axial chromatic aberration can be reduced by stopping down the lens, but transverse chromatic aberration cannot. Both can be reduced if you purchase lenses with low diffraction index glass and which incorporate elements that cancel the chromatic aberration of other glass in the lens. For example, a strong positive lens made of low-dispersion crown glass (made of a soda-lime-silica composite) may be mated with a weaker negative lens made of high-dispersion flint glass, which contains lead.

- **Symptom: lines that bow outward.** Some wide-angle lenses cause straight lines to bow outwards, with the strongest effect at the edges. In fisheye (or *curvilinear*) lenses, this defect is a feature, as you can see in Figure 8.11. When distortion is not desired, you'll need to use a lens that has corrected barrel distortion. Manufacturers like Sony do their best to minimize or eliminate it (producing a *rectilinear* lens), often using *aspherical* lens elements (which are not cross-sections of a sphere). You can also minimize barrel distortion simply by framing your photo with some extra space all around, so the edges where the defect is most obvious can be cropped out of the picture.
- **Symptom: dark corners and shadows in flash photos.** The Sony Alpha's built-in electronic flash is designed to provide even coverage for fairly wide lenses. If you use a wider lens, you can expect darkening, or *vignetting*, in the corners of the frame. At wider focal lengths, the lens hood of some lenses (my 16mm-80mm f/3.5-4.5 zoom lens is a prime offender) can cast a semi-circular shadow in the lower portion of the frame when using the built-in flash. Sometimes removing the lens hood or zooming in a bit can eliminate the shadow. Mounting an external flash unit can solve both problems. Its higher vantage point eliminates the problem of lens hood shadow, too.

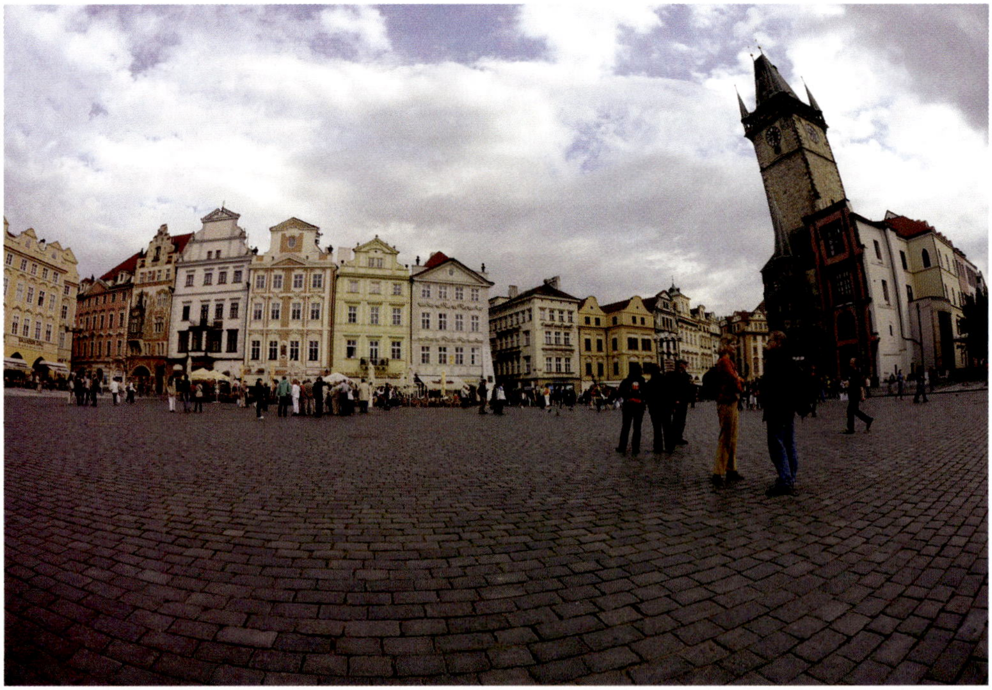

Figure 8.11
Many wide-angle lenses cause lines to bow outward toward the edges of the image; with a fisheye lens, this tendency is considered an interesting feature.

- **Symptom: light and dark areas when using polarizing filter.** If you know that polarizers work best when the camera is pointed 90 degrees away from the sun and have the least effect when the camera is oriented 180 degrees from the sun, you know only half the story. With lenses having a focal length of 10mm to 18mm (the equivalent of 16mm-28mm), the angle of view (107 to 75 degrees diagonally, or 97 to 44 degrees horizontally) is extensive enough to cause problems. Think about it: when a 10mm lens is pointed at the proper 90-degree angle from the sun, objects at the edges of the frame will be oriented at 135 to 41 degrees, with only the center at exactly 90 degrees. Either edge will have much less of a polarized effect. The solution is to avoid using a polarizing filter with lenses having an actual focal length of less than 18mm (or 28mm equivalent).

Using Telephoto and Tele-Zoom Lenses

Telephoto lenses also can have a dramatic effect on your photography, and Sony is especially strong in the long-lens arena, with lots of choices in many focal lengths and zoom ranges. You should be able to find an affordable telephoto or tele-zoom to enhance your photography in several different ways. Here are the most important things you need to know. In the next section, I'll concentrate on telephoto considerations that can be problematic—and how to avoid those problems.

- **Selective focus.** Long lenses have reduced depth-of-field within the frame, allowing you to use selective focus to isolate your subject. You can open the lens up wide to create shallow depth-of-field, or close it down a bit to allow more to be in focus. The flip side of the coin is that when you *want* to make a range of objects sharp, you'll need to use a smaller f/stop to get the depth-of-field you need. Like fire, the depth-of-field of a telephoto lens can be friend or foe. Figure 8.12 shows a lemur in its "natural" habitat (the Bioparc zoo in Valencia, Spain), photographed using a short telephoto lens and wider f/stop to de-emphasize the other foliage in the foreground and background.
- **Getting closer.** Telephoto lenses bring you closer to wildlife, sports action, and candid subjects. No one wants to get a reputation as a surreptitious or "sneaky" photographer (except for paparazzi), but when applied to candids in an open and honest way, a long lens can help you capture memorable moments while retaining enough distance to stay out of the way of events as they transpire.
- **Reduced foreground/increased compression.** Telephoto lenses have the opposite effect of wide angles: they reduce the importance of things in the foreground by squeezing everything together. This compression even makes distant objects appear to be closer to subjects in the foreground and middle ranges. You can use this effect as a creative tool.

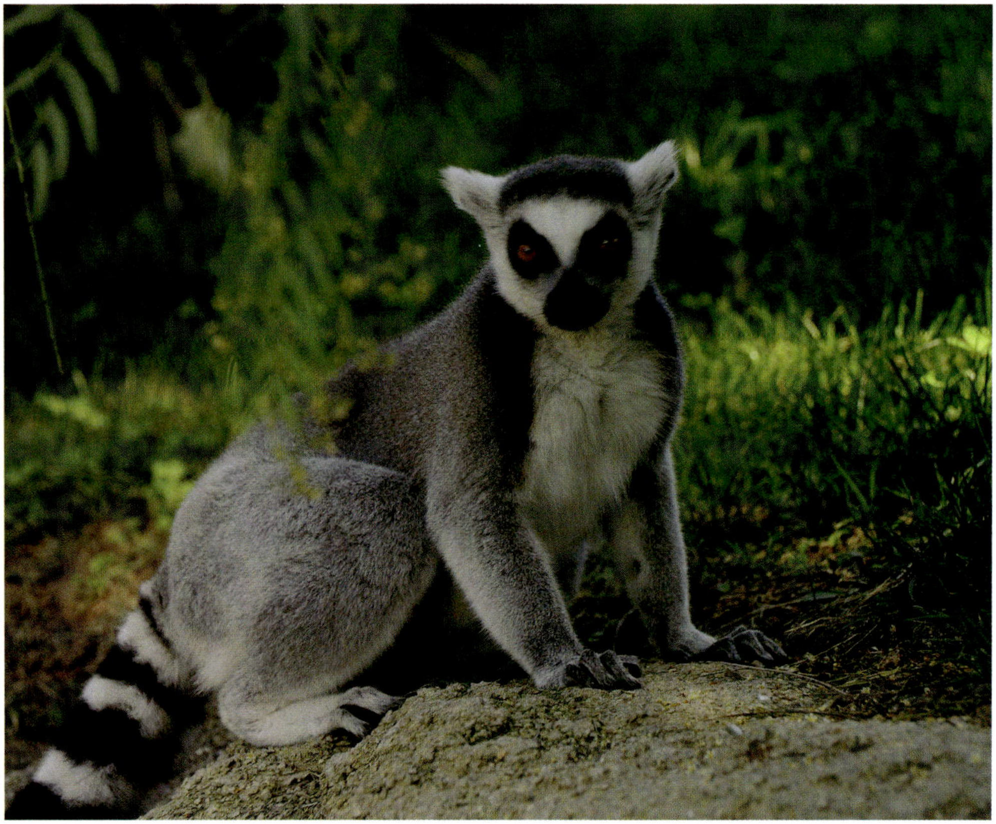

Figure 8.12
A wide f/stop helped isolate this lemur from its background.

- **Accentuates camera shakiness.** Telephoto focal lengths hit you with a double-whammy in terms of camera/photographer shake. The lenses themselves are bulkier, more difficult to hold steady, and may even produce a barely perceptible seesaw rocking effect when you support them with one hand halfway down the lens barrel. Telephotos also magnify any camera shake. It's no wonder that Sony's image stabilization feature is popular when using longer lenses.
- **Interesting angles require creativity.** Telephoto lenses require more imagination in selecting interesting angles, because the "angle" you do get on your subjects is so narrow. Moving from side to side or a bit higher or lower can make a dramatic difference in a wide-angle shot, but raising or lowering a telephoto lens a few feet probably will have little effect on the appearance of the distant subjects you're shooting.

Avoiding Telephoto Lens Problems

Many of the "problems" that telephoto lenses pose are really just challenges and not that difficult to overcome. Here is a list of the seven most common picture maladies and suggested solutions.

- **Symptom: flat faces in portraits.** Head-and-shoulders portraits of humans tend to be more flattering when a focal length of 50mm to 85mm is used. Longer focal lengths compress the distance between features like noses and ears, making the face look wider and flat. A wide angle might make noses look huge and ears tiny when you fill the frame with a face. So stick with 50mm to 85mm focal lengths or zoom settings, going longer only when you're forced to shoot from a greater distance, and wider only when shooting three-quarters/full-length portraits, or group shots.
- **Symptom: blur due to camera shake.** First, make sure you have SteadyShot turned on! Then, if possible, use a higher shutter speed (boosting ISO if necessary), or mount your camera on a tripod or monopod, or brace it with some other support. Of those three solutions, only the second will reduce blur caused by *subject* motion; SteadyShot or a tripod won't help you freeze a race car in mid-lap.
- **Symptom: color fringes.** Chromatic aberration is the most pernicious optical problem found in telephoto lenses. There are others, including spherical aberration, astigmatism, coma, curvature of field, and similarly scary-sounding phenomena. The best solution for any of these is to use a better lens that offers the proper degree of correction, or stop down the lens to minimize the problem. But that's not always possible. Your second-best choice may be to correct the fringing in your favorite RAW conversion tool or image editor. Photoshop's Lens Correction filter offers sliders that minimize both red/cyan and blue/yellow fringing.
- **Symptom: lines that curve inwards.** Pincushion distortion is found in many telephoto lenses. You might find after a bit of testing that it is worse at certain focal lengths with your particular zoom lens. Like chromatic aberration, it can be partially corrected using tools like Photoshop's Lens Correction filter.
- **Symptom: low contrast from haze or fog.** When you're photographing distant objects, a long lens shoots through a lot more atmosphere, which generally is muddied up with extra haze and fog. That dirt or moisture in the atmosphere can reduce contrast and mute colors. Some feel that a skylight or UV filter can help, but this practice is mostly a holdover from the film days. Digital sensors are not sensitive enough to UV light for a UV filter to have much effect. So you should be prepared to boost contrast and color saturation in your Creative Style menu or image editor if necessary.

- **Symptom: low contrast from flare.** Lenses are furnished with lens hoods for a good reason: to reduce flare from bright light sources at the periphery of the picture area, or completely outside it. Because telephoto lenses often create images that are lower in contrast in the first place, you'll want to be especially careful to use a lens hood to prevent further effects on your image (or shade the front of the lens with your hand).
- **Symptom: dark flash photos.** Edge-to-edge flash coverage isn't a problem with telephoto lenses as it is with wide angles. The shooting distance is. A long lens might make a subject that's 50 feet away look as if it's right next to you, but your camera's flash isn't fooled. You'll need extra power for distant flash shots, and probably more power than your Alpha's built-in flash provides unless you increase the ISO setting to ISO 3200.

Telephotos and Bokeh

Bokeh describes the aesthetic qualities of the out-of-focus parts of an image and whether out-of-focus points of light—circles of confusion—are rendered as distracting fuzzy discs or smoothly fade into the background. *Boke* is a Japanese word for "blur," and the h was added to keep English speakers from rendering it monosyllabically to rhyme with *broke.* Although bokeh is visible in blurry portions of any image, it's of particular concern with telephoto lenses, which, thanks to the magic of reduced depth-of-field, produce more obviously out-of-focus areas.

Bokeh can vary from lens to lens, or even within a given lens depending on the f/stop in use. Bokeh becomes objectionable when the circles of confusion are evenly illuminated, making them stand out as distinct discs, or, worse, when these circles are darker in the center, producing an ugly "doughnut" effect. A lens defect called spherical aberration may produce out-of-focus discs that are brighter on the edges and darker in the center, because the lens doesn't focus light passing through the edges of the lens exactly as it does light going through the center. (Mirror or *catadioptric* lenses also produce this effect.)

Other kinds of spherical aberration generate circles of confusion that are brightest in the center and fade out at the edges, producing a smooth blending effect, as you can see at right in Figure 8.13. Ironically, when no spherical aberration is present at all, the discs are a uniform shade, which, while better than the doughnut effect, is not as pleasing as the bright center/dark edge rendition. The shape of the disc also comes into play, with round smooth circles considered the best, and nonagonal or some other polygon (determined by the shape of the lens diaphragm) considered less desirable. Most Sony lenses have near-circular irises, producing very pleasing bokeh.

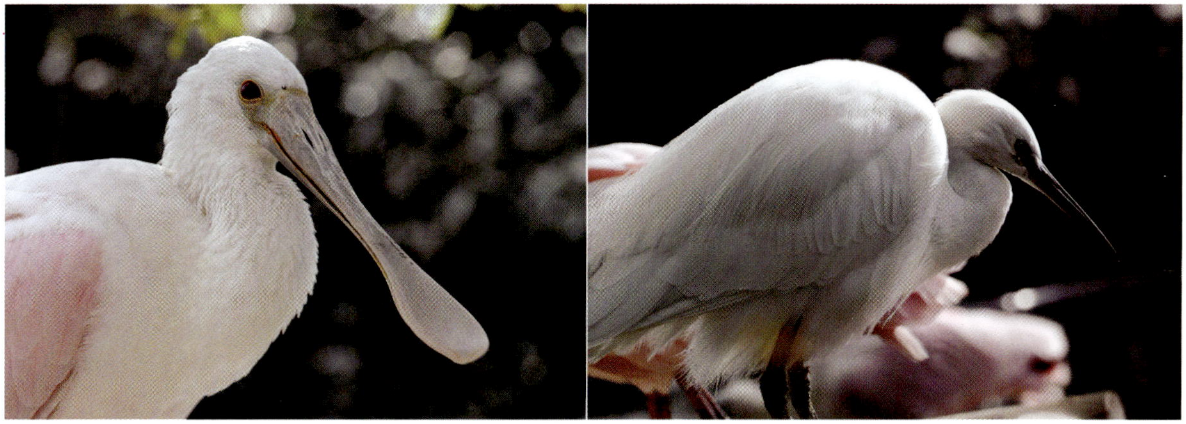

Figure 8.13 Bokeh is less pleasing when the discs are prominent (left), and less obtrusive when they blend into the background (right).

If you plan to use selective focus a lot, you should investigate the bokeh characteristics of a particular lens before you buy. Sony user groups and forums will usually be full of comments and questions about bokeh, so the research is fairly easy.

Add-ons and Special Features

Once you've purchased your telephoto lens, you'll want to think about some appropriate accessories for it. There are some handy add-ons available that can be valuable. Here are a couple of them to think about.

Lens Hoods

Lens hoods are an important accessory for all lenses, but they're especially valuable with telephotos. As I mentioned earlier, lens hoods do a good job of preserving image contrast by keeping bright light sources outside the field of view from striking the lens and, potentially, bouncing around inside that long tube to generate flare that, when coupled with atmospheric haze, can rob your image of detail and snap. In addition, lens hoods serve as valuable protection for that large, vulnerable, front lens element. It's easy to forget that you've got that long tube sticking out in front of your camera and accidentally whack the front of your lens into something. It's cheaper to replace a lens hood than it is to have a lens repaired, so you might find that a good hood is valuable protection for your prized optics.

When choosing a lens hood, it's important to have the right hood for the lens, usually the one offered for that lens by Sony or the third-party manufacturer. You want a hood that blocks precisely the right amount of light: neither too much light nor too little. A hood with a front diameter that is too small can show up in your pictures as vignetting. A hood that has a front diameter that's too large isn't stopping all the light it should. Generic lens hoods may not do the job.

When your telephoto is a zoom lens, it's even more important to get the right hood, because you need one that does what it is supposed to at both the wide-angle and telephoto ends of the zoom range. Lens hoods may be cylindrical, rectangular (shaped like the image frame), or petal shaped (that is, cylindrical, but with cutout areas at the corners that correspond to the actual image area). Lens hoods should be mounted in the correct orientation (a bayonet mount for the hood usually takes care of this).

Telephoto Extenders

Telephoto extenders, like the SAL-14TC 1.4X C-series tele-converter lens and SAL-20TC 2.0X C-series tele-converter lens multiply the actual focal length of your lens, giving you a longer telephoto for much less than the price of a lens with that actual focal length. These extenders fit between the lens and your camera and contain optical elements that magnify the image produced by the lens. Available in 1.4X and 2.0X configurations from Sony, an extender transforms, say, a 200mm lens into a 300mm or 400mm optic, respectively. Given the Alpha's crop factor, your 200mm lens now has the same field of view as a 450mm or 600mm lens on a full-frame camera. At around $450 each, they're quite a bargain, aren't they?

Actually, there are some downsides. While extenders retain the closest focusing distance of your original lens, autofocus is maintained only if the lens's original maximum aperture is f/4 or larger (for the 1.4X extender) or f/2.8 or larger (for the 2X extender). The components reduce the effective aperture of any lens they are used with, by one f/stop with the 1.4X extender, and 2 f/stops with the 2X extender.

Macro Focusing

Some telephotos and telephoto zooms available for the Sony Alpha have particularly close focusing capabilities, making them *macro* lenses. Of course, the object is not necessarily to get close (get too close and you'll find it difficult to light your subject). What you're really looking for in a macro lens is to magnify the apparent size of the subject in the final image. Camera-to-subject distance is most important when you want to back up farther from your subject (say, to avoid spooking skittish insects or small animals). In that case, you'll want a macro lens with a longer focal length to allow that distance while retaining the desired magnification.

Sony makes three lenses with official macro designations, in 30mm, 50mm, and 100mm focal lengths. You'll also find macro lenses, macro zooms, and other close-focusing lenses available from Sigma, Tamron, and Tokina. If you want to focus closer with a macro lens, or any other lens, you can add an accessory called an *extension tube*, like the ones shown in Figure 8.14. These add-ons move the lens farther from the focal plane, allowing it to focus more closely. You can also buy add-on close-up lenses, which look like filters, and allow lenses to focus more closely.

Although I use extension tubes for extreme close-ups, Sony's macro lenses, like the 30mm f/2.8 lens shown in Figure 8.15, do the best job for most subjects, providing close, automatic focus and a wide enough maximum aperture to allow selective focus for shots like Figure 8.16.

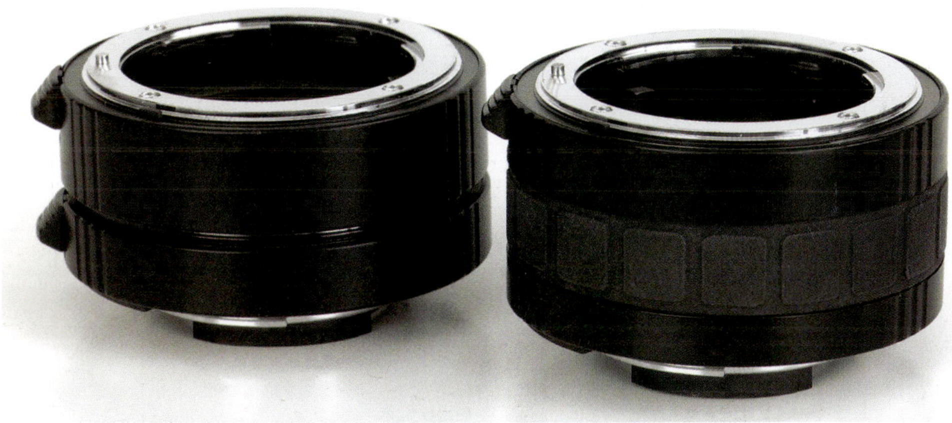

Figure 8.14
Extension tubes enable any lens to focus more closely to the subject.

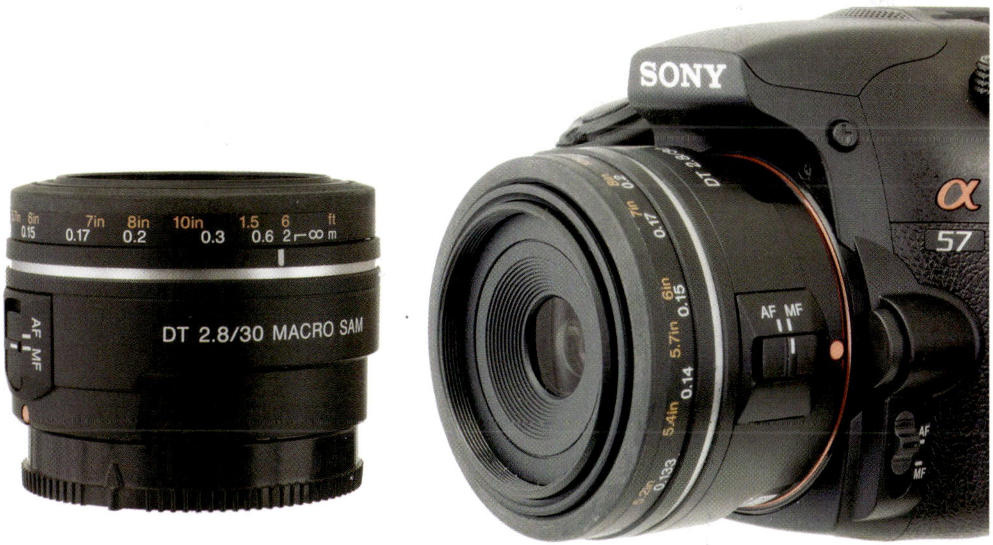

Figure 8.15
Sony's 30mm f/2.8 macro lens.

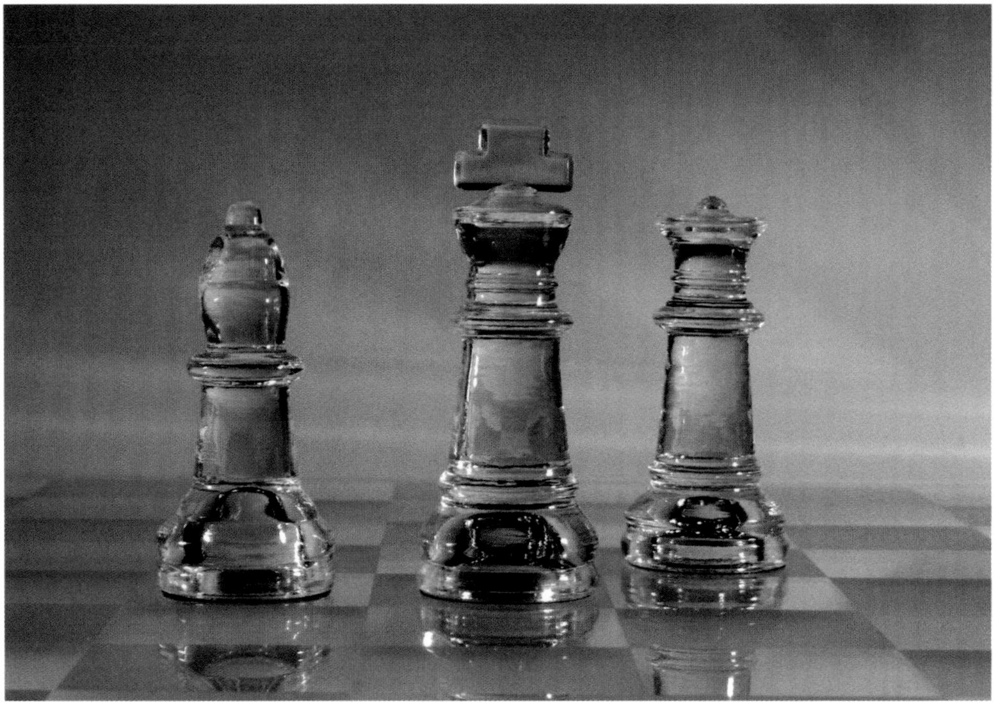

Figure 8.16
Close focusing and a wide maximum aperture allow for selective focus effects.

Using the Lensbaby

The Lensbaby, which comes in several varieties, including the Composer Pro shown in Figure 8.17, uses distortion-heavy glass elements mounted on a system that allows you to bend, twist, and distort the lens's alignment to produce transmogrified images unlike anything else you've ever seen. Like the legendary cheap-o Diana and Holga cameras, the pictures are prized expressly because of their plastic image quality. Jack and Meg White (formerly of the White Stripes) are, in fact, selling personalized Diana and Holga cameras on their website for wacky *lomography* (named after the Lomo, another low-quality/high-concept camera). The various Lensbaby models are for more serious photographers, if you can say that about anyone who yearns to take pictures that look like they were shot through a glob of corn syrup.

Lensbabies are capable of creating all sorts of special effects. You use a Lensbaby by shifting the front mount to move the lens's sweet spot to a particular point in the scene. This is basically a selective focus lens that gets very soft outside the sweet spot. There are several different types of Lensbabies.

- **Macro.** A Lensbaby accessory makes it possible to use this tool for macro photography.

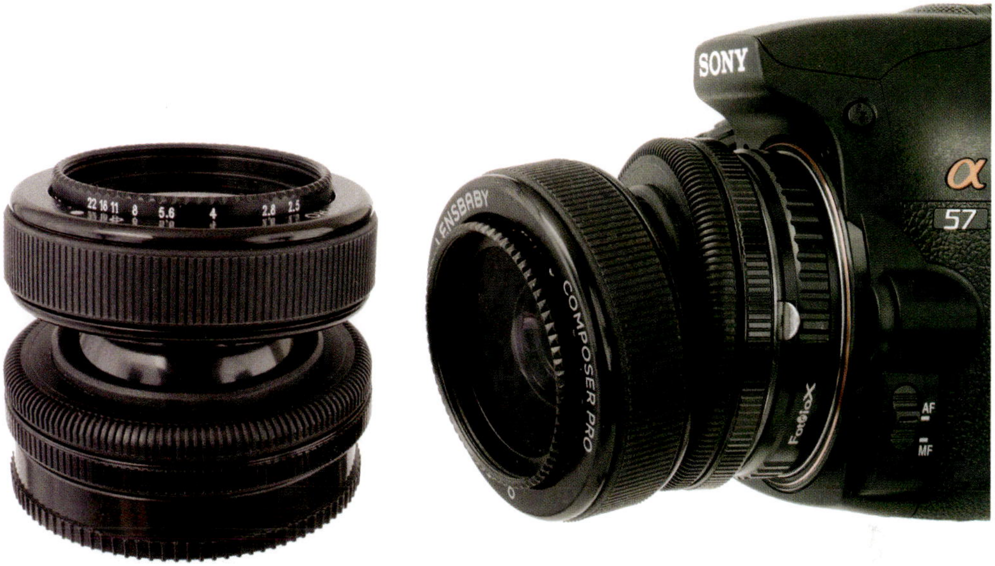

Figure 8.17
Lensbabies are specialized lens replacements with some special soft-focus features.

- **Wide-angle/telephoto conversion.** Add-on lenses convert the basic Lensbaby into a wide-angle or telephoto version.
- **Creative aperture kit.** Various shaped cutouts can be used in place of the regular aperture inserts that control depth-of-field. These shapes can include things like hearts, stars, and other shapes.
- **Optic swap kit.** This three-lens accessory kit provides different adapters that include a pinhole lens, plastic lens, and single glass lens.

The latest Lensbaby models, like the Composer Pro, have the same shifting, tilting lens configuration as previous editions, but are designed for easier and more precise distorting movements. Hold the camera with your finger gripping the knobs as you bend the camera to move the central "sweet spot" (sharp area) to any portion of your image. With two (count 'em) multicoated optical glass lens elements, you'll get a blurry image, but the amount of distortion is under your control. F/stops from f/2 to f/22 are available to increase/decrease depth-of-field and allow you to adjust exposure. The 50mm lens focuses down to 12 inches and is strictly manual focus/manual exposure in operation. At $300 or so, these lenses are not cheap accessories, but there is really no other easy way to achieve the kind of looks you can get with a Lensbaby.

Figure 8.18 is an example of the type of effect you can get, in a photograph crafted by Cleveland photographer Nancy Balluck. She also produced the back cover photography of yours truly, and one of her specialties is Lensbaby effects. Nancy regularly gives demonstrations and classes on the use of these optics, and you can follow her work at www.nancyballuckphotography.com.

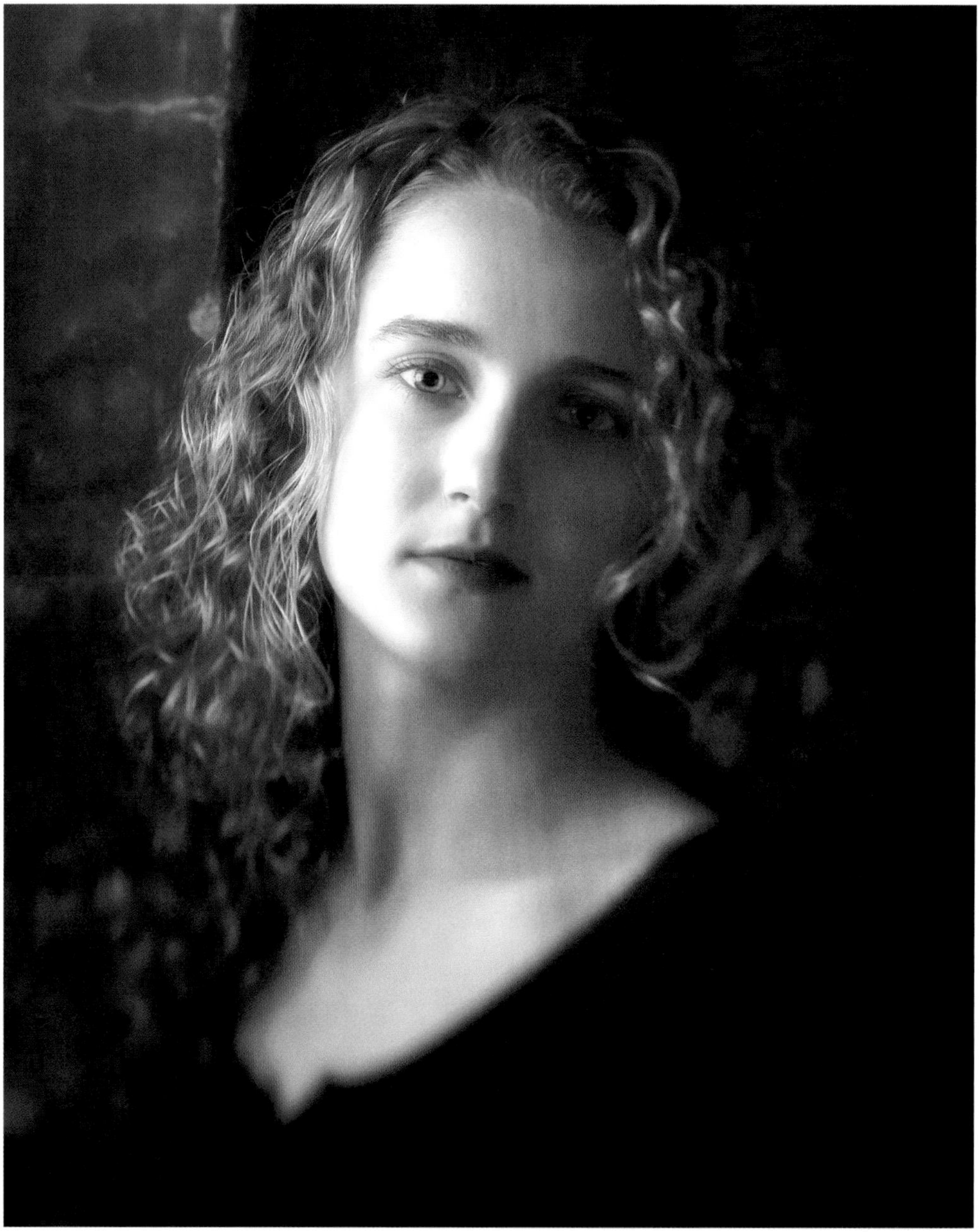

Figure 8.18
Everything is uniquely blurry outside the Lensbaby's "sweet spot," but you can move that spot around within your frame at will. They can be used for selective focus effects, and can simulate the dreamy look of some old-style cameras.

SteadyShot and Your Lenses

Vendors like Nikon and Canon sell special lenses with anti-shake features built in. With your Sony Alpha A57, *every* lens you own has image stabilization. SteadyShot provides you with camera steadiness that's the equivalent of at least two or three shutter speed increments. This extra margin can be invaluable when you're shooting under dim lighting conditions or hand-holding a long lens for, say, wildlife photography. Perhaps that shot of a foraging deer calls for a shutter speed of 1/1,000th second at f/5.6 with your lens. Relax. You can shoot at 1/250th second at f/11 and get virtually the same results, as long as the deer doesn't decide to bound off.

Or, maybe you're shooting a high-school play without a tripod or monopod, and you'd really, really like to use 1/15th second at f/4. Assuming the actors aren't flitting around the stage at high speed, your wide-angle lens can grab the shot for you at its wide-angle position. However, keep these facts in mind:

- **SteadyShot doesn't stop action.** Unfortunately, no stabilization is a panacea to replace the action-stopping capabilities of a higher shutter speed. Image stabilization applies only to camera shake. You still need a fast shutter speed to freeze action. SteadyShot works great in low light, when you're using long lenses, and for macro photography. It's not always the best choice for action photography, unless there's enough light to allow a sufficiently high shutter speed. If so, stabilization can make your shot even sharper.
- **Stabilization might slow you down.** The process of adjusting the sensor to counter camera shake takes time, just as autofocus does, so you might find that SteadyShot adds to the lag between when you press the shutter and when the picture is actually taken. That's another reason why image stabilization might not be a good choice for sports.
- **Use when appropriate.** Sometimes, stabilization produces worse results if used while you're panning. You might want to switch off IS when panning or when your camera is mounted on a tripod.
- **Do you need SteadyShot at all?** Remember that an inexpensive monopod might be able to provide the same additional steadiness as SteadyShot. If you're out in the field shooting wild animals or flowers and think a tripod isn't practical, try a monopod first.

9

Making Light Work for You

Successful photographers and artists have an intimate understanding of the importance of light in shaping an image. Rembrandt was a master of using light to create moods and reveal the character of his subjects. The late artist Thomas Kinkade's official tagline was "Painter of Light." Dean Collins, co-founder of Finelight Studios, revolutionized how a whole generation of photographers learned and used lighting. It's impossible to underestimate how the use of light adds to—and how misuse can detract from—your photographs.

All forms of visual art use light to shape the finished product. Sculptors don't have control over the light used to illuminate their finished work, so they must create shapes using planes and curved surfaces so that the form envisioned by the artist comes to life from a variety of viewing and lighting angles. Painters, in contrast, have absolute control over both shape and light in their work, as well as the viewing angle, so they can use both the contours of their two-dimensional subjects and the qualities of the "light" they use to illuminate those subjects to evoke the image they want to produce.

Photography is a third form of art. The photographer may have little or no control over the subject (other than posing human subjects) but can often adjust both viewing angle *and* the nature of the light source to create a particular compelling image. The direction and intensity of the light sources create the shapes and textures that we see. The distribution and proportions determine the contrast and tonal values: whether the image is stark or high key, or muted and low in contrast. The colors of the light (because even "white" light has a color balance that the sensor can detect), and how much of those colors the subject reflects or absorbs, paint the hues visible in the image.

As a Sony Alpha photographer, you must learn to be a painter and sculptor of light if you want to move from *taking* a picture to *making* a photograph. This chapter provides an introduction to using the two main types of illumination: *continuous* lighting (such as daylight, incandescent, or fluorescent sources) and the brief, but brilliant snippets of light we call *electronic flash.*

The Elements of Light

Unless you're extraordinarily lucky, or supremely observant, great lighting, like most things of artistic value, doesn't happen by accident. It's entirely possible that you'll randomly encounter a scene or subject that's bathed in marvelous lighting, illumination that perfectly sculpts an image in highlights and shadows. That's what happened when I encountered the stark geometric shapes of the fountain in the infrared shot shown in Figure 9.1. All I really needed to do was walk around the fountain until I found the best angle. The light was already there; I just needed to be lucky enough to encounter and recognize it.

But how often can you count on such luck? Ansel Adams, producer Samuel Goldwyn, and golfer Gary Player have all been credited with originating the phrase, "The harder I work, the luckier I get." If you work at learning what light can do, and how to use it, you'll find yourself becoming luckier too.

Knowledge, patience, and the ability to use the lighting tools at your disposal are the keys to great lighting. Ansel Adams was known for his patience in seeking out the best

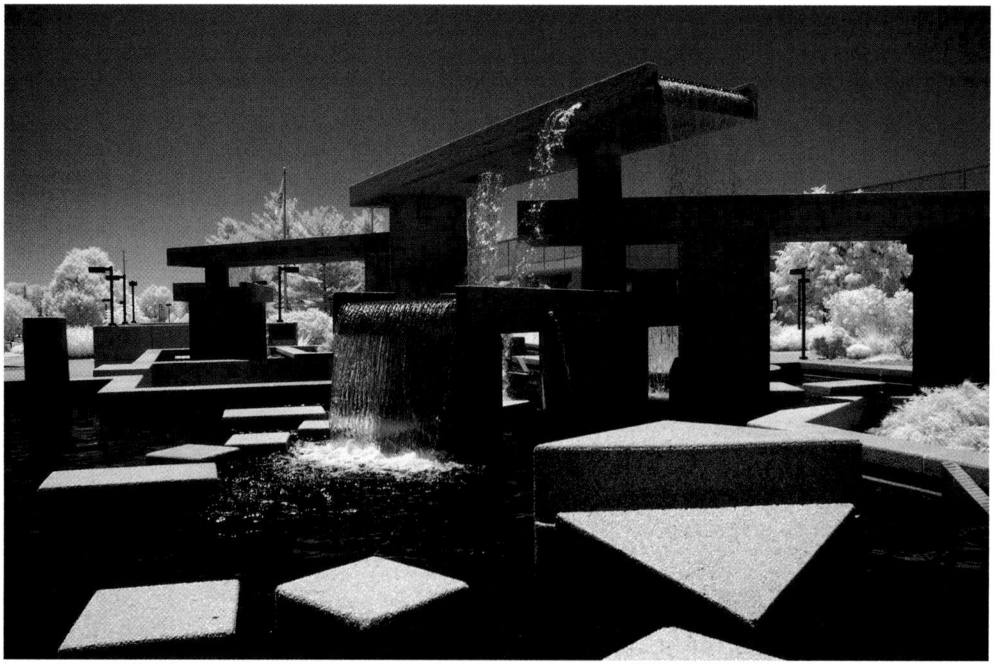

Figure 9.1
Recognizing and using interesting illumination allows you to sculpt your photographs with light.

lighting for a composition, and he *did* actually say, "A good photograph is knowing where to stand." You have to possess the ability to *recognize* effective lighting when it is already present, and have the skill to manipulate the light when it is not.

One of my favorite stories is about photographer George Krause, who spent the early part of his career shooting photographs *only* on overcast days, under diffuse, low-contrast illumination. That kind of lighting can be exceptionally challenging, because there is no interplay of highlights and shadows to add depth to a composition. Only when Krause was convinced that he understood soft lighting did he move on to work with more dramatic applications of light. Check out Krause's *Shadow*, taken in Seville, Spain more than 40 years ago at http://www.gallery339.com/html/Detail.asp?WorkInvNum=2209&artistname=George%20Krause&whatpage=artistfull. Does the photo show an old woman—or an old woman followed by a dark secret?

Continuous Lighting—or Electronic Flash?

Continuous lighting is exactly what you might think: uninterrupted illumination that is available all the time during a shooting session. Daylight, moonlight, and the artificial lighting encountered both indoors and outdoors count as continuous light sources (although all of them can be "interrupted" by passing clouds, solar eclipses, a blown fuse, or simply by switching off a lamp). Indoor continuous illumination includes both the lights that are there already (such as incandescent lamps or overhead fluorescent lights indoors) and fixtures you supply yourself, including photoflood lamps or reflectors used to bounce existing light onto your subject.

The surge of light we call electronic flash is produced by a burst of photons generated by an electrical charge that is accumulated in a component called a *capacitor* and then directed through a glass tube containing xenon gas, which absorbs the energy and emits the brief flash. Electronic flash is notable because it can be much more intense than continuous lighting, lasts only a brief moment, and can be much more portable than supplementary incandescent sources. It's a light source you can carry with you and use anywhere.

Your Sony Alpha SLT-A57 incorporates a flip-up built-in electronic flash. (See Figure 9.2.) You can also work with an external flash, either mounted on the Alpha's accessory shoe or used off-camera and linked with a cable or triggered by a slave light (which sets off a flash when it senses the firing of another unit). Studio flash units are electronic flash, too, and aren't limited to "professional" shooters, as there are economical "monolight" (one-piece flash/power supply) units available in the $200 price range. Those with some cash to spare can buy a couple to store in a closet and use to set up a home studio, or use as supplementary lighting when traveling away from home.

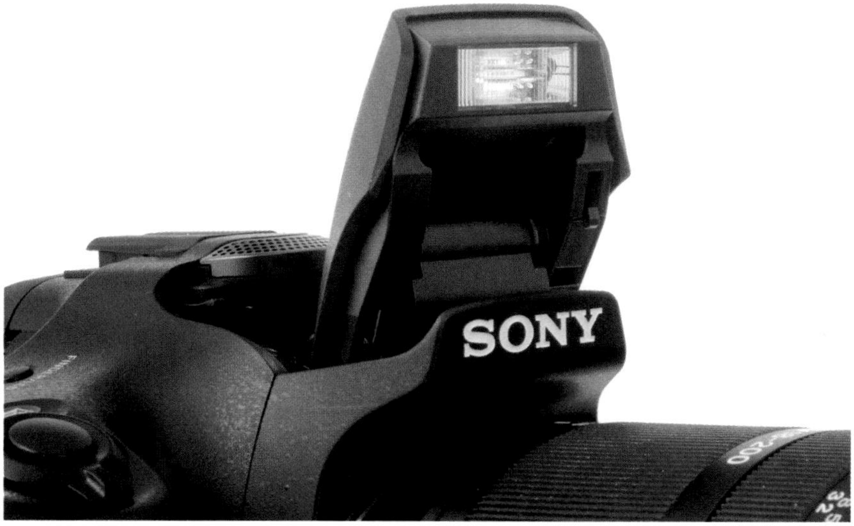

Figure 9.2
Your camera's built-in flash is always available.

There are advantages and disadvantages to each type of illumination. Here's a quick checklist of pros and cons:

- **Lighting preview—Pro: continuous lighting.** With continuous lighting, such as incandescent lamps or daylight (see Figure 9.3), you always know exactly what kind of lighting effect you're going to get and, if multiple lights are used, how they will interact with each other. With electronic flash, the general effect you're going to see may be a mystery until you've built some experience, and you may need to review a shot on the LCD, make some adjustments, and then reshoot to get the look you want. (In this sense, a digital camera's review capabilities replace the Polaroid test shots pro photographers relied on in decades past.)
- **Lighting preview—Con: electronic flash.** Some external flash have a modeling light function (consisting of a series of low-powered bursts that flash for a period of time), but this feature is no substitute for continuous illumination, or an always-on modeling lamp like that found in studio flash. As the number of flash units increases, lighting previews, especially if you want to see the proportions of illumination provided by each flash, grow more complex.
- **Exposure calculation—Pro: continuous lighting.** Your Alpha has no problem calculating exposure for continuous lighting, because the lighting remains constant and can be measured through a sensor that interprets the light reaching the viewfinder. The amount of light available just before the exposure will, in almost all cases, be the same amount of light present when the shutter is released. The Alpha's Spot metering mode can be used to measure and compare the proportions of light in the highlights and shadows, so you can make an adjustment (such as using more or less fill light) if necessary. You can even use a hand-held light meter to measure the light yourself and set the camera manually.

- **Exposure calculation—Con: electronic flash.** Electronic flash illumination doesn't exist until the flash fires, and so it can't be measured by the Alpha's exposure sensor until the exposure. Instead, the light must be measured by metering the intensity of a pre-flash triggered an instant before the main flash, as it is reflected back to the camera and through the lens. The Alpha cameras actually have two exposure measuring modes using the pre-flash: the ADI (Advanced Distance Integration) flash mode, which adds in distance information to calculate flash exposure, and Pre-Flash TTL, which uses only the information from the pre-flash reflected back to the camera from the subject. (These can be set under Flash Control in the Still Shooting 2 menu.) If you have a do-it-yourself bent, there are hand-held flash meters, too, including models that measure both flash and continuous light.

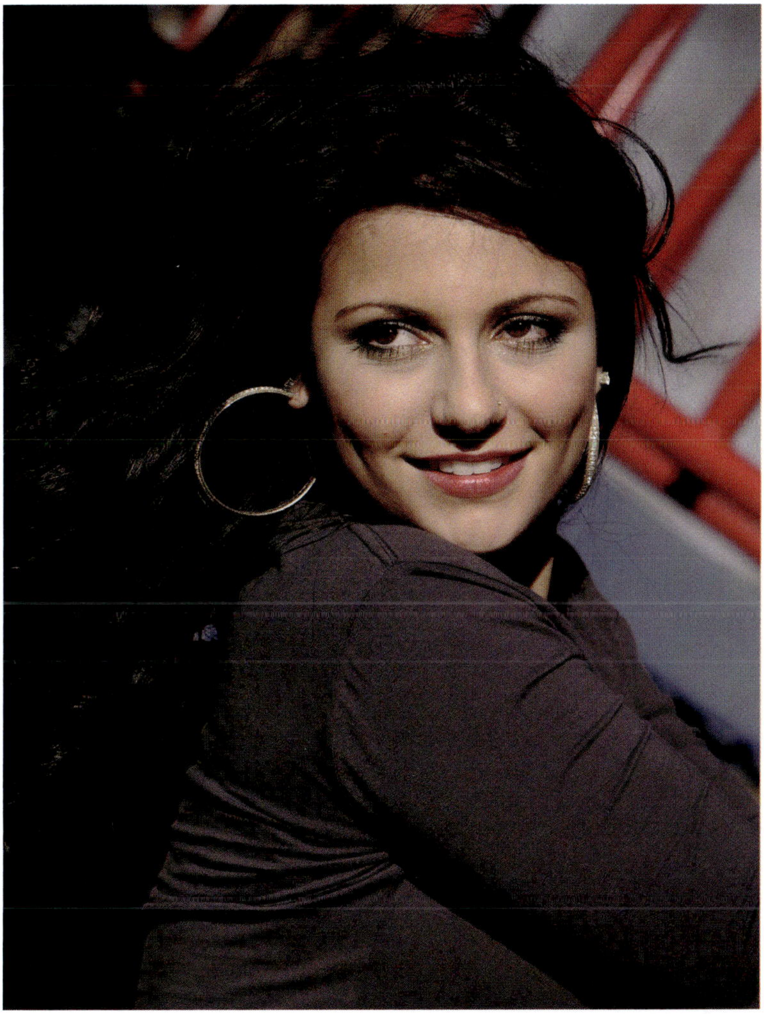

Figure 9.3 You always know how the highlights will look, and how the shadows will fall, when using continuous illumination.

- **Evenness of illumination—Pro/con: continuous lighting.** Of continuous light sources, daylight, in particular, provides illumination that tends to fill an image completely, lighting up the foreground, background, and your subject almost equally. Shadows do come into play, of course, so you might need to use reflectors or fill-in light sources to even out the illumination further, but barring objects that block large sections of your image from daylight, the light is spread fairly evenly. Indoors, however, continuous lighting is commonly less evenly distributed. The average living room, for example, has hot spots and dark corners. But on the plus side, you can *see* this uneven illumination and compensate with additional lamps or reflectors.
- **Evenness of illumination—Con: electronic flash.** Electronic flash units, like continuous light sources such as lamps that don't have the advantage of being located 93 million miles from the subject, suffer from the effects of their proximity. The *inverse square law*, first applied to both gravity and light by Sir Isaac Newton, dictates that as a light source's distance increases from the subject, the amount of light reaching the subject falls off proportionately to the square of the distance. In plain English, that means that a flash or lamp that's eight feet away from a subject provides only one-quarter as much illumination as a source that's four feet away (rather than half as much). (See Figure 9.4.) This translates into relatively shallow "depth-of-light."

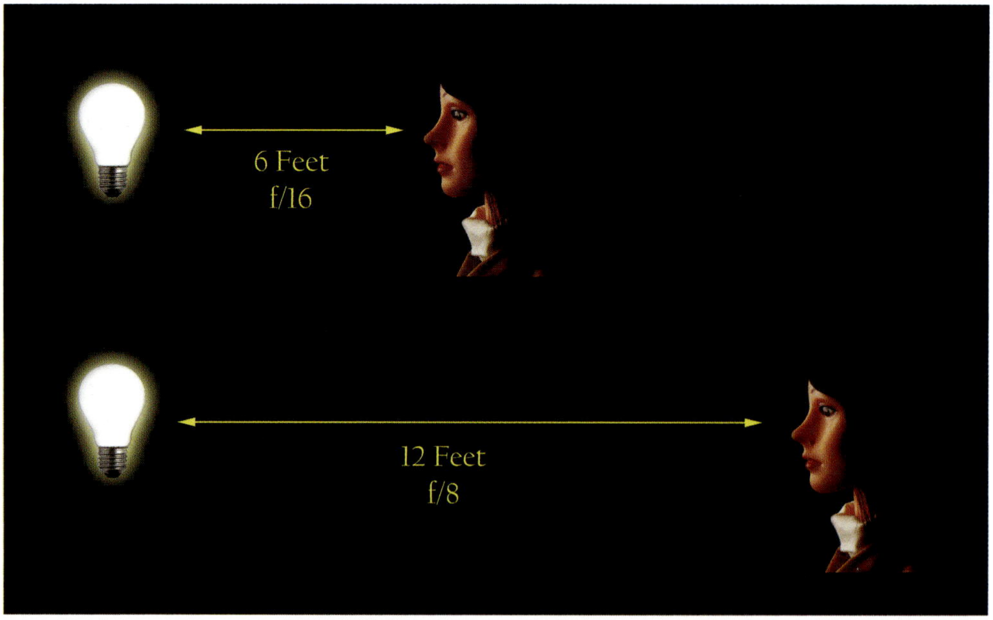

Figure 9.4
A light source that is twice as far away provides only one-quarter as much illumination.

- **Action stopping—Con: continuous lighting.** Action stopping with continuous light sources is completely dependent on the shutter speed you've dialed in on the camera. And the speeds available are dependent on the amount of light available and your camera's ISO sensitivity setting. Outdoors in daylight, there will probably be enough sunlight to let you shoot at 1/2,000th second and f/6.3 with a non-grainy sensitivity setting of ISO 400. That's a fairly useful combination of settings if you're not using a super-telephoto with a small maximum aperture. But inside, the reduced illumination quickly has you pushing your Sony Alpha to its limits. For example, if you're shooting indoor sports, there probably won't be enough available light to allow you to use a 1/2,000th second shutter speed (although I routinely shoot indoor basketball at ISO 1600 and 1/500th second at f/4). In many indoor sports situations, you may find yourself limited to 1/500th second or slower.
- **Action stopping—Pro: electronic flash.** When it comes to the ability to freeze moving objects in their tracks, the advantage goes to electronic flash. The brief duration of electronic flash serves as a very high "shutter speed" when the flash is the main or only source of illumination for the photo. Your Sony Alpha's shutter speed may be set for 1/160th second during a flash exposure, but if the flash illumination predominates, the *effective* exposure time will be the 1/1,000th to 1/50,000th second or less duration of the flash, as you can see in Figure 9.5, by Cleveland photographer Kris Bosworth, because the flash unit reduces the amount of light released by cutting short the duration of the flash. The only fly in the ointment is that, if the ambient light is strong enough, it may produce a secondary "ghost" exposure, as I'll explain later in this chapter.
- **Cost—Pro: continuous lighting.** Incandescent or fluorescent lamps are generally much less expensive than external electronic flash units, which can easily cost several hundred dollars. I've used everything from desktop hi-intensity lamps to reflector floodlights for continuous illumination at very little cost. There are lamps made especially for photographic purposes, too, priced up to $50 or so. Maintenance is economical, too; many incandescent or fluorescents use bulbs that cost only a few dollars.
- **Cost—Con: electronic flash.** Electronic flash units aren't particularly cheap. The lowest-cost dedicated flash designed specifically for Sony cameras (the HVL-F20AM) is less than $129. Such units are limited in features, however, and intended for those with entry-level cameras. Plan on spending some money ($499) to get the features that a sophisticated electronic flash such as the HVL-F58AM offers.

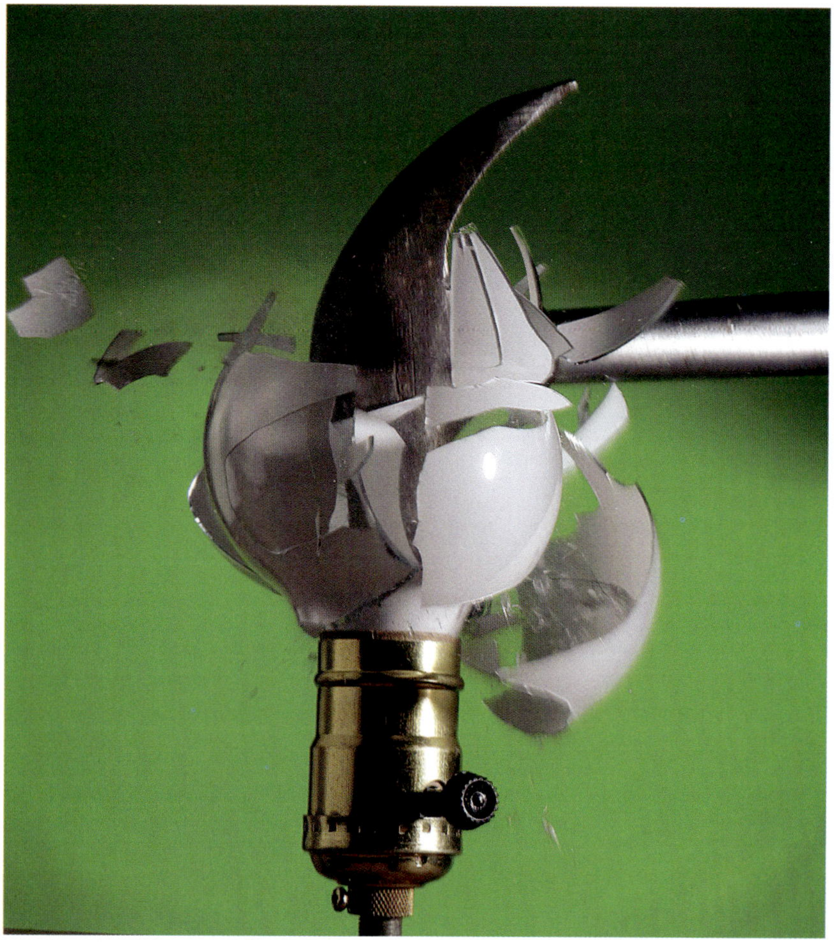

Figure 9.5
Electronic flash can freeze almost any action.

- **Flexibility—Con: continuous lighting.** Because incandescent and fluorescent lamps are not as bright as electronic flash, the slower shutter speeds required (see "Action stopping," above) mean that you may have to use a tripod more often, especially when shooting portraits. The incandescent variety of continuous lighting gets hot, especially in the studio, and the side effects range from discomfort (for your human models) to disintegration (if you happen to be shooting perishable foods like ice cream).
- **Flexibility—Pro: electronic flash.** Electronic flash's action-freezing power allows you to work without a tripod in the studio (and elsewhere), adding flexibility and speed when choosing angles and positions. Flash units can be easily filtered, and, because the filtration is placed over the light source rather than the lens, you don't need to use high-quality filter material. For example, theatrical lighting gels, which may be too flimsy to use in front of the lens, can be mounted or taped in front of your flash with ease to change the color or quality of light falling on a scene.

Continuous Lighting Basics

While continuous lighting and its effects are generally much easier to visualize and use than electronic flash, there are some factors you need to take into account, particularly the color temperature of the light. (Color temperature concerns aren't exclusive to continuous light sources, of course, but the variations tend to be more extreme and less predictable than those of electronic flash.)

Color temperature, in practical terms, is how "bluish" or how "reddish" the light appears to be to the digital camera's sensor. Indoor illumination is quite warm, comparatively, and appears reddish to the sensor. Daylight, in contrast, seems much bluer to the sensor. Our eyes (our brains, actually) are quite adaptable to these variations, so white objects don't appear to have an orange tinge when viewed indoors, nor do they seem excessively blue outdoors in full daylight. Yet, these color temperature variations are real and the sensor is not fooled. To capture the most accurate colors, we need to take the color temperature into account in setting the color balance (or *white balance*) of the Alpha—either automatically using the camera's smarts or manually using our own knowledge and experience.

Color temperature can be confusing, because of a seeming contradiction in how color temperatures are named: warmer (more reddish) color temperatures (measured in degrees Kelvin) are the *lower* numbers, while cooler (bluer) color temperatures are *higher* numbers. It might not make sense to say that 3,400K is warmer than 6,000K, but that's the way it is. If it helps, think of a glowing red ember contrasted with a white-hot welder's torch, rather than fire and ice.

The confusion comes from physics. Scientists calculate color temperature from the light emitted by a mythical object called a black body radiator, which absorbs all the radiant energy that strikes it, and reflects none at all. Such a black body not only *absorbs* light perfectly, but it *emits* it perfectly when heated (and since nothing in the universe is perfect, that makes it mythical).

At a particular physical temperature, this imaginary object always emits light of the same wavelength or color. That makes it possible to define color temperature in terms of actual temperature in degrees on the Kelvin scale that scientists use. Incandescent light, for example, typically has a color temperature of 3,200K to 3,400K. Daylight might range from 5,500K to 6,000K. Each type of illumination we use for photography has its own color temperature range—with some cautions. The next sections will summarize everything you need to know about the qualities of these light sources.

Daylight

Daylight is produced by the sun, and so is moonlight (which is just reflected sunlight). Daylight is present, of course, even when you can't see the sun. When sunlight is direct, it can be bright and harsh. If daylight is diffused by clouds, softened by bouncing off objects such as walls or your photo reflectors, or filtered by shade, it can be much dimmer and less contrasty.

Daylight's color temperature can vary quite widely. It is highest (most blue) at noon when the sun is directly overhead, because the light is traveling through a minimum amount of the filtering layer we call the atmosphere. The color temperature at high noon may be 6,000K. At other times of day, the sun is lower in the sky and the particles in the air provide a filtering effect that warms the illumination to about 5,500K for most of the day. Starting an hour before dusk and for an hour after sunrise, the warm appearance of the sunlight is even visible to our eyes when the color temperature may dip to 5,000-4,500K, as shown in Figure 9.6.

Because you'll be taking so many photos in daylight, you'll want to learn how to use or compensate for the brightness and contrast of sunlight, as well as how to deal with its color temperature. I'll provide some hints later in this chapter.

Incandescent/Tungsten Light

The term incandescent or tungsten illumination is usually applied to the direct descendents of Thomas Edison's original electric lamp. Such lights consist of a glass bulb that contains a vacuum, or is filled with a halogen gas, and contains a tungsten filament that is heated by an electrical current, producing photons and heat. Tungsten-halogen lamps are a variation on the basic light bulb, using a more rugged (and longer-lasting) filament that can be heated to a higher temperature, housed in a thicker glass or quartz envelope, and filled with iodine or bromine ("halogen") gases. The higher temperature allows tungsten-halogen (or quartz-halogen/quartz-iodine, depending on their construction) lamps to burn "hotter" and whiter. Although popular for automobile headlamps today, they've also been popular for photographic illumination.

Although incandescent illumination isn't a perfect black body radiator, it's close enough that the color temperature of such lamps can be precisely calculated (about 3,200-3,400K, depending on the type of lamp) and used for photography without concerns about color variation (at least, until the very end of the lamp's life).

The other qualities of this type of lighting, such as contrast, are dependent on the distance of the lamp from the subject, type of reflectors used, and other factors that I'll explain later in this chapter.

Fluorescent Light/Other Light Sources

Fluorescent light has some advantages in terms of illumination, but some disadvantages from a photographic standpoint. This type of lamp generates light through an electrochemical reaction that emits most of its energy as visible light, rather than heat, which is why the bulbs don't get as hot. The type of light produced varies depending on the phosphor coatings and type of gas in the tube. So, the illumination fluorescent bulbs

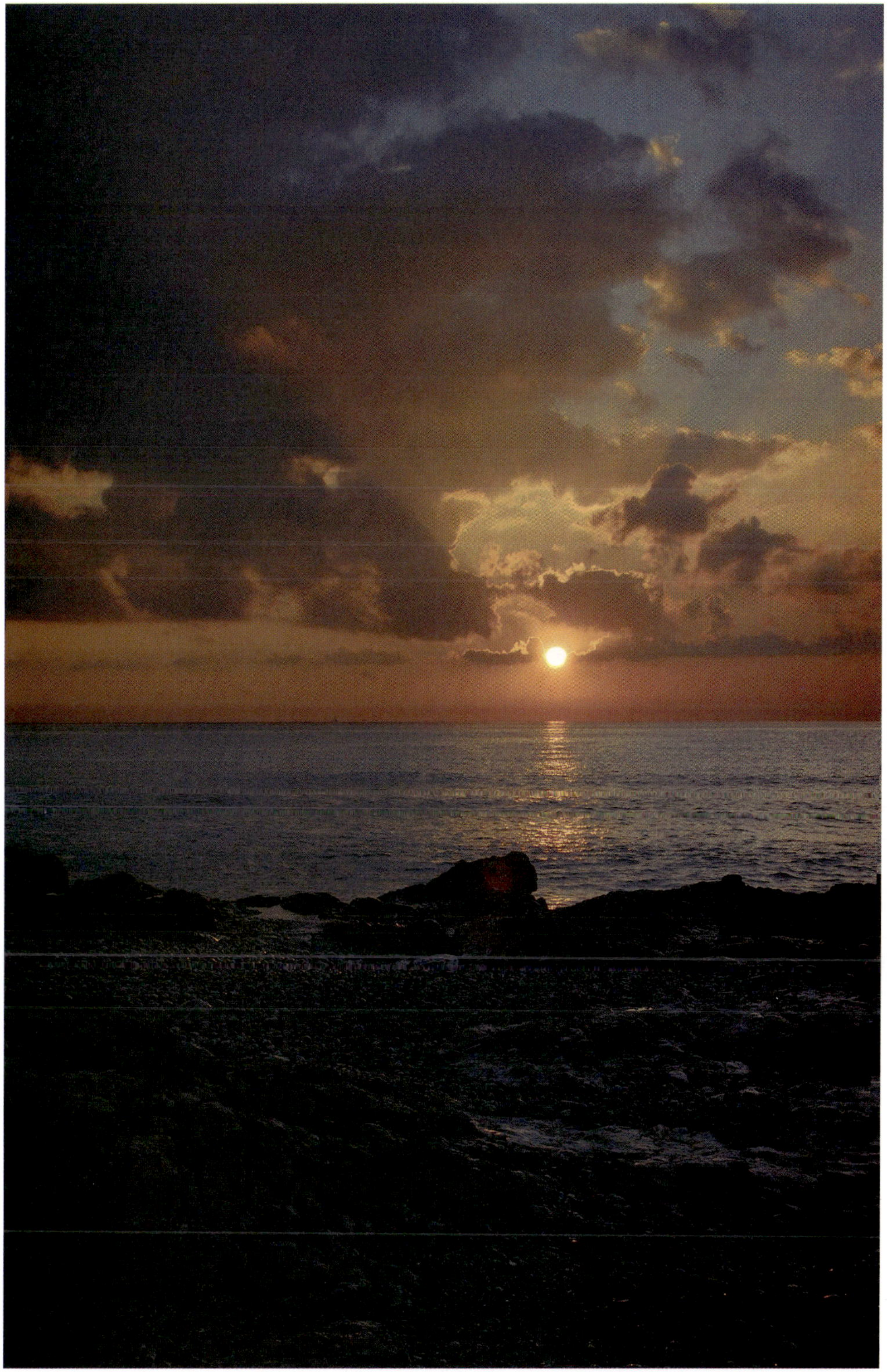

Figure 9.6
At dawn and dusk, the color temperature of the sky may dip as low as 4,500K.

produce can vary widely in its characteristics. Fortunately, the A57 has settings for several different types of fluorescent lamps.

That's not great news for photographers. Different types of lamps have different "color temperatures" that can't be precisely measured in degrees Kelvin, because the light isn't produced by heating. Worse, fluorescent lamps have a discontinuous spectrum of light that can have some colors missing entirely. A particular type of tube can lack certain shades of red or other colors, which is why fluorescent lamps and other alternative technologies such as sodium-vapor illumination can produce ghastly looking human skin tones. Their spectra can lack the reddish tones we associate with healthy skin and emphasize the blues and greens popular in horror movies.

Adjusting White Balance

In most cases, the Sony Alpha will do a good job of calculating white balance for you, so Auto White Balance, described in Chapter 3 and explained in more detail in Chapter 4, can be used as your choice most of the time. Use the preset values or set a custom white balance that matches the current shooting conditions when you need to. The only really problematic light sources are likely to be fluorescents. Vendors, such as GE and Sylvania, may actually provide a figure known as the *color rendering index* (or CRI), which is a measure of how accurately a particular light source represents standard colors, using a scale of 0 (some sodium-vapor lamps) to 100 (daylight and most incandescent lamps). Daylight fluorescents and deluxe cool white fluorescents might have a CRI of about 79 to 95, which is perfectly acceptable for most photographic applications. Warm white fluorescents might have a CRI of 55. White deluxe mercury vapor lights are less suitable with a CRI of 45, while low-pressure sodium lamps can vary from CRI 0-18.

Remember that if you shoot RAW, you can specify the white balance of your image when you import it into Photoshop, Photoshop Elements, or another image editor using your preferred RAW converter, including Image Data Converter SR. While color-balancing filters that fit on the front of the lens exist, they are primarily useful for film cameras, because film's color balance can't be tweaked as extensively as that of a sensor.

Electronic Flash Basics

Until you delve into the situation deeply enough, it might appear that serious photographers have a love/hate relationship with electronic flash. You'll often hear that flash photography is less natural looking, and that the built-in flash in most cameras should never be used as the primary source of illumination because it provides a harsh, garish look. Available ("continuous") lighting is praised, and built-in flash photography seems to be roundly denounced.

In truth, however, the bias is against *bad* flash photography. Indeed, flash has become the studio light source of choice for pro photographers, because it's more intense (and its intensity can be varied to order by the photographer), freezes action, frees you from using a tripod (unless you want to use one to lock down a composition), and has a snappy, consistent light quality that matches daylight. (While color balance changes as the flash duration shortens, some Sony flash units can communicate to the camera the exact white balance provided for that shot.) And even pros will cede that electronic flash has some important uses as an adjunct to existing light, particularly to fill in dark shadows.

But electronic flash isn't as inherently easy to use as continuous lighting. As I noted earlier, electronic flash units are more expensive, don't show you exactly what the lighting effect will be, unless you use a second source called a *modeling light* for a preview (some flashes, such as the HVL-F58AM have pulsed light rudimentary modeling light capabilities built in), and the exposure of electronic flash units is more difficult to calculate accurately.

How Electronic Flash Works

The electronic flash you use will be connected to the camera by slipping it onto the hot shoe, or linked by a cable connected to an adapter mounted on the shoe. In all cases, the flash is triggered at the instant of exposure, during a period when the sensor is fully exposed by the shutter.

As I mentioned earlier in this book, the Alpha has a vertically traveling shutter that consists of two curtains. The first curtain opens and moves to the opposite side of the frame, at which point the shutter is completely open. The flash can be triggered at this point (so-called *first-curtain sync*), making the flash exposure. Then, after a delay that can vary from 30 seconds to 1/160th second, a second curtain begins moving across the sensor plane, covering up the sensor again. If the flash is triggered just before the second curtain starts to close, then *second-curtain sync* is used. In both cases, though, a shutter speed of 1/160th second is the maximum that can be used to take a photo.

Figure 9.7 illustrates how this works, with a fanciful illustration of a generic shutter (your Alpha's shutter does *not* look like this, and some vertically traveling shutters move bottom to top rather than the top-to-bottom motion shown). Both curtains are tightly closed at upper left. At upper right, the first curtain begins to move downward, starting to expose a narrow slit that reveals the sensor behind the shutter. At lower left, the first curtain moves downward farther until, as you can see at lower right in the figure, the sensor is fully exposed.

When first-curtain sync is used, the flash is triggered at the instant that the sensor is completely exposed. The shutter then remains open for an additional length of time (from 30 seconds to 1/160th second), and the second curtain begins to move downward, covering the sensor once more. When second-curtain sync is activated, the flash

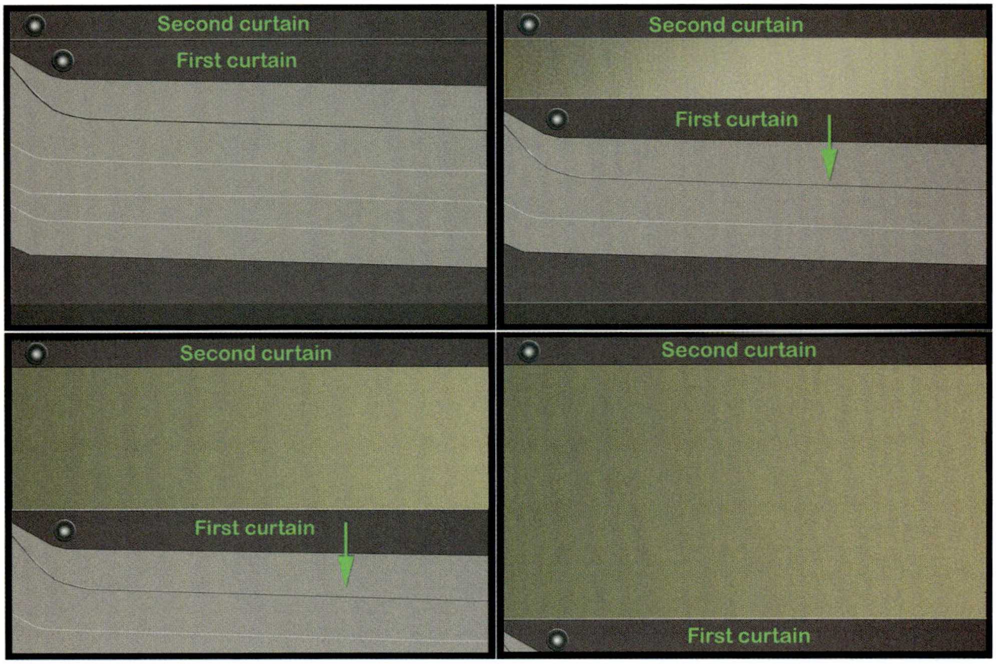

Figure 9.7
A focal plane shutter has two curtains, the lower, or first curtain, and an upper, second curtain.

is triggered *after* the main exposure is over, just before the second curtain begins to move downward.

The Alpha cameras always default to front/first-curtain sync unless you explicitly select another mode using the Fn button. Autoflash mode is blocked when using P, S, A, or M modes.

Avoiding Sync Speed Problems

Using a shutter speed faster than the maximum sync speed can cause problems. Triggering the electronic flash only when the shutter is completely open makes a lot of sense if you think about what's going on. To obtain shutter speeds faster than 1/160th second, the Alpha exposes only part of the sensor at one time, by starting the second curtain on its journey before the first curtain has completely opened. That effectively provides a briefer exposure as the slit of the shutter passes over the surface of the sensor. If the flash were to fire during the time when the first and second curtains partially obscured the sensor, only the slit that was actually open would be exposed.

You'd end up with only a narrow band, representing the portion of the sensor that was exposed when the picture is taken. For shutter speeds *faster* than the top sync speed, the second curtain begins moving *before* the first curtain reaches the bottom of the frame. As a result, a moving slit, the distance between the first and second curtains, exposes one portion of the sensor at a time as it moves from the top to the bottom. Figure 9.8 shows three views of our typical (but imaginary) focal plane shutter. At left is pictured the closed shutter; in the middle version you can see the first curtain has moved about

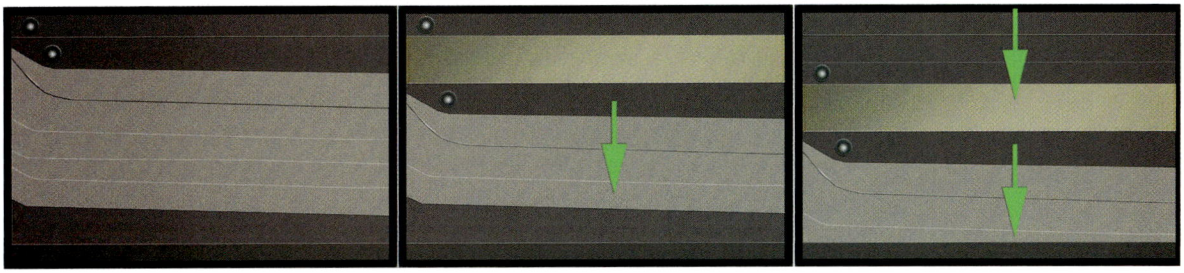

Figure 9.8 A closed shutter (left); partially open shutter as the first curtain begins to move downwards (middle); only part of the sensor is exposed as the slit moves (right).

1/4 of the distance down from the top; and in the right-hand version, the second curtain has started to "chase" the first curtain across the frame towards the bottom.

If the flash is triggered while this slit is moving, only the exposed portion of the sensor will receive any illumination. You end up with a photo like the one shown in Figure 9.9. Note that a band across the bottom of the image is black. That's a shadow of the second shutter curtain, which had started to move when the flash was triggered. Sharp-eyed readers will wonder why the black band is at the *bottom* of the frame rather than at the top, where the second curtain begins its journey. The answer is simple: your lens flips the image upside down and forms it on the sensor in a reversed position. You never notice that, because the camera is smart enough to show you the pixels that make up your photo in their proper orientation during picture review. But this image flip is why,

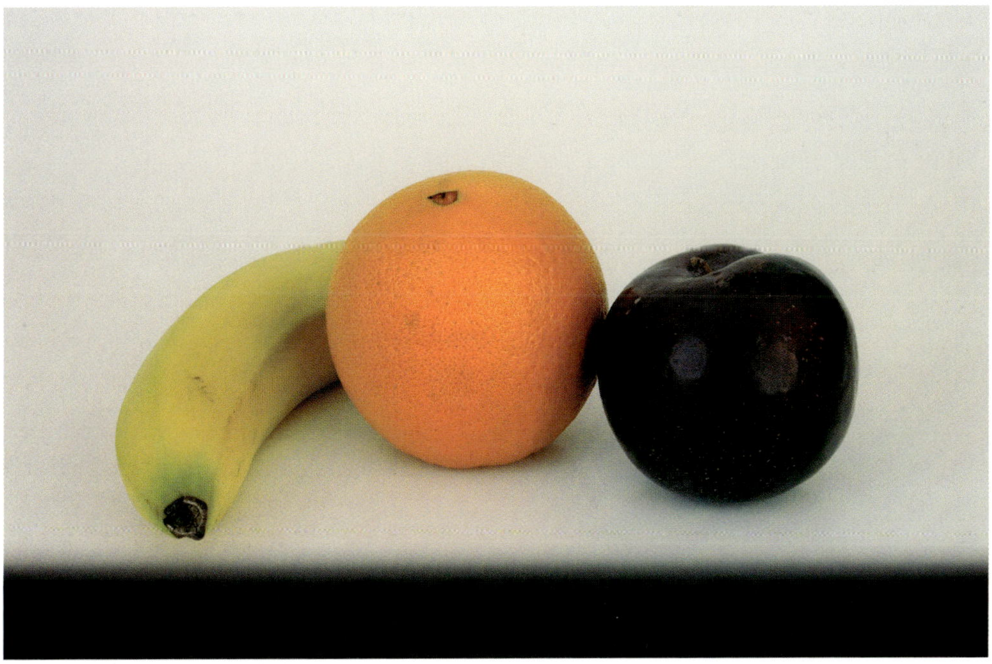

Figure 9.9 If a shutter speed faster than 1/160th second is used with flash, you can end up photographing only a portion of the image.

if your sensor gets dirty and you detect a spot of dust in the upper half of a test photo, if cleaning manually, you need to look for the speck in the *bottom* half of the sensor.

I generally end up with sync speed problems only when shooting in the studio, using studio flash units rather than my Sony dedicated unit. That's because if you're using either type of "smart" flash, the camera knows that a strobe is attached, and remedies any unintentional goof in shutter speed settings. If you happen to set the Alpha's shutter to a faster speed in S or M mode, the camera will automatically adjust the shutter speed down to the maximum sync speed as soon as you flip up the internal flash or attach and turn on an external flash (or prevent you from choosing a faster speed if the flash is powered up). In A, or P, where the Alpha selects the shutter speed, it will never choose a shutter speed higher than 1/160th second when using flash.

But when using a non-dedicated flash, such as a studio unit plugged into an adapter attached to the accessory shoe, the camera has no way of knowing that a flash is connected, so shutter speeds faster than 1/160th second can be set inadvertently.

Note that the Alpha can use a feature called *high-speed sync*, which allows shutter speeds faster than the maximum sync speed with certain external dedicated Sony flash units. When using high-speed sync, the flash fires a continuous serious of bursts at reduced power for the entire duration of the exposure, so that the illumination is able to expose the sensor as the slit moves.

HS sync is set using the controls that adjust the compatible external flash units, which include the HVL-F58AM, HVL-F56AM, HVL-F43AM, and HVL-F36AM. It cannot be used when working with multiple flash units. When active, the message H appears on the LCD panel on the back of the flash. You'll find complete instructions accompanying those flash units.

Ghost Images

The difference might not seem like much, but whether you use first-curtain sync (the default setting) or rear-curtain sync (an optional setting) can make a significant difference to your photograph *if the ambient light in your scene also contributes to the image.* At faster shutter speeds, particularly 1/160th second, there isn't much time for the ambient light to register, unless it is very bright. It's likely that the electronic flash will provide almost all the illumination, so first-curtain sync or second-curtain sync isn't very important.

However, at slower shutter speeds, or with very bright ambient light levels, there is a significant difference, particularly if your subject is moving, or the camera isn't steady. In any of those situations, the ambient light will register as a second image accompanying the flash exposure, and if there is movement (camera or subject), that additional image will not be in the same place as the flash exposure. It will show as a ghost image and, if the movement is significant enough, as a blurred ghost image trailing in front of or behind your subject in the direction of the movement.

As I mentioned earlier, when you're using first-curtain sync, the flash goes off the instant the shutter opens, producing an image of the subject on the sensor. Then, the shutter remains open for an additional period (which can be from 30 seconds to 1/160th second). If your subject is moving, say, toward the right side of the frame, the ghost image produced by the ambient light will produce a blur on the right side of the original subject image, making it look as if your sharp (flash-produced) image is chasing the ghost. For those of us who grew up with lightning-fast superheroes who always left a ghost trail *behind them*, that looks unnatural (see Figure 9.10).

So, Sony provides rear (second) curtain sync to remedy the situation. In that mode, the shutter opens, as before. The shutter remains open for its designated duration, and the ghost image forms. If your subject moves from the left side of the frame to the right side, the ghost will move from left to right, too. *Then*, about 1.5 milliseconds before the second shutter curtain closes, the flash is triggered, producing a nice, sharp flash image *ahead* of the ghost image. Voilà! We have monsieur *le Flash* outrunning his own trailing image.

EVERY WHICH WAY, INCLUDING UP

Note that although I describe the ghost effect in terms of subject matter that is moving left to right in a horizontally oriented composition, it can occur in any orientation, and with the subject moving in *any* direction. (Try photographing a falling rock, if you can, and you'll see the same effect.) Nor are the ghost images affected by the fact that modern shutters travel vertically rather than horizontally. Secondary images are caused between the time the first curtain fully opens, and the second curtain begins to close. The direction of travel of the shutter curtains, or the direction of your subject does not matter.

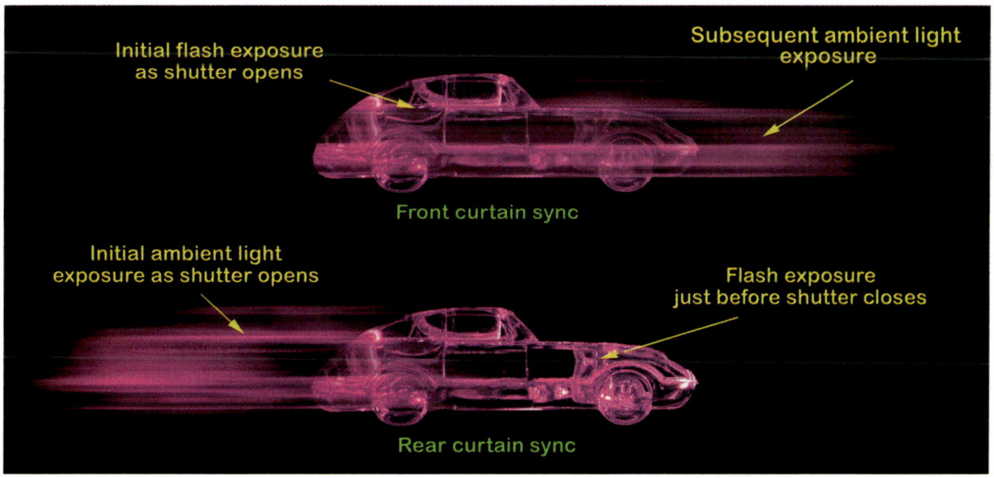

Figure 9.10 Front-curtain sync produces an image that trails in front of the flash exposure (top), whereas rear-curtain sync creates a more "natural looking" trail behind the flash image (bottom).

Slow Sync

Another flash synchronization option is *slow sync*, which is actually an exposure option that tells the A57 to use slower shutter speeds when possible, to allow you to capture a scene by both flash and ambient illumination. To activate Slow Sync, press the Fn button, navigate to the flash options, and choose Slow Sync.

Then, the exposure system will try to use longer shutter speeds with the flash, so that an initial exposure is made with the flash unit, and a secondary exposure of subjects in the background will be produced by the slower shutter speed. This will let you shoot a portrait of a person at night and, much of the time, avoid a dark background. Your portrait subject will be illuminated by the flash, and the background by the ambient light. It's a good idea to have the camera mounted on a tripod or some other support, or have SteadyShot switched on to avoid having this secondary exposure produce ghost images due to camera movement during the exposure.

Because Slow Sync is a type of exposure control, it does not work in Manual mode or Shutter priority mode (because the A57 doesn't choose the shutter speed in those modes).

Determining Exposure

Calculating the proper exposure for an electronic flash photograph is a bit more complicated than determining the settings by continuous light. The right exposure isn't simply a function of how far away your subject is, even though the inverse square law I mentioned does have an effect: the farther away the subject is, the less light is available for the exposure. The Alpha can calculate distance if you're using a lens with "DT" in its name (these lenses transmit distance codes to the camera), based on the autofocus distance that's locked in just prior to taking the picture.

But, of course, flash exposure isn't based on distance alone. Various objects reflect more or less light at the same distance so, obviously, the camera needs to measure the amount of light reflected back and through the lens. Yet, as the flash itself isn't available for measuring until it's triggered, the Alpha has nothing to measure.

The solution is to fire the flash twice. The initial shot is a pre-flash that can be analyzed, then followed by a main flash that's given exactly the calculated intensity needed to provide a correct exposure. As a result, the primary flash may be longer for distant objects and shorter for closer subjects, depending on the required intensity for exposure. This through-the-lens evaluative flash exposure system when coupled with distance information from a DT lens is called *ADI flash exposure* (ADI stands for Advanced Distance Integration), and it operates whenever you have attached a Sony dedicated flash unit to the Alpha, and a lens that provides distance integration information. (Check the documentation that came with your lens to see if it is compatible with ADI.)

Using the Built-In Flash

The Sony Alpha's built-in flash is a handy accessory because it is available as required, without the need to carry an external flash around with you constantly. This section explains how to use the flip-up flash.

Your Alpha automatically pops up the built-in flash when there is insufficient light and you are using Auto, or any Scene mode except for Night Scene and Hand-held Twilight (if you haven't disabled the flash). In PASM modes (Program, Aperture priority, Shutter priority, and Manual), you'll need to flip up the flash manually. In modes that do not pop up the flash, including Flash Off mode, the flash will not pop up. If the flash is already up, because you switched to a non-flash mode from a PASM, or if you have set Flash Off as the flash mode using the Fn button, the flash will not fire.

For example, the flash doesn't pop up in Landscape mode because the flash doesn't have enough reach to have much effect for pictures of distant vistas in any case; nor does the flash pop up automatically in Sports mode, because you'll often want to use shutter speeds faster than 1/160th second and/or be shooting subjects that are out of flash range. Pop-up flash is disabled in Flash Off mode for obvious reasons.

When trying to use flash in Scene modes that disable flash, a message appears on the LCD telling you the operation is invalid, with a suggestion to switch to Program, Aperture priority, Shutter priority, or Manual exposure modes.

When using a flash-compatible mode with the built-in flash, if you want the Alpha to issue a few additional low-light pre-flashes prior to taking the picture, turn the feature on with the Red eye reduc. option in Custom 1 menu.

When using semi-automatic or manual exposure modes (or any Scene mode in which flash is used), if Red-eye reduction is turned on in the Custom menu (as described in Chapter 3), the red-eye reduction flash will emit as you press down the shutter release to take the picture, theoretically causing your subjects' irises to contract (if they are looking toward the camera), and thereby reducing the red-eye effect in your photograph.

Setting Flash Modes

To set the various flash modes (which may or may not be available, depending on which exposure mode you're using), press the Fn button on the back of the camera to the right of the LCD, navigate to the flash options using the controller buttons, and choose:

- **Flash Off.** The flash never fires; this may be useful in museums, concerts, or religious ceremonies where electronic flash would prove disruptive.
- **Autoflash.** The flash fires as required, depending on lighting conditions.
- **Fill-flash.** The Alpha balances the available illumination with flash to provide a balanced lighting effect. See Figure 9.11 for an example.

- **Slow Sync.** The Alpha combines flash with slow shutter speeds, so that the subject can be illuminated by flash, but the longer shutter speed allows the ambient light to illuminate the background.
- **Rear Sync.** Fires the flash at the end of the exposure, producing more "realistic" "ghost" images, as described earlier in this chapter.
- **Wireless Flash.** The internal flash triggers compatible external flash units without the need for a connecting cord.
- **H (High-speed sync).** Available only when the HVF-F58AM, or HVF-F42AM flash units are attached, it allows synchronizing those flashes at shutter speeds higher than 1/160th second.

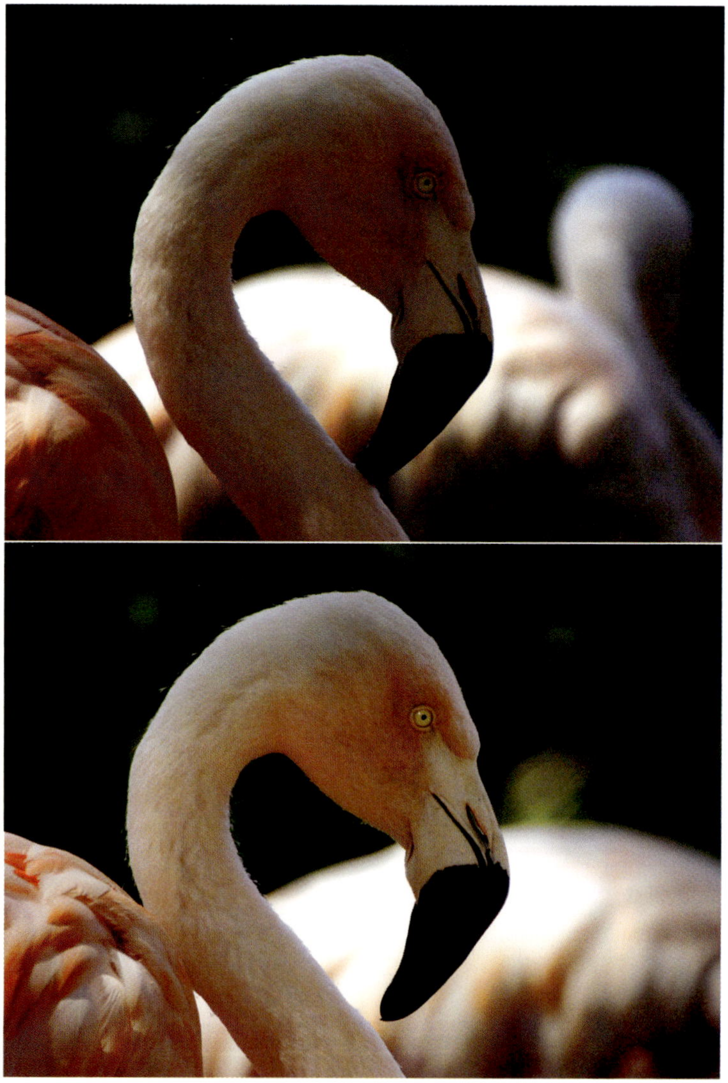

Figure 9.11
The flamingo (top) was in shadow. Fill-flash (bottom) brightened up the bird, while adding a little catch light to its eye.

> **USING WIRELESS FLASH**
>
> To work with wireless flash, attach the compatible dedicated flash unit, such as the HVL-FV58AM, to the accessory shoe on top of the camera. Turn on both flash and the camera, then press the Fn button, select Flash Mode, and choose Wireless. You can then remove the external flash from the camera, and pop up the A57's built-in flash to trigger the external unit wirelessly. The external flash can be set to one of several different channels, as explained in the directions furnished with the dedicated flash. Ordinarily, you won't need to switch channels, unless another photographer using a Sony flash is in the same vicinity, and you don't want your flash to trigger when the other shooter's flash is fired.

Flash Exposure Compensation

It's important to keep in mind how the Alpha cameras' exposure compensation system (discussed in Chapter 4) works when you're using electronic flash. To activate exposure compensation for flash, press the Fn button and navigate to Flash Comp., then press the center controller button. The Flash Comp. screen appears (see Figure 9.12), with its plus/minus scale. Use the left/right controller keys to add or subtract exposure. Pressing the right button adds exposure to an image; pressing the left button subtracts exposure. This function is not available when using Auto or Scene exposure modes, nor when you have used the Flash Off option from the Flash menu.

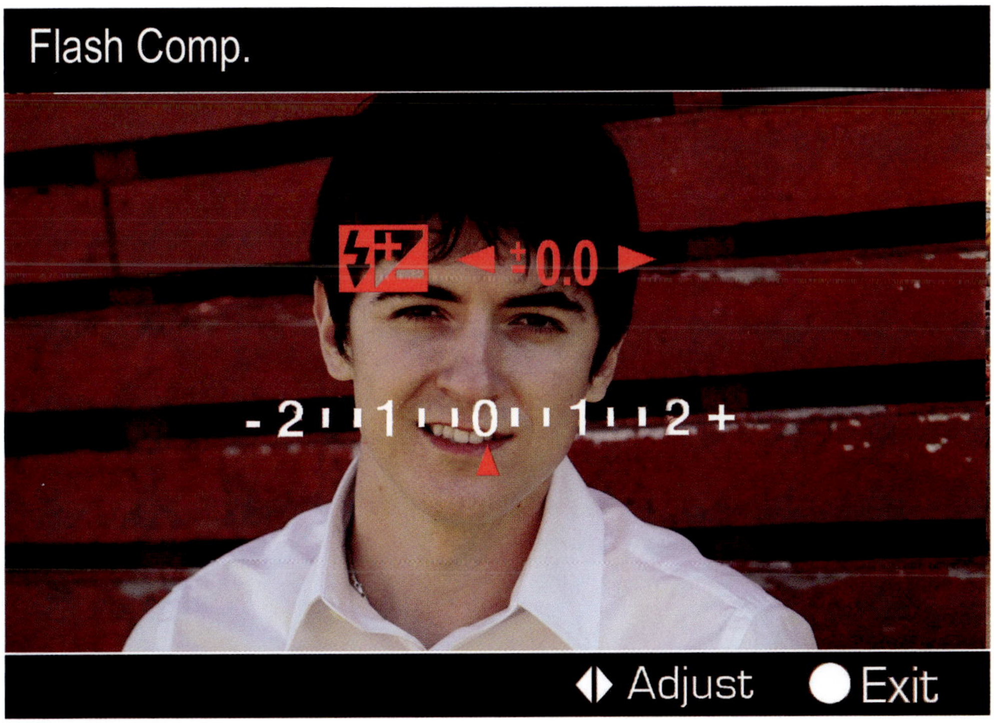

Figure 9.12 Adjust flash exposure using this screen.

Flash Control

I described the Flash Control menu setting in Chapter 3. Your choices are as follows:

- **ADI (Advanced Distance Integration) flash.** This setting takes advantage of a distance encoding feature built into many Sony lenses, which uses focusing data to provide the flash with more accurate distance information. The distance data is combined with light metering data from the pre-flash to provide more precise flash exposure control. ADI enables the camera to avoid being deceived by highly reflective or very dark subjects.
- **Pre-Flash TTL.** In this mode, only information from measuring the amount of light reflected from the subject during the pre-flash is used to calculate exposure. The system can be fooled by subjects that have highly reflective or very dark areas. You might need to use this mode when working with lenses that don't have the distance encoder feature. (Most Sony lenses do. Exceptions are the SAL16F28 16mm f/2.8 fisheye; SAL20F28 20mm f/2.8; SAL28F28 28mm f/2.8; SAL135F28 135mm f/2.8; and SAL500F80 500mm f/8 mirror lens. If you're using third-party lenses, check with your vendor.)

Red Eye Reduction

The other key flash-related control is the Red Eye Reduction option described in Chapter 3. You can turn it on or off. When activated, the Alpha's flip-up flash issues a few brief bursts prior to taking the photo, theoretically causing your subjects' pupils to contract, reducing the effect (assuming the person is looking at the camera during the bursts). This option works only with the built-in flash, and doesn't produce any pre-bursts if you have an external flash attached. In most cases, the higher elevation of the external flash effectively prevents red eye anyway.

Using the External Electronic Flash

Sony currently offers several accessory electronic flash units for the Sony Alpha cameras. They can be mounted to the flash accessory shoe, or used off-camera with a dedicated cord that plugs into the flash shoe to maintain full communications with the camera for all special features. The beefier units range from the HVL-F58AM (see Figure 9.13), which can correctly expose subjects up to 17 feet away at f/11 and ISO 100, to the (discontinued) HVL-F36AM, which is good out to 11 feet at f/11 and ISO 100. (You'll get greater ranges at even higher ISO settings, of course.) A very inexpensive and useful unit, the $129 HVL-F20AM, was introduced with an earlier Alpha series. There is also an electronic flash unit, the HVL-RLAM Alpha Ring Light, specifically for specialized close-up flash photography.

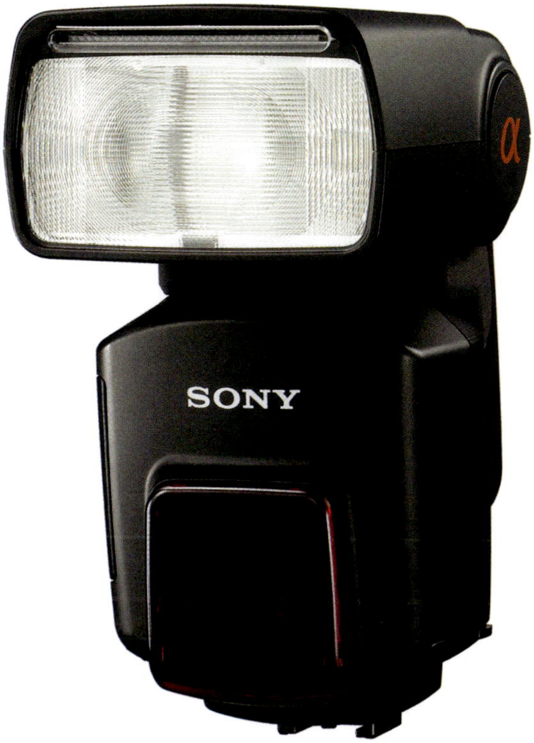

Figure 9.13 The Sony HVL-F58AM is a top-of-the-line external flash unit for the Alpha.

HVL-F58AM Flash Unit

This $499 flagship of the Sony accessory flash line is the most powerful unit the company offers, with an ISO 100 guide number of 58/190 (meters/feet). Guide numbers are a standard way of specifying the power of a flash in manual, non-autoexposure mode. Divide the guide number by the distance to determine the correct f/stop. With a GN of 190, you would use f/19 at 10 feet (190 divided by 10), or f/8.5 at 20 feet.

This flash automatically adjusts for focal length settings from 24mm to 105mm, and a built-in slide-out diffuser panel boosts wide-angle coverage to 16mm. You can zoom coverage manually, if you like. There's also a slide-out "white card" that reflects some light forward even when bouncing the flash off the ceiling, to fill in shadows or add a catch light in the eyes of your portrait subjects.

Bouncing is particularly convenient and effective, thanks to what Sony calls a "quick shift bounce" system. This configuration is particularly effective when shooting vertical pictures. With most other on-camera external flash units, as soon as you turn the camera vertically, the flash is oriented vertically, too, whether you're using direct flash or bouncing off the ceiling (or, wall, when the camera is rotated). The HVL-58AM's clever pivoting system allows re-orienting the flash when the camera is in the vertical position, so flash coverage is still horizontal, and can be tilted up or down for ceiling bounce.

The 15.6 ounce unit uses convenient AA batteries in a four-pack, but can also be connected to the FA-EB1AM external battery adapter (you just blew another $250), which has room for 6 AA batteries for increased capacity and faster recycling. It automatically communicates white balance information to your camera, allowing the Alpha to adjust WB to match the flash output.

You can even simulate a modeling light effect. A test button on the back of the flash unit can be rotated for flash mode (one test flash, with no modeling light); three low-power flashes at a rate of two flashes per second, as a rough guide; and a more useful (but more power-consuming) mode that flashes for 40 flashes per second for 4 seconds (160 continuous mini-bursts in all). This switch also has a HOLD position that locks all flash operations except for the LCD data display on the flash, and the test button. Use this when you want to take a few pictures without flash, but don't want to turn off your flash or change its settings.

The HVL-F58AM can function as a main flash, or be triggered wirelessly by another compatible flash unit. The pre-flash from the second "main" flash is used to trigger the remote, wireless flash unit that has been removed or disconnected from the camera. When using flash wirelessly, Sony recommends rotating the unit so that the flashtube is pointed where you want the light to go, but the front (light sensor) of the flash is directed at the flash mounted on the camera. In wireless mode, you can control up to three groups of flashes, and specify the output levels for each group, giving you an easy way to control the lighting ratios of multiple flash units.

Those who are frustrated by an inability to use a shutter speed faster than 1/160th second will love the High Speed Sync (HSS) mode offered by this unit and the discontinued HVL-F36AM flash. When activated, you can take flash pictures at any shutter speed from 1/500th to 1/4,000th second! For example, if you want to use a high shutter speed and a very wide aperture to apply selective focus to a subject, HSS is one way to avoid overexposure when using flash. The mode button on the back of the flash is used to choose either TTL or Manual flash exposure. Once the flash mode is chosen, then use the Select button and flash plus/minus keys to activate HSS mode. HSS appears on the data panel of the flash, and an indicator appears on the camera's LCD monitor. (Note: HSS is not available when using the 2-second self-timer or rear-sync mode.)

Keep in mind that because less than the full duration of the flash is being used to expose each portion of the image as it is exposed by the slit passing in front of the sensor, the effective flash range of this "reduced" output is smaller. In addition, HSS cannot be used when using multiple flash or left/right/up bounce flash. (If you're pointing the flash downwards, say, at a close-up subject, HSS can be used.)

Another feature I like is the HVL-F58AM's multiple flash feature, which allows you to create interesting stroboscopic effects with several images of the same subject presented in the same frame. If you want to shoot subjects at distances of more than a few feet, however, you'll need to crank up the ISO setting of your Alpha, as the output of each strobe burst is significantly less than when using the flash for single shots.

HVL-F43AM Flash Unit

This less pricey ($350) electronic flash shares many of the advanced features of the HVL-F58AM, but has a lower guide number of 43/138 (meters/feet). (By now, you've figured out that the number in Sony's electronic flash units represent the GN in meters, so the power rating of the HVL-F36AM, described next, will not come as a surprise to you.)

The shared features include high-speed sync, automatic white balance adjustment, and automatic zoom with the same coverage from 24-105mm (16mm with the slide-out diffuser). This unit also can be used in wireless mode to operate other Sony strobes using a pre-flash signal. Bounce flash swiveling is still versatile, with adjustable angles of 90 degrees up, 90 degrees left, and 180 degrees right, so you can reflect your flash off ceilings, walls, or persons wearing large items of clothing in light colors. The HVL-F43AM is a tad lighter than its bigger sibling, at 12 ounces.

HVL-F36AM Flash Unit

Although discontinued, you can easily find this versatile flash available online or in used condition. The guide number for this lower cost ($199) Sony flash unit is (surprise!) 36/118 (meters/feet). Although (relatively) tiny at 9 ounces, you still get some big-flash features, such as wireless operation, auto zoom, and high-speed sync capabilities. Bounce flash flexibility is reduced a little, with no swiveling from side to side and only a vertical adjustment of up to 90 degrees available. Like its four siblings, this one uses four AA batteries.

HVL-F20AM Flash Unit

The least expensive Sony flash (see Figure 9.14) is this one at $150, designed to appeal to the budget conscious, especially those who need just a bit of a boost for fill flash, or want a small unit (just 3.2 ounces) on their camera. It has a guide number of 20 at ISO 100, and features simplified operation. For example, there's a switch on the side of the unit providing Indoor and Outdoor settings (the indoor setting tilts the flash upwards to provide bounce light; with the outdoor setting, the flash fires directly at your subject). There are special modes for wide-angle shooting (use the built-in diffuser to spread the flash's coverage to that of a 27mm lens) or choose the Tele position to narrow the flash coverage to that of a 50mm or longer lens for illuminating more distant subjects. While it's handy for fill flash, owners of an Alpha A57 will probably want a more powerful unit as their main electronic flash.

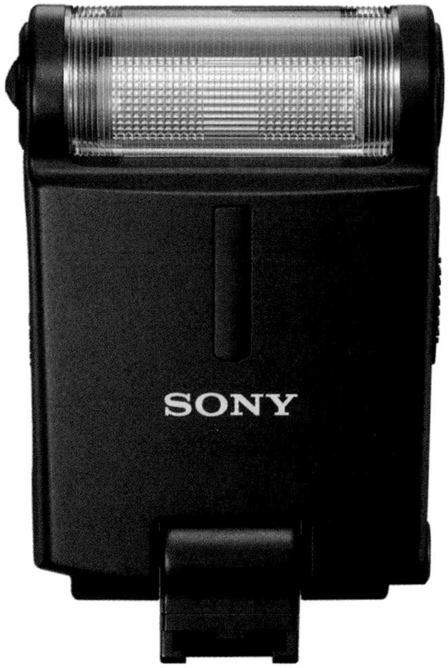

Figure 9.14 The HVL-F20AM flash unit is compact and inexpensive.

More Advanced Lighting Techniques

As you advance in your Sony Alpha photography, you'll want to learn more sophisticated lighting techniques, using more than just straight-on flash, or using just a single flash unit. Entire books have been written on lighting techniques. (If you're *really* into complex lighting setups, you might want to check out my book, *David Busch's Quick Snap Guide to Lighting*, available from the same folks who brought you this guidebook.) I'm going to provide a quick introduction to some of the techniques you should be considering.

Diffusing and Softening the Light

Direct light can be harsh and glaring, especially if you're using the flash built into your camera, or an auxiliary flash mounted in the hot shoe and pointed directly at your subject. The first thing you should do is stop using direct light (unless you're looking for a stark, contrasty appearance as a creative effect). There are a number of simple things you can do with both continuous and flash illumination.

- **Use window light.** Light coming in a window can be soft and flattering, and a good choice for human subjects. Move your subject close enough to the window that its light provides the primary source of illumination. You might want to turn off other lights in the room, particularly to avoid mixing daylight and incandescent light (see Figure 9.15).

- **Use fill light.** Your Alpha's flash makes a perfect fill-in light for the shadows, brightening inky depths with a kicker of illumination (see Figure 9.11, shown earlier).
- **Bounce the light.** All the Sony flashes have a swivel that allows them to be pointed up at a ceiling for a bounce light effect. As I noted, two of them let you bounce the light off a wall. You'll want the ceiling or wall to be white or have a neutral gray color to avoid a color cast.

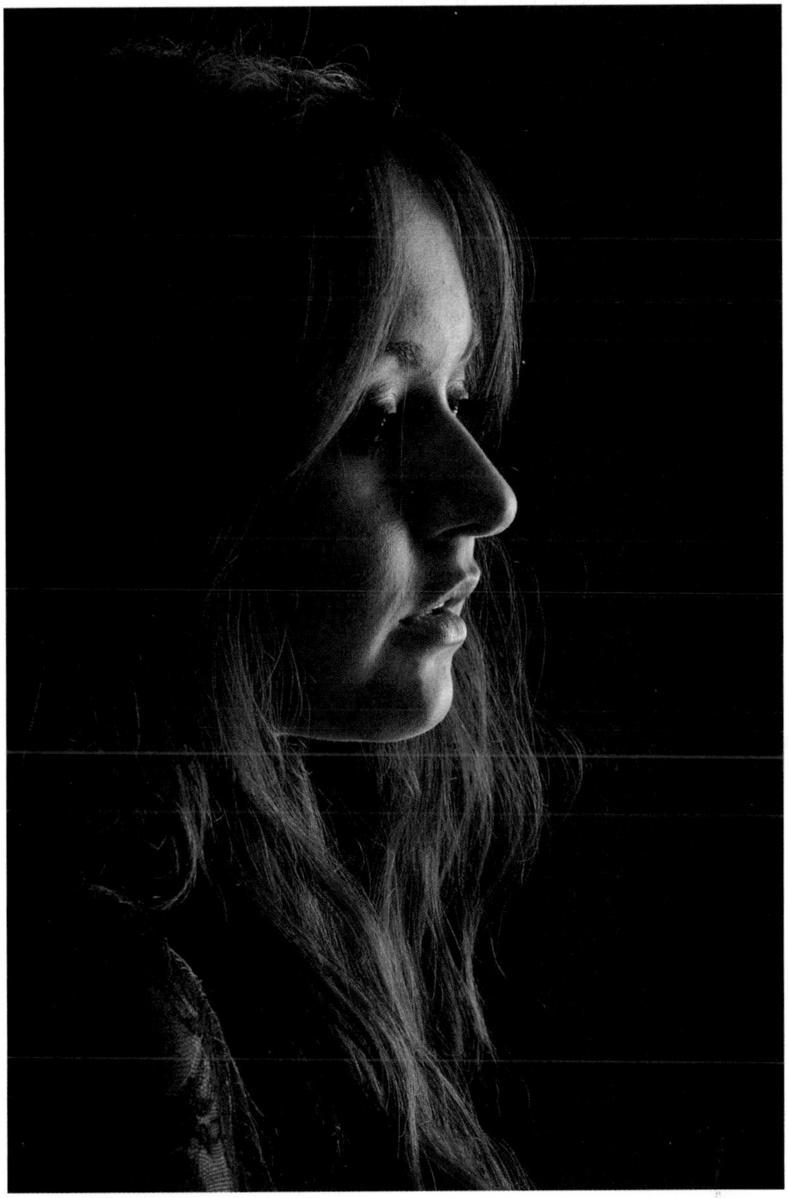

Figure 9.15
Window light makes the perfect diffuse illumination for informal soft focus portraits like this one.

- **Use reflectors.** Another way to bounce the light is to use reflectors or umbrellas that you can position yourself to provide a greater degree of control over the quantity and direction of the bounced light. Good reflectors can be pieces of foamboard, Mylar, or a reflective disk held in place by a clamp and stand. Although some expensive umbrellas and reflectors are available, spending a lot isn't necessary. A simple piece of white foamboard does the job beautifully. Umbrellas have the advantage of being compact and foldable, while providing a soft, even kind of light. They're relatively cheap, too, with a good 40-inch umbrella available for as little as $20.
- **Use a diffuser.** Sto-Fen (www.stofen.com) makes a clip-on diffuser for Sony HVL-series flash units. This simple device (see Figure 9.16) creates a softer light for direct flash or bounce.
- **Try a soft box.** Inexpensive attachments like the one shown in Figure 9.17 can provide the equivalent of a miniature photo studio "soft box," although in a much smaller, more convenient size.

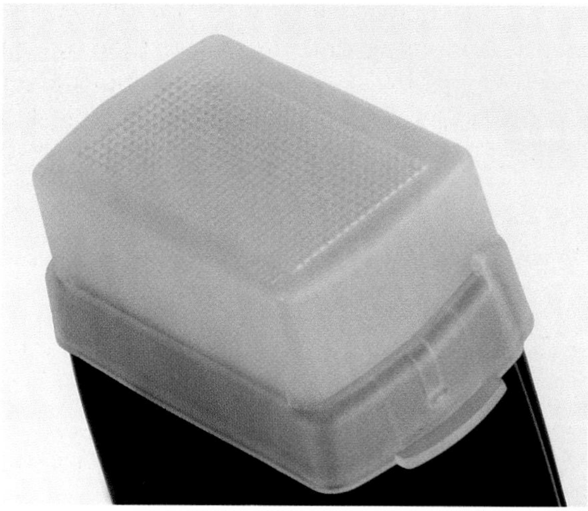

Figure 9.16 Sto-Fen's Omni-Bounce diffuser is available for Sony electronic flash units.

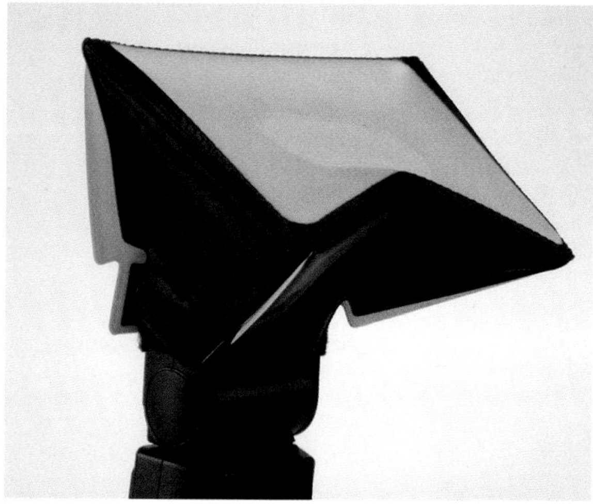

Figure 9.17 Soft boxes use Velcro strips to attach to third-party flash units (like the one shown) or any Sony external flash.

Using Multiple Light Sources

Once you gain control over the qualities and effects you get with a single light source, you'll want to graduate to using multiple light sources. Using several lights allows you to shape and mold the illumination of your subjects to provide a variety of effects, from backlighting to side lighting to more formal portrait lighting. You can start simply with several incandescent light sources, bounced off umbrellas or reflectors that you construct. Or you can use more flexible multiple electronic flash setups.

Effective lighting is the one element that differentiates great photography from candid or snapshot shooting. Lighting can make a mundane subject look a little more glamorous; it can make subjects appear to be soft when you want a soft look, or bright and sparkly when you want a vivid look, or strong and dramatic if that's what you desire. As you might guess, having control over your lighting means that you probably can't use the lights that are already in the room. You'll need separate, discrete lighting fixtures that can be moved, aimed, brightened, and dimmed on command.

Selecting your lighting gear will depend on the type of photography you do, and the budget you have to support it. It's entirely possible for a beginning Alpha photographer to create a basic, inexpensive lighting system capable of delivering high-quality results for a few hundred dollars, just as you can spend megabucks ($1,000 and up) for a sophisticated lighting system.

Basic Flash Setups

If you want to use multiple electronic flash units, the Sony flash units in wireless mode will serve admirably. The two higher-end models can be used with Sony's wireless feature, which allows you to set up to three separate groups of flash units (several flashes can be included in each group) and trigger them using a master flash and the camera. Just set up one master unit and arrange the compatible slave units around your subject. You can set the relative power of each unit separately, thereby controlling how much of the scene's illumination comes from the main flash, and how much from the auxiliary flash units, which can be used as fill flash, background lights, or, if you're careful, to illuminate the hair of portrait subjects.

Studio Flash

If you're serious about using multiple flash units, a studio flash setup might be more practical. The traditional studio flash is a multi-part unit, consisting of a flash head that mounts on your light stand, and is tethered to an AC (or sometimes battery) power supply. A single power supply can feed two or more flash heads at a time, with separate control over the output of each head.

When they are operating off AC power, studio flash don't have to be frugal with the juice, and are often powerful enough to illuminate very large subjects or to supply lots and lots of light to smaller subjects. The output of such units is measured in watt seconds (ws), so you could purchase a 200ws, 400ws, or 800ws unit, and a power pack to match.

Their advantages include greater power output, much faster recycling, built-in modeling lamps, multiple power levels, and ruggedness that can stand up to transport, because many photographers pack up these kits and tote them around as location lighting rigs. Studio lighting kits can range in price from a few hundred dollars for a set of lights, stands, and reflectors, to thousands for a high-end lighting system complete with all the necessary accessories.

A more practical choice these days are *monolights* (see Figure 9.18), which are "all-in-one" studio lights that sell for about $200-$400. They have the flash tube, modeling light, and power supply built into a single unit that can be mounted on a light stand. Monolights are available in AC-only and battery-pack versions, although an external battery eliminates some of the advantages of having a flash with everything in one unit. They are very portable, because all you need is a case for the monolight itself, plus the stands and other accessories you want to carry along. Because these units are so popular with photographers who are not full-time professionals, the lower-cost monolights are often designed more for lighter duty than professional studio flash. That doesn't mean they aren't rugged; you'll just need to handle them with a little more care, and, perhaps, not expect them to be used eight hours a day for weeks on end. In most other respects, however, monolights are the equal of traditional studio flash units in terms of fast recycling, built-in modeling lamps, adjustable power, and so forth. A remote trigger, like the one shown in Figure 9.19, can cost as little as $50-$70.

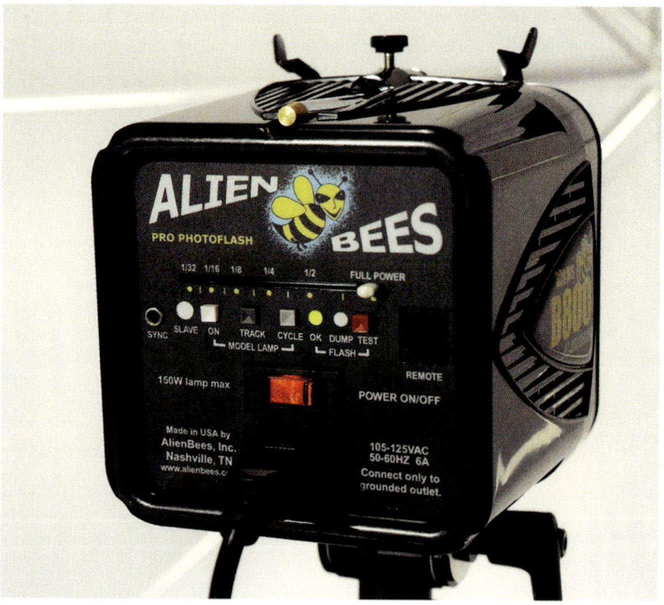

Figure 9.18 All-in-one "monolights" contain flash, power supply, and a modeling light in one compact package (umbrella not included).

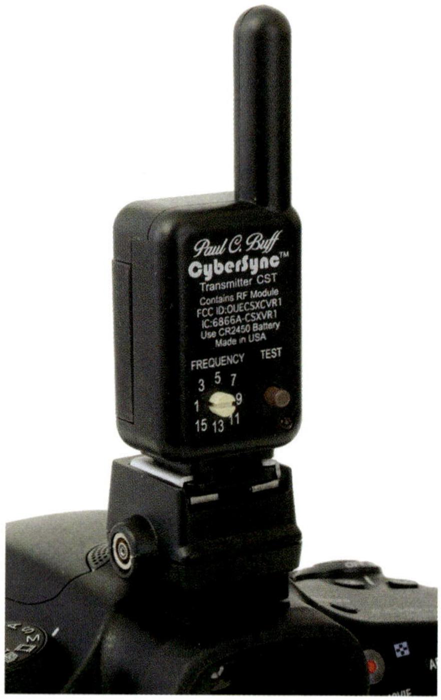

Figure 9.19 Your A57 can control external studio lights with a radio-control trigger like this one.

Other Lighting Accessories

Once you start working with light, you'll find there are plenty of useful accessories that can help you. Here are some of the most popular that you might want to consider.

Soft Boxes

Soft boxes are large square or rectangular devices that may resemble a square umbrella with a front cover, and produce a similar lighting effect. They can extend from a few feet square to massive boxes that stand five or six feet tall—virtually a wall of light. With a flash unit or two inside a soft box, you have a very large, semi-directional light source that's very diffuse and very flattering for portraiture and other people photography.

Soft boxes are also handy for photographing shiny objects. They not only provide a soft light, but if the box itself happens to reflect in the subject (say you're photographing a chromium toaster), the box will provide an interesting highlight that's indistinct and not distracting.

You can buy soft boxes, like the one shown in Figure 9.20, or make your own. Some lengths of friction-fit plastic pipe and a lot of muslin cut and sewed just so may be all that you need.

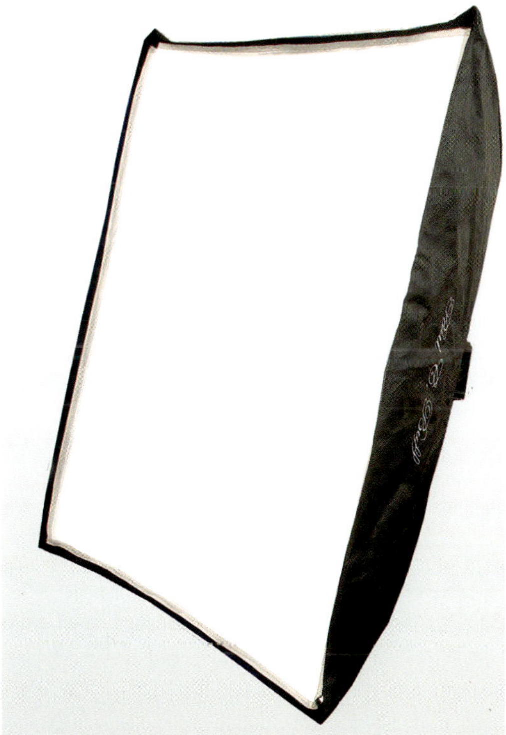

Figure 9.20
Soft boxes provide a large, diffuse light source.

Light Stands

Both electronic flash and incandescent lamps can benefit from light stands. These are lightweight, tripod-like devices (but without a swiveling or tilting head) that can be set on the floor, tabletops, or other elevated surfaces and positioned as needed. Light stands should be strong enough to support an external lighting unit, up to and including a relatively heavy flash with soft box or umbrella reflectors. You want the supports to be capable of raising the lights high enough to be effective. Look for light stands capable of extending six to seven feet high. The nine-foot units usually have larger, steadier bases, and extend high enough that you can use them as background supports. You'll be using these stands for a lifetime, so invest in good ones. I bought the light stand shown in Figure 9.21 when I was in college, and I have been using it for decades.

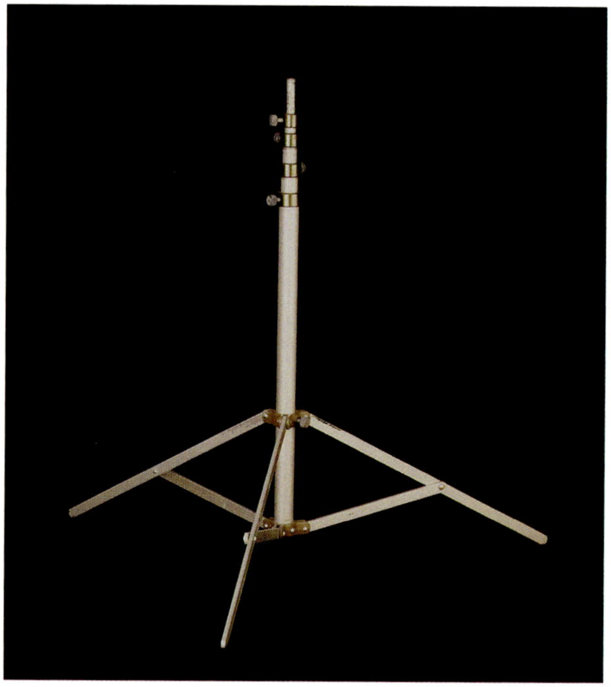

Figure 9.21
Light stands can hold lights, umbrellas, backdrops, and other equipment.

Backgrounds

Backgrounds can be backdrops of cloth, sheets of muslin you've painted yourself using a sponge dipped in paint, rolls of seamless paper, or any other suitable surface your mind can dream up. Backgrounds provide a complementary and non-distracting area behind subjects (especially portraits) and can be lit separately to provide contrast and separation that outlines the subject, or which helps set a mood.

I like to use plain-colored backgrounds for portraits, and white seamless backgrounds for product photography. You can usually construct supports for these yourself from cheap materials and tape them up on the wall behind your subject, or mount them on a pole stretched between a pair of light stands.

Snoots and Barn Doors

These fit over the flash unit and direct the light at your subject. Snoots are excellent for converting a flash unit into a hair light, while barn doors give you enough control over the illumination by opening and closing their flaps that you can use another flash as a background light, with the capability of feathering the light exactly where you want it. Barn doors are shown in Figure 9.22.

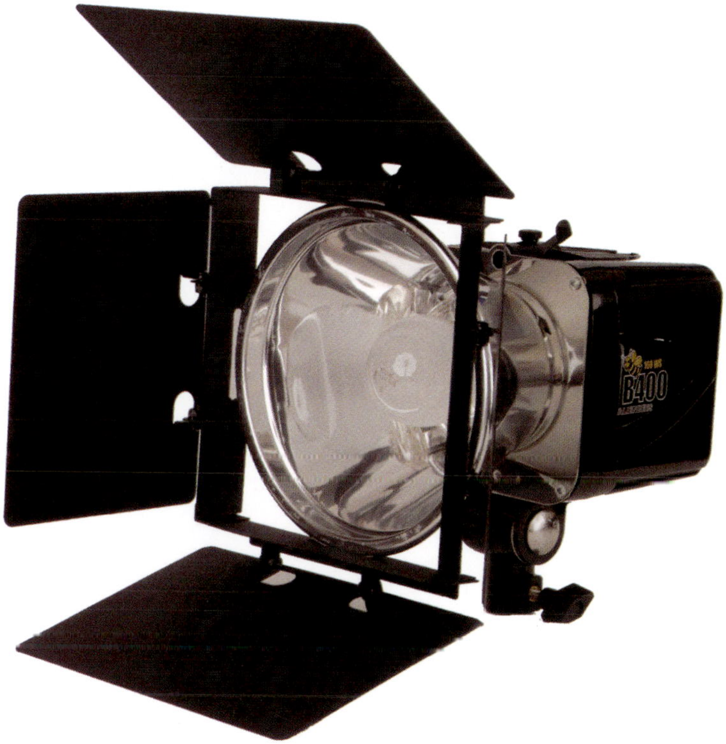

Figure 9.22
Barn doors allow you to modulate the light from a flash or lamp, and they are especially useful for hair lights and background lights.

10

Downloading and Editing Your Images

Taking the picture is only half the work, and, in some cases, only half the fun. After you've captured some great images and have them safely stored on your Sony Alpha's memory card, you'll need to transfer them from your camera and memory card to your computer, where they can be organized, fine-tuned in an image editor, and prepared for web display, printing, or some other final destination.

Fortunately, there are lots of software utilities and applications to help you do all these things. This chapter will introduce you to a few of them. Don't expect a lot of "how-to-do-it" or instructions on using the software itself. This is primarily a *camera* guide, rather than a software manual. My intent in this chapter is to let you know what options are available, to help you choose what is right for you.

What's in the Box?

Sony includes three basic software utilities with the Alpha SLT-A57. They are the Picture Motion Browser (abbreviated PMB, and compatible with Windows only), Image Data Lightbox SR (for Windows and Macs), and Image Data Converter SR (supplied for both Windows and Mac operating systems).

Install these applications using the CD supplied with the camera. Picture Motion Browser is an importing utility that collects images into folders and offers some simple editing capabilities for making minor fixes. Image Data Lightbox is a more advanced image browsing and workflow manager, while Image Data Converter SR is a sophisticated tool for importing and manipulating RAW images.

Picture Motion Browser

This tool, supplied with a variety of Sony cameras, camcorders, and other imaging devices, works with both still images and video files. It is available for Windows only, but Mac users can get most of its functions in iPhoto, and can import images to their computer by dragging and dropping image files as described in the "Transferring Your Photos" section that follows. Once you've imported/registered images with this browser, they are displayed either in Index View (see Figure 10.1), Map View, or in a calendar view that arranges the photos by the date they were taken. There is also a player included for AVCHD movies.

Double-click a thumbnail to display it in an editing window (see Figure 10.2), along with tools for trimming, rotating, adjusting brightness and contrast, enhancing or reducing saturation, adjusting sharpness, manipulating tonal curves, and activating red-eye reduction. You can also put the date on your photo. Picture Motion Browser can display all the photos in a folder as a slide show, burn them to a CD or DVD, and mark them for printing or e-mailing directly from the application. PMB lets you create Blu-Ray and AVCHD format video DVDs that can be played on compatible equipment.

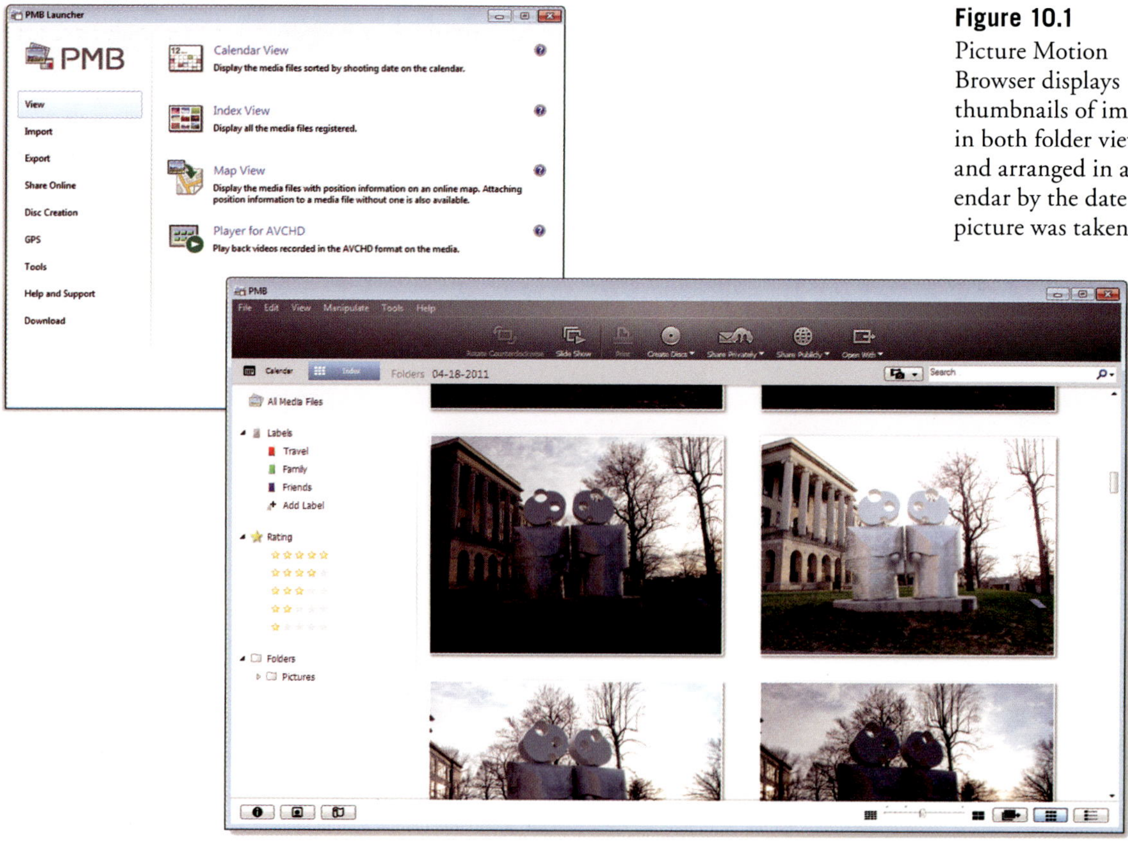

Figure 10.1
Picture Motion Browser displays thumbnails of images in both folder view and arranged in a calendar by the date the picture was taken.

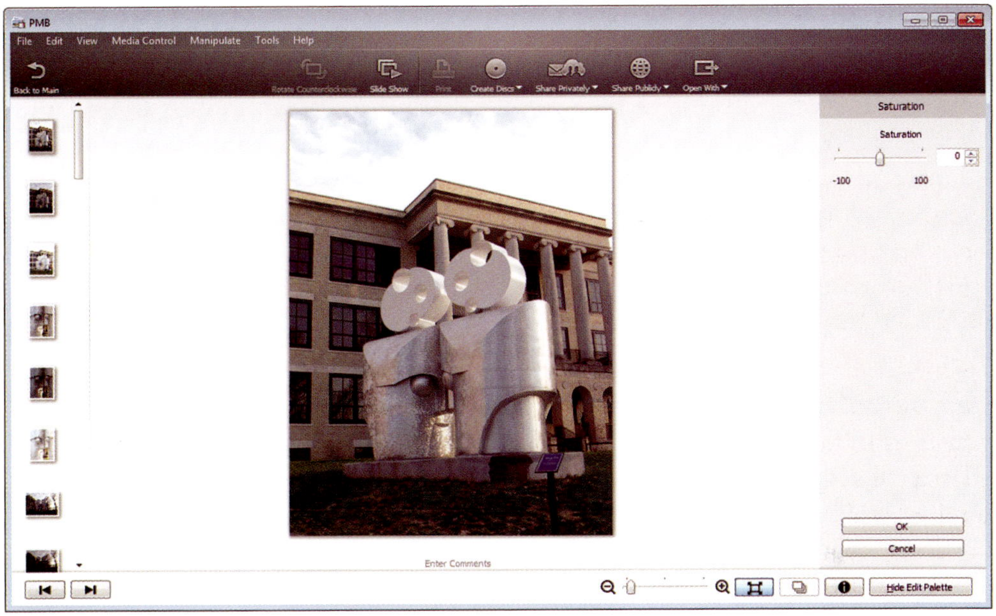

Figure 10.2
Simple editing fixes can be applied within Picture Motion Browser.

Picture Motion Browser has a photo-downloading utility that you can activate or deactivate in the Tools menu. As images are imported, they are moved into a folder within your My Pictures folder and are named after the import date, or deposited in a folder with a different name that you specify.

If you select Check for Updates from the Help menu in PMB, the utility will search for software and firmware updates on the Sony website and pop up dialog boxes that will whisk you off to the proper URL for downloading. (See Figure 10.3.)

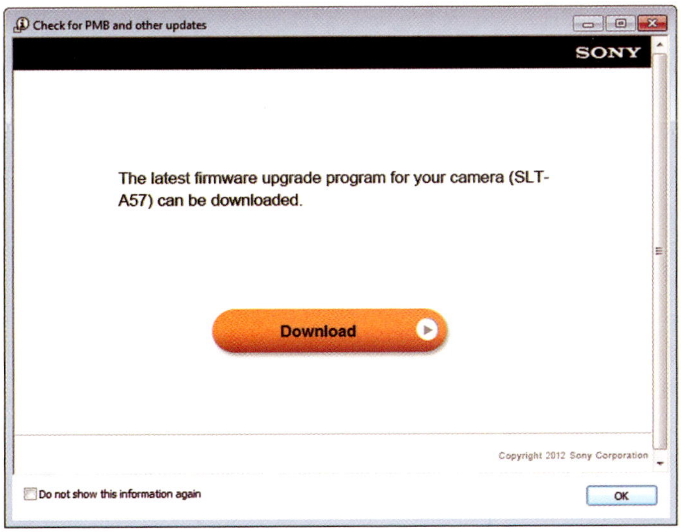

Figure 10.3
PMB will search for updates to your software and direct you to the correct URL for download.

Image Data Lightbox SR

This is a newer application than Picture Motion Browser and is better for viewing, sorting, and comparing images than the older program. It's no Adobe Lightroom (or Apple Aperture, for that matter), but the price—free—is right. The application lets you compare images, even when still in RAW format, and apply star ratings, so you can segregate your best shots from a group of similar images (as shown in Figure 10.4) while you manage your photo library. You can choose to view the images as all thumbnails or in the Preview Display format, which features a line of images and one large image. It includes tools for creating image collections, batch printing, and converting photos to JPEG or TIFF format. To manipulate RAW files, you need Image Data Converter SR, discussed next.

Image Data Converter SR

This RAW converter is Sony's equivalent of Adobe Camera Raw, except that as your .arw files are converted, they can be transferred to the image editor of your choice, such as Corel Paint Shop Pro, rather than just to Adobe Photoshop or Photoshop Elements.

Like all RAW converters, Image Data Converter SR (see Figure 10.5) enables you to change any of the settings you could have made in the camera, plus modify a selection of additional settings, such as tonal curves, that you can't normally adjust when you

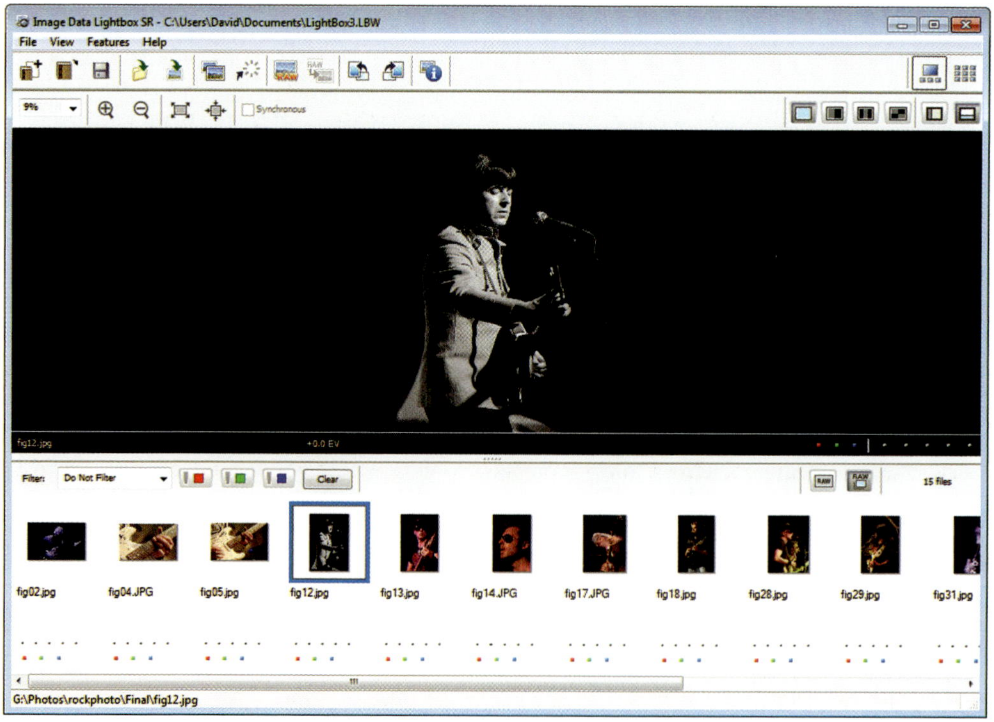

Figure 10.4 Image Data Lightbox SR helps you manage your picture collection.

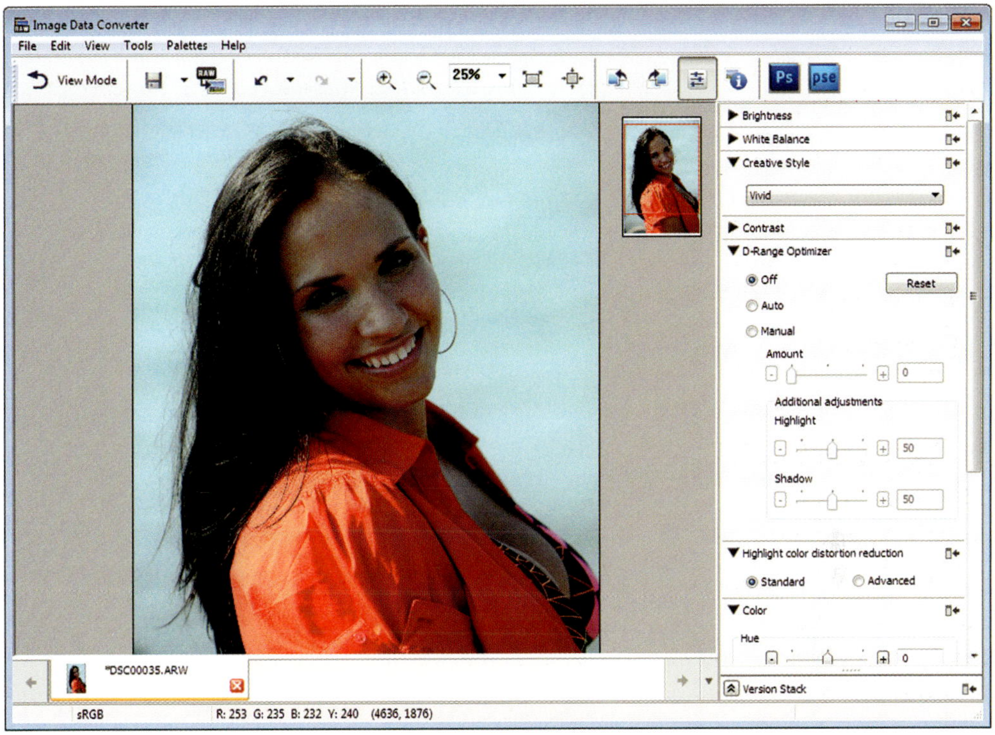

Figure 10.5
Image Data Converter SR lets you manage any of the in-camera settings as RAW files are imported—as well as many other options.

take the photo. Making these changes after the picture is taken allows you to fine-tune your images, correct errors you might have made when you shot the photo, and fix things such as color balance that the camera (or you) might have set incorrectly.

This program includes four Adjustment Palettes that enable you to invoke specific dialog boxes with sliders and other adjustments. For example, there are separate exposure value (EV) adjustment settings, contrast and saturation settings, and a three-channel histogram, which can, optionally, display separate red, green, and blue histograms rather than the simple brightness (luminance) histogram shown in the camera.

Palette 1 is used for adjusting and setting white balance, color correction, hue, and saturation; Palette 2 is used to modify exposure, contrast, D-Range Optimizer, and other settings; Palette 3 makes it easy to set Creative Style adjustments, and specify sharpness, noise reduction, and picture effects, etc.; Palette 4 is where you'll find controls for display area, histograms, and tone curves.

The Image Properties dialog box, shown in Figure 10.6, has an icon in the toolbar you can click to view a complete listing of all the settings you applied when you originally took the photo, such as lens, f/stop, shutter speed, ISO setting, and metering mode. These can all be changed within Image Data Converter SR as the files are imported for your image editor.

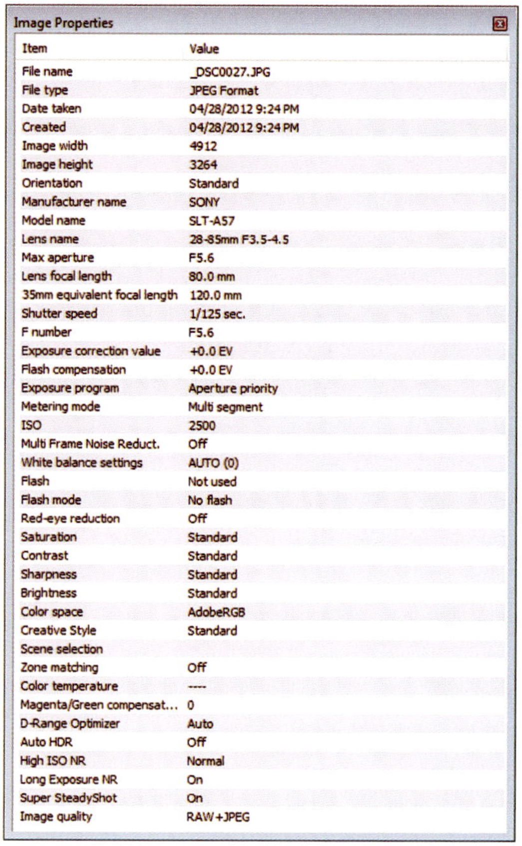

Image Properties

Item	Value
File name	_DSC0027.JPG
File type	JPEG Format
Date taken	04/28/2012 9:24 PM
Created	04/28/2012 9:24 PM
Image width	4912
Image height	3264
Orientation	Standard
Manufacturer name	SONY
Model name	SLT-A57
Lens name	28-85mm F3.5-4.5
Max aperture	F5.6
Lens focal length	80.0 mm
35mm equivalent focal length	120.0 mm
Shutter speed	1/125 sec.
F number	F5.6
Exposure correction value	+0.0 EV
Flash compensation	+0.0 EV
Exposure program	Aperture priority
Metering mode	Multi segment
ISO	2500
Multi Frame Noise Reduct.	Off
White balance settings	AUTO (0)
Flash	Not used
Flash mode	No flash
Red-eye reduction	Off
Saturation	Standard
Contrast	Standard
Sharpness	Standard
Brightness	Standard
Color space	AdobeRGB
Creative Style	Standard
Scene selection	
Zone matching	Off
Color temperature	----
Magenta/Green compensat...	0
D-Range Optimizer	Auto
Auto HDR	Off
High ISO NR	Normal
Long Exposure NR	On
Super SteadyShot	On
Image quality	RAW+JPEG

Figure 10.6
Check out your original settings in the Image Properties dialog box.

Transferring Your Photos

While it's rewarding to capture some great images and have them ensconced in your camera, eventually you'll be transferring them to your laptop or PC, whether you're using a Windows or Macintosh machine. You have four options for image transfer: direct transfer over a USB cable; automated transfer using a card reader and transfer software such as the Sony Import Media Files utility that is a part of the Picture Motion Browser and Image Data Converter SR applications; Adobe Photoshop Elements Photo Downloader; or manual transfer using drag and drop from a memory card inserted in a card reader.

If you want to transfer your photos directly from your Sony Alpha camera to your computer, you'll first need to visit the Setup 2 menu and make sure that the USB connection option is set to Auto or Mass Storage. That allows your computer to recognize the memory card in your computer as just another external drive, as if the camera were a hard drive or thumb/flash drive. While this method consumes a lot more battery power than the card-reader option discussed later, and may be quite a bit slower, it is convenient (assuming you have the USB cable handy) and easy.

Just follow these steps:

1. With the Alpha's USB connection option set to Mass Storage, turn the camera and computer on.
2. Open the door over the connector ports and plug the smaller connector of the USB cable into the camera. Then, plug the larger cable plug into a USB socket on your computer.
3. If you're using Windows, its Autoplay Wizard may pop up (see Figure 10.7), offering a selection of downloading utilities (including the Windows Scanner and Camera Wizard, Adobe Photo Downloader, and the Media Importer). Choose one. Mac OS X offers similar options.

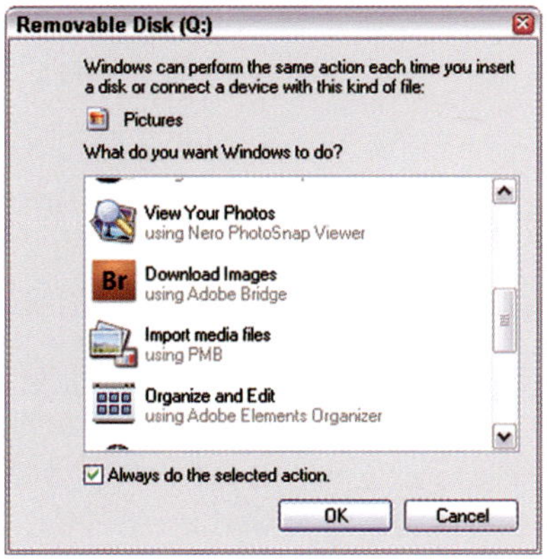

Figure 10.7 Windows Autoplay Wizard allows you to choose which utility to use to transfer your photos.

4. Use the options in the downloading utility you selected. You may be able to specify automatic red-eye correction, rename your files, place your files in a folder you select, or even view thumbnails of the available images so you download only the ones you want.
5. Activate the download process.

Using a Card Reader and Software

You can also use a memory card reader and software to transfer photos and automate the process using any of the downloading applications available with your computer. The process is similar to downloading directly from the camera, except that you must remove the memory card from the Alpha camera and insert it into a memory card reader attached to your computer.

Whereas USB-to-computer transfers are limited to the speed of your USB connection, card readers can be potentially much faster. This method is more frugal in its use of your camera's battery and can be faster if you have a speedy USB 2.0 or 3.0 or FireWire card reader attached to an appropriate port. I have FireWire 800 ports in my computer,

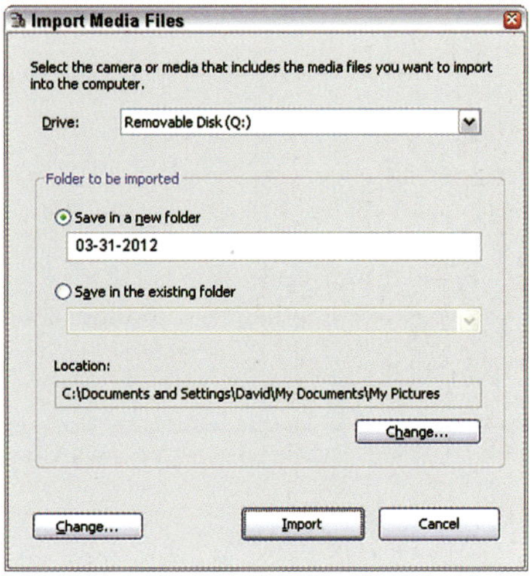

Figure 10.8 The Picture Motion Browser is installed automatically with the Sony software suite.

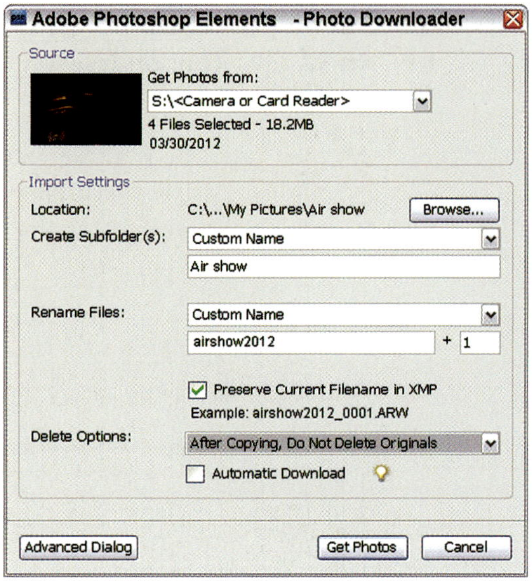

Figure 10.9 With Basic view activated, Photoshop Elements Photo Downloader allows you to choose a filename and destination for your photos.

and a FireWire 800 card reader, and I get roughly four times the transfer speed I got with my old USB card reader.

The installed software automatically remains in memory as you work, and it recognizes when a memory card is inserted in your card reader; you don't have to launch it yourself. You'll see the Import Media Files dialog box (see Figure 10.8), or, sometimes, several competing downloaders will pop up at once. If that happens, you may want to disable the superfluous downloaders so your utility of choice will take precedence.

With Photoshop Elements Photo Downloader, you can choose basic options, such as file renaming and folder location, and then click Get Photos to begin the transfer of all images immediately. (See Figure 10.8.) Or choose Advanced Dialog for additional options, such as the ability to select which images to download from the memory card by marking them on a display of thumbnails. You can select other options, such as Automatically Fix Red Eyes, or insert a copyright notice of your choice. Start the download by clicking Get Photos, and a confirmation dialog box like the one in Figure 10.10 shows the progress.

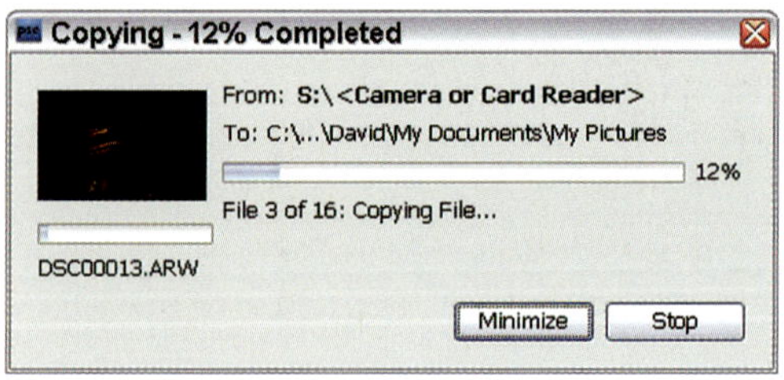

Figure 10.10 The Photo Downloader's confirmation dialog box shows the progress as images are transferred.

Dragging and Dropping

The final way to move photos from your memory card to your computer is the old-fashioned way: manually dragging and dropping the files from one window on your computer to another. The procedure works pretty much the same whether you're using a Mac or a PC.

1. Remove the memory card from the Sony Alpha and insert it in your memory card reader. (Make sure the USB connection option in Setup 2 menu is set to Mass Storage or Auto.)
2. Using Windows Explorer, My Computer, Computer, or your Mac desktop, open the icon representing the memory card, which appears on your desktop as just another disk drive.
3. Open a second window representing the folder on your computer that you want to use as the destination for the files you are copying or moving.
4. Drag and drop the files from the memory card window to the folder on your computer. You can select individual files, press Ctrl/Command+A to select all the files, or Ctrl/Command+click to select multiple files.

Editing Your Photos

Image manipulation tasks fall into several categories. You might want to fine-tune your images, retouch them, change color balance, composite several images together, and perform other tasks we know as image editing, with a program like Adobe Photoshop, Photoshop Elements, or Corel Photo Paint.

You might want to play with the settings in RAW files, too, as you import them from their .arw state into an image editor. There are specialized tools expressly for tweaking RAW files, ranging from Sony's own Digital Image Converter to Adobe Camera Raw, and PhaseOne's Capture One 5 Pro (C1 Pro). A third type of manipulation is the specialized task of noise reduction, which can be performed within Photoshop, Adobe Camera Raw, or specialized tools just for noise reduction, such as Noise Ninja (www.Picturecode.com).

Each of these utilities and applications deserves a chapter of its own, so I'm simply going to enumerate some of the most popular image editing and RAW conversion programs here and tell you a little about what they do.

Image Editors

Image editors are general-purpose photo-editing applications that can do color correction, tonal modifications, retouching, combining of several images into one, and usually include tools for working with RAW files and reducing noise. So, you'll find programs like those listed here good for all-around image manipulation. The leading programs are as follows:

Adobe Photoshop/Photoshop Elements. Photoshop is the serious photographer's number one choice for image editing, and Elements is an excellent option for those who need most of Photoshop's power, but not all of its professional-level features. Both Photoshop and Elements editors use the latest version of Adobe's Camera Raw plug-in, which makes it easy to adjust things like color space profiles, color depth (either 8 bits or 16 bits per color channel), image resolution, white balance, exposure, shadows, brightness, sharpness, luminance, and noise reduction. One plus with the Adobe products is that they are available in identical versions for both Windows and Macs.

Corel Photo Paint. This is the image-editing program that is included in the popular CorelDRAW Graphics suite. Although a Mac version was available in the past, this is exclusively a Windows application today. It's a full-featured photo retouching and image-editing program with selection, retouching, and painting tools for manual image manipulations, and it also includes convenient automated commands for a few common tasks, such as red-eye removal. Photo Paint accepts Photoshop plug-ins to expand its assortment of filters and special effects.

Corel Paint Shop Pro. This is a general-purpose Windows-only image editor that has gained a reputation as the "poor person's Photoshop" for providing a substantial portion of Photoshop's capabilities at a fraction of the cost. It includes a nifty set of wizard-like commands that automate common tasks, such as removing red eye and scratches, as well as filters and effects, which can be expanded with other Photoshop plug-ins.

Corel Painter. Here's another image-editing program from Corel for both Mac and Windows. This one's strength is in mimicking natural media, such as charcoal, pastels, and various kinds of paint. Painter includes a basic assortment of tools that you can use to edit existing images, but the program is really designed for artists to use in creating original illustrations. As a photographer, you might prefer another image editor, but if you like to paint on top of your photographic images, nothing else really does the job of Painter.

Corel PhotoImpact. Corel finally brought one of the last remaining non-Adobe image editors into its fold when it acquired PhotoImpact. This is a general-purpose photo-editing program for Windows with a huge assortment of brushes for painting, retouching, and cloning in addition to the usual selection, cropping, and fill tools. If you frequently find yourself performing the same image manipulations on a number of files, you'll appreciate PhotoImpact's batch operations. Using this feature, you can select multiple image files and then apply any one of a long list of filters, enhancements, or auto-process commands to all the selected files.

RAW Utilities

Your software choices for manipulating RAW files are broader than you might think. Camera vendors always supply a utility to read their cameras' own RAW files, but sometimes, particularly with those point-and-shoot cameras that can produce RAW files, the options are fairly limited.

Because in the past digital camera vendors offered RAW converters that weren't very good, there is a lively market for third-party RAW utilities available at extra cost. The third-party solutions are usually available as standalone applications (often for both Windows and Macintosh platforms), as Photoshop-compatible plug-ins, or both. Because the RAW plug-ins displace Photoshop's own RAW converter, I tend to prefer to use most RAW utilities in standalone mode. That way, if I choose to open a file directly in Photoshop, it automatically opens using Photoshop's fast and easy-to-use Adobe Camera Raw (ACR) plug-in. If I have more time or need the capabilities of another converter, I can load that, open the file, and make my corrections there. Most are able to transfer the processed file directly to Photoshop even if you aren't using plug-in mode.

The latest version of Photoshop includes a built-in RAW plug-in that is compatible with the proprietary formats of a growing number of digital cameras, both new and old, and it's continually updated to embrace any new cameras that are introduced. This plug-in also works with Photoshop Elements.

To open a RAW image in Photoshop, just follow these steps (Elements users can use much the same workflow, although fewer settings are available):

1. Transfer the .arw images from your camera to your computer's hard drive.
2. In Photoshop, choose Open from the File menu, or use Bridge or Elements Organizer.
3. Select an .arw image file. The Adobe Camera Raw plug-in will pop up, showing a preview of the image, like the one shown in Figure 10.11.
4. If you like, use one of the tools found in the toolbar at the top left of the dialog box. From left to right, they are as follows:
   - **Zoom.** Operates just like the Zoom tool in Photoshop.
   - **Hand.** Use like the Hand tool in Photoshop.
   - **White Balance.** Click an area in the image that should be neutral gray or white to set the white balance quickly.
   - **Color Sampler.** Use to determine the RGB values of areas you click with this eyedropper.

- **Crop.** Pre-crop the image so that only the portion you specify is imported into Photoshop. This option saves time when you want to work on a section of a large image, and you don't need the entire file.
- **Straighten.** Drag in the preview image to define what should be a horizontal or vertical line, and ACR will realign the image to straighten it.
- **Retouch.** Use to heal or clone areas you define.
- **Red-Eye Removal.** Quickly zap red pupils in your human subjects.
- **ACR Preferences.** Produces a dialog box of Adobe Camera Raw preferences.
- **Rotate Counterclockwise.** Rotates counterclockwise in 90-degree increments with a click.
- **Rotate Clockwise.** Rotates clockwise in 90-degree increments with a click.

5. Using the Basic tab, you can have ACR show you red and blue highlights in the preview that indicate shadow areas that are clipped (too dark to show detail) and light areas that are blown out (too bright). Click the triangles in the upper-left corner of the histogram display (shadow clipping) and upper-right corner (highlight clipping) to toggle these indicators on or off.
6. Also in the Basic tab you can choose white balance, either from the drop-down list or by setting a color temperature and green/magenta color bias (tint) using the sliders.

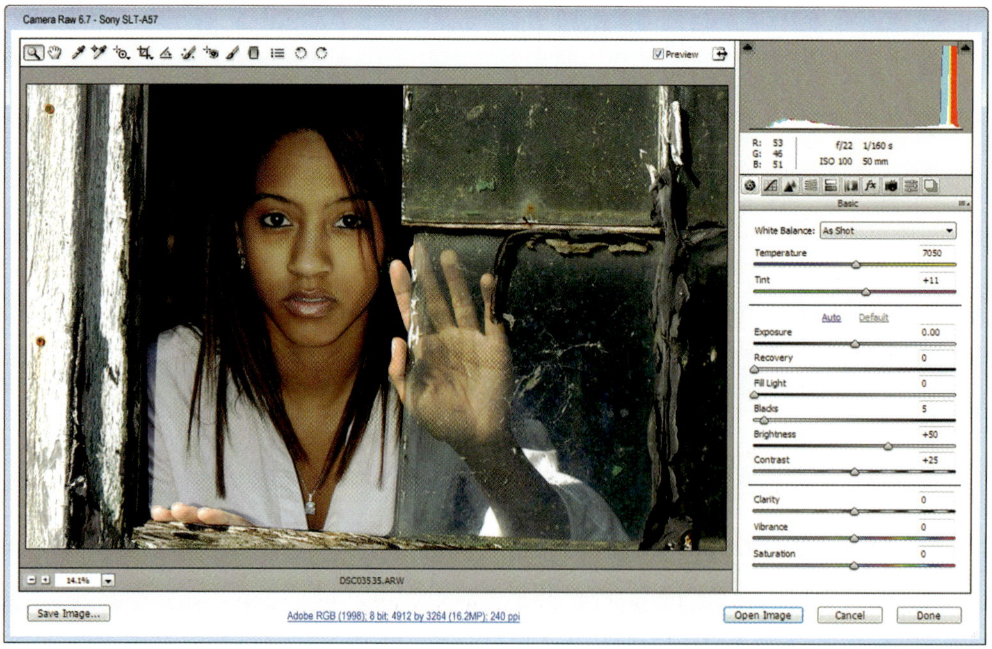

Figure 10.11
The basic ACR dialog box looks like this when processing a single image.

7. Other sliders are available to control exposure, recovery, fill light, blacks, brightness, contrast, vibrance, and saturation. A checkbox can be marked to convert the image to grayscale.
8. Make other adjustments (described in more detail below).
9. ACR makes automatic adjustments for you. You can click Default and make the changes for yourself, or click the Auto link (located just above the Exposure slider) to reapply the automatic adjustments after you've made your own modifications.
10. If you've marked more than one image to be opened, the additional images appear in a "filmstrip" at the left side of the screen. You can click on each thumbnail in the filmstrip in turn and apply different settings to each.
11. Click Open Image/Open Image(s) into Photoshop using the settings you've made. You can also click Save or Done to save the changes you've made *without* opening the file in your image editor.

The Basic tab is displayed by default when the ACR dialog box opens, and it includes most of the sliders and controls you'll need to fine-tune your image as you import it into Photoshop. These include:

- **White Balance.** Leave it As Shot or change to a value such as Daylight, Cloudy, Shade, Tungsten, Fluorescent, or Flash. If you like, you can set a custom white balance using the Temperature and Tint sliders.
- **Exposure.** This slider adjusts the overall brightness and darkness of the image.
- **Recovery.** Restores detail in the red, green, and blue color channels.
- **Fill Light.** Reconstructs detail in shadows.
- **Blacks.** Increases the number of tones represented as black in the final image, emphasizing tones in the shadow areas of the image.
- **Brightness.** This slider adjusts the brightness and darkness of an image.
- **Contrast.** Manipulates the contrast of the midtones of your image.
- **Clarity.** Use this slider to apply a hybrid type of contrast enhancement to boost midtone contrast.
- **Vibrance.** Prevents over-saturation when enriching the colors of an image.
- **Saturation.** Manipulates the richness of all colors equally, from zero saturation (gray/black, no color) at the –100 setting to double the usual saturation at the +100 setting.

Additional controls are available on the Tone Curve, Detail, HSL/Grayscale, Split Toning, Lens Corrections, Camera Calibration, FX, Presets, and Snapshots tabs, shown in Figure 10.12. The Tone Curve tab can change the tonal values of your image. The Detail tab lets you adjust sharpness, luminance smoothing, and apply color noise reduction. The HSL/Grayscale tab offers controls for adjusting hue, saturation, and lightness and converting an image to black-and-white. Split Toning helps you colorize an image with sepia or cyanotype (blue) shades. The Lens Corrections tab has sliders to adjust for chromatic aberrations and vignetting. The Camera Calibration tab provides a way for calibrating the color corrections made in the Camera Raw plug-in.

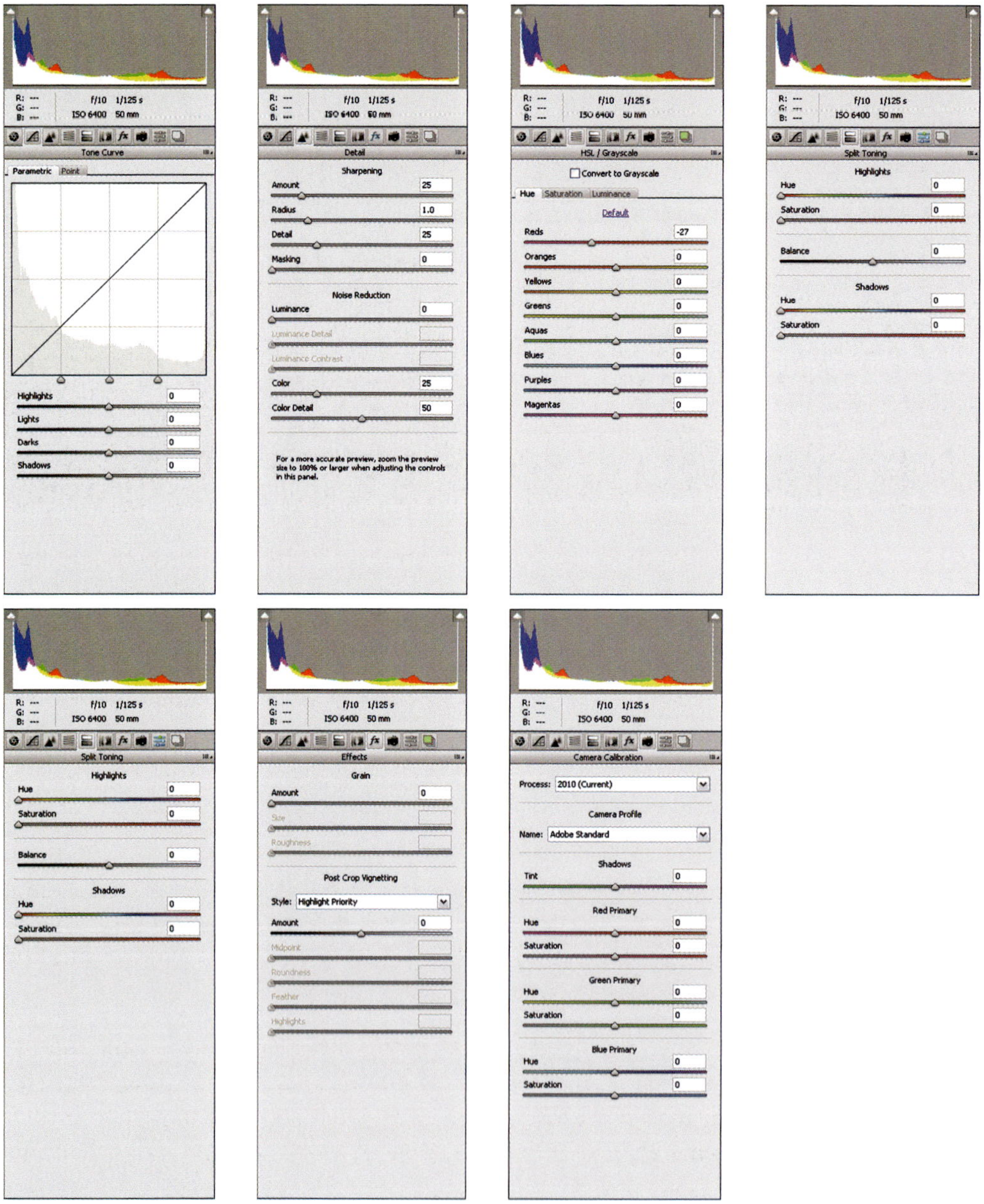

Figure 10.12 More controls are available within the additional tabbed dialog boxes in Adobe Camera Raw.

11

Sony Alpha SLT-A57: Troubleshooting and Prevention

One of the nice things about modern electronic cameras like the A57 series is that they have fewer mechanical moving parts to fail, so they are less likely to "wear out." No film transport mechanism, no wind lever or motor drive, no complicated mechanical linkages from camera to lens to physically stop down the lens aperture. Instead, tiny, reliable motors are built into each lens (and you lose the use of only that lens should something fail), and one of the few major moving parts in most other cameras is a lightweight mirror (its small size one of the advantages of the Alpha's 1.5X crop factor) that flips up and down with each shot, but which remains stationary on the A57 models (unless you flip it up manually to clean the sensor).

Of course, the camera also has a moving shutter that can fail, but the shutter is built rugged enough that you can expect it to last 100,000 shutter cycles or more. Unless you're shooting sports in continuous mode day in and day out, the shutter on your Alpha is likely to last as long as you expect to use the camera.

The only other things on the camera that move are switches, dials, buttons, the flip-up electronic flash, and the door that slides open to allow you to remove and insert the memory card. Unless you're extraordinarily clumsy or unlucky and manage to give your built-in flash a good whack while it is in use, there's not a lot that can go wrong mechanically with your Sony Alpha.

On the other hand, one of the chief drawbacks of modern electronic cameras is that they are modern *electronic* cameras. Your Alpha is fully dependent on its battery. Without it, the camera can't be used. There are numerous other electronic connections in the camera (many connected to those mechanical switches and dials), and components like the swiveling 3-inch color LCD on the A57 that can potentially fail or suffer damage. The camera also relies on its "operating system," or *firmware*, which can be plagued by bugs that cause unexpected behavior. Luckily, electronic components are generally more reliable and trouble-free, especially when compared to their mechanical counterparts from the pre-electronic film camera days. (Film cameras of the last 10 to 20 years have had almost as many electronic features as digital cameras, but, believe it or not, there were whole generations of film cameras that had *no* electronics or batteries.)

Digital cameras have problems unique to their breed, too; the most troublesome being the need to clean the sensor of dust and grime periodically. This chapter will show you how to diagnose problems, fix some common ills, and, importantly, learn how to avoid them in the future.

Updating Your Firmware

As I said, the firmware in your Sony Alpha is the camera's operating system, which handles everything from menu display (including fonts, colors, and the actual entries themselves), what languages are available, and even support for specific devices and features. Upgrading the firmware to a new version makes it possible to add new features while fixing some of the bugs that sneak in.

The exact changes made to the firmware are generally spelled out in the firmware release announcement. You can examine the remedies provided and decide if a given firmware patch is important to you. If not, you can usually safely wait a while before going through the bother of upgrading your firmware—at least long enough for the early adopters to report whether the bug fixes have introduced new bugs of their own. Each new firmware release incorporates the changes from previous releases, so if you skip a minor upgrade you should have no problems.

WARNING

Use a fully charged battery to ensure that you'll have enough power to operate the camera for the entire upgrade. Moreover, you should not turn off the camera while your old firmware is being overwritten. Don't open the memory card door or do anything else that might disrupt operation of the Alpha while the firmware is being installed.

Previous Sony models have "hidden" the firmware version number, but the A57 displays it in the Version entry at the top of the Setup 3 menu. Write down the firmware version installed in your camera, and then check to see if a firmware update is available.

To do that, visit the Sony support site at www.esupport.sony.com. The support page provides updates and information about a huge range of Sony products, but there is a Search box you can use to jump directly to the page for your particular camera. I've found that all you need to enter is "SLT-A57," or "SLT-". If new firmware is available, it will be listed as a link under the "Hot Topics" display. Follow the links and download the update. As I write this, the latest firmware for this Alpha series is Version 1.02, which was introduced only a few weeks after the camera itself hit the shelves.

The firmware will be accompanied by a list of steps to follow. The firmware update I installed on my A57 went like this:

1. **Put the firmware software in a separate directory or folder.** It will have a name like Update_SLTA57V103.exe (for Windows computers) or Update_SLTA57V104.zip (for Mac OS).
2. **Extract the firmware file.** Go to the directory/folder where the firmware download was placed and double-click to run the firmware updater utility. On a Windows PC, a dialog box like the one shown in Figure 11.1 appears. A similar screen will appear on a Mac.
3. **Follow the instructions.** When you run the Firmware Updater, you'll see a series of instruction screens. I'll run through the instructions, shown in Figure 11.2 in a clockwise arrangement.
4. **Connect the camera to the computer.** You should have USB Connection in the Setup 2 menu set to Mass Storage. Then connect the camera and computer with the cable supplied with the A57. Click Next in the dialog box.
5. **Verify the version.** Once the Firmware Updater is satisfied that the camera and computer are connected, you'll be prompted to click the Next button again to verify the current firmware version of your camera.

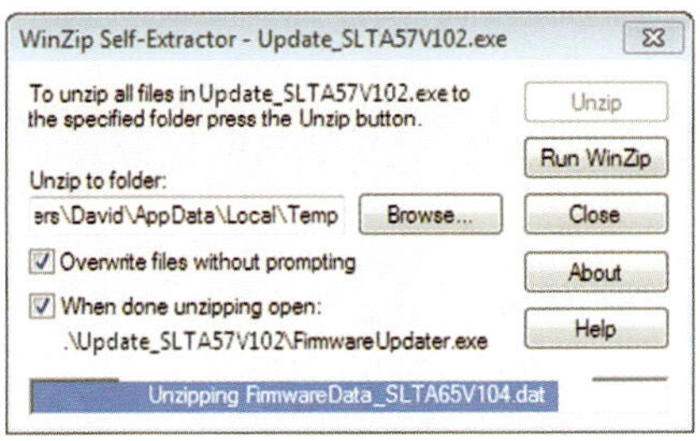

Figure 11.1
Uncompress the Firmware Updater file.

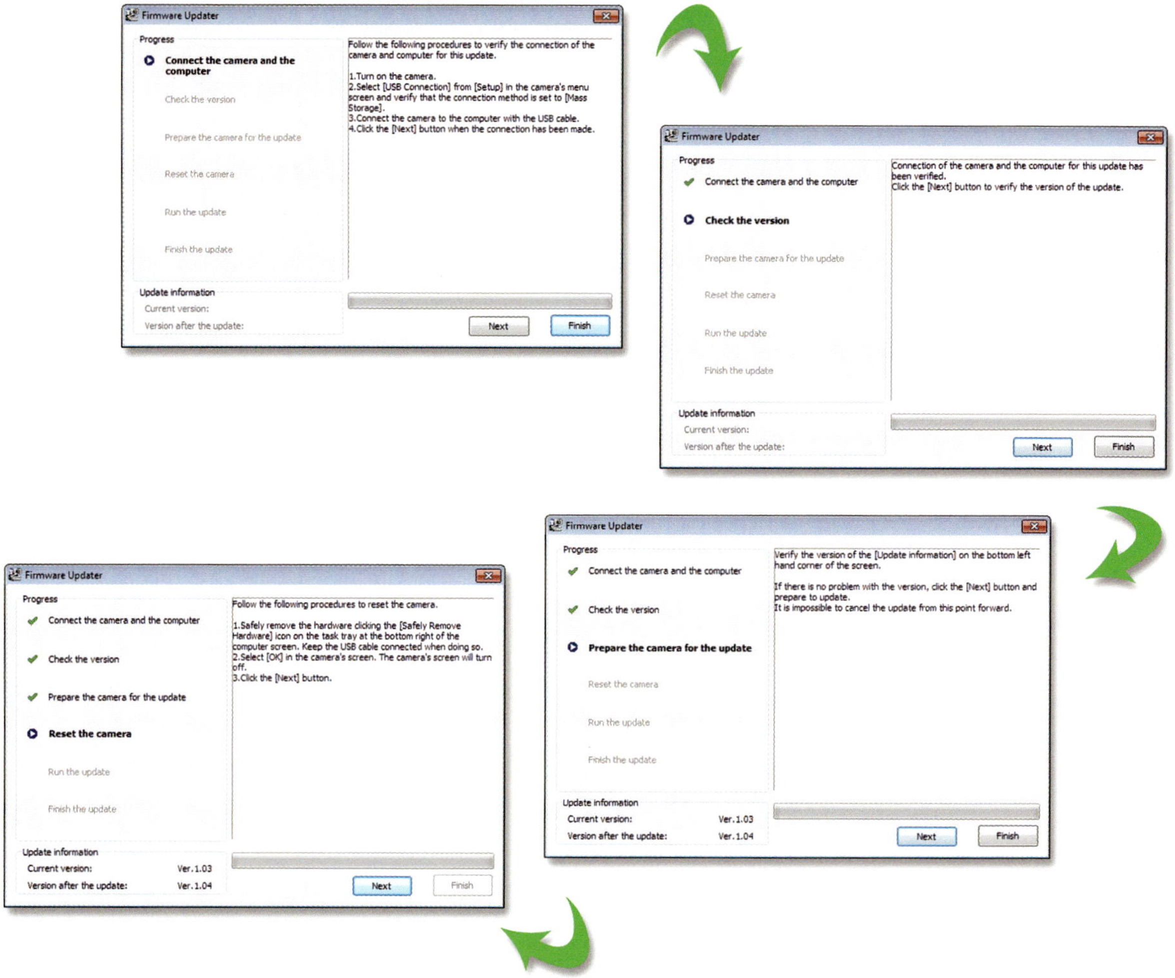

Figure 11.2 Prepare the camera for the update.

6. **Prepare for Update.** If the Updater verifies your current firmware for updating, you'll be asked to click Next once again. The update process cannot be canceled from this point onward.
7. **"Eject" (but don't disconnect) the camera.** Use your operating systems safe disconnect utility (it's Safely Remove Hardware under Windows, and usually has an icon in the Windows System Tray) to "eject" the camera from your computer's list of devices. With a Mac, drag the camera icon to the Trash. *Do not unplug the USB cable, either before or after the camera has been logically disconnected.*
8. **Reset the camera.** A screen will appear on the A57. Press the OK button on the control dial to reset the camera. Then Click the Next button on the Firmware Updater dialog box.

9. **Camera reconnects with the computer.** Once the camera has reset, the Updater will attempt to reconnect the computer with the A57. Click the Run button in the dialog box (see upper left in Figure 11.3) to begin the update. *Do not turn off the camera or unplug the USB cable.*
10. **Update in process.** While the update runs, the dialog box shown at right in Figure 11.3 displays the progress.
11. **Finish update.** When the update is done, the screen shown at the bottom of Figure 11.3 appears. Click Finish.
12. **Disconnect USB cable.** Remove the USB cable and turn the A57 off. The next time you power up, the new firmware will be in operation, which you can verify from the Version entry in the Setup 3 menu.

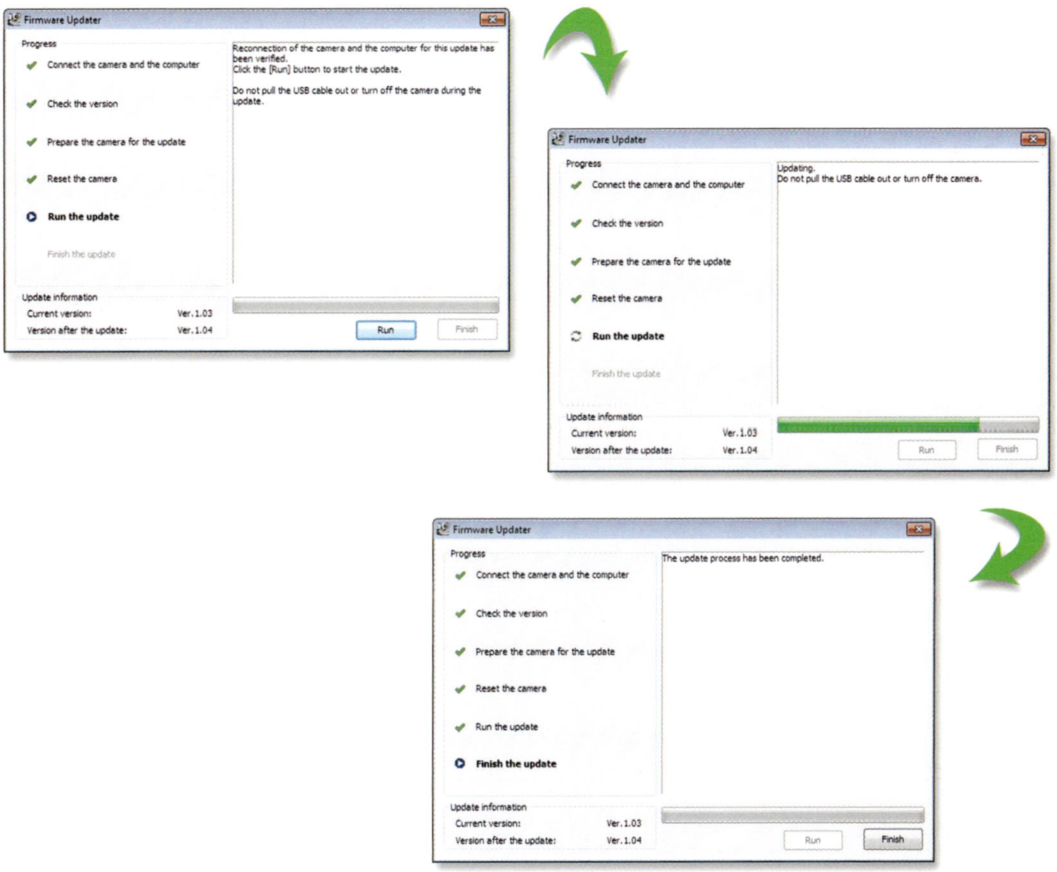

Figure 11.3 Run and finish the update.

Protecting Your LCD

The 3-inch color LCD on the back of your Sony Alpha almost seems like a target for banging, scratching, and other abuse, especially when it is swiveled up or down for viewing from high or low vantage points. Fortunately, this LCD is quite rugged, and a few errant knocks are unlikely to shatter the protective cover over the LCD, and scratches won't easily mar its surface. However, if you want to be on the safe side, there are several protective products you can purchase to keep your LCD safe—and, in some cases, make it a little easier to view. Here's a quick overview of your options.

- **Plastic overlays.** The simplest solution (although not always the cheapest) is to apply a plastic overlay sheet or "skin" cut to fit your LCD. These adhere either by static electricity or through a light adhesive coating that's even less clingy than stick-it notes. You can cut down overlays made for PDAs (although these can be pricey at up to $19.95 for a set of several sheets), or purchase overlays sold specifically for digital cameras. Vendors such as Zagg (www.zagg.com) offer overlays of this type. These products will do a good job of shielding your Alpha's LCD screen from scratches and minor impacts, but will not offer much protection from a good whack.
- **Acrylic/glass/polycarbonate shields.** Sony offers a clip-on polycarbonate LCD shield for the A57, the PCKM-L1AM, which costs about $12. A company in China called GGS makes a very popular glass screen protector for various Alpha models. (See Figure 11.4.) Unfortunately, it seems to be available only through eBay, Amazon, and a few other online retailers, so I can't give you a specific URL to visit. There are a number of different sellers offering these shields for $5 to $12, plus shipping, and I've ordered from several of them with good luck. The protectors attach using strips of sticky adhesive that hold the panel flush and tight, but which allow the protector to be pried off and the adhesive removed easily if you want to remove or replace the shield. They don't attenuate your view of the LCD and are non-reflective enough for use under a variety of lighting conditions. Thicker shields *may* interfere with your ability to reverse the LCD and close it with the glass side facing inward.
- **Hoods.** Various hood-type devices are available for the Alpha series, including a fold-up hood offered by Sony itself. My objection to these hoods is that you must close them to use the optical viewfinder, and then open them if you want to review your image. They are best suited for protecting/shielding the LCD when using the Live View feature, as you can then leave the hood unfolded all the time while shooting.

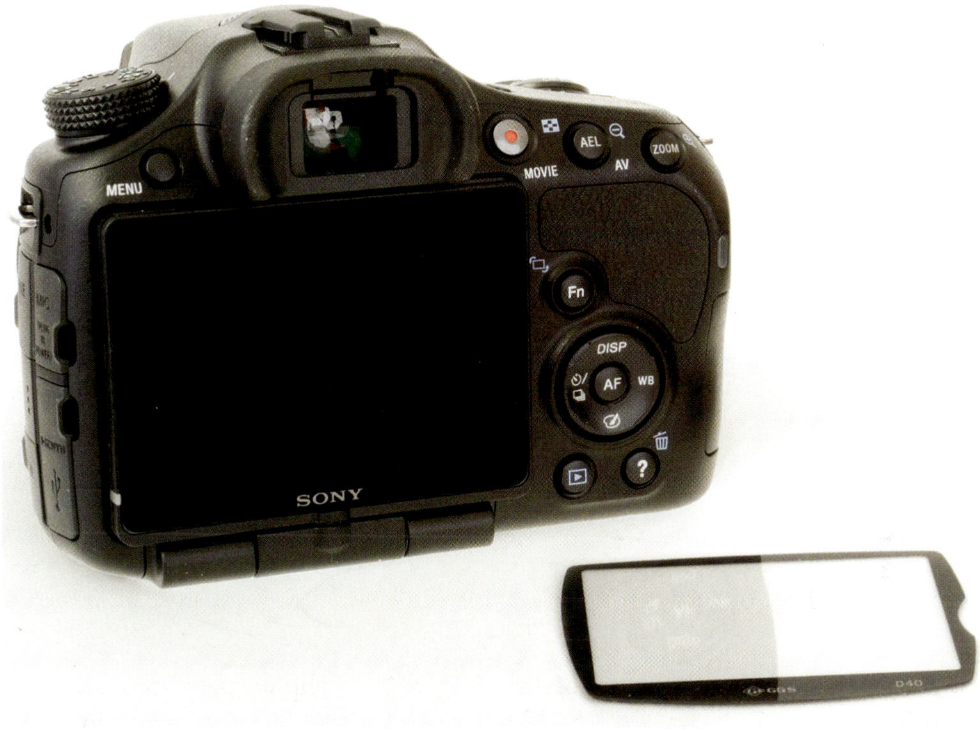

Figure 11.4
Stick-on LCD protectors can protect your viewscreen.

Troubleshooting Memory Cards

Sometimes good memory cards go bad. Sometimes good photographers can treat their memory cards badly. It's possible that a memory card that works fine in one camera won't be recognized when inserted into another. In the worst case, you can have a card full of important photos and find that the card seems to be corrupted and you can't access any of them. Don't panic! If these scenarios sound horrific to you, there are lots of things you can do to prevent them from happening, and a variety of remedies available if they do occur. You'll want to take some time—before disaster strikes—to consider your options.

All Your Eggs in One Basket?

The debate about whether it's better to use one large memory card or several smaller ones has been going on since even before there were memory cards. I can remember when computer users wondered whether it was smarter to install a pair of 200MB (not *gigabyte*) hard drives in their computer, or if they should go for one of those new-fangled 500MB models. By the same token, a few years ago the user groups were full of proponents who insisted that you ought to use 128MB memory cards rather than the huge 512MB versions. Today, most of the arguments involve 4GB cards versus 8GB cards, and I expect that as prices for 16GB and 32GB memory cards continue to drop, they'll find their way into the debate as well. I just bought two high-speed 32GB cards for *less* than I paid for a 4GB Secure Digital or Memory Stick card only 18 months ago. Because you own the 24MP SLT-A57, you'll be especially interested in high-capacity cards.

Why all the fuss? Are 8GB memory cards more likely to fail than 4GB cards? Are you risking all your photos if you trust your images to a larger card? Isn't it better to use several smaller cards, so that if one fails you lose only half as many photos? Or, isn't it wiser to put all your photos onto one larger card, because the more cards you use, the better your odds of misplacing or damaging one and losing at least some pictures?

In the end, the "eggs in one basket" argument boils down to statistics, and how you happen to use your Alpha. The rationales can go both ways. If you have multiple smaller cards, you do increase your chances of something happening to one of them, so, arguably, you might be boosting the odds of losing some pictures. If all your images are important, the fact that you've lost 100 rather than 200 pictures isn't very comforting.

Also, consider that the eggs/basket scenario assumes that the cards that are lost or damaged are always full. It's actually likely that your 8GB card might suffer a mishap when it's less than half full. Indeed, it's *more* likely that a large card won't be completely filled before it's offloaded to a computer. I often use only one quarter to one half of the capacity of my larger cards in a single session. I'm thankful that the extra room is there when I need it, but I don't always use it. So the reality is that you might not lose any more shots with a single 8GB card than with multiple 4GB cards. A bad card—of whatever size—might contain, say 3GB of images, so the size of the card won't really matter in such cases.

If you shoot photojournalist-type pictures, you probably change memory cards when they're less than completely full in order to avoid the need to do so at a crucial moment. (When I shoot sports, my cards rarely reach 80 to 90 percent of capacity before I change them.) Using multiple smaller cards means you have to change them that more often, which can be a real pain when you're taking a lot of photos. As an example, if you use 4GB memory cards with an Alpha A57 and shoot RAW & JPEG, you may get only a few dozen pictures on the card. That's almost exactly the capacity of a 36-exposure roll of film (remember those?). In my book, I prefer keeping all my eggs in one basket, and then making very sure that nothing happens to that basket.

There is really only one good reason to justify limiting yourself to smaller memory cards when larger ones can be purchased at the same cost per-gigabyte. One of them is when every single picture is precious to you and the loss of any of them would be a disaster. If you're a wedding photographer, for example, and unlikely to be able to restage the nuptials if a memory card goes bad, you'll probably want to shoot no more pictures than you can afford to lose on a single card, and have an assistant ready to copy each card removed from the camera onto a backup hard drive or DVD onsite.

To be even safer, you'd want to alternate cameras or have a second photographer at least partially duplicating your coverage so your shots are distributed over several memory cards simultaneously. Or, you might consider *interleaving* your shots. Say you don't shoot weddings, but you do go on vacation from time to time. Take 50 or so pictures on one card, or whatever number of images might fill about 25 percent of its capacity. Then, replace it with a different card and shoot about 25 percent of that card's available space. Repeat these steps with diligence (you'd have to be determined to go through this inconvenience), and, if you use four or more memory cards, you'll find your pictures from each location scattered among the different memory cards. If you lose or damage one, you'll still have *some* pictures from all the various stops on your trip on the other cards. That's more work than I like to do (I usually tote around a netbook and portable hard disk and copy the files to the drive as I go), but it's an option. (See Figure 11.5.)

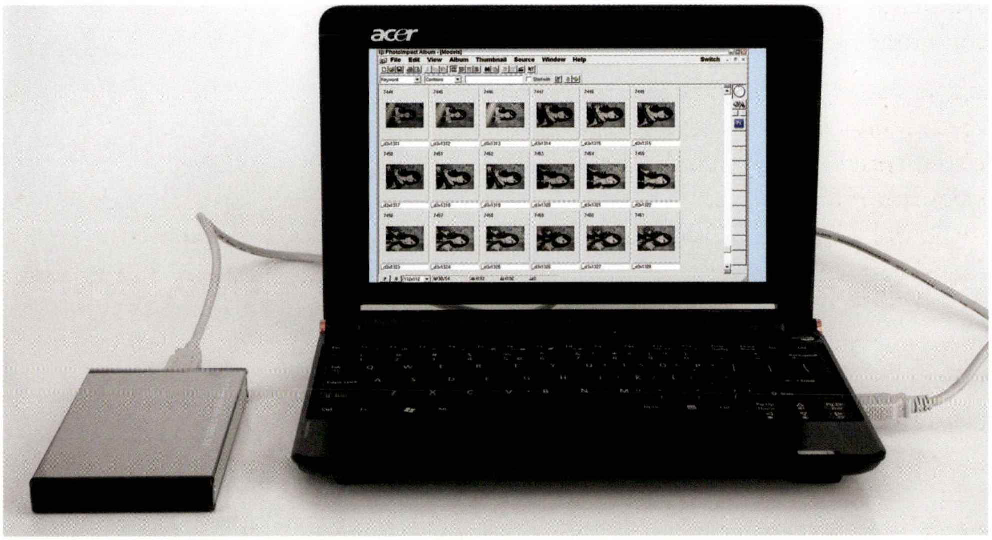

Figure 11.5
A netbook and a portable hard drive make a good backup option when you travel.

What Can Go Wrong?

There are lots of things that can go wrong with your memory card, but the ones that aren't caused by human stupidity are statistically very rare. Yes, a memory card's internal bit bin or controller can suddenly fail due to a manufacturing error or some inexplicable event caused by old age. However, if your memory card works for the first week or two that you own it, it should work forever. There's really not a lot that can wear out.

The typical memory card is rated for a Mean Time Between Failures of 1,000,000 hours of use. That's constant use 24/7 for more than 100 years! According to the manufacturers, they are good for 10,000 insertions in your camera, and should be able to retain their data (and that's without an external power source) for something on the order of 11 years. Of course, with the millions of memory cards in use, there are bound to be a few lemons here or there.

Given the reliability of solid-state memory, compared to magnetic memory, though, it's more likely that your memory card problems will stem from something that you do. Secure Digital or Memory Stick memory cards are small and easy to misplace if you're not careful. For that reason, it's a good idea to keep them in their original cases or a "card safe" offered by Gepe (www.gepecardsafe.com), Pelican (www.pelican.com), and others. Always placing your memory card in a case can provide protection from the second-most common mishap that befalls memory cards: the common household laundry. If you slip a memory card in a pocket rather than a case or your camera bag often enough, sooner or later it's going to end up in the washing machine and probably the clothes dryer, too. There are plenty of reports of relieved digital camera owners who've laundered their memory cards and found they still worked fine, but it's not uncommon for such mistreatment to do some damage.

Memory cards can also be stomped on, accidentally bent, dropped into the ocean, chewed by pets, and otherwise rendered unusable in myriad ways. It's also remotely possible to force a card into your Alpha's memory card slot incorrectly if you're diligent enough, doing little damage to the card itself, but possibly damaging the camera internally, eliminating its ability to read or write to any memory card. This almost never happens, but don't discount the ingenuity of a determined fumble-fingers.

Or, if the card is formatted in your computer with a memory card reader, your Alpha may fail to recognize it. Occasionally, I've found that a memory card used in one camera would fail if used in a different camera (until I reformatted it in Windows, and then again in the camera). Every once in awhile, a card goes completely bad and—seemingly—can't be salvaged.

Another way to lose images is to do commonplace things with your memory card at an inopportune time. If you remove the card from the Alpha while the camera is writing images to the card, you'll lose any photos in the buffer and may damage the file structure of the card, making it difficult or impossible to retrieve the other pictures you've taken. The same thing can happen if you remove the memory card from your computer's card reader while the computer is writing to the card (say, to erase files you've already moved to your computer). You can avoid this by *not* using your computer to erase files on a memory card but, instead, always reformatting the card in your Alpha before you use it again.

What Can You Do?

Pay attention: If you're having problems, the *first* thing you should do is *stop* using that memory card. Don't take any more pictures. Don't do anything with the card until you've figured out what's wrong. Your second line of defense (your first line is to be sufficiently careful with your cards that you avoid problems in the first place) is to *do no harm* that hasn't already been done. Read the rest of this section and then, if necessary, decide on a course of action (such as using a data recovery service or software described later) before you risk damaging the data on your card further.

Now that you've calmed down, the first thing to check is whether you've actually inserted a card in the camera. The Alpha cameras will actually "take" pictures with no memory card inserted, although a warning is displayed on the LCD (as a flashing NO CARD message). In Live View mode, the LCD shows a helpful No Card warning. It's hard to take photos without a memory card installed, but it is possible.

Things get more exciting when the card itself is put in jeopardy. If you lose a card, there's not a lot you can do other than take a picture of a similar card and print up some "Have You Seen This Lost Flash Memory?" flyers to post on utility poles all around town.

If all you care about is reusing the card, and have resigned yourself to losing the pictures, try reformatting the card in your camera. You may find that reformatting removes the corrupted data and restores your card to health. Sometimes I've had success reformatting a card in my computer using a memory card reader (this is normally a no-no because your operating system doesn't understand the needs of your Alpha), and *then* reformatting again in the camera.

If your memory card is not behaving properly, and you *do* want to recover your images, things get a little more complicated. If your pictures are very valuable, either to you or to others (for example, a wedding), you can always turn to professional data recovery firms. Be prepared to pay hundreds of dollars to get your pictures back, but these pros often do an amazing job. You wouldn't want them working on your memory card on behalf of the police if you'd tried to erase some incriminating pictures. There are many firms of this type, and I've never used them myself, so I can't offer a recommendation. Use a Google search to turn up a ton of them.

THE ULTIMATE IRONY

I recently purchased an 8GB Kingston memory card that was furnished with some nifty OnTrack data recovery software. The first thing I did was format the card to make sure it was okay. Then I hunted around for the free software, only to discover it was preloaded onto the memory card. I was supposed to copy the software to my computer before using the memory card for the first time.

Fortunately, I had the OnTrack software that would reverse my dumb move, so I could retrieve the software. No, wait. I *didn't* have the software I needed to recover the software I erased. I'd reformatted it to oblivion. Chalk this one up as either the ultimate irony or Stupid Author Trick #523.

A more reasonable approach is to try special data recovery software you can install on your computer and use to attempt to resurrect your "lost" images yourself. They may not actually be gone completely. Perhaps your memory card's "table of contents" is jumbled, or only a few pictures are damaged in such a way that your camera and computer can't read some or any of the pictures on the card. Some of the available software was written specifically to reconstruct lost pictures, while other utilities are more general-purpose applications that can be used with any media, including floppy disks and hard disk drives. They have names like OnTrack, Photo Rescue 2, Digital Image Recovery, MediaRecover, Image Recall, and the aptly named Recover My Photos. You'll find a comprehensive list and links, as well as some picture-recovery tips at www.ultimateslr.com/memory-card-recovery.php. I like RescuePRO (Figure 11.6), which came free with one of my SanDisk cards.

DIMINISHING RETURNS

Usually, once you've recovered any images on a memory card, reformatted it, and returned it to service, it will function reliably for the rest of its useful life. However, if you find a particular card going bad more than once, you'll almost certainly want to stop using it forever. See if you can get it replaced by the manufacturer, if you can, but, in the case of memory card failures, the third time is never the charm.

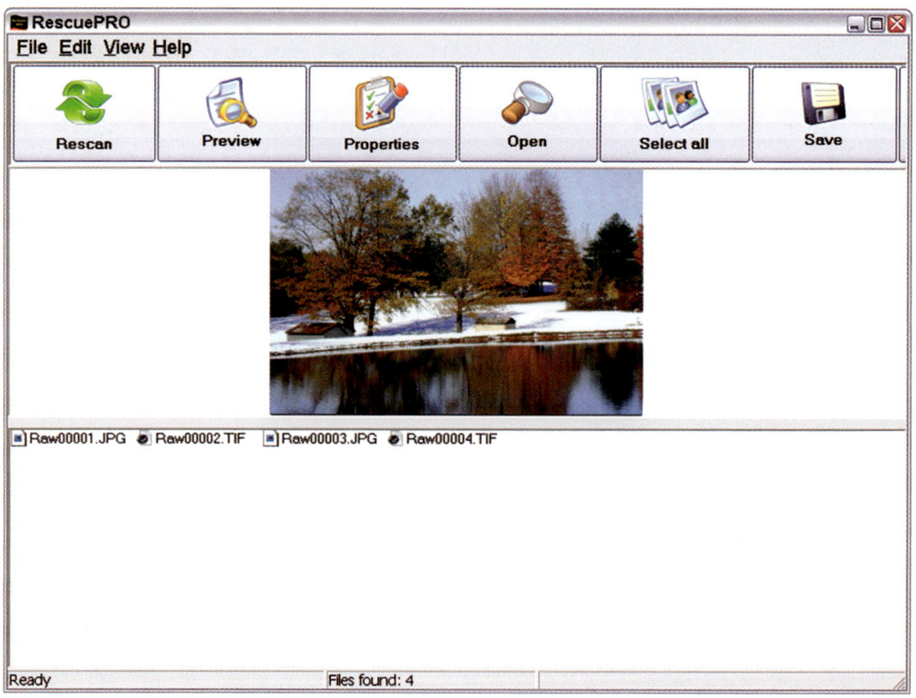

Figure 11.6
RescuePRO is an image recovery utility offered by SanDisk.

Cleaning Your Sensor

Yes, your Alpha A57 does have an anti-static coating on the front of the sensor. And it does have an automatic sensor dust removal system that activates every time you turn on the camera. And that transparent mirror doesn't flip up and down with each shot, which theoretically should reduce the amount of dust sneaking past the mirror and shutter and onto the sensor itself.

But, even with those high-tech aids, you'll still get some stubborn dust on your sensor. There's no avoiding it. No matter how careful you are, some dust is going to settle on your camera and on the mounts of your lenses, eventually making its way inside your camera to settle in the mirror chamber. As you take photos, dust manages to become airborne and eventually makes its way past the mirror and shutter curtain to come to rest on the anti-aliasing filter atop your sensor. There, dust and particles can show up in every single picture you take at a small enough aperture to bring the foreign matter into sharp focus. No matter how careful you are and how cleanly you work, eventually you will get some of this dust on your camera's sensor. But even the cleanest-working photographers using Sony cameras are far from immune.

Dust the FAQs, Ma'am.

Here are some of the most frequently asked questions about sensor dust issues.

Q. I can see dust on my mirror. How can I remove it?

A. Any artifacts that have settled on your mirror won't affect your photos. You can often remove dust on the mirror or focus screen with a bulb air blower, which will loosen it and whisk it away. Stubborn dust on the focus screen can sometimes be gently flicked away with a soft brush designed for cleaning lenses. I don't recommend brushing the mirror or touching it in any way. The mirror can be easily scratched. If you can't blow mirror dust off, it's best to just forget about it. You can't see it in the viewfinder, anyway.

Q. I see a bright spot in the same place in all of my photos. Is that sensor dust?

A. You've probably got either a "hot" pixel or one that is permanently "stuck" due to a defect in the sensor. A hot pixel is one that shows up as a bright spot only during long exposures as the sensor warms. A pixel stuck in the "on" position always appears in the image. Both show up as bright red, green, or blue pixels, usually surrounded by a small cluster of other improperly illuminated pixels, caused by the camera's interpolating the hot or stuck pixel into its surroundings, as shown in Figure 11.7. A stuck pixel can also be permanently dark. Either kind is likely to show up when they contrast with plain, evenly colored areas of your image.

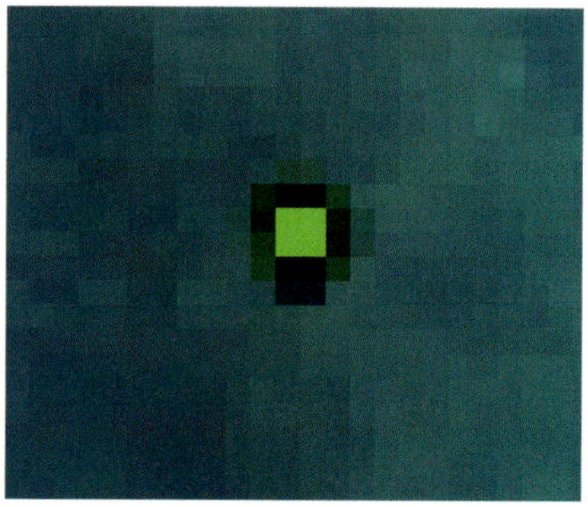

Figure 11.7
A stuck pixel is surrounded by improperly interpolated pixels created by the Alpha's demosaicing algorithm.

Finding one or two hot or stuck pixels in your sensor is unfortunately fairly common. Bad pixels can also show up on your camera's color LCD panel, too, but, unless they are abundant, the wisest course is to just ignore them.

Q. I see an irregular out-of-focus blob in the same place in my photos. Is that sensor dust?

A. Yes. Sensor contaminants can take the form of tiny spots, larger blobs, or even curvy lines if they are caused by minuscule fibers that have settled on the sensor. They'll appear out of focus because they aren't actually on the sensor surface but, rather, a fraction of a millimeter above it on the filter that covers the sensor. The smaller the f/stop used, the more in-focus the dust becomes. At large apertures, it may not be visible at all.

Q. I never see any dust on my sensor. What's all the fuss about?

A. Those who never have dust problems with their Sony Alpha fall into one of four categories: those for whom the camera's automatic dust removal features are working well; those who seldom change their lenses and have clean working habits that minimize the amount of dust that invades their cameras in the first place; those who simply don't notice the dust (often because they don't shoot many macro photos or other pictures using the small f/stops that make dust evident in their images); and those who are very, very lucky.

Identifying and Dealing with Stubborn Dust

Sensor dust that isn't automatically removed by the Alpha's anti-dust features is less of a problem than it might be because it shows up only under certain circumstances. Indeed, you might have dust on your sensor right now and not be aware of it. The dust doesn't actually settle on the sensor itself, but, rather, on a protective filter a very tiny distance above the sensor, subjecting it to the phenomenon of *depth-of-focus.* Depth-of-focus is the distance the focal plane can be moved and still render an object in sharp focus. At f/2.8 to f/5.6 or even smaller, sensor dust, particularly if small, is likely to be outside the range of depth-of-focus and blur into an unnoticeable dot.

However, if you're shooting at f/16 to f/22 or smaller, those dust motes suddenly pop into focus. Forget about trying to spot them by peering directly at your sensor with the shutter open and the lens removed. The period at the end of this sentence, about .33mm in diameter, could block a group of pixels measuring 40 × 40 pixels (160 pixels in all!). Dust spots that are even smaller than that can easily show up in your images if you're shooting large, empty areas that are light colored. Dust motes are most likely to show up in the sky, as in Figure 11.8, or in white backgrounds of your seamless product shots and are less likely to be a problem in images that contain lots of dark areas and detail.

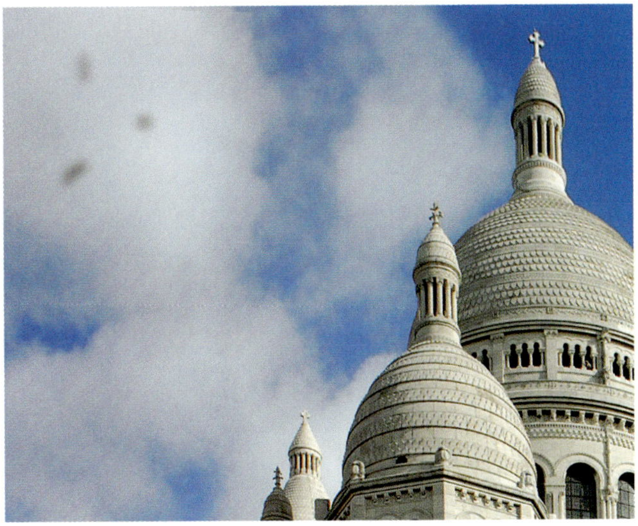

Figure 11.8
Only the dust spots in the sky are apparent in this shot.

To see if you have dust on your sensor, take a few test shots of a plain, blank surface (such as a piece of paper or a cloudless sky) at small f/stops, such as f/22, and a few wide open. Open Photoshop, copy several shots into a single document in separate layers, then flip back and forth between layers to see if any spots you see are present in all layers. You may have to boost contrast and sharpness to make the dust easier to spot.

Avoiding Dust

Of course, the easiest way to protect your sensor from dust is to prevent it from settling on the sensor in the first place. Here are my stock tips for eliminating the problem before it begins.

- **Clean environment.** Avoid working in dusty areas if you can do so. Hah! Serious photographers will take this one with a grain of salt, because it usually makes sense to go where the pictures are. Only a few of us are so paranoid about sensor dust (considering that it is so easily removed) that we'll avoid moderately grimy locations just to protect something that is, when you get down to it, just a tool. If you find a great picture opportunity at a raging fire, during a sandstorm, or while surrounded by dust clouds, you might hesitate to take the picture, but, with a little caution (don't remove your lens in these situations, and clean the camera afterwards!) you can still shoot. However, it still makes sense to store your camera in a clean environment. One place cameras and lenses pick up a lot of dust is inside a camera bag. Clean your bag from time to time, and you can avoid problems.

- **Clean lenses.** There are a few paranoid types that avoid swapping lenses in order to minimize the chance of dust getting inside their cameras. It makes more sense just to use a blower or brush to dust off the rear lens mount of the replacement lens first, so you won't be introducing dust into your camera simply by attaching a new, dusty lens. Do this before you remove the lens from your camera, and then avoid stirring up dust before making the exchange.
- **Work fast.** Minimize the time your camera is lens-less and exposed to dust. That means having your replacement lens ready and dusted off, and a place to set down the old lens as soon as it is removed, so you can quickly attach the new lens.
- **Let gravity help you.** Face the camera downward when the lens is detached so any dust in the mirror box will tend to fall away from the sensor. Turn your back to any breezes, indoor forced air vents, fans, or other sources of dust to minimize infiltration.
- **Protect the lens you just removed.** Once you've attached the new lens, quickly put the end cap on the one you just removed to reduce the dust that might fall on it.
- **Clean out the vestibule.** From time to time, remove the lens while in a relatively dust-free environment and use a blower bulb like the one shown in Figure 11.9 (*not* compressed air or a vacuum hose) to clean out the mirror box area. A blower bulb is generally safer than a can of compressed air, or a strong positive/negative airflow, which can tend to drive dust further into nooks and crannies.
- **Be prepared.** If you're embarking on an important shooting session, it's a good idea to clean your sensor *now*, rather than come home with hundreds or thousands of images with dust spots caused by flecks that were sitting on your sensor before you even started. Before I left on my recent trip to Spain, I put both cameras I was taking through a rigid cleaning regimen, figuring they could remain dust-free for a measly 10 days. I even left my bulky blower bulb at home. It was a big mistake, but my intentions were good. I now have a smaller version of the Giottos Rocket Blower, and *that* goes with me everywhere.
- **Clone out existing spots in your image editor.** Photoshop and other editors have a clone tool or healing brush you can use to copy pixels from surrounding areas over the dust spot or dead pixel. This process can be tedious, especially if you have lots of dust spots and/or lots of images to be corrected. The advantage is that this sort of manual fix-it probably will do the least damage to the rest of your photo. Only the cloned pixels will be affected.

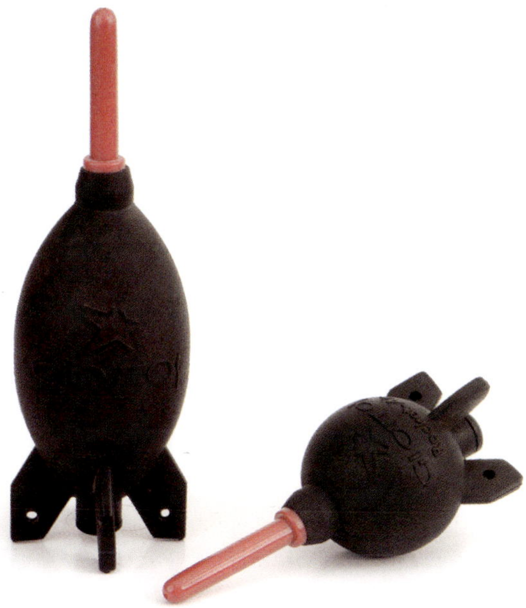

Figure 11.9
Use a robust air bulb like one of these Giottos Rockets for cleaning your sensor.

- **Use filtration in your image editor.** A semi-smart filter like Photoshop's Dust & Scratches filter can remove dust and other artifacts by selectively blurring areas that the plug-in decides represent dust spots. This method can work well if you have many dust spots, because you won't need to patch them manually. However, any automated method like this has the possibility of blurring areas of your image that you didn't intend to soften.

Sensor Cleaning

Those new to the concept of sensor dust actually hesitate before deciding to clean their camera themselves. Isn't it a better idea to pack up your Alpha and send it to a Sony service center so their crack technical staff can do the job for you? Or, at the very least, shouldn't you let the friendly folks at your local camera store do it?

However, if you choose to let someone else clean your sensor, they will be using methods that are more or less identical to the techniques you would use yourself. None of these techniques are difficult, and the only difference between their cleaning and your cleaning is that they might have done it dozens or hundreds of times. If you're careful, you can do just as good a job.

Of course, vendors like Sony won't tell you this, but it's not because they don't trust you. It's not that difficult for a real goofball to mess up his camera by hurrying or taking a shortcut. Perhaps the person uses the "Bulb" method of holding the shutter open and a finger slips, allowing the shutter curtain to close on top of a sensor cleaning brush. Or, someone tries to clean the sensor using masking tape, and ends up with goo all over its surface. If Sony recommended *any* method that's mildly risky, someone would do it wrong, and then the company would face lawsuits from those who'd contend they did it exactly in the way the vendor suggested, so the ruined camera is not their fault.

You can see that vendors like Sony tend to be conservative in their recommendations, and, in doing so, make it seem as if sensor cleaning is more daunting and dangerous than it really is. Some vendors recommend only dust-off cleaning, through the use of reasonably gentle blasts of air, while condemning more serious scrubbing with swabs and cleaning fluids. However, these cleaning kits for the exact types of cleaning they recommended against are for sale in Japan only, where, apparently, your average photographer is more dexterous than those of us in the rest of the world. These kits are similar to those used by official repair staff to clean your sensor if you decide to send your camera in for a dust-up.

As I noted, sensors can be affected by dust particles that are much smaller than you might be able to spot visually on the surface of your lens. The filters that cover sensors tend to be fairly hard compared to optical glass. Cleaning the sensor in your Sony Alpha within the tight confines of the mirror box can call for a steady hand and careful touch. If your sensor's filter becomes scratched through inept cleaning, you can't simply remove it yourself and replace it with a new one.

There are four basic kinds of cleaning processes that can be used to remove dusty and sticky stuff that settles on your camera's sensor. All of these must be performed with the shutter locked open. I'll describe these methods and provide instructions for locking the shutter later in this section.

- **Air cleaning.** This process involves squirting blasts of air inside your camera with the shutter locked open. This works well for dust that's not clinging stubbornly to your sensor.
- **Brushing.** A soft, very fine brush is passed across the surface of the sensor's filter, dislodging mildly persistent dust particles and sweeping them off the imager.
- **Liquid cleaning.** A soft swab dipped in a cleaning solution such as ethanol is used to wipe the sensor filter, removing more obstinate particles.
- **Tape cleaning.** There are some who get good results by applying a special form of tape to the surface of their sensor. When the tape is peeled off, all the dust goes with it. Supposedly. I'd be remiss if I didn't point out right now that this form of cleaning is somewhat controversial; the other three methods are much more widely accepted. Now that Sony has equipped the front-sensor filter with a special anti-dust coating, I wouldn't chance damaging that coating by using any kind of adhesive tape.

Placing the Mirror in the Locked and Fully Upright Position for Landing

Make sure you're using a fully charged battery.

1. Turn the camera on.
2. Remove the lens.
3. Push down the tab on the mirror lock lever with the tip of your finger (see Figure 11.10), being careful not to touch the mirror itself.
4. Lift up the mirror.
5. Use your cleaning method of choice to remove the dust from the sensor.
6. Clean the rear surface of the mirror gently with a puff of air, while it is flipped up.
7. Press the mirror tab downwards to lower the mirror until it clicks back into place. Note that if you don't fully lower the mirror, autofocus won't function properly.
8. Replace the lens and turn the camera off.

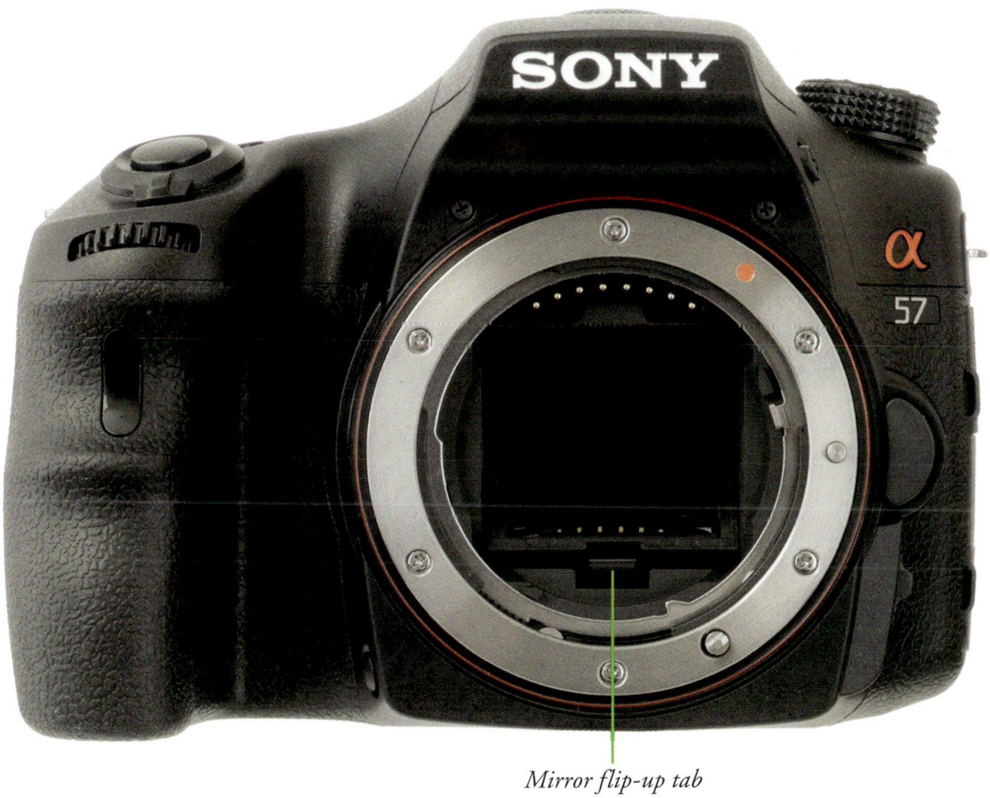

Figure 11.10
With the mirror flipped up by lifting the tab on the front, the sensor will be exposed and available for manual cleaning.

Air Cleaning

Your first attempts at cleaning your sensor should always involve gentle blasts of air. Many times, you'll be able to dislodge dust spots, which will fall off the sensor and, with luck, out of the mirror box. Attempt one of the other methods only when you've already tried air cleaning and it didn't remove all the dust.

Here are some tips for air cleaning:

- **Use a clean, powerful air bulb.** Your best bet is bulb cleaners designed for the job, like the Giottos Rockets shown earlier in Figure 11.9. Smaller bulbs, like those air bulbs with a brush attached sometimes sold for lens cleaning or weak nasal aspirators may not provide sufficient air or a strong enough blast to do much good.
- **Hold the Sony Alpha upside down.** Then look up into the mirror box as you squirt your air blasts, increasing the odds that gravity will help pull the expelled dust downward, away from the sensor. You may have to use some imagination in positioning yourself. (And don't let dust fall into your eye!) (See Figure 11.11.)
- **Never use air canisters.** The propellant inside these cans can permanently coat your sensor if you tilt the can while spraying. It's not worth taking a chance.
- **Avoid air compressors.** Super-strong blasts of air are likely to force dust under the sensor filter.

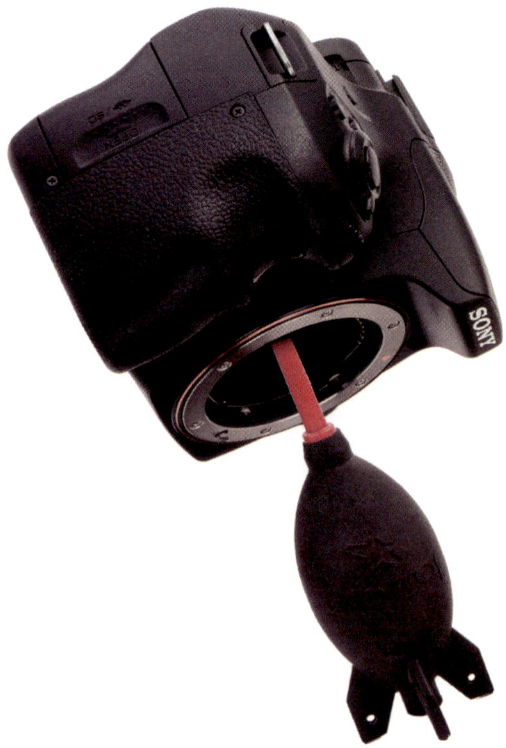

Figure 11.11
Hold the camera facing lens mount downward to allow dust to fall out.

Brush Cleaning

If your dust is a little more stubborn and can't be dislodged by air alone, you may want to try a brush, charged with static electricity, which can pick off dust spots by electrical attraction. One good, but expensive, option is the Sensor Brush sold at www.visible-dust.com. A cheaper version can be purchased at www.copperhillimages.com. You need a 16mm version, like the one shown in Figure 11.12, which can be stroked across the long dimension of your Alpha's sensor.

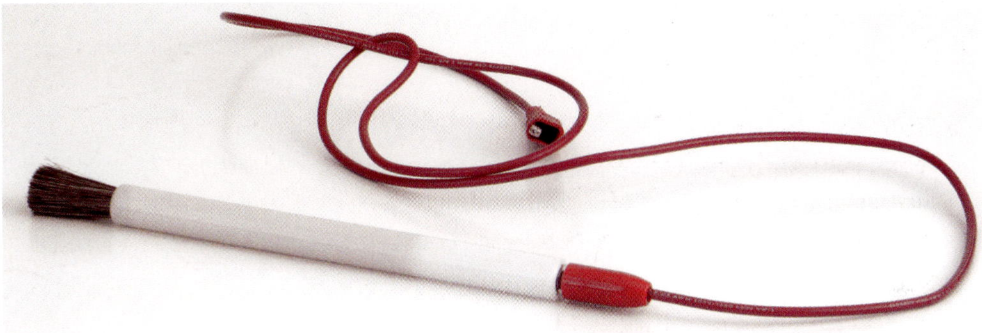

Figure 11.12
A proper brush is required for dusting off your sensor. The long cord shown is attached to a grounded object to reduce static electricity.

Ordinary artist's brushes are much too coarse and stiff and have fibers that are tangled or can come loose and settle on your sensor. A good sensor brush's fibers are resilient and described as "thinner than a human hair." Moreover, the brush has a wooden handle that reduces the risk of static sparks. Check out my *Digital SLR Pro Secrets* book if you want to make a sensor brush (or sensor swabs) yourself.

Brush cleaning is done with a dry brush by gently swiping the surface of the sensor filter with the tip. The dust particles are attracted to the brush particles and cling to them. You should clean the brush with compressed air before and after each use, and store it in an appropriate air-tight container between applications to keep it clean and dust-free. Although these special brushes are expensive, one should last you a long time.

Liquid Cleaning

Unfortunately, you'll often encounter really stubborn dust spots that can't be removed with a blast of air or flick of a brush. These spots may be combined with some grease or a liquid that causes them to stick to the sensor filter's surface. In such cases, liquid cleaning with a swab may be necessary. During my first clumsy attempts to clean my own sensor, I accidentally got my blower bulb tip too close to the sensor, and some sort of deposit from the tip of the bulb ended up on the sensor. I panicked until I discovered that liquid cleaning did a good job of removing whatever it was that took up residence on my sensor.

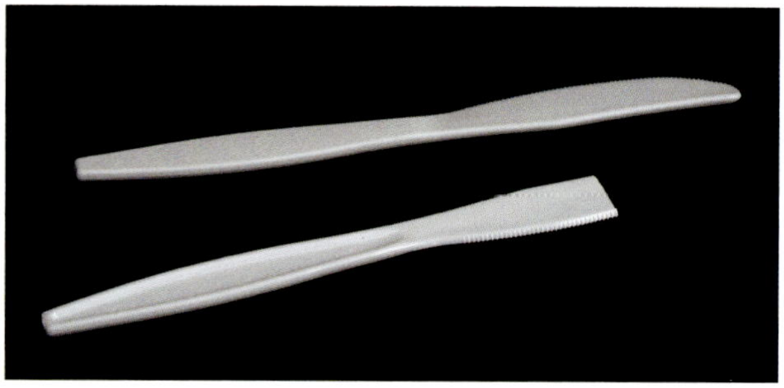

Figure 11.13 You can make your own sensor swab from a plastic knife that's been truncated.

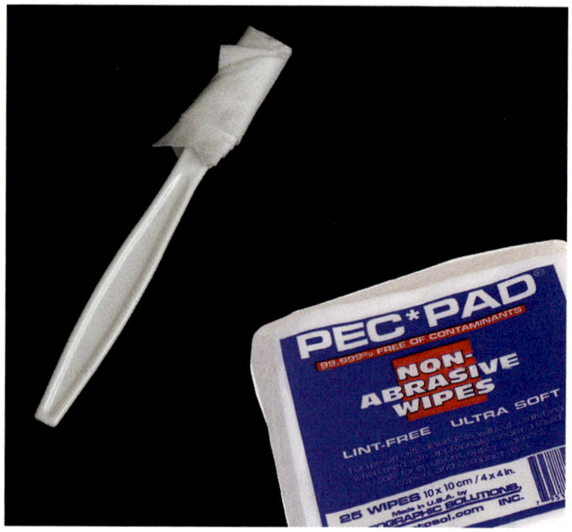

Figure 11.14 Carefully wrap a Pec-Pad around the swab.

You can make your own swabs out of pieces of plastic (some use fast food restaurant knives, with the tip cut at an angle to the proper size) covered with a soft cloth or Pec-Pad, as shown in Figures 11.13 and 11.14. However, if you've got the bucks to spend, you can't go wrong with good-quality commercial sensor cleaning swabs, such as those sold by Photographic Solutions, Inc. (www.photosol.com/swabproduct.htm).

You want a sturdy swab that won't bend or break so you can apply gentle pressure to the swab as you wipe the sensor surface. Use the swab with methanol (as pure as you can get it, particularly medical grade; other ingredients can leave a residue), or the Eclipse solution also sold by Photographic Solutions. Eclipse is actually quite a bit purer than even medical-grade methanol. A couple drops of solution should be enough, unless you have a spot that's extremely difficult to remove. In that case, you may need to use extra solution on the swab to help "soak" the dirt off.

Once you overcome your nervousness at touching your Alpha's sensor, the process is easy. You'll wipe continuously with the swab in one direction, then flip it over and wipe in the other direction. You need to completely wipe the entire surface; otherwise, you may end up depositing the dust you collect at the far end of your stroke. Wipe; don't rub.

If you want a close-up look at your sensor to make sure the dust has been removed, you can pay $50-$100 for a special sensor "microscope" with an illuminator. Or, you can do like I do and work with a plain old Carson MiniBrite PO-55 illuminated 5X magnifier, as seen in Figure 11.15. (The company also still markets the PO-25 model with a

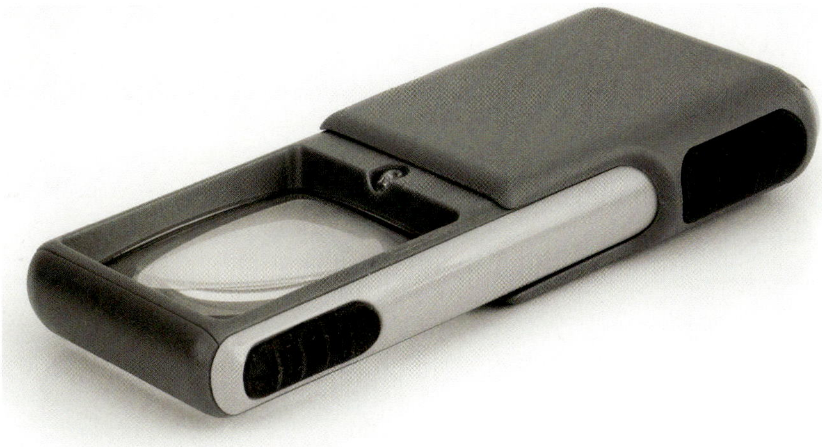

Figure 11.15
The Carson Mini-Brite is an inexpensive illuminated magnifier you can use to examine your sensor.

3X magnifier.) It has a built-in LED and, held a few inches from the lens mount with the lens removed from your Alpha, provides a sharp, close-up view of the sensor, with enough contrast to reveal any dust that remains. If you want to buy one, you'll find a link at www.dslrguides.com/carson. You can also use the SensorKlear loupe (www.lenspen.com), shown in Figure 11.16.

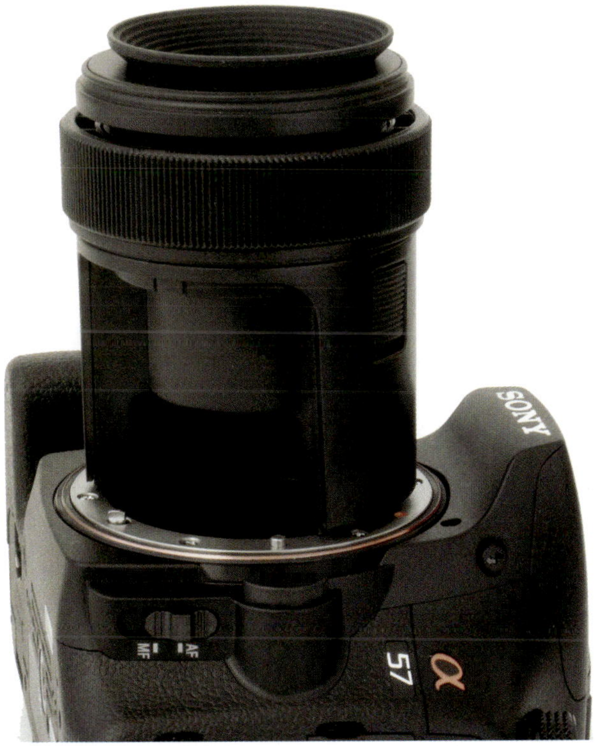

Figure 11.16
The SensorKlear loupe is another illuminated sensor viewing device.

Tape Cleaning

There are people who absolutely swear by the tape method of sensor cleaning. The concept seems totally wacky, and I have never tried it personally, so I can't say with certainty that it either does or does not work. In the interest of completeness, I'm including it here. I can't give you a recommendation, so if you have problems, please don't blame me. The Sony Alpha is still too new to have generated any reports of users accidentally damaging the anti-dust coating on the sensor filter using this method.

Tape cleaning works by applying a layer of Scotch Brand Magic Tape to the sensor. This is a minimally sticky tape that some of the tape cleaning proponents claim contains no adhesive. I did check this out with 3M, and can say that Magic Tape certainly *does* contain an adhesive. The question is whether the adhesive comes off when you peel back the tape, taking any dust spots on your sensor with it. The folks who love this method claim there is no residue. There have been reports from those who don't like the method that residue is left behind. This is all anecdotal evidence, so you're pretty much on your own in making the decision whether to try out the tape cleaning method.

Glossary

Here are some terms you might encounter while reading this book or working with your Sony Alpha.

additive primary colors The red, green, and blue hues that are used alone or in combinations to create all other colors that you capture with a digital camera, view on a computer monitor, or work with in an image-editing program, such as Photoshop. *See also* CMYK color model.

Adobe RGB One of two color space choices offered by the Sony Alpha. Adobe RGB is an expanded color space useful for commercial and professional printing, and it can reproduce a larger number of colors. Sony recommends against using this color space if your images will be displayed primarily on your computer screen or output by your personal printer. *See also* sRGB.

ambient lighting Diffuse, non-directional lighting that doesn't appear to come from a specific source but, rather, bounces off walls, ceilings, and other objects in the scene when a picture is taken.

analog/digital converter The electronics built into a camera, such as Sony's BIONZ image processing engine, that convert the analog information captured by the Alpha's sensor into digital bits that can be stored as an image bitmap.

angle of view The area of a scene that a lens can capture, determined by the focal length of the lens. Lenses with a shorter focal length have a wider angle of view than lenses with a longer focal length.

anti-alias A process that smoothes the look of rough edges in images (called *jaggies* or *staircasing*) by adding partially transparent pixels along the boundaries of diagonal lines that are merged into a smoother line by our eyes. *See also* jaggies.

Aperture priority A camera setting that allows you to specify the lens opening or f/stop that you want to use, with the camera selecting the required shutter speed automatically based on its light-meter reading. This setting is represented by the abbreviation A on the Alpha's mode dial. *See also* Shutter priority.

artifact A type of noise in an image, or an unintentional image component produced in error by a digital camera during processing, usually caused by the JPEG compression process in digital cameras.

aspect ratio The proportions of an image as printed, displayed on a monitor, or captured by a digital camera. The Sony Alpha cameras offer both the traditional 3:2 aspect ratio used by most digital SLRs, and also the 16:9 ("HDTV") aspect ratio.

autofocus A camera setting that allows the Sony Alpha to choose the correct focus distance for you, based on the contrast of an image (the image will be at maximum contrast when in sharp focus). The camera can be set for *Single-shot AF*, in which the lens is not focused until the shutter release is partially depressed; *Continuous AF*, in which the lens refocuses constantly as you frame and reframe the image; or *Automatic AF*, which allows the camera to switch back and forth between Single-shot AF and Continuous AF, based on subject movement.

backlighting A lighting effect produced when the main light source is located behind the subject. Backlighting can be used to create a silhouette effect, or to illuminate translucent objects. *See also* front lighting and side lighting.

barrel distortion A lens defect that causes straight lines at the top or side edges of an image to bow outward into a barrel shape. *See also* pincushion distortion.

blooming An image distortion caused when a photosite in an image sensor has absorbed all the photons it can handle so that additional photons reaching that pixel overflow to affect surrounding pixels, producing unwanted brightness and overexposure around the edges of objects.

blur To soften an image or part of an image by throwing it out of focus, or by allowing it to become soft due to subject or camera motion. Blur can also be applied in an image-editing program.

bokeh A term derived from the Japanese word for blur, which describes the aesthetic qualities of the out-of-focus parts of an image. Some lenses produce "good" bokeh and others offer "bad" bokeh. Some lenses produce uniformly illuminated out-of-focus discs. Others produce a disc that has a bright edge and a dark center, creating a "doughnut" effect, which is the worst from a bokeh standpoint. Lenses that generate a bright center that fades to a darker edge are favored, because their bokeh allows the circle of confusion to blend more smoothly with the surroundings. The bokeh characteristics of a lens are most important when you're using selective focus (say, when shooting a portrait) to deemphasize the background, or when shallow depth-of-field is a given because you're working with a macro lens, with a long telephoto, or with a wide-open aperture. *See also* circle of confusion.

bounce lighting Light bounced off a reflector, including ceiling and walls, to provide a soft, natural-looking light.

bracketing Taking a series of photographs of the same subject at different settings, including exposure and white balance, to help ensure that one setting will be the correct one.

buffer The digital camera's internal memory where an image is stored immediately after it is taken until it can be written to the camera's non-volatile (semi-permanent) memory or a memory card.

bulb The shutter remains open while the shutter release button is held down. This setting is available when the camera is set to Manual mode. Refers to the way an early camera was operated using a long tube and a rubber bulb to activate the shutter.

burst mode The digital camera's equivalent of the film camera's motor drive, used to take multiple shots within a short period of time, at a rate of up to 8 frames per second (with the A57), each stored in a memory buffer temporarily before writing them to the media.

calibration A process used to correct for the differences in the output of a printer or monitor when compared to the original image. Once you've calibrated your scanner, monitor, and/or your image editor, the images you see on the screen more closely represent what you'll get from your printer, even though calibration is never perfect.

Camera Raw A plug-in included with Photoshop and Photoshop Elements that can manipulate the unprocessed images captured by digital cameras, such as the Sony Alpha's ARW files. The latest versions of this module can also work with JPEG and TIFF images.

camera shake Movement of the camera, aggravated by slower shutter speeds, which produces a blurred image, unless countered by the Alpha's SteadyShot feature.

Center weighted metering A light-measuring setting that emphasizes the area in the middle of the frame when calculating the correct exposure for an image. *See also* Multi segment metering and Spot metering.

chromatic aberration An image defect, often seen as green or purple fringing around the edges of an object, caused by a lens failing to focus all colors of a light source at the same point. *See also* fringing.

circle of confusion A term applied to the fuzzy discs produced when a point of light is out of focus. The circle of confusion is not a fixed size. The viewing distance and amount of enlargement of the image determine whether we see a particular spot on the image as a point or as a disc. *See also* bokeh.

close-up lens A lens add-on that allows you to take pictures at a distance that is less than the closest-focusing distance of the lens alone.

CMYK color model A way of defining all possible colors in percentages of cyan, magenta, yellow, and frequently, black. (K represents black, to differentiate it from blue in the RGB color model.) Black is added to improve rendition of shadow detail. CMYK is commonly used for printing (both on press and with your inkjet or laser color printer).

color correction Changing the relative amounts of color in an image to produce a desired effect, typically a more accurate representation of those colors. Color correction can fix faulty color balance in the original image, or compensate for the deficiencies of the inks used to reproduce the image.

compression Reducing the size of a file by encoding using fewer bits of information to represent the original. Some compression schemes, such as JPEG, operate by discarding some image information, while others, such as RAW, preserve all the detail in the original, discarding only redundant numeric data.

contrast The range between the lightest and darkest tones in an image. A high-contrast image is one in which the shades fall at the extremes of the range between white and black. In a low-contrast image, the tones are closer together.

dedicated flash An electronic flash unit designed to work with the automatic exposure features of a specific camera.

depth-of-field A distance range in a photograph in which all included portions of an image are at least acceptably sharp.

diaphragm An adjustable component, similar to the iris in the human eye, that can open and close to provide specific-sized lens openings, or f/stops, and thus control the amount of light reaching the sensor or film.

diffuse lighting Soft, low-contrast lighting.

digital processing chip A solid-state device found in digital cameras (such as the Sony Alpha's BIONZ module) that's in charge of applying the image algorithms to the raw picture data prior to storage on the memory card.

diopter A value used to represent the magnification power of a lens, calculated as the reciprocal of a lens's focal length (in meters). Diopters are most often used to represent the optical correction used in a viewfinder to adjust for limitations of the photographer's eyesight, and to describe the magnification of a close-up lens attachment.

equivalent focal length A digital camera's focal length translated into the corresponding values for a 35mm film camera. This value can be calculated for lenses used with the Sony Alpha by multiplying by 1.5.

Evaluative metering A system of exposure calculation that looks at many different segments of an image to determine the brightest and darkest portions. The Sony Alpha uses this system when you select the Multi segment metering mode.

exchangeable image file format (Exif) Developed to standardize the exchange of image data between hardware devices and software. A variation on JPEG, Exif is used by most digital cameras, and includes information such as the date and time a photo was taken, the camera settings, resolution, amount of compression, and other data.

Exif *See* exchangeable image file format (Exif).

exposure The amount of light allowed to reach the film or sensor, determined by the intensity of the light, the amount admitted by the iris of the lens, the length of time determined by the shutter speed, and the ISO sensitivity setting.

exposure values (EV) EV settings are a way of adding or decreasing exposure without the need to reference f/stops or shutter speeds. For example, if you tell your camera to add +1EV, it will provide twice as much exposure, by using a larger f/stop, slower shutter speed, or both.

fill lighting In photography, lighting used to illuminate shadows. Reflectors or additional incandescent lighting or electronic flash can be used to brighten shadows. One common technique outdoors is to use the camera's flash as a fill.

filter In photography, a device that fits over the lens, changing the light in some way. In image editing, a feature that changes the pixels in an image to produce blurring, sharpening, and other special effects. Photoshop includes several interesting filter effects, including Lens Blur and Photo Filters.

flash sync The timing mechanism that ensures that an internal or external electronic flash fires at the correct time during the exposure cycle. A digital camera's flash sync speed is the highest shutter speed that can be used with flash, ordinarily 1/160th of a second with the Sony Alpha. *See also* front-curtain sync (first-curtain sync) and rear-curtain sync (second-curtain sync).

focal length The distance between the film and the optical center of the lens when the lens is focused on infinity, usually measured in millimeters.

focal plane A line, perpendicular to the optical access, that passes through the focal point forming a plane of sharp focus when the lens is set at infinity. A focal plane indicator (a line drawn through a circle) is etched on the top surface of the Sony Alpha to the right of the LCD button.

focus tracking The ability of the automatic focus feature of a camera to change focus as the distance between the subject and the camera changes. One type of focus tracking is *predictive,* in which the mechanism anticipates the motion of the object being focused on, and adjusts the focus to suit.

format To erase a memory card and prepare it to accept files.

fringing A chromatic aberration that produces fringes of color around the edges of subjects, caused by a lens's inability to focus the various wavelengths of light onto the same spot. Purple fringing is especially troublesome with backlit images.

front-curtain sync (first-curtain sync) The default kind of electronic flash synchronization technique, originally associated with focal plane shutters, which consists of a traveling set of curtains, including a *front curtain*, which opens to reveal the film or sensor, and a *rear curtain*, which follows at a distance determined by shutter speed to conceal the film or sensor at the conclusion of the exposure. For a flash picture to be taken, the entire sensor must be exposed at one time to the brief flash exposure, so the image is exposed after the front curtain has reached the other side of the focal plane, but before the rear curtain begins to move. Front-curtain sync causes the flash to fire at the beginning of this period when the shutter is completely open, in the instant that the first curtain of the focal plane shutter finishes its movement across the film or sensor plane. With slow shutter speeds, this feature can create a blur effect from the ambient light, showing as patterns that follow a moving subject with the subject shown sharply frozen at the beginning of the blur trail. *See also* rear-curtain sync (second-curtain sync).

front lighting Illumination that comes from the direction of the camera. *See also* backlighting and side lighting.

f/stop The relative size of the lens aperture, which helps determine both exposure and depth-of-field. The larger the f/stop number, the smaller the f/stop itself.

graduated filter A lens attachment with variable density or color from one edge to another. A graduated neutral-density filter, for example, can be oriented so the neutral-density portion is concentrated at the top of the lens's view with the less dense or clear portion at the bottom, thus reducing the amount of light from a very bright sky while not interfering with the exposure of the landscape in the foreground. Graduated filters can also be split into several color sections to provide a color gradient between portions of the image.

gray card A piece of cardboard or other material with a standardized 18-percent reflectance. Gray cards can be used as a reference for determining correct exposure or for setting white balance.

HDMI (High Definition Multimedia Interface) An interface for transmitting audio and video information between a source, such as a digital camera or television tuner, to an output device, such as a high-definition television (HDTV) monitor.

high contrast A wide range of density in a print, negative, or other image.

highlights The brightest parts of an image containing detail.

histogram A kind of chart showing the relationship of tones in an image using a series of 256 vertical bars, one for each brightness level. A histogram chart, such as the one the Sony Alpha can display during picture review, typically looks like a curve with one or more slopes and peaks, depending on how many highlight, midtone, and shadow tones are present in the image. The Alpha can also display separate histograms for brightness, as well as the red, green, and blue channels of an image.

hot shoe A mount on top of a camera used to hold an electronic flash, while providing an electrical connection between the flash and the camera. Sony cameras use a proprietary, non-standard hot shoe.

hyperfocal distance A point of focus where everything from half that distance to infinity appears to be acceptably sharp. For example, if your lens has a hyperfocal distance of four feet, everything from two feet to infinity would be sharp. The hyperfocal distance varies by the lens and the aperture in use. If you know you'll be making a grab shot without warning, sometimes it is useful to turn off your camera's automatic focus, and set the lens to infinity, or, better yet, the hyperfocal distance. Then, you can snap off a quick picture without having to wait for the lag that occurs with most digital cameras as their autofocus locks in.

image rotation A feature that senses whether a picture was taken in horizontal or vertical orientation. That information is embedded in the picture file so that the camera and compatible software applications can automatically display the image in the correct orientation.

image stabilization A technology that compensates for camera shake, which, in Sony's SteadyShot implementation, is achieved by adjusting the position of the camera sensor. Some other vendors, such as Nikon and Canon, move the lens elements in response to movements of the camera (which means that the feature is available only with lenses designed to provide it).

incident light Light falling on a surface.

International Organization for Standardization (ISO) A governing body that provides standards used to represent film speed, or the equivalent sensitivity of a digital camera's sensor. Digital camera sensitivity is expressed in ISO settings.

interpolation A technique digital cameras, scanners, and image editors use to create new pixels required whenever you resize or change the resolution of an image based on the values of surrounding pixels. Devices such as scanners and digital cameras can also use interpolation to create pixels in addition to those actually captured, thereby increasing the apparent resolution or color information in an image.

ISO *See* International Organization for Standardization (ISO).

jaggies Staircasing effect of lines that are not perfectly horizontal or vertical, caused by pixels that are too large to represent the line accurately. *See also* anti-alias.

JPEG A file "lossy" format (short for Joint Photographic Experts Group) that supports 24-bit color and reduces file sizes by selectively discarding image data. Digital cameras generally use JPEG compression to pack more images onto memory cards. You can select how much compression is used (and, therefore, how much information is thrown away) by selecting from among the Standard and Fine or other quality settings offered by your camera. *See also* RAW.

Kelvin (K) A unit of measure based on the absolute temperature scale in which absolute zero is zero; it's used to describe the color of continuous-spectrum light sources and applied when setting white balance. For example, daylight has a color temperature of about 5,500K, and a tungsten lamp has a temperature of about 3,400K.

lag time The interval between when the shutter is pressed and when the picture is actually taken. During that span, the camera may be automatically focusing and calculating exposure. With digital cameras like the Sony Alpha, lag time is generally very short; with other models, the elapsed time easily can be one second or more.

latitude The range of camera exposures that produce acceptable images with a particular digital sensor or film.

lens flare A feature of conventional photography that is both a bane and a creative outlet. It is an effect produced by the reflection of light internally among elements of an optical lens. Bright light sources within or just outside the field of view cause lens flare. Flare can be reduced by the use of coatings on the lens elements or with the use of lens hoods. Photographers sometimes use the effect as a creative technique, and Photoshop includes a filter that lets you add lens flare at your whim.

lighting ratio The proportional relationship between the amount of light falling on the subject from the main light and other lights, expressed in a ratio, such as 3:1.

Live View The ability of some Sony cameras, including the Alpha models, to provide a real-time preview image, as seen by the sensor, on the rear-panel color LCD.

lossless compression An image-compression scheme, such as TIFF, that preserves all image detail. When the image is decompressed, it is identical to the original version.

lossy compression An image-compression scheme, such as JPEG, that creates smaller files by discarding image information, which can affect image quality.

macro lens A lens that provides continuous focusing from infinity to extreme close-ups, often to a reproduction ratio of 1:2 (half life-size) or 1:1 (life-size).

maximum burst The number of frames that can be exposed at the current settings until the buffer fills.

midtones Parts of an image with tones of an intermediate value, usually in the 25 to 75 percent brightness range. Many image-editing features allow you to manipulate midtones independently from the highlights and shadows.

Multi segment metering One system of exposure calculation used by the Sony A57 that looks at many different segments of an image to determine the brightest and darkest portions. *See also* Center weighted metering and Spot metering.

neutral color A color in which red, green, and blue are present in equal amounts, producing a gray.

neutral-density filter A gray camera filter that reduces the amount of light entering the camera without affecting the colors.

noise In an image, pixels with randomly distributed color values. Visual noise in digital photographs tends to be the product of low-light conditions and long exposures, particularly when you've set your camera to a higher ISO rating than normal.

noise reduction A technology used to cut down on the amount of random information in a digital picture, usually caused by long exposures and/or increased sensitivity ratings.

normal lens A lens that makes the image in a photograph appear in a perspective that is like that of the original scene, typically with a field of view of roughly 45 degrees.

overexposure A condition in which too much light reaches the film or sensor, producing a dense negative or a very bright/light print, slide, or digital image.

pincushion distortion A type of lens distortion in which lines at the top and side edges of an image are bent inward, producing an effect that looks like a pincushion. *See also* barrel distortion.

polarizing filter A filter that forces light, which normally vibrates in all directions, to vibrate only in a single plane, reducing or removing the specular reflections from the surface of objects.

RAW An image file format, such as the ARW format in the Sony Alpha, that includes all the unprocessed information captured by the camera after conversion to digital form. RAW files are very large compared to JPEG files and must be processed by a special program such as Sony's Image Data Converter SR, or Adobe's Camera Raw filter after being downloaded from the camera.

rear-curtain sync (second-curtain sync) An optional kind of electronic flash synchronization technique, originally associated with focal plane shutters, which consists of a traveling set of curtains, including a *front (first) curtain* (which opens to reveal the film or sensor) and a *rear (second) curtain* (which follows at a distance determined by shutter speed to conceal the film or sensor at the conclusion of the exposure). For a flash picture to be taken, the entire sensor must be exposed at one time to the brief flash exposure, so the image is exposed after the front curtain has reached the other side of the focal plane, but before the rear curtain begins to move. Rear-curtain sync causes the flash to fire at the end of the exposure, an instant before the second or rear curtain of the focal plane shutter begins to move. With slow shutter speeds, this feature can create a blur effect from the ambient light, showing as patterns that follow a moving subject with the subject shown sharply frozen at the end of the blur trail. If you were shooting a photo of The Flash, the superhero would appear sharp, with a ghostly trail behind him. *See also* front-curtain sync (first-curtain sync).

red-eye An effect from flash photography that appears to make a person's eyes glow red, or an animal's yellow or green. It's caused by light bouncing from the retina of the eye into the camera lens, and is most pronounced in dim illumination (when the irises are wide open) and when the electronic flash is close to the lens and, therefore, prone to reflect directly back. Image editors can fix red-eye through cloning other pixels over the offending red or orange ones.

RGB color A color model that represents the three colors—red, green, and blue—used by devices such as scanners or monitors to reproduce color. Photoshop works in RGB mode by default, and even displays CMYK images by converting them to RGB.

saturation The purity of color; the amount by which a pure color is diluted with white or gray.

selective focus Choosing a lens opening that produces a shallow depth-of-field. Usually this is used to isolate a subject in portraits, close-ups, and other types of images, by causing most other elements in the scene to be blurred.

self-timer A mechanism that delays the opening of the shutter for some seconds after the release has been operated.

sensitivity A measure of the degree of response of a film or sensor to light, measured using the ISO setting.

shadow The darkest part of an image, represented on a digital image by pixels with low numeric values.

sharpening Increasing the apparent sharpness of an image by boosting the contrast between adjacent pixels that form an edge, using algorithms either in the camera or in an image editor.

shutter In a conventional film camera, the shutter is a mechanism consisting of blades, a curtain, a plate, or some other movable cover that controls the time during which light reaches the film. Digital cameras may use actual mechanical shutters for the slower shutter speeds (less than 1/160th second) and an electronic shutter for higher speeds.

Shutter priority An exposure mode, represented by the letter S on the Alpha's mode dial, in which you set the shutter speed and the camera determines the appropriate f/stop. *See also* Aperture priority.

side lighting Applying illumination from the left or right sides of the camera. *See also* backlighting and front lighting.

slave unit An accessory flash unit that supplements the main flash, usually triggered electronically when the slave senses the light output by the main unit, or through radio waves. Slave units can also be triggered by the pre-flash normally used to measure exposure, so you may need to set your main flash to Manual to avoid this.

slow sync An electronic flash synchronizing method that uses a slow shutter speed so that ambient light is recorded by the camera in addition to the electronic flash illumination. This allows the background to receive more exposure for a more realistic effect.

SLT Single Lens Translucent. A stationary mirror that passes 70 percent of the available in-camera light to the sensor. The technology provides a number of advantages including full-time Live View and autofocus in movie mode and high burst speed.

specular highlight Bright spots in an image caused by reflection of light sources.

Spot metering An exposure system setting that concentrates on a small area in the image, represented by the circle in the center of the Alpha's viewfinder. *See also* Center weighted metering, and Multi segment metering.

sRGB One of two color space choices available with the Sony Alpha. The sRGB setting is recommended for images that will be output locally on the user's own printer, as this color space matches that of the typical inkjet printer and a properly calibrated monitor fairly closely. *See also* Adobe RGB.

subtractive primary colors Cyan, magenta, and yellow, which are the printing inks that theoretically absorb all color and produce black. In practice, however, they generate a muddy brown, so black is added to preserve detail (especially in shadows). The combination of the three colors and black is referred to as CMYK. (K represents black, to differentiate it from blue in the RGB model.)

time exposure A picture taken by leaving the shutter open for a long period, usually more than one second. The camera is generally locked down with a tripod to prevent blur during the long exposure. For exposures longer than 30 seconds, you need to use the Bulb setting.

through-the-lens (TTL) A system of providing viewing and exposure calculation through the actual lens taking the picture.

tungsten light Light from ordinary room lamps and ceiling fixtures, as opposed to fluorescent illumination.

underexposure A condition in which too little light reaches the film or sensor, producing a thin negative, a dark slide, a muddy-looking print, or a dark digital image.

unsharp masking The process used by image-editing software for increasing the contrast between adjacent pixels in an image, increasing sharpness, especially around edges.

vignetting Dark corners of an image, often produced by using a lens hood that is too small for the field of view, a lens that does not completely fill the image frame, or generated artificially using image-editing techniques for artistic purposes.

white balance The adjustment of a digital camera to the color temperature of the light source. Interior illumination is relatively red; outdoor light is relatively blue. Digital cameras like the Alpha set correct white balance automatically or let you do it through menus. Image editors can often do some color correction of images that were exposed using the wrong white balance setting, especially when working with RAW files that contain the information originally captured by the camera before white balance was applied.

Index

A

B

C

E

F

I

M

N

Q

R

S

T

U

V

W

Y

Z